Aspects of Roman H

MW01284210

This new edition of *Aspects of Roman History 31 BC–AD 117* provides an easily accessible guide to the history of the early Roman Empire. Taking the reader through the major political events of the crucial first 150 years of Roman imperial history, from the Empire's foundation under Augustus to the height of its power under Trajan, the book examines the emperors and key events that shaped Rome's institutions and political form. Blending social and economic history with political history, Richard Alston's revised edition leads students through important issues, introducing sources, exploring techniques by which those sources might be read, and encouraging students to develop their historical judgment.

This book includes:

- chapters on each of the emperors in this period, exploring the successes and failures of each reign, and how these shaped the Empire;
- sections on social and economic history, including the core issues of slavery, social mobility, economic development and change, gender relations, the rise of new religions, and cultural change in the Empire;
- an expanded timeframe, providing more information on the foundation of the imperial system under Augustus and the issues relating to Augustan Rome;
- a glossary and further reading section, broken down by chapter.

This expanded and revised edition of *Aspects of Roman History*, covering an additional 45 years of history from Actium to the death of Augustus, provides an invaluable introduction to Roman imperial history, surveying the way in which the Roman Empire changed the world and offering critical perspectives on how we might understand that transformation. It is an important resource for any student of this crucial and formative period in Roman history.

Richard Alston is Professor of Roman History at Royal Holloway, University of London. He has been teaching Roman history for two decades. He is the author of several books on Roman imperial history, including *Soldier and Society in Roman Egypt: A Social History* (Routledge), and *The City in Roman and Byzantine Egypt* (Routledge). He has edited six books on subjects as diverse as slavery, the Greek city, and the borderlands of the Roman Empire. He has researched and published more than thirty articles on Roman history covering the period from about 150 BC to about AD 750. He is noted for his work on the Roman city, historiography and cultural history, the reception of Classical political ideals in modernity, and economic and social history.

Aspects of Classical Civilisation

Aspects of Greek History 750–323 BC
A Source-Based Approach
Second Edition
Terry Buckley

Aspects of Roman History 82 BC–AD 14
A Source-Based Approach
Mark Davies and Hilary Swain

Aspects of Roman History 31 BC–AD 117
Second Edition
Richard Alston

Classical Literature
An Introduction
Edited by Neil Croally and Roy Hyde

Aspects of Roman History 31 BC–AD 117

Second edition

Richard Alston

Routledge
Taylor & Francis Group

LONDON AND NEW YORK

Second edition published 2014
by Routledge
2 Park Square, Milton Park, Abingdon, Oxon OX14 4RN

and by Routledge
711 Third Avenue, New York, NY 10017

Routledge is an imprint of the Taylor & Francis Group, an informa business

First edition published by Routledge 1998

British Library Cataloguing in Publication Data
A catalogue record for this book is available from the British Library

Library of Congress Cataloging in Publication Data
Alston, Richard, 1965-
[Aspects of Roman history, AD 14-117]
Aspects of Roman history, 31 BC-AD 117 / Richard Alston. --
Second edition.
pages cm. -- (Aspects of classical civilisation)
Revised edition of Aspects of Roman history, AD 14-117. London ; New
York : Routledge, 1998.
Includes bibliographical references and index.
1. Rome--History--Empire, 30 B.C.-284 A.D. 2. Rome--Politics and
government--30 B.C.-284 A.D.--Historiography. 3. Emperors--Rome--
Biography. 4. Rome--History, Military--30 B.C.-476 A.D. I. Title.
DG276.A44 2013
937'.07--dc23
2013018603

ISBN: 978-0-415-61120-6 (hbk)
ISBN: 978-0-415-61121-3 (pbk)
ISBN: 978-1-315-87166-0 (ebk)

Typeset in Garamond and Gill Sans
by Saxon Graphics Ltd, Derby

MIX
Paper from
responsible sources
FSC
www.fsc.org FSC® C013056

Printed and bound in Great Britain by
TJ International Ltd, Padstow, Cornwall

For Efrossini, Sam, Josh, Vasilis, and Stefanos

Contents

Illustrations

Maps

Figures

Tables

Preface

This book has been written with modest aims. It updates and revises a text produced 15 years ago which had a narrower focus of AD 14–117. That book was written as a guide for students and focused very much on a school syllabus. With the continued decline in the teaching of Ancient History in schools, it seemed sensible to focus the text more closely for an undergraduate audience. The change in the audience has led to certain changes in style and content. The aim of the first version of the book was to introduce students to debates and provide them with a guide to ways of approaching the complex history of a century of imperial rule. Now, the market for the attention of students is more competitive. As historians, we need to explain why the periods of history we are writing about are sufficiently interesting that they might be worth studying. We now need to convince our students that what we study matters.

At first, I thought that this rewrite would be a minor issue, changing a few things here and there, adding a couple of chapters on Augustus. Yet, as I rewrote, more and more seemed to need to be changed. In part, this is because my views have changed somewhat in the last 15 years. But the changes have also been designed in part to make the text less descriptive since it seems less necessary to explain what happened, but more necessary to worry about why it happened. I have made a deliberate effort to make the chapters more questioning and more controversial. I want the reader to come away from the chapters wanting to know more and perhaps filled with doubt. Was this really the way the Empire worked? Was the Principate truly an exercise in the politics of paradox? Was the Roman Empire really so nasty? It may be that the reader will come away annoyed and wanting to debate these issues, and in that case my job is done.

There is also now more focus on the historical traditions. The ancient sources we read came out of certain traditions of thought and historical analysis. They had a certain way of understanding the world. This ideology shapes our knowledge of the period from Augustus to Trajan. We have, I think, to approach the historians with a focus not on whether they were right or wrong (for that often cannot be resolved), but on how they thought about political life. Contemporary historians have started to focus much more on political ideologies and the mentalities of politics in the Imperial period. The issues are no longer who stabbed whom and what were the immediate causes of that stabbing, but why Roman politics was so brutal generally and repeatedly. If it seems unsurprising that the Roman political class gathered themselves to rid Rome of Caligula, it is more interesting and puzzling that they suffered Claudius and Domitian for so long, and that many were so willing to acquiesce in or even to aid the murders of so many of their fellow political leaders. The shift in focus from the business of politics to the ideology of political life means, I think, that Roman politics seems stranger than it did 15 years ago. It is less easy to understand and to imagine, but as a consequence it is more rewarding and interesting.

The second half of the book has been completely rewritten. In the first edition, the idea was to have a political history to which was appended some guidance to the workings of Roman society. The history taught in schools and universities focused almost entirely on the political and institutional. This is simply no longer the case. Fifteen years ago, if I had suggested that I teach a course on social and economic history, I would have been frowned up and possibly regarded as dangerously eccentric: the business of Roman historians was teaching political history. Now, my most popular courses are on social and economic history. It is difficult to know why attitudes have changed, but changed they have. Most historians spend much more time thinking about social history than political history. As a consequence, we can think about Roman history in different ways, escape from a history centred on the emperors and their court, and look beyond, to the cities and towns of the Empire. We have a more balanced history as a result and, arguably, a more interesting history.

Throughout all the chapters of this book I have been keen to emphasise the workings of power in Roman society. In the chapters that focus on politics, I have time and time again tried to cut through the senatorial debates to look at where power lay in the discussions. I have argued that we cannot understand Augustan success without thinking about the money that the Empire brought in, the soldiers he paid, and the exceptionally violent manner in which he came to power. I have suggested that Tiberian relations with the senate were corrupted not so much by the brazen hypocrisy of the emperor, but by the difference between a conservative culture of power and the brutal imperial truth that all power stemmed from the emperor. That truth was perhaps both asserted and denied by Gaius. This most tyrannous of emperors made clear that he did not need the senators, but he was assassinated. This might seem an assertion of conservative power, but in reality it was the praetorian prefects who got rid of him and it was the soldiers who were to appoint Claudius as his successor. One has to ask why the senators suffered Claudius and Nero and Domitian, and the answer is obvious. They could do nothing about them. Power, real power, lay elsewhere.

Roman politics was vicious in a way which few modern states experience. The losers of the political game were killed. This fate befell not just those who aimed at the imperial position, but those lower down the political system who competed for honours (political offices) and authority. Modern political debates are often acrimonious, but at the end of the day, losers are not forced to commit suicide. Attempts to make Roman politics seem more polite, to make Roman emperors seem more generous and sensible, and revisit the hostile senatorial traditions that provide us with our picture of Roman political life have to take into account this institutionalised violence. Admirers of Rome and its Empire, among whom we may count some of our more prominent politicians, might like to reflect on the fatal consequences of the political game.

The chapters on Roman society also focus on issues of social power. The emphasis of these chapters is also not on description or Roman society as a system, but on domination. Roman social values maintained a hierarchy in which some were very rich and very powerful and others were not. It is those rich and powerful voices which we hear in our sources. Too often, these comfortable voices have lulled ancient historians into thinking well of Roman social values. Worse, historians have adopted the worries of these sources. What are we to make of the rise of freedmen in Roman society? What about the indiscipline of women? Was the natural order of Roman society under threat? I have tried to show that there is nothing natural about Roman social values. The task of the social historian is, I think, to get behind and beyond those voices, to try to reconstruct the lives of some of the silenced of Roman society. Of course, that is difficult. The silent are by definition (almost) without record, but the very silencing of them is an act of power which, in my view, we are obliged ethically to resist. Even if the mute cannot be made to talk, we can expose those structures of domination that rendered them silent in the first place.

The task of the social historian is get beyond the obvious representations of society by the rich and powerful, those committed to seeing their society as wonderful in large part because it makes them rich and powerful. We need to look for the lives of slaves and the poor, women and barbarians.

Why should we study this period? We should study it because it provokes questions about the nature of power and the nature of society. It provokes questions about one of the most revered and imitated institutions of world history, the Roman Empire. We should study the Roman Empire today because it is with us today and because it gave birth to Christianity and many of the ideas of the modern West. We should study Rome because by studying a period which is so different and in many ways odd, it brings into sharper focus issues of politics and power. Ultimately, we also live in an imperial age. For me, certain aspects of Roman history so often resonate uncomfortably. We might not have slavery, but we have cloth workers in Bangladesh who labour in terrible conditions, computer assembly lines in China from which people escape only by suicide, and we have an imperial system which, we are told, is natural and irresistible.

In practical terms, one of the great changes since 2008 has been in the development of the Internet. In 2008, images were not easily accessible. Information was often buried in books difficult to find, or out of print. But today, there is an abundance of high-quality information available on the web. The great museums of the world have put much of their collections online. Search for the Ara Pacis and you will find thousands of images become available. If one needs to know about Timgad, good quality information and pictures are a moment away. Nearly every important archaeological site has a virtual counterpart. One can find more images of Pompeii on authoritative websites in three seconds than we could possibly put into this book. Also, the major Classical historical texts are available online providing access as never before. Online provision also means that unfamiliar persons or concepts or events can easily be checked and holes in knowledge can be filled. Previously, information that might have taken hours and access to a high-quality library to reach, can be discovered almost instantly.

What the Internet is less good at is the transmission of ideas. History is not about what happened, but why it happened. In this version of the book, I have tried to focus not on 'the event', but on the why the event happened. The challenge of the book is not to deal with the information that I provide, but what you think about the ideas that arise from this information. I have not tried to provide an orthodox answer to every problem. Partly, I find that the orthodox answers so often seem not to work. One of the pleasures of ancient history is that the material we have is so slight. Anyone can get hold of the same basic data that I am using to write this book and make these arguments. If I was writing modern history and had ploughed through vast archives, my expertise would be such that you would not be easily able to challenge my views. But this is ancient history. I invite the challenge. I am obviously always right about everything, in life and in Roman history, but you have the obligation to decide whether or not you agree.

I have learnt much in the last 15 years. I have learnt from colleagues and friends. I have even learnt a few things from books. But I have learnt enormously from students. One of the great joys of being in a university is that every year bright, committed, and energised young people sit before me, eager to learn and challenge. As a result, I learn. From the first-years to the PhD students, they all teach me, as I try to teach them. Each time I go into a classroom, I interact with all those fresh minds. They bring to me so many new ideas and perspectives. I thank you all, past, present, and hopefully future.

I'd like to thank my publishers for asking me to revisit this text, for finding electronic versions of the original book (my own versions now rendered unreadable by the expensive upgrades in computer technology we are obliged to suffer), being patient while the text was being rewritten and various deadlines missed. I would like to thank the computer for not breaking down. In particular, the letter 't' has kept leaping from the keyboard and bouncing round the desk to the extent that at one point I thought I would have to write a history of Rome without using that letter, a challenge I leave unanswered.

Finally, the first edition was dedicated to my second son. There are now more sons. They are a team of four, all joyous. Most of the time when they are together they make some pretence of keeping me involved and informed; they are charitable like that. They even listen to me from time to time, but with the healthy disregard that one should show to an opinionated parent. It seems appropriate to treat them as a group. I get their names confused anyhow.

And to Efi. She knows.

I count my blessings and I thank them.

Abbreviations

Abbreviations of journals and authors follow the standard abbreviations of *L'Année Philologique* and the *Oxford Classical Dictionary*.

EJ = Ehrenberg, V. and Jones, A. H. M. (1976) *Documents Illustrating the Reigns of Augustus and Tiberius*, Oxford.

Campbell 1994 = Campbell, J. B. (1994) *The Roman Army: 31 BC–AD 337: A Sourcebook*, London, New York.

IGRR = Cagnat, R. (ed.) (1901–27) *Inscriptiones Graecae ad res romanas pertinentes*, Paris.

McCrum, Woodhead 1966 = McCrum, M. and Woodhead, A. G. (1966) *Select Documents of the Principates of the Flavian Emperors including the Year of Revolution, AD 68–96*, Cambridge.

Smallwood 1966 = Smallwood, E. M. (1966) *Documents Illustrating the Principates of Nerva, Trajan and Hadrian*, Cambridge.

Smallwood 1967 = Smallwood, E. M. (1967) *Documents Illustrating the Principates of Gaius, Claudius and Nero*, Cambridge.

Map 1.1 The Roman Empire in AD 60 (from Talbert 1984)

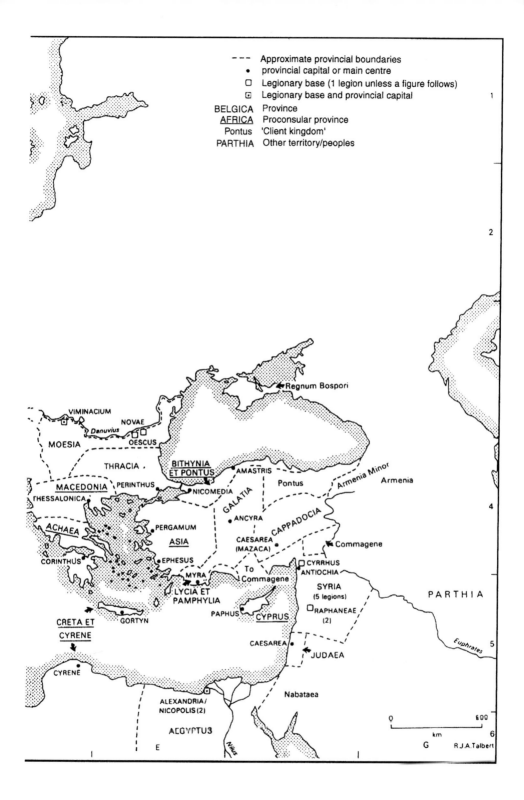

Approximate provincial boundaries
- • provincial capital or main centre
- ☐ Legionary base (1 legion unless a figure follows)
- ⊡ Legionary base and provincial capital

BELGICA Province
AFRICA Proconsular province
Pontus 'Client kingdom'
PARTHIA Other territory/peoples

Regnum Bospori

VIMINACIUM
NOVAE
Danuvius
MOESIA
OESCUS
THRACIA
BITHYNIA ET PONTUS
AMASTRIS
MACEDONIA
PERINTHUS
NICOMEDIA
Pontus
Armenia Minor
Armenia
THESSALONICA
GALATIA
ACHAEA
ANCYRA
PERGAMUM
ASIA
CAESAREA (MAZACA)
CAPPADOCIA
CORINTHUS
EPHESUS
Commagene
To Commagene
CYRRHUS
ANTIOCHIA
MYRA
LYCIA ET PAMPHYLIA
SYRIA (5 legions)
PARTHIA
PAPHUS
CYPRUS
RAPHANEAE (2)
CRETA ET CYRENE
GORTYN
Euphrates
CAESAREA
CYRENE
JUDAEA
Nabataea
ALEXANDRIA/ NICOPOLIS (2)
AEGYPTUS
Nilus
0   600
km
G   R.J.A.Talbert
E   I

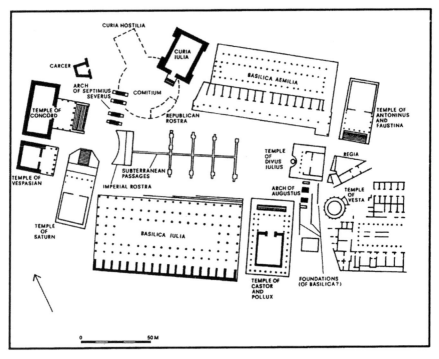

Map 1.2 The Forum Romanum (from Patterson 1992)

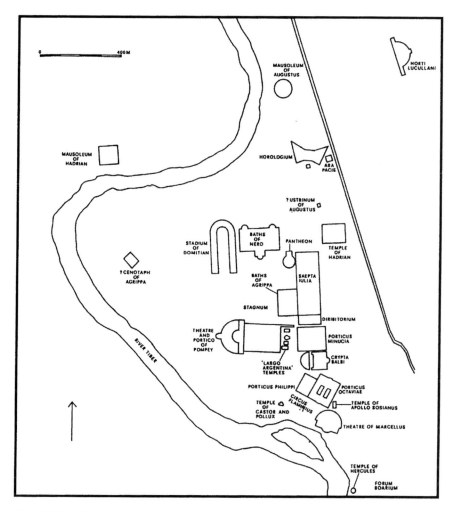

Map 1.3 The Campus Martius (from Patterson 1992)

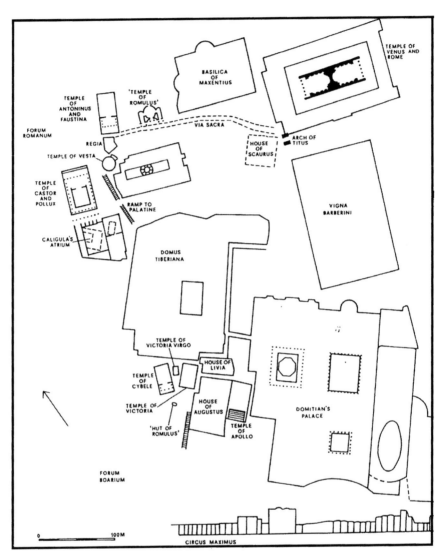

Map 1.4 The Palatine (from Patterson 1992)

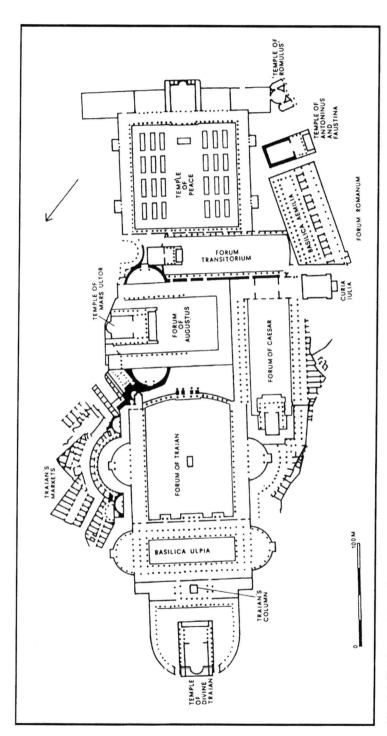

Map 1.5 The Imperial Fora (from Patterson 1992)

Chapter 1

Rome before Augustus

Introduction and issues

On 2nd September, 31 BC, the fate of the world was decided. Two fleets sailed into battle on a constricted stretch of sea between the Greek island of Lefkas and the straits of Actium in what is now Northern Greece. One fleet was led by Mark Antony and his wife and ally Cleopatra, Queen of Egypt. The other fleet was commanded by C. Julius Caesar Octavianus, heir to his uncle Julius Caesar. Octavian was supported by his experienced admiral Vipsanius Agrippa.

Neither side appear to have been ready for war when it broke out in 32 BC. Antony and Cleopatra had gathered an impressive legionary and naval force to resist Octavian. They had assembled that force at Actium in Western Greece partly to oppose any attempt by Octavian to invade the East and partly as a launch pad for an invasion of Southern Italy. Yet, Antony and Cleopatra faced considerable logistical problems in gathering their forces from across the region while Agrippa and Octavian made use of their relative proximity to Greece to strike first. They created a beachhead in the North of Greece, at Paxos, and launched naval raids across the west coast of Greece. This military activity gave Agrippa and Octavian the advantage. They took control of the sea lanes and Agrippa was able to establish a naval base at Lefkas, modern Lefkada. Octavian meanwhile advanced to make camp north of the straits of Actium.

Antony and Cleopatra were encamped to the south of the straits. Actium had looked like a sensible base. It was a good harbour, safe from summer storms. But the land route to Actium was difficult, running over mountain ranges, and there were no major centres nearby to help organise supplies for the large number of troops that Antony had assembled. Cut off from the sea, Antony could not easily feed his troops. As spring turned to summer and the temperatures rose, hunger and disease gripped the troops. Antony's army started to die. Antony offered battle, but Octavian's troops were safe behind their defences and were well-provisioned. They were almost certainly informed about what was happening in Antony's camp. Strategically, they could wait for Antony's army to weaken.

Antony and Cleopatra needed to move. Potentially, they had two choices: they could burn their fleet and retreat over the difficult land route or they could attempt a naval breakout. In reality, however, they had no choice. The fleet was their major strategic asset. Fleets were expensive and time-consuming to equip and train. If they were to continue the war, Antony and Cleopatra would need to assemble reinforcements from across their territories and that would require a fleet. A naval battle was their best chance of escaping Actium and preserving their fleet was their only chance of winning the war. And so, they sailed out to battle with the strategic objective of escaping with as many of their ships intact as possible.

There is a peculiar feature of the summer weather on that part of the Greek coast. Although the day often dawns still, the wind tends to blow every afternoon before falling as the day nears its end. The fleet could not row to freedom, it needed to sail. But raising sail required the fleet to break formation and battle lines and make a dash for the open sea. The battle was, therefore, time limited. If Antony and Cleopatra could neither destroy their opponents nor fight their way through Octavian's and Agrippa's lines before mid-afternoon, the battle would be lost. At some point in the afternoon, Cleopatra and Antony thought they saw their opportunity. They raised sail and made their escape. The fleet dispersed to catch the wind and sailed for their appointed rendezvous. When they assembled again, the terrible truth became obvious. The majority of the fleet had not escaped. The battle was lost. Without a powerful fleet, Antony and Cleopatra could not contest the sea lanes and could not assemble reinforcements. It would be near impossible to resist Octavian. Octavian was in position to make a steady and victorious progress around the Eastern Mediterranean, persuading the various cities and states and the Roman provincial governors that their only future lay with him. As the full magnitude of the disaster became apparent, everyone made the same calculation: the war might not have been over, but it had been lost. Antony and Cleopatra sailed to Alexandria for a last winter, waiting for the arrival of their conqueror and the death that was an inevitable consequence of their defeat. Their allies defected and began the process of making peace with Caesar's heir. Octavian could now contemplate his unrivalled mastery of the Roman world.

Rome had suffered civil war before and those wars had led to periods in which a single individual had held quasi-monarchic powers. After a period of civil wars that been fought intermittently from 88 BC–83 BC, Sulla had emerged victorious, appointed himself dictator and either killed or exiled all his remaining enemies. He was in absolute control and used that control to reform the Roman constitution, reinforcing the control of the senate, the traditional governing council of Rome. Sulla was to lay down his powers in 80 BC and Republican government resumed in a relatively normal form. In 49 BC, Julius Caesar had crossed the Rubicon, the river that separated his province from Italy and launched another civil war. He, too, had become dictator and effectively wielded monarchic power. His assassination on 15th March, 44 BC had brought an end to that period of government. Like Sulla's dictatorship, Caesar's rule could also be seen as an interlude (and there had been several others in remote Roman history) in a long period of Republican government.

It is conventional to divide Rome's history into these three periods: the regal period, the Republic, and the Empire. Rome was traditionally thought to have been founded in 753 BC by Romulus. The date in itself has little value and Romulus, like many of the early kings of Rome, belongs to the realm of myth. In a similarly unreliable and mythic history, the Roman Republic was said to have been founded after the expulsion of the last king, Tarquinius Superbus, in 509 BC. After that point, Rome was seen as a Republic. Whatever political system was developed in the late sixth century, it is unlikely to have been very like the Roman Republic as we know it from the first century BC. Nevertheless, and in spite of various experiments, the main components of Republican government (rule by a collective of Roman citizens and a number of magistrates whose tenure of the position was time-limited) were in place for the majority of the next five centuries. During that period, Rome was transformed from perhaps a reasonably large city-state in the heart of Italy to the central city of a vast Mediterranean empire. After 430 years of remarkably successful Republican government, the battle of Actium was to usher in a new period of imperial rule that was to last until AD 475, when the Gothic King decided that the nominal emperor of the West, Romulus Augustulus, was more trouble than he was worth and sent him into a comfortable internal exile. Actium, then, marks the beginning of this new age, an age which we, somewhat confusingly, refer to as the Empire.

The transition from Republic to Empire is one of the most controversial events in world history. It has been the subject of considerable and forceful debate from antiquity to the present. The transition is important because it makes us think about the nature of government, what government is for and what the best possible government is.

Although we live in an age in which liberal democracy is almost universally regarded as the best form of government, this is an unusual feature of contemporary political culture. In previous generations, many have argued that democracy risks corruption and that some form of monarchic rule or aristocratic rule (rule by the best men) would be more efficient and therefore better. Even today, questions are asked as to whether democratic governments can ever be relied upon to take the necessary difficult decisions, whether politicians are sufficiently expert to identify the right course, or whether the necessity of re-election is to the detriment of their management of the state since politicians will always seek to bribe their electorates or need to court alliances with business leaders and financiers who will fund their campaigns. Many of these questions have been and can still be discussed using Roman history. The focus of that discussion is frequently on the transition between Republic and Empire. The fall of the Republic appears to represent a rejection or failure of aristocratic governance. The spectre of the fall of the Roman Republic suggests that any republican system may have certain flaws integral to its workings and that if political circumstances are unfavourable, a republic might just degenerate into corruption and violence.

The transition between Republic and Empire poses certain key questions:

- Is republican government necessarily corrupt?
- Is the development of monarchic imperialism necessary to ensure the survival and good governance of states?
- What is the nature of imperial government and is imperial government in itself necessarily corrupt?
- Who is government for?

These are general political issues, which deserve endless debate. I leave it for the reader to think through these issues.

Before we can use Rome to answer these questions, we need to understand what happened in Rome in the transition from Republic to Empire. We must ask different, more precise questions. This chapter will guide us through the following historical issues:

- What was the nature of Republican government?
- How did Augustus change Rome's political system?
- Did Augustus make Roman government better?

The Roman Republic as a political system

We can analyse the Republican system in three sections, which will look at the following themes:

- constitution and law;
- Roman political culture;
- the historical operation of politics in Rome.

These three themes overlap and they need to be understood together. The first section is 'formal': it illustrates the rule book by which Roman politics was played. The second section looks at the regularities and expectations of the Roman political system. These were, arguably, more important in generating the political class in Rome than the constitution. These regularities governed political relationships, and it is relationships that make political power. The final section looks at the historical operation of the system since the experience of Roman politics in the first century influenced how individuals acted (whatever the precise balance of institutional relationships).

The Roman Republican constitution and Roman political institutions

Rome did not have a written constitution. The operation of Roman politics was governed by custom modified by occasional legislative acts (rather in the manner of the British system). The Romans valued tradition. Tradition guaranteed the rightness of actions and the 'custom of the ancestors' could be used to justify political actions. Furthermore, Roman political gatherings were also religious gatherings in which empowered magistrates would ascertain the will of the gods and seek the blessing of the gods for the decisions to be made. The emphasis placed on tradition meant that the Romans were reluctant to rationalise their political system (for that would interfere with tradition). The constitution developed a plethora of different assemblies, councils, boards and magistrates, many of which had overlapping functions or powers which were not clearly defined. For our purposes, it is not necessary to cover the finer detail of the development of Roman constitutional practices, merely to recognise that such practices were not fixed by law.

The fundamental principle of the Roman constitutional system was the sovereignty of the people. The people elected magistrates and passed laws. The power of the magistrates, which included the right to punish and the ability to lead armies, depended on the sovereignty delegated by the people to the magistrates. The 'people' (*populus*) was the collective body of Roman citizens. For the purposes of Roman political life, the political community was constituted of Roman adult males, though Roman children and Roman women were citizens and were covered by the right and protections of Roman citizens. Foreigners and slaves were not given any political rights, though foreigners had some legal protections that they could exercise in Rome (through application to magistrates) and slaves were protected, as property, from abuses by those who were not their masters. Citizens were registered in a census. The census established the property holdings of the individual citizens (which allowed the citizenry to be located in particular bands of wealth) and by tribe. Tribes were associated with particular localities within Roman territory and tribal membership was passed down the family line from father to son. The tribes were effectively hereditary constituencies of the Roman people, convenient ways of organising the population, and were not communities.

The Roman male citizenry met in two main assemblies: the *comitia tributa* and the *comitia centuriata*. These assemblies were responsible for the election of magistrates and the passing of laws. The *comitia tributa* appears to have been the main law-making assembly. It was this assembly that seems to have elected the more junior magistrates and most notably the tribunes, the people's representatives. The senior magistrates were elected by the *comitia centuriata*. The *comitia tributa* was organised by the 35 tribes of Rome and would vote by tribe. In the passing of laws and elections, the voting would proceed by members of a particular tribe leaving an enclosure and crossing specially erected bridges. Once all members of the tribe had voted, their votes would be counted and their vote declared. Once sufficient tribes had been declared, for a decision to be made (the required number of magistrates elected or the law passed), the assembly would be dismissed. The process of election for the *comitia centuriata* was similarly cumbersome. The assembly divided the people into 197 centuries. These centuries were organised by the wealth bands established in the census. The assembly was heavily weighted towards the wealthier sectors of Roman society and it was the centuries of the wealthiest bands that voted first. The very poorest Roman citizens were probably rarely consulted.

These processes of decision-making were ritualised. Magistrates presided over the assemblies and either proposed the candidates to the people or put the laws to be decided to the people. Voting would normally be preceded by public meetings (*contiones*) in which issues might be discussed. The electoral assemblies themselves were not opportunities for debate. Magistrates had considerable opportunities to manage the voting process, but electoral interference was limited by the underlying principle of popular sovereignty.

The assemblies elected the magistrates and the magistrates were the effective rulers of Rome. There were a number of different grades of magistrates of varying levels of seniority in age and position within the political system. Although there were a number of junior positions, the senior elected magistrates were, from the most junior to the most senior: the quaestor, aedile, tribune, praetor, consul and censor. The censorship was a special position and was rarely held. The two most important magistrates were the praetors and the consuls. It was these magistracies to which the *comitia centuriata* elected candidates.

Table 1.1 The senatorial magistrates

Magistrate	Number of postholders per year	Normal age	Powers/duties
Censor	2 (not every year)	Normally held by former consuls	Revising the lists of citizens
Consul	2	42	Chairing the senate and leading the Roman people in war
Praetor	8	39	Chairing courts/ governing provinces
Aedile	6	—	Running games/ maintaining Rome
Tribune	10	—	Representing the people and defending their rights
Quaestor	20	30	Financial offices/supporting praetors and consuls

The consuls and the praetors were holders of *imperium*. This allowed the magistrates to exercise military power and to discipline the Roman citizenry. Technically, the consuls and praetors were able to execute Roman citizens and the consuls were accompanied by attendants, lictors, who carried bundles of rods and axes (*fasces*) which represented this disciplinary capacity. That power was, however, limited by Roman legal practices, which prevented the execution of a Roman citizen without due process, and the possibility of tribunician intervention. The tribunes were charged with defending the rights and privileges of the Roman citizens against the powers of the magistrates. This included the right to veto the actions of magistrates and the right to intercede to protect individuals from magistrates. The tribunes were elected by the *comitia tributa*.

Before Sulla, membership of the senate appears to have depended on periodic revisions of the senatorial roll. After Sulla, it seems that the senate was automatically replenished each year by adding 20 quaestors to the senate. Once a man was appointed to the senate, he was normally appointed for life. He could not be voted out of the senate. The censors could remove senatorial status, but this seems to have been rarely done and was reserved for cases of gross immorality. At times of violent civic disturbance, men could also lose their senatorial status, but again this was unusual. It appears that the sole criterion for election to the senate was performance of the quaestorship and there is no evidence of a property qualification. It is possible, however, that election to the quaestorship depended on being a member of the *prima classis*, the first class, with a property qualification of 100,000 *sesterces*. The only condition of which we can be reasonably secure is that it was expected that a candidate for quaestor would have extensive prior military service, perhaps for as many as ten years.

The senate is the most well-known assembly of Republican (and Imperial) Rome. Most histories of the Republic give the impression (probably correctly) that the senate was the governing assembly of the city. Yet, the senate had very few powers. It operated as an advisory council for the magistrates. Nevertheless, the senate had considerable authority and that authority depended largely on custom (it was normal for magistrates to follow the advice of the senators) and the collective personal authority of the senators. Given that the senate was composed of the leading men of Rome who had exercised power through the various magistracies that they had held, their advice carried moral weight. The senate would also receive embassies from other states and communities (either internal or external to the Empire). Since the senators would advise the magistrates on war and peace, the advice that the senate gave to other states was often treated as having the force of law and it is clear that the Romans expected that senatorial advice would be followed. Individual magistrates who did not follow senatorial advice could find themselves prosecuted in the courts.

Once elected to the quaestorship, the next positions in the senatorial career structure were only marginally competitive. Senators would normally hold either the tribunate or the aedileship, but not both. Of the 20 men entering the senate, 16 would be elected to the next stage. Only half of those would progress to the praetorship, though we must make some allowance for individuals dropping out of the political race and for deaths in the peer group (probably a significant factor given high levels of mortality in a pre-industrial society and, of course, extended periods of military service). The consulship was, however, truly competitive since the original 20 entrants were reduced to two. Furthermore, although it was uncommon to hold a second consulship, in the pre-Sullan period, appointing leading generals to repeated consulships was a way of dealing with military crises. Even after Sulla, a second consulship was possible (though rare). Holding the consulship was the greatest political honour for a Roman politician.

Before Sulla, the praetors and the consuls would command Rome's armies. As the Empire expanded, it became more difficult to combine chairing the senate and running Roman political life with military command. After Sulla's reforms, the consuls tended to stay in Italy during their consulship. After their magistracy, they would be given a province, normally either by ballot or by decision of the senate. The former consuls would be invested with consular powers in the provinces in which they served and were known as proconsuls. The powers of the proconsuls were rigorously limited to the territories over which they had been given command. A second level of governors was composed of propraetors. The propraetors were of lesser status but had exactly the same powers in the provinces. Once proconsuls and propraetors had fulfilled their duties in the provinces (which were normally limited to a year, but frequently extended should Rome need to pursue an extended campaign), the governors would return to Rome and take up normal senatorial duties.

The Roman people were divided into various status groups. The Roman senators were the most important group. The second group were the equestrians (the knights). This was in many ways an archaic division of Roman society. The equestrians had been the traditional cavalry of Rome. By the late Republic, the technical definition of an equestrian was someone who had a 'public horse', and reflected the military origins of the status grouping. In reality, it seems as though the equestrians were a group within the *prima classis*, the richest band of the Roman people with property worth more than 100,000 *sesterces*. The term is often used of the minor aristocracy of Rome and Italy but the son of a senator who did not take up senatorial office would, it seems, normally have been an equestrian.

The Roman population was divided into six wealth bands, as assessed by the census. These bands were adjusted over time, in part to reflect changes in Roman coinage. The lowest category was the *capite censi*, those who were counted only by head (i.e. having no property). Formally, these were individuals who had property worth less than 375 *sesterces* and who were very poor. Before the first century BC, the *capite censi* were not allowed to join the

Roman army, but after the Marian reforms of the late second century this property qualification was dropped.

There were two further archaic status groups: the patricians and the plebs. The patricians were the original senators of Rome (the fathers of the city). This group originally exercised a monopoly of magisterial power. Gradually, however, in the fifth century BC, that monopoly was broken and magistracies became open to plebeians. The distinction survived in certain priestly offices, which were reserved for patricians, and in the tribunate, which was closed to patricians, but outside the religious sphere the distinction was not obviously important. The term 'plebs' referred to those who were not patricians and gradually came to be applied to the population of the city of Rome itself, as distinct from the Roman *populus* who could and did reside throughout Italy or even in the provinces.

The qualification for Roman citizenship was hereditary: Roman citizens were descendants of Roman citizens. There was no particular residential qualification. Roman citizenship gradually spread from Rome and its immediate hinterland to encompass the other communities in central Italy. After the Social War in 88 BC, citizenship was extended to all communities of peninsular Italy. In 49 BC, Julius Caesar further extended citizenship to many of the communities of Northern Italy. Roman citizenship was effectively the citizenship of all the freeborn of Italy by the end of the Republic. Roman citizenship could also be acquired by grant of magistrates, and this appears to have been used as a reward from time to time. The most significant source of new citizens, however, was former slaves. The Romans were unusual in granting their slaves full citizenship (see pp. 279–84).

The constitution provided a rule book for Roman political life, though these rules were often broken in the last century of the Republic. Rome worked with what was recognised in antiquity as a mixed constitution. Ancient political theory divided constitutions and states into three formal categories: monarchy, aristocracy, and democracy. These categories were in a perpetual state of flux and each category was in danger of corruption. As each system had its own weaknesses and a mixed constitution offered to blend the benefits of all three types of government, operating a system of checks and balances in which no one part of the state could overwhelm other parts. This theory has, of course, come down to modern states in the form of the separation of powers within the state (political, administrative, military, judicial). In Rome, the assemblies provided the democratic element, the senate the aristocratic, and the magistrates (and especially the consuls) the monarchic. Since ultimate sovereignty lay with the people, Rome was in the last instance democratic. But this democracy was managed by the aristocratic and monarchic elements. In this balance, the Romans thought that they had achieved the ideal constitutional mix. The Greek historian Polybius, who wrote in the later second century BC, viewed the constitutional system as being close to ideal and it was these constitutional arrangements which largely explained Rome's great political achievements (Polybius, 6.11–19). Yet, Polybius set the achievement of that perfection in the last decades of the third century, a century before his writing.

Roman political culture

If the constitution provided the rule book for Roman politics, the business of politics was conducted in personal relationships. These personal relationships were governed by conventions. These conventions, in turn, shaped behaviours. Roman historians, such as Livy and Sallust (who were both writing at the end of the first century BC), placed more emphasis on behaviour than on constitutions and attributed Rome's success to moral values. Sallust and Livy, in common with many of their contemporaries, associated Roman political and moral virtue with the past. A decline in adherence to approved behaviours was responsible for the political turmoil that marked the fall of the Republic. For Romans, political culture was at least as important and probably more important than constitutional forms.

We can understand political culture in two ways. Firstly, we may think of political culture as the way in which the business of politics is conducted. It is in this sense that we normally use the phrase today. We expect our politicians to behave in certain ways, to talk in certain ways and to have a certain type of appearance. Politicians know this. They even manipulate it. In most democratic countries, political parties manage their candidates and present those candidates in such a way that they conform to the values of the political culture. Mavericks, the anti-establishment figures, the unusual thinkers tend to get deselected in the process of party approval so that our politicians often seem to be very similar. A political culture can then operate to create a homogeneous class of political representatives (which does not, of course, mean that they always agree with each other).

Roman politicians were all educated in Greek and Latin literature. They were all trained in rhetoric and would almost certainly have adopted similar patterns of speech and self-presentation. Although the political disputes in the late Republic were vicious and, indeed, politicians even killed each other, viewed from the outside, the Roman political class were remarkably homogeneous. It was a club to which outsiders could not gain access.

The second way we can understand political culture is different from the situation of modern politics. Rome was a political culture in the sense that political and social structures were identical. Roman politicians were rich and powerful men. They were expected to be wealthy. This meant that wealth was an informal qualification for being a Roman politician. Roman politicians were in charge of the judiciary. Roman politicians also led the army into battle. The priests who represented Rome to the gods were also politicians. In many modern societies, there is a difference between social power and political power. A person may have power in a local community or a local organisation (they may run a school or a business, etc.), but have no real political influence outside that community. In Rome, there was an identity of those who held social power and political power. More importantly, this appears to have been the dominant expectation in Roman society. It was natural that the wealthy would be the politicians, that the politicians would lead the army, and that generals would be priests or offer sacrifices on behalf of the community to the gods, and that those who represented the people would also support the arts in the city.

Roman political culture worked in such a way as to generate a homogeneous political class. There were no political parties as such in Rome, no political manifestos and not much in the way of political debates, and no mass media. A young man who wanted to get on in the Roman political world and be elected to the first magisterial post needed to secure for himself a reputation so that he would be recognised come the election. If the young man was the son of a distinguished family, he would have that all-important name which would ensure that he was recognised. If a candidate could secure the support of senior and well-known figures in the political system, then he could trade on their reputations rather than his own. This meant that political connections were essential in commencing a political career and, indeed, in advancing through its stages. As a politician became more senior, although he could secure for himself a reputation he would still need the support and help of senior political figures who might give him, for instance, opportunities to serve as an officer in the army, where one could distinguish oneself on the field of battle. For those who were voting and thus making the careers of the politicians, voting for someone who seemed to be well-supported was a sensible strategy. Faced with a group of virtually anonymous young men, the voter had little information on which to base his decision. If the candidate's father had been a good leader, one could hope that his son would be a good man. If the young man was supported by senior figures, one could hope that he would listen to their advice, be sensible and take counsel when necessary. One has to remember that the electoral decisions were important: the Romans were electing leaders who might lead them into battle or represent them to the gods. The consequences of electing an incompetent general or a man who could not secure the goodwill of the gods could be fatal.

Such a system was normative: it tended to reinforce certain shared characteristics on the part of politicians. The aspiring politician needed to court his seniors and peers for their support, since they would provide him with the reputation necessary to ensure electoral success. Furthermore, politicians needed to honour the collective wisdom of their fellow senators. In the best circumstances, this meant that politicians would make the 'right' decisions. If a decision went wrong, magistrates who had taken advice would spread the blame. This is one of the reasons why the senate was so powerful. It represented the collective political power of the Roman elite and thus individual politicians spent their careers trying to ensure the support of that collective.

The Roman political class was also very small. There seems to have been a view that there should be 300 senators for the period before Sulla. The number of senators in the late Republican senate was likely somewhat larger, at just over 450 (assuming an average life expectancy for a quaestor of 25 years after appointment). The political class bound itself together in a network of friendships and associations. These were men likely to share many common cultural interests and, of course, to have stood alongside each other in the many ceremonial events that dotted the calendar of Republican Rome. They would also have fought together. Rome officered its armies from the aristocracy and so many of the young men of the political class would have found themselves serving alongside each other in the legions. The senior officers would have selected the junior officers from the promising youths, building up a network of friendships and obligations. As the young men's careers progressed, they would have co-operated in courts and in politics. The aristocracy chose their wives from the daughters of the aristocracy, establishing another level of associations and ties. Roman dinner parties would have brought together these aristocrats, allowing the formation of friendships. It seems very likely that everyone in the Roman political class knew everyone else, and what is more, those relationships lasted for considerable lengths of time. A senatorial position was for life, as were one's senatorial colleagues.

Roman politics worked in a culture of friendship (*amicitia*) and respect for the worth (*dignitas*) of the various members of the political class in combination with an adherence to the authority (*auctoritas*) of the collective body of experience and wisdom that was the senate. In such circumstances, politics was personal. A man who did not hold office might still hold considerable power because of his individual authority and standing. Roman politicians rarely retired into private life. They might lay down office and then become a *privatus*, a private individual, but they would still sit in the senate and exercise authority as a senator.

There were three key results of this system.

1   The political class tended to be culturally and politically uniform. There was almost no opportunity for outsiders to make any impact within the political system. The result is that Roman politics tended to be very conservative and lacked new ideas.

2   Political culture tended to be highly personal. Instead of discussing ideology and disputing over ideas, political debate had a strong personal focus. Manners and moral status were essential political qualities. Political invective concentrated to an extraordinary degree on the personal since the judgement to be made was whether an individual had the right personal qualities to be a political leader. Furthermore, when disputes did arise and someone was portrayed as not adhering to the norms of social convention, the debate could quickly escalate from questioning whether that person was unsuitable for power to whether they were a danger to

Rome. The nature of the invective meant that animosities frequently became very violent.

3   Roman politics was hierarchic. Although there were perhaps 450 senators, the really important people would be those who had held senior political office at some point in their careers or who were expected to hold senior political office. These would be the people who could support the junior members of the senate as they rose through the ranks, but also would be able to control those who gained access to the lesser posts. Perhaps only 50 or so senators would ever have individual authority.

Although membership of the Roman political class was never formally hereditary and there were always men from new families who were able to enter the system, the senior figures in Roman politics were often the sons of the great families of Rome. These men were known as the 'nobiles', not in the sense that they had any formal titles (as had the nobility of medieval Europe), but because they came from families that had political had reputations and those familial reputations affected the standing of particular individuals. The reputation of a great man was personal, but could be passed down to his sons and grandsons. The personal nature of the operation of political life made 'nobility' a familial trait. Furthermore, as Rome was a traditional society, the successes of previous generations resounded to the benefit of subsequent generations of the family. One's ancestors were a significant element in one's social standing and the busts of ancestors would be displayed in houses and at important family events, notably funerals. In the traditionalism of Roman social thinking, it made sense to trust the sons of great families who had produced able leaders in the past.

If the *nobiles* tended towards the conservative, the new men (*novi homines*) were not necessarily any more radical. The two most famous new men of the late Republic were Gaius Marius, who was the political opponent of Sulla, and M. Tullius Cicero, the great orator. Both men were exceptional in different ways. Marius has some claim to be an outsider in Roman politics in that he clashed violently with the establishment, especially with his former patron, Metellus. But Marius owed his rise to extraordinary prominence (he held more consulships than anyone else before the Imperial period) to a very particular set of circumstances. Marius was elected in the face of a military crisis in North Africa and seemingly ineffectual management of that war. Once he had ended that war, he was a military hero and the obvious man to deal with another major crisis, the invasion of two Germanic tribes, the Cimbri and the Teutones, in the last years of the second century BC. Marius was an isolated exception and his prominence did not open the door to a stream of new men, quite the opposite.

M. Tullius Cicero, about whom we know a great deal, was a brilliant orator and owed his political success to that facility with words. Cicero was, however, certainly not a radical reformer, nor did he seek to challenge the authority of the *nobiles*, however much he may have felt excluded from and snubbed by their charmed circle.

New men faced jibes at their lack of distinguished ancestry and probably had to work much harder to build the political friendships which were inherited by their more high-born contemporaries. But they were in no sense from poor backgrounds. Rome had originally been a city state with a limited territory. It was only in the middle of the first century BC that citizenship had been extended to the majority of Italy. New men were often landed aristocrats from these new communities (what are sometimes called *domi nobiles*, 'nobles at home').

Republican Rome may have had democratic elements, but its political culture was aristocratic. Rome was governed by a largely hereditary class of politicians. This class was culturally uniform. What is more, the operation of political culture was such that it excluded any who were potentially outsiders to the aristocratic clique: such men would not, unless circumstances were very unusual, achieve high political office. The dominance of the hereditary aristocracy was honoured by tradition and by a record of considerable political and military success. Furthermore, it was reinforced by the completeness of Roman political culture. Since the political class were also the leaders of the army, the priests, the judiciary, the most wealthy, and the cultural leaders in the city, there was no source of political or cultural authority that lay outside their remit: their control, collectively, was absolute. There was no competing group to challenge their authority.

The only limitations on the authority and power of this elite stemmed from the rights and privileges of Roman citizens. Rome was a citizen community and the citizens had certain protections from the arbitrary violence of the magistrates. Roman political culture balanced the enormous authority vested in the magistrates with an obligation to the people as fellow citizens. As we shall see, in practice, that obligation was often over-ridden by the demands of the senate. The senators clearly regarded themselves as being by right the ruling class of Rome and any attack on that right was seen as revolutionary. It was revolutionary both in the narrow sense of attempting to change the system of government, but also in a wider sense of overthrowing the socio-economic order which guaranteed the stability of the state and the pre-eminence of the senators. In defence of this pre-eminence, many in the senate believed that they were justified in the exercise of extreme violence and it was this violence that marked the last century of the Republic.

The last century of the Republic

From the Gracchi to Caesar

The last century of the Republic is marked by a number of major outbreaks of civil violence. This violence extended sometimes into civil war. In addition, there were wars in Italy against the Italian allies and against slaves which further disrupted the peninsular.

The history of violence in the late Republic was the background to the reign of Augustus and formed an element in the 'world view' of the Augustan age. As we shall see, Augustus is said to have offered Rome 'peace' (*pax*) or 'restfulness' (*otium*) in exchange for his political dominance. The alternative was not the civil conflict of the kind that we see with Antony and Cleopatra – for that war was short-lived and the disruption was relatively contained and remote from Italy itself – but the episodes of major civic unrest that disfigured the last century of the Republic. The Augustan promise was to end the violence that had brought death and destruction on an enormous scale to Italy over the previous century. One should also bear in mind that the upper classes of Rome would have suffered disproportionately in these wars: they were the known figures who were the targets of political murders and they were the individuals of wealth whose riches were sequestered by the violent regimes that from time to time took control of Rome.

Table 1.2 Major outbreaks of violence in the last century of the Republic

Date (all BC)	Event
133	Murder of the tribune Tiberius Gracchus during rioting in Rome
121	Murder of the tribune Gaius Gracchus during rioting in Rome
104–101	Slave War in Sicily
100	Marius leads troops against the tribune Saturninus and kills him
91–89	Social War between Rome and her Italian allies
88	Sulla stages coup in Rome
87	Marius stages counter coup in Rome
83	Sulla launches civil war against enemies in Rome
81	War ends and Sulla appointed dictator
79–71	War in Spain between Sulla's supporters and the remnants of the Marian opposition
78–77	Death of Sulla. Insurrection and civil war between Lepidus and Catulus, supported by Pompey
73–71	Revolt of Spartacus
63	Conspiracy of Catiline results in brief civil war
58–57	Rioting in Rome
53	Rioting in Rome
52	Prominent politician Clodius killed in rioting: the senate house is burned down
49	Julius Caesar launches civil war
46	End of the civil war
44	Assassination of Caesar
44–42	Civil war
43–32	The Triumvirate

The unrest of this period was severe. Many countries may have periods of civic violence (rioting and the like), but casualties from the political violence of the last century of the Republic were extreme. For example, for the war of 83–81 BC, the sources, which are far from ideal, give casualty figures from the various battles which amount to 89,000 soldiers. The sources tend only to mention the dead of the defeated, not the 'victorious' dead. So, we could assume that actually 150,000 or more were killed in this war, perhaps as many as 5% of the total free population. That war followed on from the Social War, a war between Rome and her allies in Italy. It was a long and brutal war, though we cannot get close to reliable casualty figures for the conflict. The revolt of Lepidus in 78 BC can be seen as a continuation of the Sullan conflicts. Together, these three wars must have struck down a high proportion of the total free population of Italy.

The scale of the conflicts between 91 and 78 BC would not be replicated until Caesar's civil war of 49 BC. But there were other periods of major violence. The revolt of Catiline may have been short-lived, but Catiline did raise an army and a battle was fought. In addition, we have periods of street violence in Rome, of which only the major outbreaks are listed in Table 1.2. The regularity of such outbreaks suggests that the Romans had become accustomed to resolving political problems through violence, though we cannot say that street violence was ever the norm in Roman political life. Nevertheless, the Romans knew that the business of politics could result in corpses in the street, and the use of violence was not necessarily to the detriment of a politician's political reputation. Indeed, in some instances, the perpetrators of violence were treated as heroes of the Republic.

The violence of the late Republic established a mode of political life that is completely unfamiliar to Western democracies. The repression of the two brothers, Tiberius Sempronius Gracchus and Gaius Sempronius Gracchus in the late second century marked an escalation in civic violence. The brothers were opposed by men in the senate who objected to their programme of distributing public land to the Roman poor and, perhaps more strenuously, to their attempts to extend the political power that they had secured through their tenure of the position of tribune. Tiberius Gracchus was killed when an assembly turned violent. First, his supporters took control of the assembly, then, their opponents, perhaps reinforced by members of the aristocracy and their retainers, counter-attacked and drove the Gracchans across the centre of Rome. The aristocracy were perhaps shocked by the initial outbreak of violence and saw it as confirmation that Tiberius Gracchus was aiming for revolution and attempting to establish himself as a tyrant. It seems probable that the rioters laid hold of what they could (there were wooden benches in the assembly that could easily be broken up and turned into staves), and there were fatalities: Tiberius Gracchus himself was caught and beaten to death.

One might imagine that the murder of a tribune and the son of one of the great families of Rome would give the Roman political class reason to reflect.

But there is no evidence that the aristocratic factions doubted the rectitude of their behaviour. There was no sense of shock or of the need to heal the political wounds after the event. In fact, the victors celebrated their triumph and the losers mourned their losses. It was a brutal political world. This lack of shared communal values was exposed a decade later when Gaius Gracchus, Tiberius's younger brother, revived the Gracchan programme. Gaius had more success, but eventually he ran up against a consul, Opimius, who was determined to reverse the Gracchan legislation. This time, when the conflict came, everyone was expecting street violence. The Gracchans seem to have been reluctant to fight, perhaps thinking that the odds were against them and that the aristocracy could mobilise their supporters more effectively. Nevertheless, they entered the forum prepared for a riot. What they did not know was that the consul had taken the precaution of securing the services of a band of archers. The rioters may have equipped themselves with staves and perhaps even knives, but they did not carry armour and the unexpected intervention of the archers was decisive.

This time, the murder of the tribune was not an unfortunate consequence of the rioting, but a planned outcome. The consul even offered a reward for Gaius Gracchus's head: the weight of the head in gold. When the head was presented, it was found to be surprisingly heavy. The brain had been removed and the skull filled with lead. The reward was paid.

There were other major outbreaks of violence. In 100 BC, the consul called upon the leading general of the day, Gaius Marius, to repress the tribune Saturninus. Saturninus had been one of Marius's allies, but, in a testament of the political conservatism of the great general, Marius obeyed the instruction, gathered his veteran troops, and marched on Saturninus. A decade later, the consul Sulla was driven from Rome by a riotous mob and then deprived of a command promised to him. He responded by gathering his legions and marching on the city. A battle was fought through the streets of Rome and many of Sulla's enemies were killed. In the fluctuating fortunes of the next years, whichever power was in charge of Rome made use of their power to purge the city of their opponents. Sulla invented the process of proscription whereby a list of enemies was published; the lives and property of these individuals were forfeit and rewards were given to any who brought in evidence of the murder of the proscribed.

After the suppression of Lepidus in 78 BC, the sequence of civil conflicts in Italy was brought to an end, temporarily. The civil war, however, continued outside Italy, where a refugee from the Sulla, Quintus Sertorius, led a long and mostly successful resistance in Spain until the Sertorians were eventually defeated by Gaius Pompeius in 71. Italy, however, was not at yet peace since a Thracian slave by the name of Spartacus launched a rebellion in 73 BC and defied and defeated various armies sent against him until 71 BC, when Licinius Crassus crushed the most famous slave revolt in history. The ending of these wars may have led to a new sense of optimism in 70 BC, a year which saw the consulships of the two great generals of the conflicts, Crassus and Pompey. But the civic peace was to last only seven years.

In 63 BC, the consul Cicero detected a conspiracy to overthrow the state. It is difficult to reconstruct the form of the conspiracy from our partial sources, but its key component appears to have been to murder Cicero and replace him with Catiline. This coup was to be supported by military forces raised by Catiline and his allies. Detected at a relatively early stage, the Rome segment of the conspiracy was easily defeated and Cicero was able to arrest most of the leading figures in the conspiracy. There then followed a debate as to what to do with these prisoners. Cato, a paragon of moral rectitude, favoured immediate execution. Julius Caesar favoured imprisonment until after the end of the war and then trial. Cicero favoured the Catonian option. The debate turned on fundamental principles of Roman politics: was it right to revoke the civil rights of citizens and summarily execute those who were perceived to be a threat to the Roman state or should the rights of the citizens, even of those who were seemingly attempting to overthrow the political order, be maintained? Caesar's argument was not that violence could not be used to defend the state (of all men Caesar was not a pacifist), but that these individuals, secured as they were, did not present a clear and immediate danger to the state, and thus could, for the moment, be spared. Caesar lost the debate. Cicero executed the prisoners and after the subsequent crushing the army raised by Catiline, Cicero was honoured as a 'parens patriae', a parent of the state.

The execution of the Catilinarians would come back to haunt Roman politics. Although Cicero celebrated his victory and the conservatives in the senate were reinforced in their hold on political authority, some Romans were dismayed at the ease with which magistrates killed Roman citizens and there was a political reaction from at least some of the citizens. That reaction resulted in the temporary exile of Cicero following a violent campaign led by the tribune Clodius. Cicero was soon to return, but the impression that the conservative senators were disposed towards the violent removal of their enemies was reinforced by the subsequent murder of Clodius.

The most serious consequence of Cicero's actions, however, and one which was eventually to bring an end to the Republic itself, was on the position of Julius Caesar. Caesar was a politician prone to taking risks. As a young man in the aftermath of Sulla's victory in the civil wars, Caesar had refused to repudiate his Marian connection, causing his temporary inclusion on the list of the proscribed. In the debate on the fate of the Catilinarians, Caesar had stood for civil liberties in the most difficult of circumstances. He was in considerable danger of being seen as a sympathiser of Catiline and finding himself swept up in the anxieties and paranoia that follow on from such events. That he managed to come away from that debate with his life and that he continued a form of friendship with Cicero are testament to his very great political skills.

Nevertheless, in 59 BC, when Caesar was consul, he formed a powerful political alliance between himself, Licinius Crassus, and Gaius Pompeius. This alliance has come to be known as the First Triumvirate, but it was unlike the (Second) Triumvirate proper in that was not a formal or magisterial arrangement, but a convenient pooling of political resources to achieve certain clearly defined political aims. This alliance was deeply unpopular with the more conservative senators and Caesar forced through certain laws against the bitter but ultimately ineffectual opposition of many senior senators.

After his consulship, Caesar left Rome for a decade. His ten years in Gaul brought Caesar military glory, many friends and allies, and enormous wealth. But the key question that Rome faced was how to accommodate Caesar on his return. Caesar feared that his many powerful political enemies in Rome would act against him. He sought protection, but the senators were unwilling to provide him with guarantees and Pompey, perhaps the leading power in Roman politics at the time, appears to have been determined that Caesar would have at least a period in which he was subject to the laws (as was the constitutional custom). Negotiations broke down and the tribunes who had been representing Caesar's cause fled the city, fearing violence. Caesar, presumably seeing no other means by which his security and status, and the security and status of his supporters, could be guaranteed, crossed the small river dividing his province from Italy, the Rubicon, and another civil war commenced.

Caesar's civil war was the direct result of the continuous violence of Roman politics and especially the way in which the Roman political elite had confirmed their pre-eminence by the use of violence over the previous century. Caesar could not be confident that should he return to Rome without his army that he would not suffer the same fate that had befallen the Gracchi, Saturninus, the Marians, Lepidus, Catiline, and Clodius. In the absence of credible protection, Caesar launched a civil war.

Caesar's enemies were in a similar political bind. Caesar was a mighty politician with a track record of violence and constitutional improprieties (to put it no more seriously). To allow him to return to Rome with special privileges would have been to acknowledge that he was in some way above the law, but it would also have given credence to the idea that at least some in the political elite were predisposed to violent politics. The constitutionalism of Roman civic life may have been something of a myth, but it a myth that held together the Roman political order. The senators probably felt that they too had few choices.

Of course, Caesar won the war and went on to establish his political control of Rome. He took the title of dictator, but he forgave many of his enemies. Caesar's problem was that his position was politically unstable. In March 44 BC, the conservative senators responded in a traditional way to someone who threatened their hegemony: they assassinated Caesar and in so doing, they hoped, restored the Republic. They were proved entirely wrong.

After Caesar's death

The history of the Republic and, indeed, of the Empire is normally told through the eyes of the senators. The senators were, as we explored above, the leading members of a political class in a social system in which political, social and economic power were closely intertwined. Since the upper classes of Roman society were the ones who produced and consumed the literature of the period (most of the historians of the period were senators, though the poets tended to be from less elevated backgrounds), it is only the perspectives of the elite that have come down to us. That is no reason in itself to reject those views, but we must recognise that senators had a particular position within Roman society and had, as we have seen, been brought up to view certain aspects of the organisation of their society as part of the natural order. We may take a different position.

The common-sense view of reading historical sources is that we gather the relevant sources together, read and compare them all, and decide which is most truthful. The problem with such a view is that sources may be blind to particular aspects of their society. They take certain arrangements as obvious, true, and, indeed, as common sense, when they are nothing of the sort.

The Roman political classes regarded it as natural that they should be in charge. Crucially, they identified the success of the Roman Republic with their political authority. Liberty was, for them, the fundamental attribute of the Roman Republic system, but liberty meant that the senators were acknowledged in their authority, an authority which they saw as vested in a history that stretched back over five centuries. The people's contribution to the system was the election of magistrates, but it was the senators and the senatorial magistrates who governed.

For many of the senators, the assassination of Caesar was a restoration of liberty. Caesar clearly exercised unusual power within the Roman state and there were issues as to whether he respected the senators and their views and whether his political power was compatible with the traditions of the Republic. Of his assassins, Brutus especially has been lauded by tradition and throughout the Roman Imperial period, he was seen as a hero who lost his life in defence of Republican liberty. The propaganda of the assassins made great play on liberty, picturing the freedman's cap and a dagger on their coinage.

Yet, not everyone took the same view as the assassins. Caesar's assassination was represented very differently by Mark Antony, Lepidus, and Octavian (the triumvirs) in 43 BC. In that year, they issued a decree in which they condemned the assassins for their murder of Caesar. Julius Caesar was portrayed as a hero. He was a magistrate of Rome, a great general, the *pontifex maximus* (one of the more important priests in Rome). Caesar was a man who spared many of his enemies and should have secured their gratitude. He had not engaged in a reign of terror. He had not murdered his enemies, seduced their wives, or abused his power. He was a man about to engage in a great campaign against the Parthians in the East. Yet, he had been murdered in the senate house. This was an offence against normal political relations in which friends should support each other (not kill each other), against the honour that should be given to a magistrate, and against the dignity (*dignitas*) of Caesar himself as a man who had performed great services for the city. Furthermore, the murder of Caesar was one further example of the senators using violence rather than legal or constitutional means to rid themselves of a threat to their power. The triumvirs represented the murder of Caesar as evidence that these particular senators could not be trusted and needed to be crushed before normal politics could be resumed.

Of course, the triumvirs' presentation of their righteous anger simplified political reactions to the death of Caesar. Although many of the senators themselves were jubilant, the senate was divided. Crucially, Caesar's deputy, Mark Antony, was consul at the time and thus effectively in control of the formal meetings of the senate and much of the governmental machinery. He had many friends and allies among the senators, and they certainly had support among the governors of the provinces (men who controlled large armies). Yet, the immediate aftermath of Caesar's death was notable for its lack of action. The senators who had been supporters of Caesar did not rally to his cause. There was no Caesarian party that gathered to revenge themselves on the assassins. The assassins and Mark Antony regarded each other with great suspicion, but they were not at war, at least not initially. The generals in the provinces did not gather their troops and march on Rome.

This inaction tells us something fundamental about Roman politics. It is difficult to imagine that in the face of such a coup, there would not be immediate violence consequences in most modern states. But Rome paused. There was no Caesarian party. What had bound together the supporters of Julius Caesar was a personal loyalty to the man. Crucially, that loyalty did not go beyond the exchange of friendship and favours with the great dictator. Once Caesar had been removed, the social and political relationship was broken. There was no institution or ideology to which these men could give their loyalty. Caesar's programme of reforms, such as they had been, was focused on administration and religion and were far from a radical political agenda, and certainly did not represent an ideology. With Caesar dead, the politicians started remaking their political relationships and forming new alliances.

There are two central examples of this process. Decimus Brutus was one of the foremost of the assassins (he was not a close relation of the leading figure in the conspiracy, Junius Brutus). Decimus Brutus was a trusted friend of Caesar. At the time of the assassination, he was about to be posted to the militarily crucial province of Cisalpine Gaul (Gallic territory on the Italian side of the Alps). Honoured by Caesar, it might have been expected that Decimus Brutus would respect his friendship with the dictator. Yet, Decimus Brutus was both involved in the assassination and was then to take a leading position in the military operations that followed. His loyalty to the senatorial cause was unquestioned.

Munatius Plancus was governor in Gaul when Caesar was assassinated. He was leading legions which were certainly well disposed to the Caesarian cause, but as the political tensions of 44 BC turned into military confrontation, Plancus was to show himself loyal to the senatorial cause. Even when the military situation seemed to have turned against the senators, in the West at least, Plancus remained loyal. Yet, at the end, when faced by overwhelming Caesarian armies, Plancus made his peace with the Caesarians. Having shown no loyalty to Julius Caesar or his heirs, one might have expected that Plancus would be deposed and spend the rest of his life in quiet retirement (if he was lucky), but instead he remained a central political figure and leading general throughout the triumviral period.

Yet more surprising are the actions of the young Octavian, who was to become the emperor Augustus. Octavian was the nephew of Julius Caesar and was named as heir in Caesar's will. In the personal world of Roman politics, this was a somewhat ambivalent position. He was heir to Caesar's personal estate, but that brought no political office, nor, in fact, any particular expectation of political office. Nevertheless, as Caesar's heir, Octavian was responsible for meeting the various bequests listed in Caesar's will, which included bequests to the Roman people. Octavian set about securing the means by which to pay those bequests and also establishing a personal relationship with Caesar's veterans who had been settled in communities (colonies) throughout Italy. The payment of the bequests was an offer of political friendship that established a relationship between the plebs and Octavian and between Caesar's veterans and Octavian. Yet, there is no suggestion that Octavian inherited the loyalty of the plebs or of the veterans and, indeed, it is clear that many veterans especially showed no loyalty to Octavian and preferred to support Octavian's enemies.

Octavian was born in August 63 BC and was a youth when Caesar was assassinated. He was certainly not regarded as sufficiently mature to embark on a political career. Yet, from his arrival in Rome, he started making political speeches and claiming that he was Caesar's heir in a more than personal context. Nevertheless, his alliances seem to contradict this political position. His closest initial ally was the senator Cicero. When the assassins had left the bloodied body of Caesar, they had supposedly cried out, 'For Cicero!' Cicero had not, in fact, been part of the conspiracy, but after the assassination he identified himself with the assassins' cause and worked in their interests.

However, Octavian and Cicero were to co-operate closely. Cicero lavished praise on the young man and Octavian paid court to Cicero. Cicero appears to have hoped that he could negotiate a resolution of the differences between Junius Brutus and Octavian, and Octavian was to lead an army against Mark Antony. Clearly, neither Octavian nor Cicero regarded Octavian's position as being in any way paradoxical. Caesar's heir could fight alongside Caesar's assassins.

What does this tell us about Roman politics among the elite?

We can conclude that

- Roman politics was personal rather than ideological
- Personal alliances were flexible
- Alliances were not inherited

In light of these assumptions, the expectations of the assassins become clearer. Once Caesar was dead, it was expected that Caesar's political group would dissolve. It was expected that, perhaps after a period of uncertainty, the normal workings of the Republic (which meant senatorial government) would resume. To a certain extent, they were right. Senators remade their political positions in the aftermath of the assassination. Yet, this view of politics was crucially and fatally limited. It took no account of other actors on the Roman political scene.

Soldiers and plebs

In the shocked aftermath of Caesar's assassination, it was the plebs of Rome who were first to show their violent feelings: they rioted. The political motivations of the plebs are not easily understood, since we never have any representative opinions from them. The plebs has shown in 44 BC that they were not monarchists. When Mark Antony had offered Caesar a diadem at a festival, the assembled plebs had expressed their displeasure. Caesar's reforms may have offered some support for the plebs, through an improvement in the distribution of grain, but he had himself acted roughly towards the tribunes when they had opposed him. Caesar had, nevertheless, consistently courted popular support throughout his career and in that sense he could be seen as a 'friend' to the plebs. The demonstration of the plebs may have been as much a demonstration against the assassins as for Caesar and, significantly, it was suppressed by Mark Antony as consul.

The attitude of the plebs raised the political temperature in Rome and may have been sufficient for Antony to be able to persuade the assassins to leave Rome. He assigned Junius Brutus and Cassius duties outside the city and Decimus Brutus left to travel to his province.

Perhaps more significant was the attitude of the veterans. Yet here again the actions of the veterans are surprising. We are often told that the legions were ferocious in their loyalty to Caesar. We might have expected men who had fought with Caesar in Gaul and had campaigned with him in the civil war would seek immediate revenge on Caesar's assassins. Although they had no obvious political leadership, Caesar had probably settled his veterans according to the legions in which they served. The new communities will have preserved something of the military organisation of their service. They had leaders. But they did not move. The legions of the provinces, many of whom had served under Caesar, similarly did nothing. Nobody moved. Later, when war broke out, many of the legions did not declare.

This can again lead us to certain fundamental conclusions. However loyal the soldiers and the plebs had been to Caesar in life, this loyalty did not extended to Caesar in death. They had no political position or cause to which to rally. The death of Caesar may have given rise to considerable uncertainties, but the soldiers showed no immediate interest in exploiting those uncertainties.

Nevertheless, the veterans did eventually decide that their interests were at stake and they did rally to the Caesarian cause. Their contribution to the political events of the next months was crucial, but it was not consistent. The veterans struggled to identify where their interest lay. Yet, it was clear that they had no particular loyalty to the senators and the assassins, and indeed were suspicious that the senators would work against their interests. The veterans were anxious to secure the land that they had been given by Caesar. Soldiers serving in the legions of this conflict were similarly eager to win rewards promised by their generals. They pursued political courses designed to achieve those goals. Since it was to become apparent that senatorial government threatened those goals, the soldiers encouraged their leaders in the overthrow of senatorial government.

Such actions have traditionally been denigrated and the motivations of the soldiers have be seen as ignoble when compared with Brutus's actions in favour of liberty and Cicero's defence of the Republic. However, we must take account of the realities of the soldiers' lives.

The soldiers were probably mostly recruited from the rural poor of Italy. The archaeology of poverty is, of course, much more limited than the archaeology of wealth. The poor simply had less material that could be preserved in the archaeological record. One would even presume that much of the housing of the rural was poorly constructed, perhaps made of rough stone and wood, and thus very difficult to spot in an archaeological environment. When we do find the rural poor, it is sometimes because of state intervention: the land settlement programmes of the late Republic not only laid out the divisions of land, in a process known as centuriation, and designed the urban centres of the new communities, but also sometimes provided at least the basics of the rural housing. The concrete foundations of these houses (regular and far better built than we would expect from the pottery and other material culture that survives) can be detected archaeological. What they show is that the plots on which the rural poor were settled were extraordinarily small, barely enough to support a family. For all the schemes of poverty alleviation through the provision of land for the poor, it seems that most land redistribution policies (there are exceptions in Northern Italy) were designed to provide subsistence level support. The absolute poverty of the rural poor meant that it was essential for families to secure additional resources and income, and one of the most obvious resources was military service.

The majority of Italy was politically unified only in the first decade of the first century BC after the Social War. This political unification did not, of course, mean that the communities were unified in feeling. Long into the Imperial period, there is good evidence of strong local identities. One struggles to imagine that the myths and history of Rome itself had much emotional hold on the residents of many Italian communities. Furthermore, Rome did little to welcome the new citizens of Italy. As we have seen, Rome was hardly a democracy and the political structures of Rome remained those of a city state. For a citizen to exercise their vote, they needed to travel to Rome and be present in the assemblies. Furthermore, Italians would have to know what was happening in Rome and to decide whether it was worth the journey. One imagines, then, that to the extent that any non-Roman residents exercised their vote in Rome, there would be a strong bias towards those with sufficient wealth and leisure to inform themselves of events and to make the journey. It is clear from the physical spaces available for voting in Rome that if anything more than a tiny proportion of the Roman citizenry decided to turn up to vote, the Roman assemblies would have been swamped. We need to understand the accounts of politics in the late Republic in the context of the actual and effective voting public as being potentially very small. Of course, the smaller the voting public, the more easily controlled they are.

The majority of the Italian population had little or no political or emotional stake in the Republic of Rome. Citizenship brought certain protections from Roman magistrates and probably altered the relationship between the citizens and levy of troops for the army. But other than those very important practical issues, it did not make the Italians members of the Roman political community.

The soldiers who served in the Republican Roman legions served not for patriotism or duty (however much later elite authors made of such qualities), but for money and to secure a livelihood for themselves and a future for their families. Their political actions in the aftermath of the death of Caesar focused not on revenge for their former leader and still less on any programme that he may have represented, but on securing the interests of the soldiers themselves. They had little or no loyalty to the senate. The senators themselves were an obvious threat to the property the veterans had managed to secure from Julius Caesar.

Rome's revolution: the triumvirate

After Caesar's murder in March, it took nearly until the end of the year for the political situation to clarify. A central character in the story is Mark Antony, who had been consul in Rome on Caesar's death. As consul, he was legally at least the senior magistrate in the city and he made every effort to draw his fellow consul, Dolabella, into his camp. At first, relations between the assassins, the senators and Antony and his supporters were tense, but neither side took action against the other. By the summer, however, Antony was seeking military support, securing the legions that Caesar had gathered for a campaign in the East and bringing them back to Italy. At the same time, the assassins were arming themselves: Junius Brutus and Cassius went to the Roman provinces in the East and Decimus Brutus went to Gaul. Once Antony had legionary forces in Italy, he moved against Decimus Brutus, passing a decree of the people to depose Decimus Brutus from his province. The province was transferred to Antony's control. This would provide Antony with a military base within striking distance of Rome.

Decimus Brutus was unwilling to give up such a strategic prize and decided to resist Antony from the city of Mutina in Northern Italy. Antony gathered the legions from Brundisium in the South, and prepared to march to claim his province. On the way, however, he suffered a mutiny and lost a legion. He more than compensated for this loss by recruiting from Caesar's veterans, but the mutinous legion was to form the core of the army that Octavian was seeking to raise. In December 44 BC, Antony laid siege to Mutina.

From December 44 and through the early months of 43, Antony's political enemies were mobilising in Rome. They were led by Cicero, who was one of the most experienced politicians of the city. Cicero had considerable trouble persuading many of the senators of the danger posed by Antony. Antony was, after all, a friend to at least some of them; he had been in effective control of Rome since March 44 BC without there being any catastrophic breach in Roman law and order, and, probably, most importantly, the Roman elite feared the civil war which would inevitably follow any move against Antony. Cicero's task was to persuade the political elite that Antony was such a danger to the safety and position of the Roman political elite that they should risk all on a civil war. Yet, the elite had experience of losing civil wars and were understandably reluctant.

Cicero wished Antony to be declared a public enemy and for the consuls of 43 BC, together with Octavian, to march on Mutina and save the city from Antony. Cicero's argument was that Antony needed to be deprived of his civic rights because he posed a threat to the civic rights of the Roman people. Yet, it was Cicero himself who had the track record of extra-judicial executions. The great orator had set himself a difficult rhetorical task. This task he carried out through a number of viciously vitriolic personal attacks on Antony, which are known collectively as the *Philippics*. These have some claim to be Cicero's greatest rhetorical works.

Nevertheless, it seems unlikely that the senators would have been naïve enough to be persuaded by Ciceronian brilliance. The choices were stark and relatively simple, as they often are in civil war. The senators needed to decide whether Antony posed a serious threat to their political hegemony and a threat sufficient to justify violence. They would have been aware that, legally, Antony was in the right. He was empowered to deposed Decimus

Brutus by a decree of the people and the people were sovereign. However much they might dislike it, a decree of the senate was not sufficient to overturn a decree of the people. Antony was, of course, not shy in pointing this out, nor in pointing to Cicero's track record of violence. Perhaps more to the point, they needed to be persuaded that if they went to war with Antony, they would win.

Octavian's presence in the alliance was probable crucial. He brought with him Caesarian legions and some of Caesar's veterans. Although we cannot directly know the motivation of the Caesarian troops who had joined Octavian's cause, we may imagine that they were persuaded that Antony, ultimately, did not have their best interests at heart (Antony had been notably authoritarian when he had met his legions in late 44 BC, executing several soldiers who had expressed opposition) and that they had more to gain from the young Octavian. Octavian had been assiduous in courting the veterans and firm in his support for their cause. It was clear that Octavian's power depended on the troops. Octavian needed them and could therefore be relied upon to act in their interests. Octavian had also promised lavish payments to those who supported him. Octavian's Caesarians, then, could be used as a counter to Antony's veteran troops.

Equally important was the indecision of Caesar's old generals. None of them had declared. The legions in Gaul, Spain, and North Africa would tip the strategic balance. If they had declared for Antony, the senators would be outnumbered. Yet, in December 44, those generals had individually to make the same calculation as the senators: the consequences of being on the wrong side of a civil war were fatal.

Whatever the thought processes of the senators, eventually they were persuaded to move against Antony. They declared him and his troops enemies of Rome and instructed the consuls and Octavian to defend the Republic. At the same time, they legalised the armies being raised by Junius Brutus and Cassius. War was declared.

In March 43, Octavian and the two consuls led armies into battle against Antony at Mutina. After two battles, Antony broke camp and marched North. The senatorial generals declared victory. Cicero led the celebrations in Rome; the senators announced a thanksgiving to celebrate the end of the war. Their celebrations were premature.

The two consuls had been killed in the battles of Mutina. After the battle, Octavian retreated into camp with his legions and would not move again until after the summer, during which time he continued to attract soldiers to his cause. Decimus Brutus gathered the senatorial forces and set off after Antony, but he was a long way behind. Antony met up with reinforcements gathered from Italy by his friend Ventidius and marched into Gaul to meet the legions gathering there.

The governor Lepidus, a close associate of Caesar, failed to decide which side to back. He marched very, very slowly on Antony and sent reassuring letters back to Cicero. Antony, however, had connections with the officers in Lepidus' army. One evening, after Lepidus had gone to bed, messages were sent to Antony. Lepidus woke in the morning to find Antony in his camp talking with his troops. As Lepidus approached, Antony welcomed him and offered him an alliance.

By May 43 BC, Antony was the dominant power in Gaul. His legions were more experienced and stronger than those of the senatorial armies. He appears to have been reluctant to move against the senate in this period, perhaps hoping for further defections that would make fighting unnecessary.

The balance of power shifted decisively towards the end of July. Octavian's troops sent an embassy to the senators in Rome, asking for the money that was promised to them. The senators sent some money, but not all that had been requested. Another embassy followed which demanded that Octavian be made consul, the two vacancies having yet to be filled. The senators refused and the debate became heated. The soldiers returned to the camp. Their colleagues were informed of the attitude of the senators. Octavian divided his troops into two columns and they set out to Rome.

There can be little doubt that the soldiers' embassy to the senate was an attempt to secure for themselves political power: with Octavian as consul, they would obtain their rewards and security in the benefits offered to them by Octavian and those which had previously been obtained from Julius Caesar. Equally surely, the senators resisted in order to maintain their control of the levers of power in Rome. Astonishingly, it seems never to have occurred to the senators that their refusal might have dire consequences and, in the circumstances of civil war, insulting the representatives of an army of perhaps 60,000 men was unwise. The misjudgement of the senators (and they were led in this by Cicero) would seem to reflect their absolute confidence in their political authority and their right to rule Rome.

As soon as Octavian's army appeared on the outskirts of Rome, the political reality dawned. Whatever the histories and traditions of Rome, however the Roman elite chose to dress up their political hegemony in the language of constitutionalism and tradition, they had maintained their political power over the previous century through irregular but frequent violent interventions. Political power came at the point of a sword and, in late 43 BC, those sword points were directed not by the senators, but at them.

The military coup brought Octavian to power and the soldiers established their control over Rome. There could, however, be no doubt that a lasting settlement would require Octavian to hold power for longer than the remaining months of the year. The conservative senators would hardly forgive the young man for his actions. He needed to reconcile himself with Antony. In a similar fashion, Antony needed to work with Octavian. Brutus and Cassius had enjoyed a period of military and political success in the East and had gathered substantial armies. Antony and Octavian needed to face that challenge together. The scene was set for a reconciliation.

Lepidus, Antony and Octavian met at Mutina. There they agreed to bury their differences and prepared the ground for a political alliance that would reshape Roman politics. On 27th November 43 BC, the tribune Titius passed a law which brought into being three new magisterial positions. The *Lex Titia* created the *triumviri rei publicae constituendae*. We may translate the magistracy as the 'Three Men for the Constitution of the Republic'. Although we have little idea of how long the law was, it is perhaps most likely to have been brief. It granted Antony, Lepidus, and Octavian absolute authority, above and beyond the law, for a period of five years. This was justified as an emergency position, as dictatorships had been justified in the past. The Republic was broken and needed to be remade. It was this emergency that required the suspension of all constitutional laws and civic rights.

The triumvirate was, in fact, to last for a decade and only ended as Antony and Octavian began the political disputes that led to the battle of Actium. Table 1.3 lists the main events of this period.

Table 1.3 Political events: 43–31 BC

Date	Event
43 January	Hirtius and Pansa become consuls
43 February	Senate declares war on Antony
43 April 14th	First Battle of Mutina
43 April 21st	Second Battle of Mutina; Hirtius killed
43 April 22nd	Antony leaves Mutina
43 April (late)	Pansa dies
43 May 5th	Antony joins forces with Ventidius
43 May 30th	Legions of Lepidus defect to Antony
43 July–August	Octavian's legionaries send embassies to Rome
43 August (early)	Octavian's march on Rome
43 August 19th	Octavian elected as consul
43 August to November	Decimus Brutus murdered in Gaul
	Senatorial resistance in Gaul ended
	Antony, Lepidus and Octavian meet at Bononia
43 November 27th	*Lex Titia* established the Triumvirate
43 November 28th	Proscriptions begin
42	Julius Caesar deified
	Battles of Philippi (October)
	Suicides of Brutus and Cassius
41	Consulship of Lucius Antonius
	Mark Antony meets Cleopatra
	Outbreak of the Perusine War
	Lucius Antonius besieged in Perusia by Octavian
40	Fall of Perusia
	Antony returns to Italy and war with Octavian averted
	War between Antony and the Parthians

Table 1.3 continued

Date	Event
39	Antony marries Octavia
38	War between Octavian and Sextus Pompeius
	Antony campaigns against the Parthians
36	Octavian invades Sicily and Sextus Pompeius defeated
	Lepidus deprived of triumviral office
35	Death of Sextus Pompeius
34	Antony celebrates victory over the Parthians at the
	'Donations of Alexandria'
33	Octavian consul
32	Consuls for the year flee Rome to Antony
	Antony and Octavia divorce
	War between Antony and Octavian
31	Octavian and Antony consuls
	Battle of Actium (3rd September)
30	Octavian Consul
30 August 1st	Octavian captures Alexandria
	Antony commits suicide
30 August 10th	Cleopatra commits suicide
29	Octavian Consul
29 August	Octavian celebrates triumphs in Rome; Temple of Divus
	Julius dedicated; new senate house dedicated
28	Octavian and Agrippa Consuls

The triumviral period causes historians problems. These problems are fundamental to the understanding of this period and relate very closely to the formation of the Principate in 28 or 27 BC, which will be discussed in the next chapter. These problems are:

- What is the relationship between the events of the triumviral period and the Republic?
- What is the relationship between the triumviral period and the Principate?

These problems relate to issues of periodicity, meaning the manner in which historians divide historical periods. The triumvirate is often seen as the last of the bloody events of the Republic and an intermediate or transitional period between Republic and Empire. In 28 and 27 BC, Octavian set about a radical revision and reform of the political order. As part of this reform, Octavian took a new name, Augustus.

Historians have traditionally praised the Age of Augustus, valuing its political and cultural achievements. Yet, the triumvirate has been subjected to no such praise. Even when one reads the account of Augustus in Suetonius' biography, there is a strong sense that the young Octavian's career is marked by extremes of violence and hostility towards Rome's established order, whereas the career of Augustus is that of a conservative and moral statesman beloved of his peers, and trusted to provide the order that Rome seemed to so very much need. The historian Cassius Dio divides his account of Roman history between the world of Republican violence and the world of monarchic imperial order. The transition occurs in 27 BC (perhaps 30–27 BC). Octavian/ Augustus emerges as an almost schizophrenic figure, brutal in his youth and conservative in his maturity.

Yet, there can be no such absolute division. When the senators of 27 BC voted Octavian his new name, they did not forget the triumviral leader and the astonishing violence of the previous decade. Furthermore, the triumviral period was remembered as a trauma of Roman history. The historian Appian, who wrote a history of Rome's civil wars, devoted page after page (Appian, *Civil Wars*, 4.8–45) to stories from the triumviral proscriptions. Cassius Dio gives similarly extensive coverage to events (Cassius Dio, 47.3–14). Valerius Maximus, a lesser-known figure who compiled a number of moralistic tales (possibly for use by orators or writers of moralising accounts) returned again and again to the proscriptions for their tales of violence and betrayal, of greed and lust, and conversely, of loyalty and familial devotion (see Valerius Maximus, *Factorum et Dictorum Memorabilium* (*Memorable Deeds and Sayings*), notably, 5.3.4; 5.7.3; 6.7.2; 6.7.5–7; 7.3.8; 9.11.6–8). The senators and indeed everyone else will have remembered the violence of Octavian whenever they were in the presence of Augustus.

We need to think about the significance of the violence. Rome may have been at the heart of a great empire, but the Roman elite was a small political community. The aristocracy was a tightly-knit group, bound together by ties of friendship and family and the shared experiences of lives spent working closely together. When Antony, Lepidus, and Octavian arrived in Rome, they posted lists of men they counted as public enemies and rewards for the delivery of their heads. Numbers vary. Appian (*Civil Wars* 4.5) reports the number of victims as having been 2,000 equestrians and 300 senators. These numbers may be an exaggeration: it was not in the interests of the triumvirs to keep accurate records of those that they killed. Livy (*Periochae* 120) has an initial list of 130 proscribed, but there was a second list of 150 (Dio, 47.3) and the listings were subject to regular revisions.[1] There are various figures given for the number of men in the senate, and the traditional numbers of the late Republic may have been boosted when Caesar elevated some of his supporters to the senate, but it seems unlikely that the number of senators would ever have crept much above 600. Some escaped, but many, including Cicero, did not. The proscriptions turned slave against master, wife against husband, son against father, neighbour against neighbour. Stories circulated that personal enmities could be settled by asking a triumvir to include someone on a list. Antony supposedly removed someone from the list when the victim's wife offered herself to Antony. One man was included because he had refused to sell an apartment block to Antony's wife Fulvia. Others were listed because of their wealth since the triumvirs were desperate for money and the easiest source of cash was to confiscate the estates of the wealthy.

The deaths and displacement caused by the proscriptions were just one part of the civil conflicts that were to grip Rome. The proscriptions brought an end to a phase of the civil war that had begun with Antony at Mutina and opened another phase in which the triumvirs came into conflict with the assassins. That was to end at the Battle of Philippi in 42 BC, when 200,000 men lined up to fight. After the defeat of Brutus and Cassius, Octavian had personally condemned to death many of the elite who had fought alongside Brutus and Cassius (Suetonius, *Augustus*, 13). After Philippi, a further civil war broke out when Octavian fought Lucius Antonius, Mark Antony's brother, in a dispute which probably had at its heart the colonisation programmes by which Octavian and Antony gave land to their veterans. The Perusine war ended with a siege. Octavian again massacred the Perusines and the equestrians and senators who had sided with Lucius Antonius (Appian, *Civil Wars*, 5.48–49; Dio, 48.14.4; Suetonius, *Augustus*, 15). Stories of human sacrifice circulated.

With the defeat of Lucius Antonius, Octavian was able to go ahead with a programme of land settlement that displaced unknown numbers of Italians from the land. In the aftermath of the Perusine war, Octavian turned his attention to Sextus Pompeius, the son of Pompey the Great. Sextus had continued his father's war against Caesar and had established quasi-autonomous zones, first in Spain and later in Sicily, from where he could launch naval attacks on the Caesarians. Sextus was probably reinforced by those who fled Italy in the late 40s, but from 38–36 Octavian drove him from Sicily.

We cannot know how many Romans were killed or displaced in these wars. Yet, it is obvious that the losses were great and that the social disruption was enormous. There was also a huge transfer of resources from the landed and wealthy to the soldiers. There are not many numbers in Ancient History and those that do exist cannot be easily understood, but it is worth thinking about some of the financial values reported during of the triumviral period. The rewards promised to the 43 legions would suggest a distribution of about 3,870,000,000 *sesterces*. This amount is likely to have been about 43 times the normal military pay budget (see pp. 316–18) and since paying for troops was the major drain on Rome's treasury, wealth equivalent to many times the total budget of the Roman state was distributed to the troops.[2] In a society in which wealth was very unevenly distributed, the wealth of an average senator probably fell somewhat below 5,000,000 *sesterces*. The rewards promised to individual soldiers (20,000 *sesterces*) were far greater than the annual wage of a soldier (900 *sesterces*) which was probably a reasonable but low income. It would take a soldier more than 22 years to earn that amount. The payments made to individual soldiers transformed their standing.

The triumviral period was one of revolutionary change. In 43 BC, Octavian's troops seized control of Rome. In alliance with Antony and Octavian, the dominance of the soldiers was further enhanced. Although generals had taken control of Rome previously, and the soldiers had been beneficiaries from purges of the Roman elite, the Sullan, Marian, and Caesarian periods of dominance were short-lived and temporary affairs. Under the triumvirs, the overthrow of elite power was allied to a sustained and violent campaign in which many were killed and much property transferred. The soldiers effectively maintained their political control for a decade and ensured that they would be well rewarded for their efforts on behalf of the triumvirs. The soldiers did not, it is true, form a new aristocracy, nor were all elements of the old system done away with, but the interests of the soldiery in the Roman state were maintained and to a great extent the political system was reshaped by the interests of the soldiers, who were fully aware of their political power. Whereas Sulla used his political position to reassert the power of the nobility and Caesar had sought reconciliation and peace with his former enemies in a restored but Caesar-dominated government, the realities of power in the triumviral period meant that it was the soldiers, above all, who counted and wielded authority.

One of the paradoxical issues of the triumvirate is that all the constitutional and institutional infrastructure of the late Republic remained in place. The senate continued to meet under the chairmanship of the consuls. It continued to pass decrees. It continued to supervise the actions of its magistrates. Laws were passed. The triumvirate itself was a legally-constituted entity. Nevertheless, our sources see the period as one of unprecedented revolutionary violence which gave rise to a new age and a new imperial power.

Traditionally, ancient historians are trained to watch for constitutions: they decide whether (using the language of Aristotle) states are democratic or oligarchic or monarchic. Yet, the triumviral period is a warning against constitutional approaches to history. It mattered little that the senate and consuls continued to meet, and that is in part why they were allowed to continue to meet. What mattered was power: who had power and on whose behalf. As we shall see when we look at the political history of the early Empire, it was not the constitutional frameworks (which remained almost entirely Republican) that gave political life its meaning, but how power operated within society.

The violence of the Republic was in part carried over into the Imperial period, emerging notably from the reign of Tiberius onwards. Imperial power may have little constitutional or legal form, but it made itself felt in the conspicuous displays of imperial power that we see with Augustus and Nero, in the near deification of emperors that we see from Tiberius onwards, in the celebration of the relationship between emperor and plebs and between emperor and his troops, that we see with Claudius and Domitian, and in the overwhelming deployment of murderous violence that is such a feature of many of the reigns from AD 14 onwards.

Augustus was no different. He got his killing in first, in the triumviral period. Having worked so hard and killed so many, he was not about to give up power. No source ever suggests that he laid down real power. The soldiers had put Octavian in power and by 28 BC had maintained him there for 15 years. Although the military dependence of his regime may have slipped somewhat into the background (though military imagery still abounds in the Augustan period), he never gave up that gift.

Notes

1 The *Periochae* of Livy is a very brief summary of the contents of the books of his history. One would expect key events to be only partially reported.
2 Appian, *Civil Wars*, 4.3. The calculation is 43 legions of 4,500 men gives us 193,500 soldiers and at 20,000 *sesterces* each makes 3,870,000,000 *sesterces*.

Chapter 2

Augustus (31 BC–AD 14)

Main events of the reign of Augustus

Date	Event
31 BC	Actium.
30	Deaths of Antony and Cleopatra. Annexation of Egypt.
29	Closure of the doors of the temple of Janus. Triple triumph.
27	First Constitutional Settlement.
27-24	Augustus campaigns in Gaul and Spain.
23	Return of Augustus. Second Constitutional Settlement. Death of Marcellus.
22	Conspiracy of Caepio and Murena.
22-19	Augustus in the East.
20	Peace with Parthia.
19	Third Constitutional Settlement.
18	First moral legislation.
17	Adoption of Gaius and Lucius. Saecular games
16	Imperial expansion in the North. Augustus in Gaul.
13	Augustus returns to Rome. Voting of the Ara Pacis. Agrippa leads Augustus' armies on the Danube. Death of Lepidus. Augustus made Pontifex Maximus.
12	Death of Agrippa.
9	Death of Drusus. Dedication of the Ara Pacis.
6	Tiberius made Augustus' colleague and goes into retirement on Rhodes.
5	Gaius Caesar introduced into public life.
2	Lucius Caesar introduced into public life. Dedication of the Forum Augusti. Augustus receives the title *Pater Patriae*. Exile of Julia (the elder) on adultery charges.
AD 1	Gaius sent to the East.
2	Tiberius returns from exile, but takes no official role. Death of Lucius Caesar.
4	Death of Gaius Caesar. Tiberius adopted.
6	Massive revolt in Pannonia. Tiberius leads the Roman forces.
7	Exile of Agrippa Postumus.
8	Exile of the Younger Julia on adultery charges. Exile of Ovid.
9	Varus' legions destroyed in Germany. Tiberius leads Roman reply.
14	Death of Augustus.

Introduction: problems and methods

Augustus is generally regarded as the first Roman emperor and is perhaps the most studied of all Romans. We are fortunate in having an abundance of source material for his reign, some of which is contemporary. Yet, the main narrative account of the reign of Augustus comes in Cassius Dio's history and is not only fragmentary in places but dates from two centuries after the death of Augustus. The major biographical account is that of Suetonius, which was composed a century after Augustus' death. From the time, we have Augustus' own testament to his achievements, *Res Gestae Divi Augusti* (*The Achievements of the Deified Augustus*), which gives an account of his reign, listing donations, awards, successes, priesthoods, constructions, conquests, and many other things, but it is not a narrative account. It is also quite clearly composed to present its author in the best possible light. We also have the writings of a number of contemporary poets who touch on political themes, notably Virgil, Horace, Propertius and Ovid. Augustus or those in his inner circle built numerous monuments in the city of Rome. There is also a considerable number of surviving inscriptions which illustrate different aspects of Augustan Rome. Yet, the abundance of source material does not solve the problems of the reign and, indeed, at least some of the material appears contradictory or paradoxical.

The very importance of Augustus has made the task of interpreting his age more difficult. As the first of the Roman emperors, it is difficult to disassociate his period of power with what we know came later. Augustus is often read with the benefit of hindsight. That hindsight can be used to contrast Augustus with later emperors, a process which can raise Augustus to the status of an ideal against which other emperors are judged. The generally favourable accounts of our ancient sources contrast markedly with the generally hostile accounts we have for virtually every later emperor from Tiberius to Domitian, with the exceptions of Vespasian and the short-lived Titus. Further, since there is very limited evidence of opposition or conspiracy against Augustus over the 44 years of his sole hegemony, it is tempting to understand his reign as having been popular or at the very least having secured the acquiescence of the Roman people and political classes. There is considerable temptation to accept Augustus' self-presentation as a universally popular and respected leader.

Our most influential historian from the early Imperial period, Tacitus, comments only briefly on Augustus, beginning his history of the Julio-Claudians with Tiberius (for reasons which have long escaped modern historians). The exclusion of Augustus from the rather depressing catalogue of political corruption that we find in Tacitus' *Annales*, may have encouraged others to a positive evaluation of the reign. As we shall see, however, Tacitus was critical of Augustus.

A second problem comes from Augustus' position as a founder of the Roman Empire. This identification is, in itself, peculiar. Rome had an empire long before Augustus, and the technical transformation between Republic and Empire has little to do with our usage of the word 'empire'. Whereas we associate 'empire' with a state that has established its political control over a number of formerly-independent states, 'the Empire' for the Romans was the system of rule by emperors. There is an etymological link here through the Latin word 'imperium', which meant authority or power, and *imperator*, someone who wielded power, normally a general. *Imperium* also appears to have been used rather more loosely to mean the territory over which the Romans held power and that, of course, leads to our conception of empire. Augustus is seen as the first emperor and thus the founder of the Imperial period, but he has also been regarded as the man who established a system for governing the empire, setting Rome's empire on a regular administrative course after the rather anarchic Republican period. Yet, there is little evidence to suggest that Augustus was engaged in any radical programme of administrative reform or improvement. Instead, the changes in the administration of the empire appear to have been irregular and piecemeal. Augustus worked with what he found and invented and reformed only when he hit a problem. The result was that the administration of the Roman Empire only gradually became more systematic over the next century. Augustus' reputation as the architect of the Roman Empire seems undeserved.

Nevertheless, the evaluation of Augustus is often confused with the evaluation of Empire. For those historians who view the Roman Empire as a 'good thing', there is a tendency to see Augustus as some form of hero. His political successes brought order to Rome and did bring an end to much of the civil conflict and violence that had afflicted Rome throughout the previous century. A bargain was struck in which the liberties of the Republican period were exchanged for order. The sense of a grand bargain is already present in Tacitus' description of Augustan politics:

> He seduced the army with bonuses, the people with food, the rest with the sweetness of leisure and little by little he took to himself the duties of the senate, the magistracies, and the law, without opposition, since the most fierce had been killed in battle or through the proscriptions, the remainder of the *nobiles*, who were somewhat more ready for servitude, were raised by wealth and honours and, having benefitted from the new order, preferred safety and the present to the old and dangerous. Nor did the provinces reject this state of affairs since they distrusted the imperium of the senate and people on account of the contest of the powerful and the greed of magistrates since the protection of the law were invalidated by force, intrigue and finally money.
>
> Tacitus, *Annales* 1.2

Tacitus emphasises the corruption of the Republic and contrasts it with the security of the Imperial period. Leisure replaced dangerous uncertainties. But the price was the loss of the functions of the senate, magistrates and law, and the political independence of the leading men.

How historians read the Augustan period depends very much on how they read this bargain. Like much in Ancient History, there is not a right or wrong answer here and one's approach will very much reflect one's understanding of how political relationships work. Such bargains have been made throughout history. The great modern political tradition of liberalism turns on the issue of the extent to which the individual should give up his or her innate freedoms to the state in return for protection from disorder. The great dictators of the twentieth century made the same bargain, more or less conscious of their Classical predecessors: the disorders of democracy were replaced by the order of dictatorship, always, obviously, as they claimed, to the benefit of their people.

These resonances affect modern interpretations. Perhaps the most influential of modern accounts was published in 1939 by the New Zealand-born historian Sir Ronald Syme. Syme called his book *The Roman Revolution*, a title which suggested that his readers think of these events in the same light as the communist revolutions and fascist revolutions that dominated contemporary politics. Syme was deeply hostile to both communism and fascism and in a conscious use of these parallels he argued that the revolutionary nature of all these regimes was false: what happened was that one elite was replaced by another elite without there being a social or political transformation. Augustus was explicitly compared with Mussolini, and their politics exposed as vicious claims on power, and little else.[1] This image of Augustus as quasi-fascist dictator had considerable appeal, in part because Mussolini himself made use of the political and cultural imagery of the Roman Empire and, in particular, Julius Caesar and Augustus.

The same associations can be felt throughout the twentieth century, with Paul Zanker's extremely influential lectures and his book, *The Power of Images in the Age of Augustus,* published in 1988, seeing a parallel between the Augustan manipulation of opinion and its self-representation in culture (poetry, architecture, art) and the way in which modern totalitarian regimes managed their public images and produced a 'total' regime which stretched beyond the realm of the political into the houses of the people.[2]

Older tendencies survived in the interpretations of Augustus. There is a long tradition of analysis that focuses on constitutionalism and the balance between the various powers of the state. This is associated with the nineteenth century German historian Theodor Mommsen, a great historian of law, who saw in the Augustan period a constitutional division between monarchy and oligarchy, and in that there was a grand bargain which was very similar to the 'bargain' Mommsen and his friends were trying to negotiate in contemporary Prussia. The English historian A.H.M. Jones in his 1971 biography of Augustus placed considerable emphasis not on Augustus the man, but on the political and legal systems that supported Augustan power: power within administration rather than in politics narrowly defined.[3] To an extent, this emphasis on administrative system has remained important, and many recent historians, such as Fergus Millar and Peter Brunt, have argued that there was no radical change in the Augustan period precisely because the administrative systems of the Republic appear to have remained in place (perhaps extended somewhat) and the same type of people seem to have been engaged in more or less the same roles of running the Roman state. After all, the senate continued to meet, the consuls continued to be appointed, and the magistrates continued to serve.[4] But this perspective also raises the substantial difficulty of what it is that Augustus actually did. It is evident that Roman political life changed dramatically between Republic and Empire and that there was thus a new political system: all our post-Augustan sources recognise this as a fundamental change. Yet, pinpointing the changes has proved remarkably difficult.

More recently, historians have come to recognise much more explicitly a paradox at the heart of Roman imperial power.[5] It is obvious that Rome, as a conservative society, invested a great deal in its traditions, including traditions of personal and political behaviour. To some extent, to be Roman was to be a member of the Roman political body, to have a vote, and to be governed by the senate. This is the culture of Rome as discussed in the previous chapter. Yet, in the Imperial period, there was no doubt that the senate no longer acted as the leading political authority. We thus have imperial or monarchic politics in a Republican culture. Arguably, the repeated political disturbances of the first century of the Imperial period grew out of this paradox. It is also evident that, as we shall explore in the next section, the paradoxical nature of imperial power emerged specifically under Augustus.

Historians and political thinkers, of course, like matters to be straightforward and clear. We find ourselves uncomfortable with paradox. But if we look around at other forms of political ideology and belief at the heart of particular states or systems of government, we can find plenty of other examples in which political ideology and political behaviours appear to be in considerable tension. In the cold light of rational analysis, many regimes have ideologies which are fundamentally in contrast with the operation of power in their societies. From recent history, ideas such as equality under the law and equality of opportunity seem in remarkable contrast to the persistent inequality of much modern Western society. In a similar fashion, communist regimes maintained the paradox of the democratic dictatorship and many revolutions have defended the liberty of the people by political terror (and extreme violence).

Such paradoxes raise the question of why people seem to support political actions which are in marked contrast to the political ideals those acts claim as their inspiration. There are three possible explanations.

1   People accept political contradictions in part because they recognise the great complexity of the world.

2   It is in the interests of people to adopt certain ideologies and not question
    them.
3   People have no choice.

The Romans were fully aware of these problems. They knew that they do not
live in an ideal state and sometimes it was necessary to do things even if they
seemed wrong, morally or politically. The philosopher Seneca, in his discussion
of the rights and wrongs of anger (*De Ira*, 2.33), asks whether it is right to
speak truth to power. So when a man dines with an emperor who has just that
day killed the man's son, should he reprimand the emperor? Seneca's answer
reflects the political realities of the time: if he has another son, the man should
restrain his righteous rage. The anecdote is given an added force since the
story is, as far we can tell, real and involves a certain Pastor, whose son was
killed by the emperor Gaius. Many had much to lose by speaking the truth to
those in power, and much to gain through peddling the paradoxes that the
powerful maintain. Finally, the emperor had a great deal of power at his
disposal: military, financial, judicial. If politics is ultimately about power, we
may imagine that in Imperial Rome, as in other states, what people chose to
believe might be heavily influenced by the brute materiality of political
power.

The very fact that historians have not been able to agree on the nature of the
Augustan regime and, indeed, of the regimes that followed, points to the
complexity of the political world of the late first century BC and the century
that followed the Augustan revolution.

The continuing debate on the nature of the Augustan principate suggests
the following conclusions:

- Our understanding of Augustan history is very closely related to our
  understanding of how all political relationships work (ancient and
  modern).
- The issues at stake within our interpretation of Augustan history are
  profound.
- As there is no consensus today on Augustus, it is very likely that there
  was no consensus in antiquity: the opinions of Augustus' contemporaries
  probably differed fundamentally.

Augustus is a problem.

There is always a temptation to read modern and ancient historians for the
facts (which are obviously important), but the crucial issue is not to know
what happened, but to understand *why* it happened. Therefore, if we want to
get further than a superficial understanding of historians' arguments, we need
to analyse the reasons why historians come to their respective conclusions.
This is not a simple issue of bias within historical sources (favouring one side
of a political argument), but of ideology (the world view of a particular writer).

Every writer and every thinker has an ideological position and that ideology affects the way that writer understands history.

In what follows, we will look at Augustan constitutionalism and politics and, the organisation of opinion. In later chapters, we will return to Augustus and look at his military policies, religion and the imperial cult, and administration.

Politics and constitutionalism

Much of the historical debate concerning Augustus turns on constitutionalism. Greek political theory emphasises constitutional form and that theory was influential on the modern development of political theory from the Renaissance onwards. We are very used to thinking in terms of a tripartite division of types of government (democracies; oligarchies; dictatorships/ monarchies/ autocracies). Augustus has provoked so much debate in part because Augustan government does not adhere to these categories.

The problem starts in 28 and 27 BC. The crucial events are summarised by Augustus himself:

> In my sixth and seventh consulships, after I had extinguished civil wars, and when with universal consent I was in control of all matters, I transferred the Republic from my power into the judgement of the senate and people of Rome. For this service of mine by decree of the senate I was named Augustus, and the door-posts of my house were wreathed with laurel by public order and a civic crown was fixed over my door and a golden shield was set in the Curia Julia (the Senate house), granted by the senate and people of Rome, which witnessed through the inscription thereupon my virtue, clemency, justice and piety. After this time I excelled all in influence (*auctoritas*), although I had no more power than others who were my colleagues in the magistracies.
>
> *Res Gestae Divi Augusti*, 34

This passage comes from the *Res Gestae* of Augustus. This document was written by the emperor himself and inscribed on two bronze pillars which were placed outside the family mausoleum in Rome. Copies were then sent round the empire and inscribed in various places. The text as we have it comes from Ankara in Turkey, though it can be supplemented by various fragments from other locations. The text reached its final form in AD 14. It was a last testament of Augustus to his people, especially to those in Rome. It can be seen as Augustus' statement as to how he would like to be remembered.

The passage quoted comes from almost the end of the *Res Gestae*. Chronologically, the actions narrated should have come have come towards the beginning of the inscription, after Augustus' account of the triumviral period. This section (and the chapter that follows it) is a conclusion to

Augustus' summary of his own career. The presentation suggests that his actions in his sixth and seventh consulship were, therefore, among his greatest achievements.

The sixth and seventh consulships of Augustus were held in 28 and 27 BC. They marked a regularisation of his position. Whereas in the previous year, Octavian had exercised greater power than his colleague, in 28 BC, Cassius Dio (53.1) tells us that Octavian performed his duties according to the old traditions of Rome, sharing the symbols of his supreme magistracy with his colleague in the consulship, his long-standing friend and leading general, Marcus Agrippa. The friendship between the two men was cemented by marriage: Agrippa married his fellow consul's niece, Marcella. Octavian forgave all debts to the state accumulated during the triumviral period and then rescinded all the triumviral laws with effect from the end of his sixth consulship (Cassius Dio, 53.2). A gold coin was issued which showed Octavian seated on his consular chair with a box at his feet from which he had taken a scroll. The scroll was being handed to a grateful citizen. The legend reads, 'He restores the rights and laws of the people of Rome'. Octavian declared that the triumvirate and its associated state of emergency were over, and there could be a return to normality.

At the end of 28th December 28 BC, he laid down his consular power and 1st January 27 BC, he took up his seventh consulship. On 13th January the senate met. Octavian made a speech in which he resigned his extensive authority in the provinces. On 16th January, Octavian was granted the honours listed in the *Res Gestae* and from that point onwards was named Augustus. Furthermore, a whole series of provincial commands was voted to him.

These events are regarded as the first constitutional settlement. Cassius Dio, writing from two centuries later, gives Octavian a speech in which he renounces sole power and lays down all authority. He proclaims his desire to become a private citizen, but the senate force certain residual duties upon him. Dio clearly did not believe what he reads in his sources. He did not believe that Octavian ever wished to lay down his power and instead saw the speech as a clever way of maintaining constitutional form; the whole episode was a charade and the truth that lies behind that charade was represented in Augustus' first act which was to regularise the privileges granted to his personal guard. Given that the praetorian guard was the instrument by which future emperors were to assert their power in Rome, the regularisation of the guard was seen by Dio as primary evidence that Augustus never sought to restore Republican rule.

Here is the fundamental historical problem. We know that Augustus was the first emperor in a sequence of imperial monarchs that was to last five centuries. This succession of emperors was obvious to most subsequent Roman writers (with one interesting exception). It is thus obvious that there could have been no restoration of the Republic. Yet, Dio is faced with accounts of the events of January of 27 BC that proclaim just such a restoration. So bemused is Dio by the record of events and its obvious difference from what he knows happened (the meaning of the events), that he concludes that he has been tricked: the whole event was an elaborate charade. But if Augustus was engaged in this charade, who was he intending to fool? Who was his audience for these acts?

The *Res Gestae* itself has a focus on Rome and its management. It seems very likely that the primary audience for the *Res Gestae* were the citizens of Rome. The actions in the senate in 27 BC were directed towards the senators. Augustus was, therefore, addressing himself to the most politically informed groups in the Empire, and those who were most likely to care about the constitutional reforms (and detect any untruths in Augustus' presentation).

Furthermore, Augustus himself represents the events of 28–27 BC as key moments in his career. He emphasised the importance of events in those years and more than 40 years later, when Rome had experienced 40 years of post-settlement 'guidance' from Augustus and was on the verge of the transfer of power from Augustus to his successor. If Augustus meant to disguise his power in 27 BC, then by AD 14, when he gave instructions for his career and achievements to be inscribed on bronze pillars outside his tomb, by far the largest tomb that Rome had ever seen and at a time when Rome had been reshaped by the building of monuments that inscribed that greatness of Augustus into the very fabric of the city, there seemed little point in disguise.

The exception to the general perception of Augustan monarchy is Velleius Paterculus. Velleius served in the army with Tiberius (Augustus' successor) and appears to have been fiercely loyal to his former general. He was not from one of the more distinguished families of Rome and this, together with his fondness for Tiberius, means that there has been a tendency not to take him seriously. But Velleius was a near-contemporary of these events and closer to them than any of our other historians. What he tells us (Velleius Paterculus, 2.89) is that Caesar 'recalled the original and ancient forms of the Republic'. This seems to be an explicit reference to the restoration of the Republic from an author writing in the reign of the second emperor, Tiberius.

We are thus faced with a paradox. We can accept the possibility that people can, when they wish, acquiesce in their political leaders telling them things that they know to be untrue, but here we have a political discussion that goes beyond that familiar tendency of politicians to 'improve' on the truth. The paradox is very obvious and difficult to avoid. Unless we accept that Augustus was telling us an enormous, spectacular untruth that any contemporary would have instantly seen through (which is Dio's solution), we have to believe that the obvious meaning of the Augustan settlement (the establishment of Imperial government) was not what was actually seen to be happening. How can we reconcile the predominant historical interpretation of Augustus as the founder of imperial monarchy with the expressed sentiments of Augustus himself and Velleius Paterculus?

Two of our other sources are calendrical listings of important events, known as *Fasti*. The *Fasti Praenestini* was, like several other *Fasti*, inscribed on stone and is unfortunately incompletely preserved. In the following translation, the parts in square brackets are what the editor of the text guessed was in the gap on the entry for 13th January.

> corona quern[a uti super ianuam domus imp. Caesaris] Augusti poner[etur
> senatus decrevit quod   ] p. R rest[i]tui[t]

> [The senate decreed that] an oak wreath should be placed [over the door of the house of imperator Caesar] Augustus [because] he restored [   ] to/of/for the Roman people.

As is the way with many inscriptions, the restorations are reasonably obvious and unquestionable. The same event is described by Dio and is in the *Res Gestae*. But the main question is what was restored that justified these honours? The key piece of information is lost in the gap (lacuna) in the inscription.

We do, however, have a second *Fasti*, a poetic version of the Roman calendar produced by the poet Ovid. Under the entry for 13th January, Ovid, *Fasti* 1.589–90, tells us that 'The whole *provincia* was restored to our people, and your grandfather was given the name of Augustus'. The poem is addressed to Germanicus, who was the grandson of Augustus. Ovid is in error here, since the name was not given to Augustus on 13th January but on 16th January (as stated in the *Fasti Praenestine* and the *Fasti Cumanum*), but Ovid is explicit in linking the granting of the title of Augustus not to a restoration of the Republic, but to a return of the provinces to the control of the senate and people of Rome. It is perfectly possible to follow Ovid and restore 'provinces' into the *Fasti Praenestine* above. Both sources would then suggest that on 13th January, Octavian returned his provinces to the control of the senate and people of Rome and for that service he was named Augustus. Our explicit references to events in January 27 BC discuss the return of the provinces from Octavian's control to the senate and people of Rome.

Although traditional readings of the Roman politics and constitutional changes pay too little attention to the provinces, it is difficult to think that this rapid exchange of control over the provinces was enough in itself to justify the emphasis placed on January 27 BC in the Augustan tradition. Whatever happened was sufficiently important to be regarded by Augustus as one of the most important events in a glittering career and to have provoked considerable attention from contemporaries and later writers.

There is one further explicit contemporary source and that is Augustus himself (again). Suetonius (*Divus Augustus*, 28.1–2) writes of the constitutionalism of Augustus in the following way:

He twice thought of restoring the Republic; first immediately after the overthrow of Antony, remembering that his rival had often made the charge that it was his fault that it was not restored; and again when wearied by a lingering illness, when he even summoned the magistrates and the senate to his house to submit the account of empire. Reflecting, however, that as he if he were to become a private citizen, he himself would not be without danger, and it would be hazardous to trust the state to the control (*arbitrio*) of more than one, he maintained it in his hands; it is not easy to know whether his intention or his actions were better. His intentions he not only expressed from time to time, but put them on record as well in an edict in the following words: "May it be my privilege to establish the Republic in its place, firmly and safely, and reap from that act the fruit that I desire; so that I may be called the author of the best government (*status*), and have the hope when I die that the foundations which I have laid for the Republic will remain unshaken."

Suetonius, *Divus Augustus*, 28.1–2.

Suetonius is clear that even though Augustus thought of restoring the Republic in 28 BC and when he was ill (in 23 BC), he never did so. However, he quotes an edict of Augustus himself in which Augustus claims to have put the Republic on a firm footing. There is a fundamental contradiction in this single paragraph.

There is an ambiguity in the Latin word *res publica*. We use 'republic' to refer to certain states which have particular constitutional forms. We talk of the Roman Republic to mean the political system of the period from 509 BC–49 BC. The Latin words, however, mean 'public business'. Could we understand Augustan claims to have restored 'public' government as opposed to the private government of monarchy and tyranny that had been in place since the *lex Titia*? Such a solution has a certain appeal, but it does run up against the second usage of the term in this very passage. It is clear that Suetonius and indeed others understood 'res publica' to mean the Roman Republic, in the same sense that we use it. Suetonius denies that Augustus restored the *status quo* from before the Caesarian civil war. Yet, Augustus' own usage of the term seems more complex, since he acknowledges that he has changed the *res publica,* but there is nothing in Augustus' own words to suggest that his constitutional reforms were incompatible with the Republic: indeed, quite the contrary, Augustan reforms were necessary to protect the Republic. We should take Augustus' own words seriously and understand Augustus as presenting the Republic as fully functioning.

The question that arises is the nature of the 'government (*status*)' that Augustus claims to have founded. The contemporary and near contemporary sources (Octavian's *aureus*, the *Res Gestae*, Augustus as quoted in Suetonius, Velleius Paterculus) see in the events of 28–27 BC a major reordering of political relationships tantamount to a restoration of the Republic. Cassius

Dio places considerable emphasis on the events of early January 27 BC, but it is clear that this, and the award of the title of Augustus, was merely the culmination of the reforms and therefore (as Dio in fact suggests), many of the senators must have been fully prepared for Octavian's actions in January 27 BC. We are looking at a process, rather than a single political event.

Velleius Paterculus describes this process:

> There is nothing that man can desire from the gods, nothing that the gods can grant to a man, nothing that prayer can conceive nor fortune produce, which Augustus did not present the Republic, the Roman people, and the world, after his return to the city. The civil wars were ended after 20 years, foreign wars suppressed, peace restored, the madness of arms everywhere rested; power was restored to the laws, authority to the courts, and majesty to the senate; the power of the magistrates was reduced to its former limits, except for the addition of two praetors to the existing eight. The original, ancient form of the Republic was restored. Cultivation returned to the fields, honour to religion, safety to men, and rights of possession over property; laws were usefully emended, and passed for the general good...
>
> Velleius Paterculus, 2.89

It might be tempting to dismiss this passage as verbose and hyperbolic, since the 'wonders' that followed from Octavian's return do not seem to belong to the political sphere (for instance, the return of cultivation to the fields) and there is a strong emphasis on the divine, yet the passage offers a sort of description of the restoration of the Republic.

- The laws and courts are restored: this echoes Dio's claim that the triumviral legislation was repealed and the gold coin issued in 28 BC by which Octavian recorded the return of laws and rights.
- Majesty was returned to the senate: Octavian and Agrippa held a census and removed various members of the senate who were thought to be unfit for office.
- The power of the magistrates was reduced to its former limits: this would seem to reflect Octavian's laying down of the powers of the triumvirate which were uncontrolled and unlimited.

Velleius' exception here is of interest. The increase in the number of praetors, which might be thought of as a means of boosting the control of the senators (who served in such positions) is seen as a minor increase in the power of the executive arm of the Roman state and to be (broadly) anti-Republican.

Security of property and the individual were restored, as was the worship of the gods. Velleius identifies the Republic as being something far more extensive than the relationship between the senators and political power:

there are a range of political and religious relationships involved in the Republic, including, most obviously, those that protected the individual citizen. It is these relationships which were restored and which go beyond any narrow constitutional definitions.

This takes us back to what Augustus actually says in the *Res Gestae*, as quoted above. Augustus is explicit that, in 28–27 BC, he restored Republican government. It was this deed that was lavishly rewarded and gave rise to his new name. He further claims that the legal and constitutional powers that he held in the years subsequent to 27 BC were the same as those of other magistrates (and, broadly speaking, this appears to have been an accurate claim). Yet, Augustus does not claim that he thereby returned to a 'normal' position among his fellow citizens and senators. He excelled all in influence (*auctoritas*). We need to read that claim in conjunction with previous 33 chapters of the *Res Gestae* which lists the extraordinary achievements of Augustus throughout his career. We also need to take into account the near megalomaniac monumentalisation of Augustus, his family, and his career throughout Rome. Augustan authority was visible and exceptional, both in contemporary political life and in the history of the Rome.

The word Augustus uses, '*auctoritas*', is, like many moral terms, difficult to translate. Its most obvious translation is 'influence' or 'authority', but in a traditional, conservative, hierarchical, face-to-face society such as Rome, where the elite all knew each other, *auctoritas* was a powerful quality. Men were expected to acknowledge authority and to respect it. Augustus' claim in the *Res Gestae* was to have exercised power, but that power was not expressed through unusual magisterial authority (as had been the case in Caesar's dictatorship) or under the triumvirate, but through an individual moral quality. What we see is a difference between constitutional form and political power.

Augustus' claim could then be supported. He had restored many of the constitutional forms and practices of the Republic (forms and practices which went well beyond the narrow question of senatorial government), but that did not mean that he had thereby loosened his political control of Rome.

Tacitus sums up the situation in the passage quoted above and which I give again in a slightly extended version:

> He gave up the title of Triumvir, proclaiming himself content to hold the consulship and the powers of a tribune. He seduced the army with bonuses, the people with food, the rest with the sweetness of leisure and little by little he took to himself the duties of the senate, the magistracies, and the law, without opposition, since the most fierce had been killed in battle or through the proscriptions, the remainder of the *nobiles*, who were somewhat more ready for servitude, were raised by wealth and honours and, having benefitted from the new order, preferred safety and the present to the old and dangerous [...] At home matters were peaceful; the

magistrates held the same titles; the younger were born after the Actian victory, and even many of the elders had been born during the civil wars. How many remained who had seen the Republic? Thus the state had been revolutionised, and had nothing of the original and sound morals remained. All, stripped of equality, looked up to the orders of a princeps.

Tacitus, Annales, 1. 2–4 (excerpts)

In Tacitus's view, the revolution was political and not constitutional. Augustan power rested in a series of political relationships, with the soldiers, the people, and the *nobiles*. The constitutional forms remained the same. The magistrates continued to do their duties and the senate continued to meet, as it had throughout the triumviral period. But all were now dominated by Augustus.

This brings us to two sets of conclusions. The first set is about the nature of the Republic and the second is about constitutionalism and politics.

If we think that the nature of the Republic meant senatorial government, then we face a problem in understanding events in 28–27 BC. In the first place, the senate had never stopped meeting nor had magistrates ever stopped serving over the previous decades of political turmoil. If we think that the nature of the Republic meant senatorial government, there was nothing to restore in 28–27 BC, because nothing was in abeyance. The events of 28–27 BC did not mean the restoration of government by the senators but a restriction of the powers of the magistrates to their former boundaries. Alongside this, there was a restoration of the protections and rights of the ordinary citizen (protections that defended the citizens from the magistrates). The senators had never ruled in a conventional sense: they had simply exercised influence over the magistrates and it was the magistrates who ruled, constrained by customs and laws. It was those constraints which were restored in 28–27 BC.

This raises a fundamental historical and political problem of the relationship between constitutional form and political power. The Roman Empire was, as we shall see, a despotic system in which vast power was concentrated in the hands of a single individual. Yet, that power was structured constitutionally around the oligarchic and democratic elements of the Republican constitution and was, fundamentally, very similar to that prior constitutional system. The constitution clearly did not determine political activity.

Constitutions tend to provide the institutional structures in which political debates and political decisions are made, but if political power is concentrated in the hands of an individual or group of individuals, and they control the decision-making and the content of political debates, does it matter whether the institutions that frame that debate are democratic, oligarchic or autocratic? Many authoritarian regimes have surrounded themselves with councils, committees, assemblies, parliaments, senates, traditional gatherings of elders, but the decision-making functions of the state remain firmly under the control of a very limited number of individuals. In 1939, Ronald Syme argued that 'In all ages, whatever the form and name of government, be it monarchy, republic, or democracy, an oligarchy lurks behind the façade'.[6] But was Syme right?

The second set of issues concern political power. In the Republic, much power was vested in the people, who were sovereign, but much political influence appears to have been concentrated in the hands of the senators. Under Augustus, magisterial power was concentrated in a limited fashion. In Rome, the *princeps* was merely one magistrate among many. The key to Augustan power was political.

This emphasis on the political made Augustus both more and less powerful than he seemed, from a superficial level. He was more powerful since whatever his exact constitutional and legal position, he could ensure that what he willed would happen. Although the legal powers of later emperors were reinforced in subsequent years, there was a rawness to the power exercised by Augustus and later emperors: it depended not on law as much as their ability to oblige people to do their will. It is this obligation that is emphasised in Tacitus, not in a negative way (as if Augustus threatened those he wished to work for him), but in a positive way. Augustus obliged people to do his will through the offer of rewards. Later emperors, such as Gaius, were to put much more emphasis on the threatening nature of power.

The weakness in the Augustan reliance on politics over law was that politics was a matter of debate whereas law is (relatively) fixed. In practical terms, this meant that Augustan power could be challenged through political debate. In fact, this is what we see throughout the reigns of Augustus and Tiberius; ongoing political debate. That process of political debate allowed Augustus and Tiberius to exercise and display their political power, but it also allowed the possibility of challenge and subversion. The debate happened, but the result was decided before the debate. Neither Augustus nor Tiberius felt that they could close down political debate, for if they had closed the senate, they would have been presenting their power as legal and magisterial rather than resting on the politics of *auctoritas*. To do so, would have been to return to the politics of the Caesarian and triumviral periods and to risk accusations of tyranny. Nevertheless, the continuous assertion of imperial political authority through debate risked the perversion of the political process itself since that *auctoritas* set the agenda, determined the outcome, and influenced the conduct of those debates.

The political process dressed itself in the conservative clothes of the Republican political culture and worked through Republican institutions. Nevertheless, there was an emerging difference between the form of political activity (Republican) and its substance (Imperial). However much they may have talked as if they were Republicans, the very fact that the emperor won every political debate differentiated the politics of the Republic from the politics of the Empire. As Tacitus points out, the form of political activity remained the same, but the substance was transformed: no vestige of the old Republican behaviours remained ('Tacitus uses the word '*mos*', meaning customs) and this was not the Republic of old. Tacitus' challenge to the Augustan regime (and one that, we shall see, was central to his account of Tiberius) was that matters were not as they seemed and that the process of political debate was unreal.

We can, as Tacitus does, take seriously Augustan claims to have restored the Republic: much looked, and indeed was, the same as in the previous age. Yet, it is precisely through Augustan dominance of the Republican political processes that the Republic ceased to exist. The politics of the Augustan period was completely unlike that of the early age. The restoration of the Republic provided a set of constitutional and governmental means by which Augustus could rule. The reality of Augustan rule allowed no real debate.

The politics of the constitutional settlements

Politics 30–26 BC

Between the news of Octavian's victory at Actium and his return to Rome, the senators voted Octavian a range of honours for which it is difficult to find parallels in Roman history. The honours are listed in Cassius Dio, 51.19–20, though there is some question as to accuracy of the list. Most of the honours had little practical value, but served to represent and monumentalise Octavian's acts. He was voted triumphal arches to be built in Rome in the Forum and at Brundisium and although we are familiar with the triumphal arch as a Roman monumental form and eventually arches were to spread across the empire, permanent triumphal arches appear to have been an innovation of the Augustan period. A triumph over Cleopatra was voted (which was to be celebrated in 28 BC), the Temple of the Deified Julius, which was either complete or nearing completion in the very centre of the old Forum of the city, was to be adorned with the rams of the captured warships from Actium. A festival was to be held in Octavian's honour every five years. Statues were dedicated. The day of the fall of Alexandria was to be declared lucky. This not only meant that it would be treated as a good day for doing business, getting married and the like, but also it would be noted in the calendar and every year Romans would be reminded of Octavian's victory. Prayers were to be offered for Octavian alongside those offered to the gods. The day of his return to Rome would be made sacred, an occasion for public festivities and sacrifices. The Alexandrians were ordered to start their year from the day on which Octavian entered Alexandria. Octavian was given the right to enlarge the priestly colleges which ran Rome's religion. An altar of victory was established in the *Curia Iulia*, the new senate house of Rome. Octavian was given the right to wear the triumphal crown at all public festivals (a privilege similar to that awarded to Julius Caesar). Such public honours extended into the private sphere and Dio tells us that libations (offerings of wine) were to be made at private banquets.

Octavian was also to enjoy certain political benefits. Dio mentions the award of tribunician power (the powers enjoyed by a tribune) for life, but in this he is clearly confused. The confusion may relate to Octavian receiving powers similar to the tribunes in the right to intervene in support of a Roman citizen (*ius auxilium*) and it would seem possible that this grant is the origin of the much disputed right of appeal to Caesar, famously exercised by Saint Paul. Together with *sacrosanctitas*, which declared it a religious crime to attack Octavian's person and which had been granted to Octavian in 36 BC, this grant meant that several of the key rights and privileges of the tribunes had already been amassed by Octavian.

It was obvious to the cities of the Greek East how the politics of Rome was moving. In the aftermath of Actium, several cities asked permission to establish cult centres to Octavian. Sanctuaries to *Roma et Caesar* were established in Ephesus and Nicaea and similar sanctuaries were dedicated in Pergamum and Nicomedia. Although there were many precedents for ruler cults in the East, ranging from the Ptolemaic ruler cult in Egypt, the semi-divinity of kings in Persia and cultic offerings to Hellenistic kings and even Roman governors in Asia Minor, the development of Roman ruler cult was an innovation that reflects a perception that Octavian was in a position unparalleled in Roman history. This was not just an Eastern representation of Octavian's power, but part of a more general attempt to differentiate Octavian from other Romans and Octavian himself was required to give his permission for such developments (he clearly could have stopped them).

In 28 BC, Octavian celebrated an unprecedented triple triumph for his conquest in Dalmatia before the Actian war, his victory at Actium, and his victory in Egypt on the 13th, 14th and 15th August. There is some ambiguity as to whether the victory at Actium was celebrated by a formal triumph or by a triumph-like event.[7] Whatever the case, Octavian's celebrations of the victory were on a grandiose scale. The poets weighed in as well, though some of the poems were written and published sometime after the triumphs. Propertius treats the victory of Actium in two separate poems (3. 11 and 4. 6). The first portrays Actium as a contest between East and West, between Egypt and Rome, and between the feminine Eastern morality of Cleopatra and the manly virtues of Rome. The second poem is one of epic confrontation in which the gods contest over the fate of the world and in which Apollo stands alongside Augustus in a divine war. Virgil takes a similar position, choosing Actium and its aftermath for the central scene on the shield of Aeneas (*Aeneid* 8.675–723), a prophecy and culmination of Roman historical greatness. Horace suggests that the victory of Actium is an occasion for general celebration (*Epode* 9; *Odes* 1.37).

Octavian was not shy about celebrating Actium and reminding everyone of his triumph. The altar of victory in the senate house may have come to be associated with Actium. Similarly, the dedication of a victory arch in the Forum was a reminder of his triumph in the ceremonial and political heart of the city. Octavian was to remove an obelisk from Alexandria and transport it to Rome. It was erected on the Campus Martius, close to Octavian's mausoleum and Pantheon and the site of the future Ara Pacis. Octavian was building a house on the Palatine hill. This house came to be associated with a large marble temple of Apollo, opened in 28 BC: Apollo had been regarded as Octavian's patron deity in the triumviral period and he was later to be associated firmly with Actium. References to Egypt appear to have marked the décor of the house and temple (Propertius, 2.31; Suetonius, *Divus Augustus* 29.3). It was this house which was decorated with laurel and on which a civic crown was placed in honour of Octavian's victories and his saving of the lives of citizens (Cassius Dio, 53.16). The house was much more than a place to live; it was symbol of Octavian's political dominance.

There was a moderation of Octavian's self-presentation in the aftermath of Actium. Octavian ordered that all gold and silver statues (precious metal statues being associated with the gods) should be melted down (Cassius Dio, 53.22). The Pantheon was being constructed by Agrippa. The plan appeared to involve a statue to Octavian being the centre-piece of the temple, suggesting worship of the new young god, but the plan was changed and a statue of Caesar located in the centre of the temple with the statue of Octavian relegated to the ante-room. Octavian was avoiding an outright assertion of his divinity even though his iconographic representation prior to Actium was pointing in that direction.

The politics of these events is obscure. There is nothing to suggest that Octavian was seeking to cloak his power or to underplay his political achievements of the previous decade. Nor can we detect much of an attempt to draw a veil over the war with Antony as an unfortunate episode and look for reconciliation in the Roman state. Octavian had won the war, as he had won previous civil wars. Unlike his adoptive father, he appears not to have been persuaded of the political virtues of *clementia* (clemency). His dominance of the political scene could only be challenged by those eager to surrender their lives.

However, it is clear that the presentation of a unified city and people in the *Res Gestae* and in Velleius in the aftermath of the war, could hardly have been accurate. On the eve of the war between Antony and Octavian, the triumviral arrangement had come to a planned end (its time had run out). The consuls of 32 BC had been Antonians and they had fled the city. This left something of a legal and constitutional lacuna in Roman politics. Octavian filled this void by arranging that the communities of Italy take an oath to follow him in the coming war. It was this oath that allowed Octavian to claim in the *Res Gestae* (1; 34) that he acted in the name of 'all Italy' and that in 28 BC on his return to Rome that he controlled all things 'by universal consent'. Nevertheless, there was clear evidence of opposition.

In 30 BC, when Octavian was campaigning in the East, Marcus Lepidus was suddenly removed from the political scene. Marcus Lepidus was the son of the disgraced *triumvir* and was thus no minor political figure. He was supposedly involved with Junia, the sister of Marcus Junius Brutus and who thus carried some of the prestige of her noble brother and family line. There was supposedly a conspiracy, though we have no details. Velleius Paterculus (2.88) tells us that Maecenas, Octavian's close friend, was in charge in Rome at the time, and that he removed Lepidus and Junia, without disturbance to men and property, quietly and with concealment. It suggests that they were killed without trial or publicity. It is, of course, likely that there were others involved and removed (Roman conspiracies tended to be large for reasons to be discussed in later chapters), but that those other individuals were not sufficiently significant to be remembered by our sources.

Velleius represents the speed and concealment of the purge as a good action since it crushed the spectre of a renewed civil war. In itself, this gives us an insight into the political mentalities of the period in which an act of non-legal murder was not seen as an infringement of the basic liberties of the Roman people, but as a decisive act to prevent civil strife and the terror of a public purge. Velleius' report suggests that memories of triumviral violence were raw. There was to be no resumption of the triumviral proscriptions, but to guarantee that level of civil peace Rome had to accept that the emperor's associates wielded unlimited power.

The actions of the senators in 30–28 BC were political. Many of the senators would have been connected to Antony and we may suppose that if Antony had emerged victorious, he would have been received with similarly lavish honours. Octavian would have known that the senate contained many who were hostile to him and who would have preferred an Antonian victory. Yet, the inventiveness of the senators appears to have been designed to send a message to Octavian, one of loyalty and one in which Octavian's pre-eminence was recognised and accepted.

The supposed conspiracy of Lepidus showed that not all were prepared to accept quietly Octavian's victory; the crushing of the real or suspected conspiracy symbolised the brutality with which Octavian would treat potential opponents. Yet, the senators' honouring of Octavian would seem to deny any residual opposition and make the assertion that the senate as a body would remain loyal to the new master of Rome. If the war was recognised to be over when Antony and Cleopatra were defeated, it did not mean that anyone expected the victor to submit himself to the decisions of his fellow senators. The senate opened the door to the settlement of 28–27 BC, but there can be little doubt who was in the stronger position in any such settlement.

In modern constitutional debates there are many precedents, lawyers and formally constituted parties and interests who become involved, but in the circumstances of 28 BC, there was no body or group with whom Octavian could negotiate. There were no organised parties to challenge Octavian's decisions and we should assume (as indeed Cassius Dio does) that the ideas behind the settlement of 28–27 BC largely sprang from Octavian's associates.

The events of 28–27 transferred Octavian's power from a legal and constitutional basis to a political sphere and this was a fundamental change as noted in the *Res Gestae*, by Velleius Paterculus, and Tacitus. Nevertheless, there could be no resumption of politics as it had been practised during the Republic. The very power and presence of Augustus was to undermine any restoration of normality in politics. The political dominance of the emperor meant that no groups or factions could challenge his power. Of course, the political manoeuvre that Augustus performed with the senators in 28 and 27 BC would always have had detractors. The settlement established a peculiar dynamic in which Augustan 'Republicanism' could be undermined by those who wished to represent Augustan power as more monarchic. The dynamic established a vulnerability in Augustus' position. Any non-Republican actions on his part risked exposing his regime as monarchic; intervening outside the normal conventions of Republic authority similarly exposed his monarchism and weakened the power of his regime. Yet, the real power that he held (to which we will turn in a moment) inevitably concentrated political authority on his person and meant that decision-making was restricted to the Augustan inner circle. Political opposition was perpetually marginalised and excluded, unable to attain the positions of power that would give the discontented more than marginal influence.

This left two possible courses for opposition:

- Opposition could treat Augustus as a monarch (and thus undermine his claim to Republicanism). Consequently, we can suspect that contemporary statements which seem excessive, raising Augustus to the level of the gods or proclaiming and praising his vast power, were designed to embarrass the *princeps*.
- Opposition could take him at face value and behave as if the Republic was restored, daring Augustus to intervene in his own political interests.

Ultimately, however, neither course of opposition was particularly effective, in part because the concentration of power in the hands of Augustus was such that challenging Augustus was difficult. Further, many people had an interest in supporting his regime. Also, neither course of action really threatened the emperor. To behave as if in the Republic would merely reinforce the paradox that Augustus was maintaining and to behave as if it was a monarchy simply recognised Augustan power. Although there are incidents of opposition, it is difficult to find any serious political challenge to the Augustan regime from disgruntled Republicans. There was no attested serious attempt to change the nature of the regime (a revolution or counter revolution) by overthrowing the emperor.

In the immediate aftermath of the settlement of 27 BC, the paradox of an imperial presence in a supposedly Republican system was made somewhat less obvious by Augustus absenting himself from Rome. From the summer of

27 BC, Augustus spent much of his time away from Rome. In late 27 BC, he was in Gaul, but then led campaigns in the Alpine region and in Spain. He did not return to Rome for his daughter Julia's wedding (to her cousin Marcellus) in 25 BC and it was only after victory in Spain in 24 BC that he was to return to Rome for any lengthy period.

Yet, there is still evidence of political opposition, though much of it is obscure. In 27 BC, Marcus Licinius Crassus returned to Rome from his provincial command. Crassus had been in Thrace and Macedonia and with considerable success. He was, it seemed, due a triumphal procession through the streets of Rome. Crassus had personally taken a role in the fighting (which seems to have been unusual for Roman generals) and when his troops met the Bastarnae in battle (a Thracian tribe), Crassus had himself killed their king, Deldo. A special honour was reserved for such an act of valour, the dedication of the *spolia opima* (the best spoils) in the Temple of Capitoline Jupiter (Cassius Dio, 51.24–25). Augustus could not compete and a technicality was found to deny Crassus the honour.

Crassus was governor in one of the provinces under the legal and religious authority of Augustus himself and it was claimed that the *spolia opima* could not be awarded to the person who merely commanded the army, but only to the individual who had ultimate legal and religious responsibility for the army. Yet, this sparked a further debate about the status of one the previous recipients of the honour, a certain Cossus, whose career is lost in the mists of archaic Roman history. Every authority listed Cossus as a military tribune, which would suggest that he was under the authority of a senior magistrate. As the debate raged, a linen scrap was found in the temple of Jupiter Capitolinus that explicitly stated that Cossus was consul when the *spolia opima* were awarded. The convenience of the discovery of such a document from the depths of Rome history provoked considerable scepticism. When Livy (4.20) reports the deeds of Cossus his sarcasm is palpable: he reports that all authorities stated that Cossus was tribune, but the linen record was solid evidence of his consulship and no one could believe that anyone would forge such an important religious and historical artefact. Livy's treatment of lies as truth undermined the regime. The controversy suggests Augustan insecurity.

In 26 BC, there were two similarly opaque episodes. One involved a prominent aristocrat, Messala Corvinus. With Augustus away from Rome on campaign, he appointed Corvinus *Praefectus Urbi*, Prefect of the City of Rome. The post had been initially employed for Maecenas when Octavian was fighting the civil war and it appears to have had the responsibility of maintaining order in Rome. It was, however, an unusual post and within a few days, Corvinus resigned. On resigning, he supposedly said 'imperii pudet' ('I am shamed by my power'). What was shaming about the *imperium* would seem to be that it was outside the norms of the Republican system and it was an imperial appointment to govern the city. One can imagine that those senators wishing to make trouble pointed to the appointment as clear evidence that the Republic had not been restored and that this forced Corvinus to resign (Tacitus, *Annales*, 6.10–11; Seneca, *Apocolocyntosis*, 10). Notably, the post became regular and uncontroversial under later emperors.

The second case involved Cornelius Gallus, a noted poet, who had been Antony's commander in Cyrenaica, modern Libya. He had defected to Octavian to 30 BC and led his armies in an invasion of Egypt co-ordinated with that of Octavian. Once Egypt had been annexed, Gallus was left in charge of the province, a clear example of the lack of any fundamental differences between the Antonians and Octavian's supporters. Other than Gallus' prior history, the appointment was controversial since Gallus was an equestrian and although equestrians were used in less important administrative roles, Egypt was a major province and everyone must have expected that it would have been given a senatorial governor.

Gallus initially served in the province under the authority of Octavian in which role he completed a major building project in Alexandria, which involved the reuse of an obelisk.[8] The obelisk ended up in Rome, moved by Gaius Caligula. The inscription that recorded Gallus' activities was obliterated but can be reconstructed from the holes left by the nails that secured the bronze letters in place. The inscription reads 'By the order of the Imperator Caesar, son of the Deified, Caius Cornelius, son of Gnaeus, Gallus, *Praefectus Fabrum* of Caesar, son of the Deified, made the Forum Iulium'. *Praefecti Fabrum* seem to have been equestrian officers in charge of works and the role appears to have been one of the most senior in an equestrian career. When Octavian left Egypt, he promoted Gallus to Prefect of Egypt, effectively the governor of the province. It is not clear whether promoting an equestrian was a policy decision by Octavian or simply a matter of administrative convenience, given that Gallus was in place and a man of administrative skill. Whatever the initial justification, the appointment of equestrian governors to the province was enshrined in law when Egypt was formally made a province (probably by a law passed through an assembly in Rome).

Gallus had a busy time in Egypt, suppressing a rebellion and campaigning to the south of Egypt. He recorded his victories in inscriptions set up at various places in Egypt, notably at Philae in the very south and at the pyramids in Giza.[9] There were, however, complaints. One Valerius Largus reported back on Gallus's actions and Augustus very publicly withdrew his friendship from Gallus.

At this point, the enemies of Gallus moved in. He was put on trial (though on what charge is not obvious), convicted, his estates confiscated and granted to Augustus, and then Gallus killed himself. The aftermath of this suicide is yet more puzzling. Augustus is said to have shed tears on hearing of Gallus's death saying that only he could no longer fall out with his friends (Suetonius, *Augustus*, 66) and Cassius Dio (53.23–4) reports that a certain Proculeius, whom we know to have been very close to Augustus and prominent within the regime, went out of his way to be rude to Largus. Such events are very difficult to interpret and we may just have to accept the obvious reading that Augustus was distressed by the arrogance of Gallus and the senate loyally over-reacted, but then one must wonder why Augustus was moved to tears over his death (he was notably unconcerned about killing his political enemies) and Proculeius was so bitter.

I think we can propose another reconstruction in which Gallus got himself into trouble (perhaps by campaigning outside his province without permission); Largus reported this and Augustus came under pressure to act. He removed his support of Gallus and then the senators showed their 'loyalty' by attacking this former friend of the emperor, much against the wishes of the emperor and his friends. One may suspect that Augustus was caught in the dilemma of maintaining his friendship to protect Gallus in the face of the law and thereby appearing to act as a monarch, or of not intervening and thereby sacrificing Gallus and maintaining his Republican posture.

Such events suggest that individuals set out to discomfort the emperor, but they hardly amount to serious opposition. If the fall of Gallus was, ultimately, the result of the machinations of those who were ill-disposed towards Augustus, that opposition was cloaked in excessive loyalty to the regime. Augustus may have been upset and angered by such events (he may even have been reduced to tears), but he was not threatened. If there was a serious challenge to the Augustan regime, we will find it in the political crises of 23 BC and following years.

The Crisis of 23–22 BC

Augustus had returned to Italy into 24 BC after his campaigns in Spain. He was consul for the tenth time in that year, exceeding the number of consulships held by any figure in Republican history. Augustus' return was an opportunity to reassert his political position. He provided a gift of 400 *sesterces* (see below) to each member of the Roman plebs. The senators voted him a new series of privileges. He was granted exemption from all laws (an almost useless privilege in 24 BC, but one that may have opened the way to his laying down the consulship in 23 BC). Perhaps more significantly, privileges were granted to Augustus' step-son Tiberius (who was to be allowed to stand for office early) and to Marcellus. Marcellus was the son of Octavia and Claudius Marcellus. Marcella, the sister of Marcellus, was married to Agrippa, and Marcellus himself was married to Julia, Augustus' daughter. He was, therefore, the most obvious heir to Augustus. Marcellus was given the right to stand for the consulship ten years early (Cassius Dio, 53.28).

These events very obviously began the process of establishing a dynasty by associating the younger members of the Augustan household with the honours and power which Augustus himself had. Neither magisterial nor political power was directly inherited in Rome. Prominent fathers could give enormous support to their sons, but being the son of a great man was no guarantee of political success. The prominence of these youths suggested that Augustan power would outlive Augustus.

Augustan dynastic plans were laid to waste in 23 BC. That year, Rome was hit by a summer disease, possibly cholera, possibly typhoid. Augustus and Marcellus were both taken ill. On the point of death, Augustus had summoned his fellow consul, Calpurnius Piso, and his closest associates. He presented Piso with an account book which listed the revenues of empire and the disposition of military forces. He presented his signet ring to Agrippa. Augustus himself was saved by his doctor who decided to employ cold plunge baths (and thus probably reduced the fever). However, Marcellus did not respond to the same treatment, and died (Cassius Dio, 53.30–32).

The political meaning of this anecdote, as recounted by Dio, is complicated. The passing of the accounts to Piso reflects the paradoxical Republicanism of Augustus. In a true Republic, whatever business was being conducted by one consul would inevitably pass to the other on the death of the former. But it seems clear that there was no equal partnership here: the information, financial and military information necessary to govern the empire was held by Augustus. Legally, Piso may have been Augustus' equal, but politically he was not.

Agrippa was given the ring by which was symbolised a future role in managing Augustus' personal affairs. The position of Agrippa in a putative post-Augustan era is not clear. He held no official position, though would have had considerable political influence. One may wonder, however, whether that would have been enough to establish Agrippa in a position similar to that enjoyed by Augustus. Of course we will never know, because Augustus lived, but had he died in 23 BC, there was a possibility that the Republic really would have been restored, if only in default of any alternative.

The missing element of these events is Marcellus. No role was given to the young Marcellus. Perhaps he was already ill and also thought to be dying

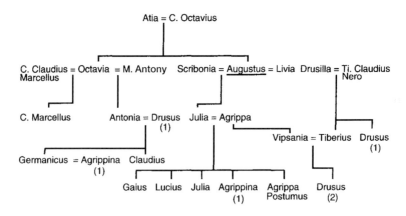

Figure 2.1 Augustus' family in 23 BC

(though the story of the doctor's interventions makes little sense unless Marcellus fell ill after Augustus had sickened). Marcellus was passed over in favour of the older and vastly experienced man: Marcellus could not have been expected to assume the leadership role that Augustus had undertaken. Yet, after Augustus' unexpected recovery, he came to the senate and offered to read them his will. The senators refused to listen. The machinations here must relate to an on-going political rumour and the only reason for Augustus to offer to read his will to the senators was to prove that he had not left Marcellus his political position. In other words, there was no imperial dynasty in Rome.

However, at least some of the senators clearly took a different view, and with good reason. The death of Marcellus became a moment of great public mourning. He was buried in the mausoleum of Augustus. The great stone theatre that was being built at the foot of the Capitoline Hill at the time was designated as the Theatre of Marcellus. It seems, therefore, that the death of a promising young man who had held no major political office and whose career was cut short before he could accomplish anything worthy of honour, became a great public spectacle. Virgil, whose great Augustan epic, the *Aeneid*, was being composed through this period, provides us a 'prophecy scene' from the hero Aeneas' visit to the Underworld. There, he is shown the history of the community he is about to found, but that history does not end in triumph instead it culminates in the sadness of national mourning at the death of Marcellus (Virgil, *Aeneid* 6. 788–883). The ceremonial and perhaps even the popular reaction to the death of Marcellus speaks of a different political order than that represented to the senators. Constitutionally, Augustus continued to maintain the republicanism of his position and the forms of magisterial power, but in the politics of the city, the Augustan family was becoming a dynasty. Whatever Augustus said to the senators about his intentions for Marcellus, the reaction to his death does suggest that Marcellus was the heir designate of Augustan (imperial) power.

Yet, the traumatic events of Augustus' illness and the death of Marcellus seem to have marked not the culmination of crisis, but its commencement. At the centre of the crisis was Marcus Primus. Primus had been governor of Macedonia, a key military province, and it is likely that Primus was a trusted figure in the Augustan circle. While he was campaigning in Macedonia, he waged war against the Odrysae (probably in 24 BC or earlier).[10] On his return to Rome, he was brought to trial for campaigning outside his province. There is no doubt that he was guilty but the defence he offered was that he had been instructed by Augustus or (his story seems to shift later) by Marcellus. The problem was that Macedonia was a 'senatorial' province and was not under Augustan authority. Marcellus, whatever his personal qualities, had no authority in this matter at all. It was clear that Augustus was over-stepping his very considerable authority and if Marcellus was acting in such a way, Augustan power was openly dynastic rather than Republican. During the proceedings of Primus' trial and much to everyone's surprise, Augustus turned up in the courtroom. The defence, Licinius Murena, asked him his reason for being there and Augustus replied, 'The Republic'.[11] Supposedly, the defence was furious. His case was lost. Nevertheless, many of the jurors voted to acquit, suggesting that they simply did not believe Augustus (Cassius Dio, 54.3).[12] By appearing at the trial, Augustus was condemning Primus. He was denying his imperial power, but Primus was paying the price. This was a friendship betrayed.

The trial of Primus was perhaps not dissimilar to the difficulties surrounding Cornelius Gallus, but whereas Gallus was an equestrian, had been Antony's man and was probably not part of the Augustan inner circle, Primus was a senator and clearly trusted and well connected. The anger of the defence counsel led to a conspiracy and a purge that went right to the heart of the Augustan regime. The conspiracy was led by Licinius Murena and a certain Fannius Caepio. Caepio was prosecuted by a young Tiberius and condemned to death (Suetonius, *Tiberius*, 8). Murena appears to have been removed without trial.

Dio tells us that Licinius Murena was the brother of Proculeius (who we came across earlier in connection with Gallus) and Terentia. Terentia was the wife of Maecenas and thus very close to Augustus. The relationship between Terentia and Augustus may, in fact, have been closer than that between Maecenas and Augustus. There were persistent rumours that the two were long-term lovers. There were stories that Augustus had made Livia and Terentia compete in a contest of beauty (perhaps playing 'Paris' to his 'two goddesses') (Cassius Dio, 54.19). Dio even goes as far to suggest that Augustus engineered an opportunity to leave Rome in 16 BC so as to be able to pursue his affair with Terentia out of sight of the city gossips. Yet, we are told that relations between Maecenas and Augustus soured after Maecenas told his wife that her brother was in danger (Suetonius, *Augustus*, 66).[13]

The events surrounding Primus and the conspiracy of Caepio and Murena are dated to 22 BC in Dio's narrative, though there have been attempts to date these events to 23 BC. The redating is largely to associate the changes with a constitutional adjustment in mid 23 BC. Augustus resigned the consulship and was to take the office only irregularly throughout the rest of his career. The senate gave him tribunician power in Rome. This enabled him to call together assemblies and probably to collate all previous grants of powers associated with the tribunes (Cassius Dio, 53. 30–31). He thereby maintained his association with the plebs and popular politics. He also seems to have gained authority in the provinces over which he had previously had no official influence (*imperium maius*) (Cassius Dio, 53.32), a grant which one might associate with the political events surrounding Primus.

The conspiracy reflected an on-going dispute from the prosecution of Primus (which may well have been in 23 BC) to the death of Murena. The connections of Murena were such that he clearly sat at the heart of the regime. His fall was a major political event and the first major breach in the Caesarian group since Actium. The removal of a senior and trusted advisor was politically damaging for Augustus and his group and the events have some claim to be the worst political crisis faced by Augustus in the period from 30 BC until his death in AD 14.

It seems unlikely that this constitutional adjustment was an emergency measure. Its significance is a matter of some debate. Augustus lost some powers and gained others. In terms of what he was able to do through official powers after June 23 BC, he was, in fact, probably equipped with slightly more legal authority than before. Yet, as we have seen, politics is not just about laws and constitutions; it is about perceptions and traditions and authority. There is no doubt that the consulship was the major magisterial position in Rome and the holders of the consulship were at the heart of Roman political business. Stepping down from the position was a major step back for Augustus and it is difficult to believe that it was an entirely voluntary step. The events surrounding Primus and the scandal over the position and role of Marcellus attest to an increase in political tension. It seems likely that the presence of the emperor in Rome from 24 BC onwards brought the senators face to face with their diminished power relative to Augustus. Augustus' decision to retire from the consulship was undoubtedly an attempt to affirm the 'normality' of the constitutional system and to deny that he was in a quasi-monarchic position. In such a context, we could see the laying down of the consulship as a retreat for Augustus and a further victory for his opponents.

But Augustus was far from beaten. The year 22 BC was the first in a decade that Augustus had not been consul. It was also a year of plague, flood, storms and lightning strikes on temples and statues, and famine (Cassius Dio, 54.1). The plebs responded by rioting. The senators were shut up in the senate house and the plebs approached Augustus to ask him to become dictator. The senators were intimidated into acquiescence by a threat to burn down the senate house with them still trapped inside. Augustus refused the honour (*Res Gestae* 5), dramatically throwing off his toga and bearing his breast to the people: the symbolism would suggest that they were plunging a dagger towards his heart. He did, however, accept the role of *curator annonae* (Manager of the Grain Supply), and he supposedly resolved the famine in a few days. He then made the post of *curator annonae* a regular office which would be held by members of the senate. Tiberius, the son of Augustus' wife, appears to have taken on this role (Suetonius, *Tiberius*, 8).

The events of this year saw an upswing in the violent undercurrents of Roman politics and the re-emergence of some of the basic fault lines in Roman society. The plebs supported Augustus against the senators and whatever the senators felt about it, if we are to believe Dio, it was Augustus' intervention that prevented the senators being burnt alive in their own meeting house. The senators could not control the streets. Nor, it seems, could they control the supply of food to the city. The actions of the plebs would seem at first to be irrational (and to a certain extent that is how they are presented) since it could hardly have been Augustus' removal from the consulship that caused the bad weather and the plague. But the problem is more subtle: whatever the religious anxieties of the plebs, the senators were either unwilling or unable to intervene to provide the plebs with a proper supply of food. Augustus, however, could and did solve the problem. In so doing, he showed himself the friend of the plebs and demonstrated that the senators needed him to restrain the revolutionary forces in Roman society.

The plebs may, in fact, have been right to blame the senators for at least some of their woes. One of the more notable features of the story is Augustus' claim in the *Res Gestae* to have resolved the issue within days. Even assuming that Augustus was very efficient, this is a somewhat puzzling achievement for a society dependent on pre-industrial communications. One would assume that a *curator annonae* would need to identify supplies of grain (probably outside Italy), write to those who had control over those supplies and instruct them to be delivered to Rome, await the loading, shipping, and unloading of that grain, and only then would the city be delivered from famine. In the best of circumstances, such processes would take more than a few days. Alternatively, one could assume that there was, in fact, plenty of grain local to Rome that Augustus was able to extract and get onto the Roman grain market. It is the latter which seems more likely.

There is a possible political-economic explanation for this remarkable success. If there is a famine the cost of grain rises, as everyone knows. Because everyone knows this, people act on the expectation of price rises. So, if the weather had been bad, everyone would expect the price of grain to rise. In such circumstances, the profits of those who had grain to sell would also rise (per unit of grain). It was, then, in the interests of the seller to wait, if possible, for the grain to reach the highest price before selling. If the harvest was bad and everyone was expecting a famine, then those who had grain would hang onto it in the hope of price rises. Grain would thus disappear from the market. The plebs would then be faced with a situation in which everyone knew or suspected that there was grain, but no one was selling it in the hope of making a profit. The intervention of Augustus would thus be crucial for two reasons. In the short term, he could apply political pressure or use his own money so that grain would be released onto the market. Further, those holding grain might make the calculation that a man as powerful as Augustus would quickly secure a fresh supply of grain for the city, which would mean that prices would fall. The opportunity to make high profits would then disappear and thus there was no point in hanging on to the grain. Whatever Augustus did or did not do, the blame for the famine was likely to be laid at the door of the landowners, and the largest landowners of Italy sat in the senate, while the credit was likely to further enhance Augustus' reputation with the plebs.

The politics of the famine of 22 BC were likely to further divide the Roman state. Conservative senators saw Augustus enhancing his political reputation with the plebs and that the plebs were in a position to threaten the senators. As the hostility of the plebs to the senators was likely worsened, so the senators were probably more threatened by the accumulation of power by Augustus and the potential for violence of his supporters. Augustus' refusal of the dictatorship was symbolically important, and much emphasis has been placed upon it, but the fact that he was offered the dictatorship in itself suggests that the plebs desired him to overthrow the constitution and return to the days of the triumvirate. The refusal was political theatre, showing the senators that he stood by the restoration of the Republican norms of government, but it also made the senators aware of the ever-present possibility of an Augustan *coup d'état*.

Augustus was, however, to head East to deal with political and military problems. The trip may have been in the planning since 23 BC when news of troubles in Armenia reached Rome. It is very tempting, however, to see Augustus' keenness to direct events in the East himself as a response to the difficulties of his tumultuous three years in Rome. The presence of the emperor in the restored Republic had indeed proved difficult. His absence, however, did not resolve the tensions at the heart of Roman politics.

The crisis of absence: Politics 21–19

Piecing together the events of these crucial years is complicated by the fact that we don't have a clear narrative for this period. To understand why things happened as they did, we have to first establish exactly what happened. The chronology is imprecise, but I summarise it here.

22 BC: Augustus leaves Rome and heads to Sicily. Marcus Lollius is elected consul for 21 BC. The people hold open a consulship for Augustus, who refuses to take it.

21 BC: Lollius takes up a sole consulship. Elections are held for the vacant position but are contested violently. Augustus summons the main candidates to him in Sicily. Quintus Lepidus eventually elected. Agrippa is sent to Rome, where he marries Augustus' daughter Julia. Further rioting takes place in the city. Augustus establishes colonies in Sicily and sails to Greece. He rewards Sparta for loyalty during the civil war, but disagrees with the Athenians. The statue of Athena supposedly turns its face against him and spits blood. Augustus deprives Athens of control over Aegina and retreated to Samos for the winter (Dio, 54.6–7).

20 BC: Augustus settles the East without a war and retrieves Roman standards captured in 53 BC. He appoints kings to various territories and returns to Samos (Dio, 54.8–9). Elections in Rome are once again violent. Sentius Saturninus is elected and a position held open for Augustus. Egnatius Rufus sets up fire brigades while acting as aedile. These appear to be violent. But Rufus wins popularity and is elected praetor for 19 BC.

19 BC: Augustus appoints Quintus Lucretius to the vacant consulship.
Saturninus is given a bodyguard by the senate and murders take place
in Rome (Dio, 54.10). Rufus runs for the consulship, but his
candidature is refused by Saturninus. Rufus is then detected in
conspiracy, arrested and executed, together with some of his followers
(Velleius Paterculus, 2.91–2). Saturninus disappears from the record
(his fate is uncertain) and on 12th October Augustus returns from the
East. The senators, led by the consul Quintus Lucretius come to
Campania to welcome Augustus back and a new temple is built to
mark the day of his return (Fortuna Redux) (*Res Gestae* 11–12).

The story of the period from 22–19 BC is one of continued violence and
political uncertainty. Every year was marked by violence and that violence
sometimes seems to have been extreme: Agrippa himself could not control it.
Some of that violence appears to have been generated by competition among
the political elite and in this regard, what we see in this period is reminiscent
of the Republic and its violent elections. It is clear that election to the
consulship was competitive and valued by members of the senate. There is no
sense that Augustus was in control of political events in Rome or that the
elections were a sham. Yet, Augustus was also powerful in his absence and his
supporters appear to have engineered elections in 22 and 20 BC so that one of
the consular positions was not filled. One might imagine (though there is no
positive evidence) that something similar would have happened in 21 BC. The
holding open of the consulships was a powerful demonstration of Augustus'
popular support and his continuing pre-eminence in Rome.

One of the peculiarities of this period is the rise and fall of Egnatius Rufus.
Rufus appears to have had an accelerated career moving straight from
aedileship to praetorship and then running for the consulship. That political
trajectory was based on support among the plebs, whom he organised into
gangs. Such actions were reminiscent of the Republican politician Clodius,
who fought for control of the streets of Rome using similar gangs. Rufus thus
deployed a recognised political technique. In a city in which the poor had no
organised political representation or voice, such groups (sometimes called
collegia) could be powerful influences, providing some basic level of support
for the poor and mobilising them either on behalf of their patrons or in voicing
certain political grievances. Rufus ran up against the traditional forces of the
senate and it would seem that the senators were able to defeat Rufus, though
it is unclear from our accounts whether the 'conspiracy' was detected after
Augustus had returned to Rome or before. Whatever the case, street violence,
electoral violence, political murders, and the political purge that marked the
end of Egnatius Rufus are ample testament to political turmoil in the Imperial
city.

The return of Augustus appears to have been a watershed in Roman political
life. The narrative account in Dio becomes more sparse and more focused on

events outside Rome. Opposition appears to be treated in general terms, as in Dio, 54.15 which mentions 'many people' who were accused of plotting against Augustus and Agrippa 'at this time', but provides very little detail that would allow us to consider who these many people were and, indeed, when 'this time' might have been. The very anonymity of the conspirators suggests that opposition was likely to have been disordered and desperate. Augustus' return was not just marked by the distribution of honours, such as the new temple of Fortuna Redux, or ceremonials, such as the senate leaving Rome to accompany Augustus into the city, but by a consolidation of Augustan power and a renewed drive for political reform. Measures which appear to have been somewhat half-heartedly broached before were now implemented with vigour. The regime acted with a confidence which would seem to reflect a renewed and unchallenged political power.

Augustan reforms: politics and the renewal of society

The events of the next few years can be divided into two separate accounts, that of politics and that of social reform. But they are not discrete areas. They are linked by a political ideology that is manifested in the reforming activities in these years. Further, the reforms depended on Augustan political control. Yet, Augustan political control was in many ways supported by the process of reform, which further cemented the dominance of the regime in part by offering a vision of the Roman state and of Roman history in which Augustus was necessary for the survival of Rome and Roman society. Augustus represented his pre-eminence as the means by which Rome could rediscover her traditions and disciplines and face the challenges that lay before her. Although clearly his position in the state was anomalous, his exceptional position was justified by the guarantee of social and political order that he brought.

This is, of course, the bargain referred to by Tacitus that we discussed above (see pp. 47–50). That bargain entailed a take-over of the Roman state, perhaps little by little, in which the old Roman Republic (or those parts of it which had been restored) was absorbed and managed by the emperor. Augustus established a form of protectorate in which the anomalous position of emperor was necessary to protect and preserve the political values of Rome, values which were traditionally incompatible with the elevation of an individual to such a position. This is the paradox of the imperial settlement. We cannot assume that people of the time were unaware of the contradictions in Augustus' role and position in the Roman state or that they acquiesced happily. Behind the emperor lay his wealth and his legions. Power and political ideology were mutually supportive and those who did not accept the ideology were bound to reflect on the power of the regime. To a considerable extent, that power had been displayed in its absence from late 22–19 BC: only Augustus could bring peace to Rome.

The constitutional settlement

On Augustus' return in 19 BC, he arrived as if in triumph. The standards were to be housed (either then or later) in the temple of Mars Ultor, which was at the centre of Augustus' great new Forum in the heart of the city. An arch was built to remember the victory (Dio, 54.8).

The political honours were equally significant. Tiberius, the older son of Livia, was given the rank of a former praetor and Drusus, Livia's younger son, was given the privilege of running for office five years ahead of the normal age. The two brothers were thus rewarded for their membership of the dynasty, very much in the same way that Marcellus had been marked out five years earlier. They were probably not being designated as political or personal heirs, however. Agrippa remained on the scene and his marriage to Julia had put him at the heart of the dynasty. Furthermore, in 19 BC, Julia had given birth to a son (Dio, 54.8), Gaius, and it seems likely that this first grandson to Augustus would be the eventual heir.

Augustus also received the power of a consul and he was allowed to sit on a curule chair in the senate between the two consuls. He was attended by lictors and thus had all the marks of consular power without actually holding the consulship (Dio, 54.10). The senate appears also to have suggested that he hold a censorship or take the role of *curator morum* (Manager of Morals), but he refused and the actions he was to take subsequently to restore the morals of the city were carried out using his tribunician powers (*Res Gestae* 6).

In 18 BC, Agrippa returned from a war in Spain. He was awarded a triumph, but he refused to take it and from this date onwards no one who was not a member of the imperial family was ever to hold a triumph. Agrippa took on the duties of civic improvement, paying for and managing the construction of a new aqueduct for Rome (the Aqua Virgo) (Dio, 54.11). As a modern society we perhaps take the supply of water too much for granted, but water was a scarce commodity in pre-industrial cities. For a city as crowded as Rome, a new aqueduct was as vital as the provision of food.

Augustus' tribunician power was time-limited and came up for renewal in 18 BC. He asked for a colleague in the role and Agrippa also received the power. This power was to be renewed in 12 BC (Dio, 54.28).

The constitutional arrangements of 19 –18 BC restored the constitutional powers that Augustus had lost in 23 BC. They also appear to have continued the practice of constitutional invention that had begun in 28–27 BC with tribunician powers. Augustus secured for himself all the privileges of magisterial power without actually holding the magistracies concerned. Furthermore, he secured for himself a partner in power. Agrippa's position was enhanced and the two men were now securely dominant in the Roman state. The dynasty was emerging and perhaps for the first time, it seemed likely that the power of Augustus would outlast the *princeps*. Should the emperor die, Agrippa was in place to continue his role.

Reforming Rome

The period after Augustus' return from the East saw a flurry of social and political reforms. This was not a new agenda. Perhaps as early as 28 BC, Octavian had an interest in social reform, in particular with regard to religious matters (he claims in *Res Gestae* 20 to have restored 82 temples in 28 BC) and the functioning of the senate, and there was also a flurry of activity when he returned to Rome from Spain in the mid-20s BC. But it was after the return from Parthia that such measures were pursued with considerable vigour and against significant opposition.

The background to these reforms lay in the problems that had beset Rome for more than two generations. The violence of Roman politics and the various civil wars tell of a period of social instability and the Romans were aware that major, long-term historical changes, such as the rise and fall of empires, required long-term structural explanations.

Livy can be considered a case in point. In the preface to his long history of the Republic, he divides his history into three periods. He fears that his readers will rush through the first parts and reach more contemporary times for in those sections they will come to understand contemporary woes. The more remote history (as if of a different age) will seem to his readers irrelevant to their contemporary concerns. But for Livy, those periods had a value. He recognised that the stories of the remote periods are less than credible in many cases and there is considerable doubt as to the historical veracity of the legends surrounding the early history of Rome, but the stories of how Rome grew and achieved greatness and of the achievements of the ancestors have considerable value and interest. In part, the value of those stories lies in their contrast with Livy's contemporary world. There is an element of escapism in this contrast: Livy imagines himself being transported back to the remote past. But Livy's expressed task is to recount the life and morals of Rome, the qualities that led to imperial expansion and the decline of those qualities and the character of Romans. Slowly, according to Livy, the Roman character slips from its virtuous position, declining bit by bit but at an ever increasing rate until it plunged into ruination. For Livy, neither the disease nor the cure (and here he must be referencing Augustan reforms) seem bearable.

Livy is certainly not alone in relating the political problems at the end of the Republic to a gradual decline in morality. We can read Sallust and even the second-century BC historian Polybius in the same way. For Livy (and indeed for Sallust), the decline seems cataclysmic and as the preservation of Roman customary values was central to the rise of empire, so the loss of Roman values will entail a loss of imperial power.

There is in such a stance a fundamental contradiction. Rome under Augustus was not quite at the height of her power: later, further territories would be added to the empire and campaigns in Spain and Germany and the lands south of the Danube were features of Augustan imperial expansion. At the start of the Augustan period the Roman Empire was not the same empire that we know it to be later. Nevertheless, Rome was unchallenged in her mastery of the Mediterranean. There was no power from the old Classical world that threatened her. The Gauls, a historic enemy of Rome, had been crushed. The Germans, whose tribes had threatened Roman power in the early second century BC, were pushed back. The war in Spain, which had been on-going intermittently for nearly two centuries, was clearly coming to a victorious end. Only the Parthians would appear to have been any sort of strategic threat to Rome and they were a remote people, who had been defeated by Augustus.

Further, not everyone appears to have taken the pessimistic stance of Livy and Sallust. Virgil, for example, in a long prophetic passage from the *Aeneid* (1.261–96) has Jupiter promise Venus that the Romans will have empire without limits (*imperium sine fine*) in time and space. A later prophecy, delivered to Aeneas in a visit to the Underworld (*Aeneid* 6. 788–883), promises a new golden age under Augustus in which the world from its most remote fastnesses of East and West will fall under Roman control. There are, however, ambivalences in both passages and an unease that allow us to question the obvious meaning of the jingoism. Both passages have unsettling images of death and violence in which there is a shadow of a very different future, perhaps a future without Augustus.

Virgil's contemporary Horace seems similarly positive in places. In a series of poems in *Odes* III, he offers a patriotic reading of the Roman present, discussing the nature of virtue (*virtus*) and envisaging conquest of Parthia (*Odes* 3.2), an unending empire (*Odes* 3.3), victory in Britain and Persia (*Odes* 3.5). Yet, even here the confidence of the poems is punctured. The virtues that will lead to conquest in *Odes* 3.2 are not those shared by the crowd; the unending empire is leavened by a brief account of the fall of the great city of Troy (ancestral home of the Romans), which suggests a different possible outcome of Roman imperial adventures; victory in Britain and Persia is measured against the defeat of Crassus at Carrhae in 53 BC and the supposed moral shame of the defeated Romans making lives for themselves in Parthia and taking Parthian wives to their beds. One can hardly think that a Roman could have read this passage without thinking of Mark Antony and realising that some Roman men at least willingly married 'barbarian' women. More fundamentally, in *Odes* 3.6, Horace reflects on a decline in religious practice, military defeats, sexual promiscuity, and adultery (and dancing), and a decline in peasant agriculture, which, for Horace, seems an inevitable trajectory of destruction.

This last poem captures key elements of the moral crisis gripping the Roman state. Horace links an increasing urban sophistication of Roman society with a deterioration in sexual morality, a falling away of religious practice, and imperial decline. That imperial decline involves civil dissension. Horace's *Odes* were probably published around 23 BC. We can assume that the diagnosis of Rome's ills that we see in Horace and Livy and Sallust was common among the Roman political class. It was on this diagnosis that Augustus acted.

The laws that Augustus passed are not easily understood. In part, this is because they are only partially preserved in later traditions. They either appear briefly in the historians or sometimes in the discussions of the jurists with more detail. Yet, the jurists were all writing much later and were interested in contemporary applications of the law in particular instances. They avoided giving detailed accounts of particular laws and would not discuss clauses which had been subsequently revised or repealed.

- *Lex Iulia de adulteriis coercendis* (18 BC). This law made adultery, which was previously a private matter, a criminal offence. Adultery was defined as an act of sexual intercourse between a married woman and a man who was not her husband. The sexuality activity of husbands was not constrained by this law except and in so far that any extra-marital sexual activity should not involve the wives of other men. The law allowed a father to kill his daughter and her lover if they were caught in the act of adultery. A husband had no rights of violence against either party. After an accusation of adultery, a husband had 60 days to bring a case against his wife. After that point, it was open to anyone to prosecute the wife. A husband was obliged to divorce a wife found guilty of adultery. If he did not, he was liable for punishment as a pimp. The penalty for adultery was relegation (exile). Women lost half their dowries. Men lost half their property (Paul, *Opinions* 2.26.1–8, 10–12, 14–17).
- *Lex Julia de maritandis ordinibus* (18 BC) and *lex Papia Poppaea* (AD 9). These two laws relate to similar issues and as the later law amended the earlier, it is not always easy to understand what was in each law. The laws laid down that senators and their children were not allowed to marry freedwomen, actors, prostitutes, or adulterers. Women were encouraged to marry again within a year after being widowed and six months after divorce. This was modified by *Lex Papia Poppaea* which doubled the time allowed to two years after death and a year after divorce (Ulpian, *Rules*, 13–14). Other sources are more vague. We are told that penalties were imposed on unmarried men and women and rewards for those who had children. The penalties are obscure and these may have been revoked by the later law. The benefits appear to relate to inheritance, limiting the rights of the unmarried and childless, especially women. The privileges for men allowed men with children to run for office early while free-born women with three children and freed women with four children were allowed to act in legal business without a tutor (see the account in Dio, 54.16–17; 55.2; 56.1–10; Suetonius, *Augustus*, 34; Gaius, *Institutes*, 1.144).
- *Lex Iulia de Theatralis* (18 BC or AD 5): This law designated seating at the theatre. The front row was to be reserved for senators and further rows

reserved for equestrians. Soldiers and boys were given their own places. Women were restricted to the back of the theatre for gladiatorial shows, though there was an exception made for Vestal Virgins. Senators and equestrians may have been banned from performing in the theatre.

- *Lex Fufia Caninia* (AD 2) and *lex Aelia Sentia* (AD 4): These laws limited the ability of masters to free their slaves by will and established certain categories of slaves, normally those who had been punished for criminal acts, who could not be freed into full Roman citizenship (Gaius, *Institutes*, 1.13–46).
- *Lex (Iulia?) de sumptuariis*: Little is known about this law other than it limited 'extravagance'.
- *Lex Iulia Maiestatis*: This law cannot be dated. We know more about the law from the Tiberian period, when the law was 'revived'. It appears to condemn those who in word or deed diminished the majesty of the Roman state and it seems to have been directed against any who might conspire against a magistrate (notably the emperor himself) or slander leading figures.

This cluster of legislation, extending over two decades, represents a major extension of the powers and interests of the Roman state. Roman political leaders had exercised some control over matters which would traditionally have been regarded as private and apolitical through institutions such as the census. The census did not just count Roman citizens, but also assigned them to the particular orders of Roman society. In earlier times, the holding of the census would have been the mechanism by which men were recruited into the senate, though that had changed in the first decades of the first century BC. But the censors still had the ability to demote a Roman citizen for moral failings (as happened to the historian Sallust). Nevertheless, the interference in 'private' matters reflected in these laws was both unprecedented and controversial.

Some of this legislation appears to have been focused primarily on the political elite, but the laws and the sentiments behind them were far from limited to the elite. Augustus appears to have been concerned to elevate the birth rate in Rome. The Roman poet, Propertius (2.7), responding to what must have been an early discussion of proposals to enforce marriage wrote 'How should I produce sons for national triumphs, none of my blood will be a soldier'. Dio's account also emphasises the perceived importance of the production of children for the future of the Roman state. Such concerns have a long history (and that is clear from the historical parallels that Augustus himself drew, according to Dio), but can also be seen in earlier perceived crises in Roman power such as that of the mid second century BC, which inspired the Gracchan reforms (see pp. 16–17 and below).

The Romans did not have good demographic information. They conducted a regular census and the figures from the census. Augustus held a census in

28 BC in which 4,063,000 citizens were registered. At the end of his reign, 40 years later, he again held a census and counted 4,937,000 citizens, a spectacular increase that Augustus himself associates with a restoration of the traditions of the ancestors (*Res Gestae* 8). The accuracy of such figures is probably very low, but they represent a concern over population levels that was, in fact, long-lasting.

The cause of low-population growth (according to the Romans) was both moral and economic (Plutarch, *Life of Tiberius Gracchus*, 8; Appian, *Civil Wars*, 1.9 for economic discussions). There was some recognition of the economic imperatives even in Augustan policy, since Augustus used his wealth to sponsor children. On at least one of his periodic tours of Italy, he distributed 1,000 *sesterces* for each legitimate child (Suetonius, *Augustus*, 46), a sum sufficiently large that it would easily support a child for several years. Yet, the majority of the discussion is set in moral terms. The accusation is that men do not wish to marry so that they do not burden themselves with wives, and wives do not wish to burden themselves with children. Not marrying could be seen as a familial strategy to preserve landholdings since in the Roman inheritance system an estate should be divided between the children equally. A man with more than two children, then, risked diminution of status. There may also have been 'lifestyle' issues that lay behind a reluctance to marry. Against such reluctance, Augustus deployed the rhetoric of duty: men and women were obliged to serve the Roman state with their bodies and offer to the Roman state a fresh generation of citizens. In a fundamental way, the legislation designed to encourage the procreation of children (and it is unclear whether this was an explicit title in the law) was about discipline and duty.

The legislation in general focuses on discipline. The legislation concerning the theatre established the theatre as a form of ceremonial centre. The theatres of Rome were enormous and almost certainly were the largest assemblies of the Roman people (probably larger than most electoral assemblies). Therefore, it was a perfect opportunity to put the Roman people on display to themselves, and the law ordered that display into particular ranks and status groups. There may even have been pressure to ensure that Romans turned up to the theatre appropriately dressed in white togas rather than dark cloaks (which were associated with Greek costumes).

The legislation on freedmen would again appear to reflect social discipline. There was a prejudice among the Roman elite about freedmen having power (pp. 289–98), but Romans freed their slaves in such numbers that it is difficult to believe that freedmen were in themselves regarded as a social problem. Indeed, the legislation focused primarily on the freeing of slaves by testamentary bequest and the freeing of slaves who were criminals. Testamentary freeing of slaves appears to have been an opportunity for the dead person to display his or her wealth and generosity at no cost to him- or herself. It was the heirs who would lose out. It confused the ordered passing of an estate from generation to generation, but it was also an extravagant display and in that it offended conventional Roman social values.

The legislation on *maiestas* falls into the same pattern. The law is a treason law, but was applied and was probably intended to be applied to deal with a much greater range of offences and issues than any contemporary treason legislation. In particular, the limitations on freedom of expression, which were taken to great lengths under later emperors, could be seen as an attempt to calm the vitriolic and vicious nature of much Roman political discourse. In a world without newspapers and libel and in which 'rumour' was perhaps the most effective way of spreading 'news', scandalous gossip could be very damaging. The *maiestas* law was designed in part to still tongues.

And finally we come to the law on adultery. Within a Judaeo-Christian-Islamic tradition, adultery is considered to be a 'sin', but the Romans had no such concept. Adultery was a social crime, an offence against the husband, and perhaps against the ordering of families. Relations between husbands and wives were not, in this period, necessarily romantic, nor was it expected that men would be sexually exclusive (see p. 69). The legislation concerning remarriage after death or divorce points to a very practical approach to marital relations: women were to be married to produce legitimate children. Men were to marry to have legitimate children. A marriage was a social relationship to achieve certain social functions. Love had little to do with it (see pp. 387–400). For this reason, divorce was not a particular issue. It simply meant that the social relationship was not achieving its goals and no particular moral stigma attached to the divorced. Moral stigma did associate itself with adultery, however, since adultery on the part of a woman showed her willingness to violate her duties to her husband (for sexual desire or pecuniary gain) and that would show her to be an unsuitable woman to be a wife.

For a man caught in adultery, the position was more complicated since his offence was against the family of the woman (husband/father). In taking an active part in the violation of the domestic-social relationship of marriage, the adulterer was offending those who had invested in that relationship. But the crime was also political since the duty of the husband and wife was to have legitimate children and the intervention of the adulterer made that impossible. Although we may think that adultery would be likely to increase the birth rate rather than reduce it, Roman men tended to believe that a woman engaged in adultery would take measures to prevent or abort pregnancies. The law was, once more, an issue of social discipline.

It is in this context of a disciplining Roman society that we can extend our understanding of the Augustan reforming agenda. In 29 BC, Augustus and Agrippa set about the reform of the senate. The aim of the reform was to reduce the number of senators from the nearly 1,000 who were now honoured by that position. There was, as far as we can tell, no ideal or canonical figure for the number of senators. Under the Republic, the number likely varied. Senatorial membership was for life and so although there was a regular in-flow of senators, the out-flow, through death, was irregular. One would expect, assuming that few senators would survive into their seventieth year, that the senators would normally number little more than 350. The 1,000 senators of 29 BC must either be an exaggeration or, as our sources suggest, reflect gifts of senatorial membership during the civil war period (Suetonius, *Augustus*, 35; Dio, 52.42). The withdrawal of such 'gifts' was likely to be controversial and what is more is likely to have affected more those who had benefited from the patronage of the triumvirs and Julius Caesar. Agrippa and Augustus were, therefore, seemingly acting against their own interests. Yet, they pressed ahead and one can only explain their determination as resulting from a desire to be seen to restore Roman order and social discipline: those who were not deserving of status were to lose it.

A similar purge took place in 18 BC, when Augustus organised an extraordinarily elaborate system of selection by election by colleagues and by lot to reduce the number of senators. The result was predictably chaotic with distinguished generals finding themselves relegated and dishonoured and several sons volunteering to step aside to make room for fathers who had been similarly offended. Augustus was forced to intervene to 'correct' the lists. The whole flawed process was evidently designed so that no one could accuse the emperor of removing his political opponents and to attempt to ensure that only those generally regarded as the best and most honourable men were sitting in the senate (Dio, 54. 14–15). The failed reforms of 18 BC, however, encouraged Augustus to another attempt in 13 BC. This time Augustus established a special census level for senators of 1,000,000 *sesterces*. Again, this was a controversial measure since some distinguished families could not make the new census level, but it would also seem to reflect not political management but a desire to differentiate senators from 'ordinary' members of the landed aristocracy. It also, and incidentally, reflects a Roman view that wealth and honour were closely correlated (Dio, 54.26). Such a desire to differentiate the senators from the rest of society can also be seen in the legal limitations placed on senators' rights to marry whom they pleased.

Augustus also invented a tradition by which the second order of Roman society, the equestrians, was also disciplined. Equestrians were expected to parade past the emperor on horseback, a ceremonial that recalled the origins of the order as the Roman cavalry, but which was also clearly designed to suggest that equestrians had duties to perform (Suetonius, *Augustus*, 38–39).

The laws and regulations of Roman society reflect the consistent application of an ideology. Rome had become undisciplined and Augustus' reforms were designed to return to a prior age of Roman morality. To an extent, one might wonder who could object to such an aim, and it certainly fits with the predominant flavour of Roman moralising texts. Further, later modern historians have often looked upon Augustan reforms with approval. If we associate these reforms with Augustan restoration of temples and religious actions, then much of Augustan political activity would appeal to the socially conservative.

But the reforms were contested, and with good reason. The Roman conceptions of public and private were very different from those of today. Yet, what went on in a Roman's house was, largely, a matter for the residents of that house. After the Augustan reforms, it was a matter of state interest, what the sexual relations were within the house. The pressure from Augustus was to subjugate individual desires to the wishes of the state. In that discipline, freedom was threatened.

The head of the state would, obviously, be the major beneficiary of a new culture of subservience, but also the enforcing of those disciplines required a head of state. Augustus' position was justified by measures which disciplined the Roman people. In this new dispensation, a citizen had to face the situation that the state was now interested in whether one is married, has children, or engaged in adultery; how one disposed of one's property at death; and where one sits or what one wears in the theatre. Further, we have to wonder whether a state dominated by an emperor has any right to demand the loyalty of its citizens.

If the politics of the Augustan reforms give us pause for thought, a further problem lies in the practical results of these laws. There were few in Roman society who would openly support adultery, though, and perhaps in response to the authoritarianism of the Augustan regime, Propertius and Ovid were aware of the oppositional implications of their romantic liaisons. Ovid's *Ars Amatoria* (*The Art of Love*) very obviously runs against the moral tide in his advice on seduction, a poetry of love that was necessarily politicised. Yet, even Tacitus (*Annales*, 3.25), whose histories do not suggest a man prone to moral levity, criticised the laws, not because the faults that were being addressed were not faults, but because the laws opened a door into the private lives of every Roman and exposed every Roman to malicious charges. Law was transformed from an instrument by which the rights and privileges of Romans were protected to become a tool of imperial repression. As Tacitus puts it, the laws put guards over all and became 'chains' that were a terror to Romans (*Annales*, 3. 28).

Nevertheless, Augustan confidence appears to have been high. The new laws were a cause for celebration. In May 17 BC, Augustus and Agrippa presided over a huge festival in which the Romans proclaimed a new age. There were sacrifices and games and processions and Horace composed a hymn that was sung on the occasion. The games represented a fresh start for Rome after the civil wars. The new age was at least intended to be one of moral discipline and imperial vigour. In the years before the celebration, Virgil had provided Rome with its great epic. At the centre of the poem was a hero, Aeneas. Aeneas had a predominant moral characteristic: he was, pius (pious). That piety drove Aeneas to fulfil his mythical destiny in devotion to his people. But such devotion came at a considerable cost. He founded Rome, but had to abandon his own city, Troy, losing his wife in the process. He deserted Dido, his Carthaginian lover, since his relationship with her was incompatible with his designated destiny. Aeneas is hero who is difficult to admire partly because his duty forces him to give up so much and his devotion to the Roman state is absolute. Our ambivalence in the face of such devotion seems also to be shared by Virgil (see below).

Not everyone was persuaded by the new golden age. Ovid advised those who wished to seduce a girl to bring presents, not poems. He wrote, *Ars Amatoria*, 278–9.

> Truly, now is the Golden Age: with gold
> comes many offices, with gold love is won

For Ovid, the age was 'golden' because all could be bought by gold. His use of the phrase highlights the moral hypocrisy of a state which trumpets its moral foundations, but in which money can buy everyone.

Politics, poetry and propaganda

The Augustan age saw a flourishing of Roman cultural life. There are five major poets associated with the period: Virgil, Horace, Tibullus, Propertius, and Ovid. Augustus also presided over an extended period of urban renewal in Rome. The programme led to the remodelling of the Roman Forum, the traditional political centre of Rome, large-scale construction on Palatine Hill, on which Augustus had his house, the building of a new Forum, the Forum of Augustus, the construction of various theatres and porticoes across the centre of the city, many named after members of the Augustan household, and an extensive series of related buildings on the Campus Martius which was built in collaboration with Augustus' close associate, Agrippa. The most famous surviving monuments from Augustan Rome are probably the Ara Pacis and the Mausoleum of Augustus, but the scale and number of buildings erected in the Augustan period is truly impressive and must have led to a complete transformation of the city. The major monuments are, however, but one element of the Augustan impress on the city. Statues of Augustus and his family and close associates were common.

Many of the monuments, much of the art, and many of the poems were avowedly political and it is tempting to describe them as propaganda. Yet, this is something of an anachronism. Propaganda is associated with the deliberate organisation of opinion through mass media, normally via a state agency. The definitive propagandists have been associated with twentieth-century totalitarian regimes or with ideological struggles which required the organisation of opinion. The Roman situation was different. There was no ministry of propaganda.

The relationship between the regime and the generation of particular political images is opaque. Some of the poets, notably Virgil and Horace, wrote of their close relationships with Maecenas, who was perhaps the third-ranked man in the Augustan regime, at least in the early decades. Propertius also wrote as if Maecenas was his patron, though the relationship is less clear. Nevertheless, there can be little doubt that, with one exception, there was a distance between the Augustan grandee and the production of poetry.

It seems unlikely also that Augustus or those close to him spent much time with the moneyers deciding what image to stamp on the coins. At least some of the definitive 'Augustan' buildings, such as the Ara Pacis, were, in fact, senatorial buildings. The creative process that lay behind the art, such as portrait statuary, is also obscure. We cannot detect an administrative or straightforward political relationship between a work of art and the political masters.

Nevertheless, much of the art of the period (including architecture and literature) consistently embraced political issues in ways which are perhaps uncommon in modern artistic production. At least some of that art appears to have been directed to secure the favour of the imperial regime. It seems pointless to read a monument such as the Forum of Augustus, which had a statue of Augustus at its centre and which displayed a version of Roman history that would appear to have been that favoured by the regime in its décor, without acknowledging that the politics of the regime were directly inspirational. Even if the process by which the ideology of the regime found its artistic expression may be opaque, there can be no doubt that the regime discovered ways in which its ideological perspectives could be represented. If a ministry of propaganda works to build belief in a set of ideas that support a particular political regime, then much Augustan art and architecture shares features with propaganda.

Poetry

Yet, the looseness of the relationship between the political regime and at least some artistic production leaves room for analysis. A case in point is poetry. The poetry of Horace and Virgil reflect many Augustan themes. The *Aeneid,*, in particular, is seen as an Augustan epic. The story is one of the foundation of the Roman people after the sack of Troy. The treatment of Augustan themes is evident throughout the work. The hero of the epic, Aeneas, is described throughout as *pius* (dutiful). That duty is manifest in his relationship to the gods, his family, and his people. From the first scenes of the epic, when Aeneas and his band wash up on the shores of Africa, we are presented with a driven hero, conscious of his manifest destiny to found a great city in the West. That destiny is advertised in various prophetic monuments in the text, notably when Venus secures a prophecy from Jupiter in Book 1, 261–96, at the opening of the epic, which promises the reader that there will be a happy ending, that Rome will be founded, and that Romans will enjoy an 'empire with end' that will culminate in 'Trojan Caesar' (clearly Augustus), conqueror of the East (which Augustus claimed as his achievement in 19 BC, just two years before the presumed publication date of the *Aeneid*). A similar prophecy, delivered this time directly to Aeneas in his visit to the Underworld (6. 788–883), offers a summary account of all Roman history, with a focus on conquering heroes and an ending with Augustus. A third prophecy begins in 8.675 in which we have described a divinely-made shield delivered to Aeneas with which he will finally triumph over his enemies in Italy. That shield has at its centrepiece a depiction of the battle of Actium and Augustus' subsequent triumph. In the *Aeneid*, Augustus is an 'end of history'.

There is little ambiguity about the pro-Augustan depictions in the *Aeneid*. It is a patriotic epic of Roman myth-history which celebrates a certain representation of Roman history and identity: it tells the Romans who they are and from whence they have come, and at the centre of that narrative is Augustus. One can try to envisage what a contemporary equivalent might look like, but away from the great cinematic epics and nationalistic histories of the early twentieth century, there are no obvious parallels and that in itself should give us pause for thought.

Yet, if there is no ambiguity, there is ambivalence, an ambivalence which has allowed the detection of 'other voices' in the *Aeneid*. This 'other voice' is more doubtful and less triumphant, more aware of the costs of Rome, and cautious about the outcomes of Rome's imperial success. This voice is not necessarily more truthful than that which expresses the superficial and obvious meanings of the text, but it does express a nuanced approach to Augustan culture. In that nuancing, of course, there is an enormous difference from the state-sponsored propaganda (however beautifully done) of the twentieth century.

The ambiguity runs through the text and I will give only a few examples. The most obvious comes in the relationship between Aeneas and Dido, queen of Carthage, which dominates books one and four. Dido, who has sworn to remain unmarried after the death of her first husband, is forced by Venus and Cupid to fall in love with Aeneas. Their relationship is consummated in a cave to which they are driven to take shelter during a convenient rainstorm. Dido supports the Trojan refugees and gives them shelter in Carthage. Eventually, though, Mercury is sent to remind Aeneas of his duty, and he starts to pack, arrange his fleet, and prepare to sail (all by night). Dido notices that her lover is leaving and is somewhat upset. There is a confrontation between the two in which Aeneas excuses his behaviour and Dido levels accusations at him. Aeneas leaves. Dido kills herself, swearing eternal enmity between her city and Rome.

The story provides the mythic background for Rome's struggle with Carthage, but it also raises fundamental moral questions. Primarily, does Aeneas behave badly towards Dido? It is possible to construct an argument that Aeneas is only doing his duty and that Dido is remiss in breaking her oath to stay unmarried. But, however one reads the story, the facts are that

Dido is manipulated by the gods, seduced, and abandoned. Aeneas does not have any obvious compunction in abandoning a woman who regards him as her husband and with whom he had been co-operating in developing her city. There is a further question as to whether Aeneas loved Dido. The purposes of the city of Rome are such that the feelings and lives of individuals are as nothing.

Rome's founding is in blood and loss. And not just that of Dido; the key figure of the later books is Turnus, who leads Italian resistance to the Trojan invaders. Turnus is also the plaything of the gods, driven on in a reckless war. In the culminating scene of the *Aeneid*, Turnus, defenceless, is slaughtered. Although Aeneas might be right to kill Turnus (and in so doing avenge the death of a friend), the closing of the epic on such an angry and vicious note darkens the story. At that moment, Aeneas is Achilles, the morally questionable hero of the *Iliad*, and by association Turnus is Hector, a man of family. It is difficult not to feel for the Italian hero and although we might think that Romans would shed few tears, the whole episode brings home the plot device of founding the Roman people in a war fought between future Romans and Italians: a war which in the late first century BC could not help but recall the civil wars.

The presence and rejection of Dido in the story had other contemporary resonances. Dido, a powerful female figure, can be read as an allegory of Cleopatra, but she can also be read (as can Cleopatra) as a parallel of another central figure in the Roman literary culture of the period, the elegiac *puella* (see Chapter 15 for further discussion). The *puella* was the 'girl' of Roman erotic poetry and was a character that had been developing since her effective invention by the poet Catullus in the mid-first century BC. Whereas Catullus celebrated his relationship with Lesbia, we find various manifestations of the elegiac *puella* in the writings of Gallus, Tibullus, Propertius and Ovid through the Augustan period. The *puella* is in many ways a literary construct, a girl who is part muse and part symbol of poetry itself, but she also poses as mistress to the poet and in that guise has more concrete character. The poets' devotion to their mistresses ran counter, sometimes explicitly as in Propertius, 2.7 and Ovid's *Ars Amatoria*, to the moral and political values of the emperor. The relationship was incompatible with marriage, seemingly adulterous and without children. The poets refused to write of martial affairs because of their devotion to the girl; they wrote instead of battles of a narrow bed. The poets proclaimed their subservience to love, a slavery that ran counter to the traditional values of citizenship and masculinity. Moreover, the poet could not serve in the army or take in political office since both would distract from the far greater service of love. However seriously this was intended and however grounded in social reality, the poets present us with a picture of an alternative set of values to the traditional service to the state and with a life that finds its meaning in the private sphere of love and erotic passion and not in the public sphere of politics and duty.

There is thus a thread that runs from Dido to the historical Cleopatra and the depiction of Antony's passion for Cleopatra, to the literary *puella* and an alternate lifestyle. In this way, we can come to understand the ambivalence of Aeneas' rejection of Dido. It is not just a man finding an unsatisfactory way of leaving a lover, but it is a rejection of whole way of life in favour of a life of duty in which, in Aeneas' case, there is a fulfilment of a historic destiny, but precious little evidence of personal emotional satisfaction. Dido's suicide in book four remains a looming presence in the text, darkening the story as much as the slaughter of Turnus, and offering the question or the possibility of an alternative to the life of a dutiful (*pius*) Roman.

If the relationship between regime and poetry in the most patriotic of Augustan poetry (the *Aeneid*) is often ambivalent, the position of the elegists is yet more difficult to understand. The last of the Augustan elegists, Ovid, is often classed as an opposition figure and with reason. His later poetry, the *Tristia* and *Epistulae ex Ponto* are poems from exile and often about exile. Ovid plays with our expectations in these poems, never quite confessing, but always exploring his relationship with the imperial family. Ovid's exile was likely real but also figurative, a separation from the political world that was Augustan Rome and its increasingly limiting ideologies. Ovid never finds himself at home in exile, but one wonders whether he was already an exile in Augustan Rome.

The exilic pose that made Ovid a stranger in the barbarian world and in the unfamiliar world of Augustan Rome continues a literary trajectory already obvious in his own Augustan epic, the *Metamorphoses*. This is a collection of strange and wonderful, frequently violent and sexual stories of transformation. The *Metamorphoses* depicts a world in which gods will attempt to rape girls who will be turned into trees, in which boys become flowers, and in which a hunter is transformed into his prey (for the crime of seeing the goddess Diana naked) and ripped apart by his own hounds. In a world of strange of capricious gods, which memorably includes Julius Caesar in a final concluding metamorphosis from man to god, in which laws of physics and nature were routinely by-passed, no one could be sure of their place. Ovid was thus alienated from a world that was strange, obeyed few laws, but was definitively Augustan.

Yet, Ovid's later work, in which we must include his poem on the Roman calendar, the *Fasti*, was political in the broadest sense. There are elements of the poetry that would seem to praise the imperial family (sincerity is always an unresolved issue) and it is hard to describe Ovid's political stance. Conditioned as we are to a world of political parties and groups which offer either relatively coherent ideological stances or at least a clear sense of belonging to a defined faction, understanding a political world in which there were no parties and no defined political groups, in which ideologies were ill-defined and the regime was not changeable through a political process, presents considerable problems to our imagination. This is a problem which we will face in later chapters. Opposition to the emperor in theory was difficult and in fact limited. The emperor was a political given and however much individuals might wish the empire away, they could not. Politics was a matter of negotiating a relationship with the political certainty that was government by emperors. One might object to particular actions or particular individuals, but the emperor was a very powerful fact of life.

It is perhaps in this light that we should understand the poetry of Propertius and the early poetry of Ovid. Both wrote elegiac love poetry. Propertius frequently engaged with political issues in a tangential way. In 2.31, for instance, he devotes a poem to celebrating the opening of a portico of Apollo. This portico was part of a monumental complex on the Palatine Hill that created a unified complex of a new temple of Apollo, the house of Augustus, the house of Livia (Augustus' wife), libraries and, though this is less obviously linked, the temple of Vesta. It was therefore one of the major projects by which the regime advertised itself to the people of Rome and Propertius describes the décor of the temple in reverential tones. Yet, the purpose of the poem is in part to excuse the poet who was late (again) to meet his girlfriend, Cynthia, who, again, took offence at his tardiness. The portico was praised in part because Cynthia would be more reluctant to leave the city if it were there.

Yet, in spite of this ironic twisting of religious values to the interests of illicit love, Propertius dedicated the first poem of his second book to Maecenas, the close associate of the emperor and the man who sponsored Horace, a more explicitly pro-Augustan poet. By convention, the first poem of a collection was dedicated to the poet's patron. Propertius, then, would have us believe that he was close to the regime, sponsored by one of its leading figures and although Propertius produced poems refusing assumed requests from Maecenas to turn his hand to epic, there was a complex and multiple relationship with the regime.

There is no such question with the early poems of Ovid, the three books of elegies (*Amores*), and the guidance on love affairs in *Ars Amatoria*, the *Art of Love*, and *Remedia Amoris*, *The Cures of Love*. In a context in which the emperor had passed legislation on adultery, poetry which proclaimed how to seduce women could hardly avoid a political context. And Ovid uses the illicit nature of his advice to add verve to his verse. In the first book of the *Ars Amatoria* (1.32–4), Ovid excuses his project 'We sing of safe sex and allowable secrecy; there will be no crime in my verse'. The object of his lustful intent is, it is presumed, a girl of lower status, a courtesan or prostitute, perhaps a freedwoman. But the advice in the *Ars* (comically inappropriate in many cases) does not seem to be status-specific. Two hundred lines later, he forgets the safeness of his lusts (1. 269–70), 'All women are able to be caught', and 300 lines after that he is advising the lover to 'let it be your prayer to please the husband of your girl' (579–80). At the very least, the suggested relationship is adulterous and there is no reason to believe that the lover is not attending respectable dinner parties given by members of the political elite at which he can try out his seduction techniques.

Such poetry is, indeed, political, but it is hardly damaging to the regime. Ovid and Propertius were self-consciously marginal to the political mainstream and characters who were unconventional in their morality. They might irritate the morally censorious emperor and his associates, but they could not threaten him. The irony and wit was in many ways a withdrawal from the front line of politics and as a challenge to the regime, it was individualised. They were saying that they did not conform as individuals, but they were not a political movement. Yet, even so Ovid found himself exiled.

Building the Imperial City

The Augustan rebuilding of the city of Rome was extensive. Many buildings were erected in this period and many restored. The centre of Rome, the old Roman forum, was remodelled completely. One end of the Forum, leading out towards where the Colosseum now stands and away from the Capitoline, was closed off by triumphal arches and a temple to the Divus Caesar, now destroyed. At the other of the Forum, the site of the senate house, burnt to the ground in rioting in the late Republic, was adorned by a new senate house, the *Curia Iulia*. Statues and victory monuments celebrating Octavian's victory at Actium and over Sextus Pompeius at Naulachos dominated the central sectors of the Forum. On one side, a new or remodelled portico provided a formal coherence to what had been a fairly disordered space. On the other flank, lines of temples led up the Palatine hill to the house of Augustus and the new bright, white temple of Apollo. Behind the Forum, from the Palatine, Augustus constructed a whole ceremonial centre, following in the wake of Julius Caesar's constructions, and paving the way for future forum builders, Vespasian and Domitian, Nerva and Trajan. But it was not just in the heart of the city that there were new buildings. New buildings appeared all across the city and, indeed, all across Italy and spilling out across the provinces.

Some of those buildings carried a distinct architectural or artistic message. The mausoleum of Augustus, for instance, was the intended tomb of the emperor. Its construction on the banks of the Tiber reflected a commitment to Rome which differentiated Augustus from Antony (who famously expressed his request to be buried alongside Cleopatra in Alexandria). That narrow political point, important at the moment when the Mausoleum was being designed and constructed, obviously lost its relevance as Actium receded in people's political consciousness. More obvious was the scale of the monument. In the same period, a Roman aristocrat built himself a pyramid just outside the Ostian gate of the city, but that grandiose (and perhaps politically questionable) statement was dwarfed by the scale of the Augustan tomb. There had never been anything like it in Rome before. In antiquity the tomb was crowned by a statue of the emperor and after Augustus' death, his *Res*

Gestae were inscribed on bronze pillars at its entrance. The tomb (and text) marked Augustan achievement and commitment to the city. The scale was more than human, recalling the hero cults of Greece. In so doing, the tomb reflected a consciousness of the historical significance of Augustus, and this was manifest during his own lifetime.

The Ara Pacis is another monument loaded with symbolic significance. Although not particular large, the monument is adorned with spectacular and detailed friezes. These represent the fertility of Italy in the new era of Augustan peace. The foliage runs a disciplined riot around the monument. On one of the panels, an unidentified goddess (possibly Italia, possibly Pax, possibly Venus, but the identification hardly matters) suckles infants as symbols of abundance and agricultural vitality surround her, an ox and a sheep sit peacefully at her feet, and she is attended by two bare-breasted nymphs/goddesses, one sitting on a swan and the other on a dragon. Other friezes may depict Mars, and father Aeneas, and Romulus and Remus, though not all these identifications are certain. Around the outside of the temple are two long friezes representing a procession for sacrifice. Notable is the realism of the portrayals. At least some of the characters are recognisable or their identities can be reconstructed and we can see male and female members and the children of the Augustan house. The other frieze represents the senators, coming to attend the same sacrifice.

The monument is fascinating in the manner in which we can read it as representation of the regime. Most obviously, we have a presentation of harmony in the coming together of the community's leaders for the sacrifice. That community is represented by the senate and the imperial family. We have perhaps the earliest representation of a family in Roman public art and in itself it shows that the Augustan family had made that transition from being a 'normal' familial unit to being identified with the state: this is a monument that establishes and reflects an imperial dynasty, but one which exists within the confines of the traditions reflected in the presence of the senators. Moreover, the radical nature of Augustan dynastic representation finds a historical and religious context in the representations of the mythic origins of Rome and the blessings of the gods associated with the new Augustan age which adorn the monument.

We could, of course, multiply the readings of particular monuments, though few are as obvious and easy to read as the two I have selected. The broader issue, though, is why Augustan invested so much effort in the urban fabric of the city and what the overall meaning of the Augustan building programme was. To an extent, even a relatively neutral building, such as the Theatre of Marcellus had a wider meaning. Further, some of the major and probably most expensive Augustan projects, the aqueducts, were primarily functional, though they had a monumental value.

The Augustan project, we are told, was to turn Rome into a city of marble, from the city of brick it was before. But we need to ask ourselves why Augustus undertook this project. It is all too easy to see in this aim a programme of civic renewal and improvement akin to that of modern city planners and, of course, there are similarities. Agrippa, in particular, devoted considerable attention to the infrastructure of the city, its water supply and, equally important, its water management strategies: we should remember that Roman sewers were primarily concerned with the drainage of rain and flood waters and were not built to deal with human waste, which was removed from the city in soil carts.[14]

Yet, the Augustan project was not (just) one of civic improvement. The 'marbling' of the city reflected a shift in the city's representation. Rome, by far the largest city of antiquity, was a 'city of brick', crammed with a disorderly crowd whose political and economic demands from time to time had erupted onto the streets of the city and provided a dynamic to Roman politics. The city of brick was a city of tenements, of shops, of small and disordered buildings. The city of marble would be monumental and religious: temples and civic monuments, theatres and arcades were to mark the new imperial centre. Turning the city of brick into a city of marble was an act of power and wealth: Augustus spent vast monies to leave his imprint on the city. In this way, he could be seen as a second founder of Rome, building Rome anew, as it had been built by Romulus. In its newness, the city broke from its past and Augustus offered it a fresh start. In his association with Romulus (and back to the original founder of the Roman people, Aeneas) Augustus gave his leadership of the Roman people a justificatory association and a mythic foundation. Augustan monarchy invented the traditions of a very old Rome, in which monarchy was the preferred system of governance and it also built that myth into the ordered representation of the new city.

Further, the building of a new city raised the question, what kind of city would this new Rome be? Here, again, the marble is significant. The building of the temples reflected a new contract with the gods and a renewal of the honours that the Romans had given to them. The restoration of temples and religious buildings, then, was compatible with a renewal of the city and its religious traditions. It was those traditions that had provided the historic blessing of the gods which had brought Rome her empire.

The 'marbling' of Rome also reflected a new social discipline and a newly-enforced hierarchy that was of political import. The Ara Pacis, for instance, shows a marble procession of the senators and the imperial family, but missing from this portrayal of Rome are the crowds, the observers who must have watched the processions through the streets. Such ceremonials were of great importance in antiquity as they marked out political divisions. In a similar way, Augustan legislation (*lex Iulia theatralis*, passed after AD 5) organised the seating in the theatre (the largest and most important assembly in Rome) so that the wealthy sat at the front. In the theatre, the Roman people were on display to each other. Augustus also reorganised the local administration of the city, dividing into regions and *vici* (streets or perhaps neighbourhoods), each of which had a *vicomagistratus*. Among the duties of the *vicomagistratus*, though perhaps not formally defined, was the worship of the emperor (see pp. 409–12).

Augustan Rome represented itself as an Imperial city, adorned by monuments that reflected and represented Rome's imperial wealth and triumphs, notably in the obelisks looted from Egypt, the arches of victory, the statues, and the Forum of Augustus. The city represented itself as devoted to the gods and blessed by the gods. The city was also built to represent a relationship with history (the city's heritage), the political hierarchies of Rome, the imperial family, and, most of all, Augustus himself. The marble represented a permanence of the shape of the city, a monumentality that set in stone a particular set of ideas and social relations. The marble city was a city of Augustan order and in claiming to have found the city in brick (in a form of popular, unofficial, plebeian chaos) and left it in marble, Augustus was representing more than an architectural change, but a political transformation of the city of Rome.

Death of the emperor: birth of an empire

The death of Augustus was long foretold. As a young man, his health was far from robust. He was ill throughout much of the crucial year of 42 BC. Sometime in the 30s BC he began construction of his monumental tomb. If poets such as Horace wondered what would happen should the leader take his rightful place among the gods, one has to presume that others looked on the prospect of the demise of Augustus as an opportunity. After all, Sulla's death had left no succession in place and led to the assumption of power by the senate. For a brief period after Caesar's death, there had been the prospect of a restored Republic. In 23 BC, the succession became a political issue, with Augustus' near death. Marcellus was his closest male relative and was marked out to succeed him, but it was less obvious what Marcellus would succeed. There does not appear to have been any generalised discussion of what succession to Augustus meant, perhaps until after Augustus died in AD 14. Nevertheless, it is clear that some sort of succession was intended, and we can observe the management of that succession in Augustus' management of his family.

Augustan family politics

Octavian owed his political career to a posthumous adoption. Caesar had made him his son and from March 44, Octavian was referred to by contemporaries as Caesar. Romans were careful about succession. They often left elaborate wills and were anxious to secure a continuation of their reputation into the next generation. Yet, although there were some exceptional families, a successful father could not guarantee political success for his son, though he could help. Roman sons inherited their father's property and their network of friends. That network enabled an ambitious son to gain prestigious offices and appointments to important campaigns. The network allowed the son to stand out from his peers, and there can be little doubt that an adult son of a powerful father could benefit from those anxious to win favour from the father. A powerful father also planned his family. He would marry his sons and daughters to prominent individuals, cementing friendships in familial ties and those ties would prove useful for the next generation.

We see exactly this policy with Augustus, but Augustus also used marriage alliances to bind his family closer together. Augustus had only a daughter, Julia; his marriage to Livia produced no children. His closest other relative was his sister, Octavia. Octavia had been married to Claudius Marcellus, a prominent aristocrat, and then to Mark Antony. With Marcellus, she had a boy, Claudius Marcellus, and two girls, both called Marcella, and with Antony she had two girls, both called Antonia. Livia had two children, Tiberius Claudius, the future emperor, and his younger brother, Drusus Claudius. From this generation, Augustus made a range of marriages, which death shifted round.

- The most important pawn in this game was Julia, daughter of Augustus. Claudius Marcellus married Julia. After Marcellus' death, Julia was married to Agrippa (Augustus' closest political associate) and after Agrippa's death, she was passed on to Tiberius.
- The elder Antonia, daughter of Octavia and Mark Antony, was married into the important family of the Domitii Ahenobarbi, which went on to produce Nero.
- The younger Antonia was married to Drusus, the younger son of Augustus' wife and they had three children, Germanicus, the future emperor Claudius, and Livia Julia.
- The elder Marcella, daughter of Octavia and Claudius Marcellus, was married to Agrippa and later to Iullus Antonius, a son of Mark Antony.
- The younger Marcella was married into the Aemilii Paulli, another very prominent family in Rome.
- Tiberius Claudius, the elder son of Livia (from an earlier marriage), was first married to Vipsania, daughter of Agrippa, and then to Julia, daughter of Augustus.

These marriages produced a further generation with which Augustus could make his dynastic arrangements. The marriage of Agrippa and Julia proved successful with five children, Gaius, Lucius and Agrippa Postumus (born after his father's death), and the daughters, Julia and Agrippina.

- Gaius married Livia Julia, daughter of the younger Antonia and Drusus.

- Julia was married to Lucius Aemilius Paullus, son of the man who married the younger Marcella.
- Agrippina was married to Germanicus, the son of Antonia and Drusus.

These marriages represent a strategy of endogamy, marriage within the family, rather than exogamy, marriage outside the family. For instance, Germanicus was the grandson of Antony and Octavia and of Livia; he was also the nephew of Tiberius and was married to the granddaughter of Augustus. Such strategies are frequently employed in relatively traditional societies in which social networks are built around familial relationships.

The Romans used marriage to reinforce relationships and among the political classes, women and men were pawns in the socio-political game, given in marriage (normally with the consent of those involved) to further the aims of the family. As we have already seen, marital relationships in Roman society were not expected to be romantic: they were social and political, and everyone understood the reasons for marriage. Anthropologists call such alliances 'lineage marriages'. But lineage marriages are not necessarily endogamous: a family might decide to draw another family into its circle, making a strategic alliance that might be of use to the family members. We see this in the marriages to Aemilii Paulli. Augustus' use of marriage is distinctive in that it reinforces the unity of the family. We see that Agrippa and the sons of Livia are closely bound into this familial unit by marriage. The family was effectively constructed around two lines of descent, one through Augustus and his sister (the Julian line) and the other from Livia's children (the Claudii) and in each generation, these two lines were matched.

This process created the dynasty that we know as the Julio-Claudians. But we should not take this process of creation for granted. Augustus manipulated the members of his family to create a strongly defined unit, a royal house, in which the most suitable marital partner for a member of the extended household was another member of the extended family. This strategy looks like the plan of royalty, creating links among those of equal status and, although we cannot and should not think of the Augustan family as a royal family at this date, the process of inter-marriage worked to separate the family and ensure that it was distinctively placed in the Roman aristocracy. Augustus was progressively making his rule a family matter. As he had inherited from Julius Caesar, so those close to him in the family, Marcellus, Agrippa, Tiberius, Drusus, Gaius, Lucius and, eventually, Germanicus, were his associates in power. On the walls of the Ara Pacis, Augustus had depicted this new political force in Roman society, the *domus Augusti*.

The *domus Augusti* operated in such a way that Augustus was able to bring in close friends and family as his associates in power. The advantage of such a system was that the most important provinces and roles in the state could be dominated by those who were closest to the emperor. Further, the distribution of power and offices in the imperial family allowed the concentration of political and administrative resources in the imperial household. There was no Roman state bureaucracy to speak of and administrative tasks tended to be performed by the households of magistrates. The imperial household became a form of bureaucracy itself, gradually concentrating governmental functions. All Roman households were, in one way or another, multi-generational enterprises in which the interests of the family rather than the individual drove on the household. The *domus Augusti* started to take on the form of a family enterprise in which all members of the family were expected to work under the head of household for the benefit of the whole family.

The familial nature of Augustan dominance needs to be taken into account when thinking about the nature of Augustan power and the break with the Republican era. Further, Augustan familial strategy developed over the period of his power.

Octavian had inherited from Julius Caesar. That inheritance had not brought political office, though it had brought political power. The power came from an alliance that Octavian was able to build with Caesar's veterans and the plebs of Rome. This alliance was cemented by Octavian's strategic distribution of favours and money to build a network of support. There was no requirement for that network to survive the death of its leader, but by association, Agrippa and the other members of the imperial house had leadership positions within the network and soldiers, veterans, and plebs, as well as those senators who showed loyalty to the imperial family, would expect to benefit from continued loyalty to the Augustan household.

If political power could survive the death of the leader of the imperial household, there remained a question about political office and the exact relationship between the power that was concentrated in the imperial household and the legal institutions of the Roman state. This problem may not have been obvious nor easily resolved in the early years of Augustan dominance. In 23 BC, for instance, the illness of Augustus and the death of Marcellus were an indication of the uncertainties that would follow Augustus' death and it seems likely that Augustus was forced to show unruly senators that he was not establishing a dynasty. But the death of Marcellus brought Agrippa closer into the family. His marriage to Julia put him at the heart of the Augustan household and confirmed his position as the leading figure in the Roman state after Augustus himself. Although there was no constitutional recognition of his power at that point, when Augustus returned in 19 BC he was able to associate Agrippa with his tribunician power (in 18 BC) and after that point, other members of the Augustan family always held offices and powers similar or identical to those held by Augustus.

The distribution of offices to the leading members of the imperial family meant that although office could not be inherited, there would be no repetition of the uncomfortable and dangerous period that followed the death of Caesar. The senate would not step into any political vacuum, because there would be no political vacuum. Augustus established the framework for a smooth transition of power from one generation to the next. Although much that Augustus did had some form of Republican precedent, especially in the offices that he held, the association of his family with his political offices was unprecedented and a remarkable transformation of Rome from a state led by elected magistrates whose office was time-limited to one which was dominated by a single family.

Yet, Augustan family strategy would hit many obstacles. Such obstacles were inevitable when a strategy was extended over more than 30 years. Furthermore, we are dealing with individuals within a household and there would inevitably be tensions and difficulties. Imperial history can always, as Suetonius shows, become biography.

The most obvious difficulties were caused by death. Marcellus died in 23 BC and robbed Augustus of his most obvious heir. Agrippa replaced him, and he and Julia provided Augustus with grandchildren. Gaius and Lucius were adopted by the emperor as his sons. They were marked out to succeed him, but there was a long period of their childhood and youth that was to be negotiated. In the meantime, Agrippa, their father, along with Tiberius and Drusus, were Augustus' assistants in power. Agrippa's death in 12 BC led to the further elevation of the sons of Livia. Both campaigned extensively in Germany. Tiberius divorced Vipsania, Agrippa's daughter by an earlier marriage, and married Julia, the twice-widowed daughter of Augustus. The death of Drusus in 9 BC left Tiberius as the sole adult male in the imperial family.

As the leading general, Tiberius had slipped as easily into the shoes of Agrippa as he had been slipped into the bed of Agrippa's wife. But then, for reasons which are far from clear, the family began to fracture. In 7 BC, Tiberius was consul. The following year he assumed tribunician power and was given extensive duties in the East. Yet, he chose to step down from office. He retained tribunician power until the grant ran out five years later, but he left the political scene (Dio, 55.9).

It is difficult not to associate the voluntary exile of Tiberius with the emergence into public life of Gaius Caesar, Julia's eldest son, in 5 BC. Still a youth, he was far too young for major political office, yet it would have been clear that he was being groomed for eventual succession, perhaps jointly with his younger brother Lucius. We must assume that this plan cannot have been a surprise to Tiberius: these boys were after all the adopted sons of the emperor. But perhaps we are too hasty in understanding the dynamics of the imperial household. After all, this was not yet a royal family and it certainly did not have the established rules of succession with which we are familiar from Medieval and Early Modern History. Tiberius was the senior figure in the family after Augustus and the only other member of the family with extensive military and political experience. If Rome needed to choose a successor based on experience and office holding, then Tiberius was the obvious man. A dispute between Tiberius and the young men was not a dispute between equals.

We must presume that the quarrel was conducted at higher levels in the family and involved the emperor and perhaps his daughter. But it involved more than family politics. If Augustus intended Tiberius to succeed, then the position of emperor would move the leading man of the day, the *princeps*, to the leading man of the next generation. The *princeps* could pose as a quasi-magisterial figure who could exercise a paternal authority over the state. But if the position was to pass to Gaius and Lucius, there could be no pretence that this was not a form of monarchy. One may wonder, as many did under the early years of Tiberius, whether there was a real difference between a Tiberian principate and a monarchy, but for Tiberius the difference was his subordination to the younger men or his leadership of the imperial family and the Roman state. It is to be presumed that Tiberius' exile reflected his loss of that political discussion.

Augustus was, for perhaps the first time since 23 BC, without an obvious adult successor in Rome. In 2 BC, he was consul once more. He dedicated the Forum of Augustus and he was voted the title of *Pater Patriae* (Father of the Native Land). Lucius was introduced into public life and the two boys were now being prepared for major office. At this point, it looked as though the uncertainties surrounding the succession were at an end. But then events took an extraordinary turn. Julia was caught up in a sex scandal.

Dio (55.10) tells us that Julia was involved in drinking sessions in the Forum and on the speaker's platform itself. As soon as Augustus became aware of this, he sent her into exile. She was accompanied by her mother, Scribonia, voluntarily. Some of her lovers were put to death, including Iullus Antonius, the son of Antony, while others were sent into exile. One of the exiled was Sempronius Gracchus (Tacitus, *Annales*, 1.53) who was later executed under Tiberius. Velleius Paterculus (2.100) gives us other names: Quintius Crispinus, Appius Claudius, a Scipio, and 'other men of both orders'. Sempronius Gracchus, Scipio, and Appius Claudius were among the most aristocratic names of the Republic. Julia chose her lovers from the highest echelons of the Roman political order.

But the story is not complete. In AD 2, Lucius Caesar died, seemingly of natural causes, in Marseilles. In the same year, Tiberius returned from exile, but did not yet return to political office. Two years later, in AD 4, Gaius was wounded in Armenia. The wound became infected and he died. The stage was set for a major restructuring of the imperial house. Tiberius was restored and adopted by the aging emperor. He was no longer outside the direct line of descent. At the same time, Augustus adopted Agrippa Postumus, the only surviving son of Agrippa and Julia, and Tiberius adopted Germanicus (Velleius Paterculus, 2.102–104). But the problems of the imperial house were not over. The younger Julia, granddaughter of Augustus, was also caught in adultery. She was exiled and her husband executed for conspiracy (Suetonius, *Augustus*, 19), probably at the same time. Agrippa Postumus, the sole surviving son of Agrippa and Julia, was also sent into exile, his crime is never revealed

(Velleius Paterculus, 2.112; Dio, 55.32). Dio (55.13) preserves a story of a riot from about this period in which the people urged Augustus to restore his daughter. The crowd threw firebrands into the Tiber. The symbolism is not clear, but the Roman populace were perfectly aware of the similarity in sound between Tiber and Tiberius.

As with the stories about Cleopatra, the connection between sex and politics in these stories is uncomfortable for the serious historian. Historians think they should be analysing politics, not the sex lives of the princesses of Rome. There can be no doubt that the removal of Julia the Elder and Julia the Younger were political. The list of lovers shows that the accusations were a purge of the high Roman elite. The fall of Julia's husband on a charge of conspiracy in itself suggests political motivations, since he could hardly be accused of adultery with his own wife. But as with Messalina, the wife of Claudius, the political context of the accusations of sex should not lead us to dismiss the importance of sex in politics. Julia had been married to Marcellus, Agrippa, and Tiberius. These were not love matches, but political relationships. The bodies of leading men and women were not their own, they were political resources. We can interpret Julia's alleged sexual proclivities in four ways:

1   Julia was sexually promiscuous, a princess unable to control her passions.
2   Julia was virtuous, but she was attacked by her political enemies who used traditional misogynistic accusations.
3   Julia reacted against the moral conservatism of the regime and, in keeping with the more liberal and oppositional atmosphere among some of the artistic circles of the period (witness the elegists), was liberal in her affections.
4   Julia was engaged in building a political alliance with many of the leading men of the state. That alliance was cemented by sex.

Julia needed friends in the years before 2 BC. Her sons were young and the emperor was old. Tiberius may have been in exile, but should Augustus die, the future would be uncertain. The senior men in the state were in a position to undermine any authority that her sons might have and Tiberius was unpredictable. The logical and secure policy was to build an alliance with the powerful outside the *domus Augusti* to ensure that many would have an interest in the continued hegemony of the family and her sons. Yet, political alliances, especially those which were semi-discrete, gave rise to hostilities and jealousies, especially from those excluded from the inner circle.

Julia's fall was far from fatal to her political hopes. The deaths of her sons, however, left her political hopes shattered. The elderly emperor needed Tiberius. There can be little doubt that Tiberius extracted his price, which was to become the designated successor. The interests of the household meant that there could be no internal divisions. Agrippa was exiled. The younger

Julia was exiled. Germanicus was fiercely loyal. All internal opposition was crushed. The stage was set for Tiberius' unopposed succession.

In AD 14, the elderly emperor Augustus grew ill. He was 75 years old, ancient for a Roman. Stories circulated around his death, as they did about nearly all the emperors who died in their beds, but there is no reason to believe anything other than the official story: a very old man grew sick and died. Augustus' death served the interests of Tiberius only, but Tiberius was already in charge of the Roman state and the designated successor. There was no alternative to his power if the Augustan house was not to tear itself apart in civil war and Augustus had consistently over the previous 40 years defended the interests of his house above all other concerns. Tiberius had nothing to gain by advancing the old man's death.

After nearly six decades in which Rome had been under the shared or sole rule of Octavian, later to become Augustus, the first Roman emperor passed away. With his passing, a new age began.

Notes

1 Ronald Syme, *The Augustan Revolution* (Oxford, 1939).

2 Paul Zanker, *The Power of Images in the Age of Augustus* (Ann Arbor, 1988).

3 A.H.M. Jones, *Augustus* (London, 1971).

4 F. Millar, 'The First Revolution: Imperator Caesar, 36–28 BC', in A. Giovanni (ed.) *Le Révolution romaine après Ronald Syme: Bilans et Perspectives* (Genève, 1999), 1–38; F. Millar, 'Triumvirate and Principate', *Journal of Roman Studies* 63 (1973), 50-67; P.A. Brunt, *The Fall of the Roman Republic and Related Essays* (Oxford, 1988). See also K. Galinsky, *Augustan Culture: An interpretive introduction* (Princeton, NJ, 1996).

5 A. Winterling, *Politics and Society in Imperial Rome* (Malden, MA, Oxford, 2009).

6 R. Syme, *The Roman Revolution* (Oxford, 1939), 7.

7 The *Fasti Triumphales Barberini* records only two triumphs (for Dalmatia and Egypt), whereas the *Fasti Antiates* record three triumphs, but in an abbreviated form. The description of Actium and its aftermath in Virgil's *Aeneid* 8. 675 and following culminates in Octavian's 'threefold triumph'.

8 IUSSU IMP CAESARIS DIUI F / C CORNELIUS CN F GALLUS / PRAEF FABR CAESARIS DIUI F / FORUM IULIUM FECIT.

9 *ILS* 8995 = *CIL* 3.14147⁵

10 One would expect any new governor to arrive in March of the year of appointment. The last point at which Primus could be on trial is 22 BC, which would mean that he would need to have returned from his province, be charged, tried, and a conspiracy result all before the end of 22 BC. It seems more likely that Primus returned to Rome in early 23 BC and he could claim to have been advised to launch the campaign in 24 BC or earlier.

11 Cassius Dio, of course, wrote in Greek, but the words τὸ δημόσιον appear to be a direct translation of *res publica*.

12 Cassius Dio recounts these events under 22 BC. Some historians have suggested that the events should be dated be to early 23 BC so as to relate them to a constitutional reform of that year. There is also reference in a fragmentary inscription (*Fasti Capitolini*) to a consul of 23 BC by the name of Murena who appears to have died or been condemned in office. There is an understandable tendency to want to identify the consular Murena with the defence counsel. Nevertheless, other than it making an even better story, the evidence for redating is not compelling. Velleius Paterculus (2.93) dates the conspiracy to about the

time of the death of Marcellus. The fact that Marcellus was not involved in the Primus trial provides negative evidence that the trial came after Marcellus' death. Further, Cassius Dio gives us the name Licinius Murena, and the name of the consul on the inscription was Aulus Terentius Varro Murena and so one would have to assume a spectacular error on Dio's part to allow the identification.

13 Given that Terentia's brother should have been called Terentius, there are also good grounds for connecting the mysterious consul of 23 BC to the family as the third (though perhaps the eldest) of Terentia's brothers.

14 Part of the business of being a historian is to give public lectures and afterwards, many people have told me that in their current incarnations they can remember past lives. I have met several ancient queens and pharaohs, but I am yet to encounter someone whose previous life was as a driver of the soil cart.

Chapter 3

Tiberius (AD 14–37)

Main events of the reign of Tiberius

Date (AD)	Event
14	Deaths of Augustus, Julia, Agrippa Postumus, Sempronius Gracchus. Mutinies in Pannonia and Germany. Germanicus campaigns in Germany.
15	War in Germany. Treason law revived.
16	War in Germany. King of Parthia deposed. Trial of Libo for treason. Revolt of Clemens.
17	Triumph of Germanicus. Deaths of kings of Cappodocia (executed), Commagene and Amanus. Unrest in Syria, Judaea and Armenia. Germanicus receives *imperium maius* and sent to the East. Revolt of Tacfarinas in Africa.
18	Germanicus settles Armenia, Cappadocia and Commagene, but quarrels with Piso.
19	Germanicus visits Egypt, but returns to Syria to depose Piso. Germanicus dies.
20	Agrippina returns to Rome with Germanicus' ashes. Trial of Piso. Tacfarinas resumes revolt in Africa. Emergence of Sejanus (Dio).
21	Revolts in Africa, Thrace and Gaul. Successful prosecution of the poet Priscus for treason.
22	Drusus given *tribunicia potestas*. Tacfarinas defeated. Sejanus given a statue in the theatre (Dio).
23	Emergence of Sejanus (Tacitus). Death of Drusus.
24	Prosecutions of Calpurnius Piso, C. Silius, Cassius Severus, Plautius Silvanus and Vibius Serenus. Death of Tacfarinas.
25	Prosecutions of Cremutius Cordus and Fonteius Capito.
26	Rebellion in Thrace. Prosecution of Claudia Pulchra. Tiberius leaves Rome for Campania.
27	Collapse of the amphitheatre at Fidenae.
28	Entrapment of Titius Sabinus.
29	Trial and death of Sabinus. Death of Julia. Revolt in Germany. Statues dedicated to Tiberius and Sejanus. Altars to Clementia and Amicitia associated with Tiberius and Sejanus.
30	Death of Livia. Charges brought against Drusus (son of Germanicus) and Agrippina. Images of Sejanus receive sacrifices. Death of Fuflus Geminus. Death of Mucia.

Date (AD)	Event
31	Fall of Sejanus. Rise of Macro. Gaius Caligula made heir.
32	Trials and deaths of the supporters of Sejanus.
33	Deaths of Agrippina and Drusus. More treason trials. Credit crisis in Rome.
34	Political trials. Rumours that the governor of Germany threatened revolt if summoned back to Rome.
35	War in Parthia and Armenia. Treason trials.
36	War in Cappodocia. Treason trials. Tiridates crowned in Parthia. Fire in Rome.
37	Political trials. Death of Tiberius. Accession of Gaius Caligula.

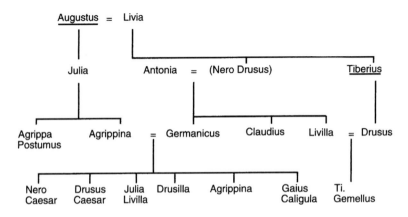

Figure 3.1 The family of Tiberius in AD 14

Tiberius and Tacitus

All the major literary sources for the reign of Tiberius, with the exception of Velleius Paterculus, are hostile. Most attention has been given to Tacitus' depiction of the reign and his portrayal has dominated modern perceptions. In part, this is due to the literary quality of Tacitus' work, which is generally regarded as being far greater than that of other writers, and his influence is a tribute to his compelling portrait of the political events of the period.

Like many Roman historians, Tacitus was an annalist. His history was written within a fairly rigid framework in which the events of each year were recounted in order. Thus, a narrative which a modern historian would usually collate might be fragmented in Tacitus and described under several years. This structure has certain strengths in that it allowed Tacitus to describe the events as they unfolded and to establish chronological links and coincidences which might escape a more thematically organised work, but it also has certain weaknesses in that it provides few obvious opportunities for summation and conclusions. Where a modern historian might spend pages in analysis, Tacitus moves on. Yet, the very process of moving on to the next event generates conjunctions of events. These events often comment upon each other. Thus, when we read any event in Tacitus, a trial or a debate, we need to be aware of the events that surround it: context is key in Tacitus.

Although Tacitus' opinion of Tiberius is clear from the start, the methodical relating of events gradually lends support and credibility so that the stated 'facts' of Tiberius' reign seem to rule out other interpretations. Any assessment of the reign of Tiberius must start from Tacitus' devastating depiction and from an acceptance that the *Annales* are a work of literature, carefully shaped and constructed by its author to represent his opinions and historical viewpoint.

All history-writing is an art in which the truth of the historian's understanding of the past is depicted through language and arguments. It is an illusion to think that we can ever have an unvarnished, truthful, and objective account of history. Any attempt to unpick Tacitus' account to get back to a pure, original history faces insuperable difficulties. Tacitus was writing more than 60 years after the death of Tiberius. There will have been few who could remember Tiberius' reign and Tacitus must have been dependent on literary sources whose identity, quality, veracity and significance cannot normally be assessed. Since Tacitus rarely discusses his sources, it is virtually impossible to detect or evaluate interpretations borrowed from earlier writers. Biases, lies, misunderstandings and rumours were integrated with the facts by the time they reached Tacitus. We, as modern historians, have few tools by which to reconstruct the processes that led to the formation of Tacitus' historical account. Our other extended accounts of Tiberius' reign, notably that in Cassius Dio and in the biographical work of Suetonius were either later than or contemporary with Tacitus and would also have been influenced by the same traditions of interpretation that affected Tacitus. If a 'fact' appears in three sources, all it may mean is that those three sources had read the same book.

Nevertheless, we are not dealing with fiction with Tacitus. The process of historical writing demands a deep and thoughtful engagement with the past. Tacitus' view of the Roman Empire is shaped by his historical research and when we read Tacitus, at the very least we are reading the account of a man who devoted much of his life to thinking about Roman history, and a man who was enormously better informed about the nature of Roman politics and society than we will ever be. Of course, Tacitus, like every other writer, was 'situated' in a particular context and that context will have affected his judgements.

Tacitus was a senator. His history concentrates on the relationship between the senatorial aristocracy and the emperor. Rome and the senate are presented as the crucial areas of political activity, as they had been during the Republic. Tacitus' history writing was fundamentally conservative in that it focused on the traditional nexus of power between the aristocracy and the emperor. We may compare this with the rather different perspective offered by Velleius Paterculus, a writer who had followed an equestrian career before entering the senate. The notably positive presentation of both Tiberius and Sejanus in Velleius suggests that some, at least, may have had a rather different perspective on political events from that of the senators. In fact, neither Velleius nor Suetonius show the same obsessive interest as Tacitus in the relationship between the senate and Tiberius. One could also envisage other types of history that might have been written of the reign, histories that focused on matters military or administrative, on the empire, or on social history, but although such matters often figure in Tacitus' account, it is to the politics of the senatorial class to which Tacitus returns again and again.

Tacitus lived through the reign of Domitian, which was marked by a deterioration in the relationship between emperor and senate culminating in what is now known as 'the reign of terror', a period vividly described by Tacitus in the *Agricola* (1–2, 45) (see pp. 247–48). There were superficial similarities between the reigns of Domitian and Tiberius which were probably generally recognised at the time: Suetonius (*Domitian*, 20) tells us that Domitian 'read nothing except the journals (*commentarii*) and register of deeds (*acta*) of Tiberius'. Both emperors became reclusive. Historians who wish to offer a revisionist view of the reign of Tiberius argue that the experience of the Domitianic period affected Tacitus' account, making him more pessimistic than any 'fair' reading of Tiberius would allow. Puzzlingly, as we shall see later, revisionist historians would also like to see the 'reign of terror' under Domitian as being grossly exaggerated by our contemporary writers. But the relationship between Tacitus' political experience and his depiction of the regime of Tiberius was much more subtle. There were major differences in the way in which the emperors presented themselves and behaved towards the senate; most notably, Tiberius presented himself as the servant of the senate while Domitian may have seen himself as the senate's master. Tiberius appears to have regarded the plebs with aristocratic hauteur, while the plebs were an audience for Domitian's greatness. The reign of Tiberius was not a blueprint for that of Domitian.

Like all historians, Tacitus writes with the benefit of hindsight. If we date the formation of the monarchy to 31 BC, then Tacitus was writing after more than 130 years of monarchic government, when the imperial throne had had 13 incumbents and there was no realistic alternative to imperial monarchy. Tiberius became emperor less than 50 years after the formation of the monarchy and when there had only been one previous incumbent. Tacitus knew that the principate would develop and that the senate would suffer the tyrannous rules of Caligula, Nero and Domitian without there ever being a serious bid for a return to Republican government. Tacitus knew how this story ended and he could not escape that knowledge. He had a certain understanding of the Principate derived from his experience and his historical research, and that understanding informed his historical interpretations.

Furthermore, Tacitus was writing for a knowledgeable audience. His contemporaries, even if not historians, will have known something of the reign of Tiberius. This shared knowledge lends the account a certain irony and a sense of inevitability. Let us take a modern parallel: any modern account of the international developments of 1910–1914, or 1933–1938 must be overshadowed in the minds of readers and the historian by the eventual outbreak of the World Wars. Thus, for Tacitus and his contemporaries, the events of the reign of Tiberius are a prelude to the history of the rest of the century, and the respect paid by Tiberius to the senate in the first years of the reign especially becomes bitterly ironic when writer and audience know what is to happen. Further, the historian's task is always to explain what will happen in the narrative, which requires that Tacitus always is aware of what will come pass and is seeking explanations for the end of the story. Tacitus writes his history not just to record events, but to explain his contemporary society. When we read Tacitus and we think about the Principate, we need to do more than just list events; we must also understand the emergence of tyranny. Yet, in AD 14, no one knew what the future held.

The accession

Velleius tells us that Tiberius was at Augustus' bedside when the old emperor made his farewells and 'returned his heavenly spirit to heaven' (Velleius Paterculus, 2. 123.2). Tacitus is not so certain. Tiberius was summoned by his mother and arrived at Nola to find the emperor either dead or almost so. Livia had taken control of the situation and managed the flow of information from the emperor's bedchamber so that news of the emperor's death was issued only when Livia and Tiberius were ready (Tacitus, *Annales*, 1.5). Immediately after the announcement was made, Tiberius issued the watchword to the praetorian guard thereby establishing control over the only significant armed force in Italy. He then set out to Rome to arrange the formalities of the funeral and to secure his accession.

Tiberius' most serious dynastic rival was the surviving son of Agrippa and Julia, Agrippa Postumus. Tacitus (*Annales*, 1.5) relates rumours that Augustus had visited Postumus in his island exile on Planasia, raising the possibility that Postumus would be summoned back to Rome. Fear of Agrippa Postumus' political resurrection allegedly led to Livia hastening Augustus' final illness. The story of an aged emperor making a secret journey to see his grandson and the allegation that Livia poisoned her husband seem far-fetched, the type of groundless rumour that enemies of the Tiberian regime might have been willing to invent so as to suggest that Tiberius was not the chosen successor of the old emperor.

In any event, action was swiftly taken to remove the potential threat to Tiberius' position. Agrippa Postumus was murdered. Tiberius later asserted that Augustus had left orders for Agrippa's death, but this was regarded with suspicion: Tacitus (*Annales*, 1.6) wonders why Augustus, who had never murdered any of his relatives, would remove his own grandson to ease the way for his stepson. Tiberius' motive was more straightforward. Nevertheless, Tacitus tells us that Tiberius acted with confusion when the murder was reported to him as a fulfilment of his orders: Tiberius claimed to have issued no such orders and demanded an inquiry. Yet, the inquiry was shelved. The deed had been done to benefit Tiberius and if Tiberius himself was not guilty, responsibility would be laid at the door either of his friends or his mother and Tiberius himself would hardly escape the taint.

Tacitus places the story of Agrippa's murder immediately after the death of Augustus, moving straight from Tiberius' assumption of control into a sentence starting 'the first crime of the new Principate'. The new regime is introduced to us as murderous and the impression we are given is that Agrippa was to be the first of many. We are also given the impression that Tiberius is struggling to control events. The regime itself has a logic that requires the death of Agrippa and whatever Tiberius might wish, the accounts of empire must be settled.

On arrival in Rome, Tiberius convoked the senate to decide arrangements for Augustus' funeral. This was the only business that he allowed to be discussed. There was a pause in the business of state. The funeral was conducted with due solemnities. Augustus was deified. Only after this, did the senate turn to the accession of Tiberius.

The accession debate seems to have been long. Tiberius refused to receive the powers that Augustus had held. The senate demanded that he should assume Augustus' role and powers. Tiberius ordered a document to be read which summarised the military and financial status of the Empire: obviously providing the senate with crucial information if it was to take over the administration of the Empire. The senate again appealed to Tiberius to take on the burden. Tiberius weakened. He stated that he would not take on all aspects of the state but would accept any cares the senate chose to entrust to him. The senate pressed him and asked him to make his wishes clear. Tiberius claimed he desired none of the responsibility. There were signs of frustration and the senators pressed him again. Eventually, Tiberius was persuaded to accept Augustus' powers (Tacitus, *Annales*, 1.11–12). Velleius (2.124) writes that Tiberius 'almost struggled longer to refuse the principate than others had fought to obtain it'. Whereas Velleius sees in this debate Tiberius' modesty, Tacitus portrays it as an example of Tiberius' hypocrisy.

The senatorial debate itself parallels events in 27 BC when Augustus established his constitutional position. There may have been a certain ritualistic quality to the debate: the prospective emperor had to be seen to be reluctant to accept the burdens thrust upon him. Yet, clearly, the staunch resistance of Tiberius was something of a surprise and led to frustration. Even Velleius seems somewhat bemused. Was Tacitus right, therefore, to dismiss the debate as an elaborate charade?

Tiberius was the senior figure in the state. He had been Augustus' partner in power and was the leading and most experienced general. The political conflicts within the imperial family over the previous 20 years reflect the intention that the Augustan system would survive the first emperor's death. On Augustus' death, Tiberius had acted to secure his position: Agrippa Postumus was killed. Tiberius had assumed control of the imperial guard. Arriving in a Rome publicly grieving the loss of their *princeps*, Tiberius was accompanied into the Forum by the guard, a potent symbol that imperial power had already passed into his hands. Tacitus (*Annales*, 1.7) also places before his account of the senatorial debate a ceremonial occasion at which the consuls, prefects of the guard, prefect of the corn supply, the senate, the army, and the people all swore allegiance to the new emperor. This oath of loyalty reinforced the supremacy of the emperor and gave a religious authority to his position. Yet, if we are to believe Tacitus, the same senate that had sworn loyalty to the *princeps* then engaged in a lengthy debate over whether he was to become *princeps*. If Tiberius had received oaths of loyalty from the consuls and senate, what was the point of seeming reluctant to take a position he had already in large part assumed? If the debate was really about whether Tiberius would retire into private life, then the charade must have been so obvious that one wonders at its purpose.

The politicians of Rome were dealing with a new problem: there was no established procedure to deal with the succession to the imperial position. We have epigraphic evidence for the accession of Vespasian that seems to show that the assumption of the imperial position would be ratified by the passing of a *lex de imperio*, which granted the emperor all the powers and privileges that went with the position. These powers and privileges had been gathered by Augustus in a series of constitutional settlements (see pp. 41–50, 66–67). There was no precedent to which Tiberius or the senate could turn and no single enabling bill which the senate could pass. There was also the issue of which powers and titles were peculiar to Augustus and whether Tiberius would fulfil exactly the same role as the old emperor. Indeed, although it was recognised that Tiberius was in some sense the political successor of Augustus, as Augustus had succeeded Caesar, we need not assume that it was clear to all or any of the participants to what exactly Tiberius had succeeded. For Tacitus, and most of the later writers, the constitutional and political role of the emperor was established and known, but in AD 14 the matter was not so clear-cut. Asinius Gallus, one of the most influential figures in the senate asked Tiberius which part of the state he wished to control. The question, so he later claimed, was intended to make obvious the conclusion that the state could not be separated and needed to be ruled by the mind of a single man.

This was the central issue of the debate: the nature of the imperial position (Tacitus, *Annales*, 1.12).

Even given these constitutional difficulties, we might have expected the senate to have recognised Tiberius as the political heir of Augustan supremacy and that Tiberius would have allowed them rapidly to establish his constitutional position, following the Augustan model. This was, after all, the decision the senate reached eventually. By forcing the senate to discuss the issue at length, the senators were driven to give Tiberius their public support. Tacitus (*Annales*, 1. 7) explains this convoluted process (typically) by reference to Tiberius' twisted character, but he also provides us with another, more interesting explanation: fear of Germanicus.

Tiberius was in a dominant position on the death of Augustus and was the most obvious and credible candidate to be Augustus' successor. This does not, however, mean that his position was secure. Augustus had secured the principate on the battlefield. Tiberius had secured his position through dynastic politics. The dynastic squabbles had created tensions in the imperial family which were probably still reflected in divided loyalties among the senators. The rumour of Augustus' visit to Agrippa Postumus, unlikely though it may have been, illustrates these continued tensions. We are hampered by the lack of good chronological data, but as he sat in the senate in AD 14, Tiberius probably had little solid information about the attitudes of the armies on the Rhine and Danube. He may already have had reason to fear that he would not secure the German and Danubian legions as easily as he had secured the praetorian guard. Until the loyalty of the troops and their commanders was assured, Tiberius was threatened by overwhelming military force. The political realities of the first months of his principate meant that Tiberius could not afford to alienate the senate. He needed all the political support he could muster. This uncertainty more than anything else explains Tiberius' cautious approach to the senate. He needed his accession to appear legitimate to minimise potential disaffection among the generals and governors and their friends in the senate.

In the end, Tiberius was not challenged by Germanicus, nor by any other of the prominent men of Rome. In retrospect, his position in AD 14 appears to have been remarkably secure, but there is no reason to believe that Tiberius himself was aware of this security. Augustus tells us in the *Res Gestae* that his power was a matter of *auctoritas*, personal authority. In *Annales* 1.3–4, Tacitus emphasises his view that the Principate did not depend on a constitutional or legal framework, but on the personal political power wielded by the emperor. In the previous chapter, I suggested that Augustan power depended on the old emperor's ability to build a network of loyal and powerful followers among all classes of Roman society. There was no guarantee that Tiberius would be able to depend on a similar authority, that the networks that had supported Augustus would not fragment once the great leader was dead, or that Tiberius would achieve the personal dominance of his adoptive father. There had been more than four centuries of Republican government, followed by about 50 years of Augustan rule. Augustus provided a model for Tiberius to follow, but no one in Rome had any experience of this sort of transfer of power.

What Romans did have was a political culture. I mean by this that the Romans had a system for getting things done in Roman political life. Roman political culture was historic in that it looked back to historical times. It also emphasised the collective values of the aristocracy. In a time of political uncertainty, Tiberius could look to the old ways of maintaining his power. He could consult the senate and seek to involve the senators in his political activities. He could attempt to build a consensus. In so doing, Tiberius was looking to a pre-imperial political culture and much of the institutional framework of that culture (the senate, the magistrates) remained in place and the values of the political culture were in all the history books and the speeches in which the Roman aristocracy were educated. Tiberius could, quite feasibly, seek to explore and exploit that system of power without stepping down from his imperial office: he took advice, honoured his fellow senators, behaved as a fellow senator, and adhered to the behavioural patterns of the Republic.

But, in retrospect, Tacitus could see that the Republic was over. There was no one alive who had experience of the Republic (*Annales*, 1.3). The senators were also befuddled. Their political reality was of imperial dominance. Tiberius was expecting them to behave as if it were the old days, but they knew from their experience of Augustus that all power stemmed from the emperor. They knew from the death of Agrippa Postumus that the regime had its own logic (its own culture) whatever Tiberius might claim. There was a paradox to the imperial situation in which all the cultural values and institutions of the Principate were derived from Republican models, but it was in truth an imperial system. That paradox was the focus of political debate and negotiation throughout the first century and a half of imperial rule, and when those negotiations broke down, people died.

Tacitus uses the accession debate in a literary way to develop his portrayal of Tiberius and the issues that were to determine the history of the Tiberian principate. The debate is a work of literary artifice, but it is possible that many of the themes that were to haunt the reign were already on display: the great historian can find the historical moment that exemplifies the political crisis. The problem on which the debate foundered was a gap between rhetoric and the reality of power. Whatever Tiberius might say, the reality of his power remained obvious. His words risked becoming meaningless in the face of what everyone knew: that Tiberius had secured imperial authority and all the mechanisms of imperial control. Tiberius became irritated by those senators who behaved as if that truth was the truth and acknowledged imperial power. However conservatively Tiberius might behave and however delicately he might seek to build a consensus, it was not the agreement of the senators that mattered, but whether Tiberius could take control of the state, unchallenged. The logic of imperial power over-rode any Tiberian self-presentation.

One of the key lessons of the debate as it is rendered in Tacitus, is the difference between words and meaning. People did not say what they meant, nor did they mean what they said. To understand the doublespeak of Roman politics required skill and training, and that is what Tacitus offers us. But the gap between words and meaning is made worse since it is not clear that the participants in historical events understand what is happening. Understanding, as Tacitus will tell us later, is not easy and comes from historical study, and without historical study one cannot tell right from wrong (Tacitus, *Annales*, 4.32). Already in these first scenes, there is uncertainty on all sides and contrasting viewpoints are offered. The Tiberian principate is shrouded in uncertainties: no one knows what Tiberius means or intends. The senators speak loyally and enthusiastically about the new emperor, but their loyalty and enthusiasm are in question. The most loyal statements raise or seem to raise questions about the regime. Tiberius appears the most Republican of senators, though, as we have already been told by Tacitus, in reality he is the most imperial of men, brought up within the imperial house, honoured as a member of that house, and possessed of the arrogance that comes from such an aristocratic origin. Tacitus sets up a gap between what seems to be happening (a debate about accession) and what is *really* happening (since Tiberius is already emperor) and thus challenges his readers. We may know what happens, but we are challenged as to whether we understand it. We can see what is happening, but we need to read more to be educated enough to understand these events, the meaning of which is hidden from view. There are no simple answers in Tacitus: his project is, in part, designed to explain how complicated political life was and is under the Principate.

Germanicus

Germanicus is very much the hero of the early years of Tiberius' reign. As we have seen, it was Germanicus, not Tiberius, who stood at the centre of the revised Augustan family (see pp. 84–85). His early death in suspicious circumstances may have enhanced his reputation. The rifts that opened in the imperial dynasty subsequent to, and in part resulting from, Germanicus' death made his reputation and family a focus for the disaffected. Even though he died in AD 19, he was a central figure in Tiberius' principate. Although Germanicus only emerges as a character in his own right with the mutinies on the Danube and in Germany and his entry into the narrative of the *Annales* is delayed, his importance to the story is apparent from the first, both as a potential rival to Tiberius' son Drusus and secondly because he was in Gaul, near the legions stationed along the Rhine (*Annales*, 1.3–4; 1.7). The implication of Tacitus' discussion is that whatever was happening in Rome, attention should be focused in Germany for it was in Germany that the fate of empire would be decided.

Germanicus in Germany

Soon after the news of Augustus death and Tiberius' accession to the throne, the legions in Germany and on the Danube sought to take advantage of the weakness of the new regime to obtain better conditions, including provision for retirement after the appropriate number of years of service and an increase in pay.[1] The revolt broke out in Pannonia (Tacitus, *Annales,* 1.16–30), but was paralleled by a mutiny in Germany (Tacitus, *Annales*, 1.31–49). The Pannonian outbreak was dealt with quickly. Tiberius sent his son Drusus, Aelius Sejanus (joint prefect of the praetorians), and a detachment of praetorians to Pannonia. A lunar eclipse convinced the soldiers their mutiny was doomed. Storms and floods reinforced the belief of the soldiers that the gods disapproved of them. Drusus took advantage of the collapse in the morale of the mutineers to execute their leaders and was able to leave the camp before a delegation that had been sent to negotiate with Tiberius could return.

The German mutiny was more serious. When Germanicus returned to the legions following the news of Augustus' death, he found four legions mutinous. Germanicus attempted to restore their loyalty but they proffered their complaints and offered to support Germanicus in an attempt on the throne. If Tacitus' story is true, the offer may have been tempting. Most of Tiberius' military career had been spent commanding the legions in Germany or on the Danube. He had had little contact with the legions in the East. Clearly, these German forces did not have sufficiently fond memories of the new Emperor to bind them in loyalty to him. The mutinous legions in Pannonia, though Drusus was with them, may have come over. Tiberius would not have had time to summon legions from the East, and it is far from certain that they would have been loyal. Nevertheless, Germanicus stood with his uncle and adoptive father. Family loyalty determined his attitude.

According to Tacitus, it was Germanicus' family that ultimately saved the day. After the first outbreak of the mutiny, a measure of order was restored and two legions marched to their winter camp. Two legions remained. After rioting, Germanicus sent Agrippina (who was pregnant) and his son Gaius Caligula to safety with the Gallic people, the Treviri. The sight of the granddaughter of Augustus and her son, who seems to have been adopted as something of a mascot by the troops, ignominiously retreating from the mutinous legions who should have been their protectors, was too much for the troops and the two legions were brought round. The ringleaders were executed. Germanicus was confident enough to threaten the legions at Vetera (modern Xanten). Before he arrived at the camp, the leading mutineers were overpowered and killed, and the legions' loyalty was secured.

Ultimately, the episode of the mutinies turned out to be a sideshow, but it tells us something about Roman politics. The episode also has something quite unusual in Roman historiography, a speech by a poor person, a certain Percennius. Tacitus (*Annales*, 1.16–17) introduces the speech, which was almost certainly his own invention, with various remarks intended to make us think badly of Percennius, portraying him as a man of the theatre (and therefore untrustworthy and not a decent Roman soldier). But there is an oddity about Percennius' speech. He complains about the terms and conditions of military service, the low wages, the extended period of service (more than 16 years), the long campaigns, and the poor quality of the lands given to them on discharge. He asks why the soldiers have been so quiescent for so long and claims that the new regime presents them with a political opportunity. He compares the soldiers' lives to the 'manner of life of slaves'. The puzzle is that everything Percennius complains of appears to be true. Indeed, the soldiers respond to Percennius' speech by showing the wounds inflicted on their bodies by the centurions and the greying hair of the elderly soldiers, physical proof of extended and brutal service (*Annales*, 1.18). Later, Tacitus (*Annales*, 1.23) tells us that the centurion Lucilius was killed by the troops. The soldiers knew him as 'Bring Another' for his habit of breaking his stick on the backs of the soldiers under his service. If everything that Percennius says is true, we need to explain why Tacitus disparages his oration.

The mutinies in Germany were contemporaneous with those on the Danube and, it seems, driven by the same factors (or at least so Tacitus represents the situation). Here, unnamed soldiers are made to proclaim that it was they 'who held the Roman state in their hand'. The mutineers were aware of their political power. When Germanicus arrived, the soldiers were far from cowed. Some made to kiss the hand of the young prince, but instead took his fingers into their mouths so that he could witness their toothlessness. Germanicus ordered them into their ranks: they refused (Tacitus, *Annales*, 1.34). When he addressed the troops, his speech was notably ineffective. The soldiers listened, but took the opportunity to display their scars and the veterans, men of more than 30 years service, complained about pay, about the extractions of expenses from their pay, and about the corruption of their officers. The soldiers then offered Germanicus the throne. Germanicus responded to the offer by unsheathing his sword and threatening suicide. One of the soldiers (Tacitus has a name, Calusidius) offered Germanicus his own sword, claiming that it was sharper. Germanicus had to be hurried from the tribunal (*Annales*, 1.35).

However we read this, Germanicus' intervention is hardly a great success and this might lead us to doubt Germanicus' heroic character. In fact, the mutiny is only quelled by accident, and through the soldiers' loyalty to Agrippina and Gaius Caligula, and not by anything that Germanicus himself does (*Annales*, 1.35–45) and the soldiers extracted considerable concessions from Germanicus. The mutineers were eventually executed, but the troops also purged the centurions, removing those cruel and corrupt. Further, the mutiny was eventually completely suppressed by violence, when the soldiers turned on the ringleaders, a violence that seemed like a re-emergence of the civil war from which Augustus had restored the Roman state (Tacitus, *Annales*, 1.48–49).

At many levels the soldiers were right. They were treated like slaves although they were Roman citizens. The terms and conditions under which they laboured were brutal. The rights of the soldiers appear to have been systematically abused. Yet, in the soldiers' hands lay the fate of the Roman state. The Empire would be decided by them. Their swords were sharper than that of Germanicus, but we are invited by the narrative to see them as wrong and we are similarly invited to read Germanicus as heroic and correct. The issue must be something other than the factual accuracy of the account provided by the mutineers.

We could read Tacitus as exhibiting class prejudice, suggesting that anything the common soldier thought must, by definition, be wrong. Perhaps we could also see the wrongs done to the soldiers as diminished in importance by the far greater wrong of indiscipline, mutiny and threatening of the political order. But although class prejudice is exploited, the Tacitean account is sympathetic to the plight of the soldiers. We are allowed to see the issues from their point of view and the rhetoric that they employ is powerful. Tacitus opens the possibility of his audience identifying with the soldiers. But there is a characteristic Tacitean paradox here. The mutineers may be correct, but they do not fully understand the situation. Germanicus understands something that they do not and that only emerges in the narrative of the mutinies. The price of mutiny is civil war. Germanicus remains fiercely loyal to Tiberius, and he remains fiercely loyal to Tiberius until almost his last breath. That is not because Germanicus has any illusions as to the virtue of the new emperor, but because the alternative is too terrible. Eventually, the soldiers come to experience civil war and pay the price in the conflict in the camp. Ultimately, as readers, we see that the soldiers' demands would have led to civil war. The same deal that Augustus made with the senators applied: peace and principate in exchange for liberty and war. Loyalty to the imperial family prevents civil war, but the ghosts of the civil conflicts past stalk the mutinous camps of Germany.

Germanicus goes East

Germanicus' reaction to the mutinies was to launch campaigns into Germany. The first raid was destructive and punitive. Although his troops were attacked returning to base, the mission was accomplished successfully. The attack was a preliminary to an extended series of victorious and destructive raids in AD 15 and 16, somewhat marred by a naval disaster in 15 (Tacitus, *Annales*, 2.24). No substantial territory was won in these battles and Roman losses were heavy. Tiberius recalled Germanicus. Tacitus (*Annales*, 2.26), who may have had access to at least some of the correspondence between Tiberius and Germanicus, claims that Germanicus was reluctant to leave since he believed that the Romans were on the verge of significant gains. Tiberius, however, thought that the frontier had been stabilised and that diplomacy offered more immediate gains. Germanicus returned to Rome and in AD 17 he celebrated a triumph. In the next year, Germanicus was consul with Tiberius and was sent to the East. He was given *maius imperium*, a power greater than that of the provincial governors, a power that marked Germanicus as imperial deputy (and heir): the same honour had been previously granted by Augustus to Agrippa and Tiberius.

In the same year, a new governor was sent to Syria, which was the most powerful province in the region. Gnaeus Calpurnius Piso was a trusted and experienced politician. He had been consul with Tiberius in 7 BC. His wife Plancina was a friend of Livia, Tiberius' mother. Tacitus depicts him as something of a monster, arrogant and violent. His relationship with Germanicus was disastrous. Even by the time he arrived, Piso's behaviour on the journey to Syria had suggested that he was hostile to Germanicus. After Germanicus provided a diplomatic resolution to the brewing Armenian crisis, relations between Piso and Germanicus worsened, but open confrontation was avoided. In AD 19, Germanicus visited Egypt. On his return to Syria, there was another disagreement with Piso. Germanicus fell ill and Piso, who had been leaving the province, delayed. Signs that magic was being employed against Germanicus were found in the dying man's room (Tacitus, *Annales*, 2. 69; Dio, 57. 18.6–10). Germanicus, apparently convinced that Piso was behind the black magic and his illness, formally renounced his friendship with Piso and ordered him to leave the province. The former was a serious act: it was a public declaration of hostility. Germanicus died.

At this stage, Piso behaved in an extraordinarily odd manner. He had been expelled from Syria, but had not rushed back to Rome to defend his cause. He heard of Germanicus' death when on the island of Kos. Allegedly, he publicly celebrated the death of his enemy, the emperor's son, a death for which, as he must have known, some would blame him. He then returned to Syria to challenge the new governor. He bribed some troops and raised an army. He was not, however, able to dislodge Germanicus' friends. After being besieged and defeated, he was sent back to Rome under escort (Tacitus, *Annales*, 2.74–81).

The death of Germanicus was a great shock. The transportation of his ashes from Syria to Rome gave rise to an outpouring of national grief. Agrippina was at the centre of the ceremony. She disembarked at the South Italian port of Brundisium carrying the ashes. The praetorians met her at the port. They carried the ashes in procession across Italy. As the ashes reached each town, the populace and the leaders of the community would show their respect by public sacrifice and mourning. Drusus (the son of Tiberius), Claudius (Germanicus' brother) and the consuls journeyed to meet the ashes and accompany the mourning procession into Rome. The ashes were laid to rest in the mausoleum of Augustus. Tiberius and Livia did not appear (Tacitus, *Annales*, 3.1–5).

Piso slowly returned to Rome. His suspected aide in the death, a woman named Martina who was a friend of Plancina and who had been arrested in

Syria, died in mysterious circumstances at Brundisium on her way to Rome (Tacitus, *Annales*, 3. 7). A public interview between Piso's son and Drusus led to Drusus expressing his hostility to Piso (Tacitus, *Annales*, 3. 8). A trial followed and is reported in detail by Tacitus. Piso was accused of inciting rebellion, corrupting the troops, magic and poisoning. Only the poisoning charge was defended stoutly. The case was lost, and Piso committed suicide. His son survived and, more surprisingly, so did Plancina, after a plea from Livia (Tacitus, *Annales*, 3. 12–19).

Tacitus (*Annales*, 3. 16) adds an allegation concerning Piso's death. Some said (Tacitus deliberately distances himself from this rumour) that Piso had an incriminating document: a letter from Tiberius. Piso held on to the letter, hoping to secure his acquittal, but the document disappeared after his death. Both this disappearance and the 'suicide' were said to be the work of Sejanus, the praetorian prefect. Tacitus does not suggest that he believes the story to have been true, but its inclusion, backed by certain unnamed contemporary witnesses, suggests to the reader that Piso was murdered and that Tiberius was behind the death of Germanicus.

The Germanicus story is dramatic, tragic and mysterious. It is given an added quality by the inclusion of magic and poisoning. The 'evidence' is, of course, mixed and from a distance of 2,000 years perhaps not such as would satisfy a court of law. The discovery of curse tablets and human remains in Germanicus' room and the other evidence of a magical conspiracy to kill Germanicus played on traditional Roman fears. Leading Romans could protect themselves against the obvious threats: they were men and women of considerable wealth and resources. Germanicus was surrounded by slaves, friends, and troops, all dedicated to his protection. But the Romans also believed in a world of spirits and gods, an unseen and dangerous world. Roman religious practices maintained the relationship between the people and the gods (the *pax deorum*), but if such religious practices were about maintaining order, Romans were aware of the possibility that religious practices could create disorder. Curse tablets were a recognised means of exacting supernatural revenge and are attested from across the Roman Empire. Human remains, especially those of premature infants, were also associated with curse magic. There is every reason to accept that that the Romans believed in their efficacy and, to a certain extent, all that magic and religion need to 'work' are for people to believe in them.

Poisoning, like magic, was also seen as the weapon of the weak. It is no coincidence that women are associated with both magic and poisoning. While men could fight, the weapons open to women were more limited. But the defences against poisoning and magic were uncertain and the powerful were fearful. In an era of very limited medical knowledge, of very poor hygiene, of infected water supplies, of malaria, of no effective measures against septicaemia and many other infections, people frequently died suddenly of no obvious cause. Such swift snatching away of life was a fact of life, but that does not mean that Romans were accepting of these losses and did not feel the suddenness of bereavement. Sudden death demanded explanation. Even in our days of forensic and medical science, conspiracy theorists flock to unexpected deaths. Whereas we might consign magic to an irrational, non-scientific sphere, poles apart from our world (becoming a special category of explanation), for the Romans that irrational world was part of their everyday life: religion and magic had real effects and could explain how the world worked. For us, magic requires a suspension of disbelief and is only justifiable in very particular circumstances (e.g. the positive decision taken by religious people to believe in miracles); in antiquity, magic was a satisfactory explanation for an unforeseen, seemingly inexplicable event.

Although Plancina and Piso could not be directly connected to the 'magic' and poisoning of Germanicus, the very absence of evidence merely added to the febrile atmosphere surrounding the death of Germanicus, and the sense that unseen forces were at work. Of course, the 'conspiracy' that surrounded the relationship between Piso and Tiberius and Plancina and Livia and into which Sejanus was dragged with the death of Piso similarly rested on an absence of evidence. But the stories give a sense of politics behind closed doors, of unseen deals and rivalries, and deep personal hostilities. To understand the *real* story of politics in the Imperial period, we must always account for what has happened behind closed doors. But what happens behind closed doors is, by definition, secret and can only be reconstructed through fictionalisation. As we know from our own politics, the 'facts' in the public domain are less than half the story. The problem, of course, is that the stories we spin, and likewise those spun by the Romans, to make sense of the known 'facts', could lead to us believing in magic.

Yet, even if we extract the magical elements, the story is extraordinary enough and its centre is Gnaeus Calpurnius Piso, a distinguished member of one of the great families of Rome. Piso's father had followed the Republicans, Pompey, Cassius and Brutus. He had held a consulship in that crucial year in Augustus' early reign, 23 BC, perhaps as a gesture to the traditional aristocracy of the city. Piso's brother, Lucius, appears to have set out to offend the imperial family: he publicly announced that he was fleeing the moral corruption of Rome and was only persuaded to return by Tiberius' personal intervention. He prosecuted Urgulania, a woman closely connected to the imperial family, seriously embarrassing Tiberius and Livia (Tacitus, *Annales*, 2.34), and was himself to be prosecuted for treason in AD 24 (Tacitus, *Annales*, 4 21). Gnaeus Piso had served in Spain (*Corpus Inscriptionum Latinarum*, 2.2703) and possibly Africa before his appointment to Syria. He had won for himself a reputation for brutality (which he may have seen as old-fashioned severity) such that he was used by Seneca, *De Ira*, 1.18 as an example of the moral failings of anger. He had opposed a motion of Tiberius and Drusus in the senate in AD 16 (Dio, 57.15.9) and in a debate of the same year argued that senatorial business should continue to be transacted in the absence of the emperor (Tacitus,

Annales, 2.35). He made deliberate show of his independence, even of his Republicanism. Not only were the Pisones leading members of the Roman aristocracy and thus very well-known figures, but Gnaeus Piso and Tiberius had served together as consuls in AD 7, which would have required at least some collaboration, and the evidence points to a close friendship between the Pisones and Tiberius (and Livia).

It is difficult to believe that Piso's elevation to the governorship of Syria was a coincidence, or that Piso acted without an understanding that Tiberius would support him in any clash with Germanicus and it is possibly this confidence in Tiberius that encouraged Piso to return to Syria after the death of Germanicus and assert his authority against the friends of the dead prince.

Although sending Piso to Syria could be interpreted as a sign of hostility towards Germanicus, and was later interpreted as such, if we examine the relationship between Germanicus and Tiberius, there is little other evidence to support this thesis. The withdrawal of Germanicus from Germany may have caused differences, but Germanicus had reasserted Roman power in Germany after the Varian disaster of AD 9 and almost ten years of campaigning. Whatever Germanicus' instincts, Tiberius' judgement that he would be better deployed elsewhere cannot be dismissed as merely a convenient excuse. Germanicus returned to a triumph: the greatest military honour available. He progressed through the streets of Rome honoured by the population. This was also a political triumph for the imperial house. In his absence, Germanicus he had been associated with Drusus in public games, at which Drusus had obviously presided (Tacitus, *Annales*, 1.76). On his return to Rome, Germanicus had a victory arch erected in his honour near the temple of Saturn in the Forum, and the emperor gave 300 *sesterces*, a significant sum for the Roman poor, to the plebs in Germanicus' name (*Annales*, 2.41–2). In the following year, Germanicus held the consulship with the emperor, a very great honour. Tiberius was later to hold the consulship with Drusus in AD 21 and with Sejanus in 31. By the January of that year, Germanicus had already been sent to the East as imperial deputy. To all appearances, there was no division in the imperial house.

Germanicus was granted great honours following his death. The *Tabula Hebana* (EJ 94a) notes that a statue was to be set up to Germanicus and his father on the Palatine Hill near the temple of Apollo in which meetings of the senate were often held; his name was inserted into the hymn of the Salii; five of the voting centuries were to be named after him; a curule chair was to be placed for Germanicus at the games held in honour of the Divus Augustus and that chair was to be kept in the temple of Augustus. Temples were to be closed on the day that Germanicus' ashes were interred and sacrifices were to be made on that day each year at his tomb. On the same day, the equestrians were to parade in Germanicus' honour. In public, all due honours were granted to Germanicus. The only oddity was that Tiberius and his mother did not attend the internment.

Tacitus (*Annales*, 2.43) argues that the imperial court was divided between Germanicus and his supporters and those of Tiberius and Drusus. It is, however, difficult to find evidence of this. Drusus had acted with Germanicus to have Haterius Agrippa appointed praetor. Agrippa was a relative of Germanicus and had caused controversy in AD 15 by vetoing a proposal to beat a troupe of pantomime actors who were held responsible for inciting a crowd that had attacked some soldiers. Since one presumes that these soldiers were praetorians, a source of loyal support for Tiberius, it may be seen as a veto directed against Tiberius. We would therefore have expected Tiberius and Drusus to have opposed Agrippa. That they did not shows the unity of the imperial family (Tacitus, *Annales*, 1.77, 2.51). After Germanicus' death, Piso's son approached Drusus in order to secure his support in the forthcoming trial, Drusus being potentially the greatest beneficiary of Germanicus' death. He was refused a private audience and publicly rebuked. Drusus then left for Illyricum. There is no evidence of any division between Drusus and Germanicus, though Germanicus' relationship with Tiberius appears to have been more complex.

We might view Piso as a maverick, a throwback to the days of the fiercely independent Republican nobility and consider his actions in the East as those of an autonomous Republican. He was irritated by the regal honours granted to the young man by the Easterners. Germanicus appears to have been comfortable in the East and to have adapted his behaviour to the cultural values of the cities that he visited, notably the great cultural centres of Athens and Alexandria. The clash with Germanicus would then become a manifestation of Republican sentiments. Yet, the Piso brothers were well connected, and it is difficult to see how they could have risen so far if they had been openly subversive. Piso's closeness to Tiberius may have been a more important factor in the hostility between him and Germanicus than any 'Republicanism'. The brothers were willing and able to play the game that Tiberius was no more than a leading senator, but it was a game that Tiberius was also playing (and Germanicus appears to have ignored). Their closeness to the emperor meant that the brothers were likely beneficiaries from the Tiberian principate and Gnaeus' reward was the important role of governor of Syria. Opposition to the imperial house, which was manifest in Lucius' behaviour towards Livia and his expressed desire to leave the city, came only after the suicide of his brother.

But if there was no innate hostility between Piso and the imperial system, nor an obvious division within the imperial house, whatever later writers imagined, then we are left with a puzzle: how can we explain the hostility between Piso and Germanicus?

There is some sign that Tiberius may also have been unhappy at the ease with which Germanicus accepted the various quasi-regal honours. There was open criticism of Germanicus for a visit to Egypt (Tacitus, *Annales*, 2.59) on the grounds that the province had been 'closed' by Augustus to visitors of senatorial status and for the honours and courtesies that Germanicus showed the people of Alexandria. In itself, this episode is easily passed over, but Alexandria was the home and final resting place of Alexander the Great, the great young conquering hero and Roman leaders in the East had (and were to continue to have) a record of explicitly comparing themselves with the great conqueror (notably Pompey the Great and Augustus). Further, Alexandria was still a city that was associated with Germanicus' grandfather, Mark Antony. The association had already been made in Tacitus' account (*Annales*, 2.53) of a visit by Germanicus to Actium, scene of Octavian's defeat of Mark Antony and Cleopatra where, we are told, Germanicus viewed the scene from both the camp of Octavian and that of Antony. Germanicus' association with Antony hints at very different traditions of imperial rule. Notable, though, is the rebuke itself, which Tacitus tells us was strongly worded. Yet, Germanicus was far from being just an ordinary senator: he was heir-designate and deputy emperor. He was married to Augustus' granddaughter and, through a series of adoptions, he was also the grandson of Augustus (as well as Antony). It was a reasonable assumption that any limitations on senatorial travel imposed by Augustus would not apply to Germanicus and would be over-ridden by Germanicus' extensive legal authority. The rebuke thus did not reflect the reality of Germanicus' political and legal authority, but was in keeping with Tiberian self-presentation of himself and his family as merely leading senators.

The growing hostility between Piso and Germanicus is represented as personal, though there was clearly an ideological element. On Piso's journey to the East, he showed hostility to the Athenians who had so recently honoured and been honoured by Germanicus, attacking them as people who had no right to the glorious cultural and historical traditions of Athens, were historical enemies of Rome, and supporters of Antony against Augustus. Rumours circulated that Plancina, Piso's wife, gossiped about Agrippina (Tacitus, *Annales*, 2.55). In public, Piso and Germanicus maintained cordial relations, but Piso appears reluctant to accept the authority of the younger man. At a banquet for the Nabataean king, when the Nabataeans sought to assure the Roman leaders of their friendship through the gift of golden crowns, Piso seemed offended that the crown he received was lesser than those offered to Germanicus and Agrippina and consequently made remarks about luxury and moral decline. Piso's self presentation as a moral conservative led to him having difficulty in accepting the pre-eminence of the young prince.

One imagines that type of problem was not unusual. Augustus and Tiberius presented themselves as first citizens and had to negotiate their political superiority over aristocratic men of considerable importance in the Roman state without causing offence. Yet, younger members of the imperial household would inevitably find such situations more difficult (and we can compare Germanicus' situation with that faced by Gaius and Nero, both very young emperors). Germanicus probably had little choice but to tolerate Piso, and such toleration would ultimately enhance his reputation. But the two men were forced to work together by the situation on the Eastern frontier (which had led to Germanicus being sent East in the first instance). Piso was reluctant to give up control of his legions to Germanicus. Furthermore, neither man was alone. The friends who supported Piso and Germanicus in their various tasks worsened the hostility between the two men.

The relationship between the two men deteriorated to the extent that Piso planned to quit his province and return to Rome. He was delayed by Germanicus' illness. When a report circulated that Germanicus was recovering and sacrifices of thanks were to be made in Antioch, Piso supposedly used his authority to clear the streets. At this point, the breach between the two became open and Germanicus wrote to Piso renouncing their friendship: in Roman politics this was a declaration of political enmity (Tacitus, *Annales*, 2.69–70).

Germanicus' recovery was illusory. He was dying. He met his friends and supposedly accused Piso of his murder. He met his wife and supposedly warned her of the political dangers facing her. Tacitus appears to know the substance of the last, private conversation between a dying man and his wife (*Annales*, 2.71–2).

In Rome, politics was personal. Politics was about friendships and behaviour. With Piso and Germanicus, we have an instance in which politics goes wrong. There were underlying causes for the hostility that emerged and these are closely related to tensions in the imperial system itself. A system which grounds its politics in a Republican culture of equality but which in fact is monarchic, risks frictions of the kind that we see in this episode. No doubt those frictions were worsened in this case by the confidence of Piso both in his own status and in his friendship with Tiberius. There can also be little doubt that those who surrounded these two men, their friends, were jockeying for power and influence, competing against each other and seemingly for their 'man'. The situation appears to have developed a dynamic of its own and that dynamic continued after the death of Germanicus. Germanicus' friends saw many of their political hopes failing with the death of the prince, but they were also aware on the enmity of Piso. Their promise to Germanicus to destroy Piso was political. Further, Piso was reluctant to allow his enemies to take control of Syria, which he regarded as rightfully under his authority, and his return to the province after Germanicus' death was an attempt to assert his authority and weaken his enemies. Factional disputes among the aristocracy moved towards the brink of civil war.

Tiberius was far away. Although there were rumours of his involvement and his support for Piso, it is difficult to see any political gain in these events for the Princeps. He had lost his deputy, who was, of course, a potentially challenger, but nothing suggests that Tiberius feared that Germanicus would cease his obvious loyalty and launch a coup. If Tiberius had been fearful, giving Germanicus the political, economic and military resources of the Eastern provinces from which to construct a bid for the throne would have been unwise. Tiberius did continue to show his support for Piso's brother, and for Plancina, but Piso himself was doomed. Tiberius seems to have been an almost passive and probably very ill-informed spectator of the events in Syria, events which were a disaster for his regime and the imperial house.

Tiberius had never enjoyed universal popularity. Dio has a story dated to AD 15, before Tiberius had paid the legacies given by Augustus to the Roman plebs. A corpse was being carried through the Forum when a man stopped the bearers, bent over and whispered a message in the corpse's ear. When he was asked what he said, he replied that he had sent word to Augustus concerning Tiberius' failure to pay the legacies. Tiberius had the man killed so that the message would be delivered directly (Dio, 57.14.1). Another sign of the weakness came in AD 17 with the emergence of a pretender. Clemens, a slave of Agrippa Postumus, had made a futile attempt to save his master. He then stole Postumus' ashes and retreated to Cosa. After some time, he re-emerged declaring himself to be Postumus, miraculously saved. Word spread and Clemens eventually made his way to Ostia. Tiberius supposedly had him secretly kidnapped and murdered (Tacitus, *Annales*, 2.39; cf. Dio, 57.16.3–4).

But after Germanicus' death attention focused on Agrippina. Agrippina had returned with her children to a nation in mourning. The passing of the cortège through Italy was an opportunity to unite the people in grief. The torch-lit procession in Rome, a procession with military honours, to the mausoleum in which Augustus had been laid to rest just a few years before and the silent placing of the ashes in the family tomb brought the community of Italy and Rome together, a community which had so recently united to celebrate Germanicus' triumph over the Germans.

Ceremonials are important and here was a great ceremonial, orchestrated around and centring on Agrippina, not on the emperor. Consciously or otherwise, Agrippina's role in these ceremonies and her position as grandchild of Augustus and the mother of Augustus' great-grandchildren made her a central political figure. The tensions that had divided the imperial family for almost 30 years were once more obvious and Agrippina was a natural, if vulnerable, focus for a growing opposition to Tiberius. The death of Germanicus and the subsequent trial of Piso cannot have eased relations between Agrippina and Tiberius, even if they had managed to maintain a measure of cordiality in spite of hostility between Tiberius and her late brothers. Yet, as with the relationship between Piso and Germanicus, Tiberius and Agrippina were not the only two actors in this game. Some would have seen benefit in attaching themselves to Germanicus and later to Agrippina: they would have felt the hostility of those close to Piso and perhaps those around Tiberius. The Roman elite had always been fractious and the divisions of the imperial family offered a potential breach in the Roman political community around which factions could form. The in-fighting of the imperial house and of the senatorial families led to an increasingly tense political atmosphere. Tiberius presided over this fraught political period, and we should remember that political failure could result in exile or death. Tiberius' response was unconventional: he came to rely more on a close friend and less on his family. The death of Germanicus created the conditions for the rise of Sejanus.

Sejanus

Tiberius' first prefect of the guard was L. Seius Strabo. He offered Tiberius crucial support at his accession and his loyalty was rewarded with a posting as Prefect of Egypt, the senior equestrian magistracy (see pp. 345–46). Although an equestrian, Seius Strabo was connected to several prominent senatorial families through his mother and wives and his career brought him considerable wealth. His son was adopted, probably into a prominent senatorial family, and his name was changed to L. Aelius Sejanus, but instead of pursuing a senatorial career, Sejanus followed his natural father and became joint prefect (with his father) and then sole prefect of the praetorian guard.

Sejanus first appears in our historical record in AD 14 when he was sent with the young Drusus to quell the mutinous legions on the Danube (Tacitus, *Annales*, 1.24). He had been among the friends of Gaius Caesar (Augustus' grandson) (Tacitus, *Annales*, 4.1), but had become an associate of Tiberius. Although Tacitus mentions him briefly in the story of the trial of Piso, we next see him in AD 20 when he betrothed his daughter to Claudius' son (Tacitus, *Annales*, 3.29). By AD 21, he was an emerging power and Tacitus (*Annales*, 3.35) alleges that Marcus Aemelius Lepidus, a member of one of the most aristocratic families of Rome, stepped aside to allow Sejanus' uncle to assume a command in Africa. The following year, after Sejanus was praised for prompt action to prevent a fire that burnt down the theatre of Pompey spreading to other areas, a bronze statue was erected to him in the theatre, a notable honour (Tacitus, *Annales*, 3.72). Tiberius had allowed him to concentrate the praetorian guard in a single camp in the city, so that the entire guard would be under his direct authority.

Sejanus was becoming prominent in the imperial government and Drusus is said to have become hostile and complained at the trust that his father placed in this interloper (Tacitus, *Annales*, 4.7). Sejanus was, however, only remotely connected to the imperial family. Drusus was his father's natural political ally and successor. Drusus' hostility seriously weakened Sejanus' position. Tiberius may have called him *socius laborum* (ally in my work) in early AD 23 (Tacitus, *Annales*, 4.2), but his position was clearly subordinate.

In 23, however, his prospects were transformed. Drusus died, allegedly poisoned by Sejanus and Drusus' wife Livilla (Germanicus' sister). Tiberius was left without an adult male member of his family on whom he could rely. The closest male surviving members of the imperial family were Claudius, who was regarded as unsuitable for high office, and the sons of Germanicus and Agrippina. Drusus appears to have acted as a guardian for these children and his loss left them and their mother vulnerable. Sejanus was now in a similar position to that of Tiberius following the death of Agrippa. He was the closest collaborator of the emperor and the second most powerful man in the state, but he was not ultimately expected to succeed.

The truth of the poisoning allegation is impossible to substantiate. The allegation of poisoning surfaced when Sejanus fell. His former wife, having seen her and Sejanus' children killed, returned home and alleged in a suicide note that Sejanus and Livilla had murdered Drusus (Dio, 68.11.6–7). Tiberius had the slaves of the household tortured until confessions were extracted. Sejanus was the obvious beneficiary of Drusus' death and there may have been rumours of foul play at the time, some of which connected Tiberius himself to the death of his son, though Tacitus regarded them as ridiculous. Sejanus' wife's allegation was made at a time of the intense personal distress and Tiberius may have found the allegation credible or convenient in AD 31 (Tacitus, *Annales*, 4. 10–11).

There was no immediate threat to Sejanus' position after Drusus' death. Ultimately, however, the young sons of Germanicus and Agrippina would usurp his position. The next few years appear to have been marked by increasing hostility between Sejanus and Agrippina and her sons. Sejanus' power over the emperor was far from complete, as was demonstrated in AD 25 when his request to marry Livilla, and thus become a member of the imperial family, was refused. (Tacitus, *Annales*, 4.39–40). Such a request reflected the importance of the women in the imperial family in establishing political status and alliances. Livilla may have been willing: Sejanus was a power in the land and she might benefit from such an alliance now that Drusus, the emperor's son and her husband was dead. The suggest alliance would have a certain logic with Livilla exchanging one heir for the next. If the gossips were right, the refusal of the request did not prevent the two from establishing a sexual relationship, which was effectively an illegitimate political compact.

Yet, in spite of this setback, continuing dissensions in the imperial family were working to Sejanus' advantage. Relations between Agrippina and Tiberius became so bad that Agrippina apparently refused to eat food at Tiberius' dinner parties for fear that it had been poisoned. She also petitioned Tiberius to be allowed to remarry, a request Tiberius refused (Tacitus, *Annales*, 4.53).

These two blocked marriages illustrate the growing political crisis in Rome. Sejanus' bid to marry Livilla offered a means for Sejanus to be brought within the family and therefore provided Tiberius with an alternative route to an heir. The implications of such an alliance were clear. In AD 25, Tiberius was unwilling to turn aside from his own grandchild or the children of Germanicus and contemplate Sejanus as imperial heir or guardian of any such heir. Agrippina's remarriage could not be allowed either, for any husband of Agrippina would similarly be elevated to a prominent position in the imperial house and would become a potential heir. It is difficult to believe that her alleged appeal was more than rhetorical. She requested male protection for herself and her children, but the request was also an implied rebuke. Tiberius himself should have been the protector of the imperial family.

One ought, however, to be cautious. These stories were obviously of dramatic importance, but dealt with matters internal to the imperial family and one must wonder how they reached the historians. They do not reflect well on Tiberius or Sejanus and their publication may be part of a hostile tradition. Certainly, the circle around Agrippina might have leaked the stories, or they could have emerged at the time of the fall of Sejanus. The stories are plausible, but not certainly true.

Faced with conflict in his family and an increasingly restive political class in Rome, Tiberius left Rome and retired to Capri, an island in the Bay of Naples. If one were to choose a place of retreat close to Rome, Capri has much to recommend it. Rising out of the Bay of Naples, the island has considerable natural beauty and sea breezes for the warm summer months. The remains of Tiberius' villa suggest that the aging emperor did not stint on his own comforts. It is easy to see a personal motive for the retreat. Tiberius cut himself off from the day-to-day politics of Rome. Politically, distance isolated him from the factions and the requirement to take a position on political issues. His interventions could be more careful. The senators, unable to take clues from the presence of the emperor, were forced to change tactics and it may have been hoped that his relative absence would mean that the emperor could not be held responsible for all that happened in the city.

The results of his retreat were, however, perhaps unforeseen. The senate was ultimately further marginalised as a political body since the real centre of power remained within the imperial court, now at Capri. The major conduit of information to and from the court was the praetorian prefect. It would be difficult for the senators not to regard the word of the prefect as being endorsed by the emperor. Further, Tiberius retained political interests in Roman and these needed to be managed, a task which further raised the mighty prefect.

In AD 28, the senate voted altars to *Clementia* (mercy) and *Amicitia* (friendship). The former was an 'imperial virtue', for only the powerful may show clemency. It may suggest a nervousness about the political situation and the increasing blood-letting that marked imperial political conflicts. The emperor (through Sejanus) controlled significant military forces in Rome and there was always a possibility that these troops would be used. The altar to *Amicitia* was flanked by statues of Sejanus and Tiberius (Tacitus, *Annales*, 4.74). Sejanus' birthday was to be honoured, a privilege normally reserved for members of the imperial family. According to Dio, various groups in Roman society erected statues to Sejanus and he was included in the usual prayers and sacrifices for the fortunes of the emperor (Dio, 58. 2.7). Sejanus was thus associated with Tiberius in the symbols and rituals of imperial power, which must have suggested to the people that Sejanus was to be further elevated.

The very next year saw a direct attack on Agrippina. Her son Nero Caesar was accused of shameful sexual activity and Agrippina's attitude was criticised. The senate, however, refused to act. It would not launch highly unpopular prosecutions of members of the imperial house without clearer direction (Tacitus, *Annales*, 5.3–4). We do not have a complete narrative for the following years and do not know what Tiberius' reaction was to this rebuff, but Nero and Agrippina were eventually exiled, presumably after a clear statement of the emperor's wishes. Nero was killed or encouraged to kill himself in AD 31 (Dio, 58.8.3–4; Suetonius, *Tiberius*, 54). Drusus Caesar was to follow into exile and eventually to death, also accused of sexual misdemeanours (Dio, 58. 3.8).

Sejanus' rise now looked inevitable. His principal enemies were exiled and it seemed that the emperor, who already relied on him, would eventually elevate him to the imperial position. He was, however, still an equestrian – not a suitable candidate for imperial office. Tiberius changed this. Sejanus was appointed to the consulship of AD 31. He was to have the very rare honour of sharing his consulship with Tiberius himself. Dio dates Tiberius' use of the phrase *socius laborum* (ally in my work) to AD 30, a phrase that might suggest that he would become an ally in his title as well. The senate voted that Sejanus and Tiberius would hold joint consulships every five years and similar ceremonies were to be conducted whenever either of them entered the city. Dio tells us that sacrifices were made to images of Sejanus, suggesting his integration into the imperial cult (Dio, 58.4.1–4). He was by this time betrothed to a daughter of the imperial house, probably Julia, who was the daughter of his supposed lover Livilla and Drusus, the emperor's son, and who had been married to Nero Drusus, the son of Germanicus and Agrippina.[2] The betrothal opened the door for Sejanus to be formally adopted as Tiberius' heir or co-emperor by the grant of tribunician power. Most must have expected both these developments. Neither happened. Instead, Tiberius decided to destroy Sejanus.

The reasons behind this change of heart are obscure. The Jewish historian Josephus (*Antiquities* 18.6) relates that Antonia, who had been married to Drusus, Tiberius' brother, and was the mother of Livilla, laid information against Sejanus. Even in the convoluted sexual politics of the imperial house, Antonia moving against her daughter's lover *and* her granddaughter's betrothed is startling. If Antonia warned Tiberius of an impending coup (as Josephus suggests), one has to wonder what Sejanus would have had to gain from taking such a risk and why Antonia would act in support of the old emperor (her former brother-in-law) and against her daughter. Cassius Dio has a completely different narrative in which Tiberius gradually let it be known he was displeased with Sejanus and Sejanus was forced to see his power gradually melt away (Dio, 58. 7–9). But even Dio (58.11) alleges that Antonia played a significant part, eventually, after the fall of Sejanus, imprisoning her own daughter, Livilla, and starving her to death. It is not clear what sparked this dramatic and implacable anger; even by the standards of the Julio-Claudians and the rumours that circulated around them, starving one's daughter to death was an extreme act. We cannot know whether the story is true or whether it later circulated as a way of sensationalising Livilla's disappearance and death. Dio's story of a diminishing of Sejanus' reputation also makes little sense in the context of the detailed account of the dramatic means by which Tiberius was eventually to rid himself of Sejanus: it smacks of interpretations after the fact when the wise might proclaim that they could see the fall of Sejanus coming. Neither narrative is persuasive, and both stories seem to speculate on the detailed motivations of those behind the palace doors with little obvious insight.

Tiberius' potential choices were limited in AD 31: he could either make Sejanus emperor, a decision which would certainly mean the death of Gaius Caligula, the third son of Germanicus and Agrippina, who had remained with Tiberius on Capri and who had perhaps threatened Tiberius' young grandson, or he could kill Sejanus.

Ridding himself of his mighty prefect was no easy task. Sejanus had control of the praetorians, the major military force in Rome. He did not, however, control the *vigiles*, the night watch, a kind of military police force stationed within the city. Tiberius sent a letter to the city through Macro, the prefect of the *vigiles*. Sejanus was summoned to the senate and led to expect further honours: he must have believed that the moment of his elevation had come. But when he entered the senate, the praetorians were ordered to barracks and the *vigiles* took control of the streets of Rome. Instead of honours, the letter condemned Sejanus. He was taken from the senate-house and imprisoned. The senate met again on the same day and had him executed. (Dio, 58.8–11; Suetonius, *Tiberius* 65).

Sejanus was more than prefect of the praetorian guard. He was a politician of some importance with influence and support in the senate. When the fateful letter was read, the consul Memmius Regulus, who was in on the plot, did not immediately propose the death penalty or put a proposal before the senate that Sejanus be arrested for fear that Sejanus' supporters, including the other consul, would cause a disturbance. He took advice from a single senator (Dio, 58.10.8). In the aftermath of the fall of Sejanus, his most prominent supporters were tried in the senate for various charges. Sejanus' uncle, Quintus Julius Blaesus who had campaigned successfully in Africa and had been awarded great honours, was probably executed. Publius Vitellius, a prominent ally, killed himself. Livilla, his presumed lover, disappeared. A Publius Pomponius was arrested, but was able to drag out proceedings until the death of the emperor. One Sextius Paconianus was accused of complicity with Sejanus and brought down Lucianus Latiaris (Tacitus, *Annales*, 5.8–9; 6.4). Others, whose names we do not have, also perished.

Sejanus' fall reverberated through Italy, and the town of Interamna in Umbria erected an inscription in AD 32 to commemorate Tiberius' saving of the state from the threat posed by Sejanus (EJ 51). Even among the legions, there must have been shock. All the legionary armies, with the exception of those in Syria, had consecrated images to Sejanus in their camps (Suetonius, *Tiberius*, 48.2). The assumption that Sejanus would be the next emperor must have been general. This was not just the death of a courtier, but the removal of a powerful political group. We can never truly know why they were removed.

The savagery of the assault on Sejanus and his followers (Sejanus' children were brutally murdered) suggests that as a group they were held responsible for the actions against senators, members of the imperial family and others in the preceding years. In AD 32, Haterius Agrippa, a relative of Germanicus, (see p. 110) attacked the consuls of the previous year for not prosecuting the adherents of Sejanus sufficiently vigorously (Tacitus, *Annales*, 6.4). The supporters of Agrippina were exacting revenge. Yet, if we examine the ultimate result of these dramatic events, the fall of Sejanus appears in a rather different light. Tiberius remained on his island retreat. Agrippina remained in exile and in 33 killed herself, supposedly having been savagely beaten and tortured. Drusus died in the same year. He was starved to death. Tiberius apparently felt able to make the details of the manner of their deaths known (Dio, 58. 22.4–5; Tacitus, *Annales*, 6.23–5; Suetonius, *Tiberius*, 53–4.). The divisions in the imperial family were not healed and Tiberius remained murderously hostile towards Agrippina and one of her sons. The death of Sejanus saw a radical shift in imperial dynastic politics, but no reconciliation with Agrippina and her sons .

The continuities in Tiberian policy suggest that Sejanus had been useful, a political tool: he had managed to enrich himself, harm his enemies, and garner political authority, but the reality of the situation was that imperial power was concentrated on Tiberius. In one way, Sejanus was an illusion, a sleight of hand by which Tiberius concealed his power. It seems likely that Tiberius either acquiesced in or encouraged the violence inherent in politics under Sejanus' ministry and, indeed, after the fall of the praetorian prefect. This was not the political violence of the street, but of the law court. It was a violence of accusations of various political crimes, crimes which were judged on political grounds and which resulted in the disgrace, exile or death of the political figures concerned. It was a politics of institutionalised violence, but it was violent nonetheless. His fall seems quixotic, without rationality, and in its violence expressive of the extreme and absolute power concentrated on the emperor.

The Fall of Sejanus became the subject of a tragedy by Ben Johnson, performed in 1603. The rise and fall of a mighty subject was suitable material for tragic drama and the violence of his end, the death of his lover and his children were a gruesome retribution in keeping with the *mores* of the stage of that time. The true historical tragedy was the violence and feuding that beset the senatorial aristocracy throughout the later Tiberian period and gave rise to the vicious political passions that rendered killing someone's children an acceptable act of political revenge

The senate

Tacitus depicts the relationship of the senate and the Emperor as starting badly and getting progressively worse. To a large extent this picture can be accepted. It is not contradicted by our other sources and is confirmed by the failure of the senate to vote Tiberius the posthumous honours his adopted father and many subsequent emperors received. Tacitus may have exaggerated the hostility; but he did not fabricate it.

Modern historians have tended to emphasise this exaggeration and to point out that Tiberius himself initiated few prosecutions of senators, that many senators were undoubtedly guilty of the crimes of which they were accused, and that the number of senators killed during Tiberius' reign was quite small. This is to miss the point. At what point do we condemn a dictatorial regime for killing its opponents: after three deaths, or after 20? All our sources present a depressing catalogue of prosecutions and trials from almost the first days of Tiberius' rule. There is no guarantee that we have a complete list of all those tried during the period and indeed it is more than likely that the less spectacular cases were omitted from the litany.

To focus on numbers (or guilt) is to miss the tyrannous nature of the politics. The senate was a relatively small body. The senators were also a close-knit group. Political marriages, remarriage, the frequent use of adoption (even of adults), and such sociological features of Roman society as *amicitia* (see pp. 297–300) meant that senators depended on an extensive network of family connections and friendships, which were inevitably politicised. The fall of any politician would not just affect that man but also his friends and family, sending ripples of fear and grief and anger through Roman society.

The tight-knit nature of Roman political society allowed for the escalation of violence. Exile or death would lead to a desire for revenge. The removal of any politician would leave a residue of supporters and friends hostile and fearful. Further, the emperor never acted alone. He nearly always had prosecutors and informers. These men benefited from the fall of others, but in their victories, secured themselves long-lasting enmities. The violence, even if a judicial violence, raised the political stakes. People were struggling for their lives, not just their careers. Fear bred desperation. As the situation worsened and as more were killed or exiled, few would have been under illusion that their enemies would show them mercy.

Under Tiberius, we seem to see just such an escalation. Sejanus and his supporters seem to have initiated prosecutions against the friends of Agrippina, tacitly supported by the emperor. The friends of Agrippina initiated prosecutions following the fall of Sejanus. With the growth in political trials, there came to be an increasing use of *delatores*. These were people who received substantial rewards for providing information leading to prosecution. It was not just treason that produced these trials but corruption and sexual misdemeanours, the very stuff of gossip and rumour in small communities.

The trials dominate our accounts in part, one assumes, because of the traumatic nature of the trials for the political class. It would not take many trials to produce an atmosphere of paranoia. Tiberius' political standing fell as a result and his relationship with the senate worsened.

It is easy to understand the process by which support could be alienated, but less easy to see how Tiberius could have allowed this to happen. He seems to have started his reign with good intentions and to have made every effort to honour the senate. He was Augustus' choice: the most obvious man for the job. What went wrong?

Our ancient sources emphasise character. Tiberius is depicted as a secretive, cruel man, masking his true nature and desires. He did not assert his policy and when others produced decisions different to Tiberius' preferred but unstated option, he stored up the memory of his defeat. Those who caused offence did not know, perhaps could not know, until Tiberius' hostility manifested itself on a different, unrelated and perhaps more dangerous occasion. In circumstances in which the political class needed to negotiate complicated political relationship and in which all real power stemmed from the emperor himself, understanding the emperor was crucial for not just a successful political career, but to be able to manage the business of politics. Yet, the senators appear not to have established a firm view of him and or to have gained a sense of what he required. With the goodwill of the emperor so crucial, inevitably senators would focus on any information that emerged that might give them a clue to the imperial character, and thus they were sucked into a maelstrom of gossip, innuendo, and rumour.

Evidence of Tiberius' cruelty abounds in the ancient sources. His perversions were rumoured, such rumours reported to us mainly by Suetonius. The retreat to Capri removed Tiberius from the direct view of the senatorial elite, and rumours of his indulgence in sexual perversions circulated.

Sex is a peculiar political issue. In contemporary politic life, sex plays differently in different societies from a relatively relaxed attitude in France and Italy to relative prurience in the US and UK. Attitudes towards homosexuality show yet greater divergences. In Roman culture, the patterns of power and sex varied in complex ways. We have seen that the bodies of the women of the imperial family were subject to political calculation and 'conspiracies' and 'adulteries' were intertwined. With men, the issue was different. Romans were relatively unconcerned about what went on within households: slaves of whatever age or gender belonged bodily to a master. Yet, sexual appetites became political when they were seen to reflect moral weakness or a rapaciousness that extended beyond the safe confines of the household. A master who was a slave to his desires was unlikely to be able to show self-discipline in public life. The danger was thus analogical, very much as the contemporary press claims that adultery on the part of our political leaders must be of interest since it shows that they are dishonest. Rapacious sexual appetites were different since if the emperor used his power to seduce or to sexually abuse aristocratic women in Rome, it would reflect on his relationship with other members of the political class. Seduction and rape of aristocratic women was the mark of the tyrant (the man who abused the free bodies of the citizens). The gossip that surrounded Tiberius in his retreat (the truth of which cannot be assessed) was, then, political and important: not to be dismissed as mere court gossip. Such gossip was treason and the stories reflected a view of Tiberius as tyrant.

These stories reflect a tendency to personalise and psychologise history: the failings of the Tiberian reign come to be the manifestations of the personal psychological failings of the emperor. Roman imperial history can be read in this way: thus we have Tiberius the hypocrite, Gaius the mad, Claudius the fool, Nero the licentious, Vespasian the mean, and Domitian the cruel. Yet, the repeated patterns of hostility between emperor and senate and the frequent collapse of that central political relationship into institutionalised violence require a deeper explanation. To have one bad emperor may seem unfortunate, but to have the four bad emperors of the Julio-Claudian period looks like a systemic failing.

Tiberius and the senators were caught in a quandary. Roman politics and the cultural and moral values on which it depended elevated notions of freedom for its citizens and equality for its political elites including the right and perhaps the obligation to speak openly. But the concentration of power in the hands of an individual, military, financial, legal established an imperial reality incompatible with those Republican values. Furthermore, Tiberius inherited the imperial position from Augustus. He was committed to Augustan policies and values, a commitment underlined by his deification of Augustus and his reading of mandates from Augustus to the senate at the debate on accession. Yet, Augustus had represented his regime as preserving the cultural and political values of the Republican era and of the Roman people through the establishment of the new constitutional arrangements. One of those core values of the Roman tradition was the adherence to law.

Tiberius offered the senators independence, but the senators realised that their safety and security and the furthering of their careers depended on the securing of the good will of the emperor. The imperial grant of freedom could not be exploited because the reality of the political arrangements which gave Tiberius the power, which allowed him to give the senators their freedom, meant that they were dependent on him and therefore not free. The situation was so frustrating that Tiberius famously remarked that these were 'men ready to be slaves' (Tacitus, *Annales*, 3. 65), and the narrative in Tacitus makes clear that the senators themselves were indeed willing participants in the processes which eroded their freedom. The regime (meaning the system of power rather than just the reign) had its own logic and however Tiberius sought to manipulate that regime, he was himself caught up in its system of power relations.

The situation was made worse by the divisions in the senate. The last years of Augustus had been marred by the problems in the imperial family and we must suppose that groups within the aristocracy offered their support to one or other of the family groups. The imperial family may have been united briefly following the accession of Tiberius but, as we have seen, there were probably residual tensions between Tiberius and certain members of the Roman elite. Some of these may have surfaced in factional disputes between groups who offered support to Germanicus or to Drusus, but until Germanicus' death the unity of the imperial family probably reduced senatorial conflict. Divisions within the imperial family were manifested following the death of Germanicus and were probably worsened after the death of Drusus (see, for example, Tacitus, *Annales*, 4.53). Yet, the prosecutions that marred the reign of Tiberius were not all, or perhaps even in the majority, related to the bitter politics of the imperial court. The early trials of Vibius Serenus and Cremutius Cordus for instance (Tacitus, *Annales*, 4. 28–32) while connected to the authority of the emperor and related to the charges of *maiestas* (treason) appear to have no very obvious imperial interest. The trials were brought about by competition within the senate and among the senators, competition that was for political status between senators and their friends and also competition for the patronage and support of the emperor. A *delatator*'s prosecuting of an enemy on a treason charge was a gratuitous display of loyalty and an assertion of the disloyalty of the enemy (and his friends). Yet, if treason was the trump card to play in such competition, other charges could be as effective: adultery would assert the untrustworthy immorality of the lover; corruption the unsuitability for high office.

Tiberius could have crushed these trials, and in some cases he appears to have done so. Yet, in refusing to allow charges to come to court, he would effectively have abrogated the law that he was in post to protect. He could exercise clemency (*clementia*) after the fact, but *clementia* in itself was an exercise of sovereign power beyond the constitutional. He was bound to protect the law and the legacy of Augustus, which meant maintaining laws. Furthermore, the law was associated with the Republic and with freedom itself: the great division in political regimes was between those who respected the law and ruled by laws openly published and those who ruled by the arbitrary judgement of the sovereign power. The latter were tyrannies. The rule of law and by law was the protection of the rights of the citizen. If Tiberius were to abrogate the law on *maiestas*, he would face the problem of what to do about charges of corruption or adultery. Tacitus (*Annales*, 3.28), in a long excursus on the history of law, describes the return of civic rights in 28 BC under Augustus but instead of these rights guaranteeing freedom, they were a 'tightening of the chains' and the laws, particularly that relating to adultery, set 'guards' among the people and initiated a terror for all. Tacitus sets up a moral–ethical problem familiar to modern states: if the rule of law is the foundation of civic life, should one obey the law in a despotic or evil regime? And, perhaps with greater subtlety this problem suggests that even laws designed to end social evils (such as adulteries) could in themselves produce social evils far worse than those they were designed to repress. The law under the Principate became not a symbol of citizenship but a means of oppressing the population.

The process of using the law to further political disputes had a long history: it had been used by Republican politicians to harm their political enemies. But with the Principate, and faced with a single judge, the law courts became yet more dangerous places. As early as AD 16, with the trial of Libo (Tacitus, *Annales*, 2.27–31) senatorial inventiveness was exploiting the law for political purposes: Tacitus describes the charges and the trial as absurd, though it is not necessarily the case that Libo was innocent. In Libo's case, he appealed to Tiberius for pardon, but Tiberius told him to appeal to the senate: in so doing, Tiberius reflected the proper working of the judicial system since it was the senators' responsibility to judge their own and in not interfering he honoured the law and customs of the Roman state, but Libo was left without hope, since the political reality of the situation was that no senator was likely to risk the animosity of the emperor or being portrayed as a friend of the enemy of the emperor by intervening. Libo killed himself, and at that point Tiberius announced that he would have exercised *clementia*, but, of course, he was too late.

As it became clear that Tiberius would allow prosecutions, senators brought test cases on the charge of *maiestas* (treason). This was an ill-defined offence that came to include offences, verbal or other, against the person of the *princeps*, his predecessor or family. A prosecution in itself was a demonstration of loyalty to Tiberius and the alleged offence may have been personally insulting. He could block these prosecutions, but he was in a more difficult position with offences against the *Divus Augustus*. By not blocking all prosecutions, Tiberius gave senators the means of pursuing their competition. Since the charges often related to the emperor's person, the emperor himself would carry some of the blame. Tiberius was in an invidious position. The very freedoms he allowed the senate were reducing his political standing and making him seem a more autocratic figure.

Tiberius was far from an innocent figure in this process and he exploited the situation by using exactly these mechanisms to rid himself of his political enemies. He was, of course, also part of this political culture and there is no reason to believe that Tiberius was immune to the increasingly vitriolic political atmosphere in Rome. A man who killed so many of his relatives and former friends would hardly be squeamish about the removal of those he perceived as his political opponents. Eventually, there could be no pretence that Tiberius preserved Republican freedom and more than a hundred people were charged with *maiestas* during his reign.

We need not see in Tiberius' dealings with the senate the actions of a malicious or perverted character. The tensions of the relationship between the senate and the imperial regime were overwhelming. Tiberius failed to resolve this defect in the Principate. Tacitus' Tiberius is cruel and vindictive, but he is aided, even encouraged, by a pliant senate ever eager to ruin one of their colleagues. For Tacitus, the most depressing element in the catalogue of prosecutions, executions and suicides was the senators themselves who were at the forefront of these prosecutions. This is history played out as tragedy: there is an inevitability about the institutionalised violence that swept through the Roman state. Furthermore, the grand bargain that had been struck by Augustus, freedom for peace, started to look unworkable. We could read these events as the senators exerting increasing authority (freedom) and see in the violence and lack of security the consequences of such freedom; we might think that the peace offered by the Augustan settlement was, ultimately, illusory: the Tiberian violence showed how close to civil war the Romans remained.

Administration

Our major ancient literary sources tended to view the world from the perspective of Rome and from the perspective of the senatorial elite. Their judgements are not, therefore, primarily motivated by the administrative efficiency of emperors, though this does play a part in assessments. Modern historians have been far more concerned with the issue and have here, as elsewhere, sought a fresh perspective on the emperor. Assessment of administrative efficiency of any emperor is hampered by the very nature of our sources. Extreme results of administrative failure, such as bankruptcy or revolts get reported, but the absence of such is hardly adequate grounds for categorising an administration as efficient. Tiberius remained solvent during his reign, but the quality of his administration of Rome and of the provinces is questionable.

While in Rome, Tiberius appears to have been assiduous in the performance of his administrative and legal duties. He passed as much business as possible to the senate for consideration and the evidence of these senatorial debates suggests that Tiberius and the senate were careful administrators. The situation does not seem to have altered significantly after his departure for Capri. Technically, since the imperial position was a creation in addition to and an amalgamation of pre-existing administrative positions, the emperor's presence was not necessary for the proper functioning of Rome's administration. Indeed, since Augustus had also spent many years away from the city, there is no suggestion that the imperial presence was intended to be integral to the administration's daily functioning. Tiberius still retained influence over Roman affairs through the employment of ministers and could have the cases he wished to hear transferred to Capri for his personal attention. Indeed, the retreat to Capri must have freed Tiberius from the daily ceremonials, the formalities of regular attendance at the senate, and allowed him to delegate much legal business which, in theory, might have allowed him to concentrate on the most important issues. Nevertheless, Suetonius (*Tiberius*, 41) claims that Tiberius ceased to pay any attention to administrative issues following his retreat (though it is unclear how Suetonius would he have known this). Tiberius did not neglect Roman business entirely. In AD 27, Tiberius provided compensation for those who had lost property in a fire on the Caelian Hill (Tacitus, *Annales*, 4. 64) and he did the same in 37 when fire destroyed part of the Aventine and the Circus Maximus (Tacitus, *Annales*, 6. 45). In 32, he wrote to the senate asking them to issue a stern proclamation against the people who had been rioting because of a threatened failure of the corn supply (Tacitus, *Annales*, 6. 13). The following year Tiberius enforced a pre-existing law on interest rates and inadvertently caused a financial crisis, which he stabilised by prompt and generous action (Tacitus, *Annales*, 6. 16–17; Dio, 58. 21.4–5). This is admittedly quite sparse evidence for administrative intervention in the affairs of the city, but it is probably sufficient to suggest that Tiberius remained concerned with administrative matters and managed the affairs of the city quite competently.

There is more information concerning policy in the provinces, but even here it is difficult to reach evaluative judgements. One of Tiberius' most famous phrases was 'I want my sheep to be shorn not shaven' (Dio, 57. 10.5) referring to the Prefect of Egypt's unexpectedly large transfer of revenues from the province. This shows some concern for the state of the province, but firmly from the point of view of the sheep farmer and not the sheep.

Another notable feature of Tiberius' reign is the between eight and eleven trials for *repetundae* (corruption). This evidence may be read in two ways: either as showing Tiberius' determination to prevent governors of provinces unduly oppressing the provincials, or as demonstrating the level of corruption during Tiberius' reign. Tacitus and Dio treat them as political trials, though Tacitus is quite willing to admit that several of the accusations were well founded (Tacitus, *Annales*, 6. 29). There were two cases in which corruption led to revolt. A major revolt in Gaul led by Florus and Sacrovir in AD 21 seems to have been caused by oppressive Roman taxation and the burden of debts (Tacitus, *Annales*, 3. 40–6). The Frisii revolted in AD 29 due to Roman extortion: the Romans had taxed the Frisii in hides but the size of the beasts had not been specified in the treaty. A senior centurion (*primus pilus*), who was in charge of the region, specified that very large hides were required and, in so doing, bankrupted the Frisians, causing a major revolt. The Romans suffered a military setback but Tiberius refused to commit to a major campaign (Tacitus, *Annales*, 4. 72–4).

The other major characteristic of Tiberius' provincial administration is the length of time he left the governors in office. Dio tells us that praetorian governors served for three years while consular governors served for six (Dio, 58. 23.5). Suetonius (*Tiberius*, 41) produces a litany of military disasters due to Tiberius' administrative mismanagement of Armenia, Moesia and Gaul. It is unclear to what events in Gaul and Moesia Suetonius' précis was referring.

Tacitus' account of the problems in Armenia and Parthia suggests rather that Tiberius, through the effective diplomacy and military tactics of Lucius Vitellius, was initially successful in supporting the Roman's preferred candidate for the Parthian throne (Tacitus, *Annales*, 6. 31–7) until the puppet's support dissolved (Tacitus, *Annales*, 6. 41–4). In any case, Rome was to secure a peace treaty and brought stability to the borders, though this had to wait until the reign of Gaius (Dio, 59. 27.3–4; Suetonius, *Gaius*, 14.3). Tiberius did detain governors appointed to Spain (Dio, 58. 8.3) and Syria in Rome, the reasons for which are unclear. Aelius Lama had remained in Rome after his appointment to Syria but was sufficiently trusted to be given the urban prefecture by Tiberius (Tacitus, *Annales*, 6. 27; Dio, 58. 19.5).

Tiberius followed a very conservative policy in the provinces. He seems to have dealt with those military problems that arose with reasonable efficiency but to have avoided any major expansion, especially in the latter years of his reign. There is no evidence to suggest that his government was any more or less efficient than that of other emperors. His policy of leaving governors in place for extended periods and his rather strange decision to detain the governors of Syria and Spain in Rome were probably not conducive to administrative efficiency in the long term. His largely pacific policy left the empire undamaged and avoided the military disasters that had marred the final years of Augustus' reign.

Conclusion

If we were to accept the ancient judgement on Tiberius, we would see his reign as a failure and judge Tiberius himself a tyrant. We must, however, recognise that Tiberius' position in AD 14 was far from easy. Although it is easy to lapse into moral judgement and a ruler who presided over the levels of political violence that marked the reign of Tiberius must carry moral responsibilities, attributing political failure to questionable character or personal moral weakness merely distracts from deeper issues. Tiberius was, as much as anyone, trapped in his time, a creature of the circumstances of society and political structure. That political structure was paradoxical. Tiberius was the first to inherit the imperial position and was clearly the most powerful man in Rome in AD 14. But he inherited the role of a monarch within an oligarchic political culture. Augustus manipulated his formal and informal power to control the empire with reasonable success, but Tiberius was unable to manage the contradictions between Republican values, a competitive and combative senatorial class, and the monarchic realities of power. Tiberian hypocrisy, that he seemed to say one thing and either mean or do another, was not so much a character failing as an integral feature of the paradoxical nature of politics in the period: the manifest contradictions in the imperial position generated uncertainties and a crisis of political ideology This is the triumph of the Tacitean portrait of the reign: the gradual emergence of the 'real' monarchic nature of imperial power from the falsities of the Augustan restorations and failed memories of the Republic. If people did not know what Tiberius intended or was, if they could not read him, it was largely because of the ideological uncertainties inherent in his position. Notably, later emperors were to dispense with at least some of those uncertainties and they would adopt a more absolutist style of governance. It is that absolutism that we see emerging in the later years of Tiberius' reign. Politically, Gaius' inheritance was very different from that of Tiberius. The Augustan political system had largely collapsed. In some ways, the imperial position was much stronger. There were none of the doubts that marked the debates in AD 14. Tiberius had established a hereditary monarchy.

Note

1 Roman legionaries were recruited to serve for 20 years in this period. As most soldiers appear to have been recruited about the age of 20, this effectively set an age of retirement from the army. Yet, it seems that this provision could be ignored by their generals who (and perhaps this was a response to unsettled military conditions on the Danubian and Rhine frontiers) may have avoided discharging the troops and paying those troops their discharge bonus. Length of service was later pushed up to 25 years, but discharge appears to have been much more systematic in later periods. Army pay was set by Caesar and was to remain at Caesarian levels until the reign of Domitian.

Chapter 4

Gaius Caligula (AD 37–41)

Main events of the reign of Gaius Caligula

Date	Event
37	Death of Tiberius.
	Accession of Gaius.
	Payments made from wills of Tiberius and Livia and on behalf of Gaius.
	Honours for Antonia, Drusilla, Agrippina, Julia.
	Repatriation of the ashes of Agrippina (the elder) and Gaius' brothers.
	Abolition of maiestas.
	Consulship of Gaius and Claudius.
	Illness of Gaius.
	Deaths of Tiberius Gemellus, Marcus Silanus, Afranius Potitius.
	Gaius marries Cornelia Orestilla and divorces and exiles her.
38	Publication of public accounts.
	Games given.
	Deaths of Macro and Ennia.
	Death of Drusilla.
	Gaius marries Lollia Paulina.
39	Gaius consul.
	Loss of some popular support.
	Building of the bridge from Puteoli to Baiae.
	Trial of Calvisius Rufus and Cornelia.
	Deaths of Titius Rufus and Junius Priscus.
	Attacks on Domitius Afer and L. Annaeus Seneca.
	Gaius goes to Gaul.
	Deaths of Lentulus Gaetulicus and M. Lepidus.
	Exile of Agrippina and Julia.
	Divorce of Paulina and marriage to Milonia Caesonia.
	Banishing of Ofonius Tigellinus.
40	Gaius consul without colleague.
	The British 'campaign'.
	Deaths of Anicius Cerealis, Sextus Papinus, Betilinus Bassus and Capito, Scribonius Proculus killed in the senate
	Raising of taxes.
41	Assassination of Gaius by Cassius Chaerea and Cornelius Sabinus.
	Murder of Caesonia and the baby Drusilla.

Accession and problems

The death of Tiberius must have come as a great relief to many in the senate and elsewhere. Tiberius appears to have been unpopular with virtually everyone in Rome; Gaius was a welcome change. He was the son of Agrippina and the beloved Germanicus, and great-grandson of both Augustus and Antony. In him, the imperial house, so long divided, was united. The friends of Agrippina would have been pleased at the accession of her son. The friends of Tiberius could console themselves that he had been chosen by the old emperor. He was a young man, 24, and great things could be expected of him. The senate accepted him enthusiastically and voted him all imperial powers. Unlike Tiberius who had held all the formal powers of emperor before his accession, Gaius had held no office: his elevation may have been the first moment the Romans established the exact legal powers associated with the imperial position. The senate also set aside the will of Tiberius which had made him co-ruler with his cousin, Tiberius Gemellus (Tiberius' grandson), who was still a minor. The people had supported Gaius' family in the face of imperial persecution. The troops probably also welcomed him as the son of Germanicus. It is to the troops that we owe Gaius' nickname (by which he is now more familiar), since as a child he had wandered the camps of his father's armies dressed in a miniature version of military uniform and the troops named him Caligula (little boots). Supported by the senate, people and army, Gaius assumed power smoothly. Within six months his support was ebbing away. Within four years, he was dead.

The standard modern explanation for the rapidity with which Gaius' fortunes declined is that he was insane. Gaius suffered an illness that could be associated with a change in the nature of the reign: he suffered from insomnia, from vivid nightmares, from fainting fits and from headaches (Suetonius, *Gaius* 50); his moods changed rapidly; friends suddenly became enemies; he killed without compunction. He apparently talked to gods and made attempts to seduce the moon (though everyone has days like that).

Yet, insanity is too easy an option for historians. At this distance, we cannot ascertain whether he was suffering from a serious mental disorder. No reasonable psychiatrist could collect the correct medical information from the surviving accounts to be able to pronounce on his mental health. Further, 'sanity' is in itself a difficult term. Different cultures have different means of assessing what is normal and healthy in their society. In Soviet Russia dissidents were regarded as insane; surely no right-thinking person could possibly regard the Soviet state as anything but paradise. Insanity is too often a means of classifying behaviour that does not fit into the 'nice' norms of society: it is what sociologists would call a 'normative concept', establishing and enforcing a view of what was expected. In many ways, Gaius did not conform to the expected norms of behaviour, but the problem is to explain that non-conformity: to attribute it to a malfunction of the chemistry of the brain is to ignore the rather obvious fact that there was much in Gaius' social and political position that was irreconcilable with the norms and values of traditional Roman society. Before opting for the easy answer, which we have no hope of supporting from the available evidence, we should consider more complicated and difficult possibilities which we can at least discuss in the light of what we know of the imperial position and Roman social values.

There are many reasons for re-evaluating Gaius. His contemporaries may have had difficulty coping with his behaviour, but he was emperor for nearly four years. He must have been able to function within society, interact with those around him, and negotiate at least some of the social and political issues that affected his regime. If there was a mental illness, it was not sufficiently severe as to cripple his interaction with others or to prevent his basic social functions. By the standards of the time, his outward appearance and behaviour cannot have suggested to all that he was unfit for office. Philo's *Legatio ad Gaium*, an eyewitness account of Gaius' behaviour, suggests a man who refused to give a fair hearing, who cruelly set out to humiliate, but not someone who was incapable. All our main sources are hostile: Suetonius and Dio were working with a senatorial tradition, a tradition which depicted Gaius' acts against the senatorial elite in extreme terms. Our Jewish sources, Josephus and Philo, saw him as a persecutor of their people and thus cursed by God. All were content to display Gaius as a tyrant, irrationally cruel, driven by insatiable desire for pleasures, be they food, wine, sex or money. Although in later traditions, Gaius was supplanted by Nero as a model tyrant and exemplification of all that could go wrong when absolute power was entrusted to one man, there was already a literary model of tyrannical behaviour, derived from Greek and Roman sources, which provided clear literary guides on how to describe and present a tyrant. Gaius, as he is depicted in our sources, conforms to the model.

In Roman traditions, two of the key features of the tyrant were a disrespect for citizens and a willingness to disregard the rights and privileges of those citizens, and an uncontrolled sensuality and desire which might manifest itself in greed, but most often and most spectacularly would be seen in sexual behaviour. There are various models. Tarquinius Superbus, the last king of Rome, was brought down through a sexual scandal, the rape of one of the ladies of the Roman aristocracy. Mark Antony also was depicted as a man of tyrannous appetites, both in his desire for alcohol (which echoed that of the great king-tyrant Alexander) and his desire for women (notably Cleopatra). Such desires were not in themselves socially damaging, but with tyranny came the ability to enact those desires. In a more philosophical sense, the increasingly important contemporary philosophy of stoicism taught that one who was a slave to the sensual and not in control of his desires was not fit to rule: ruling oneself was a pre-requisite for ruling others.

Yet, although it is clearly difficult to credit that policies represented as wholesale slaughter of the aristocracy or practically genocidal assaults on the

Jewish people could have an intelligent rationale, however morally disreputable, there is a discernible logic to Gaius' behaviour. We can look for that logic to try to understand what, if anything, Gaius was trying to achieve.

In that attempt, we are, of course, hampered by the mythology that surrounds Gaius. Almost more than in any other reign, fact and fiction are blended in our accounts and there is no convincing method for reversing the process and separating the factual information from the mythical. Further, some of the better-attested stories concerning Gaius suggest that the emperor himself was concerned to surround himself with a mythology, representing himself as something more than human, and this argues against simply dismissing the more colourful stories of the reign. One must, of course, be cautious and try to identify later inventions or additions to the tradition but, with Gaius, the myth is a fundamental part of the history of the reign. In the longer term, it is the myth of Gaius the mad emperor which has become influential, a tale with which to frighten monarchists.

The family

Gaius' position on accession was strong but his claim to power was rather different from that of the two previous emperors. Whereas Augustus had fought to obtain his position and Tiberius had been without doubt the leading man in the state, Gaius' claim for the imperial position rested solely on his birth. He had held no office, he had had no experience of military or magisterial responsibilities, and although most senators might have been well disposed towards him, few if any were bound in loyalty to him through previous favours and all were older and more experienced. Gaius' political education had been to watch the last years of Tiberius, when Tiberius had dominated a frightened aristocracy. Augustus' claim that his rule rested on personal authority rather than on constitutional or legal powers emphasises the difference between his position and that of Gaius (see p. 47). Gaius had no *auctoritas* on which to rely. He had his family (see Figure 4.1 for his family and ancestry). He also had legal and military power.

His first steps were cautious. He relied on the advice of Macro, Tiberius' praetorian prefect, and probably Silanus (his former father-in-law), and attempted to build a consensus with the senate, deferring to their authority and experience in the first days of his reign. The nervous were reassured when Gaius burnt the letters relating to the persecution of his mother and brothers (Dio, 59.6.1–4). Exiles were recalled. At the same time, Gaius set about establishing his credentials and securing the support of key elements of the Roman state. The praetorian guard had been secured through the good offices of Macro. Their loyalty was assured by the payment of 2,000 *sesterces* (Dio, 59 2.1–3). The loyalty of the plebs was similarly cemented by the payment of generous legacies on behalf of Livia and Tiberius and by payments made by Gaius himself. The rapid resumption of public games and festivals sponsored

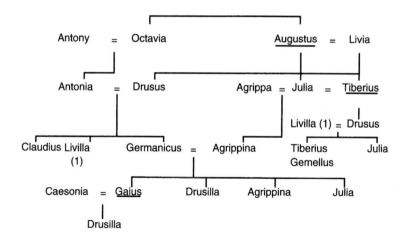

Figure 4.1 The family of Gaius

by the emperor was also popular. Most notable, though, was the treatment of his family. Antonia, Gaius' grandmother, was granted extensive honours, equal to those that had been enjoyed by Livia. His mother's and brothers' ashes were returned to Rome and interred in the mausoleum of Augustus. His sisters were honoured by association with Gaius. They were included in the public oaths taken to the emperor and appeared with Gaius at the games (Dio, 59 3.4–5). Most surprisingly, Claudius was plucked from obscurity and was awarded the consulship with Gaius (Dio, 59 6.5).

The implications of these actions ran deeper than just demonstrating Gaius' family loyalty: it was a claim to power. Power did not come from the constitution, from the legal grant of the senate, still less from the will of Tiberius (which was overturned on the grounds, ironically enough, of insanity), but from birth. This is, of course, a monarchic ideal. From the first, Gaius' position depended on the idea that he ruled because of his inherent qualities, not because of achievements or law. Family was the cornerstone of his legitimacy.

In AD 38, Gaius' sister, Drusilla, died. Her death provided Gaius with another opportunity to emphasise the status of his family. She was granted a public funeral. Gaius associated her with the goddess Venus. Statues were placed in the Forum. A senator claimed he had seen her rising to heaven, a sure sign of divine status. He was well rewarded (Dio, 59 11.1–4). The deification of his sister pre-figured Gaius' own growing association with the gods and was a further representation of the peculiar status of his family.

Like so much else in Gaius' brief reign, relations with his family soured. We can only guess at the reasons for this. The emperor's family associated with other members of the aristocracy who must have made up their social circle. They were in a position to be aware, probably more aware than the emperor himself, of the intolerable strains under which the aristocracy was placed. We need not assume that Gaius' family was insensitive to the pressure of their aristocratic friends or even approved of Gaius' policies. The difficulty of living with an absolute monarch who revelled in his ability to inflict sudden death may also have begun to tell. Antonia, Gaius' grandmother, killed herself (Suetonius, *Gaius*, 23.2). In 39, while on campaign in Gaul, Gaius claimed to have discovered a conspiracy which involved the governor of Germany, Lentulus Gaetulicus, who had served in the post for ten years, M. Lepidus, and his sisters Agrippina and Julia (Dio, 59 22.5–7). Lepidus was killed; the women were exiled. Gaius claimed it as a great victory and the senate were made to congratulate him. The senate, hundreds of miles away and probably deeply concerned and mystified at the fall of Gaius' beloved sisters and Lepidus, with all of whom he was rumoured to have had sexual relations, chose Claudius to forward congratulations (Dio, 59.23). This was a mistake. The fall of his sisters marked a change of policy: Gaius had turned against his family. He marked Claudius' arrival by having him thrown into a river and the emperor's uncle was perhaps fortunate to escape with his life. This change of policy may be related to his marriage plans. His mistress, Caesonia, was pregnant. Gaius married her and she bore him a daughter. Gaius had a child and the prospect of more.

Perhaps to compensate for this change, Gaius chose to lay further emphasis on his divinity and to make what may have been an implicit part of his representation explicit. The imperial house was effectively reduced to the nuclear family of Gaius, Caesonia and the baby Drusilla, with the addition of uncle Claudius. However, the unfortunate Caesonia and her daughter were to share Gaius' fate (Dio, 59 29).

Popular support

The people had demonstrated against Tiberius when Agrippina and her children were threatened. They had celebrated when Sejanus fell from office and when Tiberius died. Gaius inherited the popularity of his mother and brothers and, in marked contrast to his predecessor, made efforts to maintain his popularity with the masses and preserve his political control over them. He did this through lavish displays of generosity and through expensive and extended games. According to the tradition, he made no effort to conceal his pleasure in the games and theatrical displays. He surrounded himself with actors, notably Apelles and Mnester (Dio, 59 5.3; Suetonius, *Gaius*, 33; 36; 54), whom he was seen to kiss as friends (a normal Roman form of greeting) while senators were obliged to kiss his hand or foot (Dio, 59 27.1–2). Gaius himself is said to have performed in both theatrical productions and as a gladiator at the games (Dio, 59 5; Suetonius, *Gaius*, 54; 32.2). He further associated himself with popular opinion by becoming an active supporter of one of the circus teams, the 'greens' (Dio, 59 14.6). This interest in dramatic performance and the theatre as an arena for the display of imperial power and the person of the emperor before his people foreshadowed the much more extensive use of theatrical display by Nero (indeed one might suspect that the stories were created later in order to attack Nero), and one presumes that many of the same factors that influenced Nero would have affected Gaius (see pp. 183–89). Gaius' supposed wish to act in a tragedy and his prolongation of a festival by three days to make time for this theatrical extravaganza may have spurred the conspirators to action (Dio, 59. 29.6–7).

Gaius sought to increase the political authority of the people by restoring popular elections (Suetonius, *Gaius*, 16.2; Dio, 59. 20.3–5), which appear to have been effectively brought to an end in the late Augustan period when Augustus ceased to attend the elections. Tiberius had allowed the senate to co-opt its own members. Throughout this period, the electoral assembly continued to meet, though it had merely ratified the election of the candidates placed before it. One supposes that Gaius removed the right of the senate to nominate candidates and officially allowed competition, though Suetonius tells us that normally there was the same number of candidates as posts.

The relationship between Gaius and the people also soured. In 39, there were demonstrations against Gaius' treatment of the senate. The people were becoming concerned at the number of killings. Gaius is supposed to have responded by wishing that the people had but one neck to be cut (Dio, 59. 13.3–7). Gaius responded to demonstrations by use of force. His power was shown in other ways. He closed the public granaries that provided the people with the free grain supplies and thus threatened the people of Rome with starvation. On summer days, he withdrew the awnings from the theatre and closed exits so that the crowd were roasted under the Italian sun (Suetonius, *Gaius*, 26.5). These were conspicuous displays of his power.

Gaius also lost support through his attempts to raise taxes. He failed to publicise the tax regulations so that many found themselves subjected to heavy fines. There was a popular campaign to force publication of the regulations, and when Gaius eventually succumbed to pressure, the material was inscribed in lettering so small and on a notice placed so high that no one could read it. The outcry may have resulted in deaths (Suetonius, *Gaius*, 40–1; Dio, 59. 28.10–11). The story, though, stretches credibility and one suspects that it has been immensely simplified to show the emperor as insane: it is difficult to see how or why a change in tax law would be secret and the Romans were notably unwilling to countenance changes in tax, no matter how slight.

The divine emperor

More attention has been focused on Gaius' pretence of divinity than almost any other aspect of his reign. This is, of course, understandable since his divinity poses a problem for both ancient and modern religious traditions. For us, it is very difficult to concede that a man could become a god. It seems self-evident that a man does not possess the necessary attribute of the divine. For the ancients, the position was more complex. Worship of the emperor was established under Augustus and continued throughout the period (see pp. 51–2 and 408–12). It was, however, only the 'bad emperors' who went so far as to declare themselves to be gods and there was still a distinction between the mortal human and the immortal divine.

Gaius' own religious beliefs cannot be assessed. Suetonius (*Gaius*, 51.1–2) tells us that although he mocked the gods and stories of their miracles by day, he was afraid of thunder (a sign of divine displeasure) and Mount Etna, though these are hardly sufficient grounds to describe him as religious. The many stories (some of which may have been invented) of Gaius showing disrespect for the statues of gods suggest that he had no profound religious belief. Some of the elite might have shared this view. Yet, it is difficult to escape the conclusion, derived from the consistency and number of anecdotes, that Gaius presented himself as a semi-divine figure, and, towards the end of his reign, apparently demanded the public acknowledgement of his divinity.

Although both Augustus and Tiberius had been superior in authority to members of other senatorial families, they had taken care to behave as if they were among equals. They were *principes*, the leading men, but the senate contained many *principes*, men of authority and political stature to whom respect needed to be shown. Gaius was not, however, a *princeps*. He was inferior in political stature and experience. He was notably sensitive about his comparative youth (Dio, 59. 19.1–6). He needed, therefore, some way to assert his superior status over the nobles in the senate.

Suetonius provides an anecdote explaining Gaius' development of divine aspirations (*Gaius*, 22.1–2). At a dinner party, Gaius listened to several client kings disputing among themselves as to who had the most glorious ancestry. Gaius had been experimenting with titles. He had tried 'pius', 'castrorum filius' (son of the camp), 'pater exercituum' (father of the army) and 'optimus maximus Caesar' (best and greatest Caesar), but none were satisfactory. To display greater authority, to rise above the level of the client kings and the rest of the Roman aristocracy, he decided to assume divine status, a status that would reflect his pre-eminence.

The great advantage of divine status was that it allowed the development of new ways of representing imperial power and of forcing others to displays of loyalty, ways normally reserved for the gods. Gaius remodelled the entrance to the imperial palace so that visitors would pass through the temple of Castor and Pollux, two divine gatekeepers for the house of the living god. He built temples to his *numen* (his divine spirit) on the Capitoline and Palatine hills (Suetonius, *Gaius*, 22.2; Dio, 59. 28.5). He instituted his own priesthood into which Caesonia and Claudius were enrolled (Dio, 59.

28.5–6). He appeared in the guise of Apollo, Neptune, Hercules, Bacchus, Juno, Diana and Venus (Dio, 59. 26.5–10). The senate and court were forced to acknowledge his divinity and statues were altered so that the gods would have Gaius' features.

By rising above the level of the human, Gaius could also rise above the normal constraints of social behaviour. Indeed, as the ways of the gods were beyond human comprehension, so Gaius' capricious cruelty became an attribute of his great power. Like the gods, Gaius could strike at any moment and, like the gods, Gaius must be feared and obeyed.

He rose above normal social *mores* in his sexual life. While Tiberius' alleged perversions had been dark secrets hidden by his island retreat and were only matters of gossip in Rome, Gaius' sexual misconduct was a matter of public display. His sexual promiscuity rivalled that of Jupiter and, like the father of the gods, he had relationships with both men and women. Women were seized at banquets or at their own marriages, dragged from the feasts and, one presumes, raped (Dio, 59. 8.7). What we see here is a form of sexual terrorism. Gaius may have become somewhat more controlled after his marriage to Caesonia (Suetonius, *Gaius*, 25), yet in being sexually predatory Gaius was conforming to the traditional features not only of the gods, but also of the tyrant.

Gaius was also said to have had sexual relations with his sisters (Suetonius, *Gaius*, 24; Dio, 59. 3.6, 11.1, 22.6). The Olympian deities were promiscuous and incestuous. The Ptolemies, the Hellenistic rulers of Egypt from 323–30 BC, had similarly formed incestuous relationships. Incest in royal families could symbolise status in two ways:

• Royal behaviour was to be governed by the practice among the gods.
• Royals, as divine figures, were expected to form relationships only with people of similar status, which meant their own families provided the only suitable marriage partners.

We cannot know whether Gaius did have sex with his sisters, but the manner with which he associated with them in public and the deification of Drusilla as Venus was suggestive of a sexual relationship. Gaius was thus seeking to advertise the suggestion that he had sex with his sister. Myth and historical reality blend in stories of Gaius' sexual behaviour and it is probable that the myth originated with Gaius himself, whatever the reality.

Gaius' assumption of divinity was an extreme reaction to his problems, but it was not, in itself, the act of a madman. His religious representation may be seen as a means of displaying authority. We must remember that Gaius numbered among his ancestors Venus, Mars, Romulus, Hercules, Divus Julius and Divus Augustus. When interpreted in the context of contemporary religious practice and attitudes towards the imperial position, Gaius' policy may have been misconceived, but it was not revolutionary.

The senate

Gaius was remembered for the hostility he showed towards the senate, but it is important to reconstruct events carefully for, by paying attention to Dio's account especially, we can see that Gaius' policy changed during his brief reign and we can attempt to understand the factors that motivated such a change.

On accession, Gaius acted to secure his political position. As a young emperor, he needed to develop a way of dealing with the senior men of the state, most of whom were in the senate. He seems at first to have attempted to build a consensus. The burning of the papers relating to the deaths of his mother and brothers was a declaration of amnesty after the political disputes of the previous years. He also temporarily abolished the charge of *maiestas* (see p. 72; Dio, 59 6.1–4). In other ways, his behaviour was also exemplary. It was expected that Gaius would assume the senior constitutional office, the consulship, immediately after his accession. The consulship was not just an important political and ceremonial office, but it conferred status on all holders and former holders of the office. As Gaius had not held the office, he needed a consulship in order to join the elite within the senate. Instead of deposing the two consuls who already held the office, Gaius delayed his assumption of the consulship until the end of their normal period of office (six months). He then took the consulship with his uncle Claudius (Dio, 59. 6.5).

Following the lead of Tiberius in AD 14 (pp. 97–102), Gaius also published the public accounts (Dio, 59. 9.4–6). Publication of the information necessary to formulate policy and govern the empire was a declaration of his willingness to bring government out from behind the closed doors of the palace and share power with the senate. The world could see how Rome was to be financed. Secret papers were burnt. Gaius could really claim to be *demokratikotatos* (most democratic) (Dio, 59. 3.1–2).

The, consensus-building of this early policy may be related to insecurity. The young man probably turned to more experienced heads for advice, perhaps to Claudius, probably to Marcus Silanus and Macro. In some ways, this again follows his predecessor in the use of chief ministers, and it foreshadows Nero. The policy was not to last. The inevitable fate of Tiberius Gemellus had only been postponed at the start of the reign. The youth, as Tiberius' grandson, was a latent threat to the emperor since he had as good a claim to the throne. Gaius had him killed in late 37. Marcus Silanus killed himself following expressions of outright hostility from Gaius (Dio, 59. 8.4). In the following year (38), Macro and his wife Ennia were forced down the same path (Dio, 59. 10.6–8). Already in AD 38 the senate was witness to Gaius' macabre sense of humour, a feature of his treatment of the senate in later years. After his mysterious illness (see above), Gaius was informed that Publius Afranius Potitius had promised to give up his life if Gaius would be spared; Atanius Secundus had promised to fight as a gladiator on Gaius' recovery. Such grandiose gestures of loyalty were sometimes rewarded. Gaius, however, forced the two senators to keep their words (Dio, 59. 8.3). Atanius Secundus won his fight (Suetonius, *Gaius*, 27.2).

Gaius was deeply concerned with his own comparative lack of experience and *auctoritas* in comparison with many in the senate. He compensated for this by emphasising the status of his family. A natural corollary of this was to attack those other families in the senate that had claims to special status, thereby further differentiating the Julii. Some of the most noble families of Rome had peculiar traits of dress or names that recalled their places in the legends and history of Rome: the Torquati had a collar; the Cincinnati a lock of hair; and the Pompeii the name 'Magnus' (great). All these features were removed by Gaius (Suetonius, *Gaius*, 35.1).

This was comparatively mild treatment. If the stories are to be believed, Gaius emphasised his authority by humiliating individual senators. Senators were forced to attend him by running alongside his chariot for miles. Others had to wait at tables, usually the occupation of a slave (Suetonius, *Gaius*, 26.2). His posturing towards the senate became even more violent after his Gallic campaigns. He declared that he wished no triumph, but berated the senate for not granting him one. He met an embassy from the senate and threatened them with his sword. He proclaimed that he returned as a friend to the people and the equestrians (Suetonius, *Gaius*, 48–9). On his return from Gaul, he called a meeting of the senate and announced that there were only a few senators against whom he harboured animosity (Dio, 59. 25.9). The effect of such an announcement must have been electrifying since it portended death to a number of the senators and, as Gaius seems to have struck almost randomly, all must have been terrified. It is difficult to believe that this was not the intended result.

It is in this context that we should place the story of Gaius' horse, Incitatus. The horse was apparently a champion at the games and so pleased Gaius that he decided that it would make a good dinner companion. Impressing Gaius with its political insight and intelligence, he promised to elevate Incitatus to the highest office in the senate, but, in the end (and perhaps rather sadly), Gaius was killed before Incitatus became the first horse to hold high political office in Rome (Dio, 59.14.7). If taken seriously, here is a sign of madness, but surely we see here an insult, calculated and witty, aimed at the senate and their pretensions. Gaius could have a horse as social companion. He could have a horse as political advisor. The senate was without influence. The story of him suddenly laughing while at dinner with the consuls shows the same sense of humour and power. When the consuls inquired why their emperor was laughing, he said that it had occurred to him that he could, at a moment's notice, have them both killed (Suetonius, *Gaius*, 32.3).

Gaius' humour was a serious problem, as is illustrated by Philo's account of the interview of the Jewish embassy. Gaius set out to humiliate the ambassadors. They followed him through a palace as he gave orders for its redecoration, interrupting their most cogent arguments with arrangements for the hanging of pictures. He changed the subject, asking them spurious questions about their attitude towards the imperial cult and dietary laws. When the ambassadors responded that they did not eat pork as it was forbidden to them and that many peoples had similar laws, some being unable to eat lamb, Gaius responded, 'Quite right! It's not nice' (Philo, *Legatio ad Gaium*, 361–3). The ambassadors, arguing for the rights of their people to live unmolested after anti-Semitic riots in which many were killed, were reduced to discussions of the relative merits of pork and lamb. Gaius ended the interview by announcing that the Jews were unlucky rather than wicked in not acknowledging Gaius' divinity (Philo, *Legatio ad Gaium*, 367). Gaius was accompanied by both the opponents of the Jews and a crowd of servants, friends and hangers-on who encouraged Gaius' performance. It was theatre: a public humiliation of the Jews and a demonstration of the power of the emperor.

We do not have a complete list of those senators prosecuted. Calvisius Rufus and his wife were tried for their behaviour during Rufus' long governorship (Dio, 59. 18.4). Titius Rufus fell since he was rumoured to have noted a difference between the votes and thoughts of senators. Junius Priscus was unfortunately wealthy (Dio, 59. 18.5). L. Annaeus Seneca caused offence, but was spared because it was reported that he was terminally ill (Dio, 59 19.7–8). Domitius Afer was attacked because of a statue he erected to the emperor that carried an inscription which Gaius regarded as critical, noting Gaius' youth. Afer saved himself by refusing to make a speech in his defence: he simply claimed to be in awe of the rhetorical skill of his emperor and, in the face of such genius, could only beg for mercy. His friends ensured his survival and it is likely that Gaius never intended to kill him (Dio, 59. 19.1–6). In his case, even a brazen act of servility became dangerous. Fathers were killed together with their sons: Anicius Cerealis and Sextus Papinus and Betilini Bassus and Capito (Dio, 59. 25.6–26.2). The killing of fathers and sons was associated with the terrible times of civil war and especially of the triumviral period under Octavian, Antony and Lepidus (see pp. 27–30). Capito sought to revenge himself by admitting conspiracy and listing his enemies as fellow-conspirators. He over-reached himself when he named Kallistos (see below) and other of Gaius' closest associates. Cassius Longinus, governor of Asia, was slain because rumours had reached him that he should fear Cassius (Suetonius, *Gaius*, 57.2). It seems probably that men were looking for a new Cassius to remove a new tyrant, as the earlier Cassius had killed Julius Caesar. Most dramatic of all, and a symbol of the paranoia gripping the senate, is the story of the death of Scribonius Proculus. Soon after Gaius had announced that few remained against whom he retained animosity, a leading prosecutor who was supposed to be close to the imperial court entered the senate and was greeted by all the senators, who were fearful of such a powerful man. When Proculus was greeted a particular senator, he replied, 'And do you who hate the emperor so, welcome me?'. The senators responded by killing Proculus in the senate-house (Dio, 59. 26.1–2). Our sources emphasise the indiscriminate nature of the slaughter, though again we must beware of invention and distortion. The sources provide the 'true' trivial reasons for the fall of these people, while the 'untrue' real charges remain obscure. All the cases add to the depiction of a madman, a tyrant out of control.

We must set Gaius' actions in context. Gaius was committed to a theory of government in which power was inherited by the emperor who ruled on the basis of his personal authority. There was little room for a representative body such as the senate and Gaius may have been one of the few Roman emperors who seriously considered abolishing this revered political institution. On return to Rome from his victories in Gaul, Germany and on the beaches facing Britain, Gaius threatened the senate with destruction (Dio, 59. 25.5; 25.9–26.3; Suetonius, *Gaius*, 49). The fear and paranoia created among the senators was such that Gaius had no need to continue with his plan. He had seen, as he reminded the senate (Suetonius, *Gaius*, 30.2), the senators acquiesce in the persecution of his brothers and mother and the dramatic rise and fall of Sejanus. Although all united in praise of the young emperor at his accession, Gaius can have had few illusions about the senate. He must have been aware that there were many who viewed his elevation with fear and distrust and all would try to manipulate the young *princeps* to achieve their personal political ends. Many of the senior senators must have owed their political status and power to Tiberius (and Sejanus). Gaius may have been right to fear and harbour grudges against these men. Our sources do not illuminate the previous political affiliations of the killed and exiled. The attack on Seneca, for instance, seems to have no political justification, yet Seneca's son was clearly closely connected to the imperial family, especially Gaius' sisters, and was to enjoy considerable power as the tutor of Agrippina's son (see p. 171). We do not know what political roles these men played or whether these men on the fringes of our account were major political players or minor victims of Gaius' malice.

Gaius eventually fell in a palace conspiracy. Unlike Nero, he did not see his generals turn against him and his political position disintegrate. The posthumous tradition is universally hostile, but we need not assume that at the time of his death there were none in the senate who mourned his passing. If we see the reign of Gaius as a continuation of the bloody politics of the last 30 or 40 years, then our perspectives must change.

Nevertheless, there was something new about Gaius' treatment of the senate. The manner in which he humiliated the senate and elevated his own person above that of the mortal is evidence of Gaius striving for a new representation of imperial power. As Tiberius had been unable to continue the Augustan system and had resorted to a distant manipulation, Gaius also faced difficulties. He had not the rank or the experience, or the confidence in his generals that had allowed Tiberius to take so distant an interest in the doings of the senate. Gaius needed a more direct role. He needed to exert authority.

All governments need a narrative by which they assert their legitimacy and power. Most Western governments achieve that legitimacy through the workings of long-established constitutions and the operation of electoral systems which provide mandates to govern. Gaius, however, was working within a paradoxical system. His primary claim to authority was familial. This was reinforced by his self-representation as divine. This built on the concentration of power and authority under Augustus and Tiberius. Yet, many of the institutions of the Roman state and many of the ideas and ideologies of Roman governance were grounded in the political culture of the Republic. There was considerable resistance to changing that culture. This resistance did not just derive from a senatorial fondness for power or nostalgia for the Republic. To a considerable extent, to be Roman was to be a citizen and to enjoy the civic rights and privileges that came with citizenship (see pp. 287–88). To be Roman was to be the product of a cultural tradition that was Republican and in which those rights and privileges had been secured over generations of struggle. There was thus a 'cultural memory' of Rome that identified the Roman community with its Republican past. Augustus and Tiberius had both honoured that memory. Gaius did not and could not.

The imperial position was paradoxical since it existed contrary to the values that made Rome Roman. It was further paradoxical since Augustus had represented the necessity of monarchy in terms of the defence of traditional Roman values. Those values did not allow for a young monarch. Gaius was an anomaly. He needed a different justification for his imperial power. The history to which he looked for inspiration and role models was not the Republican history of Rome, but that of Hellenistic Greece, and especially to Alexander the Great. It may have been a possible mode of government. We cannot assume, however misguided the policy proved to be, that this policy was not a rational choice of a troubled politician.

The political culture of Rome was a set of rules for conducting politics (see pp. 10–14). The political culture determined the relationships between members of the elite. It affected the way people respected each other and the rules of inter-personal relationship. It reflected long-established hierarchies within Roman society. It determined marriages and sexual relations. Effectively, the political culture was a relational system: it told people who they were and what they were to do, what their relationships to others should be and what status they had in the social hierarchy. Gaius declared war on all that. It is in this light that we can begin to understand Gaius' cruelty, his blood-lust, and his psychopathic sense of humour: 'Let them hate me as long as they fear me' is reported as a favourite phrase (Suetonius, *Gaius*, 30.1). He was an anomaly within the traditions of Rome and so he rejected them. His extravagant breaches of social norms, his reckless behaviours, his sexual terrorism, his violence, his incestuous relations all displayed his hostility to the paradigms of Roman society.

Of course, once he broke from the traditions of Roman political culture, his regime had few claims to legitimacy: all he could depend on was power. When he told the consuls he could have them killed, he was displaying the ultimate source of his authority: the ability to kill his opponents. As tyrants through the ages have found, their power might allow them to kill many, many people, but it only takes one knife, one person determined enough and close enough, to reverse the power relationship. His subjects may have hated him and feared him, but once one of those subjects was reduced to such a state of fear that his own life seemed in imminent danger, the logical solution was to kill the emperor.

Administration

The practical side of imperial government is said to have dissolved into chaos during Gaius' brief rule. The most obvious symbol of this chaos is the financial prodigality of the emperor which took the treasury from an extremely healthy surplus to bankruptcy. Dio (59 2.6) suggests that there were 2,300,000,000 or 3,300,000,000 *sesterces* in the treasury, while Suetonius (*Gaius*, 37.3) opts for 2,700,000,000 *sesterces*. These are huge figures, perhaps five to six times the normal annual budget of the state (see pp. 316–18). Even after raising new taxes and reducing the bonus paid to the troops on discharge (Suetonus, *Gaius*, 44), Gaius was apparently in such financial straits by the end of his reign that he was selling heirlooms to the Gauls and prosecuting the richest in the empire in order to obtain their wealth. The ancient sources, however, produce no figures for the state of the treasury at this stage and it became a standard criticism of 'bad emperors' to note their financial mismanagement. The financial position of his successor does not appear to have been particularly bad, suggesting either that Gaius' emergency measures were successful or that tradition has distorted the situation (see pp. 155–56).

Another feature of Gaius' government was his treatment of the provinces. Gaius seems to have had a policy of favouring the use of client kings to govern Roman territory in the East. This was a standard technique of Roman imperial policy (see pp. 368–69), but emperors varied in the emphasis they placed on this method of government. For Gaius, client kings offered several advantages. The greatest threat to Gaius' position sprang from the Roman aristocracy, and relying on client kings meant that he had fewer governors to worry about. The kings were dependent on Gaius, who could remove them at a whim. They could not hope to challenge him militarily or for the position of emperor, nor to build a political alliance among the Roman notables with which to oppose the emperor. Client states continued to pay taxes to Rome and send the emperor extravagant gifts to retain his favour. Arguably, since the kings knew that they needed the emperor's favour, they were likely to be more loyal and more generous to the emperor. The use of kings also reflected and emphasised the monarchic principle at the heart of Gaius' government and enhanced the status of the emperor. Gaius appointed kings, and kings were also his servants. He was, therefore, greater than a king.

Most attention has been focused on Gaius' treatment of the Jews. There were two main areas of conflict: Alexandria and Judaea. In Alexandria, the prefect Flaccus presided over a period of increasing tension which resulted in a violent anti-Semitic outbreak when the Greeks in the city, tacitly or openly supported by Flaccus, attacked the Jews and drove them from most of the city. Our sources suggest that when news of the violence and Flaccus' behaviour reached Rome, through the agency of the newly appointed Herod Agrippa, Gaius acted. He sent a centurion to Alexandria who walked into a dinner party, arrested the prefect, put him on a boat and sailed off to Rome. Flaccus was tried, exiled and eventually executed (Philo, *In Flaccum*). One may believe that Gaius acted to save the Jews, but Flaccus' position had already been fatally undermined. Flaccus had been somehow involved in the prosecution of Gaius' mother and brothers. The reward for this had been his posting to Alexandria. Although at first insulated from Gaius' revenge by the support of Macro, his fall was inevitable.

Gaius had supported the Herodian dynasty (the Jewish royal family) by appointing his friend Agrippa to the Tetrarchy of Trachonitis and Gaulanitis. As a result of feuding within the Herodian dynasty, the history of which makes the Julio–Claudians seem a model of harmony, Agrippa received yet more territory (Josephus, *Antiquities* 18. 237–56), though the Jewish territories of Judaea and Samaria remained under direct Roman rule. Agrippa is depicted as a close friend of Gaius and a man who could exercise some influence over the emperor. He also had some claim to represent all the Jewish people of the region.

As monotheists, the Jews could not worship Gaius, yet worship of Gaius was an essential mark of loyalty to the emperor (see p. 412). Gaius, therefore, instructed the governor of Syria, Petronius, to build a statue of the emperor and install it in the Jewish temple in Jerusalem. This was the most holy of places in the holy city. The population had rioted when non-religious images of eagles had been brought within the temple complex. The conflagration that would have been caused by the installation of a cult statue of the emperor within the temple can hardly be imagined. Petronius delayed. He sent for clarification. He made every attempt to obstruct the project, but also to avoid seeming to refuse an imperial instruction. In this latter aim, he was unsuccessful. Gaius wrote an angry missive and further conflict between the governor of one of the most powerful provinces of the empire and the emperor was only avoided by Gaius' timely death. In the former aim, however, he enjoyed some success. Agrippa, who was in Rome, petitioned repeatedly and, frustrated by the various delays, Gaius rescinded his order, though he still regarded the Jewish refusal to worship him as a peculiarity (Philo, *Legatio ad Gaium*, 207–333; Josephus, *Antiquities*, 18. 261–309). Gaius managed to avoid a catastrophic war in the East but his own anti-Semitism and in particular his elevation of his own status to that of a divinity, which, of course, Jews could not worship, encouraged outbreaks of violence in the cities of the Eastern Mediterranean, many of which had large Jewish minorities.

One further aspect of Gaius' administration deserves recognition, partly because it looks forward to the government of Claudius. One of the shadowy characters of the reign was Kallistos, Gaius' freedman minister. It is difficult to know what duties Kallistos performed, but he was certainly influential. He was allegedly at least partly responsible for saving Domitius Afer (see p. 140) and supposedly chided Gaius for allowing the prosecution to be brought. A man who could save others from the wrath of such an emperor and even criticise the emperor to his face must have been powerful. Kallistos was also involved in the plot to kill Gaius (Dio, 59. 25.7–8; 29.1; Josephus, *Antiquities*, 19 64–9). We glimpse in Kallistos an influential bureaucrat who made sure that the wheels of government turned, perhaps in spite of the emperor.

War and Alexander

Many Roman aristocrats appear to have had an Alexander fixation and a typical portrait style of the Late Republic imitated depictions of Alexander. Roman military policy was frequently shaped by a desire to emulate the achievements of Alexander in conquering the East. Gaius' most splendid display of this Alexander fetish was the bridging of the Bay of Naples, an amalgamation of the Alexander myth with the story of Xerxes' bridging of the Hellespont, but the Romans were unconcerned about historical accuracy in their reconstructions of such remote and mythologised events. The display in AD 39 was at least in part for the benefit of Darius, a visiting member of the Parthian ruling dynasty. The Parthians had concluded a peace with Gaius on the death of Tiberius. Their reasons for such a generous act towards the new emperor are unclear but the treaty may have been connected with Parthian respect for Germanicus and perhaps even some doubt as to whether the generally restrained policy of Tiberius would be transformed by a young, vigorous ruler out to make a name for himself. If so, such a display of Roman power before the eyes of a Parthian prince had a diplomatic purpose. The bridge was, of course, recklessly extravagant and Gaius' charge across the bridge wearing what he claimed to be Alexander's breastplate seems almost farcical (Dio, 59. 17.1–11; Suetonius, *Gaius*, 19.1–3). Yet, we should not underestimate the impact of the display. Such a mobilisation of resources by the new Alexander could one day be real and it was no doubt a message that was transmitted back to the Parthian capital.

Gaius' sole military adventure was on the Western frontier. This is again probably significant. It was on this frontier and with these troops that Gaius won his nickname and these troops could be expected to be loyal to the boy whose retreat had once quelled their mutiny (see pp. 102–105). The Gallic expedition can be seen in part as Gaius returning to the men on whose support he relied for his political and personal survival. It came at a particularly difficult point in his reign. He was possibly running out of money and friends and it must be significant that, while in Gaul, he put aside his sisters and Lepidus and took an increasingly hard line with the senate. He returned a man with an army, reassured of their support and prepared to demonstrate his control over the military through elaborate ceremonials, such as a triumphal entry into Rome. It is almost irrelevant that his major triumphs in Gaul had been a quick trip to the seaside, the killing of a governor, and chasing a few Germans through the forest.

Much attention has been focused on the 'trip to Britain'. Gaius appears to have completed preparations for a major expedition in the West, either against Germany or Britain. Suetonius (*Gaius*, 43.1) tells us that the decision to visit Gaul was sudden, but Gaius levied large numbers of troops (Dio, 59. 21–2) and it is possible that new legions were raised for the invasion. It is difficult to know whether Gaius was ever serious about invading Britain. There were numerous reasons not to go: he had just executed an experienced commander, the troops may have been extremely reluctant. Gaius himself may not have realised the problems that invading Britain posed and it is possible that the logistical infra-structure, the boats especially, was not ready or that Gaius himself did not feel he had time to engage in such a campaign. Some have suggested that he was distracted by problems in Northern Gaul or that the whole episode was merely an elaborate training exercise. In any case, he did not go and we are told that the soldiers were left to pick shells from the beach.

Gaius' military policy may have been underestimated. Claudius' accession was marked by a spate of military activity in Germany and Africa (Dio, 60. 8.6–7.) and it seems very likely that Gaius commenced these campaigns. Claudius also launched the invasion of Britain very early in the reign, leaving open the possibility that he benefited from Gaius' preparations.

Assassination

The assassination of Gaius may hardly be described as a surprise. He had bullied and offended, threatened and killed. Dio (59. 25.7–8) has a story that perhaps provides some of the background to the conspiracy, though its neatness raises suspicions. In his paranoia, Gaius summoned the prefects of the guard and Kallistos and, standing unarmed before them, offered the three an opportunity to kill him: there was an implicit or even explicit suggestion that Gaius had heard of a conspiracy involving these men and here demonstrated that if he had lost their loyalty, his friends were to kill him. They did not, but once Gaius' suspicions had been aroused, these men may have felt that their life-expectancy was reduced.

The conspiracy (Josephus, *Antiquities* 19.37–113; Dio, 59. 29) was led by Cassius Chaerea, Cornelius Sabinus and Sextus Papinius, tribunes of the praetorian guard, Kallistos, the influential freedman, M. Arrecinus Clemens, the prefect of the guard, and Minucianus, a friend of the recently killed Lepidus. Many others were involved. In addition, large numbers must have known about the conspiracy and the prompt actions of the consuls on the death of Gaius may suggest their fore-knowledge.

The conspiracy appears to have leaked badly, but this was a risk that Chaerea and the others were prepared to take. Modern conspiracies tend to be small affairs, lone gunmen and the like. Although conspiracy-theorists like to imagine long back-stories, many conspiracies do appear to be the work of individuals or very small numbers of individuals. But Chaerea wished to ensure his own survival. To that end, he needed to be sure that his actions would receive the support of the political class of Rome and that after Gaius' death, Chaerea could secure the peace. As with the assassination of Julius Caesar, the conspirators were a political group: they acted as a political body, not as a criminal or terrorist band. Many of their friends and allies would be ready when the blow was struck.

Gaius, however, walked down a private corridor oblivious to the threat. He met first Chaerea who stabbed him and as Gaius fled, he ran into the other conspirators. Dio is at his best reporting this: 'Gaius, having done these deeds as related, over three years, nine months and twenty-eight days, himself discovered that he was not a god.'

Chapter 5

Claudius (AD 41–54)

Main events of the reign of Claudius

Date	Event
41	Accession.
	Return of Julia and Agrippina from exile.
	Victories in Mauretania and Germany.
	Resettlement of client kingdoms in the East.
	Exile of Julia.
42	Victory of Suetonius Paulinus over the Moors and the founding of two new provinces.
	Work starts at Ostia and the Fucine Lake.
	Death of Appius Junius Silanus.
	Conspiracy of Vinicianus and Camillus Scribonianus
43	Reduction of Lycia.
	Reform of the citizen rolls.
	Deaths of Catonius Iustus and Julia (daughter of Drusus).
	Invasion of Britain.
44	Claudius' triumph.
	Reform of the treasury.
	Distributions to the masses.
46	Asinius Gallus banished.
	Mithridates of Iberia deprived of his kingdom.
	M. Vinicius prosecuted.
47	Reform of the senatorial lists.
	Death of Valerius Asiaticus.
	Campaigns in Armenia.
	Campaigns of Corbulo against the Chauci.
	Secular games.
48	Fall of Messalina and her circle.
	Enrolment of men from Gallia Comata into the senate.
49	Claudius' marriage to Agrippina.
	Failure of Claudius' policy in Parthia.
	M. Silanus killed.
	Lollia Paulina killed and Calpurnia exiled.
	C. Cadius Rufus condemned for corruption.
	Ituraea and Judaea incorporated into Syria.

Date	Event
50	Adoption of L. Domitius Ahenobarbus (Nero).
	Honours granted to Agrippina.
	Campaigns and disorder in Germany and Britain.
51	Nero assumes toga virilis and presides over lavish games.
	Burrus appointed praetorian prefect.
	War in Armenia.
52	Grant of praetorian rank to Pallas.
	Revolt in Judaea.
	Problems in Cilicia.
53	Nero marries Octavia and takes more active public role.
54	Death of Claudius.

Accession

Claudius was born in 10 BC, the son of Antonia and Drusus (see family tree, Figure 5.1). His mother supposedly had a low opinion of him. He suffered from certain physical disabilities, the exact nature of which is unclear. In a culture that valued bodily perfection, infirmities were taken as a sign of physical, mental and perhaps moral weakness. There was probably some debate as to whether he should have a public role or even whether he should be allowed to become legally independent (Suetonius, *Claudius*, 2–4). He lived in the shadow of his brother Germanicus and engaged in scholarly pursuits, research which he was happy to share with the senate and others during his reign. Under Tiberius, he was given consular regalia, but no office, perhaps in part because of the hostility between Tiberius and Claudius' sister-in-law, Agrippina. He developed a public role as patron of the *equites*, and he seems to have had some support in the senate (Suetonius, *Claudius*, 6). His fortunes improved suddenly with the accession of his nephew Gaius. Claudius was made consul and achieved a certain prominence in the presentation of the imperial house. Nevertheless, although not plucked from obscurity by the praetorians in AD 41, as has sometimes been suggested, he was an improbable candidate for imperial office.

The death of Gaius led to an outbreak of anarchy. Caesonia, Gaius' wife, and their baby Drusilla were killed, suggesting that some wished to remove all the Julio-Claudians and perhaps restore the Republic. Crucially, they missed Claudius. The soldiers rioted. They had no interest in the re-foundation of the Republic and the senators returning to power. The soldiers generally and praetorians in particular had benefited from imperial power. One of the soldiers found Claudius hiding either behind some curtains or in a dark corner. He was recognised and hauled off to the praetorians' camp (Dio, 60. 1–3; Josephus, *Antiquities*, 19. 212–21; Suetonius, *Claudius*, 10). The soldiers had found the brother of Germanicus, the uncle of Gaius, the last surviving male member of the imperial family, and their emperor.

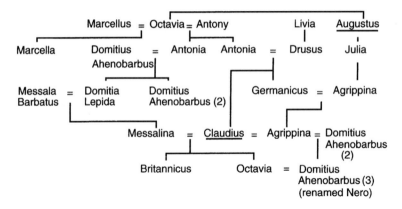

Figure 5.1 The families of Claudius, Messalina and Agrippina

Claudius was initially reluctant to accept his elevation. He knew many in the senate would be opposed to him. He had only limited political experience and no experience of military matters and he had just seen the emperor, the emperor's wife, and the emperor's child killed. It looked like a job with gloomy prospects. The senate was also reluctant to accept him. The killing of Gaius, like the killing of Caesar, was a demonstration of the power of the Roman aristocracy. Claudius had none of the personal characteristics, the political or military experience, or the political support that would have made him attractive to the senate. Many of the senators had every reason to suspect that Claudius would be hostile.

The army decided the issue. Claudius had no alternative but to accept the army's decision. Refusing their 'kind' offer would have either led directly to his death or made him a target for any new regime. The senate had no realistic alternative candidate. The very fact that the conspirators had not arranged matters to elevate a successor would seem to reflect expectation that the Republic would be restored. Nevertheless, it became apparent that the senators would need a leader and as there was no consensus nor any guarantee that a senatorial candidate would secure the loyalty and support of the people or, crucially, the soldiers, Claudius, the man who had the power to take Rome by force, suddenly seemed a reasonable choice (Josephus, *Antiquities*, 19.221–71).

The great unknown was the attitude of the troops and generals in the provinces. Some soldiers would have no doubt been loyal to the Julio-Claudians and perhaps would have even welcomed the brother of Germanicus, but the loyalty of generals whose ties to Claudius may have been slight was questionable. In AD 14, the troops had mutinied and the future of the Principate was in the balance. In AD 41, Claudius had no Germanicus and no Drusus to cement the loyalty of the troops. Even as the situation in Rome gradually became less precarious, all eyes must have looked to the frontiers.

For 30 days Claudius stayed away from the senate. He took no chances when he eventually came to meet the senators,: he brought his troops with him (Dio, 60 3.2–3). The delay was significant. It reflected a fundamental lack of security. Those who had killed Gaius and his family were insecure and feared that Claudius would seek revenge. Claudius must have feared that those who had killed his nephew would not hesitate to kill him. The memory of Julius Caesar was strong. It would take only one determined and desperate senator with a dagger to end the Julio-Claudian dynasty and the senate contained numerous individuals who would have had doubts about their future under the new emperor. Claudius moved slowly and in so doing showed his distrust of the senators. With his political and personal security reliant on the soldiers who stood behind him, obviously threatening any who might be tempted to revolution, Claudius' first meetings with the senators, whatever was said, whatever honours granted, and whatever respectful attitudes were struck, must have been difficult. In some ways, the tone for the reign was set even before Claudius reached the senate. He could not trust the senators and they would remain suspicious and hostile: they could not trust an emperor who so obviously had been chosen against their wishes.

Claudius' ultimate authority was derived from forces external to the senate, primarily the troops and secondarily the people. In these circumstances, the senators were marginalised. Given that the senate viewed political status as their due and the hierarchical nature of Roman society required that the senators held social and political authority as the leading members of that society, Claudius not only risked disaffection of the senators, but he also risked being seen to undermine of the traditions and values of Roman society. It is in the light of this tension at the heart of the regime that we need to understand dominant themes lurking behind the presentation of Claudius in sources: his dependence on his freedmen, the power his womenfolk exercised over him, and his lack of political understanding. From our modern perspective, we can detect a different Claudius within the accounts: a Claudius who was an able administrator and who sought political support from different groups in Roman society, a Claudius different from the shambling man depicted in the sources, but still an emperor who faced fundamental political uncertainties and whose attempts to cope with those uncertainties resulted in the deaths of many senators

Government and administration

Much has been written about Claudius' government and his supposed reliance on his wives and freedmen. All of the ancient sources comment on this reliance. Yet, there were other people in Claudius' inner circle who wielded considerable influence. Lucius Vitellius, for instance, seems to have been very close to the emperor. He supposedly accompanied him in the carriage on what must have been a terrible journey from Ostia to Rome once Claudius had been informed of Messalina's adulterous marriage (see pp. 164–70). In his early years, Claudius associated himself closely with his sons-in-law (Dio, 60. 25.7–8), Cn Pompeius Magnus and L. Silanus.

Nevertheless, the household is particularly prominent in ancient accounts of Claudius' reign (Dio, 60. 2; 19.2–3, 30.6; Suetonius, *Claudius,.* 28–9; Tacitus, *Annales,* 12 53; Pliny, *Epistles,* 7.29, 8.6). Claudius made little attempt to cloak the influence of his wives and freedmen. Narcissus, Pallas and Polybius took public roles. Pallas' brother was given a governorship in Judaea. Kallistos, who had survived the fall of Gaius, continued to play an important part in the household administration. Both Messalina's and Agrippina's activities have been somewhat obscured by the tradition, but we may accept that they were allowed considerable independence and Agrippina especially was portrayed almost as a partner in empire.

This use of freedmen and wives insulated Claudius from the politics of the senate. The senate was the natural forum for policy discussion for the emperors, but Claudius faced a hostile senate. He had little chance of managing the opinion of this body. By giving the freedmen so much obvious influence, he immediately reduced the authority of the senators who, in their own opinion, should have been influencing the emperor. The public acknowledgement of the power of those in Claudius' household may even have been useful. They deflected political attention. They were at once central to Claudius' political manipulations and ultimately dispensable. By moving political debate from the senate to the emperor's household, and even by moving certain judicial cases to his household rather than having them heard in the senate, Claudius took a firmer control of political life, but consequently further marginalised the senators and increased their hostility.

This might not have been a conscious policy. The prospect of leaving sensitive political issues in the hands of a hostile senate may not have filled Claudius with joy, and therefore a policy of dealing with as much business as possible within the household may have evolved. Claudius was always courteous to the senate. He made every attempt to comply with the forms of good and respectful behaviour. The senate was, however, continually made aware that real power lay elsewhere.

For a man of limited military experience, Claudius made much of his personal involvement in the British campaign of AD 43 and his other military victories. The launching of the British campaign so early in his reign was a political decision without obvious immediate military or strategic justification. The British campaign was celebrated in coins and arches, triumphs and processions. Claudius reinvented an archaic ritual in which extensions of Roman territory were reflected in an extension of the *pomerium* (the sacred boundary of the city of Rome). Claudius named his son and presumed heir Britannicus, an act that may have recalled the naming of Claudius' brother Germanicus, following their father's successful campaigns in Germany under Augustus.

His link with the praetorians was made obvious in regular donatives to the soldiers. Claudius went so far as to display on his coinage his debt to the praetorians. Such a display offers an insight into Claudian politics. Claudius did not hide his dependence on the praetorians or his elevation to the throne by the praetorians. One could argue that, from a senatorial point of view, the praetorians had staged a coup in AD 41. The senators had taken some role in the regularisation of Augustus' position in 28 BC, had debated Tiberius' accession in AD 14, had welcomed Gaius and voted him powers. Although the reality of politics may have been very different from the custom, as in the British system in which the monarch 'decides' who to invite to form her government when in reality that choice is constrained by custom and the result of the election, the very fact that the senators were involved offered the pretence that the emperor required the endorsement of his peers in the senate house. In the early empire, there was no automatic succession: one could not proclaim 'The King is dead; long live the King'. The accession of the new emperor was a matter of law that had to have some sort of legal process and the senators, as leading figures of the Roman state whose members were at the summit of the social hierarchy, were central to that process. Yet, Claudius did not even pretend that he was the senators' choice and proclaimed his debt to the soldiers.

In so acting, Claudius sought to explore and represent his power in a new way. As Gaius had sought legitimacy in family and his presumed divinity, so Claudius found legitimacy in the support offered by the soldiers and later also by the plebs. Although senators and senatorial historians from the late Republic onwards emphasised the centrality of the senate and senators to the history and politics of Rome and identified senatorial power with the maintenance of Roman values and Roman political culture, there were other interests within the Roman political system whose political understandings were often at variance with that of the traditional senators, notably the plebs and the soldiers. The ending of the Republic had seen an assertion of those interests against those of the senators. We can reconstruct a military and plebeian view of Roman politics, one in which the individual rights and freedoms of the citizen and the relationship between army and state were at least as important as the traditions of senatorial hegemony. Ever the historian, Claudius was realising an essential tension in the Roman political system between the interests of the senators and those of other groups and seeking the support of those other groups. In so doing, he was looking backwards for his model of imperial power to Augustus, who, as we saw in earlier chapters, used his ability to control the plebs and the troops to seal the grand bargain of Roman imperial politics (peace for principate). Claudius was also and, most obviously, emulating Julius Caesar whose clash with senatorial interests in 49 BC opened the final stages of the Republic's fall. Claudius effectively renewed the bargain, but there is no reason to expect that the senators were happy to accept Claudius' terms.

Claudius asserted his authority in practical ways. He reformed the senatorial roll (as Augustus had done). Those who failed to reach the census requirement were encouraged to leave of their own free will. Others were forced to go (Dio, 60. 29). He was firm with provincial governors, prosecuting the corrupt and ensuring that those retiring from office would have a period before their next posting when they would be open to prosecution (Dio, 60. 24.4; 25.4). He returned the *aerarium* (treasury) to the control of the quaestors, but in order to ensure proper financial management, he extended their office to three years. He also prevented soldiers taking part in the morning *salutatio* at the houses of senators (see pp. 341–42 for this ceremony). This measure was designed to prevent senators taking soldiers into their patronage. One might think that the fear was that senators would incite soldiers to revolt (Suetonius, *Claudius*, 25.1), but it would have taken more than the odd social event to build a coalition capable of threatening the emperor and perhaps it is more likely that Claudius wished to maintain his monopoly position in the affection of the soldiers: nobody but the emperor could be seen to have any sort of social-political relationship with soldiers.

One of Claudius' most notable reforms was an extension of senatorial membership to include prominent men from Gallia Comata, the Gallic territory north of the Mediterranean strip which had largely been conquered by Julius Caesar. The Gauls had been within the empire for approximately 100 years, but had been far from peaceful and the last major revolt had been as recent as AD 21. Many Romans would have been brought up on the myth that the Gauls were a bloodthirsty nation who threatened the very existence of the Roman state, though contemporary reality was very different. Claudius' speech is preserved both in Tacitus and on an inscription (*Annales*, 11. 23–5; Smallwood 1967, no. 369). He 'persuaded' the Senate to accept the reform through use of historical analogy, pointing out that Rome had progressively incorporated new peoples during its expansion and that in fact, few of the senators could trace their ancestry back to Romulus' foundation. It was only proper then that as the privileges of citizenship were extended, so should the membership of the Senate. The response of the unnamed senators was to argue that there was something different about Italy: Italy had been bound together by a long and shared cultural tradition and to recruit Gauls would be to break with that tradition and change the nature of the senate. There were plenty of rich and suitable persons from Italy.

It is evident that both sides were right: the Gauls would not share the same cultural traditions as the Italians. To bring those Gauls into the senate would change the nature of the senate. It would be a step towards making the senate representative of an imperial aristocracy rather than an Italian aristocracy, and an aristocracy which would have little in common other than their perceived loyalty to Rome and the emperor. Claudius was also right: Romans were never a race and always an amalgam of peoples. Rome was not a nation. Claudius won the argument, not because he convinced the senate, but because he was emperor.

It is arguable whether this shows a more liberal attitude on the part of Claudius than his predecessors or contemporaries. Claudius himself was notably fierce with citizens who showed no knowledge of Latin (Dio, 60. 17.4; Suetonius, *Claudius*, 16.2, cf. 25.3). Men of provincial origin had infiltrated the senate since the Late Republic, but these tended to be few in number. The vast majority of senators in this period were Italian. Claudius opened the door a little further, but the trickle of provincial senators did not become a flood. Nearly all these senators were from the West. It seems likely that Claudius wished to curry favour with, and demonstrate his patronage of, the Gauls. The Gallic chiefs may have been useful allies for Claudius in Gaul, but they were not enrolled in sufficient numbers nor did they have sufficient influence to become a powerful senatorial group. Furthermore, his enrolment of the Gauls must also have recalled the conquests of Julius Caesar and his very similar enrolment of the Gallic peoples of Italy into the Roman citizenship.

Claudius also increased the authority of his equestrian procurators. Two new major equestrian governorships were created in Mauretania (Dio, 60. 9.6) and, on the death of Claudius' friend Agrippa, Judaea was given an equestrian prefect, as was Ituraea when its king passed away (Tacitus, *Annales*, 12. 23). Claudius' praetorian prefects were given the ornaments of consular status (Dio, 60. 23.1–5) assimilating the honours of the highest equestrian office with those of those of the highest senatorial post. Claudius and his legates were also given powers to make treaties with the power of the Senate and People of Rome (Dio, 60. 23.6). The judicial acts of his procurators were ratified, probably increasing their authority in the collection of taxes in senatorial and imperial provinces (Suetonius, *Claudius*, 12.1). Claudius also reformed the equestrian career structure (Suetonius, *Claudius*, 25.1; see also pp. 345–47).

Claudius' reign saw reforms of the Roman administration that directly affected the Roman aristocracy, a reform carried out by a man who did not have the support of the senior element of that group. The senate officially remained at the centre of Claudius' administration. Most of the major governorships continued to be filled by senators. The equestrian role in government was enhanced, but the developments were a furthering of Augustus' use of equestrians in government. The elevation of equestrian governors was probably of greater symbolic than political or administrative importance: it demonstrated to the senators that Claudius had the support of members of the equestrian order and that these men could be deployed in the administration. It further eroded the special status of the senators at the summit of the Roman social order and the honours granted to the praetorian prefects established those equestrians as equivalent in social status to senatorial magistrates. The status of the senators was thereby weakened.

Other aspects of Claudius' administration will be considered in the relevant sections below, but it seems appropriate to comment on Claudius' financial administration at this stage. The sources on Gaius (pp. 143–45) suggest that he was almost bankrupt by the end of his reign and had to resort to desperate measures to raise money. There is no sign of any financial problems during the reign of Claudius. He promised the praetorians lavish donatives (gifts of money) and gave much smaller donatives each year to remind them and the senate of the crucial role they had played in elevating the emperor (Dio, 60. 12.4). He also made a substantial distribution to the plebs following his British victory, the preparations for which (building boats; securing equipment; providing supplies) must have been costly (Dio, 60. 25.7–8). He commenced two new huge building projects early in his reign – the harbour at Ostia and the draining of the Fucine lake (Dio, 60. 11.1–5) – and he also built a new aqueduct, having completed another already started by Gaius (Suetonius, *Claudius,* 20). He was fond of games and put on spectaculars for special occasions (Dio, 60. 33.3; Suetonius, *Claudius*, 21, 24.2; Tacitus, *Annales*, 11. 11–12, 12. 41). All this was achieved while gradually withdrawing taxes that had been imposed by Gaius (Dio, 60. 4.1). Claudius' levels of expenditure must have been high yet he is not one of those emperors accused of meanness or (often) of killing aristocrats for their wealth, though the latter charge is levelled at Messalina. Notably increased efficiency in tax collection seems improbable. Either we must conclude that Claudius was a financial genius or, and rather more likely, the financial situation in AD 41 was not as bad as the sources would have us believe.

Military and foreign policy

Claudius came to power with no military experience. As the son of Drusus and brother of Germanicus he had inherited a little of their military prestige. Great Roman leaders needed to show their military prowess as well as their political skills, and Claudius needed to demonstrate to the senate, people and soldiers that he was an effective commander-in-chief in order to bring legitimacy to his position as head of state. He would follow in the tradition of Caesar, Augustus and Tiberius in leading Roman armies effectively and conquering new territory.

He had no shortage of possibilities for new conquests. The Germans were restive and campaigns were probably already underway (Dio, 60. 8.7) and although the Roman armies were victorious in 41, there were further campaigns in 47 (Dio, 60. 30.3; Tacitus, *Annales*, 11. 16–20) and 50 (Tacitus, *Annales*, 12. 27–30). Political divisions within various German tribes and disputes between tribes provided Rome with an opportunity that the Roman general Corbulo (who was to be prominent under Nero), for one, was anxious to exploit. In Africa, Suetonius Paulinus conducted campaigns against the Moors, campaigns which brought a significant though not conclusive victory in AD 41, allowing the senate to offer Claudius a triumph. Claudius courteously declined the offer though accepted triumphal *ornamenta* in honour of the victories (Dio, 60. 8.6, 9.1–6). The Eastern frontier was also restive throughout

Claudius' reign with problems in Armenia and Iberia, and the Parthians suffered a period of internal discord and civil war, but Claudius preferred diplomacy to major conflict.

Claudius chose to invade Britain. In some ways this was an odd choice. There were internal disputes in Britain. Dio mentions a certain Berikos who had been expelled from the island and who appealed to Claudius for help. Numismatic evidence from Britain suggests that the period saw an expansion of the generally anti-Roman Catavellauni at the expense of tribes such as the Atrebates in Sussex. The Dobunni in Gloucestershire may also have been fearful of Catavellaunian expansionism. It seems unlikely that Roman interests were greatly affected by these developments. The Catavellauni could hardly pose any significant threat to Roman power or prestige and, although trade may have been a little more difficult for a time, there is no evidence to suggest that Claudius was remotely interested in protecting the livelihoods of the presumably mainly Gallic traders who transported Roman goods across the Channel. Nor does it seem likely that Claudius felt the slight to Roman prestige from Gaius' failed invasion attempt. Two factors probably motivated Claudius' decision to invade an island that the Romans had left untouched for almost a century: Britain was effectively new territory and its conquest could be guaranteed to impress. Britain was still something of a mystery and would have the benefit of exoticism. Second, Claudius' invasion could be seen to be in imitation of Caesar.

The campaign itself was a success and, with hindsight, it seems obvious that the petty kingdoms of Southern Britain, where the terrain presented few notable obstacles to Roman expansion, would have subsided before the sizeable military force collected by Claudius. Yet, the operation was not without its risks. Caesar had failed twice to make significant gains in the province. Tactically, Rome's forces would be dependent on the fleet for reinforcements, some supplies, and as a means of retreat should things go wrong; uncertainties of tide and weather were also potentially disruptive. A victory at Medway was hard fought and we need not be too cynical about Aulus Plautius' 'pause' at the Thames to await Claudius, reinforcements, and a decision as to whether to advance, a 'pause' interpreted as delaying Roman the final victory so that the emperor could be present. The Romans had used important rivers as frontiers before and the main power-base of the most significant hostile force lay North of the Thames. The arrival of Claudius inaugurated phase two of the campaign and the subsequent conquest of Southern and Central Britain seems to have been rapid.

Claudius celebrated in style. The news of Claudius' victory was transmitted to the senate by his sons-in-law. His prominent generals were rewarded with political and military decorations He celebrated a triumph. Arches were erected in Rome and Lugdunum. The victory was celebrated on coins, in sculpture (either depicting Claudius as a conquering divinity or showing a personification of defeated Britannia), and in the name of Claudius' son.

Claudius revived an archaic ceremony (previously and typically 'rediscovered' by Augustus), in which the sacred boundary of the city of Rome was extended after new territory had been incorporated into the empire (Tacitus, *Annales*, 12. 24). The final capture of Caratacus, the leading opponent of the invasion, was turned into another ceremonial. Caratacus and his family were presented to the Roman people and Claudius was able to show his magnanimity by sparing the life of his great enemy, who aided Claudian propaganda by behaving as a proud barbarian warrior rather than a man begging for his life (Dio, 60. 33.3). In both political and military terms, the invasion of Britain was a success (Dio, 60. 19.1–22.2, 23.1–2; Suetonius, *Claudius*, 17. 24.3; *Vespasian*, 4.1–2; Tacitus, *Annales* 12. 31–40).

Claudius inherited a rather disturbed German frontier, and the first years of his reign were marked by extensive campaigning against the Chatti and Chauci especially. These campaigns met with considerable success, but Claudius later changed his policy. The leading general on the frontier was told to cease any further expansion and the manpower of the legions seems to have been diverted to construction projects (Dio, 60. 30.4–6). Claudius pursued his political and military objectives in Germany through diplomatic means, and the latter part of his reign saw notable tribal conflict in Germany but only limited Roman intervention. This policy is easily explicable. Expansion into Germany in the Augustan and later periods had proved extremely difficult and had required long and bloody campaigns often for very limited territorial gains. There had also been spectacular disasters. Any consistent policy of expansion would have needed considerable resources of manpower and time. The British expedition was a major drain on manpower. In such circumstances, Claudius could not risk losing a substantial force through an expansionist policy in Germany. He had also achieved his military victory so was not as keen to win prestige in Germany. When Augustus had engaged in his major campaigns in Germany and elsewhere in the West, he had either led the armies himself or, more often, relied on his closest associates, Agrippa, Tiberius, Drusus and Varus. Claudius had fewer men he could trust to lead his armies and could not spend long and hard years on campaign himself, away from his political enemies in Rome. A major campaign in Germany would have meant entrusting many legions to his commanders and providing them with the opportunity to win glory that would have eclipsed Claudius' own triumph in Britain. Claudius did not have the political security to be so trusting.

In the East, Claudius again seems initially to have followed the lead of his predecessor, but developed his own policy as the reign progressed. He relied on client kings in much of the East and even enhanced the authority of some, most notably Agrippa I who had proved very useful in the negotiations with the senate in the first days after Gaius' death (Dio, 60. 8.1–3). These kingdoms caused problems. Rebellions were threatened and kings had to be removed (Dio, 60. 28.7). Some even revolted (Dio, 60. 32.4; Tacitus, *Annales*, 12.

15–21) but, although suppressing the revolts, Claudius was reluctant to alter fundamentally the political settlement of the East.

Judaea had been given to his close friend Agrippa in AD 41 (Dio, 60. 8.2–3), following very much the policy of his predecessor; but Agrippa's death in 44, without an adult male heir, left Claudius little alternative but to annex the province (Tacitus, *Annales*, 12. 23; Josephus, *Antiquities*, 19 343–63). The equestrian procurators introduced by Claudius initiated a long period of ineffective government in Judaea, which was to culminate in a great rebellion in AD 66.

The period also saw problems in Parthia and Armenia. The Parthians engaged in civil war with Vardanes and Gotarzes contesting the throne. Vardanes was victorious but was later murdered, leaving Gotarzes to contend with another claimant, Phraates IV, who had been a hostage in Rome (Tacitus, *Annales*, 11. 8–10). In 49, there was a new outbreak of hostilities and the Romans sent Meherdates to seize the Parthian throne. The expedition, sponsored by Rome but without Roman troops, foundered (Tacitus, *Annales*, 12. 10–14.) The situation remained disturbed. In 51, a war broke out between Armenia and Iberia and it threatened to disturb the region. The governor of Syria was reluctant to commit his forces, but the (unsuccessful) intervention of the equestrian governor of Cappadocia forced his hand. The Parthians under yet another king, Vologeses, would not allow the Romans a free hand and invaded Armenia, though disease and famine meant that the Parthian intervention was no more conclusive than that of the Romans (Tacitus, *Annales*, 12. 44–51). The defeat of the Parthians seems to have discouraged further intervention, though the possibility that there were other problems in the final years of Claudius' reign is reinforced by the next attestation of Armenia and Parthian in the historical account. In the first year of Nero's reign, the young and militarily inexperienced emperor organised a major campaign in Armenia to be conducted by his leading general, Corbulo (see p. 156).

The East was disrupted in the Claudian period and there were clear opportunities for Claudius to intervene militarily, either to take advantage of internal strife in Parthia and Armenia or to reorder the settlement of the Eastern client kingdoms. Claudius seems to have been unwilling to take such action. Again, the dangers and implications of a major campaign in the East may have been at the forefront of Claudius' calculations.

Claudius also inherited a disturbed situation in North Africa and had to fight a long war, culminating in the annexation of Mauretania. Mauretania had previously been controlled by client kings, but the last king clashed with Gaius, with predictable results. The kingdom was not, however, quickly annexed and it seems likely that the Mauretanian kings had either kept the local tribes in check or had formed a series of alliances with the various tribes, which now fell apart. Difficulties in Mauretania dragged on until 47, though even then the peace was probably fragile.

With the sole exception of his British invasion, Claudius was reluctant to commit forces to major campaigns. In Germany and the East, in spite of the obvious opportunities to take advantage of the discord among Rome's enemies, Claudius preferred to proceed through diplomacy, encouraging rival claimants to thrones. In the West, the diversion of significant military resources to Britain probably argued against a major campaign of expansion on the German frontier.

We need not see in Claudian reluctance much strategic planning: the invasion of Britain and expansion in Africa demonstrated the bellicose mentalities of Rome and a willingness to undertake large-scale military activities. In the case of the invasion of Britain, the only 'good' reason was to assert Claudius' own military authority. Policy in the East and in Germany was more nervous, perhaps fearing the danger of a general winning prestige from successful military adventurism. We should understand Claudius' policy as being driven by political needs at home

The plebs

Faced with a hostile Senate, one of the major groups in Roman society to whom Claudius could look for support was the plebs. Claudius invested considerable time and money in securing the support of the plebs. He was a notable giver of games and gave every sign of enjoying them (Suetonius, *Claudius*, 21). Presiding over the games in person, he used the opportunity to communicate with the crowds via noticeboards. Such communication allowed him to test public opinion. The cheers that greeted Domitius Ahenobarbus, son of Agrippina, were in contrast to the polite reception for Britannicus, and, since they could have been interpreted as a measure of the unpopularity of Messalina, may have significantly undermined Messalina's position. One of the major events of his reign was the secular games, an event which was supposed to mark the passing of an entire generation of the Roman people and a declaration of a new age. The games began with an announcement that nobody would ever see such games again, since in theory everyone would be dead by the time the next games would be held. Yet, the tradition had been revived by Augustus in 17 BC and Claudius held the games again in AD 47 and although there would not have been many in the audience in AD 47, there were enough to provoke a certain derision at the announcement. The games provided an opportunity for Claudius to demonstrate his links with the past (Tacitus, *Annales*, 11. 11–12; Suetonius, *Claudius*, 21.2).

In the Tacitean account, Claudius responded to the derision with a quick lecture on the history of the secular games and a suggestion that Augustus had miscalculated the date. The antiquarianism of the emperor opened him to mockery, but to some extent this is consistent with the portrayal of Claudius and becomes a dominant theme in his presentation. Claudius may have been right about Augustus' miscalculation of the date of the games, but the issue was one of religion (and thus mattered) and one of presentation of the principate to the people (and thus mattered). A great public occasion as the one in 17 BC was about bringing the people together to offer a re-forming of the relationship with the gods and to put the problematic past of civil wars behind the people. Yet, in AD 47, the same ceremony was open to mockery. Claudius' antiquarianism meant that he missed the point of the new regime and the new world in which he was living.

In addition to the games, Claudius' made spectacular attempts to secure the material well-being of the Roman people (Suetonius, *Claudius,* 18–20). He focused considerable personal attention and much money on the provision of food and water. The water supply was improved by the construction or completion of two aqueducts (one of which had been started by Gaius). Claudius attempted to secure the food supply for the city through two key but expensive measures. One was an unsuccessful project to bring more land into cultivation by draining the Fucine lake (Dio, 60. 11.5; Tacitus, *Annales*, 12. 56–7; Suetonius, *Claudius*, 21.6). The project involved the construction of a massive drainage ditch and was celebrated by a reconstruction of a naval battle staged on the lake. This descended into farce when the re-enactors refused to fight and had to be cajoled by the emperor, and the imperial family were nearly swept away when part of the canal wall collapsed. Quite what Claudius would have done with all this new land had he been able to bring into productivity is unclear, but it would seem likely that he would have returned to the age-old policy of establishing the Roman poor in colonies.

The other project was the construction of a larger and safer harbour at Ostia (Dio, 60. 11.1–5). The harbour has recently been the subject of intensive archaeological work (*The Portus Project*) and the findings have been published online (http://www.ostia-antica.org/). Like the draining of the Fucine lake, the construction was an epic display of Roman engineering and organisation, a prestige project for the imperial regime. Previously, the grain supply had been unloaded from the large Mediterranean grain ships at Puteoli in Campania and the grain then had to be transported to Rome, considerably increasing costs, wastage, and time on the road. The plan was to reshape a vast stretch of the Ostian sea front (Ostia was a small and not particularly secure natural harbour) to provided sufficient space and security from the storms to allow the grain to be unloaded there and then shipped up the Tiber by barge. This project had first been planned by Caesar, another leader in need of popular support, but was dropped because of practical difficulties. Claudius was personally involved in the construction project, and indeed personally supervised the building work at Ostia.

The harbour did not solve all the problems with the food supply. Claudius' reign was marked by several food riots in Rome (Suetonius, *Claudius*, 18.2; Tacitus, *Annales*, 12 43), possibly before the harbour was fully operational, and Trajan found it necessary to modify the harbour installation at Ostia to provide a yet more secure harbour since the fleet could still be wrecked if a storm blew in.

Claudius' efforts to secure popular support were, however, probably successful. Suetonius tells us of popular dismay following a rumour of the emperor's death (Suetonius, *Claudius*, 12.3), though the story is undated. Claudius behaved as if the support of the plebs was important. We could see in this a form of paternalism in which the emperor looked after 'his people', but although such an attitude is certainly familiar from our modern political experience, it is less obvious that paternalism was such important an element in Roman political thought. Emperors such as Augustus repeatedly provided the Roman people with gifts and sought to curry favour with displays and games and may have wanted to present their support as a generalised care for Roman citizens, but such gestures in Republican history were not read as being apolitical and charitable, but as ways of building popular political support and in some cases countering senatorial opposition. Further, although it might have suited the giver of gifts to emphasise his charitable nature, those on the receiving end may have taken a different attitude, regarding the gifts as their entitlements, part of their rights as Roman citizens and the means by which they benefited from imperial power. The relationship with the plebs was probably rather more political than many modern commentators have allowed.

After the adoption of Nero, Claudius associated the young man with his rule by giving games jointly (Dio, 60. 33.3; Tacitus, *Annales*, 12. 41). Appearing together before the people at the games was the symbolic parallel to Nero's first political speeches (see p. 171). Claudius also gave money to the plebs after his British victory, and in this he was aided by his sons-in-law, men with whom he was associating his rule at the time (Dio, 60. 25.7–8). Claudius treated the plebs as if they were important. It is not, however, easy to understand why the plebs were important. The plebs exercised no legal or constitutional authority. We could simply argue that whoever the emperor decided was important was therefore rendered important. We might imagine that the relationship with the plebs was important in the construction of a political image for the emperor as protector of his people. Perhaps more likely, we could see the plebs as a form of counterbalance to the senators, their loyalty and support marginalising senatorial opposition and asserting an old principle of the Augustan principate: the emperor spoke for the army, and plebs and offered peace by controlling these potentially disruptive forces. Further, I think we could argue that the plebs contributed to the political atmosphere of the city: they gossiped; they protested; they appeared *en masse* at the games and the theatre; they painted slogans round the city. The senators, the aristocracy and the soldiers (the other powers in Roman society) were not hermetically isolated from the rest of the city and would have been sensitive to its moods. The plebs mattered since they were an audience for Roman politics. In an era in which power was concentrated in the imperial court and there were no real institutionalised outlets for political debate or discontent, the 'mood' of the plebs was one of the few barometers of political success and failure. Ultimately, the plebs mattered because they were the Roman people.

Family and politics

Claudius' reliance on his household for policy advice and his distrust of the senate increased the political importance of the imperial family. Power rested in the imperial court and, with Claudius, we see for perhaps the first time in the history of the Principate the displacement of the politics of the senate with the politics of the court. Of course, court politics was resultant upon the creation of monarchic rule and can already be seen under Augustus when members of the imperial family, such as Livia and Julia, had ill-defined political influence. Yet, Augustus and Tiberius (and even Gaius, though to a lesser extent) worked primarily through the senate. Although Claudius showed respect for the senate and attended more regularly than his predecessors had, our sources portray a situation in which the real decisions were taken in private and political power was the ability to manipulate the emperor.

Claudius owed his political power to the loyalty of the army to his family and he laid emphasis on his family in the first year of his reign. Claudius' first major problem was how to deal with Gaius' assassins since, although few among the aristocracy would disapprove and the assassins were almost certainly popular in the senate, Claudius could hardly allow such men to survive as visible reminders of the rewards for tyrannicide. He found a compromise and punished those who had conspired to kill members of the Julio-Claudian family other than his nephew (Dio, 60. 3.4–5). Julia and Agrippina, Claudius' nieces, returned from exile, though Julia was to be exiled again in the same year (Dio, 60. 4.1; 8.5). Claudius gave games for Antonia and Drusus, for his mother and father and for Livia (Claudius' grandmother). The latter was given a statue in the temple of Augustus, which may have been a preliminary to full divine honours. Mark Antony (Claudius' grandfather) and Germanicus were also honoured. Although all Gaius' acts were annulled, he did not suffer *damnatio memoriae* whereby all record of his life would be excised from public documents and monuments, and Claudius did not allow the senate to pull down all Gaius' statues, though he arranged for them to disappear (Suetonius, *Claudius*, 11; Dio, 60. 4.5–5.2). The idea would appear to be that Gaius should be quietly forgotten, but his overthrow (with its unfortunate implication of honourable tyrannicide) was not to be celebrated

The years preceding Claudius' accession had not been kind to the Julio-Claudian family. Claudius found himself surrounded by adult female relatives, but had few close male relatives and was without an adult male heir. The women of the imperial family assumed a greater prominence and, since marriage to a princess of the imperial house brought political influence, the husbands of imperial princesses would be powerful political figures. Should anything happen to Claudius, these men would be in a good position to challenge for the imperial position.

The imperial women also had an invaluable political asset. They could gain access to the emperor and could thereby influence his decisions. These women were not merely decorative, nor were they simply 'heir-producers'; they were serious players in the political game and, given the fatality rate in the imperial family, they were playing for extremely high stakes. Livia, Julia and the elder Agrippina had accustomed the Roman elite to powerful imperial women. Claudius was married to Messalina, who had her own interests and those of her children to protect, and the tradition suggests that she was deeply involved in the politics of the period.

In outline, the history of family politics under Claudius is quite simple (see Figure 5.1). Messalina wielded considerable influence, but was caught in adultery and executed. She was replaced by Agrippina who removed any rivals and exerted significant influence over Claudius. She was able to persuade Claudius to adopt her son who, slightly older than Britannicus, became the most likely heir. When Claudius seemed to be about to reject Nero in favour of his natural son, Agrippina removed Claudius and ensured Nero's smooth succession. Behind this relatively simple if sordid tale, lurk complexities which can only be fully understood by looking at the careers of the women in some detail.

Messalina

Messalina was of noble birth, though reconstructing her lineage is complex. She was the daughter of Messala Barbatus, who was the grandson of Claudius Marcellus and Octavia, sister of Augustus. Her mother was Domitia Lepida, who was the granddaughter of the same Octavia and Mark Antony. She was, in fact, more closely related to Augustus (twice through Octavia) than Claudius (once through Octavia). She provided Claudius with two children, Octavia and Britannicus. In some ways, therefore, she was the ideal consort. The tradition, however, depicts her as the 'whore-empress' whose infidelities and promiscuity strain credulity.

Messalina was clearly a powerful woman in the early years of Claudius' reign. It seems that she held a court separate to that of Claudius and Claudius seems to have approved of this. Messalina's influence was seen behind many of Claudius' actions in the early years of his reign. The (re-)exile of Julia, who was accused of adultery with Seneca, was laid at the door of Messalina. Appius Silanus also fell victim to Messalina in an elaborate conspiracy with Narcissus (Dio, 60. 14.3–4; Suetonius, *Claudius*, 37). Silanus had been married to Domitia Lepida, Messalina's mother, and was an experienced governor. He was obviously a powerful political figure on the fringes of the imperial family. But the motive ascribed to Messalina by our sources was purely sexual and not political.

Dio links the death of Silanus to the first and probably the most serious conspiracy against Claudius. Annius Vinicianus was the prime mover of the conspiracy. He had been suggested as a possible successor to Gaius and thus may have felt that he was viewed with some suspicion. He gained the support of the governor of Dalmatia, Furius Camillus Scribonianus. But, as the legions were about to depart for Rome, a series of omens weakened their resolve and the conspiracy dissolved (Dio, 60. 15). The conspiracy involved others in the Roman aristocracy and its dissolution led to a spate of arrests and deaths (Pliny, *Epistles*, 3.16).

Messalina's authority was also seen in the death of Julia, granddaughter of Tiberius, and of a prefect of the guard Catonius Iustus (Dio, 60. 18). An alliance of Julia and a praetorian prefect would indeed have been powerful and anything that threatened the loyalty of the praetorians was to be feared. Feminine rivalry, which our sources give as the cause for the removal of Julia, may mask suspected political conspiracy and the removal of a potentially powerful group, possibly in opposition to Messalina.

Dio (60. 18) places an extended account of Messalina's growing power in AD 43. This is probably not a coincidence. Claudius was preparing to leave Rome for his invasion of Britain. He had suppressed a major revolt and wished to secure his position in Rome before he left. His trusted friend Lucius Vitellius was left in charge at Rome, but Claudius may have been willing to delegate more authority to Messalina, who was of course deeply committed to Claudius' cause. Dio presents her as building a political group, a group bound together by adultery.

Other possibly powerful leaders in Roman politics can be divined. Pompeius Magnus, who carried an extremely prestigious name, was married to Claudius' elder daughter by a previous marriage. His connection with the imperial family was paralleled by the betrothal of L. Silanus, already connected to the imperial family down the female line, to the infant Octavia, a marriage that never took place. Both men were advanced to offices at an early age. They brought the news of Claudius' victory in Britain to the senate. They also took part in donations to the plebs in 44 (Dio, 60. 5.7, 21.5, 25.7–8). These men were clearly being associated with Claudius' power. Messalina probably had little to fear from Silanus – after all he was committed to one of her children – but Pompeius was a different matter.

The position of others attacked (supposedly) by Messalina is less easy to estimate. M. Vinicius was supposedly killed for refusing to sleep with the empress, i.e. he would not join her 'group'. He was also the brother of the Vinicianus at the centre of the conspiracy of AD 42. Presumably, Claudius (or Messalina) could have removed him then. The mode of his death, poisoning, raises suspicions about the whole story (Dio, 60. 27.4).

Decimus Valerius Asiaticus was another victim, killed in 47. The political implications of this are unclear. Asiaticus was a respected senator of provincial origin and cannot easily be seen as a threat to Messalina or Claudius. The killing is explained as a convoluted sexual conspiracy and a plot to seize Asiaticus' gardens in the centre of Rome, gardens in which Messalina was herself to be killed (Dio, 60. 29.1–6; Tacitus, *Annales*, 11. 1–3). Asiaticus went to his death calmly, making arrangements for the funeral, a martyr. In the same year, in a case that cannot be convincingly related to the death of Asiaticus, Pompeius was killed.

The death of Pompeius would seem to have enhanced Messalina's control, yet there are signs of her position slipping. The instrument of her attack on Asiaticus, a certain Suillius Rufus, was himself attacked in the senate, though the debate failed to bring him down (Tacitus, *Annales*, 11. 4–7) and L. Domitius Ahenobarbus received more applause than Britannicus at the secular games of 47, which Tacitus interprets enigmatically as a gesture of sympathy for Agrippina.

Messalina's fall was sudden and the story strange (Tacitus, *Annales*, 11.26–38; Dio, 60. 31.1–5). She became involved with a certain C. Silius. This man was consul designate and the very man who had attacked Suillius Rufus in the senate. For some reason, she apparently underwent a semi-public ceremony with this man, an act of madness according to Tacitus, and then engaged in a post-nuptial revel. Narcissus, Claudius' trusted freedman, organised a concubine to break the news to Claudius while he was staying in Ostia. Claudius hurried back in a carriage with Vitellius and Narcissus, Vitellius refusing to condemn Messalina explicitly. News of Claudius' approach reached the revellers, who dispersed in a panic, but no effort was made to raise the army or to oppose Claudius. Messalina was deserted. Her only hope was to reach Claudius. She set out for Ostia to meet him on the road, but could find no carriage and travelled on the city waste cart. The meeting was brief, but she was not arrested. Claudius retreated to the praetorian camp and then the revellers were rounded up and killed, the prefect of the *vigiles* (night watch) among them.

Even Tacitus seems to have found the event incomprehensible. Modern historians have seen in it conspiracy, characteristically preferring politics to sex as an explanation and equally characteristically reversing the ancient (and Hollywood) understanding. It is difficult to see how a 'marriage' could have been kept secret and how the effective divorce of the emperor by the mother of his presumed heir could be anything less than treason. Yet, there was no organised resistance to Claudius' retribution, a retribution that affected many prominent men: were the 'conspirators' not expecting Claudius to be evenly mildly annoyed? The story is so implausible that it throws into question the whole tradition on Messalina. It must have been so easy for contemporaries to observe the political falls of so many men and blame the machinations of a woman. Ignoring the fact that Claudius had many enemies in the senate, making Messalina's responsible had the double advantage of concentrating fire on someone they might even be able to remove, and of asserting that Claudius could not even control his own womenfolk. Further, if Messalina's hand was seen behind every important decision, then the legitimacy of those decisions could be questioned.

Even the death of Messalina rebounds to Claudius' detriment. Claudius softened his sorrows with wine. He started to talk about his wife and rather than being angry, he seemed sorrowful. Then, he seemed sympathetic. Narcissus acted. He left the dining room and found a praetorian officer. He instructed the officer to kill Messalina. Narcissus could not afford Messalina returning and seeking her revenge. Claudius received news of her death without emotion. Claudius continued drinking.

We might decide to dismiss the tradition on Messalina as novelistic invention, perhaps invented retrospectively in relation to another Claudian purge of the aristocracy. The novelistic quality of the tale strains credibility. Not only do we need to believe that Messalina engaged openly in sexual relations with a number of the leading figures of Roman society, but our sources seem to know what went on at these wild parties, parties which must, on one level or another, have had a discrete clientele. We are led to imagine Messalina finding herself alone and hitching a ride on the cart filled with human excrement that was heading out to meet Claudius coming back in a panic from Ostia. That image is so perfect and so literary that only the most outrageous of novelists would have invented it. We know, according to our sources, what Messalina said to Claudius, and how indecisive Claudius was in finally consigning her to death and that the order came not from Claudius but from his freedman Narcissus. We know that Claudius reacted to her death by ordering another cup of wine and continuing with his banquet. We know, it seems, that Messalina's removal of various enemies was motivated by her desire, but quite how we can know that without a signed confession is unclear. As readers of the history, we find ourselves in the bedrooms and council chambers of the Roman imperial family and sometimes in the heads of the leading figures. We must wonder how it is that these events were recorded and passed down to the traditions. Narcissus, for example, is hardly likely to have wanted it known that he ordered the death of a princess of the imperial house and the wife of the emperor on no authority whatsoever. The historical in these accounts is buried beneath a very thick blanket of fiction.

Yet, even if truth cannot be confidently reassembled from the prevailing tradition (other than at the most basic level), the stories surrounding Messalina are widespread and contemporaneous and fascinating. This is one of those occasions when the story is all-important.

Imperial women were used as pawns in political and dynastic arrangements. They were married off as suited the emperor. It is likely that heads of other prominent families behaved in a similar way. An aristocratic woman's sexual partners were a matter of political interest. The tradition, and it is fairly uniform, suggests that the women of the early imperial period were not passive: they expected to influence their husbands and to take an active part in public life. It was also acknowledged that the relationship between husband

and wife was not necessarily romantic: a marital relationship was social and familial. Marriage had a function. An imperial princess would be expected to have a circle of friends, male and female. These were friends accumulated through social and political contacts and would not necessarily be the friends of her husband. Nor was it necessarily the case that husband and wife would operate within identical social spheres. Livia, the wife of Augustus, clearly had her own circle, and no disrepute attached to her. The elder Julia also continued to operate socially and politically even when her husband, Tiberius, was spending his life in Rhodes (and even before that when he was on his various campaigns). Roman aristocratic women had a web of friendships and social contacts.

For an emperor, those social contacts might be very useful. Friends of his wife could be relied on. The extra-political or informal nature of those ties could also pay dividends. Leaders need various circles of support and advice. Sex adds a complicating feature. It was illegal to engage in an adulterous relationship, but it is questionable whether, in the early empire at least, the political elite were very exercised by adultery. The love poets paraded their adulteries and even moralistic historians note that contemporaries considered adultery to be a matter of fashion. In a Judaeo-Christian tradition, sexuality is often problematic and associated with intimacy and privacy. Yet, for the Romans, sexual liaisons were a social matter, and the banning of adultery was not because of any concern with the sanctity of marriage (which was not sacred anyhow) but with the social bond at the heart of a household. Women and men married for social gain and thus were expected to have sexual relations for social reasons.

In a cultural environment in which sex was used to cement legitimate political links, it is possible that close illegitimate political ties could be developed through adultery. It is also possible, though this is a somewhat different issue, that romantic ties and amatory passion would be often located outside of marriage. Systematic promiscuity was a feasible, if rather odd method of creating a close-knit political alliance. It is possible, therefore, even if we dismiss the wilder stories, that Messalina was less than faithful to her husband. It is also possible that as long as this remained behind closed doors and did not pose a significant threat to the emperor, the creation of such a group was not a substantial problem. Yet, the perception can work the other way round: since women might build political relationships through promiscuity, through the use of the body, then any woman who was at the centre of a network of political relationship might be thought to have bound that group together through sex. Close political co-operation could be interpreted as signifying a sexual tie.

Such cementing of a political connection (when extra-marital) was illegitimate and illegal and when it involved an empress, it was potentially fatal. This may have added a certain *frisson* to the liaison and would have bound the adulterers more closely to each other. Yet, the easiest way to purge a queen and her circle was to suggest that they were all engaged in promiscuous sexual activity: sexual desire is a powerful passion and audiences love a good sex scandal. There was, obviously precedent for Messalina's fall in the disasters that befell the daughter and granddaughter of Augustus.

If we accept Tacitus' view that Messalina and Silius had taken leave of their senses, there is no need for further speculation, but this seems an inadequate explanation for the fall of a woman who had played the political game reasonably astutely. Dio links the fall of Messalina to her disposal of Polybius, a freedman of the emperor, suggesting that she had fallen out with the freedmen. For Dio, Claudius is forever the dupe, fooled by his wife and then fooled by his freedmen. It may be that Messalina was engaged in a reorientation of her group, an attempt to build bridges with powerful senators and in so doing, she alienated the powerful freedmen who then engineered her downfall. But there is more here than a disagreement between Messalina and the freedmen. If there was a struggle between the emperor's wife and freedmen, many would simply have stood aside. Yet, Messalina's group took in significant members of the Roman aristocracy. Messalina had created a group which could plausibly challenge the authority of the emperor and offer an alternative to Claudius. Claudius' flight to the praetorian camp may be seen as the reaction of a deluded paranoiac, but the speed with which Messalina was despatched and the summary execution of her circle suggest that we are seeing a serious conspiracy, probably intended to remove Claudius.

Conspiracies in the Roman imperial world were political movements intended to take control. They were not just focused on the removal of an individual and therefore could not be limited to a few people. The politically prominent needed to be included and arrangements put in place for an alternative government. The involvement of the consul-designate would be crucial in the manipulation of the senate in the aftermath of an assassination. Silius' 'marriage' would make him guardian of Claudius' children and place him in position to assume most of the powers of the emperor. He would also be married to Messalina and that brought her associations with the imperial family. The inclusion of a prefect of the *vigiles* brought some military force, which in itself suggests that the conspiracy was serious. But once Claudius reached the praetorian camp and assured himself of the loyalty of the largest military force in Rome, Messalina and her co-conspirators were doomed. The reality of power had not changed since AD 41 (or, indeed, 41 BC): the soldiers were arbiters of the imperial position. The narrative suggests that the conspirators were discovered before they were ready and without military force they were lost and all the evidence suggests that they knew it.

The real problem is to explain Messalina's decision to take such desperate measures. Did she fear a rival (Agrippina being the obvious threat), or that Claudius' power was disintegrating in the face of senatorial opposition, or was she becoming increasingly marginalised in the household government? Historical attention has focused on Messalina, and Claudius has been seen as essentially the passive victim of the manipulations of others, but Claudius too was in a position to sense a growing opposition to his regime. He presumably saw the display of public feeling in favour of Domitius Ahenobarbus and the story of Asiaticus, phlegmatically going to his death, a symbol of imperial tyranny, was disturbing (see pp. 165–66). Claudius appears to have been sensitive to popular opinion. To see Claudius as a Machiavellian politician manipulating those closest to him runs against the grain of ancient depictions of the emperor; our sources are committed to a depiction of Claudius as a servant of his wives and freedmen, even though they provide us with sufficient evidence to suggest a wily politician carefully manipulating a rather weak position. Perhaps it occurred to him that it was time to swap wives and neutralise the threat posed by Agrippina by marrying her. Perhaps such a strategy was being discussed by others. In detail, the politics cannot be reconstructed, but the uncertainties of court politics, the intrigues and the complexities of personal relationship led to insecurity. This is how court politics are conducted: what matters is the relationship to the emperor and not any ideological or political position. In any event, Messalina, instead of riding out any difficulties, awaiting a change in the political environment, appears to have sought a radical alternative.

If Claudius had been killed, it would seem likely that the tradition would blame him for the problems of the previous years. By disposing of Messalina, Claudius had a scapegoat who could be blamed for the deaths and the political failures of the early part of the reign. There was a cost in the judicial murders and the consequent lack of trust and the bitterness of those who saw friends and relatives slain, and, of course, in the loss of his wife, but Claudius had never been popular with the senators and showed little reluctance to kill. Roman politics remained a brutal environment.

The next move was obvious: Claudius was to consolidate the prestige of the Julian dynasty by marrying his niece.

Agrippina

The historians depict a somewhat farcical debate led by the freedmen over who should be selected as the next imperial wife. Here, again, the tradition seems dubious. Not only is it difficult to believe that the freedmen might have run such campaigns for their favoured candidates, but also one must wonder how such stories reached the tradition. As with the stories of Messalina, our access to secret discussions recalls historical fiction rather than history. There were several available noble women and Agrippina was to dispose of those thought to be her rivals (Tacitus, *Annales*, 12. 22; Dio, 60. 32.4).

Agrippina was Claudius' niece and the marriage was legally incestuous. The law needed to be 'rearranged'. These formalities were completed in early 49 and the way was then open for Agrippina to take her place at the side of the emperor (Tacitus, *Annales*, 12. 1–7; Dio 60. 31.6–32). Her son's claim to the throne, already respectable, was improved by the marriage and it was to be further enhanced. The prospective husband of Octavia, Silanus, had his long betrothal cancelled and he killed himself, probably much to the relief of the reformed imperial family (Dio, 60. 31.6–8; Tacitus, *Annales*, 12 8). This left Octavia free for the young Ahenobarbus. In AD 50, Ahenobarbus was adopted and given the name Nero (Dio, 60. 33.2; Tacitus, *Annales*, 12. 25–6). In 53, he was married to Octavia, a process which, ironically enough, required the adoption of Octavia since Nero was legally her brother. Nero emerged as the heir to the empire. Britannicus remained a threat to Nero and Agrippina (Dio, 60. 33.12; Tacitus, *Annales*, 12. 58). He was, however, still a minor and Claudius was dead before Britannicus reached an age when he could realistically assume the imperial position.

In terms of the dynasty, bringing Agrippina into the imperial household tied up a lot of loose ends. She was the only surviving child of Germanicus and the elder Agrippina, and the only surviving direct descendant of Augustus (apart from her son). In marrying Agrippina, Claudius consolidated the family and further associated his rule with the popularity of his brother and sister-in-law. The connection seemed to bring stability and unity to the imperial family.

Agrippina immediately assumed a position of remarkable prominence. She was granted the title Augusta as early as AD 50 and seems to have taken her place at Claudius' side at most public occasions (Dio, 60. 33.1–2). A colony in Germany was named after her (Tacitus, *Annales*, 12. 27). She is said to have had a hand in the appointment of Burrus as praetorian prefect, a man who proved his loyalty to Nero. Seneca also returned and became prominent within the imperial household as tutor to Nero. Already Agrippina seems to have been playing at least part of the role she was to play in the early years of Nero's reign. She was more than just the wife of the emperor, but acted as a political power in her own right.

Nero's advance was also rapid. After his adoption in 50, he received the *toga virilis* in 51, the mark of his adulthood. He celebrated lavish games in association with his new father and was declared *Princeps Iuventutis* (Leader of Youth) (Tacitus, *Annales*, 12. 41). In 53, the year of his marriage to Octavia, he spoke in public to secure grants of privileges for Ilium and Bononia (Tacitus, *Annales*, 12. 58). Both were significant places. Ilium was the original home of the Roman people from where the mythical ancestor of the Julian family led the Trojans to Italy to found the new city. Nero was thereby associated with the family myth of the Julians, surely a symbolic claim for legitimacy. Bononia was a military colony established by his great-great-grandfather Augustus. By representing the colony, Nero laid claim to have inherited Augustus' clients and, to some extent, his political position.

It is reasonable to assume that Claudius planned some role for Britannicus in the succession. The fate of dynastic rivals to previous emperors was not encouraging. Yet, advancing Nero left Claudius little room for manoeuvre. Agrippina could not allow an alternative to her son. Her timetable was quite tight. Britannicus could not be kept in the background forever and in AD 54, as the date for Britannicus' assumption of the *toga virilis* neared, Claudius died.

It has been alleged that he was poisoned by Agrippina's own hand, avoiding the many elaborate security measures. Most such accusations rest on fairly flimsy evidence. In this case, the evidence is persuasive. His death was remarkably convenient. The sources are remarkably precise. Nero is said to have quipped that mushrooms were surely the food of the gods since his father became a god through a mushroom (Dio, 60. 34; Suetonius, *Claudius*, 44–5; Tacitus, *Annales*, 12. 65–9).

Chapter 6

Nero (AD 54–68)

Main events of the reign of Nero

Date	Events
54	Accession.
	Deaths of Narcissus and M. Junius Silanus.
	Agrippina entitled 'best of mothers'.
	Corbulo sent to Armenia.
55	Prosecutions of Britannicus' friends stopped.
	Fall of Pallas.
	Death of Britannicus.
	Withdrawal of Agrippina's bodyguard.
	Supposed conspiracy of Agrippina and Rubellius Plautus.
	Cohort on guard in the theatre withdrawn.
56	Nero's gang wanders streets. Death of Julius Montanus.
	Helvidius Priscus becomes involved in dispute over debts.
57	Construction of the gymnasium.
	Cossutianus Capito condemned for corruption.
58	War with Parthia in Armenia.
	Condemnation of P. Suillius Rufus.
	Emergence of Poppaea Sabina.
	Cornelius Sulla Felix exiled.
	War in Germany.
59	Killing of Agrippina.
	Thrasea Paetus walks out of the senate.
	Private stadium constructed for Nero.
	Iuvenalia instituted.
60	Neronia founded.
	Corbulo campaigns in Armenia and takes governorship of Syria.
61	Boudiccan revolt.
	Killing of L. Pedanius Secundus.
	Dedication of Nero's gymnasium.

Date	Events
62	Trial of Antistius Sosianus. Death sentence opposed by Thrasea Paetus. Trial of Aulus Didius Gallus Fabricius. Death of Burrus. Appointment of Tigellinus and Faenius Rufus. Seneca loses influence. Assassination of Sulla. Assassination of Plautus. Divorce, exile and death of Octavia. Deaths of Pallas and Doryphoros. Seneca and Piso linked in conspiracy charge; charge rejected. Caesennius Paetus appointed to Armenia, but defeated. Thrasea Paetus speaks against provincial acclamations of governors.
63	Birth and death of Nero's daughter. Poppaea becomes Augusta. Corbulo brings the war in Armenia to an end. Nero's gymnasium burnt down.
64	Nero appears on stage in Naples. Decimus Junius Silanus Torquatus killed. Nero marries Pythagoras. Banquet of Tigellinus. Fire of Rome.
65	Conspiracy of Piso. Death of all conspirators and of others. Nero appears on stage at the Neronia. Death of Poppaea. Deaths of Lucius Junius Silanus Torquatus, C. Cassius Longinus, L. Antistius Vetus and family. Renaming of months. Plague in Rome.
66	Many deaths, including Petronius, Thrasea Paetus and Barea Soranus. Tiridates presented in Rome. Conspiracy of Vinicianus. Nero sets out for Greece. Revolt in Judaea.
67	Nero in Greece. Deaths of Corbulo and the governors of the Germanies.
68	Revolt of Vindex. Galba declares against Nero. Death of Vindex. Collapse of Nero's position. Death of Nero.

Introduction

With Nero, the Julio-Claudian dynasty came to an end. His reign is often seen as a culmination of tyranny, the final degeneration of the Julio-Claudians, and a period in which bad taste and immorality were in the ascendancy. Nero is portrayed as the undisciplined perpetrator and victim: a spoilt child given absolute power with predictable results, and thus a symbol of the weakness of absolute monarchy. Nero has been attacked across the ages: his responsibility (either directly or indirectly) for the deaths of his father (by adoption), mother, two wives, his brother and sister (by adoption), his aunt, and numerous other more distant relatives has not endeared him to upholders of family values. His sexual promiscuity, his bisexuality, his reckless financial extravagance, and his showmanship have horrified those who admire Roman restraint and self-discipline. To add to this weight of censure, both the Jewish and Christian traditions remember Nero as a persecutor. His murders and the violence with which he treated his subjects add to his notoriety. While Gaius has been seen to be mad, Nero was just bad.

We can make some attempt to understand why Nero went so completely wrong that, in the end, aided by only a few of his closest and lowest status associates, with the guards closing in, he completed a clumsy and rushed suicide. As elsewhere in Julio-Claudian family history, there are times when our sources have a novelistic quality (see pp. 164–70) and Nero the myth seems to overwhelm any historical veracity. Yet, when we gain some insight into the available source material, as with the Pisonian conspiracy (see pp. 201–202), it seems plentiful and trustworthy and it is highly likely that there was a considerable body of evidence available to our main sources. In the end, there seems little reason to dismiss the various and manifest immoralities of the reign or believe that Nero's reputation has merely fallen victim to the hostility of his successors. His was an extraordinary reign in which extraordinary things happened. But the myth of Nero is at least as important as the underlying reality.

Accession and early years

Agrippina had planned Nero's accession with care, and it seems likely that it was the mere possibility that Nero might have a rival that brought a sudden end to Claudius' life. Nero and Agrippina had brought new lustre to Claudius' regime. Their presence re-emphasised the relationship of the family to Augustus (since Agrippina, unlike Claudius, was a direct descendant) and also further associated the regime with the ever-popular Germanicus. Britannicus was confined to the background, yet it was to be expected that he would be joint heir with his adopted brother, who was also his brother-in-law. With Agrippina wielding power within the imperial household, Britannicus' position would always be tenuous. With Claudius dead, it must have been expected that Britannicus too would soon depart. Although there can have been little doubt that Nero would become emperor, his position does not seem to have been as clearly superior to that of Britannicus as in other cases of possibly contested claims to the throne: the differences of age, experience and popularity were not marked. Nero's rival was a more realistic threat and when Nero left the imperial palace to the acclaim of the praetorian prefect, there

was (according to the hostile and possibly inventive Tacitus (*Annales,* 12. 69))
a moment of hesitation, an implicit or even explicit request for Britannicus,
before Nero was acclaimed alone.

Burrus, the sole praetorian prefect and the appointee of Agrippina, had
secured the support of the praetorians. The support of the senate was obtained
and maintained at least in part through speeches prepared by Seneca
(apparently) but delivered by Nero (Dio, 61. 3; Tacitus, *Annales*, 13. 3). Much
of the success of Nero's early years is attributed to Seneca and Burrus and their
loss of influence is seen to have led directly to the degeneration of Nero's
regime. This is consistent with ancient standards of historiography and
biography which tended to perceive character as fixed and perceptible changes
due to a loss or acceptance of discipline which restrained immoral tendencies.
Thus, for our ancient sources, Nero's early success could not be of Nero's own
doing, but rather was a feature of the competent management of Nero by
those around him (Tacitus, *Annales*, 13. 2). Also, although Dio is clearly
hostile towards Seneca (Dio, 61. 10) and Tacitus seems quietly to enjoy
elements of the philosopher's corruption, there may have been a largely lost
historical tradition that lauded Seneca and saw him as a philosophical martyr
to Nero's tyranny, glorifying the years of his influence as if they represented
rule by a philosopher-king. Thus, Nero is written out of the political history
of the early years of his reign: a few acts of notable brutality excepted.

Yet, the emergence of Seneca and Burrus as leading figures is in itself
something of a surprise and suggests that Nero may have taken a keen interest
in politics right from the beginning of his reign. Agrippina had prepared the
way for Nero and had been largely responsible for his elevation, and there is
little doubt that both Burrus and Seneca owed their prominence to her, but,
in spite of initial votes of honours, her appearance on coins alongside her son,
and the prominence of the slogan 'best of mothers' (Tacitus, *Annales*, 13. 2;
Suetonius, *Nero*, 9; Dio, 61. 3), Agrippina quickly lost influence. As early as
AD 54, when an Armenian delegation was being presented to the emperor,
Agrippina was prevented from joining the emperor on the tribunal (would she
have done so in the reign of Claudius?) by Nero's sudden descent (Dio, 61.
3.3; Tacitus, *Annales*, 13. 5). In 55, her favourite at court and alleged lover,
Pallas, was forced into retirement and her bodyguard was withdrawn
(Tacitus, *Annales,* 13. 14; Dio, 61. 8.6; Suetonius, *Nero*, 34.1–4). In terms of
presentation, Nero was happy to associate his reign with his mother and give
her a remarkable prominence, but in our historical accounts she is firmly
prevented from assuming the position of co-ruler.

Nero played a sophisticated political game. He owed his position to his
mother and Claudius and he officially honoured both. Claudius was deified,
much to the amusement of all concerned. Seneca, so closely connected to the
court, produced a satirical version, the *Apocolocyntosis* ('Pumkinification'), in
which Claudius is not only refused divinity on the motion of Augustus,
significantly enough, but also chastised for his crimes and his elevation of

freedmen. Nero's speech at Claudius' funeral, allegedly also written by Seneca, caused laughter in the senate according to Tacitus (*Annales*, 13. 2–3), hardly a suitably reverent attitude on the occasion of the elevation of one so recently departed to the status of divinity. The cultural sophistication of Nero's court was already evident. Nero and his court were capable of playing to two audiences: a traditional audience and another more sophisticated audience ready to see and appreciate the subversive elements of Neronian culture. Even when raising Claudius to the skies, Nero and his court demonstrated their contempt. This may have had a certain appeal to an audience of senators who had become so skilled in dissimulation that it had welcomed each new horror with praise of the emperor. Such obvious hypocrisy allowed Nero to distance himself from the previous regime while honouring its actions, especially, of course, his own elevation.

Perhaps unsurprisingly, therefore, Nero invoked the example of Augustus rather than Claudius as his ideal: it was Augustus' memory he recalled in his first speech in the senate. Nero's triumphal entry into Rome after his 'victories' in Greece was in Augustus' chariot (Suetonius, *Nero*, 10, 25). His building was on a scale unmatched by any of his predecessors except Augustus. His closing of the temple of Janus following the celebration of a victory over Parthia may have been intended to recall Augustus' similar acts (Suetonius, *Nero*, 13). Nero was the great-great-grandson of Augustus through Agrippina and the great-grandson of Augustus' sister Octavia through his father Cn. Domitius Ahenobarbus. This association with Augustus gave him a claim to the throne separate to his adoption by Claudius. The association with Augustus may have suited Nero in other ways in that his seizure of the throne at just 17 could be paralleled by Augustus' acceptance of Caesar's legacy aged 19. If the divine Augustus could do it, why should Nero be excluded from power on the basis of his age?

Agrippina was, therefore, central to his dynastic claim. He needed Agrippina to give his regime an air of legitimacy. Yet, he also had an audience in the senate. Nero's distancing of himself from Agrippina and the obvious signs that she would be subordinate to him were probably popular with the senate. Nero's initial behaviour towards his mother in the public sphere was, in this respect, conservative, pointing to a resumption of the politics of the imperial senate and a move away from the politics of the court practiced by Claudius.

Nero appears to have tried to win over the senate in his first years. He allowed them considerable freedom and they responded with a bout of legislation, mainly concerning administrative matters (Tacitus, *Annales*, 13. 5). Nero rejected a proposal from the senate to amend the calendar so that the year would start on 1st December, his birthday (Tacitus, *Annales*, 13. 10). He also prevented the factional disturbances that had marred earlier reigns. Those who had been enemies of Agrippina were probably pleased at her apparent loss of influence and delighted at the withdrawal of Pallas, her freedman-supporter. Nero's accession saw only one notable victim, Narcissus, a freedman whose fall would have caused few senators to weep (Dio, 60. 34.4; Tacitus, *Annales*, 13. 1). M. Junius Silanus was allegedly poisoned by Agrippina, which is always a charge that raises suspicions (Dio, 61. 6.4–5; Tacitus, *Annales*, 13. 1). Silanus was a great-great-grandson of Augustus, through the maternal line and his brother had been betrothed to Octavia until he was forced to make way for Nero. Others of his family survived until the later, bloodier years of Nero's reign. More significantly perhaps, Plautius Lateranus, a supposed lover of Messalina, returned from exile and a prosecution aimed at two friends of Britannicus was stopped (Tacitus, *Annales*, 13. 10–11). Nero did not allow tensions within the imperial family to spill over into feuding. He even showed deference to his fellow consul who was not obliged to swear an oath by Nero's *acta* (deeds).

In AD 55, Nero poisoned Britannicus. His killing was unsubtle, poisoned at the emperor's own dinner table. The immediate motive for this action is rather implausibly given as threats from Agrippina to elevate Britannicus in Nero's place (how long would she herself have survived such a coup?). An account of Britannicus winning sympathy after being bullied into a recitation by Nero, and managing to recite creditably a piece that recalled the loss of his patrimony seems to provide a more likely cause for his removal; it showed that Britannicus was capable of securing sympathy and was sufficiently mature to make a public impression (Suetonius, *Nero*, 33.2; Tacitus, *Annales*, 13. 14–17; Dio, 61. 7.4). The killing did not bring about any change in policy. Nero maintained reasonable relations with the senate. Few can have been shocked by Britannicus' death.

Nero continued to suppress factional disputes and there may have been attempts to strike at the heart of the imperial court. Tacitus records accusations against Agrippina, a Rubellius Plautus, Faustus Cornelius Sulla Felix and Burrus (Tacitus, *Annales*, 13. 19–23) and Dio records an accusation against Seneca (Dio, 61. 10.1). None of these cases came to anything. Nero maintained his court and together they avoided conflict with each other and the senate. It was not until 61 or perhaps 62 that Nero came into conflict with elements of the senatorial aristocracy, but by then Nero's policy had changed and the court of his first years had disintegrated.

The end of the beginning

Although Nero continued to allow the senate notable freedom, which led to some political activity reminiscent of the Republican period (a dispute between a tribune and a praetor which resulted in the senate – not the emperor – intervening and rebuking the tribune and a quarrel between various members of the senate and Helvidius Priscus – of whom we shall hear more – over Priscus' zealous administration of the treasury (Tacitus, *Annales*, 13. 28)), there were signs that Nero was looking for new outlets for his energy. The story of

Julius Montanus illustrates Nero's own behaviour. Nero had taken to wandering the streets in disguise, accompanied by a band of his friends. This gang visited taverns and brothels and got involved in fights. On one of these outings, the gang met Julius Montanus, his wife, and (one presumes) a group of his slaves or friends. Montanus' wife was insulted and Montanus reacted by attacking the gang. Nero himself was beaten up and apparently had to stay out of sight for several days because of his bruises. Nero would have let the incident pass (indeed, what else could he have done? To let everyone know that he had been roaming the streets and had assaulted a senator's wife would not bring him credit, and to admit that his gang had been beaten up by the said senator and his followers would also bring dishonour), but Montanus wrote a note apologising. Nero could not then pretend that he had not been involved nor maintain the illusion that his disguise had fooled Montanus. By admitting knowledge of what he had done, Montanus changed his offence from having embarrassed his emperor, to having committed treason by knowingly assaulting him. Nero replied, 'So he knew he was hitting Nero'. Montanus killed himself (Dio, 61. 9.4; Tacitus, *Annales*, 13. 25).

Nevertheless, the senate continued to gain confidence. C. Cassius Longinus amended a proposal concerning the celebrations for Nero's early successes in Armenia by noting that there was a danger that no work would be done in Rome if the number of holidays continued to increase (Tacitus, *Annales*, 13. 41). This same Cassius was sent as a senatorial representative to sort out feuding in the Campanian town of Puteoli, though his mission was unsuccessful and, on his request, two brothers, P. Sulpicius Scribonianus Proculus and P. Sulpicius Scribonianus Rufus (see p. 203 for the later career of these brothers) were sent out to replace him (Tacitus, *Annales*, 13. 48). Thrasea Paetus attacked the over-indulgence of Syracuse in applying to stage more sets of games than were currently allowed (Tacitus, *Annales*, 13. 49). The senate appears to have conducted trials free from overt imperial interference; some trials were even removed from Nero's jurisdiction. Pomponia Graecina, wife of Aulus Plautius, the conqueror of Britain, was accused of foreign superstitions. Since Plautius was prominent and Graecina was connected to the imperial family, the trial was political, but Nero allowed the trial to take place in a family court, according to ancient custom (Tacitus, *Annales*, 13. 32). Corruption trials took place with varying results and among these trials a certain Cossutianus Capito (who became prominent later) was condemned for corruption and exiled (Tacitus, *Annales*, 13. 33).

Storm clouds were, however, gathering. In 58, P. Suillius Rufus was tried on a charge of accepting payments for advocacy, which was regarded as a form of corruption (Tacitus, *Annales*, 13. 42). He responded with an attack on Seneca's corruption. Since Suillius was one of the best orators of the period, it is likely that the speech had some impact. Suillius and Cossutianus Capito had come under attack during the reign of Claudius and were probably both associates of Messalina (Tacitus, *Annales*, 11. 6).

Tacitus also dates the first appearance of Poppaea Sabina to this year (Tacitus, *Annales*, 13. 44–5; Dio, 61. 11.2). Poppaea was well connected. Her father had been a friend of Sejanus and her grandfather one of Tiberius' generals (Tacitus, *Annales*, 1.80; 4. 46–50; 5. 10; 6. 39). She married an equestrian, but had an illicit relationship with Otho, the future emperor and one of Nero's close associates. Otho married Poppaea and this brought her into the imperial court where she became involved with Nero. Otho was packed off to Lusitania, which he governed with some skill. Nero, however, was faced with a problem. He was married to Octavia. The relationship between the two was probably not close, yet there would be a political price to pay for her removal. It seems possible, as our sources suggest, that Agrippina and Burrus supported Octavia, but this is one of the places in the tradition that invention must be suspected: our sources' knowledge of this intimate family business seems too good to be true. For the moment, the relationship with Poppaea remained illicit, if public.

Agrippina may have seen this new lover as a threat and she seems to have made an increased effort to exert influence over her son. It is in this period that accusations of incest are levelled against the pair. Tacitus doubts whether their relationship was incestuous, quoting two sources on the issue, though he notes that Agrippina's previous behaviour would not encourage one to believe anything but the worst about her sexual behaviour. Dio also questions the tradition, but tells us that Nero kept a mistress who looked like Agrippina (Dio, 61. 11.3; Suetonius, *Nero*, 28.2; Tacitus, *Annales*, 14. 2).

In 59, Nero decided to murder his mother. Such an action surely demands a psychological rather than a political explanation even in the strange world of Claudian family relationships, but we know too little of Nero's psyche to explain adequately his motivation. It was a crisis, perhaps a turning point for the regime. One can only speculate that Nero was finding his mother an embarrassment: he could not restrain her political activities, nor fend off her interference and perhaps he feared her disapproval of his relationships. Her exile would require a trial, create a powerful enemy, and would look cruel. A covert removal had its advantages.

The method chosen was unique, and I find it difficult to believe that it has ever been replicated. We could market the story as a handbook from Ancient History: 'Nero's Guide on How not to murder your mother', perhaps alongside 'Claudius' Guide to Marital Relations' and 'Caligula's Guide to Winning Friends'.

At the theatre, Nero had seen a boat built to collapse on purpose as part of the act. His admiral, Anicetus, volunteered to build another that would facilitate a fatal accident. After dinner with Nero, Agrippina was escorted in this ship towards her villa across the bay of Naples. The boat collapsed. But Agrippina was lying on her couch and the falling lead-weighted roof was supported by the couch's raised end. She ended up in the sea. One of her companions cried out for help, claiming to be the emperor's mother. The companion was clubbed to death. Agrippina swam away, incidental evidence that Roman aristocratic women not only enjoyed a level of social and political independence, but also took exercise. When it became light, she was picked up by a fishing boat and returned to her villa.

Now aware of the conspiracy, she had little choice but to ignore it and wrote to her son saying that she had survived an unfortunate accident and although not seriously injured, would prefer to rest, without a visit from the emperor. Nero panicked and summoned Burrus and Seneca. They were informed of the failed plot. There was silence. Seneca asked Burrus whether the praetorians would act against Agrippina. He informed Nero that they would not. Anicetus volunteered his disgraced sailors. Nero accepted. A dagger was planted on Agrippina's messenger and thus justification was provided for her murder. The arrival of the soldiers at Agrippina's villa can hardly have been unexpected. She asked them to strike at her belly since it was from there that her son, the emperor and matricide, had sprung. So runs the extraordinary account (Dio, 61. 13: Suetonius, *Nero*, 34; Tacitus, *Annales*, 14. 3–10).

These were dramatic moments, vividly portrayed. Yet, we must wonder. The meeting with Anicetus, Seneca and Burrus must have been secret, yet Tacitus seems to know exactly what went on and claims that confusion only arose in his sources when Nero came to view his mother's body, a moment which must have offered ample scope to historians with a taste for dramatic embellishment. Much of the life of the emperor was conducted in semi-public, surrounded by a retinue of slaves, freedmen and hangers-on, but who would know what went on in this meeting and live to tell of it? We may accept the broad outlines of the story (the collapsible boat is so ridiculous that it must be true), but the detail looks like fiction.

On the discovery of Nero's plot, the court contemplated stark alternatives. They must either connive in the crime of matricide or turn against Nero. Even if Burrus is not reported correctly, his summary of the likely attitude of the praetorians may have been accurate: Agrippina was the daughter of Germanicus and was popular with the soldiers. They could not be ordered to kill her. Also, perhaps Burrus had qualms about being the man responsible for ordering the death of the emperor's mother. Nevertheless, even if Agrippina could be controlled, the obvious divisions at the heart of the imperial family might seriously weaken its position. With Agrippina dead, there would be more chance of gaining acquiescence in a crime that could not be altered.

Having killed her, Nero wrote to the senate to inform them of the conspiracy against him and met the officers of the praetorians. Both the praetorians and senate acclaimed Nero's 'victory'. Thrasea Paetus walked out of the senate in disgust. Tacitus says that he was 'thus endangering himself without bringing freedom any nearer' (Tacitus, *Annales*, 14. 10–12), a harsh judgement. This was a crucial moment. Thrasea may have felt that there was an opportunity to overthrow Nero. If a leader emerged in the senate, there would have been a possibility that the praetorians would not defend Nero. The crime itself left no doubt as to the character of Nero. As Thrasea is claimed to have intimated later, with such a brutal leader, death was inevitable (Dio, 61. 15.3). If not at this moment of crisis, when would the senate act? Of course, the answer to Thrasea's presumed question was obvious: the senators would never act.

Nero entered Rome triumphantly. He had emerged from the crisis. He had shown that he could commit the greatest of crimes and remain in power. Nero made some attempt to regain senatorial support by recalling enemies of his mother who had been in exile, but his relationship with the senate was changed. Anyone who might have somehow forgotten that the regime was absolute in its power had been reminded of political realities by the death of Agrippina. In 60, Nero invited Rubellius Plautus to retire because of gossip about him as a possible rival to the emperor (Tacitus, *Annales*, 14. 22). In 61, a scandal involving a forged will led to the exile of three senators; political motivations may be suspected (Tacitus, *Annales*, 14. 40). Neither were momentous events, though the exile of Plautus suggests an undercurrent of uncertainty and dissatisfaction among the Roman aristocracy, but both suggest that Nero was taking a harder line with senators.

The crisis may have seriously weakened the existing powers at court (both Seneca and Burrus were originally Agrippina's men), but the end of the old court was delayed until 62. In that year Burrus died of throat cancer, though inevitably there were accusations that his death was assisted (Dio, 62. 13.3; Tacitus, *Annales*, 14. 51–2). Seneca requested permission to retire and give up his fortune, which was refused, but if this was a bid to restore his power by demonstrating his loyalty to the regime, it failed. Seneca was soon effectively retired with a convenient illness (Tacitus, *Annales,* 14. 53–6). Most significantly, Octavia was divorced, convicted of infertility. Crowds demonstrated on her behalf and attacked images of her successor Poppaea. So Nero escalated. Octavia's slaves were tortured in order to extract a confession of adultery. This failed. Nero then turned to Anicetus who had until now been kept at arm's length. He confessed to adultery and was exiled to Sardinia, a comfortable retirement considering the alternatives. Octavia was sent to Pandateria, the prison island, and then executed (Tacitus, *Annales*, 14. 59–64).

There were other deaths in this year, the increasing violence suggesting a purge or at least a considerable worsening of relations within the Roman political elite. Antistius Sosianus was charged with reciting slanderous verses about Nero at a dinner party. Thrasea Paetus managed to persuade the senate to spare his life, much to Nero's displeasure (Tacitus, *Annales*, 14. 48–9). Faustus Cornelius Sulla Felix (who had been exiled for conspiracy in 58) and Rubellius Plautus were both killed (Tacitus, *Annales*, 14. 57–9). Domitia Lepida, Nero's aunt, also died and our sources attribute her passing to the orders of Nero (Dio, 61 17.1). The freedmen Pallas and Doryphoros were killed (Tacitus, *Annales*, 14. 65). There may have been a mysterious allegation against Seneca and L. Calpurnius Piso (Tacitus, *Annales*, 14. 65). Aulus Didius

Gallus Fabricius Veiento suffered condemnation for a literary attack on Nero and his works were destroyed (Tacitus, *Annales*, 14. 50).

Burrus was replaced as praetorian prefect by Faenius Rufus (a popular appointment according to our sources since he had supervised the grain supply with some skill) and Ofonius Tigellinus (Tacitus, *Annales*, 14. 51). Tigellinus' son-in-law was Cossutianus Capito. Together, these two would conduct Nero's political trials. Both had been exiled by the senate previously and had many enemies. Their prominence gave many just cause to fear.

The court was also transformed. Nero married Poppaea Sabina. He surrounded himself with a host of courtiers, many (though not all) of whom were of relatively low status: freedmen and actors. The court no longer tried to reconcile itself with the senate, but instead searched for new ways of displaying its power and representing the greatness of its central figure. Nero began to make more direct use of his power, a power which had been made clear by the death of Agrippina. Increasingly, they broke with established precedents and transgressed moral and political laws. In so doing, they established the notorious atmosphere of artistic endeavour and moral inventiveness that characterised Nero's reign.

Breaking rules: The Emperor as artist

By AD 59, Nero was looking to take a more active part in the artistic life of the empire. He had already built an amphitheatre on the Campus Martius (Tacitus, *Annales*, 13. 31), but this represented only an indirect involvement. He had an enclosed arena constructed in which he could drive chariots hidden from public view (Tacitus, *Annales*, 14. 14). This 'private' chariot driving was mirrored by a first 'private' stage appearance at the Juvenalia. This festival of youth encouraged the participation of many among the nobility, including (apparently) a woman of 80. Some of the performers who had chosen to wear masks had their identities forcibly revealed though the festival, held in Nero's gardens, was technically private. Nero also became more interested in philosophy and began to take an interest in poetry (Tacitus, *Annales*, 14. 14–16; 15. 33; Dio, 61. 19).

In 60, Nero introduced the Neronia, which was a festival that imitated the major Greek events in both regularity and in types of competition (Dio, 61. 21; Tacitus, *Annales*, 14. 20–21; 47; Suetonius, *Nero*, 12.3–4.). Nero himself probably gave no public dramatic performances until 64 when he took to the stage in Naples (Suetonius, *Nero*, 20; Tacitus, *Annales*, 15. 33). Naples was a significant choice since it prided itself on its Greek origins and Greek culture. Nero's first appearance on the public stage in Rome took place in the following year (Tacitus, *Annales*, 16. 4–5; Suetonius, *Nero*, 21) We cannot detail Nero's subsequent appearances on stage, though he probably entertained Tigranes in 66 to a display of his singing and chariot-driving (Dio, 63. 3–6), before he crossed to Greece. In Greece, he progressed in triumph, winning every prize, even though he fell from his chariot in one race. He completed his trip by freeing Greece from Roman sovereignty and granting Roman citizenship to the judges who had so generously awarded him first place. His return was celebratory. He entered Naples first, the scene of his debut, and then marched to Rome, the conquering artistic hero (Dio, 63. 8.2–10.2; 14, 20; Suetonius, *Nero*, 22–5).

Generally, our sources suggest that stage appearances were demeaning, but even Thrasea Paetus, a paragon of conservative morality, had made a stage appearance in his hometown of Patavium, though perhaps in a semi-private event (Dio, 62. 26.3; Tacitus, *Annales*, 16. 21). This brief stage career was not sufficient to reduce his status in the eyes of Roman traditionalists. It seems unlikely that there was an objection to acting in itself, but to appear on the public stage and to pander to the pleasures of the masses was probably thought contrary to the dignity of a Roman aristocrat and unsuitable for the ruler of the world.

Many observers appear to have been confused by the exhibition (though, once more, the credibility of anecdotes must be questioned). Tiridates, for instance, appears not to have understood why the Romans would follow such a man (Dio, 63. 6.4). One soldier, observing his emperor in chains on stage, rushed to release him (Dio, 63. 10.2). Such stories demonstrate a failure of normal dramatic convention. Nero remained Nero even when on stage. In case any failed to notice, Nero was sometimes accompanied onto stage by the praetorian prefects and in particular roles was bound by golden chains rather than by the normal iron (Suetonius, *Nero* 21; Dio, 63. 9–4). The crowds observed their emperor, not the play.

Actors were often very popular in Rome. Their position allowed them to turn lines of a play into political commentary and crowds would cheer a line appropriate to contemporary circumstances. For Nero, to perform was to appear before his people. He had his own 'claque': an organised group of supporters who would clap in a certain rhythmical way in support of the emperor. The praetorians insisted on a rapturous response to Nero's performances. We can also understand his need to involve others of the Roman elite in such shows. By enforcing participation, Nero could show his artistic superiority, his dominance over the aristocracy politically, artistically and culturally, and display that dominance before the largest gatherings of the people of Rome whose cheers (enforced or voluntary) reinforced his authority.

His performance of poetry can be considered in the same light. Tacitus suggests that his verse was weak, not in its metrical correctness, but in direction and thought, since the verse was composed by committee and so lost all originality (Tacitus, *Annales*, 14. 16). Suetonius (*Nero*, 52), who refers to Nero's notebooks, suggests that Nero composed and amended the verse himself. Dio (62. 29.1–2) tells us that Nero was composing a historical epic that would cover the whole history of Rome. In some ways, however, what mattered was not content but context. Nero positioned himself at the centre of a court circle of poets asserted his status as a patron and leader of the arts.

Nero's other great contribution was in architecture. In 64, a fire swept through much of Rome. Only four of the fourteen districts survived more or less intact, while seven were badly damaged and three destroyed. Nero made the most of this opportunity and, indeed, was so enthusiastic about the task of rebuilding Rome that it was rumoured (almost certainly falsely) that he had been responsible for causing the fire in the city. Nero introduced a series of building regulations. The height of buildings was restricted and the partitions between buildings were regulated to stop fire passing so easily and quickly from building to building. The street plan may have been reorganised to produce wider streets and fewer alleys, which would also discourage the spread of fire and aid fire-fighting (Suetonius, *Nero*, 16.1; Tacitus, *Annales* 15. 38–43).

The most notable monument built was, however, the Domus Aurea, the Golden House of Nero. This was a huge construction that bridged the Palatine and Esquiline Hills. The vestibule was of sufficient size to accommodate a 120-foot-high statue of Nero. The palace was fronted by a triple colonnade that stretched out for a mile. Extensive gardens were attached to the house, including vineyards, woods and pastures, all stocked with appropriate animals and, around a pool, there were models of buildings. There were rooms of immense luxury: a dining room with an ivory ceiling, another that revolved. The baths were filled with sea water and sulphur water. It was a dominating monument of conspicuous luxury. The building monumentalised Nero's domination of the city of Rome. Here was a representation of the world within a city, all overseen by the towering presence of Nero (Suetonius, *Nero*, 31; Tacitus, *Annales*, 15. 42–3). Nero's house was a public expression of his power.

Nero also knew how to party. The most notorious party was given by Tigellinus. The gathering took place in the centre of a theatre, turned into an artificial lake. It is the kind of incident that Dio loves to relate. The waters of the lake became a giant 'wine-cooler' and around the edges of the lake were taverns and booths in which wine flowed freely. In the centre, the lords of misrule, Tigellinus and Nero, watched the unfolding anarchy. The taverns and booths were occupied by women, chosen for their beauty, prostitutes and respectable women. The result was, supposedly, a drunken orgy, a night when order was lost. Fathers watched the rape of their daughters. Slaves raped their mistresses. People were even killed (Dio, 62. 15). Dio's account is sensationalist (compare Tacitus, *Annales,* 15. 37), but not completely out of keeping with other reports: celebrations at the Juvenalia were also supposedly orgiastic (Tacitus, *Annales*, 14. 15; Suetonius, *Nero*, 27).

Nero's sexual behaviour was, like that of Gaius, unconventional. The details of his relationship with his mother are obscure. Nero's acquisition of Poppaea was adulterous. He celebrated two 'marriages' to men, Pythagoras and Sporus (who was castrated), both marriages post-dating the death of Sabina. The open nature of these relationships is more interesting than the fact of the relationships themselves. Romans worried about status issues within homosexual relationships and received Greek ideas about the 'proper' role for a man being to penetrate the object of his affections, the gender being less material. But Nero advertised himself as taking both the male (penetrating) and female (penetrated) roles. Other stories of Nero's sexual activities circulated, stories of sadistic sexual attacks on victims while he was wearing animal skins. All these stories suggest that Nero was out of control, a tyrant enslaved by his passions and incapable of ruling himself or an empire. Such stories justified rebellion (Suetonius, *Nero*, 28–9; 35.4; Dio, 62. 28.2–3; 63. 13.)

Yet, Nero's court was a place of sophistication and wit as well as debauchery. It sponsored a resurgence in the arts. The writer Petronius (Tacitus, *Annales*, 16. 17–21) was, for a short time, near the centre of the court until he became another victim of the Pisonian conspiracy (see pp. 201–202). The sophistication of his *Satyricon*, undeniably pornographic in many places, suggests that Nero's reign was not just about consumption, but concerned a demonstration of taste. The *Satyricon* plays frequently on the idea of the voyeur, trapping the narrator into accounts in which perverse sexual acts are viewed and recounted, and the moral line between the reader, the viewer who narrates the acts, and the sexual performers is uncomfortably blurred. If we transfer the moral complexities to the orgies of Tigellinus and Nero, arguably the viewers (Nero and Tigellinus), the readers (us), and the rapists are all caught in a moral morass.

One of the other great writers of the age was Lucan, whose epic poem, *Pharsalia*, which is sometimes called *The Civil War*, recounts the war between Julius Caesar and Pompey. The book opens with a paean of praise for Nero and an assertion that all that is about to be recounted is justifiable since it leads to the present good fortune. Yet, the foundational narrative of the Principate is one of blood, madness, and revolution. It gives us a lunatic Julius Caesar, bent on universal destruction, a Pompey weak and despairing, turning away eventually from public life in Rome, and a Cato, filled with nihilism, experiencing the world's end. Lucan was, eventually, to be killed in the aftermath of the Pisonian conspiracy (as we shall see), but it is in some ways surprising that such a poem could be written.

And then, there was Seneca. Seneca was, of course, politically involved and close to the court during the early years of Nero's principate. For a busy man, there is a formidable surviving literary output. His letters and philosophical treatises focused on a range of political and philosophical ideas. He was a stoic and was particularly concerned with issues of emotion. Stoics worried that emotion was potentially irrational. Rationality was what divided the human from the animal, but also provided criteria by which one can divide humans: women and barbarians were more prone to irrational passions (such as anger and grief) than proper men and the ideal philosopher/leader was someone who could regard problems without emotion. Some of this literature (notably the *de Clementia* [*On Clemency*] and the *De Ira* [*On Anger*]) had a focus on the behaviour of political leaders and can be read (and indeed has been read) as guidance for princes in which Nero emerges as an ideal philosopher-king. There is an obvious discrepancy between the historical Nero (who is in many ways the archetypical tyrant), and the image of the ideal emperor in Seneca's writing. But Seneca's writings attest a continuing sophisticated debate on politics and the nature of the imperial regime in the Neronian period.

Nero's cultural policy was a break from the achievements of his predecessors. He did not rule as army commander or as one of the senate or as a god among men, but as a cultural giant. Nero's urge to experiment with new ways of presenting his power inevitably led him to the theatre. Nero's artistic revolution created a new form of tyranny and Nero sought to establish the equivalence of that tyranny with past achievements. His triumph in Greece must be understood in this light. There are notable similarities between Nero's triumphal progression and those of the second-century BC Romans who had conquered the region. But Nero's domination of culture was a dangerous policy. Some responded in kind with ironic attacks. Thus, Petronius, informed of his death sentence, responded with a letter detailing and satirising Nero's sexual acts. More popular acts of rebellion came at the theatre. Nero's audience was coerced into reaction through the troops, but audiences could subvert by inappropriate laughter or tears. Others simply escaped, leaping from the walls of the theatre or feigning death. Nero might enforce the participation of some of the aristocracy, but others would remain unconverted. Standing in the theatre, receiving the applause of the crowd and backed by the praetorian guard, the opposition of Thrasea Paetus might seem a minor problem, but opposition was easily expressed and with subtlety: all opponents needed to do was adhere to traditional Roman values.

Inevitably, much popular attention has focused on the sex life of the emperor. Sex has been read as symbolic of moral decline, transferring a Roman concern with sexual status and sex as an expression of power into Christian moralistic concerns with sex as passion and sin and a sign of fundamental psychological and moral infirmity. But the sex acts of Nero were public: this was immorality on display. We could thus read Nero's sexual antics in the same way we can read Gaius' divinity, as an act or power and a display of power. But there is more to it. Sex with Sporus was indeed an act of power, but who would be impressed? The sex was in defiance of convention, but it seems unlikely that Nero merely wanted to shock (and we may assume that Nero's passions were common to many men of the Roman elite). Nero was above being constrained by the traditional morals of the Republican age, by the traditions of Rome, but Nero was also establishing a new convention. Presiding over the orgiastic parties, he advertised the newness of his regime and his moral approach. If to be Roman was to abide by the traditional morals of Rome, then Nero's rejection of those moral values creates a fundamental problem in Roman identity politics.

Let us see the problem from a Neronian perspective. Rome was a historical culture. Roman values had grown over centuries and the Romans venerated the traditions. Those traditions were a form of cultural memory. Cultural memory is a concept used by anthropologists and sociologists to explain why people within a particular culture behave in similar ways or believe similar things. Individuals have a memory of things that have happened to them, but they also remember important stories which form part of the cultural memory of a society. Arguably, Nero is part of our cultural memory, the immoral autocrat who fiddled while Rome burned. Cultural memories do not have to be accurate renditions of the past, just meaningful memories (or stories). Rome had a cultural memory of the long period of imperial expansion when the citizens were moral, simple folk, living without luxury and with devotion to the state. That state was based around a hierarchical system, with the senators at the top, but in which all citizens enjoyed a certain basic equality. To a great extent Augustus and Tiberius had attempted to maintain those traditions. Even Claudius had paid lip-service to the old traditions of Rome and senatorial governance, lecturing the senators on historical subjects while relying on the very untraditional and unrepublican power of the praetorians to support his regime. Since the position of emperor was incompatible with those traditions, the power of the emperor could only be maintained in contravention of those traditions, arguably through the threat of or the actual application of violent power.

Like all the other emperors, Nero had to work through this political paradox. By the Neronian period, the politics of this paradox appear to have been worked out. There was no serious Republican movement. The subservience of the senate was firmly established. Nero came a generation after Tiberius and there was little point in pretending that the emperor was the servant of the senate. Culturally, however, the problems remained fundamental. Nero's position was incompatible with what it was to be Roman, with the traditions of Rome, and the myths of Roman identity. His position was potentially in conflict with the political provision of the continued Republic. His response was to reinvent Rome. The great virtue of cultural memory from a politician's point of view is that it can be manipulated. Neronian orgies were not, therefore, just an outlet for uncontrolled passion or a violent expression of the ability of imperial power to corrupt, but a political statement of Nero's refusal to be bound by the old and the conventional. Sex was never more political than in the reign of Nero. The engagement with Greece and with Hellenistic culture marked an attempt to make a new form of identity in which to be Roman was to follow Nero. Nero's tour of Greece and his engagement with Naples also suggested that he looked to the empire and its traditions in new ways: rather than an empire solely embedded in Italian values, Nero offered a Hellenised Greek–Italian memory. It was precisely this union of Greek and Roman culture in an imperial setting that was to be celebrated in literature, speeches, games, and behaviour by the emperor Hadrian two generations later. But unlike Nero, Hadrian has gone down in history (perhaps unfairly) as one of the five good emperors of the second century. Perhaps even Seneca's political philosophy was about breaking with the old values and finding a new morality and mode of governing in Greek philosophical teachings. The whole point of Nero's reign was to remake the culture of power, to break with the political culture of the past, and to invent a new cultural politics. Although that project failed, we need not consider it misconceived.

The counterpoint to Neronian revolutionary activity was to establish an opposition. The weakness of cultural memory as a tool of political manipulation is that memories are not easily controlled. People can choose to remember different things. As Nero celebrated his new culture, his opponents celebrated the old. For them, what it was to be Roman was to adhere to a certain set of moral values embedded in tradition. Tempting though it might have been, it would be difficult for Nero to persecute someone for living conservatively. Nostalgia for a lost past (which is psychologically comfortable) could become an easy oppositional stance, and it is from the Neronian period that we see an increased prominence of a philosophical and intellectual opposition which drew on Republican traditions without ever seriously attempting a Republican revolution.

When modern politicians announce that history will be 'on their side', they mean that the future will inevitably show that they are right; for ancient politicians, history being on their side meant that their moral and political values were embedded in the past. History was not and never would be on Nero's side.

Administration, government and foreign affairs

Nero's reign eventually collapsed into an anarchy that resulted, in part, from his administrative failings. We shall consider his policy at home and abroad separately, though, as we shall see, the two areas were interrelated.

Home affairs

As with several other regimes, Nero started by promising to break with the past, to behave as a good emperor should and refer matters to open debate in the senate. The particular targets of senatorial ire were Claudius' freedmen. Nero did break with 'freedmen government'. Kallistos, Gaius' influential freedman, had died during the reign of Claudius. Narcissus and Pallas, two of the more prominent of Claudius' freedmen, were both removed from power very quickly. Yet, administrative structures were unaltered. The same offices continued to be filled by freedmen and, although these men were initially less prominent, they were probably influential. Nero was generous towards some of his freedmen: Doryphoros received extravagant gifts (Dio, 61. 5.4–5) and Pythagoras became prominent, though it is unclear whether his talents were sexual. When Nero went on his grand tour of Greece, he supposedly left his freedman Helios in effective control though, as in the reign of Claudius, it is impossible to reconstruct the inner workings of government to ascertain who was making the decisions (Dio, 63. 12.1).

Nero was, perhaps surprisingly, concerned with social status and adopted a conservative policy in this regard. He restricted social mobility by attacking the privileges and wealth of freedmen and their descendants (perhaps also breaking with Claudius). Sons of freedmen were prevented from joining the senate and those already in the senate saw their careers blocked by a ban on them holding office, a measure which can be interpreted as increasing the dignity of the senate and magistrates (Suetonius, *Nero*, 15.2). Nero also picked on freedmen when he grew short of money, claiming five-sixths of their estates on death (Suetonius, *Nero*, 32). They were an easy target: the Roman elite would not be affected by the measures and many might even have approved. Social status was reinforced in privileges granted to equestrians. The *equites* were to enjoy reserved seating at the circus as well as the theatre (Tacitus, *Annales*, 15. 32). Thus, in both arenas, the Romans would sit by status group.

The most violent example of this concern with social order came with the case of L. Pedanius Secundus. In 57, the senate had passed a law which decreed that if a master was killed by his slaves, those freed by his will who were within the household were to be killed (Tacitus, *Annales*, 13. 32). This reinforced the law that laid down that all the slaves within the household of a master murdered by a slave were to be considered guilty and executed. This measure seems to reflect a general concern about the disciplining of the servile and can also be seen in a proposal to limit the independence of freedmen, which had been rejected (after detailed consideration) in the previous year (Tacitus, *Annales*, 13. 26–7). In 61, the former prefect of the city, L. Pedanius Secundus, was murdered by his slaves. Secundus was notably brutal and maintained a very large household. There was considerable public and senatorial sympathy for those slaves not directly involved in the killing, but the senators resolved to apply the law and in this they were supported by Nero. The plebs, however, had sympathy for the slaves and rioted. Nero called out the praetorians to enforce public order (Tacitus, *Annales*, 14. 42–5).

Such conservatism contrasts with Nero's willingness to defy social conventions in other areas, but may also explain another notorious aspect of Nero's reign: his persecution of the Christians. The reasons for the persecution of the Christians are a matter of controversy (see pp. 414–16), but it seems that Nero was driven to this persecution by the fire of Rome. The Christians were probably seen as subversive, but Nero's attacks on the community were savage and aroused sympathy even in those hostile to the Christians (Tacitus, *Annales*, 15. 44).

Nero frequently sat in court himself and Suetonius tells us that he took care not to come to an impetuous decision. He took advice (as was the custom among all judges) but, in order to avoid political influence and to encourage considered opinions, he insisted on advice being given secretly and in writing so that he could contemplate the case overnight before giving judgement in the morning. When dealing with a capital case, Nero seems to have signed the death warrants with a show of reluctance, a reluctance which at least suggests careful judgement (Suetonius, *Nero*, 10, 15). Such care is shown in a case of senatorial corruption when Acilius Strabo was prosecuted in 59. Strabo had been presented with a complex legal problem concerning tenure of estates that had belonged to the king of Cyrene before the kingdom had passed to Rome. Strabo's investigation had found that the current holders of the land had no legal right to the land. Though illegally acquired, this land may have been in private hands for 150 years and the landowners took Strabo to court. Nero, to whom the senate passed the case, found in favour of Strabo but offered compensation to the landowners (Tacitus, *Annales*, 14. 18).

Nero appears to have curbed the activities of informers. The system whereby informers were rewarded with a portion of the estate of their victim was unpopular since it encouraged malicious prosecutions. Nero did not remove the incentive altogether; he merely significantly reduced the portion of the estates that could be claimed by the informer (Suetonius, *Nero*, 10). Care was also taken in the collection of taxes. Helvidius Priscus first rose to prominence over his assiduous collection of taxes at the treasury, possibly a matter of some controversy, since it was often the politically powerful who avoided taxes. Nero published regulations concerning the farming of taxes since the activities of tax farmers (see Glossary) had been causing complaints and he toyed with the idea of abolishing certain taxes altogether in order to end corruption (Tacitus, *Annales*, 13. 31, 50–1).

Nero also resumed the policy of founding military colonies in Italy that had been discontinued after the early years of Augustus' reign. Military colonies were established at Capua and Nuceria (in 57) (Tacitus, *Annales*, 13. 31), Antium and Tarentum (in 60) (Tacitus, *Annales*, 14. 27). Puteoli (also in 60), Pompeii and Tegeanum also received the title of colony, though it is unclear whether any veterans were sent to these towns. Antium was Nero's birthplace and marked out for particular honours. It was a favourite haunt of the imperial family. Pompeii was connected with Poppaea Sabina. Tacitus (*Annales*, 13.31; 14.27) tells that the veteran colonisation failed since most of the veterans wandered back to the provinces in which they had served.

Nero's personal generosity probably led to the depletion of the treasury. Suetonius (*Nero*, 30) has fantastic stories of his gifts. A more serious blow to state finances was probably the extravagance and number of his games and shows. For example, to encourage the actors, when staging a play in which a house burnt down, Nero allowed them to keep all the costly furnishings they rescued from the house. He also used such occasions to distribute largesse to the people by throwing precious objects into the audience (Suetonius, *Nero*, 11–13). One guesses that the Neronia and the entertainments offered for the state visit of Tigranes were expensive. The trip to Greece and the huge entourage must also have weakened the finances of the imperial household. Donatives to the people and to the praetorians also drained the treasury.

Nero's building plans were huge. The Domus Aurea was the highlight of an extensive programme that, as previously mentioned, included amphitheatres and baths, a *macellum* (a food market), the Domus Transitoria (a precursor of the Domus Aurea burnt down in the fire), and a gymnasium. The fire may have destroyed more than half of the city and Nero used the opportunity to widen streets and build porticoes. It is likely that many public buildings were damaged and, in addition to these longer-term costs, disaster relief must have drained the treasury (Dio, 62.16–18; Tacitus, *Annales*, 15. 38–41). Public response to Nero's rebuilding of the city was generally favourable, though the Domus Aurea seems to have been something of an exception. Nero's reconstruction of the city may also have been hampered by a plague that broke out in 65.

As ever, the exact state of imperial finances is rather difficult to establish, and the hostility towards Nero is such that any explicit statement by our sources has to be regarded with suspicion, but we have evidence which strongly suggests that Nero was in financial difficulties: the coins themselves. In AD 64–5, following the fire of Rome, the coinage was reformed. Nero's artistically successful moneyers started getting 5 to 12% more coins from a pound of gold bullion and 14% more coins from a pound of silver. It seems that the income derived from imperial estates and taxation was insufficient to meet the demands of expenditure and the only way to meet the shortfall was to get more coins from those that came in. Nero also started to issue some low-value token coinage, again probably because he could not collect sufficient bullion to meet his needs.

Conventionally, historians have regarded such a debasement as a bad thing, reducing trust in the coinage and being potentially inflationary. Yet, a debasement is not a devaluation. It is far from certain that those who used the coin would have been aware of the debasement. Unless they were skilled at assessing the purity of the metal or wanted to turn the coin into gold or silver (and this seems both an unlikely and specialised use for money), there would be no reason to devalue the coins and thus increases prices. We have no evidence of sudden losses of confidence in the coin. The main economic effect would have been to gradually increase the amount of coin in circulation and if anything that was likely to have beneficial effects since coin could be used for more transactions.

The debasement did ease a shortfall in taxation. A fiscal crisis may have encouraged imperial agents to squeeze provincials for new revenue. People may not have liked paying old taxes, but they hated paying new taxes. Taxation was an issue in Judaea where the financial demands of the governor provided the spark that led to the revolt of AD 66–70, and may have substantially contributed to the destabilisation of Nero's regime in other provinces.

Foreign affairs

Provincial governors

The early years of the reign of Nero are marked by a number of corruption trials involving governors (see Table 6.1) and other officials about which, unfortunately, we know very little. Most are briefly recorded in Tacitus (*Annales*, 13. 30; 33; 52; 14. 18; 46).

Unlike the corruption cases under Tiberius, these cases are not seen as examples of factional strife within the senate. The seeming end to the sequence in Tacitus need not suggest that trials for corruption ceased. Tacitus' pages become filled with more dramatic matters as Nero's relationship with the senate worsened after 60. Such trials may suggest either widespread corruption or a willingness of the authorities to stamp out corruption.

Josephus' history of the administration of Nero's procurators (governors) of Judaea before the great revolt is not encouraging. Felix (brother of Pallas), Festus (who is praised for suppressing political bandits), Albinus (a personally corrupt governor who undid all Festus' work), and Gessius Florus (who made the people long for the return of Albinus) were either corrupt or incompetent. The governors made attempts to raise taxes; illegal charges increased the burden on the Jewish population. Social unrest seems to have been a prominent feature of the period, and in Judaea this was tied to religious divisions which led to a very violent situation. The governors proved not only unable to remedy the ultimate source of the rising tension, Roman maladministration, but also failed to take effective measures to secure the province (Josephus, *Bellum Judaicum*, 2. 249–408).

The weaknesses of provincial administration are also demonstrated by the Boudiccan revolt. The story of the revolt is detailed in *Annales*, 14. 29–39 and by Dio, 62. 1–12. Dio and Tacitus differ in their accounts of the causes of the

Table 6.1 Trials of governors in Tacitus

Date	Province	Verdict
AD 56	Sardinia	Condemned
	Achaea	Acquitted
57	Asia	Died before case comes to trial
	Cilicia	Condemned
	Lycia	Acquitted
58	Africa	Acquitted
	Africa	Acquitted
59	Cyrene	Condemned
	Cyrene	Acquitted
60	Mauretania	Condemned

Note: We should probably add to this list Pollio and Laelianus, who served in Armenia (Dio, 61 6.6).

revolt, but both attribute the problems to financial and political maladministration culminating in a bungled attempt to reorganise the territory of the Iceni in East Anglia. The Iceni joined with another major tribe in the area, the Trinovantes, and, under the leadership of Boudicca, burnt Colchester, London and St Albans to the ground. They defeated the Ninth Legion, before succumbing to an army headed by the Fourteenth and Twentieth Legions led by the governor Suetonius Paulinus. Problems faced by the commander of the Second Legion in the south-west suggest that the revolt was supported by tribes other than those mentioned in the literary account. The financial pressure placed on the British, either due to the rapacity of the procurator Catus Decianus or of Seneca (whose greed was a major factor in the revolt according to Dio), was probably the major cause of the revolt and it is likely that such pressures would be felt by all provincials and not just those in the East of Britain. Paulinus conducted a winter campaign against the rebels who had failed to harvest the summer crops, which resulted in great hardship and conflict between Paulinus and the new procurator Classicianus. Eventually, a pretext was found for the recall of Paulinus, who was granted the great honour of a second consulship in 66, and the war was brought to an end.

In spite of this evidence of corruption, Tacitus' account of the trial of Claudius Timarchus of Crete in 63 suggests that the relationship between governors and provincials may have been changing (Tacitus, *Annales*, 15. 20). Timarchus was tried because he was said to have claimed that he arranged the votes of thanks on the governor's term of office. Timarchus claimed that he had such authority in the provincial assembly that governors who wished to be recognised and thanked for their administration of the province were dependent on his favour. Such votes would be communicated to the senate and emperor and it is to be assumed that a governor who failed to win the endorsement of his subjects would find it difficult to secure another appointment. Although the governor still wielded considerable power and had plenty of scope for corruption while in his province, the state of affairs is rather different from that of the Republic where a governor's power was only limited by the faint possibility that the provincials would be able to bring a successful corruption case once he had left office. The result of the Timarchus trial was that such votes of thanks were banned on the proposal of Thrasea Paetus, which was accepted by Nero: a boost for the powers of governors.

Towards the end of Nero's reign, there is evidence of some disruption in Egypt. Nero may have encouraged Greek groups within Egypt by granting additional privileges early in his reign, further encouraging the changes in Egyptian society brought about by the Roman conquest. Nero planned a visit to Egypt, perhaps to lead an expedition up the Nile against the Aithiopians. He had already sent two military officers to reconnoitre the area. The Prefect Caecina Tuscus was exiled, supposedly for the crime of swimming in the baths that had been built for Nero's prospective visit (Dio, 63 18.1), but there must be a possibility that our sources trivialise a more serious charge. The tax records of an Egyptian village suggest that the last years of Nero's reign saw a sudden increase in tax avoidance, perhaps a sign of economic difficulties, though such evidence must be treated with caution since it might reflect administrative rather than economic problems. An edict of Tiberius Julius Alexander is equally difficult to interpret (Smallwood 1967: no. 391). This edict was issued in 68 on the accession of the new emperor, Galba. Alexander made allusions to a whole series of petitions and complaints with which he had been presented and the decree was meant to reassure Egyptians of their privileges and stamp out abuses of power. This could be read as a response to real problems and part of a dialogue between prefect and people, but the circumstances of its promulgation, at the start of a new reign, also suggest that it had a propagandist value: the old bad times are over and new, just rule can be expected from Galba.

Armenia and Parthia

The problems of Rome dominate Tacitus' account of Nero's reign, but, as a contrast to these inglorious events and to the depressing listing of deaths, Tacitus also presents an extended account of the campaigns in Armenia. In so doing, Nero is contrasted with a more heroic and praiseworthy figure, Corbulo. Corbulo had been one of Claudius' leading generals and had been recalled by Claudius after a series of campaigns in Germany (p. 152).

In 54, the Parthians adopted a more interventionist policy in Armenia, though they were prevented from making significant gains by internal difficulties. Corbulo was sent to Armenia as a precaution against resumed hostilities (Tacitus, *Annales*, 13. 6). Armenia was a 'buffer state' between Parthia and Rome. Both states claimed authority over the region and some compromise normally prevailed.

Corbulo gathered his forces and worked closely with the governor of Syria. Open war may have been delayed until 58 when Armenia was invaded and secured by the Parthians (Tacitus, *Annales*, 13. 34–41). Corbulo invaded and conducted a long campaign without bringing about a decisive battle. He was, however, finally able to capture and destroy the Armenian capital, Artaxata, and drive the Parthians from Armenia. Campaigns continued into 60 with significant Roman victories in Armenia and neighbouring territories. The Romans were in a position to impose their own candidate on the throne and secure the area under Roman control (Tacitus, *Annales*, 14. 23–6). The governor of Syria died and Corbulo concentrated all troops in the region under his own command. In 61–2, war broke out with renewed intensity. By this time Corbulo had relinquished control of Armenia to a new governor, Caesennius, retaining control of Syria. The main action had been on the frontier between Syria and Parthia and although Corbulo again did not bring the Parthians to a decisive battle, almost impossible given the far greater mobility of the Parthian cavalry, he managed to prevent an invasion of Syria. A Parthian strike into Armenia brought notable success and the defeat and surrender of a Roman army under Paetus. Corbulo's relieving army arrived too late (Tacitus, *Annales*, 15. 1–18). Corbulo once more took charge of matters in Armenia and in 63 launched an invasion with a fresh army. The Parthians faced the prospect of another bitter struggle with Corbulo, who had the means to drive them once more from Armenia, and were willing to settle. A temporary settlement of the conflict may have appealed to Nero after a major Roman defeat and almost a decade of conflict. Corbulo negotiated. The Parthians accepted Nero's authority over the province and bowed down to his image. In return, the Romans agreed to appoint the Parthian nominee to the throne provided he journeyed to Rome to receive the honour from Nero personally (Tacitus, *Annales*, 15. 24–31).

Both sides could claim victories. The compromise that emerged, a Parthian ruler of Armenia who needed the blessing of the emperor, was to preserve the peace. Nero is said to have had plans for a further campaign in the East (Suetonius, *Nero*, 19), but the strains of the Jewish revolt meant that these came to nothing.

The West

Germany appears to have been comparatively quiet in this period. Indeed, commanders felt the situation was sufficiently secure that they could devote their attention to major civil engineering projects in order to keep the troops employed. There were problems with the Frisii in 58, who had seized some unoccupied Roman land on which to settle, and with an alliance between the Ampsivarii, Bructeri and Tencteri, but Roman military and diplomatic pressure led to the break-up of this dangerous alliance. The Ampsivarii suffered severe economic difficulties and the tribe dissolved. The same year also saw a battle between the Chatti and the Hermanduri that exhausted both tribes (Tacitus, *Annales*, 13. 53–7). Effective use of Rome's economic resources, limited military pressure and diplomacy ensured that the borders remained peaceful for much of the reign.

Nero inherited a half-conquered province in Britain. There had been significant unrest in the province and the governors had pursued an active military policy, pushing the boundaries of Roman political and military control further north and into Wales. Nero is supposed to have openly considered withdrawal from Britain, but rejected the idea (Suetonus, *Nero*, 18). Such a withdrawal was probably politically impossible and it is unlikely that it was ever seriously envisaged. Nero continued the Claudian policy of expansion until the Boudiccan revolt, after which a more cautious policy was adopted.

The Jewish revolt

The complete mishandling of the province of Judaea in this period is a notable indictment of Roman government. Our source for the revolt is in some ways excellent. Flavius Josephus was a leading figure in the revolt and commanded Jewish forces in Galilee, as well as being a member of the Jewish elite. He was well aware of the diplomatic and political background of the revolt. However, his close involvement clearly prejudices his account. The Jews were themselves divided and the fissures in Jewish society had been manifest long before the outbreak of the revolt. Armed gangs had roamed the countryside, though their political and religious motivations remain a matter of some dispute. Josephus was opposed to these groups, but the quality of the Roman government was such that men such as Josephus found common cause with the more extreme elements and united against the Romans. Political disputes continued between the various elements of the Jewish population and Josephus seems to have spent much of his time as general in Galilee attempting to secure his position against those who wished to revoke his command, or worse. After his defeat in Galilee, he was captured in mysterious and probably dishonourable circumstances by the Romans and then became a vocal supporter of the Roman cause. Josephus, therefore, needed to justify to his Roman audience his actions in revolting and explain his reasons for abandoning that revolt, perhaps particularly to Jewish readers. The result probably seriously distorts the position of Josephus' Jewish opponents, who continued the war and who must have regarded him as a traitor, and it confuses our understanding of the origins of the war.

Judaea had been troublesome for many decades and it was common for military forces to be sent from Syria to support the governor of the province. The Romans enjoyed significant support from the Jewish aristocracy in most periods and the aristocrats were probably able to dampen popular opposition to Rome. In 66, the procurator attempted to increase taxes and extract money from the sacred funds of the Temple. He then violently suppressed a petitioning crowd, but was unable to secure Jerusalem and a stand-off resulted that moved rapidly towards open rebellion. Cestius Gallus, the governor of Syria, marched on Jerusalem but found himself hopelessly outnumbered. Gallus withdrew, but was forced to fight a running battle with the Jews in order to extract even a remnant of his forces from Judaea. Such success encouraged a mass mobilisation of the Jewish population and the Romans were faced with a major problem.

Nero was in Greece at the time and appointed Vespasian to the command. Vespasian had served with distinction in Britain, but was of relatively humble origin and not to be feared. He set about gathering troops from across the East for his expedition. Although there was limited campaigning in 67 and 68, the civil wars that followed Nero's suicide delayed the suppression of the revolt and it was not until 70 that Vespasian's son Titus took Jerusalem (see pp. 222–23).

General policy

With the exception of the Parthian frontier, Nero seems to have been blessed with generally quiet borders. The two major revolts of the period demanded immediate attention and considerable resources. The fact that Nero never himself led a military expedition reinforces the impression of a non-military emperor. Nevertheless, there are grounds to doubt the traditional picture. Nero honoured military men such as Suetonius Paulinus and Corbulo (though the latter was eventually forced to kill himself). He may also have had more expansionist plans. He annexed the client kingdoms of Pontus and the Cottian Alps. His policy in Britain prior to 61 seems to have been expansionist. In the East, Nero conducted an aggressive campaign through Corbulo to secure Armenia, though the peace that resulted was essentially a compromise. We also have evidence of mysterious plans for expansion in the East, either to the south of Egypt or towards the Caspian Gates. These could be dismissed as wild romantic projects, but the invasion of Britain would have been placed in that category 30 years earlier. With the frontiers settled in other areas, such expeditions may have seemed a suitable outlet for Rome's military energies, and the building of baths in Egypt for Nero's visit suggests that Nero intended to lead these expeditions himself. Nero may have been aware of a political need to assert his authority as a general.

Nero and the opposition: the Emperor as tyrant

Thrasea Paetus

When Thrasea Paetus walked out of the senate on its acceptance of Agrippina's murder, he effectively turned himself into a focus of opposition. Thrasea became a symbol of old-fashioned conservative morality, a representation of the conscience of Rome and the most prominent member of what has been called the 'philosophical opposition'. Several of the figures who came out in opposition to Nero, and who suffered as a consequence, were interested in philosophical ideas and these ideas strengthened their resolution in the face of tyranny. A strong current in contemporary philosophy drew on stoicism and taught the intelligent man to free himself from emotions and not to fear death. The good man did what was right irrespective of the personal consequences; although a tyrant could take a life, he could not take a man's honour. The austere personal lives of many philosophers contrasted with the lifestyle of the emperor and court.

The view that there was a coherent 'intellectual opposition' to Nero has, however, been discredited. Although Thrasea and those around him were interested in philosophy, and it is likely that their philosophy gave them courage in facing Nero, we cannot identify these men with a particular philosophical school. Men from all parts of the political spectrum might patronise philosophers, and philosophers were active in Nero's court. An interest in intellectual matters did not lead to the adoption of a particular political position. Some took a more liberal view than others and Seneca, to give the most famous instance, was able to co-operate on exactly those issues that proved too much for Paetus.

Not only was there no consistent philosophy but the group did not form a political party that would be recognisable to modern eyes. There were prominent men and women surrounding Thrasea, such as Helvidius Priscus, L. Junius Arulenus Rusticus, Curtius Montanus, possibly Rufus Musonius and Barea Soranus, though the links between these men are sometimes a little obscure. Thrasea Paetus was married to Arria (see Figure 6.1), whose mother, also Arria, had been married to Caecina Paetus who was involved in the Scribonianus conspiracy against Claudius (see p. 165). Thrasea's daughter Fannia was married to Helvidius Priscus, who was executed by Vespasian (see pp. 235–37). The next generation was persecuted by Domitian (pp. 245–46).

The ideology of opposition passed from generation to generation within the family, and it seems likely that those who formed marital alliances with this family did so because of their approval of their style of politics, forming a dynasty of opposition. Other disaffected individuals associated themselves with the group. We do not see a political party, but a traditional Roman faction resting on ties of family and friendship as well as ideology.

Thrasea was something of an irritation to Nero. In 62, he led the senate in proposing exile rather than death for Antistius Sosianus, which provoked Nero into writing a note that confirmed the senate's right to do as it pleased, and noted that the senate could even have freed Antistius if it had so chosen (Tacitus, *Annales*, 14. 48–9). Nero's displeasure was evident. Yet, Thrasea managed to secure Nero's support in the debate surrounding the trial of Claudius Timarchus (above). Thrasea was excluded from the celebrations that

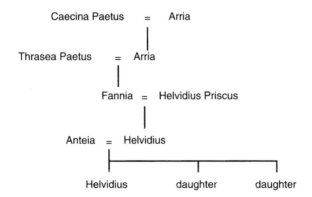

Figure 6.1 The families of Arria and Fannia

surrounded the birth of Nero's daughter in 63 (Tacitus, *Annales*, 15. 23), a sure sign of lack of friendship. Under Augustus, an admission that a prominent figure was no longer a friend of the emperor had opened individuals to attack in the courts and those from whom friendship had been withdrawn at least sometimes decided to go into exile. Even after 63, friends of Thrasea continued in their political careers and held office. Nero might not have given them important military commands, but he allowed their careers to progress.

Thrasea survived until 66. He was tried in the senate, though his general attitude towards the emperor seems to have been the issue rather than any specific conspiracy. The prosecution was launched by Cossutianus Capito, a man Thrasea had himself successfully prosecuted for corruption. Thrasea apparently debated with his friends whether he should oppose the trial, but they decided that such opposition would be useless and only dignify the proceedings. L. Junius Arulenus Rusticus, who was tribune at the time, offered to veto the trial. Technically, this would have caused something of a constitutional crisis, but there can have been little doubt that Nero would have swept aside such opposition very quickly. Thrasea killed himself when the verdict was announced, instructing his wife to carry on living for the sake of their daughter. Thus, he died a martyr (Tacitus, *Annales*, 16. 21–35).

Even though we only have Tacitus' account of Thrasea's martyrdom in incomplete form, it is clear that his career had been mythologised. Tacitus gives us another story about him, included in the account for AD 63. Nero visited Seneca and boasted to him that he had been reconciled to Thrasea (presumably after Thrasea had been excluded from the birth celebrations). Seneca congratulated Nero (Tacitus, *Annales,* 15. 23). In so doing, he suggested that Nero was the lesser man begging the friendship of the greater, a reversal of political status. The story demonstrates Nero's difficulty. Thrasea's opposition was a symbol of Nero's break with the senate and, by standing against Nero, Thrasea's status was raised far above what it would normally have been. If Nero was to reconcile himself with the senate and return to the co-operative government of the early years, he had to bring Thrasea into line. Killing Thrasea, or acting against his friends, would only further increase Thrasea's status. Thus, Nero had to allow, and was probably even pleased to see, Thrasea's friends following senatorial careers since it showed the break was not absolute and he could continue a pretence of co-operation. Even in 66, there was a tribune at Thrasea's side when the verdict was announced. Thrasea's death, however, was far from the end of Nero's problems. It was the start of a purge of AD 66–7 that marked the collapse of Nero's political position.

Rivals and plots

In 62, Nero broke with the relative restraint of his early years and killed several of those in exile. Three casualties, Octavia, Sulla Felix and Rubellius Plautus (see p. 178) were possibly dynastic threats. Two years later, another possible dynastic rival, Decimus Junius Silanus Torquatus, was killed. He was also a great-grandson of Augustus, and it was his family's relationship to the imperial house that led to their elimination. Decimus Junius Silanus was apparently accused of treason on the basis of his generosity in giving presents to his friends (perhaps he feared for his life and was seeking to dispose of his property before it was seized by the emperor), and because he gave his freedmen the same titles as were used in the imperial household (*ab epistulis*, etc., see p. 341) (Tacitus, *Annales,* 15. 35). Dio (62. 27.2) tells us Silanus was killed because his poverty was such that Nero believed his only method of restoring his fortune would be rebellion. We may suspect that our sources trivialised the charges. The Junii Silani had survived up to this point through their passivity. This studied mediocrity was not enough to prevent their deaths at the hand of an increasingly nervous Nero.

Tacitus tells us an extraordinary tale concerning Plautus. L. Antistius Vetus, who was himself to be killed in 65, wrote to Plautus to tell him of his fate and encourage him to resist, flee to Corbulo, and start a revolution. After some discussion with his philosopher friends, Plautus decided to wait on his fate (Tacitus, *Annales,* 14. 58–9). A possible source for this story is Musonius Rufus, who was himself later exiled. The story is convenient both for the philosopher, who could use it as a historical setting for moral discussion, and the historian, for whom it could be used to hint at the fates reserved for Vetus, Corbulo, and perhaps Thrasea Paetus.

In 65, Nero uncovered a conspiracy. At the head of the conspiracy was L. Calpurnius Piso, an aristocratic orator who had won fame and popularity in the law courts. He was not a Julio-Claudian and had no claim for imperial office other than his political standing. The conspiracy aimed at ridding the state of Nero and putting Piso on the throne: Piso wanted the killing of Nero to be accomplished in such a way that power would pass smoothly into his hands. When obvious opportunities presented themselves to the conspirators (such as Nero staying at Piso's house), they hesitated since they feared they would not be able to control subsequent events. Also, because of its political nature, the conspiracy had to involve a significant number of the political class in Rome. Leaks were inevitable. Tacitus (*Annales,* 15. 48–74) provides us with the full tragic story. A freedwoman, Epicharis, was implicated. She refused to give names even under torture. Then a Flavius Scaevinus obtained a dagger from a temple of Fortune or Salus (Safety) from his hometown and, after a long meeting with a certain Antonius Natalis, started behaving so oddly – organising a luxurious (final) dinner party, rewriting his will, sharpening his knife, arranging for bandages to be made ready – that his slaves and freedmen became suspicious. He was betrayed, but conclusive evidence could not be obtained. Then Natalis was brought in and the two failed to agree on what their conference had been about. Torture was applied and gradually the conspiracy was laid before Tigellinus, the praetorian prefect, and Nero. Even then, the conspirators, one of whom was Faenius Rufus, who, as the other prefect of the praetorians was present at the inquisitions, did not act. Gradually, those involved were rounded up to be executed or exiled. Tacitus tells us of suspicions that the conspiracy was a fabrication to enable Nero to rid himself of his enemies, but Nero himself published the confessions, and the details of the conspiracy were confirmed by those involved who returned from exile after Nero's death.

Many of those involved are little more than names to us. There were senators and equestrians; most of the senior officers of the guard, including Faenius Rufus, were implicated. The poet Lucan was also involved, and this brought the conspiracy close to the circle of Seneca. As the numbers of those directly involved grew, and it became clear that even those close to the emperor were also involved, more and more of the Roman aristocracy became 'guilty through association' because of their friendships and family ties with the active conspirators. Nero also struck at men who probably had little or no involvement with the conspiracy. One of these was Rufrius Crispinus, killed because he had been married to Poppaea. The philosopher Musonius Rufus was exiled. Another victim was Seneca.

Seneca's suicide is related at length by Tacitus (*Annales*, 15. 60–5) and Dio (62. 25). He played out the last hours of the philosopher in imitation of Socrates, but his body proved resilient to poisons and bleeding and finally he died after being carried into a steam bath.

Nero's confidence may have been bolstered by public demonstrations in his favour at the Neronia (Tacitus, *Annales*, 16. 4), but there was no end to the killings. The aged, respected and blind senator C. Cassius Longinus was exiled. His crime was keeping and venerating a portrait of his ancestor, as was the custom of the Roman aristocracy, but this ancestor was the Cassius who had led the conspiracy against Julius Caesar (Dio, 62. 27; Tacitus, *Annales*, 16. 7–9). Even ancestral treason had become a cause of fear. Cassius had another weakness since his wife, Junia Lepida, was related to the Junii Silani. Lepida was accused of magic and incest with her nephew Silanus, son of Decimus Silanus. Antistius Vetus, another distinguished senator, and his immediate family were also encouraged to commit suicide (Tacitus, *Annales*, 16. 10–11). A certain Publius Gallus was exiled for having been the friend of both Vetus and Faenius Rufus (Tacitus, *Annales*, 16. 12). Each exile or death made the friends and family of the deceased fear for their own security. The extent of the killings is testimony to the rapidity with which Nero's political position was disintegrating.

Nero found a new way of demonstrating his magnificence: April, May and June were renamed Neroneus, Claudius and Germanicus (Tacitus, *Annales*, 16. 12; Suetonius, *Nero*, 55). The permanence of the imperial dynasty was now built into the calendar. Six months from March (named after Mars, the divine ancestor of the Julians) honoured the imperial family.

Personal tragedy struck in the same year. Nero's beloved Poppaea died. The stories suggest that Nero flew into a fit of rage and kicked her in the stomach.

She was pregnant. The blows killed her. Nero had her deified, associating her with Venus (Tacitus, *Annales*, 16. 6; Dio, 62. 28.1; Suetonius, *Nero*, 35.3). He was now without wife or heir (his daughter had died within three months of her birth). Even reshaping the calendar could not disguise Nero's decline.

The generals

The threat posed by the Roman aristocracy was twofold. They could assassinate the emperor. They also commanded the armies and could use that military force to start a civil war. Since the generals were recruited from the ranks of the senate, and their friends and family remained in Rome, Nero's loss of support among the aristocracy in Rome inevitably led to doubts about the loyalty of the generals. By the winter of 66–7, Nero removed his leading generals.

Our understanding of events in these years is hampered by the loss of Tacitus' account, which ends sometime in the middle of 66 with the death of Thrasea Paetus, and we are forced to rely on items in Suetonius and Dio's imperfect narrative for these years. Much remains obscure, especially a *coniuratio Viniciana* (Vinician conspiracy) dated later than Piso's conspiracy by Suetonius (*Nero* 36) and located at Brundisium. Suetonius is our only source. The location, however, provides a clue: Brundisium was the port from which Nero set out on his tour of Greece and so places the conspiracy towards the end of 66. The Vinicius, or Vinicianus, is probably Annius Vinicianus who had arrived in Rome as escort to Tiridates (prospective King of Armenia) earlier in the same year (Dio, 62. 23.6). This man was Corbulo's son-in-law and had been serving with Corbulo in 63. His involvement in a conspiracy implicated Corbulo.

The threat to Corbulo illustrates the interconnection of the politics of the generals and the senate. Cassius Longinus, who had been removed in 65, was Corbulo's father-in-law. L. Antistius Vetus, also removed in 65, was the man who was rumoured to have written to Rubellius Plautus advising him to flee to Corbulo, suggesting some link between Vetus and Corbulo, even if the story was largely fiction. There were other victims in 66. Barea Soranus fell victim to the same purge that removed Thrasea Paetus. The attack on Soranus also involved Soranus' daughter Servilia, who was married to Annius Pollio, brother of Annius Vinicianus (Tacitus, *Annales*, 16. 14–15; 13. 22). The links suggest the elimination of a political group.

At some time in late 66 or early 67, Nero summoned Corbulo to join him in Greece. The governors of the two Germanies, Sulpicius Scribonius Rufus and Sulpicius Scribonius Proculus, were also summoned. All three were told of Nero's verdict when they arrived and promptly killed themselves (Dio, 63. 17). Nero's killing of these generals increased the fears of the aristocracy. If the loyal Corbulo could fall victim, all were at risk. Few were now committed to Nero's cause. The stage was set for the final act.

The death of an artist

When the end came, it was from an unlikely source. Helios, the freedman who had been left in charge of Rome, journeyed to Greece in 68 to persuade Nero to return home. He brought news of trouble (Dio, 63. 19.1). Helios' worries are not clearly stated in our sources, but they may have been rumblings of rebellion in Gaul. C. Julius Vindex, a Gallic nobleman and probably a governor of Gallia Lugdunensis had been writing to his fellow-governors to secure support. Most forwarded their letters to Nero. There were disturbances in Gaul over the next two years, and some have seen in Vindex's revolt an uprising similar to that in Judaea. Vindex's own propaganda was notably Roman and anti-Nero. He wished the liberty of Rome to be restored. Yet, although the rhetoric was imperial, the scale of local support he generated may reflect provincial discontent. It is difficult to imagine that his Gallic followers would have been motivated by the ill-treatment of the Roman senate or by Nero's capers in Greece.

Nero acted slowly. He had, after all, just appointed two new governors to control the Rhine legions, Verginius Rufus and Fonteius Capito. He might expect them to be loyal. Faced with the might of the Rhine legions, the revolt of even a major Gallic aristocrat was not a serious threat. From the first, however (and Nero may have been aware of this), Vindex was in close contact with the governor of Hispania Tarraconensis, Servius Sulpicius Galba (Plutarch, *Life of Galba*, 4).

Galba was an experienced general who had made something of a name for himself by the severity with which he treated the troops in Germany following his appointment by Gaius. He had only a single legion, however, and he needed to gather more support than that offered by Vindex before he could march on Rome. Galba delayed a formal declaration of intent, but Vindex forced his hand. He came out openly in support of Galba's undeclared candidature. Vindex's own position was probably becoming increasingly desperate. No other governor had declared with him. Plutarch describes a meeting held by Galba and his counsellors which was attended by the commander of the legion in Spain, Titus Vinius. Vinius declared the meeting a farce. The very fact that they were discussing the issue showed that they were already disloyal to Nero (Plutarch, *Life of Galba*, 4). Galba declared his hand and was quickly supported by the governors of the other Spanish provinces, including Otho, the divorced husband of Poppaea; thus Nero's misdeeds returned to haunt him.

Nero's position now disintegrated for reasons that are not altogether obvious. Galba was a major political figure, much more important than Vindex. In military terms, however, Galba was no match for Nero. He had only one legion to compare with the combined forces of the empire, and Nero not only had the praetorians close at hand, but could also quickly raise more troops and organise a substantial force. Otho's involvement suggests, however, that there were more people behind the rebellion. Politically, Nero was disturbed by Galba's rebellion (Suetonius, *Nero*, 42), but he should not have been threatened at this stage. The danger was that others would declare for Galba. At some point, however, the governor of Africa, Claudius Macer, made an independent bid for the throne (Plutarch, *Life of Galba*, 6). It looks already as if the governors considered Nero to be finished and the competition as to who among them would succeed him had begun.

Nero was threatened on two fronts. A supposed loyalist, Petronius Turpillianus, was placed in charge of forces in Italy. The exact chronology of what happened next is uncertain, but, paradoxically, the fatal blow may have come from negotiations before a defeat which should have destroyed Galba. Vindex entered into negotiations with Verginius Rufus. At the conclusion of these negotiations, Verginius' troops attacked and massacred Vindex's forces. Vindex killed himself. When Galba heard the news, he retired, fully expecting death (Plutarch, *Life of Galba*, 6). A few days later, news came of Nero's death and that the senate had called upon him to be emperor.

Verginius Rufus had been acclaimed by his troops as emperor, but had refused the honour. The later tradition, which may have been heavily influenced by Verginius Rufus himself, emphasised that he had not given the order for his forces to attack and made much of his subsequent refusal to take imperial power, yet the motivations of Rufus and his troops at this crucial moment are difficult to reconstruct. By negotiating, Rufus demonstrated disloyalty to Nero. One has to see these negotiations as evidence of a further disintegration of Nero's political position. But the troops crushed Vindex, seemingly on their own authority and seemingly demonstrating loyalty to the existing regime. To then declare for Rufus seems contradictory. We can rule out the possibility that the troops had a collective change of mind and so we must look for another motivation. It seems likely that Rufus was exploring the possibility of an attempt on the throne, either for himself or someone else. In destroying Vindex he established himself as the arbiter of Empire. For some reason (perhaps because he could not rely on the support of the other German legions), he decided not to attempt the throne himself and, by refusing the imperial acclamation, he demonstrated that he was not a threat to Galba. He was to use the same technique in 69, when Vitellius' troops pressed Rome and Otho's forces supposedly looked to Rufus to lead them against the Vitellians (Dio, 63. 24–5; Tacitus, *Histories*, 2. 51).

In Rome, Nero's position was collapsing. Grain prices rose, perhaps from fear that the supply of grain from Africa would fail (Suetonius, *Nero*, 45). Rumours of the disloyalty of Rufus may have been circulating in Rome. If Rufus turned against him, Nero's days were numbered. Turpillianus proved disloyal. The Roman political classes made their calculations. Nymphidius Sabinus, who had been appointed prefect of the praetorians after the execution of Faenius Rufus, decided that Nero would lose. The imperial palace emptied of courtiers and Nero fled the city, accompanied by only his closest associates.

The account of his last days is clearly heavily fictionalised. Vague plans of fleeing to the East or retiring to earn a living on the stage are mentioned, but the disintegration of his position was complete. Sabinus persuaded the praetorians to act. Cavalry sent after Nero found him in a suburb outside Rome. Nero killed himself. His last words were reportedly *'Qualis artifex pereo'* ('I, such an artist, perish') (Suetonius, *Nero*, 49; Dio, 63. 29.2). His final words are appropriately inappropriate, stressing his role on the stage rather than his exercise of political power, and one suspects later invention.

Conclusions: art, politics and power

Nero is possibly the most difficult of the Julio-Claudian emperors to understand. The account transmitted through our sources on Nero is almost universally hostile and certainly distorts our understanding of the emperor. Nero was not universally hated during his reign, nor in the aftermath. Otho was to make use of his association with Nero and this brought him popularity (see p. 217). Nero cannot be dismissed as a silly man who strutted about the stage for forced applause without a serious idea in his head.

Although the tradition vilifies his stage appearances, the decline in Nero's political position cannot be directly related to his artistic endeavours. Nero faced many of the same problems as Gaius and Claudius in coming to the throne with limited experience and, like his two predecessors, his style of government was inventive. He looked for new ways to display his authority and new avenues for his imperial energies. Gaius had turned to a kind of divine despotism by which to control the classes of Rome. Claudius had removed power from the senate by concentrating authority in his inner circle of close friends and household members. Nero looked to culture. In some ways, this device was remarkably successful and Nero presided over a revival in architecture and literature. His subversion of the traditional aristocratic way of life and elevation of an 'artistic ideal' as a governing principle were radical. This could be seen as a response to the changed political conditions of the Principate. The emperor appealed to a wide audience of Romans (of all social classes), troops and provincials. New media had to be found to communicate to such an audience and mass communication, such as it was in the ancient world, meant the theatre, architecture, art and literature. Portraits of the emperors are found in all provinces and, of course, coinage could be used as a vehicle for imperial propaganda. It is unlikely to be a coincidence that the art on Nero's coinage was of a very high standard. Nero met his people through art and made more use of art to display his status than any emperor since Augustus.

Yet, such excellence did not reconcile the more traditional elements of Roman society to his power. Indeed, in the very act of associating himself with subversive culture, Nero turned traditional values into the values of opposition. Co-operation with traditionalists became progressively more difficult following the death of Agrippina. The Pisonian conspiracy may not mark a turning point in the reign, since relations with the conservative aristocracy were already strained, but led Nero to fear a considerable section of the political elite. He still had 'conservatives' at his side. Vespasian later made a virtue out of his relatively humble origins, associating himself with traditional values in contrast to the extravagances of the high-born Julio-Claudians. Tacitus also claims that he was a friend of Soranus and Thrasea Paetus (*Histories*, 4. 7). Similarly, Verginius Rufus in Germany and Galba in Spain were representatives of the traditional Italian aristocracy. Nero's cultural revolution failed in that the very men he relied on to govern his empire were not affected. These men were the powerful and their obedience would not be won by a particularly fine performance in the theatre.

Given this eventual demonstration of aristocratic power, one must wonder how Nero had managed to survive so long. The lethargy of those attacked by Nero seems notable. Rudich has compared Nero's enemies to the dissidents in the former Soviet Union: a group so overwhelmed by the authority of a powerful state that they saw no hope of salvation through political action and their only hope was to hide.[1] There was no formal political organisation opposed to Nero. Opposition consisted of individuals who faced separate and individual persecution. Some may have thought that simply by doing nothing they would demonstrate that they were not a threat. Corbulo, for instance, may have calculated that, by going to Greece when summoned, he would demonstrate his loyalty and that this was the safer course, especially if he had not established the views of other governors. When Vindex finally came out into the open, the hesitation of even one so heavily implicated as Galba suggests that the Roman elite believed that the best way of surviving was to avoid open conflict, to keep their mouths shut, and to do nothing. As the Pisonian conspiracy unravelled, the passivity of the conspirators, including Piso himself, was notable. With the support of key praetorian officers and a reasonable number of the Roman aristocracy, one might have thought that open rebellion would have had a chance of success, yet the inaction that had dogged the conspiracy continued and the conspirators seem to have simply hoped that they would not be implicated.

Apart from the psychological explanation, another possibility may be suggested. The Roman aristocracy had seen Julio-Claudian domination only temporarily broken since Caesar defeated Pompey over a century before the death of Nero. There appears to have been no active republicanism at this time. There was no realistic alternative to imperial rule and if Nero was to be removed, who would replace him? As we have seen, Nero killed most of his own family and possible dynastic rivals such as the Junii Silani were also removed. Was there a realistic alternative? The Pisonian conspiracy needed to be so large so that events after the assassination of the emperor (not a substantial problem given the access to the emperor that the conspirators enjoyed) could be controlled. Any subsequent conspirator would face the same problem. A conspiracy needed to secure the future, and to do this they needed an imperial candidate who stood a realistic chance of securing the support of the senate and troops. Nero lasted so long because there was no alternative candidate. This is why Nero was not worried by Vindex. A Gallic nobleman would not be able to secure sufficient support from the Roman elite; he was not a realistic alternative. The declaration of Galba transformed the situation. He was a realistic opponent and, once Galba had declared and the aristocracy accepted the prospect of a non-Julio-Claudian emperor, other possibilities emerged. Verginius Rufus and Claudius Macer were also realistic candidates, and so were many others. All a candidate needed was the support of a sufficient number of legions; the scene was set for the civil wars of 68–70.

The crucial change that led to Galba's declaration was probably Nero's purge of his generals in 66–7. Nero had shown that even seemingly loyal supporters such as Corbulo, Nero's greatest general, could be struck down. Corbulo had brought a difficult war in Armenia to an end and presented Nero with his greatest diplomatic triumph. Killing Corbulo showed that none were safe and ultimately there was little alternative but to find an alternative. Although maladministration of the provinces may have been a contributing factor in Vindex's initial outbreak, and may have led to a greater willingness of the provincials to provide immediate support for Galba and others, Nero's fate was decided by the Roman political elite.

Epilogue: understanding Nero

Nero tests the historian. We can ask conventional questions of our sources: are they 'true'? Do they shape the material to fit their agendas? But these questions do not provide us with very sensible or useful answers. For historians, a question is only as good as its answer. We have considerable doubts as to the historical veracity of our sources and without doubt those sources are not objective. But so what? No history is objective. Instead, we need to ask more profound questions: why is Nero portrayed in this way? And how does the portrayal of Nero help us understand the nature of power in the Roman principate? Those questions may require careful judgement, but they do not require objectivity on the part of our sources. Indeed, our sources try to understand the answer to the problem of power in the Julio-Claudian era and that requires them to take an ideological position on emperors such as Nero: description is one thing; understanding another.

One of the notable features of the accounts is their scandalous nature. We cannot know whether these scandals are true. We can know that these stories circulated and formed the myth of Nero. We may suspect that at least some of those stories were in circulation during Nero's reign and were perhaps even publicised by the court. In subsequent traditions, Nero has emerged as a warning from history, an example of what goes wrong when the philosopher-king (of Seneca's imagining) turns out to be the licentious-tyrant.

This Nero is all passion and no reason. There is no measure to him. He is the anti-thesis of the good king. These features are stereotypical. The image of Nero is shaped by the tradition, probably because those who produced the tradition believed Nero to be the tyrant. Yet, there are other Neros in our sources: the Nero of culture; the philosopher-king of Seneca; the Nero beloved of the plebs; the Nero of Greece. Nero, like many leaders, manipulated his image. He was, like many Romans, playing a role. Seneca killed himself in the manner of Socrates, a staged, scripted death. But we need not doubt that death and actually there is very little reason to doubt that Seneca modelled his last hours on the death of Socrates. Just because someone chose to act out a role in his final hour does not lessen the death or make the sources unbelievable. Everyone needs scripts in life and we all adhere to certain patterns in our behaviour: it is part of our cultural memory to act in a scripted fashion. Furthermore, if there was a real story behind Seneca's death covered up by the account, what would it matter? It is the martyrdom that is important.

The accounts of Nero have these scripted elements. Nero's image was from the first carefully constructed and we have to expect that the scripted elements would be part of his story. It is very likely that later sources worked on those stories, developed them, improved them for literary purposes, but it seems unlikely that they were completely invented. Even if they were inventions, they still contribute to the myth that is Nero. When Nero died proclaiming his artistry, we need not just read the claim as delusional, but as a reflection, perhaps a representation, of a life spent on metaphorical and real stages in which his acts were scripted. His reign was a work of art; Nero was both the artist and the subject of that art. It just turned out to be a tragedy.

Our sources also appear novelistic. They have access into the secret conversations of the court and into the bedroom of the emperor. Again, we may instinctively quail before such 'knowledge', suspecting invention. But we need to ask ourselves why our sources were driven to invent and to reconstruct what happened behind those doors. Historians who claim to value objectivity and facts before all else face a considerable problem. In history as in life, the factual content of what happens is never complete. We always have to make deductions from imperfect information, being it buying a loaf of bread or voting in an election or deciding who to date. Yet, most of us are very good at filling in the blanks when we have to: we have a pragmatic understanding of the world. To understand what happened in the key moments of Nero's reign, we have to deploy that pragmatic understanding, reconstructing what went on behind those closed doors. As political pundits endlessly speculate about the secret discussion and agendas of our political leaders, interpreting the signals and signs, so ancient historians needed to know what happened in court. They needed to interpret the secrets signals and signs. If they did not, all we would have is the barest of factual and official accounts: Agrippina was discovered in a conspiracy and killed. Such a history might be factual, but it is not necessarily true. The process of understanding requires a certain amount of creative fictionalisation and that is what we see in our sources.

What that creative fictionalisation tells us is that the politics of the time were the politics of the court. Key decisions happened behind closed doors. By the reign of Nero, we had come a long way from the reign of Tiberius when the new emperor foolishly, and briefly, proposed that the death of Agrippa Postumus should be officially and openly investigated (see pp. 97–101). The nature of the Principate, Tiberius was told, would not allow such an auditing of accounts.

The myth of Nero was to effect the reigns that followed profoundly. Nero became the guide as to 'How not to be an emperor' and he remained so for centuries. The emperors who followed, and especially the Flavians, changed the mood of Rome and sought to escape the excesses of Nero and reconcile the Principate with the traditions of Rome.

Note

1 Vasily Rudich, *Political Dissidence under Nero* (New York: Routledge, 1993).

Chapter 7

Civil wars (AD 69–70)

Main events of AD 69–70

Date	Events
AD 69 January	Galba emperor and consul with Titus Vinius. Revolt of German legions in favour of Vitellius. Gaul and Britain join Vitellius. Adoption of Piso. Rising of Otho. Deaths of Galba, Vinius and Piso. Otho becomes emperor. Preparations for civil war.
February to April	Invasion of Italy by legions from Germany. Danubian legions come over to Otho. False Nero in the East. Otho's forces win victories in Gallia Narbonensis, at siege of Placentia and outside Cremona. Battle of Bedriacum. Otho commits suicide.
April to July	Vitellius marches on Rome. Flavius Sabinus administers oath to the troops in Rome. Otho's supporters among the centurions of the Danubian legions killed. The East accepts Vitellius. Vitellius wins support in Rome.
July to December	(1 July) Vespasian declared emperor in Egypt. (3 July) Syrian and Judaean legions support Vespasian. Danubian legions support Vespasian. Antonius Primus leads Danubian forces towards Italy. Mucianus leads Syrian legions to Italy. Primus invades Italy. Batavian Revolt. Revolt in Britain. Alienus Caecina defects to Vespasian. Ravenna fleet joins Vespasian. Battle of Cremona. Sack of Cremona. Collapse of Vitellian forces in North and Central Italy. Burning of the Capitol. Capture of Rome by Flavians. Death of Vitellius. Mucianus arrives in Rome.

Date	Events
July to December (continued)	Civilis defeats Roman forces.
	Siege of Vetera.
	Defeat of Legion I.
	Vocula relieves Vetera, but forced to retreat.
	Siege of Vetera continues.
	Troops in Germany mutiny.
AD 70	Creation of the 'Gallic Empire'.
	Petilius Cerealis sent to Germany.
	Cerealis inflicts defeat on Civilis and invades Batavia.
	Cerealis and Civilis battle inconclusively.
	Peace negotiated.
	Siege and capture of Jerusalem.

Introduction

The accession of Galba revealed one of the secrets of the Empire, that emperors could be made outside of Rome (Tacitus, *Histories*, 1.4). The end of the Julio-Claudians led to a period of unprecedented turmoil. In a single year, AD 69, there were four emperors. The armies competed to place these candidates on the throne and, to add to internal turmoil, there was major conflict in Judaea, on the Danube, in Germany and Gaul, and in Britain. Two major cities were sacked, Cremona and Jerusalem, and Rome itself was stormed by the forces of Vespasian.

The result of this internal strife can be explained simply. The man with the biggest army, Vespasian, won. It can be seen as a military struggle in which only those holding armies could take part, which marginalised the senate. We are guided through these events by Tacitus. We have only the first four books and the first part of the fifth book of his *Histories*. The complete work probably covered the Flavian dynasty (Vespasian, Titus and Domitian), but the surviving work concerns only the period AD 69–70. Tacitus seems to have believed that the Flavian victory was the best result for Rome. It is, however, notable that the other candidates – Galba, Otho and Vitellius – are not portrayed stereotypically and although Tacitus criticises them all, especially Vitellius, his account allows us to discern some of their better qualities.

Galba

The death of Nero left Galba in a seemingly strong position. He had replaced Nero, who was deeply unpopular with the senate. He was the only declared candidate for the throne. He had a reputation as a conservative, untainted by the excesses of Nero's reign. Galba had won his military reputation under Gaius and Claudius. He was also a member of an old aristocratic family. He owed his own prominence to a friendship with Livia, wife of Augustus, but his ancestors numbered Republican consuls and his family had a mythical ancestry to rival the Julians, since they claimed descent from Jupiter and the Minoan royal family (Suetonius, *Galba*, 2). He might, therefore, be expected to draw support from the military and from the old senatorial families. He was recognised by the senate, by the armies of the East and, after some delay, by the armies of Germany and the West. This position of seeming strength disintegrated in a remarkably short period.

Part of the reason for this collapse lay in Galba's inability to consolidate his support. Galba had made a name for himself as a fierce disciplinarian. He did not change his character when he became emperor, but more seriously, he did not bend his acts for the new political situation. Galba's self-positioning as a political and moral conservative distanced him from the previous regime, but also associated him with Republican virtue. That Republican virtue was in many ways unreal: it was part of the cultural memory of the Roman elite, but was a romanticisation of the bloody and desperate politics of the Republic. One of his favourite sayings (as we shall see) was that he chose his soldiers; he did not buy them. The expression may have been laudable, but it was political nonsense. Republican politicians had concerned themselves with securing the loyalty of their troops and had employed various means to win favour and boost morale. These may have been relatively minor favours, but generals might also allow an army to sack a city, enriching themselves in the process at a time when an army had been suffering. Sulla, Marius, Pompey, Caesar, Antony, Octavian, and Augustus had understood the importance of the troops. The soldiers had been the mainstay of the Claudian regime. To ignore the soldiers and, indeed, not seek to win over others with shows of generosity was to live in a mythical age long gone. The frequent references to Galba's age that litter the Tacitean account of his reign would appear to reflect this sense of Galba as a man who no longer understood the requirement of the era in which he lived.

The damage was done almost before Galba reached Rome. Taxes were raised to pay for Nero's reign (Suetonius, *Galba*, 12), and some of this money was extracted from Gaul. Galba wished to reward the communities that had supported Vindex and, in so doing, reorganised Gaul so that the communities closest to the legionary bases lost out. The legionaries tended to identify with those local communities. These were also the legionaries who had defeated Vindex and these troops observed communities that they regarded as rebellious instead rewarded, while loyalists suffered (Tacitus, *Histories*, 1.53–4).

Galba also continued the cycle of killings from the Neronian period. Galba killed the consul-designate, Cingonius Varro, Petronius Turpillianus (who had led Nero's army against Galba), Claudius Macer (governor of Africa), Nymphidius Sabinus (Nero's praetorian prefect) and Fonteius Capito (governor of Germania Superior who was suspected of aiming at the throne). Capito was assassinated by his legionary commanders (Tacitus, *Histories*, 1.7). There were other deaths when Galba reached Rome, such as Helios (Nero's freedman) and

Locusta (a renowned poisoner), though Tigellinus (Nero's other praetorian prefect) survived (Dio, 64. 3.3–4; Suetonius, *Galba*, 14–15).

Galba embarked on a limited reordering of the provincial commanders. Not only were governors needed in those provinces in which the previous incumbents had been executed or had accompanied Galba to Rome, but Verginius Rufus had been removed from his post: Galba held him responsible for the death of Vindex. New governors were appointed to the Spanish provinces and Africa, and also to the Germanies. Vitellius was sent to Germania Inferior and Hordeonius Flaccus was sent to Germania Superior (Tacitus, *Histories*, 1. 9; Suetonius, *Vitellius*, 7). The East was left untouched. Some of the officers of the praetorians, the *Vigiles* (watch) and the urban cohorts were also removed (Tacitus, *Histories*, 1.20).

Galba's policy made him many enemies and few friends. The killings provided evidence of Galba's brutality and did not establish the atmosphere of a fresh start that an amnesty might have offered. There was no reconciliation. Yet, not all Nero's supporters were treated in the same way and so those maltreated under Nero's reign remained dissatisfied. Justice had been denied (or so they thought). Galba also made no attempt to remove or win over former Neronians at lower levels of the military and political structure. Troops raised by Nero remained in Rome and the praetorians (for whom Galba must have been rather a distant figure) were not reorganised. Indeed, Galba offended these powerful groups. A legion raised by Nero from the sailors of the fleet petitioned Galba to be allowed to remain legionaries. Galba refused and they became disorderly. Galba charged them with cavalry and brought them to order by decimation (every tenth man killed), an archaic and brutal act (Suetonius, *Galba*, 12.2; Dio, 64. 3.1–3). The praetorians had been promised a donative by Nymphidius Sabinus for their desertion of Nero. Galba refused payment: he did not buy his soldiers (Tacitus, *Histories,* 1.5). Tacitus regarded such sentiments as admirable, but extremely foolish. Further, Galba sought the return of gifts made by Nero. Since many of these had been consumed, he threatened to bankrupt members of the Neronian court (Tacitus, *Histories*, 1.20).

Galba also managed to lose some of the friends he had. Otho had been the first to support Galba and might have expected some reward when he returned to Rome. None was forthcoming. Alienus Caecina had represented Galba at crucial moments in Germany and was responsible for the death of Fonteius Capito. He received nothing. Instead, authority was concentrated in the hands of three members of the court: Titus Vinius (who had led Galba's army), Cornelius Laco (a praetorian prefect) and Icelus (a freedman) (Tacitus, *Histories*, 1. 6; Suetonius, *Galba*, 14.2). Our sources allege rampant corruption.

In January 69, Galba's rule fell apart. It was customary for an oath of loyalty to be administered to the troops on the first day of the year. The German legions refused, mutinied, and turned to the popular Vitellius (Tacitus,

Histories, 1. 12). Galba responded to the growing crisis by adopting a young nobleman, Piso Licinianus, as his heir (Tacitus, *Histories*, 1.14–18). All authorities seem to recognise Piso as an honourable young man from one of the best families in Rome descended from the *triumvir* Licinius Crassus, but he had no military experience and was too young to have much political weight. Worse still, the troops expected a donative to celebrate such a major family event. These hopes were unfulfilled. Galba's reputation for meanness was confirmed; the praetorians became yet more discontented.

Galba was an old man and the question of the succession was one of the major issues of the brief reign. Galba may have calculated that the political problems he was facing in Germany (and possibly he was aware of discontent in Rome) were manoeuvres concerning the succession and he wished to end speculation. Adoption was the only available method. But the adoption of the young and inexperienced Piso brought no new support to prop up the regime. Galba could have looked elsewhere: Otho, himself, would have brought popularity and an ability to reconcile the old Neronians. Vespasian's son Titus would have been another possibility since this would have secured the support of his father, an influential general, and also his uncle, Flavius Sabinus, a prominent senator. Such realism seemed beyond Galba.

Tacitus gives Galba a long speech (*Histories*, 1.15–16) on the adoption of Piso in which he lambasted the Julio-Claudians for choosing family rather than the best people available. Galba praises the virtues of the young Piso, noting his distinguished Republican ancestry, but also remarks nostalgically that it would be better were he able to restore the Republic. Piso responds dutifully.

Some have seen the speech as an echo of events a generation later when a beleaguered Nerva, faced with the Praetorians in open revolt, adopted Trajan and have thus seen the speech as a disguised panegyric in favour of Nerva and Trajan. Yet, as ever with Tacitus, we need to exercise care. All Galba's talk of Piso's distinguished Republican ancestry and his proclamations of conservative moral worth are set against allegations of incompetence and corruption. Piso's distinguished ancestors in fact bring to mind not the glories of the Republic and the senators all working together, as might have happened if Piso had been descended from Cato, rather than the troublesome Crassus. Notably, the traumas of the civil wars are somehow forgotten and the lesson of subsequent years of Julio-Claudian domination are missed. We cannot, of course, know whether Tacitus' account of the speech is accurate, and one assumes it was not, but as a literary comment on Galba, Tacitus suggests that Galba had no idea of the reality of the situation, was living in a nostalgic dream of a past of which he had little understanding, and was ignorant of the corruption and violence that dogged the last days of the Republic and his own brief regime. Tacitus convicts Galba of the terrible crime of being a very bad historian. Whatever the virtues of Galba's pronouncements, they are undermined by events. What happens next is that Galba's power is swept away and Piso with it. If there is a political lesson here for Nerva and Trajan, it was not to choose the distinguished noble, but the most powerful general.

On 15th January, Otho staged his coup. It seems to have been disorganised. The situation remained unclear for most of the day. Galba's supporters tried to gather as many troops as possible, but failed to collect a plausible force. Nevertheless, news spread that Otho had been killed. Yet, as Galba and his supporters celebrated in the Forum, the praetorians arrived. Galba's guard defected, possibly by prior arrangement, and his supporters fled. The old general was decapitated, either promising money and begging for his life or offering his neck for the good of the state (Tacitus, *Histories*, 1.27–41; Suetonius, *Otho*, 6–7; Dio, 64. 5–6).

Galba had faced substantial political difficulties in Germany and the inevitable nervous opposition of those who had supported Nero. Nevertheless, Galba failed to reconcile disaffected and powerful elements. Galba's reputation sprang from his disciplining of the troops, not from political subtlety. He seems to have believed that the troops owed loyalty to their commander naturally and to have seen no need to win that loyalty. This may have been the case under the Julio-Claudians when loyalty to the family assured military support on accession, but the troops were no more loyal to Galba than to any other member of the Roman aristocracy. His failure to realise this was a failure to perceive the fundamentals of the imperial position and, indeed, the basics of the political power of any regime. A regime depends on its legitimacy and all regimes need means of established that legitimacy. The Julio-Claudians established that legitimacy through family (though Tiberius was perhaps a little different). The ultimate legitimacy of the regime depended on the deal that Augustus had struck to provide peace and the bastions of that regime were the people and the soldiers. Imperial power was legalised, but did not spring from legal authority. Galba appears to have invested his legitimacy in his personal Republican sensibilities. It is perhaps no surprise that he was not taken seriously.

Otho

Otho's accession did not alter the attitude of the legions of Germany. Otho needed to prepare for the conflict; he needed to secure the loyalty of the troops in Rome and Italy. In this, he was remarkably successful. The praetorians were allowed to choose their own prefects and other troops seem to have been kindly treated (Tacitus, *Histories*, 1.46). Politically, Otho treated the former supporters of Galba well and was able to secure the support of prominent generals. Marius Celsus (who had served in the East with Corbulo and was consul designate), Annius Gallus (an able general who later commanded troops for Vespasian in Germany (Tacitus, *Histories*, 5. 19)), Licinius Proculus (the praetorian prefect) and Suetonius Paulinus (the man who defeated Boudicca) were the main commanders of Otho's troops (Tacitus, *Histories*, 1.

87). Otho also managed to gain the support of the legions stationed along the Danube and the legions of the East.

Otho's undoubted early success may have owed much to his policy of associating himself with Nero. Although Otho's support of Galba may have been instrumental in creating the alliance that destroyed Nero, and one of his first acts as emperor was to kill Nero's praetorian prefect Tigellinus (Tacitus, *Histories*, 1.72; Plutarch, *Otho*, 2), Otho toyed with the idea of renaming himself 'Nero-Otho'. He restored statues of Poppaea and encouraged the exhibition of portraits of Nero (Tacitus, *Histories*, 1.78; Plutarch, *Otho*, 3). Nero's freedmen and procurators were restored to office and he continued work on the unfinished Domus Aurea. Suetonius tells us that he had intended to marry Nero's widow (Suetonius, *Otho*, 7; 10). A further sexual connection was established by the return to prominence of Nero's lover Sporus, who again appeared in public with an emperor (Dio, 64. 8). The continued popularity of Nero is shown by the career of a 'false Nero' who caused disruption in Asia and Greece before being killed by the governor of Galatia and Pamphylia (Tacitus, *Histories*, 2.8).

This sudden popularity of Nero questions the dominant literary tradition on the emperor. Yet, the restoration of his popularity is best seen as a response to events in 68–9. The killing of Nero had not ended the difficulties of the Roman people and the looming civil war increased political uncertainty. The candidates for the imperial position strove for legitimacy and, although none could claim to be Julio-Claudians, association with Nero, claiming to be Nero's spiritual successor, was one way of asserting that legitimacy. Many had made their careers under Nero: Otho's honouring of Nero and limited restoration of Nero's officials could be seen as reconciling the old Neronians to his rule, as well as providing him with a body of experienced administrators.

Otho also attempted to reconcile his potential enemies, the supporters of Galba or other possible contenders, to his accession. With a number of notable exceptions (Piso, Titus Vinius, Laco and Icelus) (Tacitus, *Histories*, 1.42–6), Otho pardoned Galba's supporters (Tacitus, *Histories*, 2.71). Even an extremely prominent supporter of Galba, Marius Celsus (who had attempted to organise the military resistance to Otho) was reconciled to the regime and entrusted with a command (Plutarch, *Otho*, 1). Potential enemies were accommodated by the appointment of Flavius Sabinus, brother of Vespasian, to the important post of *Praefectus Urbi* (Plutarch, *Otho*, 5; Tacitus, *Histories*, 1.46). Verginius Rufus also achieved renewed prominence and was nominated for a consulship. He was also a member of the party that accompanied Otho on campaign, since the troops turned to him once they received news of Otho's death (Plutarch, *Otho* 1, 18; Tacitus, *Histories*, 2. 51). Those who had suffered under Nero had those portions of their confiscated property that the treasury still held restored to them.

Such manoeuvres seem to have been successful in building a consensus behind Otho. We cannot know whether this would have held for any length of time but, although there may have been rumblings of discontent from the East, the fact that there was no rebellious movement until July suggests that Vespasian's bid was not yet planned.

The military position was also encouraging. Otho gathered sufficient troops in Italy to be able to resist Vitellius, and the approaching Danubian legions would have tipped the military balance in favour of Otho. However, the legions did not arrive in time. Both the Vitellian leaders and Otho followed an aggressive policy. Otho sent troops to Gallia Narbonensis where they enjoyed notable success, but the issue was to be decided in Italy (Tacitus, *Histories*, 2.14–15). Otho's camp was apparently divided over whether they should risk a battle against the Vitellian forces before support arrived from the Danubian legions, but early success encouraged the Othonians and they met the Vitellians at Bedriacum. Otho was defeated.

This defeat proved to be decisive, though the strategic situation did not appear to be lost. Otho took counsel from his friends and decided to bring the civil wars to an end. Rather than prolong the war by retreating towards the East, Otho killed himself (Tacitus, *Histories*, 2.46–50; Suetonius, *Otho*, 9–11; Dio, 64. 11–15; Plutarch, *Otho*, 15–17). The historians seem confident that the war could have been continued and that, although the defeat was significant, Otho still had resources on which he could call. His decision is widely praised since Otho's suicide is thought to have been a humanitarian decision taken to avoid further shedding of Roman blood. It may have been encouraged by an assessment of the political situation. Such a defeat often led to defections and Otho may have felt that his political support would waver as the Roman elite and the soldiers sought to back the winning side. In any case, his death brought Vitellius to the throne, but did not end the civil wars.

Vitellius

Vitellius' reign poses certain difficulties for historians, since his reputation may have been substantially damaged by later historians who were influenced by the Flavian view of events. Certainly, the historians appear to be more hostile to Vitellius than the other emperors of 69 but, in spite of Vitellius' personal weaknesses, he seems to have built a loyal and powerful following in Italy and among the German troops.

Vitellius' family became prominent under Augustus and Tiberius. Under Claudius, Vitellius' father achieved a position of extraordinary importance, holding three consulships. The future emperor enjoyed friendships with Tiberius, Gaius, Claudius and Nero, presiding at the second Neronia (p. 191) (Suetonius, *Vitellius*, 4). He had governed Africa with exceptional integrity and was appointed to Germania Inferior by Galba (Suetonius, *Vitellius*, 7). This was Vitellius' opportunity and he used his talent for winning friends to great effect. The soldiers were disaffected and Vitellius won their loyalty. On 1st January, when the oath of loyalty was to be administered to the troops in

Germania Inferior, they mutinied, refusing to accept Galba as their emperor. As in Rome, when the soldiers were asked to affirm the loyalty to the regime appears to have been a key ceremonial moment. Whereas in Rome, the murmurings had encouraged Galba and Otho to act, in Germany, the positive affirmation required pushed the soldiers into revolt.

There was no immediate declaration in favour of Vitellius; he was probably waiting to see what the governor of Germania Superior would do. The soldiers swore loyalty to the senate and people of Rome. On 2nd January, Fabius Valens greeted Vitellius as emperor and by 3rd January the legions of Germania Superior had also mutinied. Vitellius began to organise his rebellion (Tacitus, *Histories*, 1.52–8). The military side seems to have been led by Alienus Caecina and Fabius Valens. They marched into Italy in two columns with varying success but once they met outside Bedriacum in North Italy they inflicted the decisive defeat on Otho and Vitellius became emperor.

The march from Germany to Rome was slow and the Vitellians took every opportunity to extract money from the communities that they passed through. Our sources criticise Vitellius' morality, especially his eating habits (Dio, 65. 2 gives an implausibly large figure for the costs of Vitellius' dinners during his reign), and the disorder of the march through Gaul and Italy continued when Vitellius' troops reached Rome where there were clashes between the troops and the civilian population (Suetonius, *Vitellius*, 13; Tacitus, *Histories*, 2. 88).

Many of the Roman aristocracy may have regarded the approach of the Vitellians with some fear. Otho had been effective in reconciling differences, but Caecina and Valens acted sufficiently violently that there must have been doubts as to Vitellius' attitude. The death of Otho and the failure of any another candidate, such as Verginius Rufus, to take up the standard left them with little choice. Flavius Sabinus administered an oath of loyalty to the troops remaining in Rome and the armies of the rest of the empire quickly followed (Tacitus, *Histories*, 2.55). Vitellius himself delayed accepting the titles of Caesar and Augustus, though took the constitutional powers that went with the imperial position (Tacitus, *Histories*, 2.62). His reluctance to accept titles may reflect an honouring of the senate and a desire to demonstrate that he would not be an autocratic ruler. Similarly, an honouring of the principles of aristocratic government may be behind Vitellius' decision to appoint equestrians to the household offices, breaking with the tradition of employing freedmen (see pp. 340–43). Vitellius tried to reconcile the aristocracy. Flavius Sabinus retained his position as *Praefectus Urbi*. Vitellius also clashed in the senate with Helvidius Priscus, who had returned from exile, but, instead of taking action against Priscus, he merely asked the senate to excuse the quarrels of two senators (Dio, 65. 7.2; Tacitus, *Histories*, 2. 91). Although Suetonius (*Vitellius*, 14) accuses him of cruelty and killing his enemies, Dio (65. 6) contradicts this. The survival of Flavius Sabinus and

Domitian until the very end of the reign also suggests that Vitellius was not bloodthirsty.

Vitellius also tried to win the support of the Neronians. He made funerary offerings for Nero on the Campus Martius in Rome (Suetonius, *Nero*, 11; Dio, 65. 7.2–3). He tried to bring some Neronian 'glamour' to his regime by suggesting that Sporus appear on stage, taking a female part, but Sporus killed himself to avoid the shame (Dio, 65. 10.1). Nonetheless, Vitellius wooed the plebs by staging lavish entertainments (Tacitus, *Histories*, 2.94–5).

Vitellius' major problem was, however, the military. The death of Otho brought one round of the civil war to an end, but Vitellius' troops had not inflicted a militarily decisive defeat. Like the legions in Germany in 68, the Danubian legionaries who had supported Otho were potentially disaffected. Vitellius disbanded the praetorians who had shown such loyalty to Otho (Suetonius, *Vitellius*, 10), and also executed Othonian centurions in the Danubian legions (Tacitus, *Histories*, 2.60), which may have removed some of his enemies, but did not endear him to the legionaries and their surviving officers. Vitellius' military insecurity was such that he maintained a very large garrison in Rome (20,000 troops), perhaps more to intimidate potential rivals among the governors than to control the city (Tacitus, *Histories*, 2. 93). The concentration of these troops in Rome was at the expense of the garrison in Germany, which lost many of its most experienced men to the garrison. Vitellius' problems were increased by the revolt of the Batavians led by Julius Civilis (see pp. 224–29). The revolt involved the auxiliaries that Vitellius had recruited for his war effort. The forces led by Civilis and his German and Gallic allies caused havoc in Gaul and Germany and, although the chronology of these events is not altogether clear, Vitellius was unable to draw reinforcements from those areas.

The major threat was posed by the governors in the East. Initially, the Eastern armies (in Judaea, Syria and Egypt) accepted Vitellius, but it seems likely that this was only a temporary measure. On 1st July, Tiberius Julius Alexander, prefect of Egypt, administered the oath of loyalty to the legions in Egypt in the name of Vespasian. By 3rd July, Judaea and Syria had followed. The declaration seems to have been somewhat untidy, with the initiative coming from an unlikely quarter, but the speed with which the Flavians moved suggests that the declaration had been planned. Mucianus, governor of Syria, was sent West to lead the war effort while Vespasian himself went to Alexandria (Tacitus, *Histories*, 2. 79–82). Almost inevitably, the Danubian legions used the opportunity to revolt and, led by Antonius Primus, they marched on Italy without waiting for Mucianus.

Although Vitellius had a significant force at his disposal in Rome, and could call on limited support from the Western provinces, the Flavian forces were potentially overwhelming. Even as the legions crossed into Italy, it must have seemed likely that Vitellius would lose. This may explain the behaviour of Alienus Caecina, the leading general of the Vitellians, who defected to the Flavians but was unable to bring his troops over with him (Tacitus, *Histories*, 2. 100–1).

The two armies met at Cremona and fought a night battle that culminated in the rout of the Vitellians. The Flavian forces captured their camp and drove on to Cremona itself. The city was sacked. The Vitellians were effectively beaten though resistance continued (Tacitus, *Histories*, 3. 16–35; Dio, 65. 11.3–15). Once Primus could tear his troops from the looting of Cremona, he marched on Rome. There was a series of minor engagements, some of which produced successes for the Vitellians, but the overwhelming numbers of the Flavian forces led to further defections.

Vitellius entered negotiations with Flavius Sabinus (Vespasian's brother) and, probably after receiving assurances for his personal safety, Vitellius abdicated, leaving the palace and entering the Forum as a private citizen. As Flavius Sabinus organised the takeover, the situation took a dramatic turn. Vitellius was returned to the palace forcibly and there were demonstrations in his favour. The Flavian party seized the Capitoline Hill where they were besieged. During the siege, the temple of Jupiter Capitolinus, the most venerable temple in Rome, was destroyed. The Vitellian soldiers defeated the senators holding the Capitol and Sabinus was executed. Domitian, Vespasian's younger son, escaped in disguise (Tacitus, *Histories*, 3.67–74).

This extraordinary spirit of defiance continued despite the overwhelming odds. The Flavian legions arrived on the outskirts of Rome but did not receive the expected surrender. They forced their way into the city and the Vitellians fought a hopeless yet valiant rearguard action across the city culminating in the capture of the praetorian barracks. Vitellius himself fled the palace only to return later, and he was captured and killed (Tacitus, *Histories*, 3. 79–85; Suetonius, *Vitellius*, 16–17; Dio, 65. 17–21).

Vitellius had managed to win the devoted loyalty of the German troops who fought two wars for him. Many must have been killed either at Cremona and, in the last hopeless battle, through the streets of Rome. Vitellius also seems to have won the loyalty of the people of Rome who backed him until the end, though the military skill of the Roman troops was such that civilians could not offer Vitellius effective aid.

When Vespasian arrived in Rome, his position was far stronger than that of Vitellius. He had the backing of the legions of the East and had decisively defeated the legions of the West. Also, the conflict in Germany and Gaul in AD 69–70 would lead to the defeat of the remaining forces in Germany. There was no substantial effective military force that could threaten Vespasian. He had Mucianus and Titus at his side. Other generals, such as Petilius Cerealis, had distinguished themselves and some of Otho's generals were to be given positions of prominence. Antonius Primus, who had effectively delivered the empire into Vespasian's hands, may have been an effective general but his failure to preserve Cremona and his attack on the city of Rome had reduced his political standing. Vespasian could attempt reconciliation confident that he faced no immediate political threat.

'Crisis' in the provinces

The civil conflict in the Roman Empire was combined with provincial disturbances. There was continued rebellion in Judaea and fresh outbreaks in Britain, Germany and Gaul (the most notable rebellion), and along the Danube frontier. Such outbreaks seemed to threaten to overwhelm the Roman Empire but, as we shall see, Rome easily re-established control and her authority was confirmed.

Judaea

The war in Judaea (see also p. 197) had resulted in a series of hard-fought conflicts as Vespasian led his legions into the province. The course of the war was marked by long sieges in which the Romans were ultimately successful, though at great cost. The Jews had not the skill, the training, nor the technology to meet the Romans in open battle and so resistance took the form of siege warfare and sorties against the Roman forces. Vespasian's campaign was stopped when he became a contender for the throne and the campaign was resumed under Titus after Vespasian's victory in the West.

Vespasian needed a quick victory and Titus' task was to provide him with that victory. The pattern of the war was unchanged and victory could only come after the capture of Jerusalem. The Roman forces besieged the city. Josephus' account makes it clear that the siege was hard fought. Titus was unwilling to allow the war to drag on. He and Vespasian had other pressing business and it must have become obvious to all that the Romans did not intend simply to wait for the Jews' food and resolve to give out. The Flavians needed a triumph, a dramatic symbol of victory to enhance their prestige; this was especially important given the problems in the West. Storming Jerusalem was no easy task. The Romans had to bring siege equipment against the walls and force a breach in the defences. The Jews attempted to defend and repair the walls and launch attacks on the siege equipment. In this, they were notably successful, but they could not force Titus to break off the siege. There was a long period of attrition, but the Jewish forces were gradually weakened and the Roman siege became more intense. Eventually, Titus' troops breached the many defences of the city and exacted their revenge for such a bloody siege. The Temple itself was sacked and destroyed.

The Temple was the central monument of Judaism to which many Jews would travel at the various religious festivals. It was their holiest site, and it was also extremely rich since it received contributions from Jews in all provinces and those friendly towards the Jewish people also contributed to Temple funds. In AD 71, the vast wealth of the Temple was to be carried through the streets of Rome in a triumph, which was depicted on Vespasian and Titus' triumphal arch (known as the arch of Titus). The temple was never to be rebuilt and its destruction led to fundamental changes in Judaism.

Further operations continued in the region with the siege of Masada and the suppression of 'bandit' activity, yet, although this campaign was hard, Vespasian and Titus were justified in seeing the fall of Jerusalem as marking the end of the major stage of the war.

The revolt was also contained. The Jewish populations of the neighbouring provinces may have wished to support their co-religionists, but their minority position was more likely to lead to their persecution by the pagan population than any mass outbreak.

The Danube

Little is known about the outbreaks in this period. Tacitus (*Histories*, 1.79) tells us that the Rhoxolani, a tribe living north of the Danube, crossed the river during the reign of Otho and invaded Moesia, but were defeated. Similarly, in late 69, the Dacians crossed the Danube to raid. Although the garrison had been significantly weakened by the expedition to Italy under Primus, the Dacians unluckily ran into Mucianus and his legions heading west from Syria and were defeated (Tacitus, *Histories*, 3.46). However, the Dacians may have continued to pose problems for the Romans throughout 69, and later, though the detail of these wars is lost. The Sarmatians also caused problems, though again little is known about these outbreaks (Tacitus, *Histories*, 1.2; 4.54). Such outbreaks may signify growing problems in the lands north of the Danube and may be precursors of the much more serious threats to the Danubian provinces that were faced by Vespasian and Domitian (see p. 252, pp. 266–68). It seems likely, however, that these raids took advantage of the temporary weakness of the Roman frontiers but did not pose a serious threat to Roman rule in the area.

Britain

We have no significant information about events in Britain from the departure of Suetonius Paulinus until AD 69, and one must presume that the latter years of Nero's reign were occupied by a policy of consolidation and pacification of areas disturbed by the Boudiccan revolt. In 69, there seems to have been conflict between the governor and the officers of the legion, conflict which reached such a pitch that the governor fled to join Vitellius. The fact that the legions also declared for Vitellius (though they were later to declare for Vespasian who had served in Britain, perhaps urged on by the Fourteenth Legion) suggests that the issue in question was not which candidate to support in the civil wars, but may have been corruption (Tacitus, *Histories*, 1.59–60).

Vitellius returned the Fourteenth Legion to Britain in 69. The legion had been prominent among the defeated Othonian forces at Bedriacum and was mutinous (Tacitus, *Histories*, 2.66). The return of the legion may have been prompted by a fresh outbreak of anti-Roman activity. Cartimandua, the queen of the Brigantes (a tribe of northern Britain) who had proved herself a friend of Rome since the conquest, was ousted in a coup staged by her former husband, Venutius (Tacitus, *Histories*, 3. 45). Cartimandua was rescued by the Romans, but they were unable to secure the province and war continued into the Flavian period when Petilius Cerealis launched a major campaign into Brigantia (see p. 237). Tacitus' description reduces the politics of the revolt to a scandalous marriage within the royal household, but the fact that the Romans were not easily able to secure the region suggests that there may have been serious problems.

Germany and Gaul

We have already suggested that Gallic discontent fuelled the rebellions of Vindex and Vitellius. During Vitellius' reign, events took a different turn with the creation of the 'Empire of the Gauls', though this was an event subsidiary to the revolt of the Batavians.

The Batavians lived on a stretch of land along the Lower Rhine. They had long provided the Roman army with auxiliary units, which were particularly valued not just for their fighting prowess but also for their skill in fording rivers. There had been conflicts between the Batavians and other Roman troops before the outbreak of the civil wars, but Vitellius had attempted to patch together an agreement in order to secure the support of the Batavians in the forthcoming conflicts. Unfortunately, the Vitellians' demand for troops led to heavy-handed and corrupt recruitment among the Batavians. Julius Civilis led the revolt. They were joined by their neighbouring tribe, the Cannenefates, and gained support from other Germanic tribes. The Cannenefates and Batavians attacked and massacred small local garrisons. A two-legionary army was sent against them, though the legions were depleted by troops levied by Vitellius. This force was defeated and forced to retreat to the legionary camp of Vetera (Tacitus, *Histories*, 4. 12–18).

The next stage of the revolt was a mutiny staged by units of Batavians and Cannenefates within the Roman army, though their exact location at the time of their revolt is unclear (they were probably in Germania Superior heading towards Italy). Hordeonius Flaccus, governor in Germany, had to decide whether to oppose their march or allow them to join with Civilis. Flaccus was worried about the quality of troops at his disposal and the loyalty of the Gallic troops with his army. He allowed the Batavians to start on their march, but instructed Legion I to intercept them. The legion was heavily defeated and the Batavians made their way to join Civilis, adding substantially to his military strength (Tacitus, *Histories*, 4. 19–20).

Civilis' forces had defeated three legions and established control over much of Germania Inferior. Already, two more tribes, the Bructeri and Tencteri, had joined the revolt and Civilis might hope for more support. The addition of the Batavian cohorts gave Civilis a core of well-trained and experienced soldiers around which to build his army. He became more confident and launched an attack on the legionary garrison in Germania Inferior in its camp at Vetera. The Batavians and their allies did not have the equipment to storm the camp, though its fortifications may not have been strong, and were repulsed from the walls. The Romans did not have the strength to break out, however, and Civilis besieged the camp (Tacitus, *Histories*, 4.21–3).

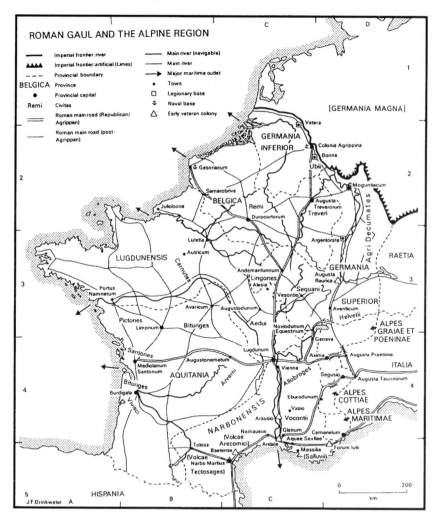

Map 7.1 Roman Gaul and Germany (from Talbert 1984)

The situation was perilous. Flaccus mobilised the resources of Germania Superior and sent his general, Vocula, north into Germania Inferior to face the Batavians and relieve Vetera. At this stage, news of the defeat of Vitellius seems to have reached Germany. The Roman troops stationed in Germany had shown great loyalty to Vitellius and the defeat of their comrades in Italy was likely to have affected morale. It may also have affected their view of their commanders. There was a suspicion that the Batavian revolt had been encouraged by the Flavians and that the legions were faced by enemies in both the Batavians and the new emperor. The smooth way in which the legions' commanders transferred their loyalty from Vitellius to Vespasian also caused the troops to doubt their former commitment to the Vitellian cause (Tacitus, *Histories*, 4.32). The troops felt betrayed.

Vocula marched on Vetera with a mutinous army. The relief column was attacked by Civilis but, not without difficulty, Vocula drove off the Batavians. The legions managed to reach Vetera. They were, however, short of supplies. The situation was so serious that Vocula was forced to retreat, leaving a garrison in Vetera. Although the expedition to Vetera had not produced a decisive battle, the campaign had ended in a further Roman defeat, increasing the prestige of Civilis and worsening the morale of the Roman troops (Tacitus, *Histories*, 4.33–7). On return to Germania Superior, the troops were openly mutinous: Vocula had to flee a lynch mob that claimed the life of Hordeonius Flaccus. Order was restored with difficulty, but the strategic situation had been made worse by the expedition. Civilis promptly besieged Vetera once more. German tribesmen now roamed across Germania Inferior and raided into neighbouring districts. There was little the Romans could do to stop them.

The anarchy that reigned among the legions, and their repeated defeat by Civilis, changed the political situation. The legions no longer seemed invincible and the Gauls looked for other means to secure their safety. Civilis had entered negotiations with Rome's Gallic allies and an alliance was formed involving the Treviri and the Lingones. The new allies appealed to all Gaul, seeking to form an Empire of the Gauls. The alliance remained secret initially, though Vocula must have been aware that his position was difficult. He decided to take the initiative by marching on Vetera once more. On the march, however, the Gallic auxiliaries defected and made overtures to the legions themselves. Vocula could not bring them to order and he was assassinated. The legions were enrolled into service with the new Gallic Empire. The troops besieged in Vetera were now without hope and surrendered. Both Germanies had fallen and at least parts of Gaul were now in rebellion (Tacitus, *Histories*, 4.54–60).

Almost as soon as the Gallic Empire was founded, it was under threat from both internal division and external intervention. The Flavians gathered a large army to invade Germany and Gaul under the command of Petilius Cerealis and Annius Gallus. The threat posed by eight legions was sufficient to force the Gauls into reconsidering their position. Gaul was not a nation state but a group of tribes politically independent of each other. Political divisions between the various tribes had been shown during the revolt of Vindex when tribes such as the Treviri and Lingones had not supported Vindex. Also, although the legionaries had come over to the Gallic Empire, their repeated defeats meant that they were not a realistic or reliable force with which to face the victorious Flavian legions. The Batavians and Gauls were more than capable, but they were no match for the legions approaching them. The chances of the Gallic Empire surviving the coming assault were slim, and many of the Gallic tribes either failed to join the Empire or quickly returned to Rome (Tacitus, *Annales*, 4.68–9).

Cerealis led the advance with mixed success. The Treviri were decisively defeated but Cerealis himself suffered the embarrassment of losing his camp in a raid launched by Civilis (Tacitus, *Histories*, 4. 71–7). The legions that had defected returned in disgrace. Eventually, Cerealis reached Vetera where Civilis made his stand. The first battle resulted in a victory for Civilis, but the legions were undaunted. Cerealis managed to out-manoeuvre Civilis and drive the Batavians back. Civilis launched a series of successful counter-attacks but was unable to halt Cerealis' advance. The Batavians retreated to a territory known as the Island. The Romans were faced with a river crossing if they were to continue their pursuit, but were able to ravage Batavian land south of the Island. The result was stalemate. The Romans had failed to bring the Batavians to a decisive battle and looked unable to dislodge them from the Island. The Batavians had lost some territory but were in a position to continue the war. Petilius entered into negotiations which appear to have resulted in peace (Tacitus, *Histories*, 5.14–26).

Conclusions

The revolts that swept the Roman world in this period can be related to problems that arose either during the latter years of Nero's reign or result from the military and political events of the civil wars. These revolts stretched Roman resources but, once the civil wars ended, there can have been little doubt that the Romans would restore the Empire. The formation of the Gallic Empire may have seemed to threaten the dissolution of the Roman Empire. The Jewish War was undoubtedly a major event, forcing Vespasian and later Titus to concentrate vast forces and leading to widespread destruction. To an extent, we know more about the Jewish War because it was so important to the Flavians and because the history of the Jewish War, written by Josephus, assumed a religious importance for Christian writers in that the destruction of the Temple was an event of major theological significance. Yet, there can be little doubt that the combination of civil conflict and major regional revolts was a significant challenge to Roman power.

The questions that arise from these revolts are important for our histories of the Roman Empire. In a previous age, it was assumed that peoples had an innate desire for national self-determination, so that the Britons would prefer British kings, the Batavians and Gauls their local rulers, and the Jews a Jewish state of some form, but historians have become sceptical about the existence of nationalism in the ancient world. Although 'national' characteristics are frequently alluded to by Greek and Roman authors and you get what are effectively ethnic stereotypes (sometimes quite different from those of modern prejudices), there was little sense that a nation or a people would be better governed if they were governed by one of their own. Nationalism is a modern phenomenon and only became of widespread political significance in the eighteenth century and later. The Romans sometimes used client kings, local aristocrats or members of a local royal family, to govern regions for them: Julius Civilis fits into this pattern. Yet, the use of established local powers was in some ways merely a convenience for Roman governments. As an administrative policy, it was easier than establishing a new power structure, a governor, a new taxation system, and new institutions in a conquered region. The Romans could turn a conquered area into a province, but they could achieve their aims and extract the troops and money they desired from a client kings as easily as from a provincial administration.

If we cannot understand the revolts in Britain, Gaul, and Judaea as nationalistic outbreaks, we are, then, forced to wonder what was really happening in this period?

One possibility is to treat the events as separate. The Jewish revolt broke out three years before the other revolts. One could understand the problems in Britain and in Gaul as a response to the civil wars and the insecurity of those wars. The demands placed on the provincial territories were probably increased as the various contending parties gathered resources for their wars. It seems also that each revolt had its own proximate causes, mostly related to the rapacity of Roman governance. The revolts all, ultimately, failed. The Gallic Empire itself was illusory and collapsed in the face of mutual hostilities and the failure to accept a unified authority. The Jewish resistance to Rome fragmented, Josephus himself defecting from the rebellion to the Flavian armies. In spite of the trauma of the civil wars, Rome was able to restore her Empire without significant territorial losses. The civil wars may have shown weaknesses in Rome's political and military organisation, but they also demonstrated the power and solidity of the Roman Empire.

There is a positive way to understand these rebellions then. We can survey the history of the Roman Empire and point to a lack of organised opposition. We see revolts from time to time, such as the revolt of Florus and Sacrovir in Gaul under Tiberius and the Boudiccan revolt in Britain, but we do not see an Empire straining for freedom. We could argue that at most times the provincial people were relatively content and acquiesced in Roman rule. There is the possibility that some rebellious events were not reported in our sources.

Some major rebellions later, such as the Jewish War of 117 and the Bar Kokhba revolt of 136 are merely reported in our source material and the surviving evidence is very slight. We might imagine that revolts in remoter areas might not have been reported at all. Yet, although the *Pax Romana* (Roman Peace) might be exaggerated, it was certainly not invented.

There is, however, a danger in our remoteness from these events. We read all the revolts through Roman eyes. Tacitus, Cassius Dio, and even Josephus represent an official view of the revolts, and the relative absence of rebellious voices might delude us into thinking such voices did not exist. The Romans were unlikely to have spent much time collecting, analysing and recording the thoughts and feelings of those who were in rebellion and to a certain extent there is a tendency to trivialise the motives of those who rebel. Further, we should not ignore the risks of rebellion. There were no international conventions to protect the rights of the defeated or to prevent violence against non-combatants. Defeat did not mean the removal of a political class and perhaps some reparations. If a Roman army stormed a city, its inhabitants would be subjected to rape, enslavement, and murder. Lives were preserved to the extent that the survivors were assets. All movable wealth was looted. Immovable wealth (houses and the like) were often burnt. Sometimes defeated peoples preferred mass suicide to what was to befall them, and this was not a romantic attachment to liberty (as reflected in, for instance, Patrick Henry's rousing 'Give me liberty, or give me death' speech on the verge of American War of Independence), but an expectation of the violence that was to come.

The Roman military machine was the most effective and brutal instrument of repression of its time. There can have been little doubt that once the legions were reorganised after the Flavian victories, the Jews and the Gallic Empire would be faced with overwhelming force. In such circumstances, many would have considered a rapid accommodation with Rome to be the only viable option. The problem with revolts against Rome is not how to explain why there were so few, but why, given the overwhelming historical experience and the potential risks, anyone ever dared to rebel.

A further feature of the civil wars in the West was the behaviour of the Roman troops. Troops fought vicious battles for Otho and Vitellius and Vespasian. Troops also defected from Rome to Civilis and his Batavians. There is nothing in Tacitus' *Histories*, which would allow us to understand why the troops fought so hard and so long. Vitellius' troops in Rome, for instance, must have known that the approaching Flavian armies would win. They were not fighting for any obvious ideal. They were not fighting on behalf of Rome. Nor was the fighting obviously in their best interests. What appears to have mattered to the troops was their loyalty to each other and perhaps to the peoples of their local communities. They had no over-arching loyalty to an emperor, especially after the death of Nero. One of the lessons of AD 68 and 69 was that the nature of the Roman troops was changing and the political attitudes and interests of those troops were complex, and not necessarily closely related to those of the masters in Rome.

In 68–9, the military came to the forefront of political life. To a certain extent, the troops developed political attitudes independent of their commanders. Their disaffection was instrumental in the accessions of Otho and Vitellius and the troops fought long and hard for both men. The inability of men like Caecina to win over his troops when he defected to Vespasian, and the reluctance of troops in Germany to accept the accession of Vespasian when their officers seem to have accepted the political inevitability of Vespasian's success shows that the troops were not simply manipulated by their officers into giving support to their chosen candidate. The secret of empire was that Emperors needed the acquiescence of the soldiers and that emperors were thus made elsewhere than in Rome.

Vespasian was able to build a coalition of powerful aristocratic supporters, men like Mucianus, Tiberius Julius Alexander, Petilius Cerealis, and his own son Titus, and it was very much in his interests to be seen as the choice of the aristocrat, bringing in a new era of peaceful, rational governance after the excess of the Julio-Claudian. But his victory was always and ultimately a military victory. It was a soldiers' victory and he was the soldiers' choice.

Chapter 8

Vespasian and Titus (AD 70–81)

There is a change in the nature of our available source material from the reign of Vespasian onwards. For the narrative history of the period we have to rely on the fragments of Dio preserved in Byzantine epitomes and it is frequently difficult to date the events mentioned. Tacitus does write about the period but his observations are contained in the *Agricola* and the *Dialogus*, neither of which provide narrative histories. Our other main guide is Suetonius, but the biographies of the Flavians are less detailed than those of earlier emperors. As a result, though we can perceive at least some of the more general developments, it is almost impossible to produce a detailed narrative of these years.

Vespasian associated his rule with his elder son, Titus. Thus, when the elderly Vespasian died, the succession was smooth and Titus took over as expected. Vespasian's reign has been generally well received by posterity but Titus' reign seems to have been regarded as almost a golden age. However, his reign was short and he was quickly succeeded by his brother, the hated Domitian (see Figure 8.1).

Politics

Friends and allies

On accession, Vespasian was the fifth emperor in two years. The Flavians were not a particularly distinguished family. In his early career, Vespasian had failed to secure the aedileship (see p. 6 for the nature of this office) at his first attempt, a sign that he did not have powerful political backing. When he eventually became aedile, he was famously dropped in mud by Gaius for not keeping the streets of Rome clean. In fact, his career may not have prospered until the reign of Claudius when he served with distinction in Britain and Germany. He was rewarded with a consulship in AD 51 and later governed Africa. He was in Nero's party that headed off to Greece, but supposedly slept through Nero's dramatic performances (which we can either read as moderate opposition or as an attempt by later tradition to disassociate Vespasian from

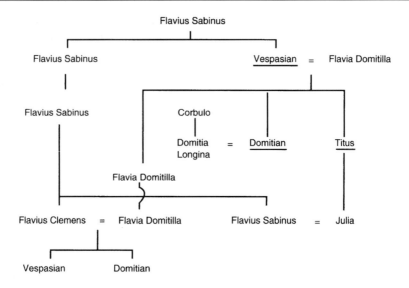

Figure 8.1 The Flavian family

Neronian revels). In spite of this obvious breach of taste, Nero chose him to command the troops in Judaea (Suetonius, *Vespasian*, 2–5). Vespasian achieved prominence with this command, but he was no more elevated socially than other provincial governors and was probably less credible as an imperial candidate than Galba or Vitellius.

Vespasian did, however, have powerful friends. He was supported by Mucianus. Comparatively little is known about this man, though his authority and leadership were amply demonstrated by the way in which he took charge of Rome following Primus' anarchic seizure of the capital (see pp. 220–23). Mucianus appointed Vespasian's first praetorian prefects and probably appointed Petilius Cerealis to the Batavian campaign. Mucianus' role in Rome during the long period before Vespasian's arrival demonstrates Vespasian's trust in the man. He was rewarded with consulships in AD 70 and 72. Holding two consulships so close was unprecedented for someone who was not emperor and in itself suggests that he was seen as central to Vespasian's regime. After his consulships, Mucianus remained in Rome, probably blending a political career with literary pursuits.

Titus was also a prominent figure during Vespasian's reign. He took charge of the war in Judaea and led the troops to a quick and bloody victory in capturing Jerusalem in 70 (see pp. 222–23). Although the war did not end until Flavius Silva (possibly a distant relative) stormed Masada in 73, Titus returned to Rome to share a lavish triumphal procession with Vespasian in 71. The triumph displayed Vespasian's power in a traditional style (by now triumphs had become the prerogative of the imperial family) and thus reinforced the legitimacy of his rule. By sharing the limelight with his son, Vespasian made it clear that he planned a dynasty. This was further marked when Vespasian and Titus held a joint consulship in 70 (Vespasian's first as emperor). Titus was *consul ordinarius* in 72, 74, 75, 76, 77 and 79, a remarkable succession of consulships. As Vespasian also held eight consulships during his reign, the two virtually monopolised the ordinary consulships, though a large number of suffect consuls were appointed (see pp. 343–44 for the differences between 'ordinary' and 'suffect' consulships). Titus was also appointed praetorian prefect (Suetonius, *Titus*, 6), possibly as early as 71, and thus took charge of the largest military force in Italy and the emperor's personal security. Vespasian's reliance on him was clear.

Vespasian's other son, Domitian, was also honoured. He was granted suffect consulships in 71, 74, 76, 77 and 79, and ordinary consulships in 73 and 80. He wielded some authority in 70 as the senior member of the Flavian family in Rome. His prominence in the consular lists shows that he was an important member of the regime.

Vespasian's brother, Sabinus, had been a popular senator (pp. 215–19) and although his death in the civil wars robbed Vespasian of his personal support, Sabinus' son, also Flavius Sabinus, was granted a second consulship in 72 (he held his first in 69).

Petilius Cerealis, a relative by marriage, also enjoyed power (Tacitus, *Histories*, 3.59). Cerealis had served in Britain in 61 when the legion he was commanding had been defeated by the Boudiccan rebels. He was in Rome when Vespasian made his bid for the throne, but managed to escape and led troops against the Vitellians. He was rewarded by being given the command against Civilis and a suffect consulship in 70. He was then sent to Britain to campaign against the Brigantes and probably returned in 74 when he was granted a second consulship.

Tiberius Julius Alexander also received due reward. He had served the Flavian cause in Egypt and had presumably cemented his relationship with Vespasian during Vespasian's rather difficult stay in Alexandria awaiting news from Italy. Alexander probably took part in the campaigns in Judaea under Titus and is recorded as being prefect of the Jews and procurator in Syria (*IGRR* III 1015). He may have journeyed to Italy soon after the conclusion of the Jewish war where he had been Titus' colleague as praetorian prefect (*P. Hibeh*. 215). The exact chronology of his advancement is difficult to establish.

There were others of less prominence who were influential in the Flavian camp: men such as M. Ulpius Traianus, the father of the future emperor, who served in the Judaean war with Vespasian and Titus and who was subsequently rewarded with a consulship, provincial governorships and a priesthood (*Inscriptiones Latinae Selectae*, 8970). We know less about the future emperor Nerva, who had risen to prominence by displaying loyalty to Nero during the Pisonian conspiracy and had been granted an ordinary consulship in 71 with

Vespasian. The domination of the consulship by Titus and Vespasian was such that only Domitian and L. Valerius Catullus Messalinus (in 73), L. Ceionius Commodus and D. Junius Novius Priscus (in 78) and Nerva were allowed ordinary consulships during Vespasian's reign. Nerva must have been close to the centre of the Flavian group.

Reconstructing the friendships and alliances at the heart of the Flavian regime is complex and hazardous and the patterns of alliances will have changed as Vespasian promoted new men and gained the friendship and trust of others. Yet, although Vespasian was clearly in charge, Vespasian seems to have avoided any of the megalomaniac representations of imperial power which had marked the Julio-Claudian period. Instead, Vespasian used a close-knit coterie of friends to establish a collectivity at the heart of the regime. The group of friends and relations which had brought the Flavians to power, held on to the reins of that power. There was to be no devolution of authority to the senators.

Manners and the senate

It may seem inconsequential to discuss the manners of an emperor, but such matters were important in Roman politics. The senators formed a small community and it mattered very much to them whether the emperor was friendly, whether he behaved as their superior or their equal, or whether he addressed them as a civilian or a general. They needed to know whether the emperor was one of them (a fellow senator) or their king.

Vespasian did not have the social status that would allow him to assert superiority over the senators: they knew he was of no better birth than them. It seems unlikely that anyone would take seriously a claim to divinity, and following the lead of Nero was problematic. Vespasian could rely on military power, but, as Claudius discovered, this would not lead to a peaceful life. Vespasian played the senator and stripped the imperial position of much of its ostentation. He did not live in the imperial palace but in a house in the Gardens of Sallust, which was a park in the centre of Rome. There, he received visitors from early in the morning. He made sure that the guard was not obvious and he gave up the practice of searching visitors. Personally, he was not above the banter of political life and rather liked to satirise his own pretensions (Suetonius, *Vespasian*, 12–13; 21–2; Dio, 66. 10–11). His most famous witticism is typical: as his last illness weakened him he is said to have remarked, 'Alas, I think I am becoming a god'. At the very moment when his physical frailty and mortality must have been most obvious, he recognised his approaching deification (Suetonius, *Vespasian*, 23).

Vespasian represented himself in the mode of the traditional Italian aristocrat and there was a certain lack of refinement to his manner. He famously revoked a military command from a man who was over-perfumed (Suetonius, *Vespasian*, 8) and he used obscenities in everyday speech. His desire for money rather than honours marked out his practicality. He may not have been what the senate wanted, but at least he was comprehensible. The regime had a utilitarian quality and the lack of cultural and political pretension was in itself a political stance: it differentiated him from the previous regimes (Vespasian had none of the terrifying unpredictability of the later Julio-Claudians) but also established a connection with the provincial aristocracies of Roman Italy rather than the old families (and traditions) of Rome. In so doing, he emphasised the realities of imperial power: Rome needed the emperor and the events of 68–70 had shown the impotence of the senate. The senators had little choice but to accept Flavian domination and be grateful for Vespasian's easy-going nature. Nevertheless, Vespasian had become emperor through civil war. He and his allies could be ruthless in maintaining their hold on power. Vespasian may not have purged the Roman aristocracy in quite the ruthless manner of the Julio-Claudians, but he was prepared to kill his enemies.

His most famous political feud was with Helvidius Priscus. Priscus had been exiled by Nero and on his return to Rome following Nero's death, became the leading member of the group that had grown up around Thrasea Paetus. The group continued its tradition of opposition (pp. 198–206). Vespasian's attitude towards them is unclear. Tacitus tells us that Vespasian had been friendly with Thrasea and Soranus during the reign of Nero (Tacitus, *Histories*, 4. 6–7). Thrasea's status as martyr and leading senator may have encouraged those favourable to Vespasian to invent such a friendship, but the behaviour of the Flavians in the first months of the new regime suggests that they may have been well disposed to Priscus and his group. Such a relationship may explain why Musonius Rufus, another member of Thrasea's group, and Arulenus Rusticus (a close friend of Thrasea, see p. 200) were chosen to lead a senatorial embassy to Antonius Primus to persuade him not to storm Rome in 69 (Tacitus, *Histories*, 3. 80–1). If this was the case, the accession of Vespasian would have raised the expectations of Priscus and his friends that they would be allowed to exact revenge on their enemies.

They did not wait long. Musonius Rufus, a prominent philosopher and senator, launched a prosecution of Publius Celer (the prosecutor of Barea Soranus) immediately after the Flavian seizure of Rome (Tacitus, *Histories*, 4.10). Flavian support for Rufus suggests friendly relations with Priscus and his circle. Helvidius Priscus then launched his attack. Priscus and a certain Curtius Montanus prosecuted Eprius Marcellus and Aquilius Regulus, who had both been prominent under Nero. Marcellus had brought the charges against Thrasea. The prosecution was blocked. The Flavians desired reconciliation and investigations into the events of Nero's reign would lead to conflict among the senators. Priscus was not to be allowed his revenge (Tacitus, *Histories*, 4. 40–4), but nor was he to be appeased.

Priscus appears never to have fully recognised Vespasian's accession, but Vespasian ignored minor slights. More seriously, Priscus launched a direct attack on the Flavian dynasty. Dio (66. 12.1) preserves an account of Priscus attacking the Emperor in the senate-house with such vitriol that the tribunes stepped in and arrested Priscus, leading him from the house. Vespasian left proclaiming 'My son shall succeed me or no one shall'. If Dio has preserved the story correctly, then it would seem that the attack had focused not on Vespasian himself but on Titus. But Titus was at the heart of the regime.

Priscus continued to attack Vespasian, though we do not know the details of the conflict. Vespasian's response was to honour Priscus' enemy, Eprius Marcellus with a provincial governorship to (*IGRR* IV 524; *Inscriptiones Latinae Selectae* 992) which removed Marcellus from Rome. But Marcellus was subjected to another prosecution on his return to Rome, probably to take up a consulship in 74. Tacitus tells us that Marcellus got the better of this conflict, perhaps suggesting that Priscus had lost the sympathy of the senate (*Dialogus* 5). Vespasian's response was to exile and then kill Priscus (Suetonius, *Vespasian*, 15; Dio, 66. 12.2).

Marcellus himself was to come to grief in 79. He was involved in a conspiracy with Alienus Caecina (see pp. 219–21). Caecina was detected with a speech that he intended to deliver to the soldiers and was struck down by Titus at Titus' own dinner table, a deed reminiscent of the ruthless killings of the Julio-Claudian period (Suetonius, *Titus*, 6; Dio, 66. 16.3–4). The background to the conspiracy and the nature of Marcellus' involvement is unclear.

Trying to understand the politics of these events is very difficult, but it doesn't prevent historians from trying. The material we have is so fragmentary that any reconstruction of the internal politics of the Flavian faction is fantastical. Some modern writers, for instance, have seen in this conspiracy a violent resolution of tensions in the Flavian camp that had been simmering since 69, tensions which had disturbed the relationship between Mucianus and Titus. They have suggested that it was Mucianus who first extended his patronage to Marcellus, saving Marcellus from the wrath of the senate, to the displeasure of Titus, and that Mucianus prevented Titus from bringing his Jewish lover Berenice to Rome. There are suggestions that Titus forced Mucianus' out so that Mucianus now had the time to be able to win renown for a devotion to literature late in life (Tacitus, *Dialogus*, 37) and the arrival of Berenice in Rome has been seen as signifying Mucianus' retirement some time before 75, a retirement which left Marcellus in a politically-exposed position, resulting in his removal in 79. The presumption that feuding between Titus and Domitian was the dominant political issue of the period has some ancient support (Suetonius, *Titus* 9–3, 10; *Domitian*, 2.3), but some of this is later literary invention that serves to contrast the good (Titus) and the bad (Domitian). Also, Domitian's comparatively minor role under Vespasian was not a mark of disrespect to the younger brother but a recognition of the fact that Domitian was not expected to succeed to the throne and that Titus was, from the beginning, a partner in his father's power. When Titus came to the throne, Domitian and Titus took the consulship of 80 together, demonstrating the unity of the imperial family.

Much else of the political history of the period is lost. Suetonius (*Vespasian*, 25; cf. *Titus*, 6) talks of many conspiracies against Vespasian, but provides no evidence, and the fact that both Suetonius and Dio note the relative paucity of senatorial and equestrian deaths suggests that these conspiracies, if they were not figments of Suetonius' imagination, were not serious. Titus similarly killed no senators, though Suetonius tells us that he was threatened by a conspiracy (Suetonius, *Titus*, 9).

Much of the opposition to the Flavians seems to have been very vocal and unafraid of the ability of the emperors to kill them. Whereas Thrasea Paetus had attempted to avoid open conflict with Nero, Helvidius Priscus welcomed public confrontations. Similar public confrontations were sought by two philosophers, Diogenes and Heras, who both spoke against Vespasian in the theatre. Diogenes was flogged. Heras, who came later, when patience had been tried, was decapitated. One might guess that their philosophy taught them contempt for the world so that they had no fear of being deprived of life, and that advertising this contempt in the face of official pressure demonstrated the strength of their conviction and attracted attention and followers. Dictatorial regimes that rely on the character of those in charge to legitimate their control (as was the case with the Flavians) find those willing to expose their moral and political weaknesses disturbing and those who do not fear death are almost impossible to control. Vespasian made public examples of Diogenes and Heras. Helvidius Priscus was more difficult, and Vespasian may have felt unwilling or unable to act until Priscus had lost senatorial support and his regime was relatively secure. Such discordant voices probably represent a much larger element of the political classes. Yet Vespasian and Titus were not dethroned by their opponents and Vespasian had his wish in that he was succeeded (peacefully) by his sons.

Military policy

Vespasian faced considerable problems when he came to the throne. There was war in Judaea, Germany and Britain and unrest along the Danube (pp. 224–31). In the East, Vespasian and Titus were mainly occupied with ending the war in Judaea. In the West, they were able to begin a process of renewed imperial expansion.

Much of this has been detailed in the previous chapter. In the East, in addition to the problems in Judaea, Vespasian annexed a number of client-kingdoms, Cilicia and Commagene being militarily significant. The annexation of Commagene involved a brief war (Josephus, *Bellum Judaicum*, 7. 220–40). In Britain, Vespasian and Titus followed an aggressive policy. Cerealis was sent from his campaigns in Germany to Britain. We know little about his campaigns but the archaeological evidence suggests that he pushed the Roman frontier to the north of Brigantian territory and established forts throughout what is modern Yorkshire. Cerealis was followed by Julius

Frontinus who campaigned in South Wales against the Silures. Julius Agricola, Tacitus' father-in-law, was sent to the province in 77–8 and campaigned throughout the next seven years. His campaigns took him from North Wales to the very north of Scotland. His victories seem to have brought much of Britain under Roman control, though Tacitus' claims for Agricola are undoubtedly exaggerated (Tacitus, *Agricola*). We know less about the campaigns in Germany after peace was made with the Batavians. The frontier needed to be secured and the damage of the Batavian revolt repaired. In addition, relationships with the German tribes that had been disturbed by the revolt had to be restored. It is clear that the frontier was reorganised with a new camp built at Vetera and legionary forces stationed close to the Batavians. At some point, the Romans went on the offensive. This can be traced in the Neckar valley between the Rhine and the Danube, where there seems to have been a Roman advance. New forts were built in this region. There may have been other military action further to the north but the territory acquired cannot have been great.

Building and finance

The treasury was empty when the Flavians took over. The excesses of Nero, gifts to soldiers and the expenses of civil war led to a rapid depletion of funds. The damage to Rome and other cities needed to be repaired and military expenses had to be met. Vespasian needed money. Taxes were raised (in some cases doubled) and new taxes invented, most notable being a tax on Jews, which was levied for the repair of the Capitoline temple and as a punishment for the rebellion, and a tax on urinals. (The latter led to another instance of Vespasian's humour. Titus had objected to the tax and was some time later summoned to his father. Vespasian gave him a gold coin and asked him to sniff it. Obviously, he could smell nothing. And then he was told that this was the result of the urinal tax.) Vespasian was not above selling minor offices and even acquittals in legal cases. He may also have used his financial resources to corner the market in certain goods and then make a profit on their resale (Suetonius, *Vespasian*, 16, 23.2–3).

This suggests financial desperation, but Vespasian met his obligations to be generous to his friends, to sponsor the arts, to entertain the plebs, and to provide emergency aid to communities in distress, and he also managed to embark on an ambitious building programme. On his death, the finances were sufficiently healthy that they could meet the very heavy expenditure of Titus' reign and the cost of the donatives paid to the troops on the accessions of Titus and Domitian.

Vespasian's major building project was to repair the damage caused by the civil war in Rome. The most notable casualty was the Temple of Jupiter on the Capitoline Hill. This was one of the oldest and most important sacred sites in the city. Its destruction was regarded as a national catastrophe and a symbol of the self-destructive nature of civil war. Vespasian himself supervised the clearance of the site, apparently carrying a load of rubble away on his head (Suetonius, *Vespasian*, 8.5).

The focus of Vespasian's building marked a radical change from that of Nero's. Whereas Nero's most notable construction had been his palace (and in this he followed the pattern set by Gaius' additions to the Domus Tiberiana), Vespasian moved out of the palace and used the area of the Domus Aurea for public building projects. His most famous construction is the Colosseum, a huge amphitheatre in the centre of Rome. Although Vespasian claimed to be fulfilling a plan of Augustus in constructing such a huge building, the Colosseum was part of an attempt by the Flavians to win popular favour. For similar reasons, he rebuilt the stage building at the theatre of Marcellus (Suetonius, *Vespasian*, 19). Vespasian rebuilt or completed a temple to the Divus Claudius. He built a large temple to Pax (Peace), which appears to have been the centrepiece of a new Forum complex: the building continued the process of extending the Forum area of Rome that had been started by Caesar and Augustus and was to be continued by Nerva, Trajan and Hadrian. Vespasian also re-erected a colossal statue (the statue of Nero from the Domus Aurea) either in or near the Forum that, Dio (66. 15) claims, had the features of Nero or Titus. The Arch of Titus at the entrance to the Forum from the Colosseum was a monument to the Flavians' great military achievement in sacking Jerusalem.

Titus' reign was marked by massive expenditure. On accession, he needed to pay donatives to the troops. He completed the Colosseum, and added a set of baths to the amphitheatre. The Colosseum was opened with lavish shows, partly to celebrate the new building, partly to demonstrate Titus' own generosity and care for the plebs (Suetonius, *Titus*, 7.3; 8.2; Dio, 66. 25). The cost of these entertainments was probably dwarfed by the expenses of disaster relief and repair incurred during his reign. In AD 79, Vesuvius erupted. Pompeii and Herculaneum were destroyed. There was probably extensive earthquake damage in surrounding communities and the debris may have affected local agriculture. The following year, a fire swept through the centre of Rome, destroying many buildings on the Campus Martius. Again, those made homeless were provided with immediate help. The emperor was also faced with the expensive task of repairing or rebuilding monuments. Titus himself is supposed to have responded to news of the fire merely by saying 'I am lost'. To economise, he used the statues from his own villas to decorate public buildings (Suetonius, *Titus*, 8.3–4; Dio, 66. 21–4). Such generosity must have drained the public purse but will have won Titus many friends, especially among the lower classes. Titus, however, did not live long enough to enjoy his popularity. He died of a fever in September AD 81, aged 40.

The building programme was a policy statement. It made clear that the Flavians were powers of historic proportions; they were not shy about advertising their success. Yet, Flavian power was not centred on the person of the emperor. We can see this in Vespasian's final joke as mentioned above. His reality, his human and frail and dying reality, was one step removed from Vespasian the emperor. The imperial position demanded that he would become a god and indeed, his sons would require him to become a god, but the man was different. Vespasian acknowledged that difference in a manner which Gaius and Nero could not have done. For them, their power was something innate to their being. In this changed attitude towards the imperial position, the Flavians marked a transition in the imperial position: the legitimacy of imperial rule rested not on the person of the emperor, but on something else. However, what that something else was is not obvious. In part, Flavian legitimacy rested on the position itself: the imperial position was a role that Rome needed and this need was now unquestioned. In part, Flavian legitimacy stemmed simply from Vespasian's victory in the civil wars. The reality of imperial power was that Vespasian was the last man standing at the end of that conflict and that no one could challenge his power. In this political realism, a utilitarianism that Vespasian openly advertised, there was a recognition of the violent reality of imperial power, but perhaps that honesty was easier to accommodate than the various constructions of imperial legitimacy of the Julio-Claudians.

Titus' reputation

History has been kind to Titus. Suetonius remarks on his personal skills and virtues, the generosity of his reign and the kindliness with which he dealt with friends and foes while he was emperor. This portrayal is in marked contrast with the treatment of his brother and it seems very likely that Titus' reputation has benefited from the comparison.

Titus' reign was sufficiently short that it avoided the gradual accumulation of animosities that marked every other reign and eventually led to conflict. There are, however, certain signs of tension between Titus and the Roman elite that give rise to the suspicion that such conflict would not have been avoided. Titus had been an active praetorian prefect and the cutting down of the conspirators of 79 showed a brutality that may have led some to fear his reign (see p. 236). His personal morality also may have led to doubts. His involvement with the Jewish princess, Berenice, was scandalous. Quintillian claims to have represented Berenice in a court case while Berenice herself sat with the judge (probably Titus), a clear abuse of power (Quintillian, *Institutes*, 4.1.19). Such behaviour recalled the relationships of Caesar and Antony with Cleopatra, and some in Rome may have feared that Berenice would wield considerable authority when Titus became emperor. Berenice had come to Rome in 75 but left again before Vespasian's death. She returned when Titus became emperor, but was sent back to the East, perhaps because of an adverse public reaction (Dio, 66. 15.3; 18; Suetonius, *Titus*, 7). Yet, such a public involvement with an Eastern princess must have reflected a tendency towards

Eastern monarchism as a mode of displaying power in which there are echoes of Mark Antony, Nero, and even Gaius.

There were elements in Titus' life that would have allowed a creative biographer to portray him as a second Nero. It is certainly possible that his interests in the Greek East and his concern to win favour with the plebs would have led to him evolving a rather different style of leadership from that of his father and that he would have come into conflict with more traditional elements of the Roman aristocracy. There were, however, no open conflicts. It seems clear though that the dismal years of Domitian's reign affected ancient perceptions of the reign of Titus and turned his two efficient and seemingly politically peaceful years into a time of tremendous hope and promise for the Roman people, ruined by their emperor's premature death.

Chapter 9

Domitian (AD 81–96)

With the sudden death of Titus, Domitian emerged from his brother's shadow to become emperor. He had played an important role in AD 69 when he had been the senior representative of the family in Rome, but had not enjoyed the same prominence as Titus during the reign of their father, nor had he come to the forefront of Roman political life with the accession of his brother. His reign was damned by tradition. Tacitus, Pliny, Suetonius and Juvenal present extremely hostile portraits of the emperor. His personal behaviour, his handling of the senate and his conduct of military and administrative affairs drew ancient criticism. Any reconstruction of Domitian's reign is hampered by this almost universal hostility. It is also hampered by the absence of a full narrative account of the reign. As a result, the chronology of political and military events is somewhat confused. Of necessity, we take a thematic rather than a chronological approach to the reign.

The imperial court

Domitian seems to have spent much of his time both before and after accession at Alba, some distance from Rome, where he is depicted in Juvenal's *Satire IV*, surrounded by a small group of intimates on whom he relied for advice. Good emperors were supposed to consult widely and take advice from the senate in public, but Domitian is depicted as secretive, concentrating power in the court. Although we cannot reconstruct in detail the operation of politics under Domitian, we do know a number of individuals who achieved prominence during the reign and in some cases we know their eventual fate. We can do little more than list these individuals. The reasons for the fall of these men and the background to their careers, remain obscure.

Domitian owed his position to his family and he continued his father's policy of elevating the family (see Figure 8.1, p. 232 for a family tree). Vespasian had been deified; Titus also became a god. Domitian was, however without the same reserve of male family to whom Vespasian had been able to delegate so much power. Domitian's niece, Julia Augusta, appeared on coins from as early as *c.* 80–1 in association with Venus and was included in sacrifices for the safety of the emperor. Julia and Domitian were rumoured to be lovers (Dio, 67. 3.1–2), though the sexual habits of emperors were always a matter for (inventive) speculation and any close relationship between an emperor and a woman, even if she was a family member, attracted gossip.

Domitian was married to a daughter of Corbulo (see pp. 195–96), Domitia Longina. Domitia was initially prominent and Domitian was probably able to exploit this connection with the popular general. She fell from grace for alleged adultery with the actor Paris, who was killed on the street by Domitian, but she returned to the emperor soon after (Dio, 67. 3).

Domitian's first consular colleague as emperor was a family member, T. Flavius Sabinus, a descendant of Vespasian's brother and husband of Julia Augusta. Sabinus apparently clad his servants in white, the same colour that Domitian used (Suetonus, *Domitian*, 12). The close relationship of these two reflected the fact that the regime continued to be a family affair. In the event of Domitian's early death, Sabinus was to continue the Flavian line with a minimum of disruption. At some point (probably early in the reign), however, an attendant became confused between the two Flavians and announced Sabinus as *imperator*, not consul. Sabinus was killed soon after (Suetonius, *Domitian*, 10).

Flavius Clemens, the brother of Flavius Sabinus, held a consulship with Domitian in 95. Two of his sons were named as Domitian's heirs. Clemens was killed, probably in late 95, and his wife was exiled on charges of atheism (Suetonius, *Domitian*, 15; Dio, 67. 14.1–2).

A more distant relative, Arrecinus Clemens, was also executed for reasons unknown (Suetonius, *Domitian*, 11).

Julius Ursus was prefect of Egypt under Vespasian. He may have been Domitian's praetorian prefect. Dio (67. 3.1) credits him with sufficient influence to prevent Domitian from killing Domitia Longina after her alleged adultery with the actor Paris. Domitian quarrelled with Ursus in the mid 80s and Dio (67. 4.2) claims that Ursus' life was saved by Julia's intervention. He was honoured with the consulship in 84, suggesting that he was no longer praetorian prefect by that date. His later fate is unclear.

Juvenal's list of courtiers in *Satire IV* is an obviously distorted picture of Domitian's court. In this poem, the courtiers summoned to consider the crucial issue of what to do with a very large fish were Pegasus (the urban prefect), Vibius Crispus, Acilius Glabrio and son, Rubrius Gallus (a military man later executed for an unknown crime), Montanus, Crispinus, Pompeius, Cornelius Fuscus (the praetorian prefect), Fabricius Veiento and Catullus Messalinus. We know very little about many of these men, but we may assume that they were senior political figures. Vibius Crispus had been consul first under Nero and held a third consulship under Domitian. Acilius Glabrio's son was consul with Trajan in AD 91 but was killed in *c.* AD 95 (Dio, 67. 14.3). Fabricius Veiento was expelled from Rome after publishing a scandalous mock will under Nero, but returned to become a close adviser of Domitian and was responsible for several prosecutions. His political skill was such that he retained prominence and power into the reign of Nerva and used that power to try and protect others who had collaborated with Domitian (see pp. 259–60). Catullus Messalinus was a notorious prosecutor of Domitian's enemies. His blindness seems to have added to the general fear he inspired. He had held an ordinary consulship with Domitian in 73 – only Nerva had preceded Messalinus in this honour – and Messalinus was to hold a further consulship in 83.

Nerva's name is absent from most ancient accounts of Domitian's reign. He cannot, however, have been invisible in this period. He had been a prominent supporter of Vespasian and held an ordinary consulship as Domitian's colleague in 90. His rapid elevation to the imperial position in 96 and his protection of the former associates of Domitian suggest strongly that he, too, was a member of the inner circle of Domitian's friends, though there is some evidence to suggest that he may have distanced himself from the regime after 93 (see below).

There was no obvious change in the composition of the imperial court between the reigns of Titus and Domitian. Domitian surrounded himself with experienced and politically astute men. The operation of the court is more difficult to understand. Juvenal portrays the *amici* (friends of the emperor) gathering suddenly and in terror. Pliny (*Panegyricus*, 48) also describes how those who visited the emperor made every effort to leave quickly. Even *amici* were intimidated by the imperial presence and the honoured were treated with suspicion. Hostile and frightened *amici* were hardly in a position to give good advice and a tyrannical emperor only heard what he was thought to want to hear. Domitian killed many of those closest to him (several in the last years of his reign) and was killed in a conspiracy of his freedmen that probably also involved both *amici* and family (Dio, 67. 15).

Much of this portrayal is clearly literary. We cannot take Juvenal's descriptions of the workings of the imperial court at face value: it was certainly not meant as history. Pliny's representation of Domitian's court was that of an enemy of the emperor and it was in a context in which he sought to contrast the idealised and equally unreal portrait of the court of Trajan with that of Domitian's era. It is unlikely that intimates of Domitian were open about their feelings nor can we believe that any representation of the court at the time, or later, could be politically neutral. Domitian's later years and his eventually assassination coloured all accounts.

Ancient accounts tended to emphasise character as a dominant feature of imperial reigns (and thus Suetonius, especially, tends to present chronologically undifferentiated accounts in which the characteristics of any emperor are seen as constant), whereas modern accounts tend to prefer politicised (rather than psychological) narrative. Modern historians also prefer to see their subjects as rational actors, concerned to do the 'right' thing and to establish power on a reasonable and sensible basis. When a reign goes wrong, the modern historian searches for the event that explains the shift.

There is much to be said for both approaches, but in rationalising Roman imperial politics, we risk losing its personal element. If modern historians at least claim to work within a politics of merit, ideas and technical skills, and treat politics as an intellectual business, ancient politics was a matter of personal relationships. An emperor who, for whatever reasons, communicated suspicions or was seen to harbour doubts, or sought to assert authority suddenly or violently, could cause fear. We know enough about the politics of modern tyrannical regimes, sometimes depicted in historical accounts, sometimes in fictional accounts, to understand that a climate of fear could build gradually and the structures of power and domination in Roman society were such that someone somewhere within the political system would see an advantage in exploiting such a climate. Thus, merely because we suspect exaggeration, we should not dismiss the ancient portrayal of Domitian as an emperor who was feared and hated.

Evidently, Domitian's relationship with his friends and family changed during his reign. Increasing conflict between Domitian and the senate led to increasing paranoia. Those to whom he may have listened in the early years of his reign might have been rather more cautious during his later years. The list of those close to the emperor who were exiled, executed, or forced to commit suicide is long. In the end, Domitian was killed by those closest to him: men who had the most to gain from the regime, but also who had most to fear from their proximity to Domitian. Killing Domitian was a major political and personal risk. It suggests that keeping him alive must have been more risky. In itself, the murder shows that Domitian's regime had become dangerously unstable.

Domitian's enemies are hardly better attested than his friends, and the picture we gain of them is equally distorted. Domitian's reign saw further conflict with the so-called philosophical opposition. This was certainly not the only group to suffer at the hands of Domitian and his supporters, but our sources are such that it is only the history of this group that can be traced with any confidence. The three most prominent victims were the younger Helvidius Priscus, Arulenus Rusticus and Herennius Senecio. The crimes of these men were literary. Helvidius published a farce which was interpreted as an allegorical attack on Domitian and his wife (Suetonius, *Domitian*, 10.2). Rusticus published a work on Thrasea Paetus (see pp. 198–206) and Domitian supposedly took exception to lavish praise of a man who had been a thorn in the side of Nero. Senecio's biography of Helvidius Priscus (the elder) (see pp. 235–37) was similarly impolitic in honouring Vespasian's enemy. These writers fell in late 93 (Suetonius, *Domitian*, 10.2–4; Tacitus, *Agricola*, 2; Dio, 67. 13.2–3; Pliny, *Epistles*, 7. 33).

Rusticus, Priscus and Senecio were not the only ones who were punished. Junius Mauricus, brother of Arulenus Rusticus, and Arria, Fannia and

Gratilla, female members of the group, were also exiled (Pliny, *Epistles*, 1.5; 3.11; 7.19). Other possible members include Maternus, a philosopher, who was killed for making a speech on tyranny (Dio, 67. 12.5) and Hermogenes of Tarsus, a historian, who was killed for certain 'allusions' in his history (Suetonius, *Domitian*, 10), and perhaps the Artemidoros whom Pliny visited in 93 and was also exiled (Pliny, *Epistles*, 3.11). Pliny himself must have come very close to being prosecuted.

We know very little of the background to these cases, but it seems likely that relations between Helvidius and his circle and Domitian had been tense for some years before 93. Domitian's connection with Corbulo (who had been on the edge of this group) may have encouraged Domitian to seek reconciliation with the circle of Thrasea and Helvidius. The accounts of the charges suggest that the opposition of these men had been clear long before their cases came to court: it is difficult to believe that these literary works were all recent publications. Nevertheless, Domitian had taken no obvious action to hamper the careers of these men and may even have aided their rise. Both Helvidius Priscus (date uncertain) and Rusticus (AD 90) held the consulship. Avidius Quietus, who had been a friend of Thrasea Paetus, received the consulship in 93, the same year in which Pliny was probably praetor, having been allowed by Domitian to stand for the praetorship a year early (Pliny, *Epistles*, 7.16). Quietus was to support Pliny's attempt to gain revenge on those who had prosecuted Helvidius Priscus (Pliny, *Epistles*, 9.13). Pliny claims that his career was subsequently blocked by Domitian (*Panegyricus*, 95), but this is difficult to substantiate. Yet, by allowing these people to advance into prominent positions, Domitian enhanced his later difficulties and the situation in 93 – when a consul and a praetor were associated with men who were tried for treasonable acts – may have been explosive.

Pliny places the events that led to the elimination of the 'philosophical opposition' in a senatorial context. Senecio and Pliny had been involved in the trial of a corrupt governor, Baebius Massa. They had effectively won the case, but Massa had not been punished. Senecio and Pliny pushed for harsh measures to be taken and Massa retaliated by prosecuting Senecio for *maiestas* (Pliny, *Epistles*, 7. 33). Treason was a worse crime than corruption and the successful prosecution of Senecio would have immediately ensured Massa's favourable treatment. Subsequent events are unclear, but Senecio was brought down by the charge and this was taken as an excuse to remove many of Senecio's circle. Priscus and Rusticus seem to have fallen victim in this outburst of senatorial faction fighting. Massa's reaction was possibly not a surprise since he was threatened by ruin if the penalties for corruption were enforced, but what is perhaps a surprise is that Domitian and his associates took Massa's allegations seriously in such circumstances. Domitian's acquiescence (and perhaps active support) is demonstrated by the involvement of men close to the emperor in the prosecutions, which he could have stopped. As in the reign of Tiberius, the prosecutions were led by senators, but the emperor stood behind them.

Domitian's relationship with the senate was probably difficult before this point. The elimination of this group of prominent senators had, however, been avoided. It is probable that they were regarded by all as a symbol of senatorial liberty and their deaths marked the culmination of a process in which liberty was destroyed. After 93, there could be little pretence of cordiality between emperor and senate, and senators needed to behave as if he was their master to survive the *dominatio*. The breach in relations with the senate may have led to an increasingly paranoid atmosphere and, although we know virtually nothing about the subsequent purges of the aristocracy, it would seem that the emperor came to fear even his closest associates.

Suetonius (*Domitian*, 10–11) and Dio's account of the later years of Domitian's reign (67. 11–14) list former consuls and others killed in this period and provide numerous examples of ludicrous charges. Aelius Lama was killed for a joke at Domitian's expense. Salvius Cocceianus was killed for commemorating the birthday of his uncle, Otho. Sallustius Lucullus was killed for naming a new type of lance after himself. Mettius Pompusianus was killed after it was predicted that he would become emperor. We cannot know whether these cases involved serious conspiracies or the destruction of political factions, and we cannot date the killings. Further, as with Nero, the trivial causes reported in our sources may misrepresent the real charges levelled at these men.

Some of the deaths of Domitian's reign cannot be connected to the 'philosophical opposition'. Antonius Saturninus, governor of Germania Superior launched a revolt in AD 89 but was not even able to gain the support of the legions of Germania Inferior, and the revolt was quickly crushed. Domitian responded to the threat by taking measures to secure the loyalty of the army. The pay of the troops was raised from 900 to 1,200 *sesterces* per year and each legion was given a separate camp (Suetonius, *Domitian*, 6.2; 7.3; Dio, 67. 11.1–3). It would be far more risky to attempt to subvert the loyalty of a provincial army if one had to take soundings simultaneously in different camps. It is not known whether Saturninus had any support in Rome for his revolt.

The atmosphere of the reign is attested by Pliny and Tacitus. In the *Agricola*, Tacitus talks of the years when all speech was impossible and the senators grew old in silence, fearing that their words would be twisted by informants in order to bring them down. In that brief description, there is an obvious exaggeration. The *Agricola* is in itself an intensely political work. Tacitus opens his account by not by talking about Agricola, his father-in-law, but by talking about the Domitianic prosecutions of those who had written eulogistic accounts in the past. Tacitus is scornful of Domitian's attempt to repress literary works and scathing in his accounts of the brutality of the regime. Books were burned: but burning books does not suppress the books, it merely makes them more valued and advertises an assumption that the stories they tell are both true (otherwise why destroy them) and dangerous. But, the burning of books was a display that worked in contrasting ways. It displayed the tyrannical power of the emperor over free speech (one of the most valued characteristics of the Roman elite) and it etched the event into the memories of all that saw it. Politicians may be able to burn books, but they cannot control memories (compare the very similar sentiments expressed concerning the trial of the historian Cremutius Cordus under Tiberius in *Annales*, 4.34–35).

Yet, Tacitus is never simple. The condemnation of Domitian is clear and absolute. But Tacitus sees the servitude of the Domitianic period as stemming in part from the senators themselves. The senators were willing accomplices in the events of the period. It was senators who brought the charges and senators who voted to condemn the opponents of the regime. Tacitus does not shirk moral responsibility.

The story of Agricola that is retold is deliberately controversial. Unlike Helvidius Priscus and Thrasea Paetus, Agricola was rewarded by Domitian with an important governorship (Britain), a duty he carried out in an exemplary fashion. After an extended period of service, he returned to Rome, where he worked on the fringes of Domitian's court. He was thus one of Domitian's courtiers. Tacitus contrasts this participation in the politics of the regime with those who sought to disassociate themselves with Domitian's court and argues that Agricola's course was better. It was better because Agricola was more useful. He was able to do good in his conquest of Britain. He was also able to mollify aspects of the Domitianic tyranny. Tacitus' argument was that it was possible to be a great Roman while working for an immoral regime: the conquest of Britain by Agricola was a great achievement. Further, Tacitus argued that open opposition was a form of self-sacrifice which benefitted no one and may even have made the situation worse. As a political doctrine, it has something in common with Seneca's view that it was better to work with or within a tyrannical regime provided one could do good, yet, if we transfer the doctrine to modern contexts, it suggests that the correct course was to work with totalitarian regimes rather than in open opposition.

This is a far from easy view to understand. In the modern West, it is not an issue, thankfully, with which are familiar and we can afford a certain moral absolutism. But if we were to ask the same questions in the 1930s in Germany or in Soviet Russia or in Ba'athist Iraq or Mao's China, the moral complexities become much more obvious. Further, after the fall of Domitian's regime, those who had been oppressed expressed and deserved moral righteousness, but Tacitus offers the view that it was Agricola's life, rather than that of Helvidius Priscus, which was the model to which contemporaries should turn as an example to emulate.

The political atmosphere of Rome as depicted in the *Agricola* was one of real or latent violence. Most contemporaries were guarded in what might be said, watching for who might be listening, and aware that the regime might strike at any minute. Others were less circumspect, flaunting their opposition and fearless of the consequences of their actions, almost daring the regime to strike. Violence was in the air and even if the violence was concentrated in the last three years of the regime, the atmosphere of paranoia and terror is likely to have considerably pre-dated Domitian's decision to eliminate his most prominent opponents.

Tacitus wrote another work that dramatised the issues of working under a tyranny, the *Dialogus*. The *Dialogus* may have been the precursor of the *Agricola* but both were written in the immediate aftermath of Domitian's murder. The set-up of the *Dialogus* is clearly fictional and the issues seem initially at least unpromising for modern historians. The *Dialogus* is a discussion of the purposes and standards of oratory, set in a villa during the reign of Vespasian. Yet, as we dig deeper into the text, serious issues emerge.

There was a custom in Latin literature of setting philosophical dialogues in the past. This allowed the philosophical discussion to be put in the mouths of respected elders. Arguably, it also gave the discussion a veneer of authority, which would be denied contemporary thinkers and writers, as if the truths being debated were transhistorical and not just of the moment. The dialogue form went back to Classical Greek philosophy. It also allowed the discussion of issues from varied perspectives and provided the audience an opportunity to differ from the opinions expressed by the speakers: the very fact that it was a dialogue suggested that disagreement was possible. One of the notable features of the *Dialogus* is that it is without obvious conclusion: we don't know who wins the argument, but we do know that the participants depart as friends.

The occasion for the *Dialogus* is a gathering at the house of Curiatus Maternus on the day after his work, *Cato*, had been read. The reason why Maternus' friends gathered was to warn him about his behaviour since it had attracted the attention of the powerful. Writing about Cato was a political act. Maternus was dramatising the life of a notable martyr to Republicanism, a man who was schooled in philosophy. In the political context of the reign of Vespasian, Cato recalls the philosophical opposition and a favourable portrayal of Cato was bound to express opposition to the imperial regime.

Maternus had also 'retired' from public life. Such a retirement could also be construed as opposition. The debate that followed turned on the manner in which individuals should participate in public life and whether oratory was a useful skill. The argument offered by Maternus was that the judge was now a single individual (the emperor) and there was no call for oratory to persuade an individual whose mind would be swayed by other factors. The very nature of the Principate meant that oratory was dead. The problem that the Roman elite faced was how they could participate in public life under such circumstances. The ability to speak, and to speak well, was an assertion of power. The art of persuasion was an art of self-representation in which status was established. If oratory was an empty art, then the traditional means of political participation were also empty. The contrary argument focused on the usefulness of oratory. It made the point that orators were able to defend their friends, but also harm their enemies. There is a suggestion that the greatest of

Roman orators, Cicero, was in fact of the same generation as contemporary orators, arguing that the division between Republic and Empire was, in fact, of little significance.

The arguments are not easy. Maternus had given up on public life and on Rome, and responded by hurling literary bombs at the regime. His retirement was a retirement into vocal opposition. It is to be assumed that Maternus' days were numbered. The raising of the issue of usefulness and duty gives this position a moral complexity: does Maternus not owe Rome and his friends the duty of care that would require him to put his undoubted talents to use for the public good? But if he does put his talents to use, rhetoric is not in itself moral. It can be used to harm and to benefit. It can be used to enrich the orator (but the orator was already rich) and to bring the orator power, but that power was in service of an immoral regime. It is perhaps no surprise that there was no conclusion to the debate.

Again, even under Vespasian's reign, the politics are repressive. A literary work could draw potentially fatal attention. Speeches in the senate were closely monitored. Prosecutions could bring down individuals but also elevate individuals to positions of power. The attitude of those in power was crucial and determined political success. Freedom, to the extent it existed, survived only in the long shadow of imperial power and under the threat of imperial violence.

Pliny's letters give us two anecdotes that offer an insight into the life under the regime. *Epistle*, 1.12 tells us of the death of Corellius Rufus. Rufus had been suffering a painful and incurable illness. We need to remember that the Romans had no effective pain-relief and very little in the way of medicine. Medical practices were mostly completely ineffective. When faced with serious and seemingly incurable illness, Romans often committed suicide to avoid the pain and suffering. Rufus did not kill himself, at least not initially. When Pliny went to visit him, Rufus sent everyone from the room, including his wife. He told Pliny that he planned to outlive the bandit Domitian.

Pliny has probably improved this story in the retelling. Rufus' death does not appear to have followed close on that of Domitian. Yet, the presentation is of a man who was willing to suffer hopeless pain over an extended period out of his hatred of the emperor. We also need to think about his behaviour when Pliny visited. Sending everyone else from the room demonstrated his trust in Pliny. It also meant that if anyone was questioned as to what the pair had discussed, they could answer quite truthfully that they were not in the room. Given the application of torture to slaves, everyone in the household was a potential informer. But sending everyone out of the room advertised the fact that Rufus and Pliny were to engage in anti-Domitianic conversation. It also advertised the assumption that Domitian had spies everywhere and would seek opportunities to persecute this dying man. Even in one's own household one was not safe and this knowledge was shared and displayed.

The second anecdote from Pliny's letters relates to Regulus. In Pliny's wonderful world of wonderful friends, there is one decided enemy: Regulus. Regulus is subject to scorn and attack in various letters throughout the collection, but in *Epistles*, 1.5, Pliny gives us his account of the origins of their conflict. Pliny was debating a case in the centumviral court, which normally dealt with inheritance matters and the like and was thus hardly a hot-bed of political intrigue. His opponent was Regulus. The case turned on the legal opinion of a jurist, Modestus. Regulus asked Pliny what he thought of the man. The question was loaded. Although the discussion was on a technicality, Regulus had suddenly turned it into a matter of politics. Modestus had been exiled by Domitian. So if Pliny praised Modestus, he risked the charge of treason. If he damned Modestus, his case lost. Pliny attempted to ignore the issue, but from that moment Pliny and Regulus became sworn enemies.

The point of these anecdotes is that you need not kill someone to terrorise. If Domitian's list of victims prior to 93 was rather short, it does not mean that many others did not fear for their lives. Tyrants survive because of fear. Others exploit that fear. Pliny and Tacitus dramatise for us the moral and political issues. They dramatise the situation in which members of the Roman elite found themselves, uncertain of their fortune, uncertain whether an unguarded remark might be used against them, uncertain who was watching and plotting. There is no reason to disbelieve Tacitus' claim that men at least felt that they were condemned to silence. There was also no alternative and no escape. One could not leave the Roman Empire and even retiring from Rome was a political act of obvious opposition. The senators had not the power to start a revolution. So, they had to live with the regime. But how does one live and behave in such circumstances? Should one co-operate and try to make life better? Should one work for the historic good of the system, expanding the empire and fulfilling one's duty as a Roman citizen? Should one stand against the overwhelming power of the regime, conscious of one's impotence and accepting of the death that would follow? These are not questions that allow easy answers. Whatever the answers, the moral and personal costs would be high. The very fact that such questions demanded to be answered on a practical everyday level in Domitianic Rome tells us that we are witnessing a history of terror and a time of trauma.

War and military policy

The best account of campaigns is limited to Roman expansion in Britain in the period 77/8–84/5. Agricola had campaigned for seven years before bringing the Britons to a decisive battle, though the literary form of the work more or less demanded a great set-piece scene in which Agricola's military and rhetorical virtues could be displayed and Tacitus may have considerably enhanced the importance of the battle. Yet the seizure of Northern Scotland was short-lived even if Agricola's success ever properly secured the territory.

Domitian withdrew a legion to meet a crisis in Germany and Rome was forced to retreat from the newly-conquered territory (Tacitus, *Agricola*).

The Rhine and Danube frontiers had been the scene of much activity during the reign of Vespasian and it seems probable that Domitian's wars should be seen as part of the same policy of gradual expansion in Germany. Domitian's German campaigns (conducted in person) were directed against the Chatti, and as early as 83 (the war probably started in the summer of 82) Domitian proclaimed victory. The literary tradition is more hostile. The Chatti were not subdued, although the defences of the frontier and communications may have been notably improved. They continued to pose a threat to neighbouring tribes and the frontier and even gave their support to Saturninus' attempted coup (Dio, 67. 3.5–4.2; 5.1; Suetonius, *Domitian,* 6).

In 84 or 85, the Dacians crossed the Danube and invaded Moesia, killing the governor. Domitian and Cornelius Fuscus intervened and restored order (Dio, 67. 6; Suetonius, *Domitian,* 6). Fuscus took the initiative and launched an invasion of Dacian territory. His army was defeated and Fuscus himself was killed. In subsequent years, there were two or possibly three major campaigns in Dacia which brought a settlement of the frontier, though the Dacians had to be bought off. Domitian did not accept a triumph: he may have been aware that, although order was restored, the frontier was not properly secured (Dio, 67. 7).

In the mid-80s, the Nasmones, an African tribe, revolted. After initial success, they were destroyed by the Roman governor. Changes in the frontier under Trajan perhaps suggest that there were other conflicts in North Africa (Dio, 67. 4.6).

Domitian seems to have followed a very similar policy to that of his father. He was interested in winning military glory and therefore pursued an active expansionist policy in Britain and Germany. He continued to make slow gains in Germany, but events on the Danube changed the military situation fundamentally, forcing the relocation of units away from Britain and a limited retreat. These long Danubian wars occupied much of Domitian's reign. Domitian's aggressive instincts are shown by Fuscus' unsuccessful attack on the Dacians and he may have intended to return to the offensive eventually. His reign was marked by defeat and consolidation rather than the acquisition of new territory.

Image

Domitian made some effort to win popular esteem. He maintained an image of personal conservatism and restraint in combination with exhibitions of largesse, especially directed towards the urban population and the military.

This conservatism was reflected in his religious policy. He collected the tax on the Jews with vigour (see p. 238). Suetonius tells that he was present at a public and humiliating examination of the genitalia of a 90-year-old man to ascertain whether he was Jewish and if he should pay the Jewish tax (Suetonius, *Domitian*, 12.2). The use of informers probably increased abuses of the law since any who had flirted with Judaism might find themselves faced with a crippling tax bill and criminal charges.

Prosecutions for atheism in this period may be connected with anti-Jewish feeling, but are also related to Domitian's use of the imperial cult as a way of displaying his authority. Dio's notice of Domitian's demand that the title *deus et dominus* (god and master) be used when addressing him is associated with the persecution of the 'philosophers' in 93 (Dio, 67. 13.4; Suetonius, *Domitian*, 13), prior to the prosecution of Flavius Clemens for atheism. Atheism could be understood as a political crime: an unwillingness to acknowledge the divinity of the emperor. *Deus et dominus* does not appear in official contexts, suggesting that its application was limited (perhaps it was only used to intimidate senators), and it is probable that it was never adopted as an official part of Domitian's nomenclature.

Domitian's religious conservatism came to the fore in the treatment of the vestals. The period saw two scandals, one involving the chief vestal. The traditional punishment for a vestal who broke her vows of chastity was to be buried alive. Cornelia, chief vestal, who had already been tried and acquitted once for failure to maintain chastity, was retried and found guilty. The traditional punishment was imposed. Three other vestals were allowed to choose their method of death. Most of those with whom they had supposedly offended were punished by death, though the former praetor who had confessed to the crime was merely exiled. The treatment of the vestals was so cruel (and the use of torture leads to considerable doubt about their guilt) that one senator supposedly expired in horror in the senate-house (Suetonius, *Domitian*, 8; Dio, 67. 3.3).

Domitian was generous to the plebs. He abolished the corn dole, but replaced it with civic banquets at which the emperor's largesse could be displayed. He also gave lavish games. He gave secular games and instituted a major new festival. He increased the number of circus teams and factions from four to six, presumably to add interest to the games. He also distributed money to the Roman plebs (Suetonius, *Domitian*, 4; 7.1; Dio, 67. 8).

Domitian, like his father and brother, had ambitious building plans. We do not know the full extent of Domitianic building, since after the *damnatio memoriae* (an official attempt to wipe out all trace of Domitian from the public records, including erasing his name from inscriptions and removing his statues from display) Domitian's name would have been removed from public buildings, and his successors associated themselves with projects started but incomplete at Domitian's death. He was engaged in major construction projects in the centre of the city. He started the Forum Transitorium, later known as the Forum of Nerva. This led from the Forum Romanum and Forum Iulii to the Forum Augusti and the temple of Pax, which is sometimes known as the Forum Pacis. This last was a Flavian construction and was probably finished by Domitian. There may have been Domitianic constructions in the huge area that later became the Forum Traiani. Alongside the Forum Romanum, Domitian completed the temple to his father and consecrated it to both Vespasian and Titus. He also remodelled the Domus Tiberiana (the imperial palace) and constructed a large three-storey structure (purpose uncertain) by the temple of Castor. He built himself a new palace near the Circus Maximus. He built a new temple to Jupiter Custos and renovated once more the temple of Jupiter Capitolinus. He constructed a new stadium and an odeion (Suetonius, *Domitian*, 5). He built many arches, presumably to commemorate his military successes (Suetonius, *Domitian*, 13.2). The list of buildings associated with Domitian is impressive (see Table 9.1) and the scale of activity can be assessed from Pliny's praise of Trajan (the oration was delivered before the building of the Forum Traiani) for his moderation in building (*Panegyricus*, 51). Such a massive construction programme was clearly meant to inscribe his name and power on the city of Rome. Numerous statues were erected in gold and silver. Domitian's domination of the city was made concrete and visible.

Table 9.1 Domitian's new buildings and refurbishments to buildings

Altar incendii Neronis	Naumachia Domitiani
Arches of Domitian	Odeion
Arch of Titus	Porticus of Minucius Vetus
Atria Septem	Porticus of Octavia and associated temples
Baths of Charinus, Claudius Etruscus, Lupus, Argentaria, Agrippa	Stadium Domitiani
	Temple of Castor
Camp of the fleet of Misenum	Temple of the Divus Augustus
Circus Maximus	Temple of Divus Vespasiani
Colosseum	Temple of the Flavian Family
Domus Augustiana	Temple of Fortuna Redux
Equus Domitiani	Temple of Isis Campensis
Forum Transitorium	Temple of Jupiter Custos
Four ludi	Temple of Jupiter Optimus Maximus
Granaries: Agrippina, Piperataria.	
Horologium Augusti	Temple of Minerva Chalcidica
Horti Domitiani	Temple of Venus Genetrix
Janus Quadrifons	Theatre and Cryptum of Balbus
Julian senate-house	Theatre of Pompey
Mica Aurea	Tiberian Palace

Finance

Our understanding of Domitianic administration is closely connected to the interpretation of Domitianic politics. As far as the sources touch on the issue, it is (normally) to emphasise Domitian's cruelty. Attention has focused on his financial administration.

The case against Domitian argues that he bankrupted the state. It can be briefly summarised as follows:

- Domitian is accused of killing senators and others in order to obtain their money.
- The administration of taxes seems to have been severe.
- Nerva established a commission to reduce public expenditure.
- The level of silver content in the coinage falls later in Domitian's reign.
- Domitian tried to compensate for the increase in the pay of soldiers by reducing the number of troops.
- Vespasian had left a full treasury.
- Taxes on inheritance were increased.

Domitian's expenditure was certainly heavy. Military pay was increased and this was probably the most significant part of the imperial budget. The building programme must have consumed large amounts of cash. He also had to pay off Decebalus, the Dacian king.

There is a counter-argument:

- 'Bad' emperors are frequently accused of financial mismanagement and greed.
- The disasters of the 70s considerably increased expenditure. Although Vespasian may have accumulated some reserves, these were depleted by the fire of Rome and the eruption of Vesuvius, as well as Titus' other expenditures and the gifts to the troops and Roman people on Domitian's accession.
- Domitian seems to have had a relaxed attitude towards debts.
- The collection of taxes was part of normal administration and Domitian's ferocious collection of the Jewish tax may be related to other aspects of Domitianic policy.
- Nerva and Trajan met the initial expenses of gifts to troops and people. It was in response to these outgoings that Nerva set up the commission on public expenditure, and although the commission saved virtually no money, Roman finances seem to have prospered.
- It is unclear whether the increase in inheritance taxes was a response to financial difficulties or simply a tightening of inheritance law.

A reduction in the silver content of coinage is evidence that the treasury was under some strain. We must not, however, exaggerate the scale of the problems and there is no evidence that Domitian seriously attempted to reduce expenditure (which he could have done comparatively easily by reducing the size of his building programme). It is also clear that although there may have been temporary problems at the start of Trajan's reign, Trajan was not short of money. This suggests that the fiscal fundamentals of the Roman state were good. The major increase in expenditure under Domitian, the army pay rise, could be met. Although the ancient sources emphasise Domitian's financial mismanagement, it seems unlikely that there was a financial crisis.

Assassination

Domitian's unpopularity with certain elements of the senate increased the danger of assassination. The elimination of the so-called philosophical opposition showed that he was unable to build a consensus in the senate and conspiracies or supposed conspiracies after 93 added to paranoia. Even those closest to him were perceived as a threat and Domitian killed members of his family and court. Domitian may have been right to fear those close to him: after all, his assassination was carried out by members of his household. Yet, once Domitian became suspicious of his closest advisers, it was almost inevitable that they would see his removal as their only chance of survival. The extent of the conspiracy is, however, difficult to assess. His assassins were all freedmen: Stephanus, Parthenius, Maximus, and several others. Others were either involved or claimed later to have been involved, such as Domitia, the emperor's wife, and the future emperor Nerva. The conspiracy was led by imperial freedmen, who one would expect had most to lose from assassinating their emperor and also, being of lowly status, would be comparatively safe from Domitian's wrath. Yet the freedmen probably felt increasingly vulnerable after the death of Epaphroditus. This freedman had served Nero before working for the Flavians and had been one of the few who accompanied Nero's flight from Rome. He had aided Nero's suicide (see p. 206), and it was this 'crime' that Domitian used to remove him. Any illusion that the freedmen of Domitian were safe was dispelled. It is very likely that the conspirators had taken steps to ensure their continued security after the assassination and had received some undertakings from Nerva. The speed with which Nerva moved to claim the imperial throne suggests that he was well aware of the conspiracy (Dio, 67. 14.4–18; Suetonius, *Domitian*, 14.4–17).

Conclusions

The history of Domitian's reign was written by his enemies. For them, Domitian was a tyrant. Although there have been attempts to react against the ancient interpretation of Domitian's reign, and we have seen areas in which the tradition has been grossly unfair to Domitian (such as in the treatment of his military activities and in his handling of the state finances), the authority of Tacitus, Pliny, Juvenal and Suetonius is not undermined. After Domitian's fall, the senate passed a *damnatio memoriae* but it was not prepared to see action taken against those who had collaborated with Domitian, with certain limited exceptions. One guesses that many in the senate deplored the treatment of Helvidius, Rusticus and others; this was a small political class in which everyone was closely connected. One can also imagine the guilt many felt when reluctantly voting for the condemnation of these men. The senators were complicit in Domitian's tyranny. It is that moral stain which is close to the heart of the *Agricola* and, indeed, the *Annales*. Few, if any, could claim moral righteousness after what had happened. This is the way with tyranny. The world is not divided into good and bad people. Tyrannies, in their absolute nature, force moral ambivalence. Either you are with the tyrant or against him. If you are against, you die. In enforcing complicity, everyone is tainted by the killings. Sometimes, modern historians complain that Tacitus' views are of the Principate were coloured by his experience under Domitian. Yet, what Tacitus and everyone else got under Domitian was a political education in the brutal realities of imperial power.

Chapter 10

Nerva and Trajan (AD 96–117)

The reign of Nerva was short. The tradition on Nerva is mostly shaped by Trajanic writers, especially Pliny, and since Nerva adopted Trajan, any criticism or praise of Nerva of necessity reflected on Trajan. The sources on Trajan tend to glorify his reign. Trajan was the conquering hero who personally led Roman armies to great victories against barbarian enemies. Politically, he shared Nerva's triumph of, in Tacitus' memorable phrase, 'integrating things previously opposed: principate and liberty' (*Agricola*, 3). Pliny's *Panegyricus* presents us with an extended speech in praise of Trajan's political and military virtues. It is the eulogistic presentation of the emperor whom the senate chose to call '*optimus*' (best) that dominates the tradition.

The legacy of Domitian

Domitian was killed on 18th September 96. On the very same day Nerva was declared emperor. It seems unlikely that Nerva's elevation was an accidental result of the conspiracy. Like other Roman conspirators, they probably concerned themselves with the issue of succession before the Domitian's assassination. They needed to find someone who could be trusted not to sweep away those close to Domitian and who would not seek revenge for Domitian's murder. Nerva had enjoyed a glittering career under the Flavians. Pliny tells us that Nerva wrote to congratulate Pliny on his bold behaviour in 93 (*Epistle*, 7. 33), which would suggest that Nerva was not part of the group that engaged in the persecution of the 'philosophical opposition' in that year. Indeed, it may have strained even the ingenuity of Pliny and Tacitus to present Nerva as the restorer of liberty had he been involved. Yet Nerva's association with the Flavian family probably meant that his closest political allies had also been prominent under Domitian and we may imagine that these connections eased his path to the throne in 96.

Domitian's treatment of the senate in the last three years of his reign led to calls for revenge. Senators who had suffered at the hands of their colleagues now looked to turn the tables. Yet, those who had been close to Domitian had been exercising influence to aid their friends as well as harm their enemies.

They had powerful support. Some had co-operated with Domitian to remove their personal enemies. Others had played less than honourable roles during the trials. It would be no easy task to bring down those who had been close to Domitian and, since some were probably still close to Nerva, such action ran considerable political risks. Nerva sought to paper over the cracks and institute an amnesty. Those who had suffered would not be allowed to continue the factional fighting into the next reign. Those who had served under Domitian were left in place. The replacement of Domitian did not lead to a purge and it was in the interests of the freedmen assassins to ensure the highest level of continuity possible between reigns.

There is no more obvious sign of continuity between the reigns of Domitian and Nerva than the career of Titinius Capito. After distinguished military service, he served in the household administrations of Domitian, Nerva, and Trajan. He was a noted figure on the literary scene and is favourably discussed in Pliny's letters (*Epistles*, 1.17; 5.8; 8.12; McCrum, Woodhead 1966: No. 347). Despite being so close to Domitian, there was no obvious stain on his character and there is no evidence that he was a controversial figure.

Nevertheless, animosities could not be laid aside. Pliny himself led one attack in 97. He threatened to bring charges against the prosecutor of Helvidius. The debate in the senate was vitriolic. The majority of the senate may have had sympathy with Pliny, but there was a reluctance to open up old wounds and Veiento led a counterattack. Pliny may have had the backing of other senior members of the senate such as Verginius Rufus, Julius Frontinus, Corellius Rufus and Avidius Quietus, though he claims he acted without seeking support in advance. Pliny carried the day in the senate in that his enemy was not allowed to hold further office, but he was unable to bring the case to court and had to be satisfied with publishing his speech in vindication of Helvidius. Before publication, his intended victim died (*Epistles*, 9. 13).

Another of Pliny's enemies from the reign of Domitian was Regulus (see p. 251). Again, Pliny may have made aggressive noises. Regulus sought reconciliation but Pliny was unwilling to come to terms: he was waiting for the return of Junius Mauricus from exile. Mauricus was the brother of one of Regulus' victims, Arulenus Rusticus, and had the moral right to launch the prosecution in person (*Epistles*, 1.5). It seems likely that this episode can also to be dated to 97 and that on Mauricus' return they were either unable or thought it unwise to launch the prosecution, probably because Regulus had powerful protectors.

Nerva himself may have been trying to maintain a foothold in both camps. The Domitianic court remained powerful, but Nerva attempted to maintain good relations with Pliny and his circle. His first choice as fellow consul was Verginius Rufus. Rufus' political activities during the Flavian period cannot be reconstructed, though his extraordinary prominence in 68–9 (see pp. 204–208) and his longevity established him as a leading senator. He had been a friend and protector of Pliny and one wonders whether he was excluded from Domitian's court. Nerva's decision to reward him with a third consulship and invitation to sit on a commission for the reduction of public expenditure suggests an attempt to associate his reign with Rufus, possibly a break with the Domitianic circle (Pliny, *Epistles*, 2.1).

The restoration of the exiled and Nerva's search for political support led to a change in the political balance. The tensions that arose were dramatised at a dinner party held by Nerva, probably in 97. Junius Mauricus and Veiento were at the table. Veiento was sitting in the place of honour, next to the emperor. Discussion turned to another notorious Domitianic courtier, Catullus Messalinus (see pp. 243–44), who had died during Domitian's reign. Someone asked where he would be were he still alive and Mauricus asserted that he would be sitting at dinner with them (Pliny, *Epistles*, 4.22). Veiento was meant to take offence. Nerva may have done so. The stresses of maintaining the peace between the two opposed groups were obvious and resurfaced even at the emperor's own table.

These tensions led to a major crisis in 97 when the praetorians rose against Nerva. Nerva's political position became virtually untenable and he turned for political support to one of the leading generals, Trajan.

The adoption of Trajan

In spite of later eulogistic treatments of Nerva, it is clear that the emperor failed to reconcile the disparate factions at the centre of Roman politics. His coinage issues proclaimed the restoration of liberty, the rebirth of Rome and the restoration of justice – themes close to the senators' hearts (*Libertas Augusta, Roma Renascens, Iustitia Augusta, Aequitas August*). Another major theme was the *Concordia Exercitum* (concord of the army). It is traditional to interpret this as a sign of Nerva's political uncertainty, a slogan reflecting more his hope than political reality, and to understand the emphasis placed on the loyalty of the army to signify that the army was anything but loyal. This is perhaps the case, but we ought to see this coinage issue in the context of the other issues of the reign. Nerva's coinage celebrated the lifting of customs duty charged on the movement of goods in Italy (*Vehiculatione Italiae Remissa*), the end of the 'wickedness of the Jewish tax' (*Fisci Iudaici calumnia sublata*), and the restoration of the corn supply (*Annona August; Plebei Urbanae Frumento Constituto*). Thus, the coinage proclaimed a fresh start with important groups: the senate, the people of Rome, the people of Italy (through the remission of taxation) and the army. We need not assume that Nerva thought the army was likely to turn against him.

In 97, the simmering discontent started to unravel Nerva's fragile consensus. The first sign of this may have been a mysterious conspiracy launched by a certain Calpurnius Crassus, descendant of one of the great Republican families. The details of the conspiracy are not known and Dio recounts an anecdote in which Nerva, once the conspiracy had been betrayed, met the conspirators, gave them all swords and asked them to assess their sharpness. The conspirators did not use them and were not brought to trial (Dio, 68. 3.1–2). The whole anecdote is suspicious. Trajan later punished the same Crassus for conspiracy. The invention of an earlier conspiracy, or the recollection of a rumour which associated Crassus with a conspiracy against Nerva, would have aided Trajan's prosecution (Dio, 68. 16.2).

Casperius Aelianus was at the centre of a more credible threat to usurp Nerva's authority. Aelianus was praetorian prefect, a post he had held under Domitian. In such a role, it is inevitable that he would have been implicated in some of Domitian's misdeeds. It is likely, therefore, that he viewed the growing influence of anti-Domitianic groups with some fear. He harnessed the discontent of the praetorians to demand action. Nerva was besieged in his palace and forced to agree to execute Parthenius and others who had been involved in the conspiracy against Domitian (Pliny, *Paneyricus*, 90; Dio, 68. 3.3).

Nerva's choices were now limited. His lack of power had been demonstrated. He needed to bring renewed legitimacy and authority to his regime in order to compete with or suppress Aelianus and his supporters. Like Galba, the aged emperor looked to establish a successor who would add lustre to the regime. He ascended the Capitoline Hill and, in the temple of Jupiter Optimus Maximus, adopted M. Ulpius Traianus (Dio, 68. 3.4; Pliny, *Panegyricus*, 7–8).

Trajan was an interesting choice. Trajan's father had enjoyed a distinguished military career. He had served with Vespasian and Titus in Judaea and had become governor of Syria. His son's career needs to be reconstructed from Pliny's *Panegyricus*, 14–15. He had started his military career with some distinction, serving with his father in Syria. Subsequently, he had been posted to Spain and from there he journeyed with his legion to aid Domitian in the suppression of Saturninus' revolt. Pliny tells us that the revolt was already over when Trajan arrived in Germany. His show of loyalty led to a transfer to Germany where he served for an extended period, though his exact role is unclear. He was consul in 91 but returned to Germany and was governor of Germania Superior when Nerva chose him as heir to the throne.

His long service in the provinces meant that he had been away from Rome during the crucial years of AD 93–6 and was untainted by association with the Domitianic terror. He and his father had been prominent and powerful Flavian supporters and had been rewarded with key governorships. The friends of Domitian could look on him optimistically. The military power at his disposal ensured that he was a force to be reckoned with and would have made him a probable contender for the throne had the discontent with Nerva become civil war. In some ways, he was an ideal choice, a man of real power who offered some hope to both sides. He was in Germany, however, not in Rome, and was not immediately able to improve Nerva's political position. Nerva's struggle with Aelianus remained the struggle of unequals, though Aelianus was now threatened by the German legions.

Nerva wrote to Trajan to inform him of his adoption. When the letter arrived, Trajan did not rush to his new father. The delay needs explanation. It is unlikely that order was restored in Rome merely by mentioning Trajan's name, as Pliny claims. We can also dismiss moralistic interpretations: Trajan not wanting to be seen to be rushing to accept the power and authority granted to him or effectively usurping the power of his 'father'. The answer is more prosaic. Trajan seems to have spent the period visiting the troops, securing their loyalty. By the time he reached Italy, Nerva was dead. Aelianus recognised his authority and came to Trajan when summoned. Trajan executed him and purged the praetorian guard (Dio, 68. 5.4). One must wonder what the tradition hides and whether Aelianus might have expected to be treated very differently. After so intimidating Nerva and establishing his domination in Rome, one might assume that the next emperor would take action against this over-mighty prefect. Yet Aelianus went to Trajan. We could assume that he was politically bankrupt, threatened by overwhelming military force and in no position to oppose Trajan, but, in fact, Aelianus may have been hoping for some reward. He had, after all, precipitated the crisis that led to the adoption of Trajan.

We can arrive at two versions of Trajan's accession. In the first, as represented by our sources, the political crisis in Rome led to Trajan being chosen from all men in the Empire as the best suited to bring peace. Order was restored. Eventually, Aelianus was killed for his undutiful behaviour towards Nerva. In the second, Nerva failed to secure general political support. Various individuals in the senate and elsewhere engaged in political manoeuvres designed to secure the dominance of their group or prepare for a bid for the throne. Aelianus moved first. Nerva, however, turned to Trajan who may or may not have been preparing to bid for the imperial position. Trajan secured the loyalty of the troops, as any usurper needed to do, and moved on Rome. There was an uneasy truce. Trajan asserted his authority by removing Aelianus and thereby disassociated himself from the former Domitianic circle. In other words, instead of an orderly succession through adoption, we have something approaching a *coup*.

A further break with the Domitianic past was signalled at games which were probably held very soon after Trajan's arrival in Rome. Informers were brought before the crowd, condemned and sent into exile (Pliny, *Panegyricus*, 34). This was a theatrical display. The status of the various informers is not stated, but it seems likely that only minor characters suffered. Powerful senators such as Regulus remained untouched and Pliny never did bring about his downfall. Trajan's assertion of authority in 98 may have been dramatic and his break with the former courtiers of Domitian decisive, but he did not allow revenge.

The Optimus Princeps

There is very little information on which to base a political history of Trajan's reign. We do, however, have varied and quite full sources concerning

Trajan's image. Much of this is related to his role as a conqueror (to be considered below). Apart from the mystery of the conspiracy of Crassus and attempts to divide Licinius Sura and Trajan by alleging conspiracy (Dio, 68. 15.3–16.2), there is no evidence of political opposition to Trajan, but it is reasonable to assume that the tensions he inherited from Nerva and Domitian continued to influence political life, and Pliny's somewhat confused depiction of the emperor suggests that Trajan was no more able to solve the various contradictions of the imperial position than any of his predecessors.

Pliny's Panegyricus

The *Panegyricus* is a fascinating work. It is a speech in praise of the emperor. Pliny delivered the original version in AD 100 as a gesture of thanks to the emperor who had just made him consul. It was later reworked by Pliny for publication and even delivered again in a public reading that lasted three days (Pliny, *Epistles*, 3. 13; 18). The composition of a panegyric posed certain fundamental problems of taste. Domitian and other emperors had received similar orations and it was felt that the whole rhetorical form had become debased: what more praise could be heaped on an emperor when so much that was insincere had been said on such occasions? Pliny faced the issue explicitly at the start of his speech (*Panegyricus*, 2–3). His solution was to claim naivety: that his speech was different simply because it was sincere. As a rhetorical device this is clearly unsatisfactory, but represents a deeper tension in the work. Pliny praises Trajan the senator but, in so doing, the *Panegyricus* shows that Trajan was more than a senator. If Trajan was 'one of us' (*Panegyricus*, 3), then the *Panegyricus* was clearly unsuitable. The very act of presenting a panegyric associates Trajan with the more autocratic aspects of imperial rule, even if the speech itself emphasises 'senatorial' or 'democratic' characteristics of the emperor. Throughout the *Panegyricus*, Pliny is faced with this irresolvable problem and it is a problem that Trajan himself faced.

I take, as an example, the divinity of the emperor though there are others that could be chosen. 'Good' emperors did not become gods in their own lifetime. Trajan could not, therefore, be a god and did not claim to be a god. In *Panegyricus* 2 this is explicit:

> Nowhere must we flatter him as a god, nowhere as a divine power: for we speak not about a tyrant but a citizen, not of a master (*dominus*) but a parent. He himself is one of us – and in this he excels and shines most since he thinks he is one of us and remembers that he is no less a man than the men he commands.

Yet, even in the same section, Pliny talks of Trajan's *divinitas*, though it is Trajan's *humanitas* which encouraged the senators to celebrate him.

Later, Pliny declares that imperial power is equal to that of the gods, the unstated logic of the argument being that the wielders of those powers should be equal (*Paneyricus*, 3). Trajan was adopted by the gods and then by Nerva (*Panegyricus*, 5). Nerva, his father, becomes a god (*Panegyricus*, 11). Trajan is compared to Hercules (*Panegyricus*, 14). His achievements were worthy of divine honours, though Trajan moderately placed bronze statues of himself in the temple of Jupiter Optimus Maximus rather than the gold and silver statues installed by Domitian (*Panegyricus*, 52).

The argument is ingenious: Trajan is not a god and does not present himself as a god, but has divine characteristics that lead to his association with gods. This is contrasted with Domitian's explicit claims to divinity. Yet, although Trajan's self-glorification had not, by AD 100 or whenever this section of the *Panegyricus* reached its final form, extended to the placing of precious metal statues of himself in the most important temple in the city, he did place other statues of himself in that temple, thus inviting his association with the divine.

One could interpret the *Panegyricus* as Pliny's attempt to impose a senatorial ideal of the emperor on Trajan's principate and, if so, much of what is said would become programmatic. It seems more likely that the confusion in the *Panegyricus* reflects Pliny's difficulties (and probably those of many of his contemporaries) in understanding and interpreting the role of the *princeps* in the first years of the second century AD. Pliny probably represents a general view that, although the emperor should behave as if he were 'one of us', the vast power that he wields and the favours that the gods have bestowed on him mean that the emperor is superior to the rest of the aristocracy and is in a quasi-divine, quasi-parental role. This intellectual acceptance of the superiority of the emperor represents not just an acceptance of the necessity of monarchy (many may have seen this as a necessary evil from the reign of Claudius), but a willingness to work within an openly monarchic system. Pliny, a conservative, seems to be saying that as long as the emperor does not actually claim to be a god, we are willing to accept that his relationship to the senate and people may be like that of a god to mortals and thus divine imagery is appropriate for presenting the role of the emperor. This allows Pliny to publish a work filled with contradictions as a coherent speech in praise of the emperor. The same man who proclaimed that none should call the emperor *dominus*, wrote as governor to Trajan from Bithynia and each time addressed him as *dominus*. Pliny, and one suspects many others in the senate, had reconciled themselves to the loss of personal and political freedom that came with the monarchic system.

At about the same time as the *Panegyricus* was first delivered, Tacitus argued in the *Agricola* that even a bad emperor can be served without bringing dishonour. Agricola was a role model of the decent man serving his country and his sacrifices are explicitly contrasted with those of the senators who had opposed Domitian's tyranny publicly and paid with their lives. Agricola's life was of benefit to the state, while the sacrifice of others brought liberty no nearer (see pp. 247–49). This would seem quite a radical agenda, but placed alongside the *Panegyricus* we perhaps see a process of transformation in the attitudes of the Roman elite.

The *Panegyricus* is in many ways a Republican text. It is very different from the poetry of Statius in praise of the emperor Domitian. For example, in *Silvae* 1.1 Statius glorifies a statue of the emperor in the most lavish terms: there is no doubt in this poem that Domitian is to be regard as a divinity. We could compare this with Statius, *Silvae*, 1.6 in which Statius finds the experience of a festival dinner given by Domitian the rival of Jupiter's bounty, or *Silvae*, 4.1 on Domitian's seventeenth consulship, or 4.2 offering thanks for Domitian's banquet, or 4.3, in which a building of a road attracts praise of epic proportions. The divinity of the emperor is not in question in these texts: it is openly acknowledged and the great achievements of Domitian, which are super-human, justify his unquestionable and beneficial rule. But the *Panegyricus* is remarkably mild in comparison and even if modern readers might find the lavish praise not to their taste, the association of Trajan with the gods is restrained.

This restraint, which emanates from Trajan himself supposedly, marks the era of Trajan as one of a restored liberty in which individuals can stop and chat freely and in which there is a normal relationship between senators and with the emperor. Even as Trajan is above them, he is one of them. But what marks Pliny's text is that the era depends on the Emperor himself: it is a result of his character and his political will. Trajan instructs the Romans to be free, to behave as if the Republic is restored, and so they do. Is the Republic restored in such circumstances? Partly, the answer must be 'yes'. Trajan uses his power to call the Republic into being and it becomes the duty of Romans to abide by that political culture. But it is a measure of the power of the Emperor that he can do this and it is only through the power of the Emperor that the Republic can be restored. In this sense, the precondition of the Republicanism of Pliny's *Panegyricus* is imperial power. The reality of that power was that Trajan could allow the Roman elite to behave as if they lived in a past world. Yet, it was a further reality that Trajan could change his mind.

The obvious contradictions of Pliny's *Panegyricus* depend on a political realisation of the near-absolute power of the Emperor. That power had been experienced under Domitian. It was that power that allowed Pliny to suggest to Trajan that he could behave in a Republican manner and that would become the imperial reality. To allow someone to be free, provided that one continues to will that freedom into being is, of course, very different from making someone truly and absolutely free. Freedom is granted as an indulgence and is always dependent on the overwhelming power of the *dominus*-emperor. Trajan's gift of allowing the senators to act as if they were free was, however, the best offer available.

From the foundation of the Principate, Rome had been faced with the paradox of monarchic power in a political culture that emphasised freedom and the role of an independently-minded aristocracy. The *Panegyricus* suggests no resolution to that paradox: freedom depends on subservience. The very fact that Pliny comes up with this convoluted political theory shows that the Roman political elite were fully aware of the contradictions of the system under which they lived.

Trajanic images

Trajan made use of all traditional means to elevate his status and win the favour of his subjects. His arrival in Rome in AD 98 appears to have been marked by games and most significant events in his reign were celebrated in a similar way. His victories in Dacia led to major celebrations (Dio, 68. 10.2, 15.1). There were also games in 109 to celebrate the opening of an aqueduct and Trajan's baths. In 112, another set of games celebrated the opening of Trajan's Forum and the Basilica Ulpia (*Fasti Ostienses*) On accession, he curried favour with the plebs more directly by providing them with grants of money and a similar gift was made again in 107 (Pliny, *Paneyricus*, 25; *Fasti Ostienses*).

Trajan also made use of divine imagery. Nerva was deified on Trajan's return to Rome. Trajan also made public reference to his wife, sister, and niece. These three all appear on coins of the period and all received the title Augusta. He deified Marciana, his sister, when she died in 112. Trajan's position was certainly not reliant upon his family's status. There was no obvious element in the background or families of these women which would honour Trajan: the situation is thus very different from Gaius liberally deifying his family members. The special status of these women sprang solely from Trajan's own authority and the divine honours granted to Marciana signify not the dominance of a family, but the concentration of power on an individual. Deifying Marciana was a substitute for deifying Trajan. Yet, the prominence given to these women calls into question the difference between Trajan and those who had preceded him: it was hardly normal senatorial behaviour to have one's sister deified.

Perhaps the most obvious way in which Trajan elevated his status was through his building programme. It was traditional for emperors to leave their mark on the central area of Rome. Trajan continued this tradition by constructing the largest of the imperial *fora*. This Forum differed somewhat from earlier imperial *fora* in that the architectural centres of the earlier fora were occupied by temples which dominated the spatial arrangements. Trajan's Forum was dominated by a basilica which separated the main court from a subsidiary court. The basilica itself, unlike the temple of Venus Genetrix or the temple of Mars Ultor, was not a natural focus for the Forum. The rather cramped secondary court had a temple at one end, but this temple was no more architecturally significant than the two flanking libraries. This secondary area was dominated by its central monument, Trajan's column. The column celebrated Trajan's Dacian war. The temple was dedicated to

Divus Traianus, presumably by Hadrian. On the hill above the Forum stood Trajan's markets, presumably constructed to house those displaced from the area of the Forum.

Its unusual design and evidence that other emperors had been involved in building projects in the area has led to disagreement among archaeologists and art historians as to how to interpret the Forum. No absolute answer seems possible since any answer must depend in part on individual artistic sensibilities. Those entering the Forum were probably not visibly aware of the column and temple standing behind the basilica. The outer court was also decorated with images from Trajan's Dacian triumph. Visitors who passed through the basilica would enter the inner court where Trajan's success was so grandly displayed with the column. The hiding of this court from those in the first courtyard may have increased the aesthetic impact on leaving the basilica. The confined space must also have enhanced the impressiveness of the column. Yet visual clues do not lead the visitor directly through the basilica into the 'inner sanctum' of the second court. The basilica effectively hides the inner monuments, suggesting that the spaces were to be interpreted differently and perhaps quite separately. The whole Forum reflects Trajan's Dacian victories and glorifies the emperor, but does so through different architectural and artistic media. Although one can still see this as part of one construction, conforming to a single plan, we perhaps see two distinct architectural elements combined. In any case, the Forum advertises Trajan and his conquests with a grandeur that certainly matches the achievements of those less popular emperors that tradition tends to see as megalomaniacs.

Trajan's military success was advertised in his Forum, his coinage and his name. It was an important part of Trajan's image. Most other emperors had made some attempt to associate themselves with the troops and military success. Trajan differed in the scale of his involvement in military matters. His campaigns were largely aggressive and, although there may have been some strategic rationale for his campaigns in Dacia, the thirst for glory appears to have been the major motivating factor. His campaigns in Germany earned him the title Germanicus in the first days of his reign, Dacicus followed in 102 and Parthicus came in 116–17.

Trajan sought to secure his own position by military feats that rivalled those of Alexander the Great. One could regard Trajan's aggressiveness as 'normal' Roman behaviour. Previous emperors had not engaged in such campaigns because of political insecurity, pressing military problems, or personal weakness. We could also see in Trajan's association with the army a continuing theme of the Principate, one which our senatorial sources tend to downplay; since Augustus, emperors associated themselves with the military and military glory. Political power and the ability of the emperors to reward their followers depended on the Empire and the wealth they could extract from it. Trajan's campaigns asserted the familiar truth that the emperor was first and foremost a general.

Wars

When Trajan was adopted, he was an experienced general, though the exact nature of that experience is somewhat obscure. He immediately adopted an aggressive policy. The two main areas of his military activity were on the Danubian frontier and in the East.

Domitian had been beset with difficulties with the tribes beyond the Danube. His victories had brought some stability to the frontier zone, but attempts to assert Roman authority beyond the Danube ended in humiliating failure (see pp. 251–53). It is unclear whether the settlement was such that further military action would have been inevitable in order to retrieve Roman honour. The Romans had, after all, accepted disadvantageous settlements in Germany and the East at various times throughout the first century.

Trajan's first intervention in the region was before AD 100. Pliny had noted that Trajan showed moderation in his recent campaign by not venturing beyond the Danube (*Panegyricus*, 16). This suggests that Trajan had been involved in suppressing a Dacian incursion, possibly as early as 97. This renewed outbreak provided a pretext for a more radical solution to this recurring problem. There is evidence to suggest a considerable build-up of forces along the Danube in 100. The war was over by 102. Decebalus sued for peace, his forces had been defeated at Tapae, and considerable territory had been lost. Trajan's willingness to accept the peace and failure to unseat Decebalus does, however, suggest that Roman successes had been mixed and the Dacians' formidable military force had not been decisively defeated (Dio, 67. 6, 8–9).

Trajan celebrated a triumph, but the very next year (103) the senate was persuaded once more to declare war on Decebalus. This time the war seems to have been extended. Decebalus explored the possibility of a diplomatic solution, but was rejected. In the end, the king was captured and beheaded by a Roman cavalryman whose military career has been preserved on a comparatively recently discovered inscription. Dacia became a province and the Dacian capital was turned into a Roman colony. The decisive defeat of the Dacians must have increased the security of the Danubian provinces and probably acted as a check on the neighbouring tribes such as the Iazyges, yet it remains an open question as to what extent Dacia was pacified. C. Julius Quadratus Bassus, who was one of Trajan's leading generals and was involved in the conquest of Dacia, was later (at an uncertain date) appointed governor of the province. There he ended his long and distinguished career. We do not know how he died, but the inscription tells us that at the time of his death he was actively campaigning in Dacia. Hadrian laid down the procedures for his funeral (Smallwood 1966: No. 214). Dacia remained a trouble spot.

In *c.* 107, Trajan expanded the empire by annexing Arabia. Details of the campaign remain obscure. Indeed, it is possible that there was only limited resistance.

Trajan's next and final military adventure was a general assault on Parthia and the East. The exact chronology of the war is a matter of some dispute but, from 112 or soon after, Trajan was preparing his invasion. The Parthians seem to have been unsure as to Trajan's motives. The region had been reasonably peaceful since the campaigns of Corbulo. There were efforts to come to a diplomatic solution along similar lines to Corbulo's settlement. The Arsacid rulers of Armenia were prepared to surrender in public and provide Trajan with the kind of ceremonial victory that had satisfied both Augustus and Nero. Instead of simply restoring the Arsacids to the Armenian throne, however, Trajan decided to turn Armenia into a province.

War was inevitable and it seems very likely that Trajan was looking to inflict a decisive defeat on the Parthians and their allies, securing the Parthian Empire for Rome. For generations, Roman leaders had looked to the achievements of Alexander the Great for inspiration, and the conquest of the Eastern Mediterranean put Roman forces in a position to emulate Alexander by defeating the successor state to the Persian Empire.

Trajan made significant territorial gains. Armenia fell and he campaigned successfully in Mesopotamia. However, the problem with the region was not securing initial military success. Roman forces were consistently able to cross the frontier and take control of Armenia and Parthian territory. The problems the Romans faced were bringing the highly mobile Parthian forces to a decisive battle and maintaining control over the disparate peoples spread over this huge territory. The Parthian military and political system seems to have been extremely flexible and the Parthians showed an ability to raise troops in spite of what would appear to have been catastrophic military defeats.

Trajan's invasion of 116 culminated in the capture of the Parthian capital Ctesiphon. It is likely that Trajan thought the war was over. Instead of consolidating his control over this territory, he advanced towards the Persian Gulf, the effective limits of Alexander's empire. Yet the Parthians proved able to put an army in the field and, although Trajan had asserted Roman military power, he still did not have political control.

In 115, a major earthquake had destroyed the city of Antioch. It has been suggested that this event precipitated a significant revolt in the East. Between 115–17, Jewish communities in Cyrenaica, Cyprus, Egypt, and probably Judaea revolted. There is no obvious explanation for this sudden outbreak of violence. The Jewish communities of the diaspora (those communities located outside the area of Israel–Palestine) had withstood periodic persecutions over the previous century without staging a revolt of this scale. There is no evidence to suggest that Trajan instituted any anti-Semitic policies. More likely, the Jewish communities were responding to a common cultural or political movement, perhaps of a messianic nature. Either the earthquake in the East or the war in Parthia, where there was a large Jewish community, were interpreted as religiously significant events which encouraged revolt. We do not have the

Jewish side of the story. In any event, the revolt forced the recall of units from Parthia.

In 116 or early 117, the recently-conquered peoples of the former Parthian Empire revolted. Major campaigns were fought to hold the territory and the cities of Nisbis, Seleucia and Edessa were sacked by Roman forces. Arabia revolted and Trajan himself was repulsed from the walls of Hatra. The Roman forces involved in the siege of Hatra were beset by illness caused by the insanitary conditions. Trajan himself became ill and died. Hadrian was unwilling to maintain control over the new provinces and came to a settlement with the Parthians (Dio, 68. 17–33).

Trajan's adventure to the East ended in failure. Trajan failed to secure control of the area. The extent of the revolt and of Trajan's campaigns in 116–17 probably forced a recognition of the difficulties in governing the region. We know nothing of the causes of the revolt, but we may speculate that Rome attempted to establish provincial governmental systems. The tasks of pacification were far from finished on Trajan's death, and further extended campaigning may have been unattractive to a new emperor unsure of his political position.

Finance

The evidence concerning the finances of Nerva and Trajan is somewhat confused. This is partly the result of a tradition that condemned Domitian for financial extravagance and saw in his treatment of the senate and other groups a rapacious desire for money (see pp. 255–56). It would seem that this interpretation was certainly encouraged by his successors and yet their own actions and generosity suggest that the finances of the state were not in too poor a situation in 96.

When Nerva became emperor Domitian suffered a *damnatio memoriae*. One of the beneficial effects of this was that Domitian's statues were destroyed and since at least some were of precious metal, they filled the coffers of Nerva (Dio, 68. 1). Nerva also created a committee to produce advice on the reduction of public expenditure (Pliny, *Epistles*, 2.1). This suggests that he was under some financial pressure. He may also have raised some new taxes: Pliny refers to *plera vectigalia* (several taxes) being created. The only detail we have is a discussion of changes in the five per cent inheritance tax. The attestation in *Panegyricus*, 37 is rather difficult to understand, but it seems that Nerva changed the grounds for exemption from inheritance tax and this had the effect of increasing income. Pliny presents this as a measure that increased the equity with which the tax was administered.

The reduction in the number of prosecutions led to a fall in state income since at least part of the property of those convicted often passed to the state (Pliny, *Panegyricus*, 36; 42). Property was sold by Trajan (Pliny, *Panegyricus*, 50), which may reflect cash-flow problems. Nevertheless, the evidence for prosperity in these years is compelling. Nerva sought to secure the loyalty of the troops and plebs through donations. He publicly proclaimed that the period of harsh imposition of the Jewish tax and a transport tax in Italy were over, though the Jewish tax was still collected. Nerva also had to meet the financial demands placed on the state by the returning exiles who reclaimed property confiscated by Domitian. Dio (68. 2) claims that land worth 60,000,000 *sesterces* was returned. Nerva's building projects were not extensive, though he completed the Forum Transitorum (or the Forum of Nerva).

Trajan was able to pay donations to the plebs, though he only paid a half donative to the troops on accession (Pliny, *Panegyricus*, 25). He gave lavish games (Pliny, *Panegyricus*, 33). He also remitted taxation from Egypt and even sent emergency aid to the province, which appears to have had a disastrous harvest (Pliny, *Panegyricus*, 30). Trajan's building programme was notable. Although Pliny praises Trajan for his moderation in building (in contrast to Domitian), he was already constructing a porticus, an arch and a temple in AD 100 (*Panegyricus*, 51). He had also commenced major and expensive building projects in Ostia to improve the harbour and provide greater protection for the grain boats. In addition, he may have been engaged in major road construction in Italy (Pliny, *Panegyricus*, 29). His greatest building works, the forum and related structures, the baths and the aqueduct were all completed much later, but it is likely that work on at least some of these projects started in the early part of his reign, before his finances were boosted by the Dacian conquest.

The evidence of Pliny suggests that Trajan spent freely throughout the early years of his reign. The *Panegyricus* does not give the impression that the Roman state was teetering on the brink of a financial crisis (though a panegyric could hardly be expected to be critical of an emperor's financial management), and Pliny's extended discussion of financial matters would perhaps have been impolitic if this were so. Unless Nerva and Trajan had worked some kind of financial miracle, it seems very likely that they had inherited a healthy financial situation from Domitian and there were no great financial problems during the reign of Nerva or the early part of the reign of Trajan.

It is normally assumed that the success of the Dacian wars transformed Trajan's financial situation and allowed him to spend freely on monuments such as the Forum. It is also impossible to estimate the significance of the money that came from Dacia, and this looted wealth, as depicted on Trajan's column, must be set against the expenses of the war and the costs of establishing a new province.

Trajan was also able to finance a new initiative in Italy. This was the *alimenta* scheme. This scheme was designed to provide a certain amount of poor relief for the children of Italy. The idea was that certain landowners would mortgage land to the state. The interest on that mortgage would be paid into a fund to provide poor relief. The landowners were encouraged by a low interest rate on the loan, though it seems that in most cases only a small part of the estate was mortgaged in this fashion. Landowners were probably able to benefit from the injection of capital (which may have been in short supply in the Italian economy) and this could be used either to improve or to extend their estates. The poor would benefit from the accumulated money and thus the population would be encouraged to grow. The financial burden of the system fell largely on the state. We do not know the extent of the *alimenta* system in Italy but it seems likely that it represented a massive financial outlay. This was a bold attempt to provide some financial security for the children of Italy. Although the demography of Italy had been a matter of some concern to the Roman state for centuries, this was a very direct and expensive intervention. Such an extension of imperial generosity (though of course the system created was nowhere near as extensive as modern welfare systems) symbolises the wealth, confidence, and power of the Trajanic principate.

Conclusions

Edward Gibbon, one of the greatest of all historians, saw the reigns of Nerva and Trajan as inaugurating a period of stability and happiness in the Roman state that, arguably, was unequalled in human history. The five good emperors of the second century all (with the exception of Nerva) had long lives. The frontiers were secure (mostly). The political traumas of the first 150 years of emperors seem to have been laid aside and the instabilities of the third century, with its multiple emperors and barbarian invasions, were a long way off. Gibbon was a utilitarian who believed not in democracy or monarchy, but in judging regimes as to whether they contributed to the sum of human happiness. He believed that the second century was remarkably successful in achieving that goal.

Centuries later, many continue to view Rome's empire in the same charitable light, as engaged in the spreading of happiness and civilisation. Yet, Gibbon's view of the secondary century was merely a preliminary dramatic counterpoint to what was to follow: the decline and fall of the Roman Empire. Further, Gibbon, working within the methodologies of his day, did not look for the voices beyond the literary record. If the voices of discontent seem to be quietened in the second century, it does not mean that there was no discontent. So many of the voices of Rome's Empire are not recorded: we have few non-elite sources, little from provincials, nothing from slaves. Even the senators largely disappear from view in the second century. Silence, as Tacitus tells us, does not mean happiness.

Chapter 11

Society

Introduction

Methods

'Society' in the Roman Empire is a complex topic. It is complex because studying societies is difficult. Sociologists of contemporary societies often disagree about fundamental aspects of the society they are studying but even if there is agreement about the facts of a particular social system, there is often disagreement about the methodologies that one should use to understand that society. The organisation of society relates closely to issues of economic structure (the material aspects of society) and issues of ideology (the intellectual or cultural aspects of society). There has long been debate as to the relationship between material and intellectual aspects of social systems and, in particular, whether the economic is determined by the intellectual or the intellectual determined by the economic. Further, the very concept of 'society' faces challenges. Our modern societies, with all that binds us together (economic structures, powerful and interventionist states, educational systems, mass media), show considerable diversity and perhaps over the last two decades most Western societies have changed so as to be more diverse and more inclusive, worrying less about difference, cultural, religious, sexual, racial, ethnic, or intellectual. But whereas three decades ago, it was easy to talk about societies identical with nation states (British society; French society; American society), it now seems less easy to define the national character of societies and one may wonder in a world in which people move so much and in which the speed and scale of global communication is so overwhelming, whether our societies bear little relationship to the spatial boundaries of nations. The globalisation of our culture makes defining society much more difficult.

As Roman historians, our problems are very different, but thinking about contemporary societies leads us to question assumptions. Can we, for example, talk about a Roman society and what do we mean by a Roman society? We can skip across definitions by simply changing some of the words, but if we were to argue that 'a society' shares a common culture or language, defining Roman culture is no easier than defining Roman society.

Outside Italy, the linguistic and cultural complexities were great. Latin and Greek became the official languages of Empire and because most of our sources are either from the high literary elite or in some way public or official texts, then local languages gradually disappear from our sight. But that does not mean that they disappeared from use. In the East, for example, virtually all the inscriptions and papers we find (hundreds of thousands of documents were preserved on papyrus in Egypt) are in Greek. Egyptian continues to be used in some specialised contexts through the first century AD and on some temple inscriptions into the third century, but Greek was the language of tax documents, of registrations, of magical texts, and, most convincingly of private letters, of which we have many from several areas of Egypt, from towns and villages. From this information, one would imagine that Egyptian had almost disappeared, being used only in certain isolated religious contexts. That is until the Christian period when Egyptian literature starts to be written once more and when it becomes clear that Egyptian was being spoken in many different regions. The reinvention of Coptic as a literary language is paralleled by the use of Syriac and both were used because the demands of Christian theology meant that ideas needed to be communicated to everyone and not just those who spoke Greek. Although this pattern of linguistic continuity is obvious in Egypt, we can just about detect it in many regions (Gaul, Syria, Asia Minor, North Africa).

Italy does appear to be more uniform than the Empire, though the political unification of Italy was a relatively late phenomenon. Although Latin was the dominant language in the Italian peninsula by the Augustan period, Greek was certainly spoken in many areas throughout the first century and other languages, such as versions of Celtic and Oscan, were, although absent from official contexts, probably still spoken in Northern Italy and Southern Italy respectively. Only two generations before Augustus, Italians and Romans had fought a long and vicious war over the relationship between Roman and Italian communities (the so-called Social War). Northern Italy had been largely conquered and colonised in the early second century BC, but citizenship was not spread to all of the peninsular communities until Julius Caesar's dictatorship. But political unification would not necessarily entail social and cultural unification: we cannot simply say that all peoples who were governed from Rome were part of the same society.

The problem is, in part, related to how we define society. We can think of a society as being the larger social group or institutional network with whom there is social interaction, real or virtual. We can map those social interactions. Thinking outwards, we start with family and friends and then we move to those we know in our immediate community. But a society is more than the people we know. We could extend social our group to include institutions which bind our society together, principally those of the state. We may think of the education system, the health services, the social services. We might even extend our range to include institutions such as the police and the army and the legal system. We might also think about virtual societies: those formed by the media that we consume. Yet, the more we extend our grouping, the less concrete our ties to those furthest away in the system seem. For instance, we tend not to view those with whom our ties are primarily economic as being part of our society: are the Chinese factory workers who produce so many of our manufactured goods part of our social system? How significant are the particular ties that are formed?

Once we transfer this pattern to Rome, we see family, friends, and acquaintances, but after that, we struggle to see the connections. If one is in Rome, one might receive the corn dole, but outside of Rome, connections to the Roman state were probably very weak for most people. There were statues of emperors and perhaps the important people in any local community might have travelled to the city. Perhaps there were economic links. Roman coin jangled in people's purses. Roman taxes were paid. In some places, one might have seen the occasional Roman soldier. Yet, in the absence of a large and intrusive state and of anything approximating mass media, it is likely that people lived, thought and worked much more locally than we do in our contemporary societies.

This requires us to think carefully about what we are talking when we talk about 'Roman society'. Most societies appear to have been conscious of difference, ethnic or otherwise: it would be noticed when people on the other side of the hill spoke a different language or dialect. But the issue is in part how significant those differences would be. If we think about the rise of national societies in the modern West, these only came about with the advent of mass media (i.e. newspapers), perhaps also thanks to improved transport technologies and the development of a modern state infrastructure. Before that, even if there was a consciousness of a shared national identity (and that consciousness does seem to go back a long way in history), the significance of that shared identity was probably very slight on an everyday basis: people lived in local societies rather than national societies and the national simply mattered less.

Nevertheless, I will suggest in a later chapter that the Roman Empire was surprising in its levels of cultural uniformity, given the limits of technology. I also suggest that Roman Italy was surprisingly uniform after the Augustan period: local identities were preserved to some extent, but only within a Roman framework. In part, the uniformity of Italy, which emerges politically in the first century BC and is perhaps most obviously and powerfully deployed first by Octavian in the war against Cleopatra (a war depicted as Italy against Egypt, in part to distract from the fact that this was in reality another civil war), may have emerged in the wake of the violence of the Caesarian period and afterwards when veteran communities were established across the peninsula and many were displaced by the war. The churning of population that came with the civil wars and the subsequent settlements (Augustus alone established 28 colonies) must have led to changes in local cultures and changes in the nature of the relationship between local towns and Rome itself.

Another way of explaining societal similarities across wide geography is in terms of social structures. Even if the Roman state was not an everyday presence in many of the communities of Italy, Rome imposed certain political structures on the conquered communities, which meant that they developed certain social structures in parallel to those of Rome. One could imagine then that when we are see social similarities across the Roman Empire we are not looking Roman society, but at Roman societies: many different localised 'Romes' spread across the Empire. The institution that spread the values of Rome was the city and these cities remained nodal points in a network of Roman cultural values. Those cities imported certain Roman cultural values, but also institutions. These included Roman law. We might envisage, then, Roman-style social relations emerging in all the different local communities as Roman institutions and that Rome law came to shape those societies.

If we were to believe this city-led model, we would have a view of society and social change which was very much top-down: the powerful and the elite establish certain social structures to which communities come to adhere. There is much to be said for such an understanding of the processes of cultural change and of cultural assimilation and I suppose this was the dominant approach to Roman society in generations past. In the next section, I will approach Roman society through its institutions.

Yet, we also need to think about issues of power in societies. How and why do people adhere to certain social rules? This is a complicated issue for all societies. Thinking about society in terms of power does not devalue thinking about society though its institutions, but does allow us to have a much more vibrant and flexible understanding of social relations. It also allows us to escape categories and to imagine Roman society in a very different way, one in which the individual plays a more important part in creating his or her society and is not a simple or passive recipient of values that come from elsewhere.

Sources

The second core issue we must face is the quality of the source material. For the political history of this period, we rely heavily on the narrative histories produced by writers who were either members of the senatorial elite or closely connected with it. The historical literature we have reflects the concerns of a very small proportion of the Italian population. We might want to convince ourselves that the views of those not represented by our source material did not matter or (even less likely) that the views of the literary elite were representative of those of all Romans.

Yet, such views are merely a convenience that allows us not to worry so much. In fact, our sources suggest that we are missing something by not having non-elite sources. For example, the actions of the soldiers were sometimes crucial, but the views of individual soldiers are very rarely even alluded to in our elite-authored accounts. Soldiers do not speak in the historical record and elite writers felt under no compunction to invent their opinions. We certainly do not have any representation of the views of soldiers which claims authenticity. Their opinions seem not to have mattered. Emperors also seem to have devoted considerable time and money to looking after the plebs, but too often the plebs are lazily dismissed by historians as being bought off by bread and circuses (evidently such historians have never had to worry about food). It is easy to see politics as an elite business, of little concern to the rest of society, yet it is precisely those others whose political support for the princeps, when Caesar was killed, when Augustus came to power, when Claudius was made emperor, and during the later civil wars, was crucial in establishing and maintaining the Imperial regime. It was, of course, the business of the Roman elite to ignore non-elite power and tell each other that their own views and status and standing were important above all else, but that does not mean that those outside the elite were entirely passive or that they shared the views of the powerful. For this reason alone, we may suspect that the views of Roman social (and political) relations delivered by our elite sources are blind (deliberately or unconsciously) to aspects of Roman society.

For social history, it matters that we cannot access the views of the urban and rural poor, of immigrants to Rome, or of slaves. It is important that we cannot get beyond the social views of the wealthy elite. Furthermore, on the odd occasion when an elite author takes us beyond the confines of elite literary salons and senatorial social groups, say when Martial produces his epigrams or Juvenal writes his *Satires* or Petronius imagines the lives of a group of itinerant chancers hustling a little money and the odd meal in Southern Italian cities, it is difficult to know whether we are in the realm of the fantastic or the realistic, whether we are being told stories so tall that they amused the elite readers or whether some echo of the everyday is preserved.

Normally, of course, people do not write about the everyday, the average and the normal since by definition the everyday is passing and not worth recording. Most likely our sources are littered with the exceptional and the unusual, the socially and sexually deviant making a far better story than the normal. Yet, for us, as historians, the 'normal' is far more interesting and far more difficult to understand.

One of the ways round this problem is to look to types of source material other than the literary. Poorer groups do appear in inscriptions. Inscriptions cover a number of varied subjects and attest individuals of many different social groups. An inscription could be expensive, especially if it ornately carved, but inscriptions depend on a simple technology. You need a stone, a chisel, and preferably someone used to carving. Inscriptions could, then, be cheap. We find slaves and freedmen in inscriptions. They also attest woman and children. There were certainly far more inscriptions in antiquity than have come down to us. Many of the stones will have been destroyed, often reused. One presumes also that many stones have been eroded to the extent that they can no longer be recognised.

Yet there are problems in using inscriptions for social history. Most of Roman inscriptions we have come from urban sites when the vast majority of the population must have lived in the countryside. The urban bias may reflect archaeological investigation, but is perhaps more likely to reflect a real preponderance in antiquity. Inscriptions were intended for an audience and that intended audience was not, unfortunately, social historians of the future. Inscriptions, thus, have a communicatory context.

This context gives rise to something modern historians call the epigraphic habit. Not all peoples in all times put up inscriptions. Secondly, what people used inscriptions for changed over time. For example, we have very many funerary inscriptions from Rome for the Imperial period. We have large numbers of funerary inscriptions from other Roman Italian cities. But, we do not have many funerary inscriptions from the Republican period. All other epigraphic data in Italy follows the same chronological pattern. Further, we do not have many inscriptions from rural communities. In the Western provinces, the epigraphic habit appears initially at least to have concentrated among the military. In many regions, the number of inscriptions falls away in the later empire (though North Africa is something of an exception). In the East, there are different and localised patterns of epigraphic use. Some areas appear to make very little use of epigraphy; in others there is a mass of epigraphic remains. In some places there is a distinct chronological pattern to the use of inscriptions; in others inscriptions continue to be used regularly both in official and private contexts to the very end of the Roman Empire. We should also remember that what comes down to us are inscriptions on stone. Some peoples may have used wood for the same purposes and official documents were sometimes painted up or even inscribed on bronze (which will have been looted at a later date).

We are then looking at fashions, but this should also give us pause for thought. In different parts of the Empire and among different social groups different cultures of commemoration applied. Further, the pattern in the use of funerary inscriptions especially but also of other inscriptions (putting up a statue to someone, dedicating an altar or religious artefact) was set by the requirements of communication within a community. Inscriptions were about assertion of identity and status.

This explains certain oddities in the epigraphic corpus. We have very many inscriptions concerning women, but more about men, when one must assume that about equal numbers of men and women died in antiquity. For the first two centuries AD, in Italy especially, we have very few inscriptions commemorating children. Yet, one must assume that in the living conditions of pre-industrial cities, children were particularly vulnerable. Older women also seem to be curiously under-represented. In Christian inscriptions though, we have far more children attested. Soldiers and veterans appear seemingly disproportionately often, especially outside Italy. In Rome and the Italian towns, vast numbers of freedman are attested. There are then obvious biases in the population attested in the epigraphic data.

Putting up an inscription is an assertion of status within a community. Most of the funerary inscriptions (a large percentage of the surviving epigraphy from antiquity) are, unsurprisingly, associated with tombs. Roman tombs were often located along the major roads leading into towns. The dead were required to be entombed outside the city walls and the roadsides were the next best spaces for display if one could not be buried within the city. A tomb could be a public monument and in a competitive culture, like that of Rome, any assertion of status was likely to produce imitations. One can see, therefore, how the culture of epigraphic commemoration would take hold: one large tomb followed another in competitive assertions of status. Making one's heirs erect a tomb was an assertion of power from beyond life. Some people put up their tombs while they were still alive, making sure that their memory would be preserved. Heirs had an interest in spending money on tombs since the expense showed them as dutiful and associated them with the deceased, especially important if the deceased was a person of wealth or importance and there might be a chance of the will being challenged. Yet, one can also see why people of lesser importance might not have tombs (elderly women, children, the very poor) since they had no social status to assert

There is, however, a positive argument: rather than worrying about groups that are disproportionately absent from the evidence, we might think of groups who seem disproportionately present: soldiers and freedmen. The very presence of these groups in the epigraphic record suggests that they played an important part in society.

Freedmen and soldiers (outside Italy) are problematic groups. The disproportionate presence of soldiers and freedmen in the epigraphic record might suggests that these groups became dominant in their particular societies. Yet, there are different possible explanations for their appearance in the epigraphic record. Soldiers might be recorded in part because of specific epigraphic practices within their military units in which status was being remembered and asserted. Notably, however, soldiers and veterans and freedmen had undergone status change during their lifetimes. The status change for freedmen is obvious. Soldiers may have received Roman citizenship as one of the rewards for military service. Another sociological feature common to freedmen and soldiers is that they must often have died in areas or communities different to, and at times far from, those in which they were born. Many 'normal' people will have lived and died in the same communities and have been part of a social continuity across the generations: in most Mediterranean societies, people carried a patronymic (father's name) and sometime a papponymic (grandfather's name). But these cross generational links were not available to slaves and soldiers. Soldiers and freedmen were to some extent 'new' people since individuals from these groups were often separated from their natal families and were the first generation of any new family. Thus, they could not rely on their place in their new community being remembered and asserted through their membership of an old familial group. If funerary epigraphy is a means of asserting memory, then the needs of these sociological newcomers to preserve memories and assert status were greater than that of ordinary indigenous peoples whose fathers and grandfathers had been known and whose children and grandchildren would be known.

The vast majority of our inscriptions are formulaic. Many of these inscriptions are undated. In terms of social information, we might be able to extract names and sometimes ages and some familial relationships, but they do not have a back-story, a reason for the inscription having been put up. Yet, the circumstances which led to an inscription being erected were crucial and it is those circumstances which we would really like to know and would make interesting history. We should not imagine that those whose names have come down to us on the inscriptions represent anything like a cross-section of Roman society.

Another key source for social history is archaeology. The excavations of Pompeii and Herculaneum provide us with extraordinary and detailed visions of how people lived in these communities. Archaeology provides a materiality to the lives of Romans. We see the houses, those of the rich and the poor. We see the shops and bars. We see the workshops. At another level, archaeology can tell us what people ate and what people ate it off and, to a certain extent, how that food got to their tables. When we have the skeletons (the Romans burned their dead), we get some idea as to how healthy they were. The remains of Herculaneum and Pompeii are, of course, extraordinary in their level of preservation. Many of the other excavated sites from Roman Italy are far less well preserved and our understanding of them is fragmentary.

Archaeology is inevitably limited as a source. The mentalities and ideologies of individuals are difficult to reconstruct from the material evidence. We can see how people presented themselves and reconstruct some of the status games that they played: we can often see how people wanted themselves to be seen and remembered, but so often the populations of Roman cities and the inhabitants of Roman houses are assumed rather than real. We have to make educated guesses as to how they used the buildings and the artefacts. Also, even at Pompeii, the material that is left in archaeological sites is not just what was dropped at some sudden catastrophic moment. Most assemblages of material were constructed over time, as people lost things and broke things. Further, it is almost inevitable that when a property was abandoned, much of value was stripped from the site. If you lose a copper coin, you might not search long for it. If you drop a gold coin, you will not stop until you have found it. We find, largely, a limited proportion of the material remains of the societies and often that material which was left behind, either because it could not be moved (walls, etc.) or because it was not worth moving.

Let us try a thought experiment. Let us imagine that our society ceased because we moved away. What is left is only abandoned material: everything that is of value and that can be carried is taken away with us. Buildings remain, though many are destroyed. All organic matter is lost (no wood, no paper, no leather, no cloth). Pottery survives. Some metal survives, but not in all places (most is corroded away or has been salvaged at some earlier point). What would a future archaeologist miss about our society?

In this chapter, I am going to take two approaches to the history of society. The first is formal: I will look at institutions and institutional structures in Roman society. These provide some of the basic conceptions with which Romans worked. This will give a fairly static and systemic picture of Roman society. The second section looks at power in society and attempts to reconstruct how Roman social relations worked. The difference between society as a system and social relations as networks of power is fundamental.

Social orders and institutions

Modern societies use very few legal few divisions to organise their populations. Most societies operate a basic distinction between citizens and non-citizens. Many pre-modern societies operated a system of legally-defined groups, often with very different political rights, known as social orders. Some historians believe that the existence of social orders with a society would mean that its social and political systems would be fundamentally different from later societies. In large part, this is due to an understanding of modern politics in which there is a correlation between social class and political activity. Whereas a social order is a defined status category, social class relates to a person's position within an economic system. In Marxist (and much non-Marxist thought) social class is defined objectively by economic position. The political actions and attitudes of an individual are, however, determined by an individual's perception of his or her interests within the dominant social order. Historians argue that in ancient society although there was consciousness of economic position and a perceived association between social orders and economic position, people were defined not by their social class, but by their social order. In these circumstances, the argument goes, the politics of individuals are not predetermined by their economic status (class politics). It is unclear, however, whether people's political acts and attitudes were determined by their social order, and we will return to this issue later. Although this is the theory, the practice for Roman society was, as we shall see, messy and complex.

Slaves and peregrini

The Romans divided the population into legal categories. A primary division was between Romans and non-Romans. The final census of Augustus counted

4,937,000 citizens. The census of AD 48 conducted by Claudius counted 5,984,072 citizens (Tacitus, *Annales*, 11.25). It is not clear whether the census counted all Romans, adult males, or just adult Romans. Estimates for the total population of the Roman empire must depend on how one judges that last question, and we will look at on the issue of Roman population on pp. 312–14. We may prejudge that discussion here by saying that it is very unlikely that Romans made up significantly more than 15% of the population of the Empire in the Augustan and Claudian periods. The rest of the population were *peregrini* (foreigners).

Although one might automatically think that *peregrini* existed outside Roman society, the position is rather more complicated. Most obviously, Rome attracted considerable numbers of immigrants, many of whom will not have enjoyed Roman citizenship. Secondly, the Romans exported their institutions and social values. The Roman system had some basic similarities with the Greek city-state organisation. It was relatively easy to map Roman social values and structures onto those of the Greek city (though Greek cities always varied and always remained distinct in some ways). In those areas in which the Greek city had not developed, mostly the West and Africa, the Romans encouraged the development of political structures which bore a resemblance to those of Rome. In particular, cities were ruled by local councils and local councils were an elite defined by wealth. The cities had a body of registered citizens and all societies maintained the institution of slavery (as far as we can tell). Peregrine communities were not separated from Roman social values and customs. Further, just as Rome imported many *peregrini*, so they exported many citizens who came to reside in various communities throughout the Empire.

Of the Roman population, the basic division was between enslaved and free. Slaves were owned. They had no control over their labour or bodies. They were property to be disposed of as their masters or mistresses pleased, subject to certain slight moral and legal constraints. They had no citizenship rights. They also had nothing we would recognise as human rights. Some small level of legal protection was extended during the Imperial period. Claudius (Suetonius, *Claudius*, 25.2) ordered that sick or aged slaves, since they were no longer economic value, were abandoned to die near the temple of Aesculapius (the god of medicine), which was on an island in the Tiber, should receive their freedom and be exempted from the patronal authority of their previous *domini*. He also equated killing a sick or old slave with homicide. Hadrian over saw a major reform of slave law (Historia Augusta, *Hadrian*, 18). He banned slave prisons, the killing of slaves by their owners was made an offence, and owners were prevented from selling slaves into prostitution or to the gladiatorial school without good reason. There are also anecdotes which attest attitudes towards slaves (some of which we will look at below). For example, the younger Pliny was distressed when his slaves were struck down with a mysterious illness (*Epistles*, 8. 16); A man named Vedius Pollio, who was one of the richer men of Augustan Rome, ordered a slave to be thrown to his collection of carnivorous fish for breaking a glass, but Augustus happened to be dining with him and the emperor intervened to pardon the slave (Dio, 52.23; Seneca, *De Ira*, 3.40).

Yet, the question that arises most often in relation to the treatment of slaves is the moral status of the abusive master rather than the legal status of the slave. The story about Vedius Pollio reflected not on the legal status of the slave or on Pollio's right to kill the slave however he wished, but on the cruelty of Pollio and the immorality of his luxurious life, and it is against this immorality that Augustus intervened. After Pollio's death, Augustus pulled down his villa since he regarded it as too luxurious. The anecdote is preserved not because Pollio was cruel, but because Augustus reprimanded him.

Claudius' intervention was even less reformist. Masters needed slaves to work. When slaves became ill they could not work and some just threw them out of the house. They would then have to beg for their livelihoods. All Claudius did was discourage this practice by freeing the slaves of any obligation to their masters. Similarly, Hadrian's actions were to close slave prisons, in part because it was suspected that such places might conceal all manner of cruelties, some of which might be visited on unfortunate free people. He also banned the forcing of slaves into the arena or into prostitution, which were seen as terrible punishments, if there was no *good* reason. This was hardly protection.

In some regards, the exposure of slaves to violence was actually worsened. There was an established law or custom that when a master was killed by a slave all his slaves were held legally responsible and were killed. Under Nero, even those who had been freed but who remained part of the same household were to be sentenced to death in the case of a master being murdered (Tacitus, *Annales*, 13.32; 13.26–27) and in the case of the murder of Pedanius Secundus (Tacitus, *Annales*, 14.42–45), the senate and emperor forced through a sentence of death on Secundus' entire slave household, even though it was clear that the murder was the action of a single disappointed slave. In similar instances (Pliny, *Epistles*, 3.14 and 8.14) a generation later, the full rigour of the law continued to be applied.

The subjection of slaves was nearly absolute. They had no rights and no property. Their bodies were their master's to dispose of as they willed. If our sources sometimes express limited qualms about the killing of slaves, the punishments of a lesser kind, beatings, the breaking of limbs, whippings etc., were no business of the state. Slaves were regarded as humans, but no rights were attached to that status.

Freedmen

The Romans freed considerable numbers of their slaves. Slaves could be freed informally, through a declaration by the master. Formally, they could be declared free by testamentary bequest or through the ceremonial of manumission. The freed were known as *liberti*. They wore a special hat and whereas, as mentioned previously, Roman names normally carried a patronymic (a Roman might be called Gaius Julius, son of Gaius, Caesar), a freedman carried the identifier of being the freedman of his former master. Under the Republic, freedmen enjoyed full Roman citizenship. The elevation of slaves to citizen status was regarded as unusual in the Classical world, though we should perhaps not see this as due to generosity but as due to a lack of other options (there was no lesser status, such as resident foreigner, to which the freed could be assimilated).

The law concerning freedmen was changed under Augustus by the *lex Aelia Sentia*. The *lex Aelia Sentia* introduced two additional categories of freedmen. Slaves who had been tortured, branded or sent to fight in gladiatorial combat were to become *dediticii* (foreigners without a state) on being freed and were not allowed to reside within a hundred miles of Rome. A slave freed informally, that is not through the ceremony of manumission, by being included in the census or by will, became a Junian Latin. Slaves under the age of 30 had to be manumitted and show just cause for the grant of freedom before a board of senators and equestrians or they would become Latins. Slaves over the age of 30 became Roman citizens on being freed.

Junian Latins rights were limited. They could not make a will or receive property through a will, but could obtain Roman citizenship by: marrying a Roman and having a son who survived for one year or by serving for six years with the *vigiles* (the watch) at Rome; (after an edict of Claudius) building a ship which could carry 10,000 *modii* (87,360 litres) of wheat and using it to transport grain supply for six years; (after an edict of Nero) investing 50% of a census level of 200,000 *sesterces* or more in a house in Rome; (after an edict of Trajan) operating a mill in Rome which ground 100 *modii* (873.6 litres) of grain each day for three years (Gaius, *Institutes*, 1.9–36).

Another Augustan law, the *lex Fufia Caninia* limited the rights of owners to bequeath freedom to slaves. This operated on a sliding scale (see Table 11.1) (Gaius, *Institutes*, 1.42–6). The testamentary rights of freedmen were limited. Freedmen who had no children were expected to leave half their estate to their patron (former owner). In addition, another Augustan law, the *lex Papia Poppaea*, obliged a freedman with an estate of 100,000 *sesterces* or more to leave property to his patron. Again this was on a sliding scale. A freedman with one child had to leave half his property to his patron, one with two children had to leave one-third of his property to his patron and one with three children was under no obligation. Freedmen with less than 100,000 *sesterces* and one child were under no obligation (Gaius, *Institutes*, 3.39–44).

Such regulations express a concern about the status of freedmen in Roman society. They reduce the freedom of the freed by establishing formal commitments on the part of the freed towards their former masters. It seems

Table 11.1 Limitations of the *lex Fufia Caninia*

Number of slaves owned	Proportion of freed that can be created by will (percentage)
2–10	50
11–30	33
31–100	25
101–500	20
501 +	No more than 100 slaves

likely that the various laws which were passed brought into law what was previously customary (that is, freedmen had obligations to their former patrons which in earlier ages they fulfilled because those times were more moral). Yet, there is no real evidence to suggest that freedmen of the Republic felt themselves any more obliged than the freed of the Imperial period and it seems quite likely that the legalisation of the obligations were effectively a new imposition. The issue that appears to trigger the concern about freedmen is an accumulation of wealth. Again, we need not see this as a new 'social problem' and a manifestation of declining standards in Roman society, as it appears to have been represented at the time: it is easy to carry over the prejudices of our sources into our thinking. Rather, it seems likely that the accumulation of wealth and power by certain freedmen did not so much reflect a decline in social hierarchy but, as we shall see, an increasing disparity in Roman society. The unintended consequence of such a disparity was the elevation of some freedmen. It was this unintended consequence that the emperors attempted to regulate.

The concern with freedmen appears not to have related particularly to numbers, but to households and status. The limitations on testamentary bequests of freedom in the *lex Aelia Sentia* make little sense as a means of limiting the number of freedmen entering the Roman population. Instead, we can see the measure as being partly sumptuary (reducing the ability of members of the elite to display wealth, which reflects a legislative concern with the issue of *luxuria*, luxury) and partly to relate to an Augustan concern with maintaining the integrity of households. Augustus passed various legislative acts concerning the family which were designed in large part to ensure that families would continue from generation to generation and that the status of particular families would be maintained. Freeing large numbers of slaves by testamentary was an act of spectacular generosity and the freed would become part of the funerary cortege, displaying the wealth of the deceased. Such a bequest could also effectively break up an existing household, leaving the heirs with little to inherit (certainly in terms of labour force). Nothing appears to have prevented a master freeing large numbers of his slaves while he was still alive.

The free

Roman citizens were divided into various groups and each had formal characteristics. During the Republic, the citizen body was divided into six status groups, five orders (numbered one to five) and a group that fell below the fifth order. These were timocratic groups, meaning that one's place in the order depended on one's wealth, assessed from property not income. Membership of a particular order was established by the Roman census at which a declaration of property was made. Originally, this process was related to service in the army, but the relationship between census levels and service was dropped by the general Marius at the end of the second century BC. In addition to these six groupings and again derived from the organisation of the army, the equestrians (knights) were recruited from the first, richest order.

During the Republican period, senators were merely those men who sat in the senate. Senators were chosen for senatorial service either by consuls (acting as censors) or censors and their names would be written down on a public list, which is why the senators are sometimes called the *patres conscripti* (the conscript fathers). In the early first century BC, Sulla established a system whereby those elected to the junior magistracy of quaestor would be also elected to the senate and senators could also be appointed by other means (especially when there was thought to be a shortage of senators). From Sulla onwards, there was a regular career structure of magisterial positions to which aspiring Roman politicians normally adhered. Senators and equestrians were distinguished by wearing slightly different togas. Senators had a wide purple stripe on their togas; equestrians, a narrow stripe.

Augustus formalised the division between senators and equestrians and the rest of the Roman population. First, he introduced separate census levels. The qualification for membership of the first order was 100,000 *sesterces*. The new equestrian status was 400,000 *sesterces*. The senatorial level was set at 1,000,000. Both groups were provided with designated seating in the theatre. The broad-striped toga was also worn by the sons of senators. Further, senators, their children and grandchildren were prohibited, by law, from marrying freed people or those who were regarded as disreputable in some way (prostitutes, actresses). By such measures, senatorial status was extended beyond the senators themselves and to their families. Through this process of establishing a hereditary element to senatorial status, senators took on some of the characteristics of being a social order. Rather oddly, at exactly the same time, the senators started to commemorate their lives by listing their offices, representing themselves as an office-holding elite rather than a hereditary order.

The creation of a senatorial order reflected an older self-representation of the senators as members of a stable, hereditary elite, some of whom could trace their ancestry back to the beginnings of Rome or even earlier. Status passed through the generations as the young males were regarded as future senators and the women as mothers and wives of senators. The truth, however, was that the senate was a more open elite than presented. Studies of consuls have shown that only about 26% of consuls during the period 249–50 BC had no immediate consular or even praetorian ancestor. In the first century AD, 46–75% of consuls had no consular ancestor. The senatorial order was not stable.

The equestrians were initially drawn from the first order comprising citizens with property worth more than 100,000 *sesterces*. Augustus gave the equestrians a defined census level of 400,000 *sesterces*. The equestrians were also given a public horse in recognition of their archaic obligation to serve as cavalry. The Augustan period saw an increase in the number of offices available to equestrians and under the early emperors a career structure developed for equestrians. The equestrians were publicly honoured with processions in which they took part and seats in the theatre and to this extent they formed a broader aristocratic status group.

The rest of the free-born population were relatively undifferentiated. Perhaps the primary differentiation was between those resident in Rome who were entitled to the grain dole (*plebs frumentaria*) and the rest, though this was not really a status issue. There were probably 200,000 plebs in receipt of the corn dole under Augustus and the number may have risen later (*Res Gestae Divi Augusti*, 15) (see also pp. 332–34 for a discussion of the population of Rome).

Roman citizens had various rights and obligations. When Octavian restored the state in 28 BC after the period of civil wars, he returned the 'laws and rights' (*leges et iura*) to the Roman people. In this emphasis on laws and rights we see a fundamental difference between contemporary conceptions of citizenship and ancient conceptions. We have certain rights which are inalienable, these human rights cannot be given away or taken away legally, except in very specific circumstances. For this reason, slavery is illegal worldwide today since one cannot sell one's own freedom nor take another person's freedom: freedom is, to some extent, integral to the modern conception of the person. For the Romans, rights were achieved and won in historic struggles. The laws and rights of the Roman people were those that had been secured over centuries during the Republic.

The struggles were represented as being against the senators and in particular against the magistrates. In the earliest days, senior magistrates had almost unlimited powers, which they could use to physically chastise and possibly even kill Roman citizens. The plebs secured magistrates of their own (tribunes) and also laws which brought them protection from the power of the senior magistrates. This magisterial arm of government was seen as potentially tyrannical. The restoration of the laws and rights of the Roman people brought to an end an emergency situation in which the powers of the magistrates, and in particular the triumvirs (Octavian, Antony and Lepidus) were unlimited. This concern with rights and a defence of those rights against the magistrates established a fundamental political division between senators (magistrates) and the people but also a sensitivity to those moments when the rights, particularly the rights of freedom from violence and freedom of property, were under threat. As the power of the tribunes was lessened, the protection of the rights of the individual from the magistrate devolved into an 'appeal to Caesar' by which a Roman citizen who was threatened by a magistrate could appeal to the emperor. Further, emperors were very concerned not to be seen to using arbitrary violence against their enemies and to employ the paraphernalia of law and trials. The plebs do appear to have reacted when the brutalities of Gaius escaped those legal limitations.

Rome was a notably violent society and the use of violence in politics suggests a relative absence of empathy between citizens: the political game was played unto death. Further, the Romans were perfectly content for criminals to be killed publicly and for the entertainment of the crowd. The treatment of prisoners taken in war was brutal and public. Slaves who rebelled were crucified and their dying bodies left on the cross. Yet, the application of violence to the individual without due process of law was a sign of tyranny in which the rights of the individual and potentially of all citizens were ignored. Citizen rights were not, then, enshrined in nature, but fragile and always capable of being repressed. This concern explains the force of the complaints of the aristocracy about *delatores* who impinged on their households (pp. 120–21) and concern over tyranny: tyranny took citizenship and all rights away from individuals and exposed them to unlimited violence.

Networks of power

The social orders outlined above suggest social groupings which were relatively closed and fixed. The use of dress to mark status again suggests an extreme consciousness of hierarchy: one needed to know the status of an individual when one met them in the street. The Romans were aware of social mobility, but the social mobility of which they approved was limited. It was possible for an individual from a relatively aristocratic background (perhaps descended from equestrians) to enter the senate and achieve high status. Similarly, many of those descended from senators probably avoided election into the senate and remained equestrians. Yet, the very fact that the Romans were deeply concerned with ancestry attests an expectation that a person's social status would be inherited.

We can see an example of this in a letter from Pliny the Younger (1.14) to his friend Junius Mauricus. Mauricus was seeking a husband for his niece (on behalf of the girl's father who had been a victim of Domitian). Pliny had just the man: Minicius Acilianus. Acilianus is recommended because he loves Pliny (as everyone did). He had a simple morality unaffected by Rome's sophistication. Acilianus' father is described as 'a leading equestrian', but one whom 'the deified Emperor Vespasian would have raised to praetorian rank'. His maternal grandmother, Serrana Procula, is seen as a model of propriety.

His uncle is also praised. Acilianus had held the offices of quaestor, tribune and praetor with distinction (and one wonders how Mauricus could not have known this). He is good looking and (though Pliny apologises for mentioning it) wealthy. Wealth, Pliny thinks, must be an issue since the status of children must be a concern.

We can find other examples. In Suetonius' *Lives of the Caesars*, for instance, there is a concern for ancestry. In the *Life of Augustus*, 2, Suetonius reports that Antony accused Octavian of coming from a freedman family, that his grandfather was a banker, and that his father also achieved his status from money lending. Yet, the Octavii claimed descent from a family that had entered the senate in the regal period, a claim which looks largely fictional. Vespasian's ancestry was similarly a matter of comment. Suetonius (*Vespasian*, 1–3) traced Vespasian's family back to his grandfather, who was a centurion in Pompey's armies. Vespasian's father, Flavius Sabinus, was a tax farmer in Asia and then a banker in Helvetia. Both his sons rose to prominence, one as prefect of the city and the other as emperor. Vespasian made a less than glorious marriage with Flavia Domitilla, whose father was a scribe for the quaestor, a junior administrative position. It seems very likely that they were relatives. Similarly, when Galba adopted the unfortunate Piso, Tacitus' speech (see pp. 215–16) makes mention of Piso's distinguished ancestry, tracing it back to the Republic.

The point of these stories is that they show that such origins were supposed to matter; they were not merely of general interest. When Pliny is looking for a suitable husband for his friend's niece, he *needs* to explain who were the father and grandmother of the prospective spouse. Suetonius *needs* to track the families of Octavian and Vespasian back over two generations. Today, it is rare to place such emphasis on our ancestry. Although modern biographies often talk about ancestry, particularly parents, who have had an influence on their subject, they are generally interested in more psychological influences. The social status of my grandparents matters to me and probably is a formative influence in my psyche and political and historical opinions, but I'd find it odd if my grandparents formed any part of an evaluation of my work and career. Further, it is almost inconceivable that anyone would decide to criticise my work because of my grandparents. By contrast, for the ancients, there was an assumed close relationship between social standing of an individual and the standing of an individual's ancestors.

Such an assumption points to an expectation of continuity of status over generations. The social structure outlined in the previous section was obviously one which allowed some mobility (as in the case of slaves becoming freedmen and the sons and daughters of freedmen and freedwomen would normally be free) and the examples drawn from imperial biographies suggest a consciousness of the possibility of families rising, yet the social hierarchy was rigid and marked and the expectation was of continuity. The Romans may have experienced some limited social mobility, but the experience was worrying for the aristocracy.

When the Roman aristocracy saw a powerful freedman or the son of a freedman serving as an equestrian, they observed an anomaly. This worried the aristocracy, in part because it was seen as a sign of disorder and of an unbalancing of the social system. We have no obligation to regard such stability as a virtue, instead we need to explain the relations of power which would allow a freedman to achieve a seemingly surprisingly high status. Further, the perception that social status should be passed down to one's descendants is an ideological position, a way of viewing society. Like all ideological understandings of society, this perception is at one step removed from the workings of power in political and economic terms that determine status, but ideology has real effects in encouraging the expectation that the world will behave in a certain way (the sons of senators will become senators) and many, especially the powerful, will behave so as to make this aspect of their ideological view of what makes a world ordered come true: thus sons of the aristocratic will continue to have the status of their fathers and mothers.

In modern terms, the best way to think of this is by analogy. Let us imagine that many powerful people think that women are not suited to high positions. A woman may achieve in her role and her success may be such that she is appointed to a high position. The powerful men around her may regard her as an exception to the rule. They may worry about her success. Yet, the occasional very talented or very lucky woman who forces who were through this barrier of prejudice will not immediately mean that the prejudice has no effects: many women who should have achieved high status will have been excluded and many men will have been 'fast-tracked' into positions of power because of the expectations that such positions be held by men.

Yet, society does not always conform to the ideological understandings that predominate. In part, this relates to the material relations of power which shape the distribution of resources and social status. In Rome, money and status went together, if imperfectly, and if someone was rich, social status would (eventually) follow. Economic inequalities underpinned social inequalities. Yet, acquiring wealth was far from easy and often required political connections of the kind that only be provided by the aristocracy. In Chapter 12, we will look at the issue of economic structure. In this section we will focus instead on the way in which networks of power operated to preserve the Roman social order and also on the issue of slaves and freedmen and their social mobility.

Ordering Rome: slaves and freedmen

Roman slavery has provoked considerable debate among historians. Slavery was a major institution in Roman society. We cannot confidently estimate the number of slaves in Roman society at any one time. Nevertheless, it is clear that slaves were widely distributed through the workforce, urban and rural. We find slaves everywhere in the literary material. Roman Egypt is the only place for which we can make plausible guesses for the servile element within the population. Census returns from Egypt suggest that the slaves made up 11–14% of the urban population and perhaps 8% of the population of villages in the first two centuries AD.

Yet, Egypt is not normally seen as a society where there would have been a high concentration of slaves. Slaves were obtained through raiding and trading and then distributed through commercial centres. Slaves were also bred. Slaves were secured in warfare. In the major Roman wars of expansion, generals enslaved vast numbers and probably sold those slaves on to traders. Although we would assume that those traders had large networks through which they distributed their slaves, we must also presume that many of the slaves ended up in Italy. Italy was, after all, rich on the proceeds of imperial conquest. Further, before the Roman conquest of Egypt, there were relatively few large landowners who might benefit from the importation of slave labour.

One can assume that slaves were a much higher proportion of the population in Italy than they were in Egypt. As the cities of Roman Italy were probably richer than those of Egypt, we can thus assume that a somewhat higher proportion of the population were servile (perhaps a minimum of 20%). If we take inscriptions as a guide, slaves and freedmen may have been up to 60% of the total population of Rome (though see the comments on epigraphic data above). Slaves were the primary workforce on at least some estates of Roman Italy whereas in Roman Egypt farms and estates appear to have been worked primarily by free workers, sometimes supplemented by slaves. It seems quite likely that slaves could have made up 25% or more of the rural population of Italy. These guesses would suggest a total population of slaves in Italy of not less than 1,500,000 and perhaps more than 2,000,000.

There can be little doubt that Roman society depended on the labour of slaves for its maintenance. Rome was a slave society.

The debate on Roman slavery has centred on the issue of the treatment of slaves and the rather more arcane issue of whether slaves formed a social class. The problem is at least in part ethical. Modern society regards slavery as an ethical abomination. The complete subjugation of one individual to another cannot be justified and is an offence against human rights. Many politicians, historians and philosophers have admired ancient Rome and its civilisational legacy. Thinkers have consistently turned to Roman for guidance in political and moral philosophy. Many of Rome's philosophers continue to be admired. Rome also later became Christian and many of the foremost moral thinkers of the Christian tradition grew up within a recognisably Roman society. How, then, can so many admire Roman society and politics when that political system depended on mass enslavement? Furthermore, what do we think of the moral philosophers, pre-Christian and Christian, who thought so hard about what it meant to be a good man and a good citizen and whose views have influenced moral philosophy ever since, when they appear to have been completely blind to the moral and social injustice of slavery? The astonishing point is that there is not a single voice from antiquity, Greek or Roman, to support or suggest the abolition of slavery.

There are a number of possible reasons for this, but firstly we must dispense with one of the least likely reasons offered. It has been suggested and it continues to be suggested that the reason why slavery was not resisted is that ancient slavery was not so bad: it was moderated by a basic decency (in most cases). There is, of course, some evidence for this 'moderate' slavery. Pliny, in the letter discussed above (8.16), expresses what appears to be a genuine concern for the welfare of his slaves. There is also no doubt that loving relationships did develop between masters and slaves. For example, Statius, *Silvae*, has several poems in which Statius writes consolations to masters who have lost beloved slave boys. An epitaph of the second century from Ostia reads 'To the Spirits of the Departed of Varia, daughter of Publius, Servanda. Ampelus and Ennychis freedmen, made this (tomb) from their own purses'.[1] Slaves formed part of a household and this established a relationship of obligation between master and slave. It was this paternalism that, in the nineteenth century, led those of the American South who wished to defend the institution of slavery to claim that slavery was better than working for wages, in which circumstances there was no obligations towards the workforce.

Yet, the evidence of affection and kindness pales against the evidence of cruelty and violence. Martial, 8.23, defends his beating of a cook for preparing a poor meal since, he asks, why else would one beat a cook? Martial regularly discusses having sex with slaves and in some instances he suggests that slaves might refuse their masters, but there is no doubt that this is the master's game and the slave who refuses is engaged in a pretence which will end in rape (see Martial, 4.42; 8.46; 4.7; 11.58; 5.83). These poems concern mostly male slaves, but female slaves were also objects of Martial's sexual desire and again these women were accused of seducing their master (6.71; 14.203). The 'game' that the epigrams play is to imagine that the slaves have some power and that they dupe and seduce their masters, but the inequalities of power underpin this relationship. The only 'power' the boy or woman has is to attract the sexual attentions of their masters. For all their lightness of tone, the poems attest an appalling sexual inequality.

Perhaps the most brutal representation of slavery in Martial's poetry comes with 11.58 when Martial imagines that his barber asks for freedom while shaving him. This was a moment of power for the slave. He carries a sharp blade. The master is defenceless. The comedic value is in that reversal of normal power relations and in the discomfort of the master. But the reversal of power is in itself reversed since the freshly shaved master intends to break the barber's legs and hands, meaning the slave will never be able to shave his master again.

Maybe this is a joke and we might imagine that the sophisticated Martial would never act so cruelly, but the first power reversal is unreal. The barber could kill the master, but the murder would mean that the barber would be hunted down and killed together with all his fellow slaves. The threat of murder was hardly real and perhaps we should understand the barber as not realising the implicit threat in his request (killing the master would have been almost unimaginably stupid). But still, the master deems the request to require revenge. Perhaps Martial would never have enacted that brutal violence, but the master had the power to do so, and what kind of joke is it when someone who has the power to do so threatens to break someone's legs and hands?

Away from perverse world of Martial's *Epigrams*, the treatment of slaves in realistic prose writing shows little kindness. Pliny's paternalism of Epistle 8.16 is limited. The kindness of freeing slaves as they were dying was hardly a great benefit to the slaves, though it does suggest that Pliny regarded that someone gaining their freedom at the end of life was a consolation. His dying slaves were allowed to bequeath their own possessions, but only within Pliny's household. Further, the whole focus of the letter is on Pliny's loss, on Pliny's kindness, on the consolation to be offered to Pliny. In another letter (3.14), Pliny discusses the murder of Larcius Macedo by his slaves. Although it was clear the Macedo was a cruel master and that only a few of the household engaged in the murder, while others tried to save him, Pliny applauds the mass killing of the slaves that followed. Only through such brutality would masters, good or bad, be safe.

In the agricultural writers, who provide us with perhaps our best insight into life on aristocratic farms, Varro *de Re Rustica*, 1.17 and Columella, *de Re Rustica*, 1.8 both advise that slave managers be granted the right to a recognised family life. The privilege is to bind the manager of the farm more closely to the master. Yet, the privilege is not to be allowed to others on the farm. The implication is not that slaves would not have partners, sexual relations, and children, but that those relationships would not be recognised. The master could decide to sell children or separate partners. The right to family is a fundamental human right, but it was not offered to slaves.

It remains true that the Romans freed large numbers of their slaves and this remains a fundamental problem in understanding Roman attitudes towards slaves and servility, but the evidence from literature and law points to the violence and enormous power inequality that shaped the life experiences of slaves and also of masters, the latter always having individuals to serve their needs and who were completely dependent upon them. The Roman were not kind to their slaves.

Although there is a conception of 'natural slaves' in Greek philosophy, Graeco-Roman slavery differed from Atlantic slavery in the absence of a racial element. A slave was not distinguished by height or weight, by eye colour or skin colour. Romans recognised that a slave could be intelligent. Romans employed slaves to read to them and to write for them, to manage their budgets, to look after their households, to cook and to manufacture, to look after them when they were ill, and to educate their children. The freedman Epictetus was to become a noted philosopher during the reign of Hadrian. A slave looked like everyone else: moreover, anyone else could look like a slave. In Roman society, there was nothing that differentiated slaves from free and indeed a slave could potentially become free as a free person could be enslaved. Romans may have defined in law the slave as a speaking tool, but that was a technical position on the legal accountability of the slave and the slave's ability to represent the master. Romans were aware of the humanity of their slaves. The social boundary between the slave and the free could thus be crossed.

The absence of any discussion about the rights and wrongs of slavery reflects a view of slavery as being part of the natural order of society. All ancient societies and many medieval societies practised slavery and it is only in the modern world that we have seen a recognition of the horror that is slavery. The debate on slavery in the modern world stemmed from the reinvention of mass slavery with the Atlantic slave trade. In the circumstance of the mass enslavement of large numbers of Africans, Europeans were forced to consider ethical issues with regard to slavery. For most Europeans, slavery was a new experience. For most Romans, it was part of the social system. Europeans had a view of natural rights, which came to be enshrined in our concept of human rights. The Romans did not. In Rome, rights depended on status.

There are thus two key reasons why slavery was not discussed as a social problem. The first is that slavery was integral to the operation of Roman society. The Romans had no experience of a society without slaves and in this sense a slaveless society could neither be imagined, nor seen as practical.

What follows from this is a different conception of the relationship of the individual to society. In our culture, we are individuals and chose to engage with society (though in reality it is not much of a choice). We are thus engaged in a social contract. For the Romans, the individual was defined by their social position. Society was a dominant force and to be outside of society was hardly conceivable. Society was also something that was, in its fundamental qualities, fixed: the Romans were aware of social change, but social change was normally seen as a decay from a natural order. In Roman political history, reform is always restoration of a pre-existing order (even if that order never really existed before) and never invention of a new society. Since society was natural and the social order was a work of nature separate to the world of the individual, where we might think of individuals who happened have a particular status (and thus be identified as a slave), for the ancient world, there was just a slave or a freeman or a senator. The individual was his or her status.

A society without slaves was inconceivable, a form of radical science-fiction for the ancients. A society without a landed aristocracy was also inconceivable. If they could conceive such a society, it would no longer be Rome. In such a worldview, it was given to some to be slaves, some to be poor, and some to be wealthy. These were facts of Roman life and were inescapable.

The problem for the Romans was not so much the existence of slavery but the particularity of the slave. If slavery was natural because that was how society was, the particular person who was made a slave was not necessarily naturally a slave. The problem was the permeability of the boundary between slave and free. If the masters thought their positions were part of a natural order, there is no guarantee that a particular slave was as happy with his or her allotted role in Roman society. Slaves were kept in place by personal and institutional violence. The beating of slaves, the killing of slaves, the sexual exploitation of slaves were, at an individual level, assertions of power that maintained a person in servitude. The slave was reminded at an everyday level of his or her subordination. Martial's threat to break the barber's legs and hands or his defence of beating his cook was perhaps meant to point to the extremity of his action but even if fictional, both poems contained a threat which could be carried out and one doubts whether the slaves saw the humour. At an institutional level, should the individualised violence not work, the state would step in to maintain slave discipline. Pliny's discussion of the murder of Macedo makes this clear. No master, however kind, would sleep safe if Macedo was not avenged: his murder was a social crime. It was an act of revolutionary madness since it threatened the whole of the Roman social order.

Yet, still slaves escaped. Still slaves engaged in petty resistance about which the Romans complained. Small acts of larceny or working inefficiently and slowly were ways of asserting some sort of revenge. In at least some cases, barbarians killed themselves and sometimes their wives and children rather than submit to slavery. We should not see in this a noble attachment to freedom (freedom or death), but an acknowledgement of the barbarity of slavery with which they were faced.

Yet, what about freedmen? The Roman freeing of slaves can be offered as evidence of Romans paternalism. It would seem to acknowledge that slavery, in spite of its horrors, was not a permanent state and that the good slave could have hopes of freedom eventually. The granting of freedom was certainly a reward. Yet, the thrust of Roman legislation on freedmen was to tie the freedmen closer to the households of their former masters, providing for minimal duties that required performing to the *patronus* (as the former master was known) and limiting the rights of freedmen to bequeath their property.

The Roman practice of freeing slaves seems at first like an act of benevolence. Slaves were a financial investment and the large-scale freeing of slaves would appear to be the detriment of household finances. Nevertheless, it seems that although a freedman was only lightly tied in law to the household of his patron, many remained within the household and continued to perform their functions for their former masters. Many were even buried within large household tombs (*columbaria*).

Most freedman remained dependent. If we think of the subordinate of individuals as being through various structures of domination (social, economic, customary, legal), then the diminution of the legal hold over the slave in his freeing did not necessarily mean that the slave was freed from obligations to the master. The patron had a formal call on the labour of his freedmen and without doubt the patrons continued to exploit the labour of their freedmen. The economic loss of freeing a slave was probably minimal (see pp. 301–303 for the economic power of households). Indeed, the Roman habit of freeing slaves shows that what mattered was not the exact legal powers that defined individual status within the social orders, but the way in which individuals maintained their position within particular structures of domination, be it through the violence that kept slaves in place or the more restrained means that maintained freedmen in dependency.

Roman aristocratic worries about freedmen achieving social prominence were not, I think, worries about social mobility in general, but about the way in which individual freedmen (notably those connected with the imperial family) achieved power in such a way as to threaten a reversal of the normal structures of domination. Like slaves revolting, a freedman who achieved independence from his *patronus* and who exerted power in unusual ways threatened the edifice of social control. Freedmen needed to be kept in place. If the Roman authorities had been worried about freedmen, the emperors could have limited the number of freedmen being made. The concern appears to have been different. It was about control. Freedmen were good, if they could be kept within their normal social bonds.

An example of this comes with the *Augustales*. These again look anomalous to a conventional understanding of the Roman social structure. The *Augustales* were priests of the imperial cult. These priesthoods grew up in various towns in Roman Italy and probably developed locally, judging from the variations in the names of the officials. Although other levels of priesthoods were taken up by members of the aristocracy, the *Augustales* were often freedmen. The *Augustales* enjoyed a relatively prominent position in their local societies and it might be thought that we are looking at the development of an alternative elite, but that would be to ignore the over-arching balance of power in Roman society. The *Augustales* gave freedmen a place in local society and integrated them into the ceremonials of the city. Their appearance in the urban ceremonials was not necessarily a reflection of the increasing power of freedmen, though as we shall see in the next section, there is reason to think that freedmen might have become more socially important, but was an integration of the freedmen into the power relations of the city and the further subordination of the freedmen to that power structure. The freedmen were given their place in the social and political order.

I make a concluding point. One of the problems about understanding the history of slaves is the silence of those slaves within the historical record. We have to guess at what the slaves thought and to a slightly lesser extent the freedmen remain silent. Our elite sources never question the institution of slavery, but we need to remember that these men were the winners of the social game. Why should they imagine that another society was possible? Those who are at the top of a society have every interest in thinking of their social order as a work of nature to which there is no rational alternative. They could not imagine a society without slavery. But the implication of that lack of imagination is that it was right and proper to use all force to keep slaves in their place. Sometimes ideology is a story that allows us to sleep at night. If the rich Roman drifting off to sleep thought about his slaves and wondered about the cruelty inflicted upon them, he might sigh and think that this was the way of the world and that there was nothing that could be done. Roman society depended on its slaves and there could be no Rome without slaves. He might reflect that to everyone was assigned a duty: some were masters and some were slaves. In this way a flickering conscience could be assuaged. There is, of course, no guarantee that the slaves were so philosophical. What looks like natural order to one, might feel like monstrous cruelty to another.

Navigating Roman society: social networks

Romans placed considerable stress on what we call networking and they called *amicitia* (friendships). It was through friendships that Romans got things done and they can be thought of as a form of social technology. Thus, if you wanted information or legal action or a posting or a business connection of even a marriage partner, it was to one's friends that one looked. Friendships were cemented by networks of favours exchanged. It is tempting to think of these networks as being a form of vertical social relationship in which the older and more powerful would lend support to the younger and less powerful and certainly that was an aspect of such social relations. A man embarking on a political career would call upon all his older and senior friends to come to his aid and to appear with him during his election. Such vertical relationships are a form of patronage. Obviously, the more powerful a man is, the more he can do for his friends, and the larger the resulting network of his friends. But power could also be acquired from a large network of friends and supporters who would arrange matters for you. Such networks can be hierarchical, but the Romans did not define the relationship in these terms. It was about *amicitia*, a relationship of equals and anyone who abused that relationship risked censure.

The circle of one's associates established social status. A powerful man would have powerful friends. One could also judge the standing of an individual by those with whom he associated. To a large extent, the network made the man. It is in this context that we can understand concerns over the friendships of emperors. Emperors who associated with actors and freedmen were not mixing with the right sort of people and did not have the right sort of friends. The networks of power within the networks of friendship could be corrupted and given that the emperor was the most powerful friend one could imagine, his friendship could create a discrepancy between the hierarchies of Roman society and the structures of power. The Roman elite worried about Domitian, who dined alone, or Claudius who stayed with his wives and freedmen (though Claudius did have his own close circle of aristocratic friends) or Gaius who associated with actors and actresses and claimed to prefer the company of his horse to that of the consuls.

Such friendships extended beyond the political sphere. Marriages cemented alliances and friends would help friends of friends in the resolution of disputes, in obtaining military office or any other favour. The interrelationship of the Roman elite is complex, as we can see by studying the family of Thrasea Paetus and Helvidius Priscus and the friends of Pliny (see pp. 235–37; 259). The top level of Roman political life was astonishingly small. In 30 BC there may have been a thousand senators, but that number was reduced by Augustus with perhaps the aim of getting the number down to 600. But these numbers were probably swelled by the packing of the senate by Caesar and perhaps later by the triumvirs. The number of senators in the Imperial period was probably determined by the number of quaestors elected (20) at aged 25. If the average life expectancy of a 25-year-old male was about 25–30 years, one would imagine the senate was composed of about 350-400 individuals. Many of these men would have been related. The political class was sufficiently small that they would all have been connected by social ties. The senate was very much a member's only club.

With Pliny, we can also observe the network stretching to the lower orders. Romatius Firmus received 300,000 *sesterces* from Pliny to raise him to equestrian status (*Epistle*, 1. 19). Pliny tried to secure a military post (*Epistle*, 2.13) and then a senatorial position (*Epistle*, 10.4) for his friend and literary adviser Voconius Romanus (see also *Epistle*, 3. 13; 6. 15; 6. 33). Voconius' father was an equestrian, but Voconius himself could not meet the census requirement for senatorial status. His mother, however, agreed to make over 4,000,000 *sesterces* for her son should Trajan decide to elevate him. Voconius was clearly not from a poor background. Pliny also gave an estate to his nurse.

Members of the Roman elite did offer patronage to communities and this was sometimes recognised with an official grant of the title of patron from a local community. Patrons were expected to invest in the civic infrastructure of their towns. Pliny is again an excellent example. Pliny makes much of his generosity. An inscription commemorating his death and benefactions (*Corpus Inscriptionum Latinarum*, 5. 5262) records that Pliny built for the town of Comum the public baths at an unknown cost with an additional 300,000 *sesterces* for furnishing them, with interest on 200,000 for their upkeep. He also left to his city capital of 1,866,666 *sesterces* to support 1000 of his freedmen, and subsequently to provide an annual dinner for the people of the city. Likewise, in his lifetime, he gave 500,000 *sesterces* for the maintenance of boys and girls of the city, and also 100,000 for the upkeep of a library. The baths were likely to be the largest single benefaction and any building for which the costs of furnishing come in at 300,000 *sesterces* must surely have cost many times that to construct.

General benefactions established Pliny's relationship with his home town. Other rich individuals appear to have been similarly generous. Often, though, benefactions were corporate and organised through the council. This established a hierarchy within Roman society and, of course, helped social unity. The greatest of such benefactors was the emperor, whose gifts to his people dwarfed those of the ordinary senator.

Yet, there is less evidence for social networks stretching to individuals outside the confines of the elite. Pliny again claims to be generous to his tenants and to those with whom he has economic relations on his estate, but these people were not his friends (see *Epistle*, 8.2 and 9.37). We do get a very unusual example from Pompeii. One of the largest buildings on the Forum of Pompeii is the so-called Eumachia building. This was constructed by a leading female member of the Pompeian aristocracy (which in itself is unusual), Eumachia. Yet, rather than construct a temple in this prime site, Eumachia built a large meeting house for the *collegium* of fullers (a guild of those who cleaned cloth).

Other guilds in the towns of Roman Italy may have been able to attract aristocratic supporters and sometimes extract gifts, but the Eumachia building seems to be exceptional and the other guild houses attested in the archaeological evidence, mostly from Ostia, are on nothing like the same scale.

It is difficult to see how ordinary Romans below the levels of the aristocracy could attract the friendship of the rich and powerful in Roman society.

Social networks probably also worked at lower levels of society. Any migrant into Rome for instance would be faced with a huge range of difficulties in establishing themselves in the city. They would need to find housing and work and it is very likely that this was achieved through some form of social network. Traders coming to the city also needed to establish a range of contacts which would enable them to work. Such networks appear to have been institutionalised into *collegia*, semi-formal groupings of citizens, such as the *collegium* of the fullers in Pompeii. *Collegia*, or similar types of institutions, were widely distributed across the Mediterranean, though some of our best information about them comes from the excavations in Ostia.[2] There various *collegia* houses have been identified were it seems trade or religious groups would gather. Probably these groups would have had regular dinners together and would have engaged in other social functions. They may have helped each other out in times of difficulty, contributed to the expenses of funerals, and probably regulated trade within the town. Around one of the squares of Ostia, the so-called Piazza della Corporazioni, there are 61 preserved offices. Many of these are identified by mosaic inscriptions laid into the pavement in the front of the office. These include offices of

- traders in flax and rope
- traders in leather
- shippers of wood
- traders in spelt
- traders in grain

- shippers from Misua (a town near Carthage)
- shippers from Miluvium (in Mauretania)
- shippers from Hippo Diarrytus (near Carthage)
- shippers from Gummo (near Carthage)
- shippers from Carthage
- shippers from Turris (Sardinia)
- shippers from Karales (Sardinia)
- shippers from Sullectum (Sardinia)
- shippers or merchants from Narbo (Gaul)
- shippers from Kurba (Tunisia)
- shippers from Alexandria (Egypt)
- shippers on the Tiber
- traders from Mauretania Caesarensis

Several of the inscriptions are lost and we are left with just images and these suggest that animals were likely also traded through these offices. Most of the mosaics probably date from the second century, but it seems very likely that the piazza was laid out in the Augustan period in order to provide facilities specifically for shippers.

The larger cities of the Roman world must have had significant markets in labour. In Rome, for example, the dockyards and the building trade must have provided considerable amount of unskilled work and it seems likely that the majority of this work was accomplished by free labourers. Cloth manufacture was probably also a major employer as was pottery and metal work. Some of this work would have been seasonal and we might imagine that there was a flow of workers into the city in the Spring and perhaps a return to the countryside for harvests.

The majority of the poorer population will have lived in apartments (*insulae*). These apartments are best known from Ostia, where they vary considerably in standard from one or two rooms (often associated with a workshop) to luxuriously appointed multi-room dwellings in which, we must imagine, the rich of the town would have lived. We may suspect the same for Rome, though there is very little preserved in the archaeological record. There is a partially preserved *insula* in the centre of the city (Insula dell' Ara Coeli), built into the hillside of the Capitoline. Mostly, it is composed of dark, small cellular structures. There is little natural light, no evidence of sanitation, and no obvious supply of water. It is very difficult to believe that any but the poor of the city would have lived there.

Pompeii offers further examples of housing.[3] The most photographed housing is that of wealthy: the grand houses such as the House of the Faun, the House of Holconius Rufus, House of Apollo the Citharist, House of Menander, and many others in which the wealthy of the city dwelled. Many of these houses had formal structural elements known from architectural manuals, such as that of Vitruvius. The entry to the house led into an *atrium* (often with an *impluvium* and with a *tablinum*, sometimes providing views into the garden beyond). Such structures were aligned to provide visibility into the house and appear to have been arranged so that the family could receive guests in a formal setting. The pattern can be seen very clearly in the House of the Vettii. We have thus archaeological evidence, built into the very structure of houses, of social networks.

Nevertheless, many Pompeian houses are far from simple in their design and layout. The House of the Citharist, for example, is built around two *atria* which are dwarfed by three peristyle courts which were in parallel to each other. The House of the Faun has two parallel *atria*, one of which leads directly through a *tablinum* into a peristyle court in typical Pompeian formal style. But behind this structure is a second enormous peristyle, larger than the two *atria* combined.

The insula Arriana Polliana (Regio VI) looks at first sight like a typical aristocratic house, but an inscription (*Corpus Inscriptionum Latinarum* 4. 138) on the house offers for rent three different types of apartments (*Tabernae* with balconies; *Cenacula Equestria* [Equestrian lodgings] and a house. These structures are not easily identifiable, but apart from the main house, there are 11 different separate structures. The renting of these structures was through a business manager and this in itself this suggests that the rentals were commercial operations rather than being given to the freedmen of the main house owner. A separate inscription advertised for tenants for a whole range of small rental properties belonging to Iulia Felix (*Corpus Inscriptionum Latinarum* 4.1136): *tabernae*, upstairs apartments, *cenacula*) built into one of the most prominent blocks of the city. It is a pattern we would expect to see repeated across the city and it is clear that in Rome the wealthy invested in urban property that they would rent out to those lower down the social scale.

The relationship between those who rented out the properties and those who lived in them is a matter of some discussion. The advertisements are unusual and might suggest an unusual situation. Iulia Felix was offering a significant number of properties on a long lease and it might be that these had just come onto the market or that Iulia Felix offered her rental properties *en bloc* every five years. Other holders of rental property may have not needed to advertise, already having available tenants. The issue was whether the relationship between tenant and house-owner was primarily contractual and economic, or whether it depending on a pre-existing social relationship.

One of the issues behind this discussion is the role of households in the Roman economy and society. The differences between the grand residences of Pompeii and the smaller sub-residences associated with them is so great that one might assume a relationship of dependency between the richer and the poorer in Pompeian society. One might further assume that many of those who actually occupied these sub-residences were freedmen of the owner of the larger house. Pompeii, which does not appear to have been a particular unusual town, clearly had a wealthy elite. As we shall see in the chapter on the economy, one of the characteristics of Roman society in the Imperial period was a wide and increasing gap between the wealthy and the poor. This increasing economic differentiation is likely to have had social implications. In particular, it must have reinforced hierarchies in Roman society.

The rise of the rich in Roman society had very clear effects. The first was a concentration of wealth and power. This meant that elite households came to be larger and more complex, often with many estates associated with them. Such households relied heavily on freedmen to administer them. The largest and most complex household was that of the Caesars. The Julio-Claudians especially used techniques of household management to run the empire. Such household administrative systems provided freedmen with opportunities and connections which were probably denied to many others in Roman society. The freedmen had access to wealth and social connections. It was almost certainly this access that allowed some to make money once they had been freed.

The rise of the freedmen was not a function of a decline in aristocratic politics and status, but an unforeseen consequence of the concentration of wealth in aristocratic houses. Yet, the appearance of powerful freedmen on the social stage caused anxieties in Roman society since there was a seeming discrepancy between the social order as theorised within Roman ideology (in which the freedmen were of lesser status than the free-born) and the observable social reality.

A further consequence of the increasing concentration of wealth was that inequalities within Roman society became yet more obvious. In theory, Rome was a community of citizens in which all had equal rights and all were equally free. Some people were more important than others, some people had higher status, and some people had achievements which gave them authority, but all were citizens. Yet, disparities of wealth caused tensions.

Martial (9.2, 3.50, 12.82. 1.23. 1.59, 2.14, 5.44) complains bitterly about his treatment in the great aristocratic houses in which he was desperate to secure dinner, which in itself would not be convincing evidence of a worsening of behaviour, but Pliny adds his voice to complaints: Pliny complains that at dinner parties the food was graded by the social status of the guest (Pliny, *Epistles*, 2.6; 1.15). This measure breached the illusion that at dinner all were equal: all were simply *amici* (friends). This was important since, although all were acutely aware of relative social status, all were free and thus had at least to preserve the illusion of independence. To provide such *amici* with poorer food than that which the host ate was to demonstrate that they were inferior and dependent, and dependency carried with it the taint of servility. Petronius provides us with an excruciating fictional account of a dinner party in the *Satyricon*, the so-called *Cena Trimalichionis* (Trimalchio's dinner party) at which the (anti-) heroes of the novel find themselves. The meal is a vision of excess in which the guests honour and despise the freedman Trimalchio. Yet, they are held in thrall to his wealth, suffering for their supper.

Dinner parties provided a microcosm of Roman social relations. The master invited people to his house and sat them in order of status. Food was served. Possibly the food was exotic and certainly it was served for display. It was cooked and brought to the table by slaves, whose invisibility (unless a glass should be broken) was assumed. It seems unlikely that feasts of the rich could be enjoyed by the poor, who were likely never invited. Other guests risked having their inferiority exposed as the rich man chose to whom to serve the best food, but the poorer man could not risk offending the rich man whose power and wealth demanded their presence.

Yet, if the dinner part was a location in which status was asserted and dependency displayed and could thus be humiliating, those who were invited to the dinners of the wealthy may have been in a better social position than those who did not. Martial wanted to dine with the rich and powerful not so much because he needed the meal, but because of the access dinner provided. Most people probably were never invited. Lower down the social scale, commensality (dining together) was also a way of establishing social bonds, but we see such dining most obviously in the *collegia*. These trade and religious groups provided networks which were perhaps only loosely connected to those of the aristocratic houses.

Conclusions

In this chapter, we have seen that the Romans had a fixed and conservative view of their society. The elites wished to maintain a fixed social order. Yet, we have also debated the best ways to think about Roman society. Should we think of society as a system of orders in which everyone had their place or should we think of Roman society as a network of power relations? I think that the data we have on Roman society makes more sense if we take the latter approach. I think we can understand better difficult and problematic issues such as the role and status of slaves, the increasing prominence of freedmen and the power of the Roman elite. In Chapter 16, I will also argue that seeing Roman society as a network of power explains better the way in which Roman society came to be exported in at least some of its aspects into various parts of the Empire. All societies are, in my view, subject to gradual change and for this reason we need to be suspicious of stable and systemised views of society. Roman society was no exception.[4]

Notes

1 See Sandra R. Joshel. *Slavery in the Roman World*. (Cambridge: Cambridge University Press, 2010, p. 45.)
2 For details and photographs, see http://www.ostia-antica.org/piazzale/corp.htm (accessed 14.04.2013).

3 For many descriptions of Pompeian houses and other buildings, see http://www.pompei-online.net/ and http://pompeiiinpictures.com/pompeiiinpictures/index.htm.

4 You will have noticed that the previous paragraph has been personalised: lots of 'I think' and 'in my view'. This is the way in thinking about societies. We all live in societies. We all have to decide how we think they work.

Chapter 12

The economy

In many ways, issues of the economy parallel the social issues discussed in the previous chapter. There are historical and methodological issues that need to be addressed. In the first instance, there is a question of what kind of history we can write about the economy and whether we can, in fact, write economic history for the Roman Empire.

Economics as a discipline is a modern invention. The great writers of what is called 'Classical economics', men such as Adam Smith, Ricardo and Malthus, worked at the end of the eighteenth and the start of the nineteenth centuries. This is no coincidence. They established the intellectual discipline of economics, or what was often called political economy, at the very point at which the industrial revolution was transforming the landscape. To an extent, all three of these writers were aware of the great changes afoot and were considering whether this represented a fundamental shift in society and its values. A generation later, Marx was arguing against the German philosopher Hegel that it was not ideas that drove history, but economics. By the mid-nineteenth century, all serious writers were convinced that the world had entered a new age of wealth and progress in which economics was a crucial factor.

If we compare these writings with Rome (and indeed Greece), the difference is notable. There is no theory of economy in antiquity. There is also an almost complete absence of economic statistics and statistics are the raw materials of economic writing. The Romans may not even have conceived of an economy as such. Histories do not consider properly economic reasons for any event (though they might comment that a people are populous or rich).

It is, however, not accurate to say that the Romans were oblivious to things we would think of as economic. There was discussion, for instance, of the development of slave estates, of increasing differentiation of rich and poor, of changes in population (cities or settlements being abandoned or growing), of increases in material wealth (especially related to *luxuria*), of the in-flow of wealth from empire (especially conquests), and fiscal issues. There is some evidence that Roman political authorities concerned themselves with economic issues as well. The Roman administration in Egypt appears to have taken active measures to improve Egyptian agriculture and to sponsor the development of the trade to the East, partly by building roads and fortlets in the Eastern desert. Domitian appears to have become concerned about the balance between grain and wine production in Italy (a dearth of grain was accompanied by a surplus of wine) and passed laws about the proportions of grain fields to vineyards (Suetonius, *Domitian*, 7). Additionally, Nerva and Trajan worried about poverty in Italy and its effect on the population, and took measures to provide some level of support. Demography appears to have been a general concern from the second century BC until at least the second century AD. The Romans worried that the free population of Italy was in decline. The geographer Strabo (4.5), who was writing in the Augustan period, provided what looks very much like economic reasons for not invading Britain: the Romans were making enough money from Britain anyhow and invading would just mean that they would have to pay for a garrison. More generally, Rome's political leaders were very aware of the potential vulnerability of the population of the city to variations in price of grain and the grain dole was an obvious intervention in the market.

In addition, there were specialist writers on what we would regard as aspects of economic life, in particular agronomy and we have three major Roman agricultural guides written by Cato, Varro and Columella. Pliny the Younger also comments extensively on the management of his estates and the inclusion of letters about such issues suggest that they were of as much concern as his other letters on the *mores* of his contemporaries.

Yet, even if the Romans were aware that matters economic affected their lives, in the literary sources available to us there was clearly not the sense that the power of the economy was a continuously shifting force possibly beyond the control of political action and determining of society and politics. There was no real economic policy and there does not appear to have been very much in the way of even of a conscious fiscal policy (balancing governmental income and expenditure). The Romans possessed few of the instruments (intellectual or political–administrative) to run an economic or fiscal policy. The government might have put money into infrastructural projects (roads, harbours, etc.) and may even have done so partly to provide employment, but there appears to have been no understanding of using government finance to stimulate economic activity. Further, although the Roman state was interested in increasing its revenues, taxes appear to have been largely customary and often inherited from previous regimes. The Romans did not have the financial sophistication that would have allowed the development of a national debt. They did not have stock markets. Financial institutions were limited and appear to have worked on a local basis for the most part. Insurance, a crucial element in the way moderns manage risk, appears to have been foreign to the Romans. Although financial institutions operated with considerable sophistication and the law was such as to allow them the flexibility to develop quite complicated financial instruments, we do not see great finance houses such as those that graced and paid for Renaissance Europe.

The absence of these institutions and ways of operating relate to a more fundamental absence in Roman economic history: there was no industrial revolution. Although that might seem so obvious that there is no need to state it, it is crucial to remember since this absence meant that the ability of the economy to change was limited. The economy continued within pre-industrial limits (which we will explore below). The inability of the economy to undergo a step change in activity raises the question of whether there can be an economic history of antiquity. Since there was no revolution, was there essential continuity in economic activity? There was obviously variation over time, but the significance of that variation is a matter of debate. Many historians think that what we are looking at in the ancient economy is an essential continuity of structure, with very little change. Thus, what we can write about the economy is broadly descriptive of the structures of economic life which remained within certain limits and were thus unable to provide the circumstances and support for a step change in economic activity that would transform Roman society.

I take a slightly different view. While agreeing that there was no radical change in economic activity, I think there is an economic history in antiquity and in the Roman period. Within the structural limitations of a pre-industrial economy, there is considerable scope for variations and changes. There can be changes in agricultural productivity, in the ways in which the land is exploited, in the labour force deployed on the land, in the distribution of wealth, in the concentration of populations in urban centres, and in the economic functioning of those urban centres. These changes mattered and had real economic and social effects.

We'll start off by looking at the structures, since it is the structures that set the ground rules for economic activity.

Economic structures

The pre-industrial economy

The Roman economy was preindustrial. Certain consequences follow from that observation.

- The majority of the population were involved in agricultural work.
- Much pre-modern agricultural production was for subsistence and not for the market. Much of the produce of a farm would be consumed on that farm for the support of workers and animals.
- Energy was overwhelmingly provided by muscles. Although the Romans did have water-wheels, most energy needs were met from agricultural products (plant and animal calories). They did not burn coal or other mineral energy sources. The Roman economy was limited by what they could grow.

- Agricultural productivity, and thus the size of the economy, comes up against natural limits. These limits (sometimes regarded as Malthusian) are set by the amount and quality of land available, climate, water, and the quality of seed. This can mean that an increase in population is not matched by a corresponding increase in agricultural productivity, since land of lesser quality would have to be brought into production and the possible surplus above subsistence on that land would be less. Put another way, an increase in the total product of the economy might correspond with a decrease in product per capita.
- Transport costs by land were very high for heavy goods. In part, this was because goods had to be moved by cart or donkey; carts move very slowly and donkeys eat a lot on the way. It follows that basic goods (grain, etc.) are likely to be cheaper if they were produced locally.
- The majority of wealth was in land.
- Trade and manufacture were, by definition, lesser elements of the economy.
- Technology was such that there were limited benefits from concentrations of activity and limited economies of scale. It was not possible to build large-scale kilns, mills, looms, foundries in part because of the quality of the building materials available. The technology did not allow the development of large factories. The benefit of concentration was mostly in retail rather than in production.

It is by these limits that economic activity has been constrained for the majority of human history and it is only in the last two centuries that we seem to have escaped to at least some extent ecological limitations.

One of the central questions of economic history is how those limits were escaped. For many historians, the fundamental institution in producing economic growth is the city. The city operates economically in several key ways.

- The city was a concentration of population.
- The city was a significant market for produce.
- The city provided a labour market.
- The city offered a concentration of labour resources.

Urbanisation provided a market for rural produce. This meant that farmers could exchange their surplus and thus had an interest in producing goods that could be sold at market. It allowed for the development of specialised agriculture in commercial goods. It also meant that a farmer need not worry quite so much about producing subsistence goods, but could produce goods that could be exchanged for what was required.

The development of an urban market also allowed the specialist production of goods. If you live in a village and are very good at producing pins, you are unlikely to sell enough to live and will then need to diversify. If you live in a city, you can guarantee a market for your pins.

A city also operates as a centre for technological diffusion. If you want an olive press, small rural communities might not have the technological skill to produce one. A city will have the smiths and craftsmen to make higher quality tools.

A city operates as an outlet for surplus labour. If you are working on a farm, there is a limit to the amount of labour you can invest in your land and it is very difficult to co-ordinate labour and land. In a purely peasant economy, there is no outlet for surplus labour, but if there is a city, someone with spare labour can move (temporarily or permanently) to the city for productive work or engage in craft production for the urban market.

In conventional development theory, cities have been seen as crucial in driving forward economic development. There has been a historically-observed correlation between prosperity and urbanisation. This has been carried to an extreme in the contemporary world where the richest societies (and the richest societies ever seen) have populations where almost all live in cities.

This relationship between economic growth and cities has long been known, but it presents a problem for Classical historians. It is generally accepted that in the Medieval West only a very small proportion of the population lived in towns, perhaps under 5% (with the possible exception of Italy). In north-west Europe, increasing economic sophistication coincided with the growth of a network of cities in Belgium, Holland, southern Britain and North Germany. But all our evidence points to the Mediterranean of the Classical period being heavily urbanised (in pre-industrial terms) and the Roman period appears to see a growth in urbanisation. This gives rise to two questions:

- Was Roman urbanisation correlated with economic growth?
- Why did Roman urbanisation not produce an economic revolution?

The German sociologist Max Weber and the historian Moses Finley came up with an answer to this question. They, in slightly different ways, argued that not all cities are the same. Finley offered a distinction between the Ancient 'consumer' city and the 'medieval' producer city. Both suggested that the modern capitalist/industrial city was fundamentally different from the ancient and medieval cities. The differences between the ancient and medieval are represented schematically in Figures 12.1 and 12.2.

These are models or ideal types which do not conform to actual reality, but are simplifications or representations of reality which allow us to examine that reality more clearly. All cities need an influx of goods from the countryside to feed their populations. In the consumer city model, members of the elite own farms in the countryside and reside in the city, which is the centre of political activity, and extract goods from the countryside mainly through taxes, rents

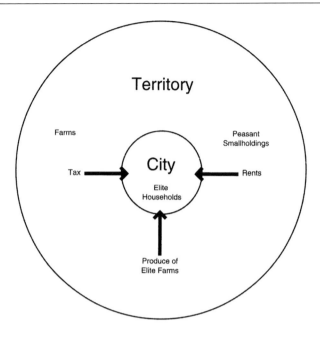

Figure 12.1 The consumer city

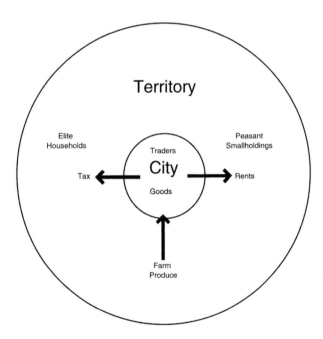

Figure 12.2 The medieval producer city

or the produce of the farms of the elite. In this model, the city offers little to the economy and to the countryside and is parasitical off the countryside, simply consuming the surplus generated on the farms. In this view, the city is a bastion of the elite, dominated by elite households and those who serve them. We may look back to the discussions of housing at Pompeii (see pp. 299–301).

In the medieval producer city, the city supports itself by trading in goods, either goods manufactured in the city itself or goods from the countryside that are marketed in the city. The elite reside mainly in the countryside and the city is not the centre of political power. The city operates as a market for goods and contributes to the economy both as a retail centre and as a centre of manufacture.

Whereas a medieval city contributes to the economic activity of the society, an ancient city does not. The size of ancient cities is governed solely by the productivity of their territories and the proportion of surplus that can be extracted from the farmers. Urbanisation would simply represent increased exploitation of the farmers (i.e. the farmers kept less of their produce). The appearance of *megalopoleis* in the ancient world, huge cities such as Rome, Alexandria, (Classical) Athens, adhere to this model since they are able to draw on very large hinterlands and indeed the hinterlands of other cities, because of their imperial power.

A further element of the Finley–Weber understanding was economic ideology. For Weber, the key moment in the development of the Western economy was the Reformation. At that point, people started to think differently about money and especially in the protestant cities, they started to use money differently. Rather than deploying excess wealth in improving their social or religious status (buying candles for prayers), people started to invest in ways of making more money. Money was a good thing in itself and a sign that an individual was hard-working, rational, and a good, blessed citizen. By contrast, according to Finley, money in the Roman world was a means to an end and that end was social status. The consequence of that mentality was that instead of sinking spare cash into productive investment, the wealthy spent money on matters which were beneficial to their social status (games, public buildings, bath houses, conspicuous luxury). Further, they managed their assets to maintain status with maximum security rather than to maximise wealth.

Is this view correct? There is, of course considerable evidence to support the Finley–Weber model. As far as we can tell, the majority of rich Romans invested the majority of their wealth in the land. If we look at Pompeii, it is the houses of the rich and powerful that so often impress. It is difficult not to see them as dominant. Politically speaking, the wealthy did control the cities. Many cities of the Roman world contained large houses. The villas that we see across the Western Empire especially provided elites with luxurious residences and testify to their wealth. We also do not seem to see many investments in speculative ventures on the part of the elites, suggesting that the elites might have been risk averse. Elites also spent considerable amounts of money on civic infrastructure and left inscriptions detailing their generosity. The councils, formed from the wealthier groups in the cities, would offer statues and honours to their leading members in return for their benefactions and in the cities of the Roman East especially these wealthy councillors appear increasingly dominant in the sources. The cities might describe themselves as democracies (as many cities did even under the Roman Empire), but it is the aristocrats who are their visible representatives. Further, if one rejects the Finley–Weber answer to these two key questions given above, one has to come up with something else by which to explain the evident truth that Rome did not undergo the economic transformations that made modern Europe.

Yet, there are reasons to question the Finley–Weber model and these are embedded in a detailed understanding of the urban and rural economies of Italy especially. But before we look in more detail at those economies, we need to continue thinking about structural issues affecting the Roman economy.

Size and scale

As we have already seen, one of the problems of Roman history is that so much basic data is missing. We simply do not know how many people there were in the Roman Empire. We also do not know how wealthy there people were. It is not just that we do not have an exact figure, but that our estimates are based on the flimsiest of material. Yet, these figures matter for understanding of the Roman Empire and its political economy.

The best population data we have comes from Italy. The Romans conducted a regular census. The sequence of the census figures we do have runs as laid out in Table 12.1. The figures make little sense as a demographic sequence. The population leaps in the six years from 131 to 125 by 24%. In a 29-year period

Table 12.1 Census figures 136 BC–AD 48

Date	Census figures
136	317,933
131	318,823
125	394,736
115	394,336
86	463,000
70	910,000
28	4,063,000
8	4,233,000
AD 14	4,937,000
48	5,984,072

from 115 BC–86 BC the population similarly leapt by 18% followed by a near doubling of the population before 70 BC and then a quadrupling of the population by 28 BC.

These rises are not natural growth but relate to the incorporation of new populations. The problem that we have is that although we can find new populations to account for the jump from 394,000 to about 910,000, we cannot find a group of people sufficiently large to account for the quadrupling of the population by 28 BC.

There are two possibilities to account for this. The one that is generally preferred by historians is that in 28 BC Augustus counted the population in a different way. The census had previously counted only adult males. The suggestion is that he started counting also women and children. The problem with such a suggestion is that there is no evidence that Augustus introduced such a radical change. Secondly, the implication of such a change is, in fact, that Roman population was falling quite rapidly from the second century BC.

The maths of this is simple. If there were 394,336 citizens in 115 BC that should make a total population of about 1,260,000 to which we need to add new citizens, both those who were freed and those who were given citizenship between 115 BC and 28 BC. These new populations would include the Italians given citizenship after the Social War and the Gauls living in Italy given citizenship by Caesar. One would assume that the Italians would be about twice as populous as the Romans. The population of Gauls can only be guessed at. Reasonable estimates would take the population total for 115 BC, including these groups, to somewhere around 5,000,000. This is about 800,000 more than the Augustan total.

There is considerable reason to worry about such a population estimate, especially since it is very likely that the population of Rome itself was increasing. The missing population must have come from the countryside and if we add to that missing population those who left the countryside and went to the big city (perhaps 500,000), the countryside must have been denuded. The trouble is the archaeological evidence does not suggest anything of the sort and in fact, points either to an increase in population in the countryside or the stability of the rural population.

In the face of the difficulties of this solution, another solution has been proposed that is equally problematic: it has been suggested that we should take the Augustan census figures to represent the male population. We can do the same maths, but make some more positive adjustments. The 394,336 male citizens of 115 BC should be a population of 1,260,000. If we assume that the census failed to count a significant number of men (and it was very easy to avoid the census count), we might assume 1,500,000 total population to which we can add new populations (3,000,000 Italians, 4,000,000 Gauls, 500,000 new citizens), to create a total in 28 BC of around 9,000,000. The Augustan figures would, however, suggest a total population of around 15,000,000. It is just about possible that a population increasing at a very rapid rate through the first century could make up that extra 6,000,000.

To these population figures, we need to add figures for non-Romans in Italy and, most significantly, slaves. If slaves were a minimum of 20% of the population, we would need to add another 3,000,000 to the population on the higher estimate or about 800,000 on the lower estimates, taking the total population of Italy up to 18,000,000 or about 5,600,000. These figures are radically different and have very different implications.

- The Augustan legions were about 5,000 strong and there were 28 in the field. The total manpower was thus 140,000, either about 11% or just over 3% of the total male free population.
- A population of 18,000,000 would be historically very high compared with what we know of the Italian population in the pre-modern period. Yet, by the end of the Augustan period, the population had risen and might suggest a total population for Italy of about 21,000,000. The low estimate by contrast, would be very low indeed for an Italian population.
- Urbanisation would be about 11% or 35% of the population. Few pre-industrial societies were urbanised to beyond 7% of the population.

We could adopt the lower estimates for the free population and opt a higher number of slaves, perhaps even taking the population as high as 6,800,000 but that would make slaves nearly 30% of the total Italian population.

Ultimately, the high estimates are, for me, implausible.

One of the conclusions of this detailed discussion relates not to the figures themselves, but what we know of the population of antiquity. The region of the Roman Empire for which we have the best evidence for population can support reasonable estimates for population which vary by a factor of 3.5. Imagine if the best estimates for the population of the UK varied from 20,000,000 to 70,000,000 or for the US from 313,000,000 to 1,095,500,000, and no one knew which figure was more likely.

Once we move from Italy to the entire of the Roman Empire, the problems multiply. Only for Egypt do we have ancient estimates for total population and these vary between 3,300,000 (in 30,000 villages) and 7,500,000 (Josephus, *Jewish War*, 2.385). Neither estimate is convincing. For all the other provinces, there is nothing in the texts on which we can base an estimate. Of course, it does not stop people trying. Sixty million is sometimes offered as a figure a range of 45,000,000 to 80,000,000 would seem reasonable.

The next question that arises is the size of the Roman economy. The basis for this calculation is the size of the population as against the subsistence rates required to support that population. We can start by looking at how much money was required to live for a year. W.V. Harris, 'Poverty and destitution in the Roman Empire', in *Rome's Imperial Economy: Twelve Essays* works from a grain price to a subsistence rate for a worker of 111 *sesterces*.[1] But that is only for food and would provide a diet so poor that it is difficult to see how anyone could live off it for any length of time. To this we need to add clothing, fuel and shelter which is likely to double the subsistence level to about 200 *sesterces*. But this was enough to support the very poorest Romans and very few Romans, even slaves, would have lived at this level. The figure for average income must have been several times this 200 *sesterces* and a reasonable estimate would be 500 to 600 *sesterces* per person.

There are a number of figures for subsistence and low-level incomes in Table 12.2. These are derived from legal sources in which Roman jurists estimated subsistence from Pliny's bequest to his freedmen and from the pay of Roman soldiers. The legal sources offer two figures of about 500 *sesterces*. Roman soldiers before the pay rise offered by Domitian were in receipt of 900 *sesterces* and we may assume that this last figure was a 'living wage', comfortably above the poverty line, but far from wealthy.

We can now estimate a range for the total size of the Roman economy by multiplying subsistence by number of people.

- Low Estimate: 500 *sesterces* x 45,000,000 people = economic size of 22,500,000,000 *sesterces*.
- High Estimate: 600 *sesterces* x 80,000,000 people = economic size of 48,000,000,000 *sesterces*.

Table 12.2 Relative wealth

Source	Income by period (in sesterces)	Annual income (in sesterces)
Subsistence (Grain price)	20/month	240
Subsistence (Digest)	40/month	480
Subsistence (Digest)	42/month	504
Veterans (Retirement bonus)	12,000 (capital)	720[1]
Soldiers (Pay before Domitian)	900/year	900
Subsistence (Digest)	83/month	996
Freedmen (Pliny's will)	18,666.66 (capital)	1,120[1]
Soldiers (Pay after Domitian)	1,200/year	1,200
Subsistence (Martial)	6/day	1,800[2]
Landowner average estate: Ligures Baebiani	79,000 (capital)	4,740[1]
Landowner average estate: Veleia	265,000 (capital)	15,900[1]
Augustan Senator	1,000,000 (capital)	60,000[1]
Pliny (Estates)	30,000,000 (capital)	1,800,000[1]

1 Assuming a return of 6%.
2 Calculated on the assumption of the client securing the gift on 300 days a year.

These figures are, of course, very broad estimates, but there is good reason to believe that they capture the range of the economy. Further, the figures have implications for understanding issues such as the role of the state in the Roman economy and the divisions of wealth in Roman society. It is to the first of these issues that we now turn.

State and economy

In nearly all modern economies the state plays a significant economic role. The state needs to draw money from economic activities in order to pay for its needs. The state also spends money that can generate wealth and economic activity. The major needs of the Roman state were to pay for:

- army;
- bureaucracy;
- buildings;
- Roman corn dole;
- Emperor.

The major sources of income of the Roman state were:

- land tax on the provinces;
- poll taxes on provincials;
- trade taxes;
- sales tax;
- inheritance taxes;
- state assets (mines, quarries);
- imperial estates;
- confiscations;
- booty.

Notably, the Roman state was very much less concerned with the provision of services than modern states. Let us start with expenses.

It is normally thought that the army was the largest single cost. The Augustan army consisted of about 140,000 Roman legionaries and about the same number of auxiliaries levied from the provincials. It is quite likely that the number of auxiliaries increased over time. The number of legions decreased under Augustus, but was increased by later emperors. It is very likely that the legions were often under strength and recruited more men as and when emergencies arose. The basic pay of a Roman legionary was 900 *sesterces*. There is considerable debate as to what auxiliaries were paid. Cavalry were paid more than infantry, since they had to support the cost of a horse. Military accounts from Roman Egypt and from Israel show that soldiers had deductions from their wages for food, clothing, and others basic charges and equipment. These were standardised charges and could amount to nearly 85% of a soldier's wages. Since that the pay of soldiers was so close to subsistence, I find it difficult to believe that auxiliary soldiers were paid less than legionary soldiers.

This gives us a basic pay budget of 252,000,000 *sesterces*. To this figure we need to an allowance for officers who were paid more and for cavalry. We also need to make an allowance for praetorians and for the fleets stationed around the Mediterranean.

The majority of materials for the army were deducted from the soldiers' wages. But the army will have had additional needs, which will have increased considerably in times of war. They needed basic materials for the camp (stone, wood, tiles), transport animals, and the like. The army tended to requisition labour from local communities, but paid for all other materials (animals and building materials).

The major additional expense was probably the retirement bonus that was given to legionaries. About 110 legionaries would have been discharged each year after 25 years' service. If legionaries were discharged after 20 years, as they appear to have been under Augustus, the number discharged each year would have been slightly higher at about 135 legionaries. This means that under Augustus 3780 legionaries were discharged each year and were in receipt of the bonus of 12,000 *sesterces* making an annual expense of 45,360,000 *sesterces*.

We cannot be precise, but the cost of the army per year under Augustus was probably about 400,000,000 *sesterces* per year.

The next major charge was the corn dole. The dole was probably paid out to about 200,000 citizens in Rome. The cost was probably about 96 *sesterces* per year per recipient, which would make a total of 19,200,000 *sesterces* per year.

The imperial bureaucracy was small but the various governors and officials were well paid. It is difficult to come to a reasonable estimate, but 50,000,000 *sesterces* is sometimes suggested.

This leaves us with the expenses of the emperor and the expenses of building. These are almost impossible to estimate and varied by emperor and by period. An emperor engaged in significant building spent a lot more than others. Emergencies, such as relief in case of volcanic eruption or earthquakes, were probably also expensive. Emperors were also expected to give generous gifts on significant occasions, such as their accessions, adoptions, and major conquests. Entertainment must also have been a drain on the treasury.

The only viable figure we have imperial disbursements comes from the *Res Gestae* of Augustus. The figure appears in the Appendix and amounts to 2,400,000,000 *sesterces*. Augustan expenditure was very large and spread over a very long period. It included the monies he spent during and at the end of the civil wars. He also dispersed various gifts to the Roman people. It does not include the money he spent on buildings, games and shows, gifts to cities and communities afflicted by natural disasters, and his gifts to colonies in Italy and to his many friends.

Table 12.3 Notional imperial budget: basic annual expenditure (*sesterces*)

Army	400,000,000
Corn Dole	19,200,000
Salaries (bureaucracy)	50,000,000
Other*	50,000,000
Total	519,200,000

*This is an entirely notional figure to cover extra expenses on army, bureaucracy and the like.

Income

Income comes in three basic forms: taxes, the management of assets, and unusual contributions and extractions.

In the ancient world (as in the modern world) it is very difficult to tax income. Taxes tend to be charged on things that can be seen and counted, which meant primarily fixed property (real estate), persons, and goods which were in transit. Italy was exempt from taxes on land and persons and had been so since the mid-second century BC. However, there were some customs duties and sales taxes. Augustus made no attempt to change this situation. He did, however, introduce an inheritance tax, from which property passed to children was exempted, and a tax on the sale of slaves. These taxes were directed in particular to the support of the army and the bonuses paid to the soldiers.

In the provinces, land was one of the two basic taxable elements. Tax rates are not clear. Sicily supposedly had to remit about 10% of its grain to Rome. Tax rates in Egypt, where there is again a plethora of evidence, were set by land type, by crop grown, and by area (rather than by product). Thus, to know what percentage the Romans took in tax, we would have to be able to calculate how much a particular patch of land grew. Unsurprisingly, the productivity of land varied, but land taxes at 8 to 12% seem normal. It seems likely that the Romans adopted pre-existing taxation systems in many of the provinces that they conquered and that taxation rates would remain the same (with the exception of poll taxes). In Western Europe, where the extraction of produce from farmers was probably not through organised taxation systems before conquest, may have seen more detailed Roman intervention.

Poll tax was also imposed on many provinces, sometimes as a punishment. The best evidence comes from Egypt, but the evidence is surprisingly diverse. The Romans adopted many of the Ptolemaic tax systems, some of which may have gone back centuries. These had made mostly small charges on adult males. But they introduced, or perhaps very greatly increased, a poll tax. The difficulty arises in that the poll tax was imposed at different rates. Romans and Alexandrians resident in the province were exempt. Priests of the traditional temples were also exempt. Those living in the various smaller cities of the province paid at a reduced rate. Villagers paid full rates, but, and the reasons for this are difficult to imagine, residents of different regions were charged the tax at different rates.

This type of diversity was probably reflected across the Empire. Poll tax was a punishment. In AD 70, a poll tax was imposed on all Jews in reparation for the war of 66–70. Notably, the tax affected Jews resident outside the Palestine region who had not been involved in the revolt. It also led to considerable abuse since up until that point the state had had no interest in defining who was Jewish and indeed Jewish identity in itself may not have been completely fixed: there were probably some members of the community whose involvement was marginal. As in Nazi Germany (but with far less horrific results), some people probably suddenly found themselves to be 'Jewish'. Some communities and perhaps whole provinces were probably exempted, but the infrastructure of poll tax, notably the census, was certainly a normal part of Roman administration and we know of its application in Gaul, Syria, and Egypt, as well as in Italy.

Taxes on the movement of goods are also attested. Some of these taxes may have been for local use in the various cities of the Empire. Rome did, however, levy a 25% tax on goods brought in from outside the Empire. On the Eastern frontier, taxes could be substantial. One papyrus, the so-called Muziris papyrus (*P. Vindob.* G. 40822), documents financial transactions relating to a single caravan coming from Muziris in India and travelling to Alexandria. The value of goods reported is just under 28,000,000 *sesterces*. The transport of goods from the East into Egypt was seasonal, but there were also trade routes running from Syria down the Euphrates and to India. There is every reason to believe that the Roman authorities saw the Eastern trade as a significant source of income. Indeed, since much of the coinage found in India is Augustan and Tiberian and is composed of seemingly unworn coins, it seems possible that those close to the imperial household were directly involved in the trade.

Other sources of income come from the management of imperial assets. The wealth from these is impossible to quantify. In Egypt, the emperor took over the estates that had been the possessions of Cleopatra and her courtiers. These were disbursed as gifts under the early Julio-Claudians but were back in direct imperial ownership by the time of Nero. These estates were indirectly managed and effectively, those farming the estates simply had to pay a rent of about 10% of the produce of the land.

Elsewhere, the emperor appears to have accumulated vast estates in North Africa. In Italy and the West, the evidence is more fragmentary. Gaius (see p. 143) may have acquired lands in Gaul. Senators who fell from power would expect to lose substantial portions of their estates as well as their lives. The emperor also expected that his wide network of friends would leave him bequests. There must have been a difficult decision for the emperor's friends to make. How much would be enough? Provincial dignitaries especially may have felt compelled to offer very significant gifts to the emperors in order to ensure a smooth succession for their heirs.

The state also had control over major mines and quarries. Mines in Spain appear to have produced considerable amounts of gold in this period.

The imperial budget

There are many uncertainties and we cannot get very close to an accurate picture of the imperial budget, but we can make some guesses. In Table 12.2, we estimated a basic level of expenditure at 519,200,000 *sesterces* per year.

We need to set this against income. Our only way of assessing income is against the size of the economy. We had two estimates above. Let us estimate poll and land taxes at 10% of produce. Let us add a figure for the Eastern trade (75,000,000 *sesterces*), suggesting that the Muziris papyrus reflects a significant proportion of the annual trade. We can make no allowance for imperial estates or mines and quarries, but the imperial estates certainly must have produced income measured in millions of *sesterces*.

Low estimate: 22,500,000,000 *sesterces* (economy):   2,500,000,000 tax
               Eastern Trade 300,000,000 *sesterces*:   75,000,000 tax
               Total: 2,575,000,000 *sesterces*

High estimate: 48,000,000,000 *sesterces* (economy):   4,800,000,000 tax
               Eastern Trade 300,000,000 *sesterces*:   75,000,000 tax
               Total: 4,875,000,000 *sesterces*

On the very low estimate, tax should produce 500% the basic needs of the Roman state. Of course expenditure must have been higher. We need to make allowance for buildings, gifts, and unusual expenditures. If we take Augustan expenditure as a guide, Augustus might have given as much as 60,000,000 *sesterces* per year through his reign. At most, that would take annual expenditure up to about 570,000,000 *sesterces*. But we also need to make some allowance for income from estates, mines, and bequests.

The implications of these figures are notable. They suggest that the Roman emperors should have been overwhelmed by income. Our evidence does suggest that they were not short of money, except in very unusual circumstances, but neither does it suggest that the treasury was full of more money than anyone knew how to spend. There appears to have been some shortages of money under Gaius, Nero, Vespasian, possibly Domitian, and Nerva. Augustus increased taxes to meet the costs of his army. Vespasian sought cash to meet the costs of rebuilding Rome. Other emperors were occasionally anxious about tax income.

We may revisit the calculations in this section. We might suggest that the economy was much smaller than in these calculations, but that would require the population to be much lower and much poorer than we have assumed, and that does not make sense. We might assume that expenditure was much higher, and that would mean imperial expenditure on buildings, games, and gifts was enormously large, multiples of the cost of the Roman army, and that also does not seem credible.

The best answer to the problem is to lower the amount of tax coming into the treasury. There are two ways of doing this. One, is to assume that tax rates were actually closer to 5% than 10%. We might also assume that the costs of tax collection were high and much tax was siphoned off to meet expenses of the collectors. Collecting tax in the Roman world was a profitable business and not all tax was collected by officials; some was commercially let to tax farmers. Even reducing tax by 75% should allow for a healthy surplus.

Finally, what follows from these considerations is that the state, although by far the most significant single institution within the Roman economy, was a very small player indeed. State expenditure probably only accounted for between 2 and 5% of the total annual production of the Roman economy. The ability of the state to affect directly economic life in the provinces was, therefore, very limited.

The agricultural economy

The vast majority of the population of the Empire were engaged in the production of food. As in all other periods of Mediterranean history, the basic crops were grains, olives, and grapes. Grain provided the staple for the Mediterranean diet. It would be eaten as bread (especially among the wealthier) or as a gruel or porridge. Vegetables were available, as were various forms of beans. Meat was probably a luxury though in the later Empire pork and beef were regarded as normal parts of the diet and included in the rations for soldiers and in the *annona* of Rome. Sheep and goats were probably also regularly consumed and their bones appear on many sites. They were probably grazed on the highlands of regions and goats are especially good at surviving on poor land. Fish was probably the most significant source of meat protein and was produced on an industrial scale. Fishing boats were common (such as the one that picked up Agrippina as she swam away from her collapsible boat, p. 181) and in at least some areas river fishing would also have been common. Fish farms, detectable by the use of large concrete pens, were a common feature of the Roman Mediterranean. The fish was either eaten unprocessed or turned into *garum*, a concoction of fish sauce that, one fears, endangered the lives of all who tasted it. Wine, sometimes used as vinegar, was the basic drink. It was normally diluted and the use of wine and vinegar probably killed at least some of the pathogens in the drinking water. A Roman man may have consumed up to a litre of wine per day. Olives were turned into oil by crushing. This enabled the easy transport and sale of the produce.

Undoubtedly, there were many other crops. Cato provides us with great lists of things you might grow on your farm. At least some of the produce will have been for durable goods: wood, reeds, leather, wool, linen, flax. Oil will also have been used for lighting and the Romans will have consumed considerable amounts of wood for heating and cooking. We need to remember also that the Roman relied very heavily on animal power and thus required enormous amounts of fodder for their beasts of burden. Hens were also probably very common, needing very little care and providing a basic and very cheap source of protein.

The agricultural regimes were probably very diverse. Many modern farms practice monocultures, often employing very large fields. They do this because monocultures provide them with certain advantages of scale and enable the mechanisation of agricultural production. These were not issues in the Roman world. Farmers practised polyculture. Typically, medium and large farmers might have had vines or olives and grow grain or another crop among the trees. They would have had a kitchen-garden which would provide vegetables, and might also seek sources of wood and building materials, grazing and fodder, and perhaps even keep small herds or flocks. Animals provided fertiliser. Multiple crops allowed farmers to spread risk in case of failure and also to feed their workforces from the produce of the farm. Small plots of land were exploitable economically in the way that they are not in the modern economy. It might be a little awkward to farm a plot of land half-way up a hillside, but humans and donkeys are very good at climbing (while tractors and other machinery are not). All over the Mediterranean, and especially in Greece and Cyprus, one is struck by the extensive evidence for terracing of hillsides to create small pockets of relatively flat land on which crops could be grown; many of those terraces are now, for one reason or another, abandoned.

Small farmers had fewer resources with which to vary their agricultural regimes. In developing countries today, small farmers tend to be very dependent on markets to supply them with the goods they cannot themselves grow and to dispose of surplus, and this means that they are more vulnerable in case of changing economic conditions. In the ancient world, the level at which farmers engaged in market production is less certain. Some farmers may have operated more as subsistence agriculturalists, growing what they and their families needed off the farm and exchanging only a small proportion of their produce for items they really could not make themselves (clothes, tools, pottery, etc.). Small farmers also had fewer resources which they could use to improve their land. Mediterranean agriculture depends often on water management and in some of the difficult environments, irrigation and water preservation strategies are essential for successful agriculture. Irrigation works and cisterns can be quite difficult and expensive to manufacture. Also, small farmers may have found it more difficult to move to specialised agriculture, spending money on vines and olives and then waiting for the trees to grow sufficiently to produce a viable crop. Nevertheless, small farmers would have had an abundance of labour and investing labour in the land could considerably increase productivity. Careful sowing of seed and weeding of the land and harvesting would ensure the best returns.

   Patterns of agricultural activity varied by region and over time as well. In Egypt, for example, grains were by far the most important crop and a vast proportion of the land was dedicated to grain production. A similar situation appears to have applied in Sicily. In other areas, there appears to have been large-scale investment in wines and olives. Italy, for example, was producing wine that was exported across the Mediterranean in the first century BC. Syria had a developing wine industry in the second century AD. Spain and Southern Gaul also developed extensive wine industries in the early Imperial period. North Africa, which tends to be associated with grain production in the early Imperial period, gradually developed an oil industry which appears to have exported across the Mediterranean in the later Imperial period. To the North and West, different balances of crops were produced in accord with environmental differences.

   Agricultural regimes were dynamic. In our consideration of the dynamism of the agricultural economy, we will divide discussion into two sections: Italy and the provinces.

Italy

Inevitably, most historical attention has been focused on the Italian economy. There is a long established historical tradition that argues for a gradual transformation in the agricultural regimes in Italy from farming by small-holders and perhaps even peasant agriculture to farming dominated by large estates (*latifundia*). The growth of the *latifundia* is often dated to the second century BC in the aftermath of the Hannibalic War. It is from this period that we get our first Latin agricultural manual, Cato's *De Agri Cultura*, which advises is readers on how to choose a farm to buy and how to manage the farm. Cato envisages a farm of about 30 hectares, which is substantial, but far from enormous. Yet, although luxury villas start to appear in the Italian landscape in the late second century BC, *latifundia* as such are difficult to find in either the literary or archaeological record until the Imperial period. Two villas in Etruria (Tuscany), La Colonna and Settefinestre, provide us with the best archaeological evidence for latifundist agriculture in the Roman period. These are both Caesarian and thus from the very end of the Republic. Settefinestre may have farmed as much as 125 hectares and housed 130 or so slaves, farming a range of products, including vines, grains, and pigs.

   In fact, archaeology reveals an agricultural landscape that is very difficult to turn into a historical narrative. There are numerous examples of reasonable small estates (perhaps on the Catonian model). A farm at Villa Regina near Boscoreale in Campania, for instance, has a relatively small set of accommodation quarters with very little sign of luxury. There is a small press on site, probably for grapes. But the site is dominated by a large court in which are buried eighteen large storage jars (*dolia*) with perhaps the capacity to store 10,000 litres of wine. This may make up as many as two vintages since the agricultural manuals suggest that ideally a farm could store a vintage for a year. Although a vintage of 5,000 litres might sound a lot (and it would be a wild party to get through it in a night), it would probably only meet the annual needs of 20 men. Two other small villas in Francolise, the Posto and San Rocco villas are so positioned in the landscape that it seems unlikely that they could have farmed more than 15 to 20 hectares, a decent size but smaller than Cato's ideal farm.

Smaller farms continued to operate into the late Republic and early Empire, though they are often difficult to detect archaeologically. Regularly dispersed farms near Cosa in Tuscany appear to have consisted of three or four small residential rooms and a work yard. They may have been farming plots of as little as three hectares. On the ridge of a hill in the landscape North of Rome (Monte Forco, though it is difficult to find on any map), the archaeologist Barri Jones found concrete platforms which had been laid to support tiny farms, about 55m^2, farming less than a hectare. It is difficult to see how the farmers survived on so little land.

Since the 1950s, archaeologists have been refining the ways in which they understand rural landscapes and gathering vast amounts of data about the Italian landscape in particular. The technique employed most often is called survey archaeology and involves assembling teams who will walk through fields looking for sherds of pottery or roof tiles or masonry which attest to ancient settlement. In spite of all the information that has been produced by this process, no clear picture of changes in the landscape has emerged. In some places, there seems to have been more farms in the early Imperial period than ever before, particularly in the environs of Rome. In other places, there may have been a small decrease in the number of farms. What is certain is that the Roman landscape was heavily exploited throughout the period.

What survey archaeology cannot tell us, however, is who farmed the land and how they farmed it. The Younger Pliny provides us with various letters in which he details his approach to the management of his estates. These are often laden with complaints about the produce he was able to extract from his estates, but it is difficult to take the letters as attesting any economic crisis in Roman farming. One of the more interesting letters concerns the failure of a grape harvest (*Epistles*, 8.2). Pliny had sold the harvest while it was still on the vine. Harvesting required a great deal of labour, more than Pliny would have on his estate, and it made sense to sub-contract to specialists who recruited gangs who would tour the local estates bringing in the grapes. The pickers probably made use of the storage facilities on Pliny's estates but then would also eventually take the wine to market.

This was quite a sophisticated operation and the sub-contracting of harvesting and marketing attests to complex economic arrangements. After all, Pliny might be able to grow his grapes, but he would not necessarily have the connections and outlets that would allow him to market his wine. Further, specialist marketers could foster connections in local towns or further afield whom they could supply. Pliny's sub-contracting also spread risk. He could sell the crop slightly cheaper and the risk of crop failure would pass to the harvesters. He would also have no need to supervise the harvest since the grapes that were coming off the vines did not belong to him anyhow.

Everything suggests that this was a standard process, but in this case, when the crop unexpectedly failed, Pliny felt the need to intervene and offer a discount on the prices offered. He probably did this because the failure was catastrophic and not just a minor failure of the harvest to meet expectations. If the harvesters had to meet their obligations to Pliny, as they would have done in law, he would have bankrupted them. It was not in Pliny's interests to put out of business those on whom he relied to harvest and market his grapes: who would bid for the grapes next year?

Pliny's procedures for refunding his buyers were complex: various fractions of the amount promised were remitted depending on how much had been offered and whether payment had already been received, but the amounts involved give us some of the idea of the scale of Pliny's enterprise (and we should remember that this involves only one the regions where Pliny held property). Those who had offered more than 10,000 *sesterces* got a higher level of remuneration than those who had bought less than that amount. What we do not know is how many buyers were involved, but the systematic nature of the refunds and the divisions into categories suggest that there were many.

In *Epistle*, 3.19, Pliny writes for advice on buying an estate. An estate neighbouring his has come up for sale. Pliny was thinking of buying it. Buying neighbouring estates had some advantages since it allowed Pliny to economise on estate management. But if a storm were to blow up at a crucial moment, the crops of both estates could be wiped out simultaneously. The letter is interesting in part because it shows how carefully Pliny planned his investment. The price of the estate is 3,000,000 *sesterces*, but Pliny reckons that with suitable investment he could return it to an earlier valuation of 5,000,000 *sesterces*. Pliny was intending to borrow the money from his mother-in-law.

Pliny's strategy for the estate was to invest in slaves and equipment. It looks very much as if Pliny was intending to rent out portions of the estate to tenants. In letter 9.37, Pliny describes how he drew rent from his tenants by taking a share from their crop rather charging at a fixed rate. In that way, both he and the tenants (who had long leases) had an interest in keeping the properties on the estate in good condition and in managing the land for the long-term rather than going for quick profits. Pliny probably provided his tenants with buildings, tools and slaves.

One wonders what Pliny's estate would look like archaeologically. It seems to me very likely that it would consist of a large villa and a number of small farm centres surrounding it. One would not be able to distinguish between a region that was controlled by a major latifundist agriculturalist, who rented out small farms within his estate and a pattern of landscape in which there were numerous independent middling farmers.

Pliny was clearly very wealthy. In a letter to his wife's grandfather (7.11), Pliny notes that he had sold an estate to his friend Corellia, sister of Corellius Rufus (see p. 250), for 700,000 *sesterces* when he could have got 900,000 for it on the open market. The estate had come to him as an inheritance (perhaps unexpected or from a remote family member). The fact that he intended to borrow 3,000,000 *sesterces* from his mother-in-law does not suggest that Pliny was lacking in wealth, but gathering up cash was a different matter. Most Romans probably kept most of their wealth in fixed assets (land, buildings, and the like). Raising money for a major purchase would be difficult and this was one of the reasons why elite Romans used moneylenders. Pliny's mother-in-law clearly had 3,000,000 in ready cash. In 10.8, Pliny asks Trajan for leave from official duties to attend to his estates in Tifernum. These estates brought in a rental income of 400,000 *sesterces*, presumably per year, suggesting an estate worth 6,000,000 to 7,000,000 *sesterces*. His major holdings were almost certainly near Como. In 5.7, he notes that he received an unexpected legacy of an estate worth 800,000 *sesterces* and we should add to that estate he granted to Corellia. The estates he inherited from his parents (and perhaps also from his uncle) are likely to have been many times larger and thus we would expect that Pliny's total worth was probably considerably more than 20,000,000 *sesterces*.

We can put this into some kind of context. Romans appear to have expected that they would secure a return of about 6% on investments. If Pliny's estate was worth 30,000,000, then it would produce 1,800,000 *sesterces* per year, which should have been enough to support 1,500 soldiers on the Domitianic pay-rate of 1,200 *sesterces* per annum. Try multiplying up a low average salary, such as might be paid to a soldier nowadays, by 1,500, which might give you some idea quite how wealthy Pliny was. Pliny was probably not exceptional, though we have no other large landowner whose business is so well recorded.

At the end of the first century AD, the emperors started to worry about the birth rate and a decline in population in Italy. We can never know whether this was a real decline or a real worry. Their response was to establish some sort of basic social provision for the poor in Italian towns. This called the *alimenta* scheme. How it worked was that members of the local elite would mortgage estates and the interest for that mortgage would be then used to support the children. Of course, this was probably a good deal for the landowners who received a cash injection into their finances. It was essential that accurate records were kept of the estates that had been pledged and in at least some cases these pledges were recorded on tables and we have inscribed tables partially preserved for Veleia in the very North of Italy and Ligures Baebiani in the South of Italy. These attest 47 and 57 estates respectively.

At Veleia, the estates are broken down into particular farms, valued normally in the region of about 42,000 *sesterces*. The estates comprised a number of such farms. The largest estate was valued at 1,500,000 *sesterces*, though the average estate was worth about 265,000 *sesterces*. At Ligures Baebiani, the estates were considerably smaller, perhaps reflecting a somewhat different stage in the development of the two towns with the largest estate being worth just over 500,000 *sesterces* and the average being about 79,000 *sesterces*. There is, of course, no reason why someone would pledge all their estates in a particular town, yet these figures suggest the levels of wealth of the aristocrats of local towns in rural Italy. At the upper end of the spectrum, we are looking at wealthy individuals and we must remember that the wealthy may have had farms and estates in multiple locations. At the middle of the scale, these locally important people may not have been particularly wealthy, with incomes four or five times that of legionary soldiers. They were all, of course, many times less wealthy than Pliny.

The processes at work in the agricultural economies of Veleia and Ligures Baebiani appear to be ones of consolidation. Multiple farms were slowly passing into single ownership and being combined into estates. To an extent, that is what we would expect in an Italian economy. The Romans practiced a policy of partible inheritance whereby properties would be dispersed among children. They also had a testamentary system in which it was expected to leave extensive bequests to one's friends. Estates would, over the generations, be in the process of fragmentation and over a lifetime a rich and powerful individual would gradually accumulate estates through processes of investment and inheritance. Yet, it looks very much as if this process of consolidation and division was over time slowly working to make the rich richer.

There are good reasons for this gradual accumulation of wealth. The Empire brought peace to Italy and with that peace came economic opportunity. Men such as Pliny were not threatened by war as they had been during the Republic. There were also large markets for the goods that they were producing on their farms, notably in Rome and the cities of Italy, but also with the legions on the frontier and perhaps the cities and elites beyond Italy. Pliny's wealth was such that he could hardly spend it all. He could and did build himself great villas on the Latian coast and in the Tuscan hills. He was generous to his home and no doubt to his friends. In 5.7, he tells us that he had already given 1,600,000 *sesterces* to Comum, but if the above is correct, that was probably only a year's income. It is very likely that Pliny and others like him effectively had money to burn and were thus able to take advantage of investment opportunities at home or in the provinces as they emerged. Unless they were very reckless or the emperor turned against them or they had many, many children, families of wealth would progressively accumulate more and more.

A measure of this can be seen in the status of senators. Augustus redefined the senatorial order (see p. 73) by introducing a census requirement of 1,000,000 *sesterces*. One imagines that the level was set to exclude those who were not of the wealthiest class and to maintain a level of prestige among the senators (money and status were closely linked). It is obviously a round figure, but it was unlikely to be a random figure. Some existing senators did not meet the grade (which was the point), but Augustus was embarrassed because some of those who did not make the grade came from the more established senatorial families, and they made a fuss until Augustus bailed them out with grants of money. But 130 years later, Pliny, who we have no reason to believe was unusual in terms of senatorial wealth (he was not from an established senatorial family, nor had he won great victories, nor did he seem to benefit particularly from closeness to the emperor), had wealth many times that minimum senatorial level. In 10.4, Pliny writes to Trajan about his friend Voconius Romanus for whom he has secured a senatorial position. Yet, there was a problem: Romanus could not make the census level. His mother, however, transferred to him 4,000,000 *sesterces* and this, we might assume, was the wealth of a poor senator.

The processes that we see at work in the Italian landscape were very gradual. We are looking at change over decades and perhaps centuries rather than anything very immediate, but the Romans do seem to have been aware of gradual change, of the slow disappearance of peasant agriculture and the rise of the great estates. They also seem to have been aware that slowly, very slowly, this development was reshaping Italian society. As the rich became richer so they accumulated more and more power.

When did this process come to an end? It probably did not. The estates of the wealthy grew into late antiquity and perhaps even into the fifth century. The wealthy of Christian Rome were fantastically wealthy and far more wealthy than Pliny had been. The processes of concentration of wealth among the rich probably only came to an end only with the great barbarian invasions of the fifth and sixth centuries. By that time, the Italian landscape had been transformed.

Provinces

The information on provinces is rather different from what we get from Italy. I have already had occasion to mention Egyptian agriculture and I will continue to discuss Egypt here in part because it illustrates trends that we see in other areas. Before the Roman conquest, the only people who seem to have had significant accumulations of land were those close to the Ptolemaic court. There were also many different types of tenure of land in Egypt. Land was held by the king and by the temples and by 'the estates'. There was also private land of various slightly different types. The Romans simplified this system by effectively making all temple and kingly land into public land and also by taking the estates under the ownership of the emperor (or those close to him). This public land was a considerable proportion of the land available in Egypt and Egypt appears to have been unique in this respect. The public land was farmed by villagers who either bid for the land or had the land assigned to them. In some cases, they may have been reluctant to take on land (and those cases generate most documentation) and in other cases they wanted to farm the land. Private land also appears to have been mostly held by villagers in the first century at least.

Egypt outside of Alexandria (which was a special case) was basically divided into cities and villages. The cities were traditional centres often (perhaps always) with large temples at the heart where the regional gods were worshipped. The Roman authorities concentrated political power in these cities, relying for some local administrative tasks on a group defined as 'those from the gymnasium', which meant those who had had a more Greek education. This class became a hereditary group. Nevertheless, there is little to suggest that they were particularly wealthy in the first century. Yet, the changes in political and economic regime in Egypt provided opportunities and we start to see larger private estates emerging during the Julio-Claudian period. The most significant landowners initially seem to have been Alexandrians and that may reflect the access that some Alexandrians had to the Roman authorities and the opportunities to make money that this provided. In a system that was relatively egalitarian in economic terms, such as very early Roman Egypt, people could only become very rich if they could access a new source of money and could not expect to build fortunes from the careful exploitation of small farms. For example, one of the families that does become wealthy is that of Tiberius Julius Alexander. His was a Jewish family that rose to sufficient prominence that a member of the family was appointed to the tax collection of customs duties in Egypt. The family continued to rise, befriending the Herods of Judaea until one of their number was appointed Prefect of Egypt and in that capacity helped Vespasian to the throne (see p. 220).

Locally, the processes of accumulation of estates appear to have been slow, taking centuries rather than decades. Egyptian agriculture remained overwhelming focused on villages. These villages could be quite large, *c.* 3,000 inhabitants, but many were rather smaller, *c.* 1,000 inhabitants. In most cases, those who had land that they could not farm themselves tended to rent out plots to those who had spare labour. There was some use of slaves, but slaves were more common in the cities than in the villages and the primary labour force remained the villagers themselves. In spite of the gradual accumulation of estates through the first century, this pattern of villager-led agriculture was maintained and free village labour remained at the centre of Egyptian agriculture throughout the Roman period and beyond.

This kind of pattern can be seen in many communities throughout the East. In Palestine and Syria, for example, the village seems to have been the major settlement form throughout the period. In Palestine, the aristocracy had tended to define themselves religiously rather than by wealth with the result that there was no obvious landed aristocracy in the late first century BC. Yet, there appears to have been a similar pattern as in Egypt, where those with some power and influence (and possibly luck) began to acquire properties.

Increasing differentials in wealth and changes in cultural values can be seen in the archaeology of the region which in places became more Hellenised and with more evidence of wealth. The gradual amassing of property and the ensuing pressures on economic and religious institutions in Palestine was probably responsible for the increasing social tensions that we see in Judaea in the early decades of the first century and which culminated in the Jewish War of 66–70. The wealthy appear to have enjoyed closer connections to the Herodian regime and perhaps also to the Roman authorities and, in increasing polarised political circumstances, sometimes appear to have been identified with the enemies of the Jewish people. Various messianic movements, of which what became Christianity was only one, often associated with charismatic figures and sometimes in revolt against the material world characterise social ferment in the region and it is difficult not to connect this disruption to changes in the agricultural world.

The position in the rest of Syria was probably more complicated, in part because of great regional environmental differences. In the environs of the great cities of the region (places like Apamea and Antioch) were Greek-style cities (*poleis*) had been established for centuries, there appears to have been a mix of larger farms and villages. In the high lands and the arid lands, exploitation of the landscape was through a mix of nomadic herdsmen and small settled villages. By the end of the first century, the settled population of the region appears to have been expanding, perhaps largely relying on the commercial farming of olives and grapes to make it viable to bring these often-difficult territories into cultivation. The stage was being set for an explosion of settlement in the region, mostly based round village agriculture.

In North Africa, the situation seems to have been very different again. Agriculture in the relatively well-watered coastal areas had been prospering for centuries and was responsible for much of the wealth of cities such as Carthage. These coastal cities provided trading access to the Mediterranean and markets for the agricultural goods being produced in the hinterlands. The gradual conquest of Mauretania was on-going through much of the early Julio-Claudian period and must have slowed developed at the western end of North Africa, but the East seems to have seen a gradual expansion of the margins of cultivation into semi-arid areas, areas where today there is now very little agricultural activity. The Roman expansion into the desert was so notable that in recent years there have been extensive surveys to understand how the near-desert was made to bloom. This appears to have been achieved by very careful management of water supplies and location of farms, often by riverbeds and the use of reservoirs and cisterns. In some instances extension into these regions was by small farms, but large-scale investment was also used to bring an area into development, possibly sometimes employing imperial money and making use of tax breaks. As with Syria, although this process was underway during the first and early second centuries, the 'golden age' of agriculture in Roman Africa lay in the future.

Spain seems to have seen extensive agricultural development in the first century AD. The Mediterranean coastal area had long been the focus of Roman attentions and had probably attracted significant numbers of Roman settlers. By the first century, trade relations between Spain and Italy appear to have been very strong. This can be seen in the pottery evidence. Just outside the Ostian Gate of Rome stands Monte Testaccio. Now degraded somewhat this 'mountain' is in fact an artificial hill built from millions of fragments of mostly Spanish transport *amphorae*. These *amphorae* appear to have been used largely for the transport of oil. Given that *amphorae* were often reused, the dump must attest a huge volume of oil being moved from Spain to Rome.

Spanish oil was also sent to the troops on the Rhine and elsewhere in the West. One has to wonder how and why Spanish oil became so important. Part of the answer may lie in official stimulus. The Roman troops needed supplies and although some of the provision for the soldiers may have been through markets, much of the trade was administered. Those orders for oil and other goods provided opportunities for merchants to make large amounts of money, but merchants would also have needed large source of supply. Once trade had started and the investments in Spanish oil production had been made then exporting to Rome may have been a logical next step.

In the North and West, the agricultural pattern was probably somewhat different again. In Britain, for example, the economy seems to have been quite primitive before the Romans arrived. There were no substantial towns and although there was some money, its circulation was probably limited and money may not have been used primarily for trade. The arrival of the Romans was probably a great economic shock. Urban settlements grew up quickly, starting in the South-East and often associated with Roman camps. In some of these sites, there is considerable evidence for retailing and manufacture of goods (notably London but also Verulamium). In the countryside, Roman style farms (villas) start to appear during the first century, almost certainly producing for the new towns. Development was, however, slow. There were palatial structures, such as Fishbourne, but the power of Fishbourne's owner was probably political rather than economic. As in the East, it took time for a local landed aristocracy to develop and that development can be mapped in the gradually increased spread and luxury of villas, again mostly through the South of Britain.

We can tell a similar story through Northern Gaul and indeed through the Danubian regions where the gradual development of Roman-style cities and the emergence of villa farms went hand in hand. Germany was probably more influenced by the presence of the military. Several urban centres appear to have been closely connected to camps and the Rhine provided a trade route along which goods could be imported from the South.

It is dangerous to be too dogmatic about the changes in rural life across such a vast swathe of territory as the Roman Empire and there were always local exceptions. Roman Greece, for instance, remains a much-debated area.

Yet, there is a consistency in the archaeology of the Empire. Rural settlements seem to be often more plentiful and more archaeologically visible in the Roman Imperial period. Part of that visibility may be due to another related trend, which is the emergence of wealthier landowners. As in Roman Italy, it appears that wealth was increasingly concentrated and that trend appears to have been maintained into Late Antiquity. It seems to be a feature of Roman imperial development.

The urban economy

We find similar variations in the urban economies of the Roman Empire and these variations are perhaps even more marked than with rural economies. In part, this results from the enormous diversity of cities. At its basic level, there is the question of population. Some cities would seem to have had populations of but a few thousand. Some cities in Greece and Italy were almost certainly tiny. Some cities in Roman Britain barely deserve the name, being walled settlements with a small number of relatively dispersed houses. And then we have places like Rome, Alexandria, Antioch, Corinth, Carthage, Lepcis (or Leptis) Magna, Athens, Marseilles, Naples, London, Cologne, Malaga, Ephesus and the list goes on. It makes very little sense economically to group all these centres into a single category.

Let us start with the largest of these cities, Rome. The key question is just how big was it? Fortunately, Rome is the only city from the Roman Mediterranean for which we can make a reasonable estimate of its population. This is in part because we have a cluster of data from the dictatorship of Caesar and reign of Augustus relating to the corn dole and gifts to the *plebs romana*. Suetonius (*Julius Caesar*, 41) tells us that Julius Caesar was faced with funding a dole which had 320,000 recipients. He introduced a house-to-house survey of the city and reduced the number in receipt of the dole to 150,000. From this, we can deduce that those receiving the dole needed to be resident within the city. Augustus, *Res Gestae Divi Augusti*, 15 lists gifts to the Roman plebs as set out in Table 12.4. The gifts are likely to include adult male citizens and perhaps only one per household in the case of the corn dole after Caesar. We need to multiply up for women and children. For the purposes of calculation, I use a multiplier of 4 for the corn dole (one male per household) and 3.2 for the other figures (all males).

The figures suggest that under Augustus there were 200,000 males in receipt of the dole, up from the Caesarian 150,000, but that there was a longer list of 250,000 + males registered in the city. It may be that some people who were not resident in the city somehow managed to insert themselves on these lists and it may also be that Rome was a disproportionately male society since it would be men primarily who travelled to the city for work. Nevertheless, these figures suggest a free resident population of 800,000 to 1,000,000 to which we need to add a population of slaves and resident foreigners, possibly

Table 12.4 Distributions to the Roman plebs and population estimates for the City of Rome

Source	Date	Recipients by type	Recipients by number	Population estimate
Suetonius, *Julius Caesar*, 41	Before c. 46 BC	Plebs in receipt of the corn	320,000	1,024.000
Suetonius, *Julius Caesar*, 41	After c. 46 BC	Plebs in receipt of the corn	150,000	600,000
Res Gestae, 15	44 BC	Gift to plebs of 300 *sesterces*	250,000 +	800,000 +
Res Gestae, 15	29 BC	Gift to plebs of 400 *sesterces*	250,000 +	800,000 +
Res Gestae, 15	23 BC	Rations to plebs	250,000 +	800,000 +
Res Gestae, 15	11 BC	Gift of 400 *sesterces* to plebs	250,000 +	800,000 +
Res Gestae, 15	5 BC	Gift of 240 *sesterces* to plebs	320,000	1,024.000
Res Gestae, 15	2 BC	Gift of 240 *sesterces* to plebs in receipt of the corn	200,000	800,000

of short-term residents and, from the time of Tiberius onwards, significant numbers of soldiers. It is difficult to believe that the population of Rome was less than 1,000,000 and it may have been significantly higher.

We are used to mega-cities, but the size of Rome is extraordinary, especially given the technological limitations. Rome had no railways to bring in goods. It had no mechanised transport. It did not even have bicycles. Its population walked to work and to market and for that reason the city (like most large pre-industrial cities) needed to be densely packed. In the Modern world, London, the biggest city in the world at that time, did not reach 1,000,000 inhabitants until after 1801. For Paris, the 1,000,000 mark was not reached until 1846. New York was getting close to this figure by 1870, but Philadelphia, the second city of the US, was still below 700,000. If Rome's population all lived within the city, which Caesar's survey would suggest, then population densities must have been very high and certainly higher than nineteenth-century London and Paris. Technologies did not, of course, allow the very high densities that can be achieved in some contemporary cities, but densities must have been similar to those in established but poor urban centres of the developing world. If these figures are accurate, life in Rome for the not wealthy would have been very crowded and very difficult.

Most of that population must have needed to work. If we assume that much of the labour of the great houses was conducted by slaves and freedmen, then the free population must have found work in commercial ventures, especially building and manufacture. An olive press required 88 separate pieces of equipment, all of which needed to be purchased or assembled (Cato, *de Agri Cultura*, 10). There were at least 160 different trades practised by free men in Rome.[2] Street and place names suggest concentrations of workers. There were lamp manufacturers in the Vatican district and bronze workers in Trastaverto. Dockyards, shipwrights, and warehouses were located along the Tiber. Butchers and cloth-workers worked out of the Forum itself, at least until they were replaced by silversmiths.[3] Careful reconstruction of the techniques necessary for Roman building suggests that somewhere between 10% and 18% of the male population may have been engaged in building work.[4] Cloth production, the weaving, dying, and fulling (cleaning and whitening) of cloth, were labour-intensive and have left considerable traces in the form of large vats across Classical urban landscapes.[5]

What was true for Rome might not have been true for the other cities of the Roman Empire. Yet, one of the most striking features of the main streets of Pompeii (Via dell' Abbondanza, for example) is the sheer number of workshops and retail facilities. Pompeii was full of bars and if one looks at the smaller houses of Pompeii, the absence of cooking facilities might explain the need for so many food-outlets. Ostia too had many workshops/shops. Bakeries and fulleries are also obvious within the urban landscape. The forum area at Pompeii was also certainly a marketing area. If one goes further afield, the huge and ornate Roman period forum at Thessaloniki was lined with large numbers of shops. The uncovered remains of Roman Corinth also show large numbers of shops along the main street and one presumes that there are many others under the fields. Alexandria was also a centre of trade and manufacturing which impressed visitors. Ephesus clearly had a dynamic manufacturing centre and the silver smiths who took against the teachings of Paul were sufficient in number to start a riot (Acts, 19: 23–41). Archaeologists working in the Mediterranean have traditionally not been very interested in retail facilities, looking for the great public buildings, temples and grand houses, but many cities were economically dynamic centres of trade and production.

Cities spread across the Roman world. One of the more notable features of Roman archaeology is the presence of cities. In Britain, there were, of course, urban centres where there had been no cities before and the same could be said of other parts of the North-West frontier. Gaul, which had been partially urbanised before the Roman conquest, developed a network of urban centres. Africa saw extensive urban growth as great cities emerged along the Mediterranean coast especially. In areas more urbanised before Roman conquest, cities often appear to have grown. Certainly many cities had expensive new buildings during the Roman period and the areas in occupation often increased. In Asia Minor existing cities, such as Aphrodisias, appear to have been wealthy and important centres. In Egypt, the small cities of the countryside appear to have been significant centres of population with 10,000 to 30,000 inhabitants and the city of Alexandria must have many times larger.

Quantification remains difficult. The levels of urbanisation in Italy, if we count in Rome, must have been historically very high. Similarly, in Egypt, where we can generate better guesses, levels of urbanisation may have been historically unusual at about 25% or more. The less developed provinces of the North and West were probably not so urbanised. It would seem possible that a higher percentage of the European and Mediterranean population lived in cities than at any time before the industrial revolution.

Not only was the growth of cities without precedent, but at the end of the Roman period many of these cities had disappeared and were never to return. For every London, where there was continuity of settlement of a sort, there is a Wroxeter or a Silchester. For every Alexandria, there is a Hermopolis Magna or an Antinoopolis; cities long gone. Cities such as Damascus survived, but other sites, such as Petra and Jerash, shrank away.

It is difficult to believe that the developments we see in the both rural and urban economies in Italy and in the provinces do not reflect real economic growth over an extended period. The cities are larger and adorned with great structures. There are far more of them. In the villages and villas, we see evidence for high-quality buildings and even some levels of luxury. Even in small houses, we sometimes find mosaics. The villages of the East, not obviously centres of elite residence, did often have some public buildings: temples in the older times, churches later. Coins are found on many rural sites and although we take coins as being part of everyday life, in much of the territory of the Roman Empire for much of its history, coinage was rare and probably concentrated in the hands of the town-dwellers and the rich. Other items travelled in the Roman Empire. *Amphorae* criss-crossed the Mediterranean carrying oil and wine and fish sauce. Roman pottery in the first century BC and first AD and later African pottery found its way onto huge numbers of sites all across the Empire. Yet, there is no obvious reason why such volumes of goods should have moved. In most regions of the Mediterranean, the same food stuffs and crops were grown. In Athens, there should have been no reason to buy African oil since oil could be made on local Athenian estates. There was long-distance trade but short-distance trade, say within a province, was almost certainly much more intensive.

All this evidence points to economic change. The Mediterranean economy became more integrated and more sophisticated and almost certainly more productive. The change in the newly-conquered provinces may have sometimes been quite rapid, but elsewhere, where economies were already more developed, change was slow. Our economies have in recent decades tended to grow at rates greater than 2% per *annum* and we expect a doubling of the size of the economy within a generation. If the Roman economy grew at just 0.66% per year, it would have doubled in size over a century.

Change theories

The pattern of urban development in the Roman world is the most obvious archaeological evidence to suggest economic growth. That growth requires explanation, particularly as it does not seem to be specific to particular regions of the Empire. One possibility is to examine the role of the state and this approach was taken in a very influential article by Keith Hopkins 'Taxes and Trade in the Roman Empire (200 B.C.–A.D. 400)', *Journal of Roman Studies* 70 (1980), 101–25. The argument was beautifully simple. One of the key areas in which the Roman state intersected with the provincials was through tax. The imposition of tax was an extra charge on the agricultural population. To meet that charge farmers needed to find more money and thus probably increased productivity. They therefore had to engage in market production. This allowed the growth of markets, forced innovation, increased specialisation, and led to economic growth. The state spent most of its money on soldiers. Soldiers spent their money in the under-developed frontier provinces where there was most need for market development. The cash thus worked to stimulate the most under-developed regions and further encouraged economic growth. There is a neatness to these ideas and it is made more neat by the fact that the majority of new coinage minted in the Empire appears to find its way to the various forts on the Empire's fringes.

There are, however, problems with the model. Outside North and West Europe, many of the economies were already quite sophisticated before the Romans came along. Further, many of the central areas of the Empire must have rarely seen a soldier, and yet these areas also show signs of growth. Secondly, although much new coin ended up with the soldiers, it looks very much as if governmental expenditure was not concentrated in the remote fringes of the Empire. The oil and wine the soldiers needed was not grown in Northern Britain, but in Gaul and Spain. Finally, one must wonder whether the state was actually large enough to influence the economy in any significant way.

My theory is rather different and actually much more difficult to establish. The keys to Roman growth are, I think, twofold. First, the Romans encouraged urbanisation by establishing certain administrative and political structures. It seems likely that the types of virtuous developments that I outlined in the first section of this chapter would have applied in the Roman Empire, provided that the cities were able to concentrate population. Second, we need to make some allowance for the Roman peace. The majority of Rome's Empire was peaceful for the majority of the time. Although far from an ideal world, that peace allowed the development of trade infrastructures and encouraged confidence in the population. Stable markets and political conditions encouraged investment and allowed returns to be made on those investments. The diffusion of technology such as mills and presses allowed the more efficient and profitable processing of food. In some areas, irrigation systems were improved. Fields were cleared and brought into production. In the most difficult of terrains, where grains were not easily grown, trees could still produce nuts and olives and if a farmer was confident of selling his product, it became worth the investment.

All those Mediterranean terraces that one sees in the Greek and Italian countryside, undatable mostly, are the product of hours of painful work, carrying stones and digging earth, persuading the donkey up the hillside. The ingenuity and labour of the farmer can, over generations, transform a landscape. If there are the incentives for long-term investment and the rewards, people will work. It is the peasants and the small-farmers who would find this investment of effort most worthwhile. In some areas, North Africa in particular, there may have been regions in which the major investment of capital would bring areas into productivity and the investors would see a fairly immediate return, but in other areas, it was probably smaller investments of money and labour that led to economic growth.

The implication is that the glory that was Rome came not from the culture of the rich and from the elites about which we hear so much, but the lower classes and their work and investments.

Notes

1 W.V. Harris, 'Poverty and destitution in the Roman Empire', in W.V. Harris, *Rome's Imperial Economy: Twelve Essays* (Oxford: Oxford University Press, 2011), pp. 27–54.
2 S. Treggiari, 'Urban labour in Rome: Mercenarii and Tabernarii', in P. Garnsey (ed.) *Non-Slave Labour in the Greco-Roman World* (*Cambridge Philological Society,* Suppl. 6) (Cambridge, 1980), pp. 48–64. See also S. R. Joshel, *Work, Identity, and Legal Status at Rome: A study of occupational inscriptions* (Norman, 1992).
3 J.-P. Morel, 'La topographie de l'artisanat et du commerce dans la Rome antique', in *L'Urbs: Esapce urbain et histoire (Ier siècle ap. J.-C.)* (Collection d'École Française de Rome, 98) (Rome, 1987), pp. 127–55.
4 J. DeLaine, 'Bricks and mortar: exploring the economics of building techniques at Rome and Ostia' in D. J. Mattingly and J. Salmon (eds.), *Economies beyond agriculture in the Classical World* (Leicester–Nottingham Studies in Ancient Society) (London, 2000), pp. 271–96. See J. DeLaine, *The Baths of Caracalla: A study in the design, construction, and economics of large-scale building projects in imperial Rome* (*Journal of Roman Archaeology*, Suppl. 25) (Portsmouth, RI, 1997), 201.
5 See A. Wilson, 'Urban Production in the Roman World: The View from North Africa', *Papers of the British School at Rome*, 70 (2002), 231–273, for a discussion of cloth production.

Chapter 13

Administration and government

Introduction and problems

This chapter considers the working of the various political institutions of the Roman Empire. We shall examine not just the administrative structures that were in place, as far as they can be discerned, but also how such structures were used by political leaders. The administrative system was a mechanism by which power was exercised and transmitted. The authority at the centre of the system was, inevitably, the emperor and it is with the emperor that we start our study. Before looking at administrative structures, we shall examine the problems the Roman administration faced, the resources available, and the nature of Roman imperial administration.

The size of the Roman Empire affected governmental systems. Telecommunications and modern methods of transport have reduced the importance of distance in the modern world, but for Roman administrators, distance was a major limitation. We can illustrate some of the problems by considering the revolt in Judaea. The revolt broke out in Jerusalem in the early summer of AD 66 and a message was sent from the city to the Roman authorities in Syria. The governor of Syria (Cestius Gallus) then needed to discuss his course of action with his friends, mobilise his troops, and march on Jerusalem. Mobilisation probably presented few problems and those troops posted to parts distant from the legionary camp could be quickly recalled or expected to meet the army on the march. Defeat followed in October 66 and Cestius retreated in some disarray. A report then had to be composed and sent to the emperor. Cestius probably wrote this report carefully: it was unusual for a Roman army to lose and Cestius would have been anxious not to be blamed.

The report was put on a boat and sailed to Greece, where Nero was at the time. Nero then had to decide what to do. He had many of the leading figures of the imperial court with him and so he could get advice quickly. The court needed to gather information. They appointed Vespasian to command the army, perhaps because he was in Greece with Nero and thus available. They then had to find him an army and recruit the senior officers for that army. Instructions were sent to the various other governors who were to provide

Vespasian with troops and a location had to be set for the army to gather. Once the letters from Nero had arrived, the various local governors had to consult with the commanders of the legions. They may have had to recruit extra troops. They needed to gather supplies and equipment and organise transport for the journey. The soldiers then had to be marched or shipped off to Syria. In Syria, the authorities must have been busy. They had to prepare for the war by gathering men and materials. Donkeys and horses would have to be found. Carts were requisitioned or even built. Preparations needed to be made in case of sieges. The logistics of supplying a major army in hostile territory needed to be considered.

Once all this was done, the army could set out. It was only in the summer of AD 67, a year after the outbreak of the rebellion, that Vespasian was able to make inroads into rebel territory, more than a year after the outbreak of the revolt. Soon, news filtered through as to the fate threatening Nero, and the campaign was put on hold.

The distances involved and the technology of transport and communications meant that the Roman Empire was something of a giant dinosaur: large, powerful, but slow-moving. The Romans relied on the fact that eventually they would win. Campaigns were not time-sensitive.

The emperor delegated considerable authority to his governors, perhaps partly as a result of the difficulties in managing remote territories, but also because this was central to the Roman conception of power. Governors exercised a personal and, in law, an almost unlimited authority in the provinces. They were holders of *imperium* and whereas *imperium* was limited by the rights of citizens in Rome, there was no such limitation in the provinces. Governors were mostly self-governing and not under direct imperial supervision.

This level of delegation reduced the need for a central bureaucracy. Most modern states have extensive bureaucratic structures and the buildings which house these bureaucrats are often visible parts of the topography of the capital city. There was, however, no Whitehall equivalent in Rome. There was central administration, as we shall see, and there must have been extensive archives, but the administration based in the city of Rome was very small given the size of Rome's Empire. This was almost empire without administration.

The power of the emperor and of the governors was limited by practical considerations and by the relative lack of administrative structures. The governor could not be everywhere at once and, although he had aides, the communities of the provinces were only subjected to occasional visitations. Yet, governors and emperors did exercise power. They did so partly through the legal system. Roman magistrates were nearly always also judges and conflicts in local communities would often escalate until the various parties appeared before the governor's court. Petitions worked their way through the judicial system and could eventually make their way to Rome. Such information flows could enable the governor to intervene.

The style of Roman government was personal. The emperor and the governors communicated directly to their people and much of the language of this communication was set in terms of personal relations: friendships rather than hierarchies. Decisions were granted as personal favours by the authorities and seem to have been treated as such by the favoured. This was a traditional aristocratic method of government, but had also to negotiate laws, edicts, and imperial pronouncements that provided a framework for governmental action.

The emperor

The emperor was the supreme authority in the Roman state. His main legal powers consisted of consular *imperium* (power) which gave him authority in Italy and Rome, *imperium maius* which gave him power greater than that of all the other governors, *tribunicia potestas* which gave him authority to intervene in legal cases and technically gave him a veto over all other magistrates, and proconsular *imperium* which gave him authority over a large number of those provinces which had significant military garrisons. Since he also enjoyed exemption from the laws, the emperor's authority was absolute.

The emperor delegated his authority to senators, equestrians, and members of his family and personal staff. All to whom authority was given could be seen as part of the administration, whether they held formal office or not. At the centre of this administrative system was the imperial household.

The women of the imperial family did not hold political office, but they helped manage imperial relations with groups in the elite. Emperors also relied on male family members and close friends, people such as L. Vitellius who was close to Gaius and Claudius. The emperor had a *consilium* (a body of advisers) with whom he would consult. Augustus established an official *consilium principis* with family members, friends, senators and the consuls, but it is likely that most emperors also had around them a less formally constituted group of friends who provided advice.

In addition to his friends and family, the emperor also relied on his freedmen. The major freedmen offices were the *ab epistulis* (who dealt with correspondence), *a rationibus* (keeper of the accounts), *a libellis* (who dealt with petitions) and the *a studiis* (whose role is not entirely clear). These officials rose to prominence under Claudius (see pp. 151–52 and 169–70), but were influential from the very beginnings of the Principate. They ran the 'imperial office'. Naturally, when the succession was dynastic, the new emperor inherited his predecessor's freedmen and tended to leave them in positions of authority. This continuity seems also to have been a feature of non-dynastic succession. The Flavians inherited some Neronian freedmen. The freedmen could thus serve a series of emperors.

The management of the imperial household seems to have been based on the methods adopted by other members of the elite to run their households though, obviously, the number of those involved, the division of duties, and the amount of work undertaken were rather different. Most members of the elite will have had a small group of family members (including freedmen) and friends who provided advice and help. Prior to the Imperial period, Roman magistrates had used their households to run their governmental business. The extension of household administration to the administration of the empire was a natural progression. Initially, no member of the elite would have thought of serving in the household of another, since this was tantamount to accepting servile status. But the situation gradually changed and the Flavians began employing equestrians in household administrative positions.

Many emperors continued to operate as if they were ordinary senators. Early each morning, at the *salutatio*, every important Roman received his friends at his house. They would crowd into the *atrium* (hall) to greet him and his family and put themselves at his service. It was a time when they could also present him with requests. The emperor, too, greeted his friends and clients at the morning *salutatio*. Much political business was conducted through a network of 'friendships' and thus accessibility and affability were highly desirable attributes. The informality of such contacts allowed transgression of normal social and political structures: imperial wives and freedmen would also be present on occasions such as the *salutatio*.

This personal and somewhat informal governmental style extended beyond the management of the Roman aristocracy. Provincial communities were often in contact with emperors and frequently stressed pre-existing ties of friendship between the emperor or members of his family and the particular community. Cities also emphasised the importance of individual citizens who had been particularly favoured by the emperor. Such communities sent petitions and embassies to ask for specific favours, but also sent greetings on the imperial birthday and congratulations on special occasions.

It was not just communities which could reach the emperor, but individuals could also deliver petitions. It is likely that this was considerably more difficult for provincials than Romans since they had to travel from the province and may have required permission to do so. The *Digest*, a sixth-century collection of legal rulings, contains many summary responses to legal problems that had been presented to the emperor. These rescripts appear to have been in response to petitions presented by members of most social groups.

The emperor was bombarded with written and oral requests and government seems to have consisted largely in responding to these problems. The emperor often responded by granting favours, and these established a personal relationship of mutual friendship between the emperor and the beneficiary. The emperor had powers to intervene in legal cases and also financial authority which would enable him to respond to specific requests. In addition, the emperor had in his direct gift most of the important appointments in the Empire. His legates (representatives) governed the military provinces, and he also influenced appointments to other provinces and to the magistracies in Rome. Patronage brought the emperor power.

The face-to-face nature of much of this exercise of patronage minimised bureaucracy.

This household administration, however, was based on an illusion. Everyone recognised the fact that the emperor's power was far greater than that of a senator. Everyone wished to be a friend of the emperor and the withdrawal of imperial friendship meant the end of an official career, exile, and possibly death. At the morning *salutatio*, it seems that all available senators would gather to greet the emperor.

Since the emperor was a friend to all senators (almost by definition) favours had to be granted to all groups. Monopolisation of favours by a particular group in the senate was likely to lead to senatorial discontent. In order to avoid open conflict or a breach with a section of the senate, favours needed to be distributed to a wide range of people, which explains why seemingly hostile senators received magisterial posts under Domitian (see pp. 245–51).

It is likely that various gradings were introduced into the *salutatio* by Claudius so that the important would join him first and the lesser grades be admitted later. Vespasian operated a similar system (though perhaps less formally) whereby his close friends would meet him in his bedchamber and he would meet the rest presumably in the *atrium*. Yet, this was still probably a ceremonial occasion. To avoid causing offence, Claudius probably decided who was going to be in the first wave of visitors by rank and not by political loyalty. Since it was quite evident under most emperors that not everyone was really a friend of the emperor, the *salutatio* ceased to have real political meaning. The ceremonial nature of much of this activity must have transmitted itself to all concerned and thus senators would have been aware that even if they received favours they might have been regarded with suspicion or hostility. To be excluded from ceremonial events meant that one was an enemy (see p. 200 for exclusions from imperial friendship). Tacitus stresses the hypocrisy of all involved and the formality of the processes eroded the seeming informality of the social custom.

This process of formalisation can be seen elsewhere. Imperial communications with provincial communities became increasingly formalised. The worship of deified emperors provided an opportunity for gestures of loyalty on the part of local elites and these gestures were communicated to the reigning emperor through embassies. Many speeches were made in praise of the emperor or Rome or both. It mattered little who was on the throne: the gesture was important and the words themselves were devoid of meaning.

One of the incidental benefits of the imperial position was that the emperor accumulated vast wealth. Formally, this money was held separately from the state finances. It is evident from the vast amounts of money that Augustus donated to the state from his private resources that the emperor was extremely wealthy and, although there were considerable drains on the private finances of the emperor, gifts, and testamentary bequests as well as the wealth that flowed in from judicious land investments boosted the private finances. It was these funds that were presumably supervised by the *a rationibus* (freedman in charge of accounts).

State finances were supervised by senators and, theoretically, were separate from those of the emperor. The financial boundaries, however, quickly became blurred with the emperor taking control over land confiscated because of legal penalties, land which had no legal owner, and mines and quarries. The mechanism behind this process is unclear, but it may have taken place more rapidly in the provinces than in Italy. Imperial freedmen were employed to supervise imperial assets in the provinces, but these procurators are also found dealing with non-imperial finances and the use of equestrian procurators, presumably initially to manage state assets, further confuses the situation. The result, however, is clear: the finances of government (both state and imperial) were effectively controlled by the emperor.

The process of 'formalisation' and transformation of a household administration into a state bureaucracy was slow and was certainly not completed by the end of the first century. One sign of the transformation was the appointment of equestrians to the major household offices. These offices had come to be considered offices of state, not offices of the emperor's household.

The senate and senators

Major reforms of the senate were introduced by Augustus. The number of senators was reduced, the required property level for enrolment was increased and a series of minor administrative posts were created in a reform of the senatorial career structure. Most senators appear to have had a regular career. They served first in a series of very minor posts (collectively called the *vigintivirate*) which involved supervision of the mint, supervision of public executions and some minor judicial duties. From there, they progressed to a military tribunate. There were normally six tribunes to a legion, one of whom was of potential senatorial status. Election to one of the 20 quaestorships followed and this brought membership of the senate. The next stage was either to become one of the ten tribunes or one of the six aediles. Members of patrician families (a higher status group within the senate) were excused this stage on the career ladder. The next stage was a praetorship. Under Tiberius, there were 12 praetors recruited from the 16 lesser posts, and so there would be some competition for office, but the number edged upwards until 18 praetors were often appointed in the Flavian period.

The consulships underwent similar inflation. Initially under Augustus there were only two consuls per year, as had been the case under the Republic, with the consuls entering on the 1st January. After Augustus resigned the consulship in 23 BC, the number of consuls was increased so that there were four consuls per year, two *ordinarii* who held office from 1st January and after whom the year was named, and two *suffecti* who took over for the second half of the year. The *ordinarii* (ordinary) consulships were the most prestigious.

This number was again increased by the Flavians so that there were between six and ten consuls per year (two of whom were ordinary). The Flavians tended to restrict ordinary consulships to family members and very close associates.

Once a man entered the senate by becoming quaestor, progression was almost automatic. The consulship seems to have been the only post for which competition would have been particularly fierce, and with the multiplication of consulships in the Flavian period, even there competition diminished. In addition to the Republican offices, Augustus introduced a whole range of new administrative positions which the senators would fulfil in between magisterial office (see Table 13.1). These ranged in type from financial offices, to caring for the grain supply, the roads, or the banks of the Tiber. Additionally, senators would often seek military experience and may well have accompanied friends to provincial postings to add support.

The role of the senate was changed by the advent of imperial power. The emperor's powers were so great that senators could not question his authority. Some have concluded that the senate was powerless and had become a shadow of its Republican precursor, but the senate was sufficiently useful that no emperor seems to have seriously contemplated closing it. The senate's power had always rested on its personnel. This did not change in the Imperial period. Most of the senior figures in the state sat in the senate. Most of the governors of the provinces, and hence the commanders of the army, were also senators. The senate contained some of the most powerful men in the empire. The emperor needed to conciliate the senate or face down those who might support its rights.

In law, the senate's status was actually improved in the Imperial period since the decrees it passed, which had before been merely advisory, were given the force of law by Tiberius. In addition, the senate started to exercise more

Table 13.1 The new administrative posts

Title	Function
Praefecti frumenti dandi	Distribution of the corn supply
Curatores viarum	Care of roads
Curatores aquarum	Care of the water supply
Curatores riparum et alvei Tiberis	Care of the banks and bed of the Tiber
Curatores locorum publicorum iudicandorum	Care of court buildings
Curatores tabularum publicarum	Care of public registers
Curatores aedium sacrarum et operum locorumque publicorum	Care of sacred temples and public works
Praefecti aerarii Saturni	Prefects of the state treasury
Legatus legionis	Commander of a legion (normally a former praetor)
Praefectus urbi	Prefect in charge of urban administration (a post held by a senior senator)

control over its membership. Popular election in some form or other continued into the late Augustan period. After this, the popular assemblies still met, but it seems probable that the senate only allowed the nomination of as many candidates as there were posts so that there was no competition and no decision for the assemblies to make.

Yet, the senate clearly lost prestige. From the Augustan period onwards, there is evidence that some men refused to embark on or withdrew from senatorial careers. People could exercise political authority without being senators and some senators probably felt that they had no political power. Augustus failed in his attempt to create a self-perpetuating oligarchic group in which father would follow son into the senate. In the period up to AD 54, only just over half of all consuls (54%) had a consular father, grandfather or great-grandfather. In the Flavian period, this figure fell to just under a quarter (24%). This compares with a Republican figure of 62%. The period also sees the gradual incorporation of men of provincial origin into the senate. Claudius supported the introduction of men from Gallia Comata into the senate and may have been encouraging men from other areas as well. Trajan himself was of Spanish origin and Flavian interest in Spain may have enabled significant numbers of Spaniards to rise in the senate. Men from the East and Africa also achieved senatorial status. By Trajan's reign, about a third of the senators were of provincial origin.

The effect of these changes is difficult to establish. Tacitus noted a change in membership in the Flavian period, and it seems possible that this brought a change in attitude towards the role of the senate and its relationship to the emperor. From the reign of Augustus onwards, we start to find funerary and honorary inscriptions for senators. The senators normally list their various offices in order. Prestige appears to depend not on birth but on office holding and access to offices was controlled by the emperor. The emperor controlled the careers of senators and it seems likely that this factor encouraged senators to conform and to tow the line. Although we see some senators acting in opposition in the Imperial period, it seems likely that the majority of senators had a strong interest in keeping the favour of the emperor and made every effort to do so. The senate slowly became a tool of government and even as early as the reign of Tiberius, was dominated by the emperor.

Equestrians

Another of the innovations of Augustan government was the integration of equestrians into the administrative structure. This was later to lead to the development of an equestrian career pattern. Most of our information concerning the equestrian career pattern dates to later periods. In the pre-Claudian period, there were irregularities in careers, and assessing them is made more complex by the fact that careers are sometimes listed in reverse chronological order, but a standard pattern is given in Table 13.2 as is the reformed Claudian structure (Suetonius, *Claudius*, 25).

Table 13.2 Equestrian career structure

Pre-Claudian career	Post-Claudian career
Centurion	Centurion
Military Tribune	Praefectus Cohortis
Praefectus Equitum	Praefectus Equitum/Alae
Praefectus Fabrum	Military Tribune
Procuratorships	Procuratorships
Great Prefectures	Great Prefectures

There were variations. In the early period, there were other offices, such as prefectures of cohorts and veterans. The post of *praefectus fabrum* (probably a staff-officer) could be held at various points in a career. In the post-Claudian period, equestrians sometimes served a fourth military prefecture as prefect of a double strength cavalry unit. In both periods, many did not enter the career structure through the centurionate and most combined a Roman equestrian career with holding several magistracies in their own communities. There appears to have been a hierarchy in procuratorships in the second century, but it is unclear when this developed. Clearly some procuratorial tasks were more important than others. Procurators collected taxes, supervised state assets, supported provincial governors, and some governed the smaller provinces. No clear distinction can be seen between equestrian and freedmen procurators. The great prefectures were those of the praetorian guard, the *vigiles* (watch), the urban cohorts, the corn supply and of Egypt. Two praetorian prefects normally held office jointly. Since these men were responsible for the security of the emperor and of Rome, the post was given to the most trusted.

Equestrian careers show a certain irregularity. People could jump posts. The mechanism for promotion is uncertain but, if we take the evidence of Pliny's letters, recommendation appears to have played an important part. The fact that some managed to combine their equestrian careers with an active role in their local communities suggests that there were periods, probably quite long ones, when these men were without an equestrian posting; thus it would appear that people did not move smoothly from posting to posting.

The equestrians were clearly an important arm of the administration, though the irregularity of the procuratorial office means that any estimate of the number of equestrians employed at any one time would be little more than a guess.

Provinces

The provinces can be divided into two basic types: those ruled directly by the emperor and those whose governors were appointed (in theory) by the senate. Apart from the titles of the governors, it is unclear whether this made any difference to the governing of the province. Imperial provinces were mostly governed by legates, either of consular or praetorian status. Some provinces were governed by equestrians, but most of these (with the exception of Egypt) were comparatively unimportant and had only small military garrisons. There was a vague hierarchy of provinces, normally based on the size of the garrison. The two Germanies and Syria appear to have been the most important provinces. The senatorial provinces were governed by proconsuls or propraetors. After the reign of Gaius, none of these provinces had any significant military garrison. The most prestigious postings were Africa and Asia.

The governor exercised supreme authority within the province. He was at once the senior financial, judicial and military officer and would probably be active in all these areas. The governors seem to have had a limited staff of advisers who were either appointed separately or chosen by them. Some provinces had a legal officer. There would also be officers dealing with financial matters and military officers, depending on the nature of the garrison of the province. There may also have been a number of other equestrian officials. In Egypt, for instance, where the administration is very well attested, large regions were supervised by equestrian officers known as *epistrategoi*. Prefects were appointed to supervise regions in other provinces. A senior centurion (almost the equivalent in status to an equestrian procurator) sparked a revolt among a German tribe through too harsh an interpretation of a tax (Tacitus, *Annales*, 4.72), and Pliny heaps praise on a prefect of the Pontic shore for the efficiency with which he administered his district (Pliny, *Epistles*, 10.86). There appears to have been some flexibility in the way in which procurators were used.

There would also be an indeterminate number of imperial freedmen dealing with taxation and the management of imperial property, and the governor may have brought with him a number of *amici* to whom he could turn for help, though the evidence for such groups is much better for the Republican period. In a province in which there was a large garrison, the governor could turn to his senior military officers for administrative support, and even in comparatively lightly garrisoned provinces there was normally a small number of troops at the governor's disposal who could be used to carry out administrative tasks.

The governor could, however, turn to local resources. The evidence from Pliny's letters from Bithynia (the most extensive archive concerning the activities of a governor) suggests that Pliny had some records at his disposal in the province, but not a complete archive of imperial documentation (Pliny, *Epistles*, 10. 56; 57; 58; 79; 108; 112; 114). Some of his material may have been found in local archives and petitioners presented copies of edicts which affected them, but it seems likely that there was a central archive.

Local authorities were important to the successful administration of the province. In all the provinces, the Romans encouraged cities to take an active administrative role. In some places, of course, cities simply continued to operate in ways similar to those which they had been employing for centuries. In others, the development of a city-based administrative system was innovative. Cities tended to be governed by councils of varying size composed of decurions, normally members of the landed elite, and the magistrates of the cities were drawn from this council. There seem to have been variations in the way that these urban centres related to surrounding communities. In some cases, the surrounding communities may have been largely independent of the urban authorities and were administered by a combination of officials imposed by the Roman authorities and members of the local communities conscripted into performing public offices. In other cases, the administration of the surrounding territory may have been the responsibility of the urban community and tax collectors and other officials were sent out from the city.

The constitutions of these cities also varied. We know that some cities were 'free', meaning that the governor had little or no legal authority over the communities, though it is likely that these communities were often forced to accept the *de facto* authority of the emperor's representative. Other cities may have had very little freedom of action. Several inscriptions have been discovered in Spain which contain fragments of the constitutions of various communities. The Flavians appear to have extended municipal status to several Spanish towns. As part of this grant, the towns were given new constitutions which were probably all adapted from a single source, possibly an Augustan that which established the framework for such constitutions. This law not only established the procedures for the internal administration of the city and the formation of the council, but also limited the powers of local magistrates. Serious legal cases were referred to the governor. It was an option, in any case, for those who fell within the remit of the council's authority to appeal to the governor, though he could refuse to hear the case or pass it down to a minor official.

Governors exercised their authority by touring the province and during their visits to the various cities they would receive petitions and hear legal cases. They would thus be closely involved in the administration of a particular community. The governor's representatives could also visit a community and would be expected to report back to the governor on any disturbing activity. The numbers of officials stationed in local communities cannot be established, but we have ample evidence for the use of centurions in this kind of supervisory role. The stationing of Roman representatives in local communities provided the governor with a valuable source of information and these men could also act as representatives of Roman authority in times of disturbance.

In addition to formal contacts with local communities, the governor probably received many less formal contacts. The visit of a governor was an important occasion and the elite of a community set out to impress. The council and people would meet the governor before he entered the city and escort him within. His visit may often have coincided with festivities. He would be welcomed and entertained by the elite and it is reasonable to expect that those who set out to befriend would, on occasion, succeed. The hospitality offered by a community created a mutual obligation that could be exploited. Not only could individual members of local elites make representations, but also the masses could probably make their voice heard at the theatre or other gatherings. The crowd could present grievances to an official at games through chants and acclamations. If a community was divided or otherwise troubled, it is very difficult to see how such information could be kept from a visiting governor.

The governor could, therefore, have been kept informed about the various communities in his charge. But was he able to do anything? It is probable that the ability of the governor to act varied from province to province. The virtual absence of the governor from the events depicted in Apuleius' novel, *The Golden Ass*, have been taken as reflecting a situation in which local authorities were largely left alone and Rome had very little administrative control. This fictional representation can, however, be compared with other evidence which shows the imperial administration at work.

We shall examine the workings of the administration in two areas: population registration and the suppression of banditry.

Population registration

The Romans introduced poll taxes into several provinces of the empire. They therefore needed a list of the taxable population. This list was drawn up by holding a census of the population. Our information on the workings of the system comes mainly from the Egyptian census, though, of course, the most famous census is described in Luke 2.1–5. All members of and property belonging to each household in Roman Egypt were registered. The names, relationships and ages of the household members were listed. This list was probably used to either draw up or amend the poll tax register. In addition, the register needed to take account of those who died or left the area, of change in residence (so that the tax collector could find the individuals involved), and of the status of the individuals, since rates of tax varied according to legal status. The tax collector would be armed with a list of those eligible to pay and would then look for those men. In the event of the men having moved away, the tax collector had to discover their location and this involved circulating lists of the disappeared. From time to time, the authorities would crack down on those avoiding the poll tax, seemingly by staging a sweep through the countryside and arresting all who did not have appropriate documentation. The success of the Roman administration is difficult to establish, though the tax continued to be collected into the third century AD, but the ambitious nature of the project is notable. The registration and subsequent monitoring of the entire population was a major task which the Romans thought they could accomplish. The administration of the census may not have been so elaborate in provinces other than Egypt and, indeed, some provinces may not have held a census regularly, but their administrative ambition should tell us something about Roman capabilities.

Banditry

Banditry was a problem throughout the Roman period, though it was a problem that often escaped the notice of our literary sources. We know that there were certain areas that were associated with bandit activity. Judaea, Galilee and the Syrian mountains suffered from such activity. Bandits were active in Sardinia and Corsica, and banditry seems to have been almost endemic in Cilicia. It seems likely that frontier areas were also subjected to bandit threats from Arabic tribes or the Mauretanians or the tribes beyond the Danube. Banditry was a problem that the Romans could not easily solve and in some areas was part of the political culture. Local aristocrats maintained armed gangs to further their interests and since it was these aristocrats that the Romans would expect to act against bandits, official action was unlikely to have much effect. Accepting that banditry could not be completely eliminated, how did the Romans control it? The Romans seem to have devoted considerable time and expense to limiting bandit activities. Watchtowers (*purgoi* or *stationes*) were built to monitor movement. Locals were recruited to guard important points. Soldiers were sent on guard duties to supervise local communities. Larger-scale expeditions were launched against bandits. As with the census, it is less the success that is important rather the ambition the activity attests. The Romans thought that their power was such that they could influence the behaviour of provincials at a local level and prevent them becoming bandits. The Romans seem to have believed that their power should be felt even by small communities.

We should not assume that Roman administration worked in the same way in all the diverse provinces of the Empire. Political, social, cultural and military factors will have influenced the administration of each province. Some provinces may have been virtually devoid of Roman administration. In other provinces, it seems likely that the governor could influence events in quite small communities and would have had considerable information at his disposal in order to make decisions. We should not, of course, compare the level of administration to that of a modern state: ancient states had far more limited aims.

Communication and control

The political imperative for most emperors was retaining control of power and thereby maintaining their personal security. The major threats to the position of the emperor stemmed from the powerful men within the political system: the senators and the governors. The emperor controlled most of the major offices of state and could ensure that his enemies did not reach powerful positions, though there were limits on the effectiveness of this policy (see above). He could avoid giving control of the major legionary garrisons to his enemies. The emperor could also manage the senate. Senators who were thought to be aware of the emperor's views were more closely regarded by their peers and their stated opinions would inevitably gain support in the senate. Since the emperor could chair senatorial debates, he could shape opinion by calling members in a particular order or by showing partiality for a particular view. The emperor could make use of intermediaries (such as the praetorian prefect) for at least some of these tasks.

Another way of controlling the activities of senators was through the use of *delatores* (informers). The extent to which informers were used to spy on the activities of the aristocracy is arguable. '*Delator*' was used as a term of abuse for those who spied on the aristocracy and those who conducted the prosecutions were tarred with the same label. Both Tacitus and Pliny (see pp. 247–49) depict the impact of *delatores* in dramatic terms and if these descriptions were even remotely correct, certain members of the elite were constrained by fear. Of course, almost by definition, the activities of spies are not fully documented. We only hear about the prosecution of the elite and cannot know whether the lower classes were subject to similar attentions. The emperor had several possible groups available for espionage. He could use the military forces stationed in Rome to report what they saw when they wandered the streets. But, in a society which still conducted its business personally, it would seem unlikely that a praetorian could infiltrate the household of a dissident without being recognised or having his background checked. Imperial intelligence relied more on the activities of amateurs, lured by the rewards of a successful prosecution to report on the private activities of the Roman population. It was such amateur espionage that led to the uncovering of the Pisonian conspiracy (see pp. 201–202). The threat to the senator stemmed from his own household, his friends and his neighbours, and from malicious prosecution.

Controlling the activities of senators in the provinces was more difficult. Authority was concentrated in the hands of the governors. To control these men, the emperors needed independent information. This could be provided from two main sources: the Romans with the governor in the province and the provincials themselves. It has often been suggested that procurators were used to check the authority of the provincial governor and could be used effectively since they were directly answerable to the emperor. There is, in fact, very little evidence for this. There were clashes between procurators and governors, as can be seen in Suetonius Paulinus' difficulties after the Boudiccan revolt (see pp. 193–96), but these problems concerned the specific issue of Paulinus' treatment of the defeated rebels and are not evidence of a general hostility between procurators and governors. The few senior Romans in a province probably worked closely together. Also, after service, the procurator would not want to have a powerful or potentially powerful senatorial enemy.

The provincial elites represented a different source of information. Emperors seem to have encouraged a flow of communication between provincial communities and the emperor, some types of which have been outlined above. The ceremonial contacts between emperor and provincials were useful since they provided the emperor with some opportunity to establish friendships with provincials and these provincials could then monitor the activities of the provincial governor. Such informing on the behaviour of the governor could in itself become formalised, as in the decrees passed by provincial councils concerning a governor's term in office (see p. 194 and 199).

The workings of the system can be seen in the fall of Flaccus, the prefect of Egypt (Philo, *In Flaccum*; see pp. 139–40). Philo represents Flaccus responding to his insecure political position by seeking the support of the Alexandrian Greeks and sacrificing the Jewish community to win that support. The thought was, presumably, that the Alexandrian Greeks would send back glowing reports on Flaccus. Flaccus was, however, brought down. The Jewish community had sent a loyal address to the emperor on his accession and this had, apparently, been suppressed by Flaccus. News of this, and probably other aspects of the mistreatment of the Jews, was passed to Gaius by Herod Agrippa. The attack on Flaccus was pressed, however, on rather different grounds by two Alexandrian Greeks whom he had previously expelled. The hostility of provincials combined with a suspicious emperor to bring down a governor.

The governor was also subject to possible prosecution on return to Rome, though prosecutions were complex and difficult. Governors had to be particularly careful when dealing with Roman citizens who could expect some protection under the *lex Iulia de vi publica* and on the whole, governors seem to have been reluctant to take action against Romans in their province and to have preferred the safe course of passing Roman citizens to the emperor for trial.

In a similar way, governors may have wished to pass difficult or potentially controversial administrative problems to the emperor. The majority of the tenth book of Pliny's letters is devoted to the correspondence between Pliny and Trajan concerning various problems that arose during Pliny's governorship. These give an insight into provincial administration and must have meant that the emperor was well informed about developments in the province (especially if we assume that he was also in receipt of considerably more information in the form of official reports). It is possible that the correspondence between Pliny and Trajan was atypical. Trajan had taken a special interest in the appointment because of financial problems in the province resulting from the corruption of previous governors. Pliny himself, though an experienced administrator, was not an experienced governor. Yet, the peculiarities of the appointment and of Pliny's previous experience did not necessarily influence the nature of the correspondence. Pliny felt it necessary to refer for guidance to the emperor on even quite minor matters.

The size of the empire forced emperors to devolve much of their authority to representatives, both in Rome and in the provinces. Imperial power depended on how closely the emperor could control his representatives and how closely his representatives could control those they administered. The key to successful administration was flow of information, and it seems that the diversity of material that flowed through the administrative system would have ensured that governors knew something of what the provincials were doing and that emperors had some independent information concerning the activities of their governors. Acting on that information may have been rather more difficult, but the knowledge that information would filter through the administrative machinery to the emperor was probably sufficient to keep governors and provincials in check.

Chapter 14

The Roman army and military policy

The Augustan army

The army of the third and second century BC was an amateur citizen militia with troops raised on an annual basis from the whole body of Roman citizen men. These troops served for the duration of the campaign (ideally a single year) before returning to their pre-enlistment professions. By the mid-first century AD, this army had been transformed into a professional force with troops serving for 20 or 25 years. Historians have traditionally placed this fundamental change in the nature of Rome's armed forces at the end of the second century BC and have associated this development with the great Republican general Marius. More recently, the extent to which Marius changed the army has been questioned and historians have pointed to continuities between the army of the mid-second century BC and that of Caesar. It seems that far-reaching changes were instituted during the reign of Augustus, who developed the framework for the later army. He established terms and conditions of service, the legal framework which governed the soldiers while in service, the benefits the soldiers received on discharge, the standing units into which the soldiers were recruited, the fiscal system to pay for the troops, the political framework in which the army was to operate, and he developed (though it is unclear quite what is Augustan) the auxiliary system (see below).

Nevertheless, Augustus was not a radical military thinker: only the political situation forced him to institute fundamental changes. After the defeat of Antony and Cleopatra, Augustus had a massive army at his disposal. The question arose as to how that military force was to be organised in the now peaceful empire and how Augustus' military supremacy might be institutionalised. It was decided as part of the political settlement of 28–27 BC that Augustus would be given authority over a huge area of the Empire. This provincial command brought with it the vast majority of the army. Augustus justified this command (which seemed to bring excessive personal power) on the grounds of the military sensitivity of these areas. As the Principate achieved political stability, so military organisation ossified.

Legions which might in theory have been recruited for a single campaign were now stationed in provinces for extended periods on the (spurious) grounds that the military situation remained insecure. The result was the birth of the standing army.

Troops had served abroad for extended periods during the Republic. Previously, such extended service could be treated as an anomaly, but Augustus was forced to face the reality of a professional army and develop the regulatory and administrative infrastructure to deal with its creation. This was a slow process and the imperial system emerged from *ad hoc* developments. The first major series of institutional reforms is dated by Dio to 13 BC (Dio, 54. 25). This was 17 years after the victory over Antony when many of the troops recruited for the Actium campaign would have retired or have been looking to retire. There was a second series of reforms in AD 5 (Dio, 55. 23), 18 years later. It was only in this year that Augustus, against much opposition, set up the *aerarium militare*, a treasury designed to meet the pay (900 *sesterces* per year) and retirement bonuses (12,000 *sesterces*) of the soldiers. The two periods of reform suggest strongly that Augustus did not have a 'masterplan' for the army, but instead reformed the army as and when he hit problems. Unsurprisingly, these problems clustered at moments when large numbers of troops were pressing for discharge.

This treasury was initially funded by direct grant from Augustus, though a new tax was developed for its long-term funding. This system was clearly not working as late as AD 14 when the soldiers of the Rhine and Danube legions revolted over their conditions. Their complaints included the prolongation of service beyond the legal maximum and improper payment of bonuses (see pp. 102–104). Again, these problems would seem likely to reflect the administrative crises that the army faced when significant numbers of their troops reached the point of discharge at the same time. Although the standing army had come into being with the political settlements of 28–27 BC, the administration to cope with this new army was not fully functioning more than 40 years later.

Military organisation

The legions

The legions remained the backbone of the Roman army during the first century AD. Historians, however, disagree about even such fundamental questions as to how many troops there were supposed to be in a legion. A legion consisted of ten cohorts. Each cohort was composed of six centuries of about 80 men. The first cohort could be of double strength. Sometimes a small body of cavalry was attached to the legion. There is some disagreement as to the number of junior officers and whether they were 'supernumerary' to the strength of a century. The theoretical strength of the legion can be estimated at *c.*4,800 to 6,000 men. There is evidence, however, that the size of the legion would vary according to military circumstances. When the legion was preparing for war, more men would be recruited. In peacetime, the legion would be allowed to fall beneath its 'paper' strength.

The legionaries were recruited for 20 years under Augustus, but this seems to have been extended to 25 years, which became the norm for the Imperial period. There was probably a physical examination to ascertain whether the recruit was fit and above a certain height, though the stringency with which the rules were applied is difficult to assess. It seems that most troops were recruited between the ages of 18 and 24 (as one would expect), though there are examples of younger and older recruits. Life expectancy in the Roman world was low and even without seeing action a large proportion of soldiers would have died in service. Although the Roman authorities retained the legal power to conscript, it seems that most of the troops were volunteers.

Legionaries were supposed to be Roman citizens. This rule seems to have been maintained during the Imperial period, but gradually the recruiting officers of the legions ceased to look to Italy for fresh supplies of troops. Legionaries began to be recruited from the provinces. Some of these provincial recruits would have been Roman citizens before recruitment. They were either descended from a previous generation of Roman soldiers who had settled in the province or from Roman settlers who had come to the province for some other reason. Some, however, were probably given citizenship on enlistment and thus the 'Romanity' of the legions was preserved. Slaves and freedmen were not allowed to join the legions.

The senior officers in a legion were drawn from the Roman aristocracy. Legions were commanded by a *legatus*. This man was appointed by the emperor and would normally be of senior senatorial rank. Six tribunes served under the legate. These were recruited from junior senators and from more experienced equestrians. Below this group was the senior centurion, the *primus pilus*. This man was either an equestrian officer starting on his career, or a man who had risen through the ranks. The next rank was the centurion. These officers would be a mixture of equestrians who had joined at centurion level, and those promoted from more junior posts.

The officering of the legion reflected the structure of Roman society. The majority of senior officers were of elite birth. Their social status gave them authority. Their ability to assume senior commands, often at a young age, does not seem to have been questioned. A minority of officers rose through the ranks. We cannot, however, know whether the original social status of those who reached the rank of centurion or above was somehow superior to those others who failed to make the grade. Reaching the rank of centurion or above, or even just becoming a junior officer, may have improved the social status of individuals. The army was, however, only a limited avenue of social mobility and dramatic progress must have been unusual. The limitations on careers can be illustrated by the career of Tiberius Claudius Maximus. This man achieved fame and the notice of the emperor when he killed Decebalus, the Dacian leader (see pp. 266–68). He fought in Parthia and received further decorations for bravery. This was a major military achievement and one might have expected that his rise would be meteoric. He was promoted, but only reached the rank of decurion (see below; Campbell 1994: 32–3). The anomalies of the third century AD, by which men could rise through the ranks to become emperor (if often only briefly), were not a feature of first-century military life.

Auxiliaries and other units

There were various types of auxiliary units. The main two were the *ala* (a cavalry unit of about 500 men) and the cohort (an infantry unit of about 500 men). In addition, there was a mixed cavalry and infantry unit of about 400 infantry and 120 cavalry. There were some double-strength units.

Like the legions, auxiliary units were distinguished by number and name. In many cases, the names of the auxiliary units referred to an ethnic origin. It seems likely that this referred to the place where the unit was originally recruited, though it is possible that in some cases it referred to its first station.

There were Republican precursors to the imperial auxiliary units. For centuries, Rome had recruited her *socii* (allies) to fight alongside the legions. These *socii* were a valuable part of Rome's military effort. Their organisation is unclear, but they were probably raised and largely officered by their native aristocracy. Caesar made extensive use of troops provided by his Gallic allies during the conquest of Gaul, and rival generals accepted help from all quarters during the civil wars. It is only after the reign of Augustus that we can identify auxiliary units of the imperial type, though Augustan units appear to have had a slightly different pattern of nomenclature from the units of the mid-first century and later: units were frequently named after a commanding officer, often a Roman.

It is unclear how many auxiliary units existed under Augustus, but under Tiberius the auxiliary forces were roughly equivalent to the legions in strength. It is likely that their organisation was somewhat irregular in this early period. Some units were probably recruited for specific campaigns and may have been discharged after those campaigns. Allied states were expected to contribute troops to Roman expeditions. Other peoples, such as the Batavians, may have effectively paid their taxes in men (see pp. 224–29) and special units of such troops retained an ethnic identity and solidarity. One may question the extent to which the organisation of such units would have been Romanised. Gradually, a more regular system of nomenclature, pay and rewards, and officering emerged and much was probably in place when Claudius reformed the equestrian career structure (see pp. 340–41).

Much of our information concerning auxiliary units comes from a series of bronze diplomas. These documents attest the grant of citizenship to those leaving auxiliary units after their term of service. We have a few diplomas from the period before AD 69, but it is only after AD 69 that these documents appear to have been issued regularly. It seems likely that there was a change in the privileges granted to auxiliaries at about that date, and this is one aspect of the steady evolution of auxiliary units during the early first century AD.

Originally, auxiliary units were mostly recruited from non-Romans, though some people with Roman citizenship did join auxiliary units. It is probable that the troops were originally recruited from one province and served in another. The link with the original province was quickly lost and the auxiliary recruiting officers turned to more convenient sources of manpower.

Auxiliaries served for 25-five years. After AD 69 they were rewarded with a grant of citizenship on completion of their service. Their children would also be given citizenship.

The units were commanded by equestrian prefects. The second grade of officer in the *alae* was the decurion. These commanded *turmae* of 30 thirty men. The cohorts were divided into centuries commanded by a centurion.

Soldier and civilian

Hostility

There is abundant evidence to attest hostility between civilians and soldiers during this period. Bullying, violent soldiers appear in Petronius' *Satyricon* (82), Juvenal, *Satire* 16, the New Testament (especially Matthew 27.26–35, Mark 15.15–19, John 19.23–4, Luke 3.14), and Epictetus, *Discourses* 4.1.79. Historians are often critical of soldiers, especially in times of civil war. The corruption of the soldiers in Britain was a major contributory factor in the outbreak of the Boudiccan revolt (pp. 193–96), and the behaviour of soldiers in Judaea brought the country on occasions to the verge of rebellion. A yet more extreme manifestation of hostility comes in the *Satyricon* (62) when a soldier turns out to be a werewolf.

The tradition of criticism of soldiers can be traced in certain texts of the first century BC and into the later Imperial period. The violence of soldiers is depicted as a feature not only of their technical ability, but also of their political power. Soldiers were able to make or break an emperor and it is argued that this resulted in not only the granting of privileges to soldiers, but also a reluctance to enforce military discipline.

Although there is no doubt that some soldiers abused their authority, we may question the extreme presentation of Juvenal and others. Roman society was conservative and hierarchical. Members of the Roman aristocracy regarded political authority as their birthright and the essential stability of Italian society meant that this ideology could be maintained. The expression of hostility to those who appeared beyond the control of the traditional elite is to be expected.

Our information about social origins is negligible, but it seems that soldiers tended to be of the lower social classes and anyone of elite status would join the Roman military as an officer. As soldiers came increasingly to be recruited from the provinces, the Italian elite may have had difficulty in seeing these men as Romans rather than barbarians. These lower-class men were, however, in a position to threaten the elite. The accession of Claudius was, to a large extent, a result of a recognition by the political elite that they could not control the soldiers (see pp. 149–51). The wars of 68–70 showed the importance of the soldiery in establishing an emperor. Even in AD 14, the soldiers on the German and Danubian flexed their political muscles in potentially revolutionary ways. The Principate was in itself the establishment of a military coup. Octavian owed his position to his veterans and rewarded them generously. The chaos that afflicted Rome and Italy from the murder of Caesar to the triumph of Octavian in 31 BC demonstrated clearly that the senators were not the real power-brokers in Roman society, it was the soldiers. What Augustus offered the aristocracy was to restrain the soldiers and in so doing, the aristocracy would be allowed to enjoy its leisure. The alternative that always hung over the Principate was that the emperor would unleash the potential of the soldiers and no-one would be safe.

Roman aristocrats did not have significant armed force at their disposal and were collectively and individually unable to defend themselves against military force. Soldiers sent by the emperor, or even soldiers acting illegitimately, could threaten or kill members of the elite. By so doing, soldiers inverted the social system and exercised authority over their social superiors.

The criminal activities of soldiers cannot be quantified and we cannot use the criticisms in the literary sources as a guide. The everyday does not necessarily get coverage and a soldier going peaceably about his duty would not be commented on. A better indicator might be the willingness of the elite to exercise authority over corrupt soldiers. Although we are hampered by a shortage of direct evidence, certain governors acted with an exemplary brutality in order to enforce discipline. Soldiers could be punished with death, with prolonged duties or with hard labour. The behaviour of martinets such as Cn. Piso, Corbulo, or Galba may reflect the indiscipline of the troops, but also shows that some Romans were able to enforce extreme disciplinary measures. Although the soldiers of the Rhine and Danube armies mutinied in AD 14, the description of their working conditions does not suggest a military force able to cow its generals and achieve excessive rewards. The Roman authorities were usually willing to promulgate edicts which attacked abuses by those in power, officials or soldiers, and although we may doubt the effectiveness of such measures, it certainly seems possible that they would be willing to act. Soldiers were punished in Judaea and people still thought it worth complaining about soldiers. Apart from in certain extreme circumstances, such as the civil wars of AD 68–69 and especially the sack of Cremona, we do not get the impression that the soldiers were out of control.

A military society?

Roman troops served for 25 years. We can find their camps across the empire, often located in frontier regions. In the West, long-term occupancy of a camp often led to the development of an urban centre nearby. In the case of legionary camps, this centre was often given the status of a Roman colony (e.g. Colchester). Land would be given to the colonists and a Roman community would be established. Although nominally civilian, such settlements had a military function in that they replaced the legion as effective garrison of the area and acted as a centre of political authority. It is normally assumed that the communities which grew up in the environs of camps, often called *canabae*, were settled by former soldiers and camp followers: 'wives' and families and purveyors of those goods and services demanded by the several hundred or several thousand men stationed in the fort.

When colonies were not established, it is difficult to assess where veterans settled. Some returned to the area from where they were recruited. Others might have been attracted to particular areas in which they had served or where they had friends and connections. Others remained near the camp. Many soldiers spent most of their careers operating out of a single camp. In such circumstances, staying in a familiar environment may have been attractive, especially if the soldier had settled his family in the vicinity. During the second century AD, there were increasing numbers of soldiers in the army who claimed not a town or province as their *origo* (place of origin), but *castris* (camp). The army was recruiting more from the sons of soldiers. The trend developed in the first century AD alongside the increased enlistment of locals into the army.

In spite of this trend, most recruits were probably drawn from areas other than the immediate environs of the camp. Even recruits who remained in their native province may have served at some distance from their homes. Legions tended to recruit from their own and nearby provinces, but a few recruits served at the opposite end of the empire from which they were born. The pattern for the auxiliary units has not been the subject of detailed study, but it seems likely that it was similar to that of the legions. There are examples of non-legionary units recruiting from distant places. A unit stationed in Egypt received 126 men (about 25% of their manpower) on a single day from the province of Asia (*PSI* IV 1063). The fleet stationed at Misenum in Italy recruited heavily, though not exclusively, from Egypt. Although trends can be observed in patterns of recruitment, they show irregularity not regularity.

The army appears to have recruited through two main procedures. First, men would volunteer. Service in the army was probably financially attractive to many provincials and offered other benefits (status and power) which would outweigh its manifest disadvantages. However, joining the army was probably not straightforward. It is likely that there was some competition in normal times. The papyrological evidence suggests that potential soldiers had to secure an introduction: their entry into the army had to be eased by influential friends and possibly by bribes. Thus, those already with military connections would stand the best chance of being recruited.

The second procedure was through the *dilectus*. The recruiting officer would visit a community and either enrol volunteers or conscript recruits. When war broke out, the army needed to recruit large numbers of troops quickly and war may also have discouraged volunteers. The first place a recruiting officer could look would be in the communities near the camp, but they could also look elsewhere, or to other provinces, or 'borrow' recruits from other armies. All these procedures would lead to irregularities in recruitment patterns. Also, once recruits had been drawn from a particular community, it established a connection between the community and the unit and those wishing to join the army might have better luck when attempting to enlist in a unit in which their former neighbours were serving. A recruiting officer might be tempted to look to those areas from where he had drawn recruits in the past.

Many of the soldiers probably returned to the village or city from which they originated. These are the least easy to spot in the available evidence since most of them will have disappeared into local communities without archaeological or literary trace. Some will have remained near the camp and these are much more visible in our records. The *canabae* (semi-urban areas that grew up outside camps) probably housed many of these veterans and their families. Some veterans will have gone to work on the land, possibly employing the skills of they had learnt as children on family farms. Others appear to have made use of their wide range of connections and went into trade, the evidence being particularly obvious for the German legions.

Although recruitment was conservative in that recruits tended to be drawn from the same areas, the irregularity of recruitment patterns encouraged a diversity of origins in the Roman army. This diversity of origins probably encouraged a diversity in settlement pattern. Veteran settlements should not be seen as 'military islands' surrounded by hostile civilian communities.

Soldiers had a rather peculiar legal status: they were not allowed to contract legal marriages; they were not allowed to own land in the province in which they were serving, except under special circumstances; they could not be summoned away from the standards to perform civilian legal business, and civil cases against soldiers were suspended for the duration of their service unless it could be shown that the soldiers had entered service to avoid their legal responsibilities; the property of soldiers was not treated as part of the property of their family under the control of the *paterfamilias* in the normal Roman fashion; and soldiers had the right to be tried on criminal charges in the camp, not in the civilian community where the offence may have taken place. This package of measures effectively isolated soldiers from many aspects of normal society.

It is apparent, however, that whatever the intention behind the regulation of soldiers' lives, soldiers interacted in many areas with civilian communities.

They formed long-term relationships with women, which they treated as marriages. The Roman authorities even came to acknowledge the existence of these relationships and, although they were not recognised as marriages during the military careers of the soldiers, the diplomas issued on the retirement of auxiliary soldiers retrospectively recognised the legitimacy of the relationship and of any children that had resulted. In addition, the Roman authorities developed extraordinary legal procedures so that the children of these soldiers could be instituted as the legitimate heirs of their natural fathers.

The work of the soldier also brought the troops into contact with civilians. Troops did not just prepare for and fight in major conflicts. They were involved in building projects (military and non-military), in supervising the state's economic assets (guarding quarries and mines, etc.), in gathering supplies and in the supervision of tax collection; they were occasionally used as a convenient labour force, and in duties which we would describe as policing. On many of these duties, soldiers must have worked closely with the civilians and, in so doing, many soldiers spent much of their time away from the camp. The stories in our literary sources which depict soldiers appearing suddenly on street corners should not be dismissed as fabrications or evidence that soldiers were allowed to roam free. At least some of the soldiers were probably at their station, ensuring the security of the province.

It should come as no surprise that we see soldiers integrating with the local population. They contracted relationships with local women, some of them may even have been born locally, and they worked with provincials throughout their careers. At Cremona, the battle was turned decisively when the Flavian forces turned to greet the rising sun (see p. 221): the German legions thought they were greeting reinforcements and fled. The greeting was non-Roman, a manifestation of the Easternisation of the legions. The Roman army developed local characteristics, and such cultural assimilation suggests interaction with and not segregation from local communities.

The extent of this interaction varied from province to province. The legions in Britain under Nero were probably faced with a hostile environment. The province was in the process of being conquered. Native cultural activities may have been scorned as barbaric by non-Britons. Integration was probably slower than elsewhere, and further slowed by major revolts which increased the mutual suspicion of the communities. In other provinces, cultures of troops and natives were probably more similar, and more peaceful circumstances allowed more rapid integration. Yet, even in a province in which one would have thought there were almost insuperable boundaries to integration, there is limited evidence of this process. In the New Testament, *Acts* 10 tells of a centurion from Caesarea named Cornelius who was perhaps the first non-Jewish convert to Christianity. Even in Judaea, a measure of integration was possible (cf. Matthew 8.5–13).

Soldiers and veterans as an elite

It is reasonable to suggest that soldiers and veterans did not form a separate society, but the nature of their relationship to the civilian community is more difficult to establish. In the provinces, most of the population did not have the privilege of Roman citizenship and were thus subjected to the full authority of Roman magistrates and their own local officials. Soldiers either had citizenship at the point of enlistment or were given citizenship when discharged. Romans in the provinces could claim protection under Roman law and limited exemptions from local jurisdiction. They enjoyed a legally privileged status. As Romans among the provincials, they could claim elite status.

Whether they were treated as an elite probably depended somewhat on political circumstances. In Britain, for instance, the province was insecure and the governors needed the support of all Romans in the province, especially those with military training. In provinces such as this, the governors were probably more inclined to take any claims of the soldiers to elite status seriously. Yet, it is notable that towns that we might expect to have been primarily military, such as Gloucester, do not show a particularly rich material culture. In more settled provinces, the governors had less need of the troops. Also, in many provinces there was an easily recognisable pre-existing native elite. This elite, often familiar with Classical culture, was entrusted with much of the day-to-day administrative business of their communities and could be relied upon politically. The Roman aristocracy probably had more in common with this group than the generally lower-class soldiers and veterans.

The annual income of soldiers and veterans was probably substantial. Before Domitian's pay increase (see p. 315), ordinary legionaries received 900 *sesterces* per year. This was raised by Domitian to 1,200 *sesterces*. If veterans lived off their discharge bonus, they would probably have had an income somewhat above 720 *sesterces* per year. In addition to this, pay records make clear that soldiers built up substantial savings which could have been invested on retirement. This probably provided a comfortable income, but unless a soldier was able to accumulate substantial savings, it would not catapult him into the local aristocracy. In Ligures Baebiani (as we saw p. 327) the average estate of the major landowners would have provided an income six to seven times larger than that provided by the retirement bonus and the wealthy of Veleia would have had average estates (and incomes) 22 times greater than that of the retired legionary. Even in Egypt, where the costs of living were quite low and the aristocracy less developed, the veterans we find in our documentary sources seem to have located to villages and there engaged in relatively small-scale farming. It seems very likely that the clustering of veterans at two particular Egyptian villages (Karanis and Philadelphia) was a result of a recruitment drive in the area and that many of the veterans we find in the texts were in fact Egyptians returning to their home villages after service. Their relative wealth in those village communities would perhaps reflect age and possibly family fields that had passed to them as much as money made through military service. The soldiers were certainly not an aristocracy, even in the provinces

The local origins of many of the troops points us to the issue of Romanisation (to be discussed also pp. 421–28). The general perception of a cultural change in the provinces of the Roman Empire begs the question of how that change came about and soldiers, as perhaps the largest group of Romans who were located in the provinces, are obvious agents for such social and cultural changes. In the West, there was an association between the location of military camps and emerging urbanisation. Soldiers were probably fluent in Latin (judging from documents such as *ostraka* from North Africa (documents scratched or penned onto pot sherds), the various writing tablets that have been recovered (notably from Vindolanda)), and the documentary record from Egypt. Latin was the primary language of the army. In the East, Greek was used extensively as well, but Greek was also a language of Empire. Linguistic fluency must have generated some level of cultural familiarity with matters Roman, though we must assume that only a few soldiers could read and even fewer would read literary texts. Nevertheless, the army life would also acculturate the soldiers, no matter where they had come from originally. Communal religious activities among the soldiers and official events would have encouraged a group identity infused by Roman cultural values. If the troops did come from mixed backgrounds, then Roman culture was probably the culture they had most in common. We may, of course, compare this with the use of English and English–American cultural references among different people (say German and Chinese businesspeople) who have no primary connection to UK or America.

The military do seem to have developed particular religious traditions, especially in the second century and beyond. Worship of the Persian god Mithras appears to have been popular. One of the more notable examples comes from the small fort at Carrawburgh on Hadrian's Wall, where a Mithraeum (a temple dedicated to Mithras) has been found. There was also a smaller and less preserved Mithraeum at Rudchester (also on Hadrian's Wall) and at Caernarfon, North Wales, just outside the fort. Five altars were found at Rudchester, three were dedicated by Prefects (commanders) of the military unit stationed at the fort, and a fourth was set up by the centurion of a legion. Even the Mithraeum in London has a military inscription within it. Soldiers from the Carrawburgh fort also worshipped at a nearby shrine to Coventina, a Celtic goddess associated with wells, suggesting a level of integration into localised religious activities (*Roman Inscriptions of Britain* 1523; 1524; 1529).

The other major cult with clear military associations is that of Jupiter Dolichenus, which also appears regularly in military contexts in the West from the second century onwards. In spite of its Latin sounding name, this particular manifestation of Jupiter comes from Eastern Turkey or Western Syria and is derived from the local god of that region, Baal. Baal was worshipped in various manifestations throughout Syria and close regions, most notably in the Temple of Bel in Palymra and at the Temple of Baal at Baalbek in the Lebanon. Little is known of the worship of the divinity, but the association with Jupiter was thorough and 'Optimus Maximus' (Best and Greatest) was frequently added to the titulature.

The Roman Empire (as we shall see) did, it seems, create the conditions for the spread of cults throughout its territories and thus established conditions for religious change in the various provinces. Yet, it is difficult to explain why individuals should engage in religious experimentation in this period (see pp. 412–19). In the case of the army, the situation is perhaps easier to interpret. The army itself provided an infrastructure of religious ceremonies and festivals which were written up into a religious calendar (*Feriale Duranum*) of which we have a late copy from the Eastern city of Dura. The *Feriale* was mostly a traditional Roman religious calendar with the aspects of the imperial cult in-built, including notably festivities honouring Germanicus. Quite how much sense frontier soldiers made of this Roman calendar is not clear. Yet, religion was a means of affirming identity in antiquity and of creating a framework by which the world could be understood. Removed from the communities of their birth, it is perhaps natural to expect that the soldiers would have been drawn to new religious cults. Both Mithras and Dolichenus appear to have been 'mystery' cults requiring initiation. Initiation established a formal structure and a sense of identity in relation to the divine. They probably enhanced the sense of community among the initiates. From the evidence we have, they certainly appealed also to senior officers who could support the building of temples and sponsor the development of the cult.

Neither of these cults were 'Roman' in a traditional sense, but the spread of the cults into the West clearly depended on the Roman Empire. What we are seeing here is a spread of cultures through the Empire, which may in turn have led to cultural homogenisation.

Yet, the other evidence of religious behaviour from Carrawburgh relates to Coventina. Coventina is local Celtic deity who comes to be worshipped along Hadrian's Wall. Water deities were common among the Celts (compare Sulis at Bath), though the iconography of Coventina shows parallels with other Roman deities and in particular with a common habit in the Northern provinces of having altars to two, three, or four mother deities. Roman soldiers in North West Britain also worshipped Mars, an obvious choice for soldiers, but in combination with seemingly local deities such as Belatucadrus and Cocidius. What we see in these instances is a process also common in Classical religion of an association being drawn between a Greek or Roman deity and deities from elsewhere in the Roman world. This interpretation is reflected the localised nature of much Classical religion in which divine personages could exist somewhat differently in different temples or sites. Furthermore, the worship of local gods was perfectly proper for Romans: they believed in local gods as much as they believed in their own gods.

There is a difficult question as to whether this type of union between two different religious traditions reflects Romanisation or a form of cultural imperialism in which Roman interpretations were imposed on local traditions. One could see the Roman element and argue for Romanisation or the Celtic element and argue for continuities within local cultures. What emerges from these contacts is clearly neither traditionally Roman nor traditionally Celtic, but a hybridised form of the two. Soldiers were responsible partly for this hybridisation since they both recorded the new cultural forms in the inscriptions but were also responsible probably for importing Roman imperial elements of the culture. What does seem likely is that whereas we see these conjunctions of religious forms drawn from different cultural traditions as unusual and surprising and needing special cultural explanations, the Romans (and probably the Celts) appear to have found such hybrid forms natural. Further, there is no obvious evidence of policy in the development of hybrid cultural forms in military contexts or in other non-military contexts elsewhere in the Roman Empire. We should not, therefore, see these hybrid deities as manifestations of an aggressive cultural imperialism, but the changes in cultic activity attested in these inscriptions do depend on the power of the imperial culture: Military officers used these cults to display their status and authority. The cults were, therefore, incorporated into the cultural and political hierarchies of the Roman Empire. The issue is not one of ethnicity, but power.

In other regards, it is difficult to see soldiers as primary transmitters of Roman culture. Where we find veterans in some numbers among communities in the East, there is little to distinguish the veterans or the communities in which they have settled in terms of the material culture as reflected in the archaeology. Only if there is an organised colonial settlement (such as Timgad or some of the Western colonies) with a Roman style constitution, do we see extensive evidence of cultural change. Certainly the process of urbanisation throughout the West led to considerable change and this cannot be disassociated from the military, but in the East there is no clear relationship between urbanisation and the presence of the military. The processes of cultural change seem much more closely associated with urbanisation than the military.

Britain was something of an exception in having a very large number of soldiers stationed in it and the province having no recognisable urban centres before the Roman invasion. Elsewhere in the Empire soldiers were neither wealthy enough nor numerous enough to generated significant cultural developments. Further, we should not regard Roman soldiers as being markedly distinct in cultural terms from those among whom they served. By the end of the first century AD, very few Roman soldiers will have had any knowledge of Italy at all and most were of provincial origins. The soldiers were, therefore, not directly responsible for cultural change in the Roman Empire.

Strategy

Discussions of military affairs normally distinguish between two levels of military thinking: the strategic and the tactical. Tactics are, in effect, what happens on the battlefield: the way a general places his troops and what he gets them to do. The placing of camps in defensible locations is also tactical. The Romans thought about and discussed tactics. Although some battles lacked obvious tactics, literary accounts make clear that the better generals employed tactics. Strategy involves the deployment of several armies and the organisation of troops over extended territories. The issue is complicated by a further level of thinking: grand strategy. This term is used by ancient historians to refer to a set of principles that govern military policy across the whole empire, or nearly the whole empire, over an extended period. For a strategy to be a 'grand strategy', it must survive changes of emperors.

There is very little discussion in our literary sources of anything that can be described as 'strategy' after the Augustan period. This is surprising. Although the focus of Tacitus, Dio and Suetonius was on affairs in Rome, there is much in these accounts which relates to military activity. Those emperors who either did not engage in conquests or limited the extent of conquests tend to be criticised, but the decision to stop expansion is nearly always represented as a political decision.

The predominance of political decision-making lies at the heart of the debate. Historians who do not see the empire as pursuing a conscious strategy usually argue that military decisions were taken for purely political reasons. They argue that if there had been any strategic discussion in Rome, it would surely have been reported by our sources. It has also been suggested that in all areas of Roman administrative and political activity the emperor tended to respond to problems: the government did not devise policy.

A third area of discussion has concentrated on the concepts that lie behind modern strategic thinking. Historians have questioned the level of knowledge available to the Romans about the frontiers. Romans tended to discuss peoples rather than land forms ('ethnography' rather than 'geography'). In a world in which political organisation was based on connections to a city, and in which Greek or Roman communities could be planted in territories that had been populated by Gauls or Syrians, the link between nation and land, so prevalent in modern thought, was much less developed. In such circumstances, an ethnographic rather than a geographic understanding of the world was more practical. It is also argued that the Romans did not even have the basic concept of a frontier. The word used in the fourth century AD and later for frontier, *limes*, seems to mean a military road, and such roads in the first century tended to lead into enemy territory rather than delineate boundaries. Yet, I think that this seriously undervalues the geographical knowledge and understanding of the Romans.

Concepts of empire

The modern word 'empire' derives from the Latin word '*imperium*'. The primary meaning of *imperium* is power. It is used to describe the power held by Roman magistrates. From this meaning a secondary usage developed, closer to our concept of empire. *Imperium* came to have implications of territoriality, so that a magistrate would have *imperium* over a particular area, an area normally referred to as the *provincia*. The Romans could understand the territorial limitations of a particular grant of *imperium* and that there was a border across which *imperium* had no legal force. Much of provincial law depends on this concept. From the sacred *pomerium* (boundary) of the city of Rome, to the River Rubicon that Caesar crossed to start the civil war, Roman history is littered with clearly defined boundaries.

Yet the concept of *imperium* allowed flexibility. The *imperium Romanum* did not merely constitute those areas under the direct control of a Roman magistrate or his representatives. Roman power extended beyond this region. Thus, the so-called client kingdoms were within the Roman Empire. 'Client kingdom' is the modern term used to describe states over which the Romans exercised influence. Client states could vary from states with which the Romans had treaty relations, but very little influence over, to states which the Romans controlled by appointing the monarch and closely supervising his or her activities. Roman power was exercised over the territory of the client state.

There was a certain elasticity of the concept of *imperium*. A state might come into contact with Rome and acknowledge Roman power through a treaty. They would become a friend of Rome, but through that treaty Rome's power would be felt in that region: Roman *imperium* was extended. Obviously the Romans would have been aware of degrees of dependence from the province to the client king to the kingdom with which there was a treaty relationship, but *imperium* allowed a blurring of frontiers so that the limits of Roman power could not be clearly established and there was room for dispute over the degree of integration.

This can be illustrated by the story of the Boudiccan revolt (see pp. 193–96). At the time of the revolt, the area of the Iceni tribe (Eastern England) seems to have been territorially within what we think of as the boundary of the province of Britain. Yet under Prasutagus, the kingdom retained some independence. It was a client state and therefore within the *imperium* of Rome. When the king died, the Romans changed the administrative arrangements of the area, but did not thereby alter its status as part of the empire. The Iceni thought otherwise and revolted against the violence with which the Romans imposed direct rule. By the same logic, the Romans could establish client kingdoms from provinces without causing an outcry in Rome over loss of territory. They could impose tribute on client states. They could impose provincial government on kingdoms that had previously enjoyed a fragile independence. They could also change the status of cities or regions within the frontiers of the Empire. Roman *imperium* was not thereby extended or diminished.

The flexibility of *imperium* meant that the boundaries of the Roman Empire (defined as the area over which the Romans exercised political authority) were in fact negotiable and uncertain. Many of the borders of the Roman world were surrounded by tribal groupings whose precise zones of influence were probably not understood by the Romans and were probably shifting and uncertain anyway. Further, Roman influence was felt in different degrees in different places and over different peoples. The Romans of the Republic had a very aggressive diplomatic mentality in which establishing networks of political relations beyond the conventional frontiers of Roman territory brought states under Roman influence and sometimes protection so that Rome would be minded to interfere in political and military issues. The flexibility of the influence exercised by Rome supported the endeavours of an aggressive militaristic state. In the Imperial period, Rome appears to have similarly extended influence beyond its defined borders (Armenia being the most obvious example, but also Arabia before the Trajanic annexation in AD 107). It would be foolish to think that Roman power stopped at its frontiers and it is only in the modern world of hard and fixed national frontiers that we like to believe in inviolate national territories.

Rome's ethnographic *imperium* made sense within a political framework of Roman hegemony and overwhelming military and economic superiority. It was a politically and technically sensible means of thinking about the extent of Roman power and influence.

We should not, however, see this loose conception of power and territory as evidence of geographical vagueness and technical inability. The Romans imposed administrative and tax-levying structures on the provinces. Since they taxed goods, heads, or land, in order to tax all three they needed to establish a boundary across which the taxable unit might cross or within which they might fall. Precise definition of frontiers was administratively desirable. Even if the collection of this taxation was devolved to local communities, they had to decide who was subjected to taxation and who was beyond the administrative boundary.

In much of the Mediterranean, Roman systems of land measurement and establishing boundaries worked with the long pre-existing processes of boundary definition. Land tenure patterns were often complex and long-established. People (and the administration) needed to know which plot of land was which, and which plot was subject to what taxes. Much of this appears to have been done through registers, sometimes topographically arranged, rather than maps, which is what is normally used today. Textual systems work very well when there are frequent emendations. On a larger scale, such techniques could be used to agree the boundaries between communities and ultimately the imperial frontiers.

There has been some disagreement as to whether the Romans had topographical maps in a form that we would recognise as maps. The Roman maps we do know of appear to have been quite primitive. Large maps were rare and notable. Augustus' colleague Agrippa was involved in geographical survey, and the resultant map was displayed in the centre of Rome. A senator under Domitian was charged with *maiestas* supposedly because he had a depiction of the Roman empire on his bedroom wall (Dio, 67. 12.2–4). It was possibly taken as evidence that the senator was planning some kind of *coup*, or perhaps that he had big ambitions (for why else would he need a map?). From the Domitianic case, it would seem clear that maps were curiosities. Yet, Strabo provides us with considerable geographical information for the Roman world and beyond, including distances between places. Pliny the Elder's *Natural History* also contains a vast amount of topographical information, including distances and sequences of places. Claudius Ptolemy's *Geography* of the second century AD provides us with sufficient information that we could draw a reasonably accurate topographical map of the Empire and the techniques that Ptolemy employed were likely to have been available to the emperors of the first century. For our purposes, it is significant that a map might be thought to have useful information for a prospective emperor.

In Late Antiquity, there were listings of places in the form of itineraries, some of which appear to have taken a map form. These representations were not really topographical maps, as we have them, but route maps, like transport maps for buses, trains, and metro systems. The best-known example of a route map is the map for the London Underground. This iconic map works so as to provide a functional means for individuals navigating the city, but it is not topographically accurate. Further, one could not easily use the map to guide a surface walker. But if we imagine the information that Roman strategists and generals needed, knowledge of every twist and turn in a road would not be necessary, but they would need to know distances between places.

Territory outside the imperial frontiers was much less well-known, but geographers did not confine their writings to the Empire and the Romans maintain records of military expeditions beyond the frontier. The invasion of Arabia Felix (South of Egypt to the West of the Red Sea) under Augustus appears to have had suffered from a lack of geographical knowledge and, indeed, understanding of the geographical conditions, which may have led to Rome's eventual withdrawal from the main city of Napata. Yet, this seems to have been an exceptional case. The Romans appear to have been very annoyed with King Syllaeus (of a neighbouring Arabian kingdom), who was supposed to have provided the key geographical information, which suggests that they had taken some precautions to gather information before invading (even if that data turned out to be poor). Arabia Felix was also remote from the Mediterranean and, indeed, from Egyptian influence: it really was at the edge of the world as far as the Romans were concerned. Agricola took some pains to survey the territory of Northern Scotland. Germanicus in his campaigns in

Northern Germany appears to have sufficient geographical knowledge to co-ordinate fleet and army. We also have, though from slightly later, topographic descriptions of routes beyond the Roman Empire. The *Periplus of the Erythrean Sea* (the Red Sea and Indian Ocean) details a journey and all the ports from Egypt to India for trading purposes. The *Parthian Stations*, written by Isidore of Charax, provides a similar itinerary for travel from Antioch to India over land.

Rome often used clear topographical markers to define the limits of Rome's territory (rivers, deserts, roads, walls, ditches). We should not think of these borders as impermeable. After all, even Hadrian's Wall had many gates that pointed to the North, but they do suggest a concern with frontiers and their definition. Rivers were, of course, very obvious markers of boundaries, on which all could agree. The use of the Rhine and Danube as frontier lines was not necessarily defensive. It was an easy way of marking the limits of Empire.

Yet, even if the Romans had the knowledge that might allow them to develop a strategy, it remains to be considered whether this potential for informed policy making was ever realised.

Statements of Rome's broad strategic policy are very few and very simple. During the Republic, Rome's empire expanded to incorporate most of the lands surrounding the Mediterranean and much of Western Europe with little obvious discussion of policy. It is difficult to imagine that there was a strategy in the Republic. In part, this is because there was no obvious body to devise a strategy. The senate met regularly, if not very frequently, but although they would discuss issues of peace and war and would decide where to deploy their armies and how many troops to recruit for particular campaigns, the extensive evidence we have for debates relating to these issues focus entirely on the particularity of issues and not strategy. They did not discuss, for instance, whether expansion in Gaul or Spain or the East should be prioritised. Furthermore, there never even seems to have been discussion of whether Rome should be expanding its territories or not. Expansion appears to have been driven by individual campaigns. Decisions were taken by magistrates and the magistrates would change every year. Campaigns were conducted initially by consuls and later by provincial commanders who had considerable scope for taking their own decisions. Sulla introduced legislation which confined governors to their allotted territories, without express permission from the senate to extend their sphere of operations, a regulation which, incidentally, must have depended on reasonably clearly defined boundaries. Sullan legislation may suggest that provincial governors had been making use of their opportunities to fight wars beyond their provinces without consultation. Yet, in spite of this legislation, Caesar appears to have been unconstrained in his rapid expansion of Roman territory through Gaul. Other, less glamorous and large scale conflicts probably also spilled beyond the defined geographical limitations. Roman military aggression appears not to have been limited by borders.

Strategic decisions must have been taken at various times. Decisions must have been taken not to extend direct Roman rule into Greece during the early second century BC. Pompey's settlement of the East in 62 BC must have been based on a series of political and strategic decisions which he needed to justify on his return to Rome. Yet, even if we understand the senate to have been a policy-making forum, it was composed of individuals and groups who probably had many different policies. With the pressures on leading politicians to achieve military glory, foreign policy was subject to rapid change. More important than any supposed senatorial policy were the social, economic, and political pressures that led Rome to adopt an extremely aggressive foreign policy from at least the third century BC onwards. The politicians wanted to lead armies in wars and the beneficial effects of successful warfare on the Roman economy and for the individuals who fought with the armies encouraged the lower classes to support aggressive military policies. The impetus for the accumulation of territory was not strategic thinking, but an aggressive disposition.

One of the reasons for this unmanaged and unplanned expansion under the Republic was a perception of instability in the regions that surrounded the growing Empire. To an extent, this created a dynamic which may have continued into the Imperial period. Roman perceptions of foreign states as weak, worrisome, or aggressive tended to lead to intervention. The Illyrian state in the third century BC, for example, was thought to be responsible for piracy in the Adriatic and the Romans invaded as a result. Cilicia in Asia Minor also came to be regarded as a pirate state and subject to mass military intervention. Caesar's expansion into Gaul was prompted by a whole series of interventions to protect other states or perceived Roman interests. There is little doubt that Caesar's expansions were inventive: if he was not looking for reasons to intervene, slight causes (real or perceived) produce dramatic reactions. The very gradual and piecemeal expansion in Spain, which went on for two centuries, was likely prompted by a whole series of local issues. In the Imperial period, Roman engagement in Armenia resulted at least in part from disputes within Armenia. The invasion of Britain appears to have been prompted by appeals from displaced British kings. Expansion in Germany and North Africa likewise reflected Rome being sucked into local problems. Of course, like other modern imperial powers who find themselves dragged into external conflicts, Rome's willingness to become involved tells us much about Rome's political and military attitudes. It also suggests that there was no strategy, grand or otherwise.

The political precondition for a strategy is relative political stability and it is only with Augustus that we get a period of coherent political leadership that might allow the development of policy. Indeed, it has been argued that we see with Augustus and especially the Julio-Claudians the development of a grand strategy, which is much more restrained than the practices of the Republican period.

The evidence for such a change is, however, decidedly mixed. There are explicit statements of strategy attributed to Augustus in Dio (54. 9; 56. 33; 56. 41), Tacitus (*Annales*, 1. 11) and Suetonius (*Augustus*, 21–25). The first is dated to about 20 BC, when Augustus was returning from the East. Consistently, and Augustus represented this at the end of his life as having been his consistent policy, Augustus claimed that he was aiming to preserve the Empire from its enemies rather than expand. His wars were, he claimed, defensive. The claim was made most obviously in Augustus' posthumous advice to the senate and his successor in which he exhorted the next generation not to engage in expansionist wars. Although these repeated claims of Augustan policy may seem like excellent evidence and provide a certainty that we lack in so many areas of ancient history, there are many reasons to be somewhat dubious about these policy statements. Most obviously, when Tacitus reports the advice, he is struck by an obvious discrepancy between Augustus' stated policy and his actions.

If Tacitus had been reading the *Res Gestae*, and there is every reason to believe that he had, there would be good reason for his puzzlement. In the text that we have, Augustus' own words are introduced by the preface 'Below is a copy of the *Res Gestae* (achievements) of the deified Augustus through which he subjected the whole world to the *imperium* of the Roman people'. In Chapters 25 to 33, Augustus lists his conquest: he freed the sea from pirates and brought peace to Gaul, Spain, and Germany, sailing his fleet and leading his armies deeper into German territory than any Roman had previously been. He was victorious in Aithiopia and Arabia Felix. He added Egypt to the Empire and could have added Armenia, but merely took it under Roman authority. He received or reasserted Roman authority all the provinces East of the Adriatic, plus Sicily and Sardinia. The Parthians restored the standards captured at the battle of Carrhae (thereby acknowledging Augustan superiority). Pannonia was conquered and the Dacians defeated. Embassies were sent asking for Roman friendship from the Scythians and Sarmatians and the Medes. Kings from Parthia and the Medes and the Britons all took refuge with Augustus, also suggesting the extension of the Roman sphere of influence. If we take the *Res Gestae* seriously, and there are reasons to be sceptical, Augustus really did have a claim to have brought the whole world under the power of the Roman people.

Similar claims are made in Augustan poetry. Virgil, *Aeneid*, 1.261–96 invents a prophecy of the greatness of Rome and puts it in the mouth of no lesser authority than Jupiter. Jupiter surveys Roman history and in this sometime eccentric reading of the future (which is the past for Virgil's audience), Rome accumulates an empire without limits in space or time which brings universal peace under Augustan rule. There is nothing ambiguous about the claim to world conquest. Another prophetic scene in *Aeneid*, 6.792–800 also proclaims Augustus' victory over the East as far as India (effectively the end of the world as far as Rome was concerned). Horace is perhaps less grandiose since he was not writing epic poetry and did not have the opportunity to voice a god, but in *Odes*, 3.5 he looks forward to the defeat of the Parthians and the Britons and in 3.14 takes advantage of Augustus' return from Spain to compare him with a conquering Hercules.

Art was also not shy about celebrating Augustan victory. The major victory monument of the city was the Forum of Augustus, enormous and triumphant. But world conquest appears in smaller forms. For example, on the breastplate of the famous Prima Porta statue of Augustus there is imagery of Augustan conquest of the sea and heavens and all in between. The Boscoreale cups, lavish silver drinking cups lost during the Second World War, depicted Augustus as conqueror of the globe (the Roman knew that the world was a globe) and the triumphs of his wife's sons Tiberius and Drusus. The Gemma Augustea, a delicate and beautiful onyx cameo and a technical triumph, now in the Kunsthistorische Museum in Vienna, shows a deified Augustus celebrating the victory of an unidentifiable figure who descends from a chariot. Personifications of Victory and Roma surround the seated emperor. On a lower tier, the other side of war is represented. Roman soldiers lift a trophaeum, a monument made from the armour of the defeated, while a bound barbarian awaits probable execution and another begs for his life. A woman ineffectively holds her torn dress in place while a soldier pulls her by the hair and nearby, another woman sits and weeps. If one is tempted to celebrate the peace brought by Augustus, one should have regard to those barbarians 'made peaceful' through these means.

If the symbols are unquestionably imperial, the reality, if one starts to map the wars of Augustus, is equally militaristic. We cannot be precise because our accounts are far from perfect, but under Augustus, Roman troops were frequently engaged in multiple fields of conquest. Wars of conquest in Egypt, Arabia and Aithiopia were almost continuous from 32 BC–22 BC. Wars in Spain were conducted from about 25 BC–16 BC. Dalmatia, Pannonia and the Danubian region saw conflicts that began *c.* 30 BC, perhaps paused after 24 BC, but resumed 14 BC–9 BC, and then again in AD 6–9. The Alpine tribes were conquered *c.* 13 BC. Warfare in Germany was intermittent from 25 BC–12 BC, but Germany became the centre of major expansion efforts from 9 BC until Tiberius called an end to the war when emperor. Augustus has some claim to have been the most expansionist Roman leader ever. Little wonder Tacitus was confused at his claims to have been restrained.

There are two ways of making sense of Augustan claims. The first goes back to the traditional Republican mode of imperial expansion. Augustus was simply very willing to get drawn into conflicts and used his army to deal with states on the frontiers repeatedly.

The second claim is more political. Augustus' power depended very heavily on his control over the military. When threatened politically, he could always rely on the soldiers. The soldiers had brought him to power and they kept him in power. Yet, the justification of Augustus' control over the soldiers was, throughout his reign, the dangers posed on the frontiers which Augustus and his legates needed to deal with. In 20 BC, very briefly, Augustus stopped fighting. It would not take much imagination to suggest that in the aftermath of his glorious diplomatic victory over the Parthians and the claims to world conquest and universal peace that were associated with it, someone somewhere suggested that Augustus need no longer command all those troops. Perhaps they even suggested that some of the legions could be disbanded. After all, the number of troops controlled by Augustus and under arms during his reign was without precedent in a period without civil war and without an obvious and immediate danger to the Roman state. In AD 14, a similar situation arose. Augustus was dead and this could have been a moment to revisit the arrangements with regard to the military and, in particular, Tiberian control over the legions. Augustus' answer was clear: the world was dangerous. Rome needed her armies to hold on to the various territories that had been acquired and everybody had better take care. The proof that the world was dangerous was, of course, the sheer number of wars that Augustus and his legates had fought. The success and wealth that the wars generated probably also quietened opponents.

Augustan strategy, then, was far from innovative or defensive. It continued the dynamics of expansion under the Republic and for the same political reasons. One of the crucial differences, however, was that the length of Augustus' reign and the continuities in political leadership meant that war could be planned and executed over a very long period. It did not matter that a campaign could not be brought to an end during the tenure of a single governor, since others would follow. It is this capacity to sustain campaigning that we see in the multiple campaigns towards the end of the Augustan period by which Roman forces drove deep into Germany and into the Danubian lands. The pace of conquest was quickened by Augustan political concerns.

After Augustus, the situation changed, but although the pace of expansion reduced, nonetheless, it continued. Tiberius was relatively pacific. Gaius was hardly around long enough to engage in large-scale military activity, though his preparations for the invasion of Britain were probably serious. Claudius was a conqueror and sought opportunities for expansion especially in Africa and Britain. Nero was not, however, so interested in military prestige and was content to use his generals in expansionist drives in the East and, indeed, in Germany. The Flavians were more traditional. Campaigns in Judaea brought Vespasian considerable prestige. Domitian was heavily involved in Germany and along the Danubian frontier and also allowed expansion in Britain. Trajan resumed large-scale expansions with enormous wars in Dacia and a serious attempt to conquer Parthia.

One of the issues that limited expansion was the availability of generals. Emperors were notably reluctant to entrust major and prestigious campaigns to men who were not close family members. Augustus had a plethora of trusted associates and it was these men who drove his expansionism. Tiberius was not so lucky. Germanicus died and for some reason Drusus was not entrusted with the army. He, too, was to die comparatively young. Tiberius needed his other potential general, Sejanus, with him in Rome. Vespasian also kept Titus close by to help him with the Roman aristocracy. We do see trusted generals in the later Julio-Claudian period, such as Corbulo, and under Vespasian, but weaker emperors were cautious about raising powers that might threaten them. The great campaigns of the period were monopolised by members of the imperial family: Germanicus in Germany, Claudius in Britain, Titus in Judaea, Domitian in Germany and on the Danube, and Trajan's campaigns. There were exceptions, such as Corbulo's campaigns in Germany and Armenia. Yet, Corbulo was closely monitored and forced to recall his troops from an expedition deep into Germany. In the East, he was notably cautious and steadfastly refused to go beyond his remit without consulting Rome. Nero still had him killed (see pp. 207–208).

One has to wonder whether anything much had changed from the Republic. Although the development of monarchy altered the political landscape, military success continued to bring popularity and acclaim and was an important way in which an emperor could establish his credentials. Wars were fought as opportunities arose and were fought for political benefit and for political reasons. It is simply that in the Empire, there were fewer men who were in a position or were allowed to win prestige through force of arms. Nero showed that it was possible to be an emperor without being a military figure, though even he may have been planning major wars towards the end of his reign.

Local and regional policies

There were general changes in Roman military organisation across the Empire during this period. These included the development of fixed camps where units were stationed for extended periods and the creation of what used to be thought of as fixed frontiers, but is perhaps better characterised as lines of defence stretching over very long distances. Hadrian's Wall is, of course, the most famous of these, though it is outside our period. There were also defensive lines in Germany, along the Rhine and between the Rhine and the Danube, and probably in Africa. In other places, roads may have marked the division between different districts of the empire.

These developments were certainly not directly contemporary and cannot have resulted from an imperial directive. The similarities between the constructions in Germany, Hadrian's Wall and the later Antonine Wall in Britain, and a fortified line in Africa are, however, notable. The situation was rather different in the East. The Romans established control over the very long frontiers by controlling the limited routes of communication in these areas. In many cases, a single fort could accomplish tasks for which a defensive line was needed in the West. Although there was not a fortified barrier, the forts of the East probably controlled access to a defined region. The marking of a boundary must represent a similar perceived need (probably to control access to the provinces). The development of these defensive fortifications shows shared perceptions and military thinking. It is certainly possible that there was transmission of ideas from one region to another, possibly through senior officers or imperial involvement. It is through developments at this local or regional level that we can see military thought and the development of military policy.

Political factors will have been important in the development of military policy in the various regions, yet we can also see a geographical and strategic rationale behind many of the decisions. Hadrian's Wall was positioned along a geographically sensible line of defence, though it may have made little sense in relation to tribal groupings (some tribes may have been divided by the Wall). The Augustan conquest of the Alpine region and campaigns into Pannonia followed what seems to have been a predetermined plan of conquest with troops invading from north and south to secure this extremely difficult terrain. Again, this showed a sophisticated deployment of military resources over a vast region. In the Flavian period, Domitian and possibly his father and brother engaged in bitter wars over an area known as the Agri Decumates, a stretch of territory between the Rhine and Danube. It is very difficult to escape the conclusion that a major aim in the campaign was to shorten the existing defensive line between the two rivers. This may have been as a preliminary to further expansion and it is clear that Roman power was felt across the Rhine, but this does not obscure the original strategic rationale.

There were military events which appear, at first sight, strategically irrational: the conquests of Britain and Dacia and the invasion of Parthia. All these were clearly influenced by political factors. Yet, if we accept that the strategic aim of Rome was world conquest, then neither the invasion of Britain nor the invasion of Parthia seem particularly irrational. Dacia is a different issue, but the Dacians had been causing problems on the frontiers for some time and, although the conquest may look ridiculous on a map of Europe, the exertion of direct military force beyond the Danube did allow the Romans to place increased pressure on other tribes north of the Danube, especially those now threatened by Roman incursions from Dacia to the East, Pannonia to the south and Germany to the west.

Conclusions: the army and politics

The Romans did not have a grand strategy. Roman policy aims remained static and simple. They aimed to conquer the world. This aim often conflicted with the political aims of emperors who wanted to stay in power. To do so, they had to restrain their ambitious generals and monopolise military prestige. This resulted in a slowing of the process of expansion. The Romans did, however, think strategically. Much of the military activity of this period made strategic sense in terms of the region in which they were operating. The Romans do not appear to have launched their armies at random, but planned military installations and campaigns with some geographical sophistication. There was certainly no Department of Strategic Studies in Rome, but the Romans did develop military policies and apply them over large areas. By our definition, this seems to be strategy.

Roman behaviour remained resolutely expansionist. The Romans valued conquest. The Romans frequently sought answers to diplomatic or political concerns by deploying the army. There was no reluctance to go to war. In part, this simply reflects the willingness of Romans to use violence for political ends and a lack of sympathy with others which seems somehow characteristic of Roman social relations. Their military violence is seen in the institutionalisation of violence towards slaves. The Romans also appear to have been little concerned with the losses of men that came with war. A great disaster caused mourning and perhaps even fear, but there is no sense that Romans would have been dissuaded from military action for fear of casualties.

There was a similar lack of sympathy for the defeated. Cremona, an Italian city, was ravaged by Flavian troops. Jerusalem was destroyed. Countless towns and cities were sacked and burned. The defeated were to be killed or enslaved. The women were to be raped. Some killed themselves rather than fall into Roman hands. This was the logic of victory and there was no reason to hide it. The suffering of the defeated appears in art in a way that is unthinkable for European imperialists. For the Romans, it was an expected consequence and an intended outcome of war. Enslaving people was good.

In Western democracies, the army is supposed to be an apolitical force concerned with the defence of the state against foreign enemies. The Roman army was also concerned with the security of the Empire and with foreign wars. This was, however, only one of the army's roles. The Augustan settlements established a constitutional framework for the monarchy. As part of that settlement, the standing army was created and most of the troops were stationed in the provinces. Since the emperors took control over the appointment of generals, much of the political feuding that had marked appointments to important commands in the Republic seems to have disappeared, or at least was contained within the doors of the palace. We should not, however, be lulled by this silence into believing that the army was depoliticised. The army continued to play an important political role.

Military units in the provinces were often dispersed. Soldiers were sent on duties which varied from supervising grain supply to building bridges to acting as the political police. Certain provinces have produced more evidence for Roman military involvement in policing than others. The involvement of soldiers in policing activities in Jewish regions of the Near East and in Egypt is comparatively well attested. Here, the soldiers dealt with bandits and other local problems. They ensured the smooth working of the local administrative and security system. They represented Roman military force and, since a soldier was potentially supported by several thousand of his fellows, he wielded considerable authority. In these regions, the soldiers were there to ensure internal security. Their stations probably related as much if not more to political geography than strategic geography. Traces of this dispersal can be found in other regions. Some soldiers are depicted on tombstones carrying writing tablets and staffs as well as swords. The staff could be used to beat the locals. The writing tablets probably represented the role of the soldiers in policing the province. Varus, the Roman general whose legions were massacred in AD 9, was criticised by Dio for sending his soldiers in small numbers to the various settlements in Germany to act as police. Dio did not criticise the dispersal itself, rather the incorrect perception on the part of Varus that the province was peaceful. Dispersal was the norm.

Roman troops were in sufficient numbers that they could bring Roman power to the smallest of communities in military provinces. They could also provide the governor with detailed information about the state of the province. They were a powerful instrument of political control.

It was not just in the provinces that the army could be deployed in this way. The praetorian guard and the urban cohorts provided the emperor with a powerful instrument of political control in Rome. There were probably around 4,000 praetorians in Rome under Tiberius. These were supplemented by the urban cohorts, about 1,300 men. Although comparatively small in an urban population of about one million, the guard was a significant military force and could certainly enforce discipline in the theatre and other areas. The fleets stationed in Italy at Misenum and Ravenna provided another nearby military resource, and it is probable that considerable numbers of troops were in transit through Italy on various tasks at any one point.

The troops in Italy were an important resource for an emperor. The praetorians were a major factor in the accessions of Claudius and Otho. Claudius openly acknowledged that his debt to the praetorians through his coinage. It was to the praetorians that he fled when news of Messalina's conspiracy broke. The praetorians obviously provided military protection for the emperor and could intimidate the senate and the urban mob. They could be used symbolically. The presence of a few soldiers with the emperor gave him status and was an implied threat. The clatter of the armour and the gleam of the weapons were obvious symbols of power. Sejanus, Macro, Burrus, Tigellinus, Titus and Casperius Aelianus used their control of the praetorians to build a power base in Rome.

The frontier armies only rarely became involved in the political struggle. Some opposed the accessions of Tiberius and Claudius. They were crucial in the events of AD 68–69 and 97–98. The emperors made every attempt to secure their loyalty The most concrete measure was the payment of the troops. Troops were paid in coin (all with the head of the emperor on it) three times a year and would also receive regular donatives (presents of money) which would encourage their loyalty. The troops also had ceremonials and symbols which would reinforce loyalty. They carried images of the emperor on their standards. It was probably to these images that they swore oaths of loyalty on 1st January each year. The imperial birthday was celebrated, as were the birthdays of other important members of the imperial family. Such ceremonials bound the troops together and cemented their loyalty. Potential usurpers had to subvert these expressions of collective loyalty to win over the troops.

The army retained a political role in the Imperial period and there was no attempt to depoliticise it. Augustus displayed his military credentials. The praetorians accompanied Tiberius. Claudius, when troubled, fled to the camp and showed his power from their secure premises. With Claudius' accession, the praetorians intervened decisively in Roman political life. The senators were given a lesson in power politics. Nero was removed by the praetorians, but they came to regret it. The senate may have hated many of the Julio-Claudians, but they retained their power because they retained the loyalty of the army. In AD 14, the soldiers offered to make Germanicus emperor: they were aware of their power and that power was real. In AD 69, Galba somehow failed to notice that power was given by the soldiers, and a soldier removed Galba's head from his shoulders. Vespasian kept Titus in charge of the praetorians and his loyal friends were sent to the legions. Domitian made sure everyone knew of his victories and he ensured the loyalty of his troops by the simple expedient of giving them an enormous pay rise. Trajan, the so-called 'Best', brought the military to the forefront of his regime. His conquests were celebrated lavishly. Trajan's Forum and Trajan's column are every bit as monumental, militaristic and grandiose as Augustan victory monuments. Trajan's campaigns in the East were another Roman attempt to emulate the greatness of Alexander the Great and another version of the dream of world conquest.

The army remained in politics because it was at the heart of the imperial position and the Roman people and especially the senators were repeatedly and forcibly reminded of that brutal political fact. The army remained at the heart of the Empire and the strategic goal of Rome remained, without embarrassment or moral qualm, the conquest of the world.

Chapter 15

Family and gender

Introduction and women

The equivalent chapter of the first edition of this book was entitled 'Women'. It has become less easy to write about Roman women in the last two decades. That is not because Roman women have changed or that a vast amount of new data has transformed our understanding, but because the way we think about women in society today has changed.

One of the fundamental changes is that actually we now talk not so much in terms of women, but of gender. The difference is subtle, but fundamental. 'Woman' is a category of being. Taking about women established women as a special category of being, differentiated from the 'norm', (that was assumed to be) 'man'. Although that category is related to certain physiological traits, what is interesting is how those physiological traits are given sociological meaning. Gender refers to those sociological meanings. The shift in language reflects a shift in social attitudes. No longer do we see the differential treatment of men and women in society as 'natural', but it now a social issue with cultural peculiarities. The debate, and it is a fundamental debate in modern society, is the relationship between physiological traits and especially those which affect behaviours, and sociological factors. The debate spills across from issues of gender into issues of sexuality.

Gender sits within a network of social relations which are imbued with power. That network of power establishes and confirms particular roles. Men and women are shaped by those roles and families are given their structures. This process of shaping is subtle and pervasive. We should not think about these structures as being imposed by external agencies. In older literature on women, there was a considerable focus on issues of law, but law does not establish the regularities of gender; it merely reinforces certain social values and expectations and employs state power to discipline individuals.

The key question is how one learns one's gender role. One certainly does not learn it from a book or from the law. One learns expectations in society as one is growing up. From our earliest years, we are plunged into a dense learning environment. We learn our social roles by observation and by copying. Boys learn what it is to be men from copying their fathers (and hence the concerns of our politicians with male role models in families). Girls learn what it is to be women from copying their mothers. One might object that we should teach our children what it is to be an adult, and not encourage specific gendered behaviour, but that will only happen when society ceases to be gendered. A non-gendered society would not be a sexless society: it would be a society in which sexual physiologies have no sociological importance. I know of no such society.

In almost every society boys are encouraged to be like their fathers and girls like their mothers. From a certain age, children are dressed differently. They are given different toys. They become aware of the different social expectations and they start to behave differently. There are subtleties to this learning. Men may walk in different ways to women; hold their bodies differently; use the spaces of the house differently. Men may spend much more time away from the house. There may be expectations that men and women will have different spheres of activity. Symbolic practices often have an effect. If a man conducted the domestic sacrifices (or cuts the Sunday roast today) or speaks first at events or is the primary greeter of guests, it suggested superiority. Then, there are the most obvious symbols of family tradition. Romans had household gods. Members of the elite had statuettes or masks of ancestors. These symbols marked the house as belonging to the man and may well also have sent the message that it is the males of the family who will have the socially significant role. One learns one's social roles from one's environment.

These social roles are not rules. It is important to make the distinction. If there were rules, no-one would vary. Social roles are more like guides to behaviour. They show you how you *might* behave: you have to choose whether you will adhere to those roles. This is one of the reasons why people often behave more conservatively at key moments. Under stress, when people do not know what to do or how to respond, formulaic behaviour becomes the way out. At funerals, everyone says the same thing, the same expressions of condolence are used, but that is what is supposed to happen. Roman funerals were elaborately ritualised semi-public events in which social bonds were remade after the death. People performed so that everyone could move on.

Social roles produce regularities. We may, as Romans did from time to time, choose to ignore those regularities and do something else. That is how social changes begin. Moreover, there is no need for uniformity within societies. If in a certain situation, I choose to behave in a certain way and you choose to behave in a different way, we are not necessarily in conflict or members of different societies, we have simply followed two different paths.

Let us take some examples. Let me imagine you, dear reader, as a young woman, purely to balance my masculinity. It is a lovely warm summer day. I decide to wear sunglasses; you decide to wear a hat. Nobody cares. Then, we decide to wear lovely matching pink sun-dresses and we go out. You get admiring glances. I get glances of a different sort. Of course, there should not be a problem and in most Western countries, but not in all countries, the law-enforcement agencies will not intervene. But by putting on a pink dress, I have made a strong statement and I am now categorised differently: I am given another name. I have become a transvestite: someone who has crossed gender boundaries. As a man in a dress, I am a source of worry to many. We can multiply examples. In most places still, I can marry a woman; you, reader, cannot. But perhaps more worryingly, there are also certain places at certain times I feel safe, but in the same place at the same time, you might be made fearful of violence. The social reactions of others are likely to shape behaviour, but there are few rules.

All societies engage in these social roles. Societies also enforce disciplines in different ways (and not everyone will agree on which behaviours to disapprove of). It is often easier to abide by those roles than to fight them. Further, those roles are often so deeply imbued into our self-expectations that we regard them as natural and simply conform. But should one choose not to conform, one is often subject to social pressures which operate to discipline the individual. Some of that disciplining may be subtle. Staring and muttering at someone who has breached convention may have little effect, but it does reinforce the social norms. Expectations are also crucial. If we define someone by the colour of their skin, for example, and we have expectations of behaviour according to that definition, then if someone does not abide by those expectations, there is likely to be sufficient reaction that the individual will become fully aware of those expectations. Roles are thus defined and enforced. Yet, even if roles are normally adhered to either through self-discipline or through mild social pressures, there are other means available to discipline those who still refuse to conform. Scandal, social disapproval, and social alienation can threaten those who challenge convention. Ultimately, the state can become involved.

Nevertheless, most societies allow considerable room for variation and that generates uncertainty. Individuals worry about the limits of social convention. What then tends to happen is that people start to talk about the issue. The result is what is called discourse. Discourse attempts to establish the norms of behaviour: sexual behaviour, for instance, is shaped by discourse that attempts to lay out what is acceptable and normal but this can shift over time. Five decades ago, homosexual behaviour was regarded with hostility in the UK (and, unfortunately, it still is in many places). Even two decades ago, discourse on the topic would often express considerable disapproval of homosexual behaviour. Such behaviours may even have, and may still produce violence from those who disapprove. Yet, whereas acknowledged homosexuals would have found themselves facing a prison sentence two generations ago, and social exclusion a generation ago, the result of the gradual social acceptance of homosexual relationships is that we talk less about such relationships: they are not an issue of social concern.

The point is if everyone in a society behaved in a certain manner, it would never be discussed in that society since it would be regarded as a 'normal'. If everyone, regardless of gender, wore pink sun-dresses when the weather was hot, it would never be discussed. It would only become an object of comment if someone from elsewhere arrived who regarded gendered dress as the norm.

When it comes to Roman society, we need to be alert to what our sources talk about. When our sources talk about sexual behaviour, they are not reporting social norms to future generations, but they are worrying about social behaviours. They are trying to decide or to assert what is normal and acceptable. Yet, our sources take for granted and thus give very little discussion as to social values which we now regard as strange, such as the inferiority of women, barbarians, and slaves. We have many sources which concern themselves with issues of sexuality and gender. We should not assume from that discussion that there was a generally held view within society, from which there were occasional deviants, but rather these were issues of social concern and issues where there was the possibility of changes in attitude over time. Discourse focuses on problems.

There is a further point about discourse and social values and that relates to origins. In the description of how we develop our social roles, I argued that we learn those roles as we are growing up and we subsequently remember how to behave. Our social roles are inherited and remembered. On a wider perspective, social values are continuously being learnt. Values are thus embedded in a past, shaped by our parents and by our grandparents and by those who became before. But values are not just familial, they are learnt and enforced by those outside the family and these values must also be embedded in the past. In a historical society such as Rome, social values are always related to traditions. Deviations from tradition (in modern cultures frequently seen as positive) were nearly always perceived as negative (immoral). There was thus an innate conservatism in Roman moral values. The consequence of this, however, is that what was perceived as moral behaviour was always assumed to be the way in which people behaved in the past. If a Roman decided that, for instance, talkative, assertive women who offered views different from those of their husbands were thereby immoral, then he would be likely to see these women as an innovation and feature of the deplorable 'our times' to be contrasted to the virtuous 'olden days'. There would thus be a tendency to project 'high' morals into the Republican period without necessarily engaging in historical research to determine the situation in that period.

The Romans were conscious of moral change and, indeed, may well have considerably exaggerated the extent of that change over time. The explanation for change is difficult. Our sources are, obviously, concentrated heavily at the elite end of society and prone to discuss the behaviours of the most prominent members of Roman society. Roman culture was also, as we discussed at the start of the book (see pp. 10–14), profoundly political. It was thus tempting to relate changes in political structure to changes in moral behaviour.

Interestingly, the direction of influence is not so clear: did immorality lead to the fall of the Republic or did the fall of the Republic lead to immorality? At least some modern writers, whose perceptions are even more centred on the elite, suggest that changes in morality were directly related to changes brought about by the advent of monarchy. It seems to me that changes in behaviour, which are, I think, detectable for the Principate, are more likely to have been generated from changes within relationships than changes in the constitutional structures of power. Discussions of changes in moral practices in more modern societies nearly always focus on sociological rather than political issues and will frequently ignore the state entirely. I see little reason for the situation to have been different in Rome.

Family

Gender relationships are primarily established within a familial context. Understanding the Roman family is made difficult by issues of definition. Yet, these issues of definition are very familiar to us. When we use the word 'family' we have a whole series of different social groups to which we might be referring and rarely are we confused. In terms of numbers my family might be six, 20, or 60 depending on whether I am talking about the household, the close relatives, or the extended familial group. The Romans were equally flexible. The Latin term '*familia*' was applied to include those within a household including slaves. Yet, there is no way in which the Romans would have confused the relationship between a *pater* and his slaves and between a *pater* and his sons and daughters. The Romans also used the word '*domus*', house to refer to an extended family. The *domus* especially was not closely defined. The best example is the imperial house that would appear to have encompassed adult men who married into the family and sons of wives (who would technically have belonged to a different family) as well as descendants and male and female relatives who were not direct descendants. The Augustan family was clearly unusual in that it was the centre of so much power, but its structure would seem to reflect the wide scope of familial links.

The concept of a *familia* would appear to have derived from the *potestas* exercised by a *pater*. In Roman law, a father had sweeping powers over those under his authority. These included the rights to punish violently and originally, the right to kill. Those rights did not normally extend to the wife of the *pater* who remained under the power of her own father (normally). Sons, daughters, and slaves would thus fall under the same authority. A child would escape from paternal authority on the death of the father or if the father went through the legal procedure of freeing the child, in very much the same way as a slave might be freed. Further, a child might be adopted into another family (which seems to have happened quite regularly among aristocrats). The patriarchy in law would seem also to be reflected in social behaviours as well. Fathers do seem to have been authority figures. That authority accumulated with age and there was an expectation that respect would be shown to the older male. Further, if we are to believe St Augustine (who came from a traditional family) then order was often asserted in the family through violence.

The younger male was in a subordinate position, which potentially gave rise to tensions. In thinking about family, however, we need to be aware of the brutal demographics of the Roman world. Life expectancy was low, perhaps lower than that of any contemporary society, no matter how poor. Men probably married quite late, possibly around aged 30. By the time a son became an adult (20+), the father was probably 55 or more. Significant numbers of fathers would have died before sons (and daughters) reached adulthood. Nevertheless, an adult son and an authoritarian father was a recipe for tension and we should perhaps take seriously Roman concerns with parricide (not something we worry about too much in contemporary societies), hostilities attested between father and son, and the occasionally attested attempts of sons to betray fathers to hostile authorities (in the context of treason trials or proscriptions).

The late marriage of Roman men appears to have been a feature of all levels of Roman society (as far as we can judge), apart from the imperial family. Marriage appears to have been delayed until the late twenties or the early thirties. This differs notably from the situation in Egypt, where again we have reasonable data and where men seem to have married in their early to mid-twenties. For Roman men, marriage appears to have been closely related to the formation of households. Marriage was certainly virilocal (women would move into the houses of men), but was probably also neolocal (women moved to form new households). This would require men to be free to form their own households: they needed to be liberated from the households of their fathers. They also probably needed some level of economic independence. Although many men married before their fathers had died, the death of the father might provide the opportunity for the creation of a new household.

As a result of these patterns of household formation, households tended to be nuclear (composed of a married couple and their children) rather than extended. In Egypt, and especially in villages, where marriage was virilocal and there was no expectation that the newly married couple would form their own household, many more families had an extended structure, often with brothers sharing the same house.

Romans appears to have regarded men as not reaching maturity until quite late, possibly as late as 30. This allowed for a long adolescence. Men did not delay sexual activity until marriage, nor did they avoid long-term relationships. Prostitution was common and brothels appear in the archaeological record from Pompeii. Men could find sexual partners among slaves and foreigners and possibly low-status women. Men also took concubines with whom they would have long relationships and these concubines may have been later maintained alongside wives. During the Republic, it is quite likely that many men would have spent many of the years between 18 and 30 on military service or possibly looking for work away from the family home. Rome and the other big cities probably had a surplus of young men and it seems likely that the youths were a disruptive influence on the streets of Rome. Nero, for example, appears to have maintained his riotous youthful pursuits even when he was emperor (p. 179), pursuits which appear to have included drinking and brawling and, one presumes, casual sex. The Roman elegists (as we shall see below) made much of their youth and differentiated themselves from the 'stern old men' who represented a more ferocious moral order that disapproved of their youthful attachment to 'the girl'.

The situation was very different for women. Age at marriage for women was low. It could be very low indeed and may have been in the early teens. Given the diet of the Romans and general health issues, marriage could easily come before menstruation. It seems, from what we can tell, that marriage was practically universal for women. Divorce and widowhood were common and there appears to have been no stigma associated with remarriage, though there is an ambivalence in our sources since the *univira* (the once-married woman) appears to have been particularly honoured. Augustus introduced legislation which encouraged divorced or widowed women to remarry (see pp. 69–70). Serial monogamy was common for both men and women.

There was no particular ethical or moral issue involved in sexual activity. Roman men had a romantic attachment to the purity of the virgin girl, which was represented in literature and poetry, but that emphasis would appear to focus on youth and possibly the erotics of a power relationship in which one partner was older and more sexually experienced than the other. Sex was not, however, in itself considered to be immoral or a 'sin' and Romans had none of the Christian concern with original sin, sexual desire, or extra-marital sexual relationships (for men). Sex becomes an issue for the Romans with regard to marriage. Marriage was a social custom and the means by which a man was to secure legitimate children and heirs. Women were expected to produce children for men. Adultery became a criminal offence under Augustus, but adultery was defined as a man and woman having sexual relations when the woman was married to someone else. The issue was not the sex, but the breach in the rights of the husband and the possible legitimacy of the resulting children.

Households centred on the conjugal couple. Yet, in this emphasis lies a problem. Traditional Roman marriages were regarded as a functional relationship between families for the production of children. Love had nothing to do with it. Augustus felt that it was perfectly proper to deploy his daughter's body as his dynastic policy required. Other emperors were similarly unromantic. The situation in the Republic seems also to have involved marriage for contingent political advantage. Yet, there is little doubt that Romans of the Imperial period valued a romantic relationship between husband and wife: they expected love.

We see this love in odd places. Pliny gives us several idealised females who were prepared to die for their husbands or were not prepared to live without their husbands. Arria, for instance, was married to Caecina Paetus who was implicated in a revolt against Claudius. Among her many other acts of personal bravery, she supported her husband to the end and encouraged him to suicide by first stabbing herself (Pliny, *Epistles*, 3.16). Arria's suicide was partly induced by her long and happy marriage. Another unnamed woman threw herself from a balcony into Lake Como where she presumably drowned. She had tied herself to her husband who had a seemingly fatal and painful disease of the genitalia (Pliny, *Epistles*, 6.24). Seneca's wife, Paulina, also took drastic actions when Seneca was forced to suicide. Although the aged philosopher was firm in his conviction that there was no moral issue as to her living on after his death, he also praised her determination to follow her husband in suicide, though in the end, she was persuaded from it (see p. 202).

Love appears also in the Greek traditions. The Greek novel, which was becoming an important genre through the Roman period, normally turned on a love story. The couple fall in passionate love, but something stands in their way and their relationship cannot be consummated. They then embark on a series of adventures, meeting all sorts of dangers (pirates, cannibals, bandits, lustful men and women, enslavement, etc.) in ever more absurd combinations. The woman normally preserves her virginity (even after being condemned to a brothel), though the man is not always so lucky. Eventually, they are reunited.

The more serious treatment comes in Plutarch's *Advice to the Bride and Groom*, which is roughly contemporary with the end of our period. What Plutarch depicts in his ideal marriage is a loving partnership. The couple respect each other, work together, and do not take sexual partners outside of the relationship. The man is also to be faithful.

Pliny is more direct about his own relationship with his wife. He displays his love for her and her love for him in his letters. Pliny's letters were not ill-considered jottings, but were meant to be published: they were consciously developing a portrait of Pliny the man. We may therefore have less confidence in their accuracy than we have in, for instance, the letters of Cicero, but we can have more confidence that Pliny is deliberately presenting an ideal version of a conjugal relationship.

Pliny's wife first appears in 4.1, in which Pliny writes to her grandfather excusing them for not having visited. The impression is given that they are newly married. The marriage would have entailed the girl leaving her grandfather's house (she was an orphan) and moving to stay with Pliny. The family came from Como, Pliny's hometown, but the couple had decided to spend time away. Pliny excuses his tardy return by, typically, referring to his other duties (dedicating a temple), and the letter enables Pliny to show that he is doubly good in honouring his grandfather-in-law and the gods.

Calpurnia comes more into focus in 4.19 when we learn about her life in some detail. This letter is written to Calpurnia's aunt. It turns out that the aunt (also called Calpurnia) was a younger friend of Pliny's mother and that she was later to become a friend of Pliny's. We should assume that Calpurnia (senior) was about Pliny's age.

Pliny was born probably in AD 61 or 62. The letters are mostly without dating material within them. The death of Verginius Rufus was in 97 and is recorded in book 2 of the letters. Book 4 probably dates several years later, to about AD 103 when Pliny would be aged 41 or 42. Calpurnia's age is not established in the text. Yet, from letters 4.1 and 4.19, she is clearly young and Pliny is her first husband. In 8.10, Pliny reports to the grandfather that Calpurnia has miscarried. He blames Calpurnia since she did not take proper precautions (whatever they may have been) since due to her youth she did not know she was pregnant. This gives pause for thought. If they were married in 103, book 8 is likely to refer to events at least four to five years later. For a miscarriage to be a notable issue, we must presume that the pregnancy was someway advanced. So, we have a girl, married and presumably engaged in sexual activity for four to five years, who at the end of that period fails to notice pregnancy. It is difficult to imagine that Calpurnia was older than 14 when she married a man probably more than 25 years her senior.

That youth provides the context for 4.19. Calpurnia is praised because she is a quick learner. She is said to be a credit to her aunt's care and upbringing. Yet, clearly she has little experience of literature, which she is trying to learn. Her devotion to Pliny is such that she is setting his poems to music (we might hope that Calpurnia had an overly developed sense of irony). She claims to love him, though for his desire for good reputation, which is more lasting than a body which will grow old, and on the recommendation of her aunt.

This is an unfamiliar sort of love, a love bound by duty and a love that operates on recommendation. Everything in the letter suggests that the Pliny is treating her as a child; in our terms she was a child. Yet, of course, he was having sex with her.

Pliny also displays his love for Calpurnia. He writes several letters saying that he is missing her and that he treasures her letters, but his affection is most notable in a very short letter, 7.5. In this letter, his wife is once more away. Pliny claims that he cannot sleep at night. He keeps thinking of her. In the day, at the accustomed hour of his visits, he finds himself outside the door of her room, but she is not there and he wanders sad and sick as a 'locked-out lover'. It is only when he is in court that he can feel at ease. What Pliny presents us with here is a love letter, and we should remember that everything is published and public. But as love letters go, there is a catch and the catch centres on the locked-out lover.

The locked-out lover is a literary allusion to elegiac love poetry. Elegy was normally directed to lovers who were in other men's house. The love was adulterous and thus the lover could be locked out. Pliny's love, though, is respectable, married. But the literariness of the letter gives it a conscious artificiality in which the passion is performance and, indeed, public performance. Pliny's letter is a prose poem. Whereas the girl can always exclude her lover and she has power, Pliny has his girl firmly situated in his house. She has no doorkeeper and no lock on the door. Further, while the poet elegist could do nothing without his love, transfixed and obsessed by his passion, Pliny could go down to the Forum and do his duty. Not only is Pliny's love respectable, but it is subordinated to duty. Whereas with the elegists, power is with the girl or perhaps in the passion itself, Pliny is ultimately in control.

Lest one doubt the artifice of Pliny's sentiments, the letter has a context. The previous letter (7.4) is a letter about poetry in which Pliny writes about his literary achievements (and excellence). He includes in the letter one of his own poems. The poem talks about another poem written by Gallus in which Gallus claims that his father (also Gallus) was a better poet than Cicero, who wrote poems about his love for his freedman, Tiro. Inspired by this, Pliny now writes of the kisses of his Tiro and the manner in which his Tiro arouses Pliny's lusts. There are layers and layers of artifice here which bury the passion, and its juxtaposition with Pliny's letter to his wife suggest that this is also a work of art, in which its creator is pretending passion in a disciplined literary framework.

Pliny's letters depict a relationship of love, but it is a love subordinated. His marriage is traditional in many ways since it represents the formation of an alliance between two families. It is also traditional in that there was no love relationship between the couple before marriage. Love is to come after marriage. Yet, Pliny and Calpurnia's love is depicted in dutiful terms. It is not physical, but intellectual. It is not of the body, but by reputation. It has passion, but that passion is shaped into literary convention (their love lies in their letters). But it is also imbued with the status differences of the two. Calpurnia never speaks in the letters. We never hear a word she says. She sets Pliny's poems to music. She reads Pliny's literary works. She lives in Pliny's house. She is visited when Pliny chooses. The imbalance of age reflects an imbalance of power. The men in 8.10 console themselves at her miscarriage. The baby is their loss. Calpurnia is to be forgiven.

In all the instances that we have cited above, love is subordinated and rationalised. The marriage remains fundamentally a lineage marriage, but the couple live in partnership and clearly the woman have an active role in those partnerships. Pliny has many female friends and he writes of them frequently. One such woman was Ummidia Quadratilla, who kept a troupe of mime artists, a form of art noted for its erotic content, and had private performances. The troupe was renowned. She built a theatre in which they could perform and they appeared at the games in Rome (Pliny, *Epistles*, 7. 24). The problem in Pliny's letters is not the status of women or women taking a social role, but seems to be love and the relationship between love and marriage, and it is to that issue which we will return later.

Yet, apart from the love, is there evidence of change in the nature of marriage in these letters? In moralistic writings of the period, notably in Tacitus in his depiction of imperial women, but also in Juvenal's misogynistic complaints in the *Satires* there is a concern about women taking a more prominent role in society and, of course, about female sexuality. This has often been taken up in modern interpretations to see within the Imperial period an increased and abnormal role for women, particularly in the court politics of Claudius, Nero, and Domitian and we saw some of this in earlier chapters. Yet, although the structures of power were new and women's roles within those structures were inevitably new as well, the prominence of women within aristocratic households does not appear to have been innovatory. There is no obvious evidence of a 'golden age' in which Roman matrons stayed at home and awaited demurely the return of their husbands. Pliny and his women are at the end of the period, but at the start we have Antony's women. His three wives (if we include Cleopatra) all enjoyed prominent social positions. They all appeared in public. They all represent Antony's interests, sometimes even militarily.

Livia, wife of Augustus, was also a prominent figure. She becomes a role model for Roman womanhood, but she was hardly confined to the home. She appears to have operated with a parallel court and prominent figures were befriended by her (notably the young Galba). We can go further back to Cicero's wife and to the mother of the Gracchi for women who had a social role and a social personality. For every Messalina in the imperial annals, we have an Agrippina the Elder or an Octavia, women who take public roles and are far from demonised in the literature.

The social prominence of women does appear to be a general phenomenon of this period. If we look beyond the Roman aristocracy to Greece, the Hellenistic and Roman periods sees an increasing number of women appearing in official contexts, sometimes even holding honorary magistracies and receiving statues from the town council. Perhaps the most noteworthy example comes from the small city of Termessos in Asia Minor in which there were two honorary statues to Atalante, a local dignitary. Both monuments were voted to Atalante by the city authorities after Atalante had spent her own money on buying grain for the city. The longer inscription notes her womanly qualities and her ancestry and the generosity of her family. Atalante was a widow and it takes little imagination to think that she stepped in during this crisis as the lead adult of a traditionally powerful and rich family. She represented family, as a man would have done should one have been available. In this broader social context Eumachia of Pompeii, who spent her money in sponsoring the fullers of the city, appears less unusual than at first sight (see p. 299).

There is, I think, social change underway in this period and it does affect gender roles. It is not, however, the rise of individualism or romanticism or a culture of conjugal love, nor is it related to the development of imperial monarchy. Nor, I think, does the development constitute a lessening of social control on women. If anything, the reverse is true. The stories of husband-wife suicides in Pliny and elsewhere may provide evidence of a close conjugal bond, but it also provides evidence for the dependency of the women. The decisions of women to kill themselves was not based on romantic passion (that she could not live in a world without him), but on the end of her identity. Suicide in these instances was applauded as being a dutiful reaction to the suicide of one's husband. The death of the husband marked also the death of the woman who was defined by her relationship to the man. The real death emphasised the social death that came with her widowhood.

This increased emphasis on the subordination of women to the conjugal role is a development in gender relations that is widespread in Roman societies: it affects Pompeii and Termessos as well as Rome and its aristocracy. It would seem to reflect a widespread social change that does not map closely on the political changes of the period. Further, that subordination was not primarily to the men. Women could express themselves and represent their families in the absence of their men and one presumes that the powerful women who appear in Pliny's letters were perfectly capable of expressing their views when their men were around. The subordination is to the partnership established by marriage, to the household and the conjugal role. Women and men represented their households.

I would like to link the change in gender relations to economics. We saw in a previous chapter that the period appears to show an increase in the wealth of the elite and an increase in the power of elite households. The rich were getting much richer and their households were becoming more powerful. The pattern can also be seen in the East and we may note that Atalante was from one of the most prominent and wealthy families in the city. This concentration of power allowed a closer identification between the individual and household and it was the household that was the primary source of status. Although wealth was closely related to status in earlier periods, status was achieved in the public sphere in male competition, be it in the senate or in the forum or in the army. In the Greek world, the pattern was similar. The politics of the council and the law courts was male dominated and status was generated in that field. But once status becomes a household and family matter and caught up in the preservation of economic power in property, then women also contributed. The family firm could just as well be managed by a woman as by a man.

Of course, the increased wealth of women and their increased prominence in society may have been a source of concern and probably this undermined traditional ways in which men maintained the subordination of women. Wealth brought power. A domestication of politics brought power to women. Pliny's letters, however, show that he was still able to subordinate his wife to his authority within his household partnership. The discourse that surrounds women in the first century AD tends to be reinforcing of the patriarchy. We need to remember that discourse focuses on what concerns people. Women taking prominent roles in society concerned men. Powerful women could threaten gender roles. They could reduce men to dependency. They could follow their own sexual instincts. The discussions that we see probably represent a reaction to changing economic structures and an attempt to reinforce a patriarchy that perceives itself to be threatened by the rise of powerful, rich households.

Patriarchy may not have worked in quite the same way as in 100 BC, but it still maintained power. Women were subject to powerful constraints. Gender was an important determinant of behaviours and status. Men still held the power.

Any desire to romanticise the emphasis on conjugality that we see in at least some of the writings of the late first century or even to think of a new and more equal era in gender relations dissipates when we think of the young girl Calpurnia setting music to the poetry of the old man to whom she had been given.

The law

Nearly all Roman children were born into a family dominated by a *pater* (father or head of family). The *pater* exercised *potestas* (power) over his family. He controlled all the family property and could punish all members of the family as he thought fit. The authority of the *pater* extended to his children, and any grandchildren born to his sons. On the death of the *pater* all his children became independent. In certain circumstances, a woman could also pass from the *potestas* of her father to that of her husband on marriage, though it seems that this was extremely rare. A woman would, therefore, normally remain under the authority of her father or grandfather even after her marriage. Her husband and his family had very little legal authority over her. On the death of her *pater*, the woman would become legally independent. The law, however, judged that women were not normally legally capable. This meant that to perform any legal action, such as marrying or divorcing or selling or buying property, a woman would need the authority of her *tutor* (legal guardian). This duty would probably normally be carried out by a close male relative or friend. This control was somewhat lessened since a woman could always apply to a magistrate to have an inefficient or otherwise difficult *tutor* removed. In addition, after legislation passed by Augustus, a freeborn woman who had three children or a freedwoman who had four children was judged legally capable and given control over her own affairs.

A woman normally had property in two forms. Her dowry was passed to her husband at marriage. This property was to be used to maintain the woman though it seems probable that husbands could make a profit from dowries. Dowries were managed as part of the husband's estate. The only difference was that such property could not be mortgaged or sold (though the woman's holdings could be adjusted), since the woman always had first legal claim on the property. At the dissolution of the marriage, the property would return to the wife. It seems that in most senses the dowry was the property of the wife though the usufruct (the right to exploit and manage the property) of the property belonged to the husband.

A woman could also hold property separate from her dowry in the same manner as property was held by a man. This could be property inherited or purchased and was in no way subject to the control of her husband.

Marriage and divorce were comparatively informal legal procedures. A man and woman were judged to be married if they cohabited with that intention. Divorce was simply the ending of that intent. Practically, a man and woman could move into the same house and announce their marriage in some way and if there was no legal impediment it would be taken to be a marriage. Normally, a dowry would be given as a symbol of that union. Divorce normally entailed notification of the end of the marriage and the restoration of the dowry. In theory, both partners were equally able to divorce, though a woman without legal independence would need the authority of her *pater* or *tutor* and the restoration of the dowry could be made difficult.

A woman was often legally a stranger within her husband's household. She could be removed or remove herself comparatively easily. She did not, however, have any rights over children or over her husband's property. Unless a woman maintained a separate household of her own (and the very wealthy probably did), divorce could render a woman homeless.

The sexual behaviour of women was controlled by law. Adultery by women was punishable by partial confiscation of her dowry and exile. Adultery was defined as sexual relations with any man who was not her husband. A man committed adultery through sexual relations with married, respectable women and an adulterous man could also be exiled. Husbands and fathers could exercise a certain amount of violence against those caught in adultery, provided that the couple were caught in the act, and the level of allowable violence increased if the male party was of low status. Husbands who killed allegedly adulterous wives could be prosecuted for homicide. In law, the husband was bound to divorce an adulterous wife. She could then be prosecuted for adultery. If he failed to prosecute a wife divorced on the grounds of adultery, after a suitable delay, any other citizen could prosecute. If he failed to divorce a wife convicted of adultery (and anyone could bring a charge of adultery), the husband could be prosecuted as a pimp.

The effect of the law on the lives of women probably depended on the manner in which it was applied. A *tutor*, for instance, may have simply acted as the woman wished, provided that nothing illegal or clearly against her interests was proposed, or he could have effectively blocked all her transactions. The independence of a woman from her husband's family could diminish her authority within her husband's household or provide her with financial and legal independence. Although the system was clearly patriarchal, recent studies have stressed how the regulations protected women's interests. The legal separation of a woman's property from that of her husband and the institution of guardianship prevented a husband from pressurising his wife into giving over management of all her property and provided some insurance against the loss of her dowry. Men who married for money could not normally take control of that money if the marriage was dissolved. Roman law provided the wife with some protection from her husband.

Love and sex

At the end of the Republic and in the Augustan we get some of the most sexually explicit poetry in Western literature. The poetry is associated with a particular form, elegy, written in a particular metre. The most prominent practitioners of this poetry were Catullus, Tibullus, Propertius, and Ovid. The poetry is seemingly autobiographical and although it tackles a variety of themes and later elegies looked for new subjects, the dominant theme of the narrative is a sexual relationship between the poet and a girl. This relationship is outside marriage, though the exact status of the girl is never made clear.

These poems are very polished literary works and the poems make frequent allusions to other contemporary poems and, indeed, to Greek models. The poems provide episodes, but offer little pretence of providing a realistic narrative of the relationship with the girl and turning the poems into biography is a hopeless task. Instead, the poems present a milieu, an atmosphere in Rome of the late Republic and early Empire.

The atmosphere is one in which young(ish) men go hunting for girls. The hunt is not one of violence, though there is sometimes violence in the relations between poet and girl, but it is a 'violence' of seduction. In Ovid's *Art of Love*, a boisterous manual of seduction methods (please don't try this at home), the reader is taught the manifold ways of seducing a girl from where to spot her to what to do with her in bed. But the seducer is not just after sex, he is also looking for love.

That love is transforming and brings meaning to the lives of the poets. It is a literary pose, but Propertius kicks off his elegies by proclaiming that he was once immune to love, but then he saw his girl and Love (a personification) stamped down upon him and he became Love's slave. Ovid, once he becomes a lover, is no good for anything else. He gives up on his ambitions and becomes committed to his girl. After the moment of conversion, normal masculine activities become impossible. The elegist will never be a soldier since service would take him away from his love. He will fight battles of a different sort, as a soldier of love in a narrow bed. He will not farm, since his girl is a creature of the city. He will not engage in politics, because the city is not the scene of politics, but of seduction.

This is a poetry of opposition, but the opposition is often subtle. Sometimes there is explicit criticism of Caesar and perhaps more often a delicate mocking of his pretensions. Often, there is explicit praise of the emperor, but praise is normally distorted, viewed from the parallel course that the elegist has taken. Opposition, though, seems integral to a poetry that centres on illicit relationships in a culture in which the emperor is passing legislation to make adultery a criminal offence. Ovid plays with this most obviously in the *Ars Amatoria*. In Book 1, when the reader might be worrying about an enterprise as evidently oppositional as seduction, Ovid is reassuring (32–4): 'I sing of safe sex: there is no crime in my verse'. Two hundred lines later, he has to admit 'all women are able to be caught' (269–70), and 300 lines after that he instructs, 'Let it be your prayer to please the husband of your girl' (579–80). Not so safe, then. Ovid doesn't forget, but he subverts. Of course, these tricks will only work on the courtesans, but by the end of the book, all women are the same.

Although the poetry may claim to be about the girl, it is mainly about the boy. We are with the boy when his girl shuts him out. We are at the side of the boy when he falls for the girl. We live his agonies and his ecstasies. Her feelings are mysterious. We see her angry, but mainly what we see is the poet fearing her anger. We see her reluctant, but only when the poet is rejected. We see her in the bedroom, but we do not know why she is suddenly there. The poet wants to seduce, but the woman is fickle and her moods cannot be predicted. But the boy lives for her, and dies for her. She is a cipher for his passion and it is that transforming passion that matters. It matters because it generates that alternate life, a life which is not political or military and which turns away from the traditional spheres. In terms of discourse, the elegies provide us with an alternative masculinity to that of the traditions and construct that masculinity in opposition to the traditions. Why worry about war and politics and status if there is love? If there is love, why should marriage get in the way?

Of course, one might argue that this is poetry not life, but if we live our lives in relation to the discourses that lay out social rules, one might wonder whether there is a significant difference. Sex lurks in the stories of the imperial age as a disruptive force. One thinks automatically of the women of the imperial household: Julia, mother and daughter, the Agrippinas, Messalina, Poppaea, Domitia Longina and others. We need not accept the stories which circulated about the imperial women. The Roman elite was prone to gossip, but the accusations in themselves carry behind them a hidden narrative (real or fictional) of wild and promiscuous parties and of a rejection of conventional moralities. Under Tiberius, a Vistilia attempted to avoid prosecution for adultery by registering as a prostitute. The emperor took a rather dim view of this evasion of the law (Tacitus, *Annales*, 2.85). But we also need to think about the men. We have seen the accusations that were levied at Gaius and Nero of unorthodox relationships and sexual adventurism. We can read these as boys having fun, but also as a public escape from convention and gender roles. If Nero really did play the woman in his sexual relations, what was he saying by so doing?

The disciplines of morality pressed on the powerful and powerless alike, confirming roles and establishing something that looked like rules. Sexuality was a marker of conformity. Sexual indiscipline was an indication of tyranny and that a man could not control his passions. The ruler was expected to conform to his sexual rules. Perhaps Gaius and Nero were merely attempting to show that they were too powerful to be constrained by conventional morality, but they were also rejecting a whole edifice of tradition and values that were rendered prestigious by their apparent age. In an earlier age, Antony and Octavian had been adventurous in their sexual *mores*, perhaps also showing that power and wealth brought freedom. But in misbehaving, Gaius and Nero were not behaving like Roman men should. They were rejecting something.

How Roman men should behave was also part of a political culture in which citizens exercised power. The disciplined citizen was also the voting citizen and the fighting citizen and the free-speaking citizen: this was a morality which was associated with the values of the Republic. Gaius and Nero could happily reject that morality. The 'Republican' schoolmasters and moralists who frowned at their antics used the traditions of morality to create a distance between them and the emperor, seeing themselves to be more conformist than the emperor himself. It was the emperors who were trying to create something new, new disciplines for a world that seemed so different from that of the high Republic.

It is in this context that we can read Petronius' *Satyricon*, a pornographic tale in which Encolpius tries to hold on to his love, Giton, through a series of sexual adventures in Southern Italy. As readers of the work, we are invited to observe the various couplings, sometimes through the narrations of other voyeurs, and trapped in complicity with the ongoing sex. How are we to read it? None of the figures in the work are admirable. Yet, there is no condemnatory narrator. There is a wildness in the text, a fantastic element, which was to encourage the Italian director Fellini into an even wilder film of the story. This is a world in which the laws are open to doubt and in which sex and lust drives the plot. It is a world of brothels and taverns and youthful indiscretion. For all its chaos, it is a world of freedoms, though far, far from being a utopia.

The treatment of sex in the Imperial period is politicised. Sex becomes a way in which the relationship between the individual and the conservative traditions of society are expressed and explored. Sex had symbolic value. The poets who expressed their devotion to the girl were representing sex as an alternative way of life and an oppositional stance, perhaps as a reaction to a society that had rejected their pretensions and was in the process of change. Later, sex became a marker of difference and of disorder, perhaps of escape from the disciplines of an old-fashioned morality. The escape was appealing at least in part because of the political stance of those who esteemed the old ways. There was a shock of the new and a freedom in the new sexualities. Yet, for Pliny, sex is controlled, disciplined, subordinate to the master of the household, to literary conventions, and to duty. What we see here is not a linear story of social change, but an ongoing debate at the heart of Roman society.

Conclusions

The changing world of gender relations reflects changes in Roman society. Gender relations were a focus of interest and discussion and even legislation in this period. The discourse of gender was sometimes violently opposed, offering different forms of masculinity and femininity. Yet, households were formed in a traditional manner, following the interests and dictates of families. Among the aristocrats, lineage marriage appears to have remained the norm. Relationships within families were firmly patriarchal. We see prominent women in various capacities, but when we are able to see the detail of the social relations, women were subordinate. There was a conjugal partnership at the heart of the family, as there had been in the Roman family of the late Republic. That conjugal partnership may have become yet more important, reflecting a shift in economic status in the households of the elite. It is in the rise of the aristocratic household that we see the most powerful economic and social force for change.

There was a debate in Roman society about gender relations and that debate projected norms of behaviour into the past: tradition was the place where the Romans found their moral guidance. There is, however, evidence that would suggest that the discourses relating to gender tended to reinforce the patriarchy and increase the disciplinary focus on women. Women were expected to commit themselves completely to the family of their spouse and their identities were closely bound to their position as wife of a certain individual. It is perhaps for this reason that the *univira* comes to be praised, for she is one who has no divided loyalties: for her, there is only one husband, ever. The issue with the *univira* was not about sex, but the integrity of the family. It is for this reason that we get spousal suicides in the Imperial period.

The debate on the status and role of women in society took into account the imperial women. They were the most famous women in Roman society and they would thus be the subject of the greatest attention. In fact, it seems likely that most of the women of the imperial house behaved in quite traditional ways. They had their friends and their social circles. They contributed to the running of the imperial household as partners of their husbands. They brought their own personal status to the imperial family. This is particularly obvious when we consider Livia's role under Augustus and the way in which Claudius worked with his wives. The power of the household inevitably did detract from the power of other social bodies which men tended to monopolise. Thus, it did cause tensions. Social pressure was brought to bear to push women into the background, successfully in the case of Trajan's almost invisible women. Such pressures built in the hostile narratives associated with women such as Livia and Agrippina the younger. Painting these women as aberrant was anachronistic. They were not aberrant in their time: if they had been, neither Claudius nor Augustus, neither of whom were fools, would have been happy to see their wives take such public roles. By the Trajanic period, and in the writings of Tacitus, these women appear out of step with Roman traditions. Nevertheless, the suppression of imperial women was out of step with a general social shift that was giving aristocratic women more prominence rather than less.

A third area on which the discourse focuses is love and sex. Augustan concerns with adultery were about the disciplining of the family and the production of legitimate children for the next generation. Yet, we see a life of illicit love being offered as an alternate to the life of politics in the writings of the elegists. This was a fundamental breach in Roman social order. It was a rejection of traditional disciplines of the self. Love was differentiated from lust. The lust the tyrant showed in his violent seductions was very different from the disciplines suffered by the lover in his pursuit of the girl. Passion is a philosophical problem for the Romans of the first century. They tended to disapprove, believing that passion impeded rationality. But love remained an attractive option. In the Neronian period, there appears to have been a conscious effort to reject the strictures of a previous generation and invent new sexualities, perhaps even as a rejection of the traditional political values associated with a restrictive sexuality. Such daring inevitably led to a backlash. When we get to Pliny, he is at great pains to show us his passion and his love, but this is a love that is disciplined and subjected to traditional authorities. It is a passion safely wrapped in letters and that never interferes with the real business of politics. It is a love that flourished on command of the family and for social not romantic reasons. It is a love tamed.

But we should end with doubt. For can love really be tamed? Should we accept Pliny at his word? Moreover what do we make of the silent Tiro and the silent Calpurnia? In Pliny's clever poem, Tiro holds off his master and lover until Pliny's passion reaches excess. What happens when a master meets reluctance in a slave? In Pliny's romance, Calpurnia is in love. But here was a girl taken from her family, perhaps aged 14, and committed to a sexual relationship with a friend of her aunt's 25 or more years her senior. Away from her family, perhaps five years later, she was to suffer a miscarriage, perhaps unaware of what was happening to her and her body. We may dress this up and argue that these were simply the *mores* of the time and explain it away by social expectations. We may point to the majority of historical societies in which romantic relationships were differentiated from marital relationships. We may suggest that we read these stories anachronistically and from our own particular viewpoints of particular socially approved moralities. We may fear imposing our own values and cultural concerns on another society. Yet, fundamentally, there is physicality to these relationships. The slave and girl are subject to a power relationship. Their bodies are not their own.

We can read Pliny's letters as clever little tales of love from a witty, urbane, educated aristocrat. But from the perspective of the silent, we can read the same letters as stories of horror.

Chapter 16

Religion

This chapter will concentrate on issues of religious change in the Imperial period. Understanding changes in religious practice in the Roman Empire in this period requires an examination of the nature of religion, and it will be argued here that the close relationship between religious, political, and social structures was central to the ancient religious mentality and that the modern distinction between sacred and secular was much less clearly drawn in the ancient world. Further, I shall suggest there was a surprising diversity in religion in this period. It is this diversity, above all, which requires explanation.

Polytheism

The religions of the Roman Empire, with the exception of Judaism and Christianity, were polytheistic. For those educated in a Judaeo-Christian tradition, there is a tendency to view polytheism as 'primitive' and regard monotheism as a more logical system of religious belief. Jewish, Christian and Islamic traditions tend to view religion as a coherent system in which all things are explained, which is why religious traditions sometimes have problems with scientific understandings of the cosmos. Monotheistic traditions differentiate themselves from polytheistic, but tend to expect those traditions to function in similar ways. Christianity opposed itself to paganism. Yet, there was no word and no single concept that we could translate as paganism. Romans thought of religion in the abstract and used 'religio' to talk about it. They also talked about the nature of the gods. There were theological texts, but before the Imperial period, there was little or no sense that the multiplicity of religious practices across the Empire (and outside) should be conceived of as a coherent unity or that one particular set of practices was inherently better than another. It was not until the advent of Christianity that the theology and belief systems of Christianity came to try to define its competition and demand that its competitors play by the Christian theological–philosophical rules. Paganism is a concept is very much the invention of the Christians. Augustine's monumental *City of God* is a fundamental text in this definition of pagan religion.

By late antiquity, we see religious movements within pagan thought, particularly in the East, which seek unifying characteristics of the divine. Neo-platonic philosophers concerned themselves with a universal divine spirit. The gods were perceived in relation to and in communication with each other. In the Hermetic tradition (derived from Egypt) powerful gods could control lesser gods and the possibility of a supreme deity was considered. Such possibilities allowed a more systematic approach to Greek and Roman religion. Yet, this is a late development. Prior to this, there was certainly interest in the religious question of why there were so many gods and what the relationship between the various manifestations of the divine was, but there appears to have been little sense that the multiplicity of gods was a fundamental problem.

In part, this relatively relaxed attitude probably relates to the very nature of the Roman relationship to the divine and the way in which Roman religion developed. The Romans were always aware of the multiplicity of divinities. From the earliest period, Rome was in contact with communities which operated with slightly different deities or represented those deities in different ways. In addition to other Italians (and archaic Italy was a diverse religious environment), Romans encountered Greeks, Celts and Carthaginians, all of whom had different gods and traditions. Greeks and Romans (and others) appear to have accepted this diversity in part because there was a localisation of divinity. Gods had their temples in which they resided. They may not have resided there all their time, but they were localised. Further, gods had aspects. The same god could have various functions and roles. Apollo, for instance, was connected to the sun, to music, and to healing, to name but three of his roles.

The localism of the gods allowed the Romans to conquer through religious means. They could transfer gods from communities to Rome and thus win the approval of the particular deity. Greeks were far more uneasy about this process, regarding it as a violation of the temple.

Localism was an important feature of Roman religious thought. Particular places had particular gods which needed to be worshipped. This is certainly not a unique feature of Roman religion. Egyptian gods also were strongly associated with places. Looked at as a whole and as an Empire-wide phenomenon, paganism could seem incoherent: Artemis of Ephesus was markedly different from Artemis in Greece, for example. But the Romans were happy not to look at religion within the Empire as whole.

Such diversity within a polytheistic system meant that an individual Roman would, as a matter of course, have worshipped different divinities. A Roman could worship Jupiter and Juno, but also offer sacrifice to Isis and, especially if he was in the provinces, to a local god of an entirely different religious tradition. There was no problem. Indeed, when a Roman visited a province, he would expect and was expected to worship the local gods: after all, those local gods were the ones with power in that particular place. Even in Egypt, where there was some divergence in the nature of the gods from the rest of the Mediterranean, Romans are depicted in worship of local gods and sponsoring local temples. Augustus, whom the tradition sees as violently anti-Egyptian, is depicted in Egyptian art sacrificing to the Apis bull. This incoherence meant that Romans could respect gods that did not conform to Roman norms. Even the Jewish god, whose worship presented very particular problems, received gifts from prominent Romans.

As a result of this incoherence, there was no system of religious authority. There was no authorised body of beliefs or practices. There were no scriptures to whose authority one could defer. There is little evidence that the Romans saw a need for such systems. There was a pantheon (group of 12 gods), sanctified by tradition. But these were not 'official' religious cults. Magistrates and prominent Romans made sacrifices to a considerable diversity of religious entities. There was an official religious calendar governing those events that magistrates and priests had to conduct, but there is likely to have been a plethora of other cults, festivals and sacrifices which took place across the Empire and which may or may not have had magisterial participation.

The absence of a separate religious authority is a notable feature of Roman religious activity. The consuls and later the emperor did concern themselves with religious matters: these were important since the future of Roman civilisation depended on maintaining the *Pax Deorum*, the Peace of the Gods, and the emperor would make rulings on issues of religious controversy. Priests were appointed to care for various aspects of the Roman people's relationship with the gods. There seems also to have been a concern to regulate religious activity within the boundaries of the city of Rome. But the senators and the priests of Rome appear to have been reluctant to extend religious authority beyond the traditional city. Religion was a local matter and remained a local matter throughout most of the Imperial period.

Local religious traditions were maintained during the Imperial period. We can detect considerable local variations and the preservation of local cults. In Syria, for example, cults of Bel and Baal remained popular throughout the pre-Christian period. Local deities, such as the Gad, Gadde, or even Had, appear in many cities and were associated with the guardian deity of the city. In Egypt, every city had its own god, worshipped in large central temples that in most cases appear to have been the dominant monument in the city. In many instances, these local manifestations became associated with Greek or Roman gods. In some cases, particularly in the East, we get a multiplication of identifications so that Zeus–Sarapis–Helios becomes a single divine manifestation. Some of these manifestations are difficult to understand. The Egyptian Baboon god, Thoth, comes to be associated with Hermes. The Ram god, Amun, appears as Zeus. The crocodile god, Souchos, seems to have been the antique father of Zeus, Chronos. The cow god, Hathor, becomes Isis and Aphrodite.

This process is known as *interpretatio Graeca*, but the significance of the *interpretatio* is not clear. Architecturally, local cults often received large Roman style temples, though local religious architectural repertoires were sometimes maintained. At Bath, for example, a local deity was given a large, classical style temple associated with an extensive Roman bathhouse. Yet, there are numerous small 'Celtic' temples. In Egypt, some cities received temples in a standard Classical style in the second century especially, but most temples to Egypt gods were built within the local architectural style and were adorned with imagery and hieroglyphic text recognisably related to those which had been in use for the previous two millennia.

At one level, what we are seeing is the preservation of local traditions in new architectural forms, but at another level we are also seeing change. The association with Classical parallels must, in some way, have changed the way in which the cult operated. The association with other gods through the *interpretatio* created a fresh series of associations. The *interpretatio* associates local cults with cultural norms of the Mediterranean, especially in terms of representation of the divine, but possibly also in terms of religious practices and the standing of particular religious institutions with the communities. But the process works two ways: association with a Greek (or Roman) deity establishes an imperial network of associations in which the localised cult is made part of a wider family of cultic associations and activity.

The temptation is to read these developments through the lens of imperialism and to suggest that this change is Romanisation, a form of cultural imperialism. But the processes are more complicated than one culture imposing its beliefs on another, and certainly the associations are not just with the culture of the imperial centre (Rome), but also with other local cultures. The process is not about conversion as religious change was in the European imperial contexts. Crucially, the same god was worshipped after the *interpretatio* as before. Nor is the issue one of ethnicity. The ethnic origins of the gods were often honoured and represented. Isis remained an Egyptian deity even as she was worshipped in Pompeii. Mithras remained Persian as he became manifest on Hadrian's Wall. The local elements of religious practice were always maintained even as the worship of the gods became extra-local. This can be seen in eccentric areas of religious activity such as magical texts. Such texts, preserved in various forms and from various regions, call upon an eclectic range of cultural traditions. The Egyptian material references Egyptian, Jewish, Persian, and Greek sources and also invents some new gods in the process. The exotic is built into local religious practices and the point is precisely that the cult was exotic.

We should, I think, not understand these processes as taking 'pure' local ethnic traditions and corrupting them by contact, but as processes of engagement and representation. To take the example of Bath again, the development of the cultic site in Roman style becomes politically and ethnically divisive if we believe that the local cult was a potential location of resistance to imperial power. But local cults appear to remain local cults. What emerges from the gradual assimilation of cultural forms is a hybrid culture, which has both Roman and local elements, and in fact this hybridisation would seem characteristic of Roman imperial cultural traditions. The result is not the transposition of an Italianate religious culture to the provinces, but the emergence of a distinctive imperial style of religious activity. Furthermore, the process was not one-way. Rome itself was changed by its engagement with imperial religious systems over time and ultimately, of course, the old traditions fell and were replaced by Christianity.

Nevertheless, this pattern of religious change is not without difficulty or without political importance. The localisation of religious authority tied religion to the city community. Although there were many local variations, the cities organised their religious activities so that the leading religious figures in the community tended also to be the leading political figures. In the cities of the Mediterranean heartlands, there was thus a unity of authority between the political and religious spheres. This unity was so thorough that there was little conceptual difference between secular and religious matters. The aristocrats represented the people to the gods as they represented the people to all other authorities. The religious authority of the priests over the people was inseparable from their political roles. Councils would discuss religious matters and the care of the temples as they would discuss the care of the theatre or the gymnasium. Moreover, many seemingly secular structures might have religious associations and associated shrines and temples. The gods were omnipresent.

In Rome, the highest religious offices were held by senators who, as they represented and led the community in political and military affairs, also led in religious matters. State-run religious practice was governed by various groups of priests organised into colleges. These colleges, often in association with magistrates, were responsible for public sacrifices and festivals. The emperor was a member of all the important colleges and also took overall authority over religious matters through his office of *Pontifex Maximus*, which came to be recognised as a supreme priesthood. Religious practice secured the *pax deorum* (the goodwill of the gods) and prevented divine retribution striking the city. In circumstances in which natural disaster, plague or the failure of a harvest could threaten even the most seemingly prosperous of communities, divine retribution may have seemed a very real threat. Since priests represented the community to the gods and led the community in public ceremonials, they acquired considerable prestige and the political elite monopolised religious authority. Religion also legitimised the political order. If the emperor or the senators were seen to be maintaining the city's relationship with the gods, then the political order would be reinforced. There was, therefore, a close interrelationship between religion and politics. But this was not a cynical process. Political authority also brought legitimacy to religious authority: the political leaders were those one wanted to represent the community before the gods, as one wanted them to lead the people in peace and war.

This integration of politics and religion affects our understanding of change factors in Roman religion. It also means that the cultural integration of various local cults was a political integration. Even if the cult maintained many of its original features, it mattered if a Roman made a dedication there and put up in an inscription in Latin. It was not about conversion of the deity, but assimilation into imperial political and religious structures. The temples of Roman Egypt remained distinctive in style and worship, but they were rapidly brought under the administrative and political control of the provincial authorities and that control was manifest in imperial sponsorship of new buildings within the temple complex, restorations, and offerings. The hybridisation that we see in the conjoining of religious traditions was often (though perhaps not always) a symbolic extension of Classical systems of knowledge and power into local cultic activity. Even if this was not part of a conscious policy of cultural imperialism (or cultural conversion), such changes reflected and responded to the power structures of the imperial world.

Religious change

Religious decline

Augustus represented his reign as being one of restoration of the political order. That restoration affected constitutional matters. It led to the state taking an interest in domestic matters. It also encouraged a focus on matters of religion. Although these issues are separate in modern cultures (though we might ask ourselves whether a non-Christian could be elected President of the US or Prime Minister of Britain), for the Romans, religion and political order were very closely interlinked. Augustan restoration was in part physical. He used the money from the Egyptian war to fund the restoration of temples. He spent considerable resources in the building of new temples throughout Rome. It was also institutional. The priesthoods were reformed and vacancies were filled. It was probably also ceremonial. Religious activity provided ceremonials and ceremonials provided the senate and the imperial family the opportunity to parade through the city.

The most obvious depiction of public ceremonial comes on the Ara Pacis. The monument is adorned with a procession of the imperial family and a parallel procession of the senators to sacrifice for the return of Augustus (and Peace). The image is a depiction (probably not accurate) of a real and repeated event. The political authorities and the imperial family united in celebration and worship.

It is tempting to take Augustus at face value and see in the restorations evidence of an underlying decline in religious practice. There are elements that might support such a thesis. Philosophers (notably the Epicureans) were thinking of new and different ways in which the universe worked and came into being, ways which problematised the nature of the gods. The gods could occasionally be treated with levity or a seeming lack of respect. The gods in Ovid's *Metamorphoses* are a strange and violent crowd, animated by passions and prone to cruel violence. Ovid's rewriting of myth tells us much about his view of the world in this period of his views of the uncertain and shifting nature of being (when girls could become trees to escape the rape of gods, when weavers would be made into spiders because of the anger of the gods, when hunters could be turned into prey and torn apart by their own hounds for the crime of stumbling onto a goddess in her bath) and in turn about the political atmosphere of Roman society. If this is 'soft evidence' (evidence of mood, not material reality) of a questioning of the authority and role of the divine, the 82 shrines Augustus claims to have restored represents more material evidence: he would hardly make up such dilapidation.

Yet, we should not think of Roman religion as fixed. It was too disorganised for that. Some rituals fell into disuse and others were developed as new religious influences were felt. Roman society, like most other societies, presented its religious beliefs as archaic. But there was a natural cycle in religious buildings. A building would be given, built, and left as a prestige monument. Over time, it would need repair. Roman magistrates would normally take on that repair, but they needed to be interested enough to do the work, know that the work needed doing, and have the money. And there is always the question of when the work should be done. Change threatened the *pax deorum* and old rituals needed to be preserved, even though sometimes the *pax deorum* needed to be secured by the invention of new rituals.

It suited Augustus to 'restore' religion by repairing and rebuilding temples to leave his mark on the city. Shrines which were no longer used became an obvious symbol of religious decline. To restore those shrines was to say to the Roman people (and the gods) that the state was back and that order was being maintained and the old disciplines would be upheld. It was central to Augustus' political message.

Yet, none of this means that there was decline in religious belief. It seems likely that in the chaotic years of the late Republic less attention was paid to the older buildings and perhaps some of the administrative tasks went incomplete, but the very fact that Augustus chose to restore the temples shows that religion retained its importance. We do not see in the literature any obvious evidence of atheism. Nor do we see evidence of apathy. Gods and worship of gods appear frequently in all literary forms. Suetonius tells us of the omens that were associated with particular emperors or particular events. Even Ovid's mad, bad gods were powerful presences in his literary universe.

A world without gods was unthinkable for the Romans (and, indeed, for the provincials). The divine was part of everyday life. It is tempting to see this presence functionally: in the absence of a scientific explanation for unforeseen events, a divine explanation was sought. But the gods were not an explanation of last resort. They were how the world worked. Shrine and temples proliferated. Street corners and crossroads had their divine spirits. Cities had their shrine, but so did farms and rural waysides. There were shrines to springs and to rivers. The Romans believed in spirits and ghosts. Wastelands and lonely roads might be walked by gods. Gods sent signs and Romans employed dream interpreters, entrail-readers, those skilled in the reading of the flight of birds, they referred to general oracular textbooks, and asked priests what the gods might mean. The senate itself kept a collection of oracular texts. Nearly every private letter we have from Roman Egypt (and we have hundreds) mentions prayers before the gods. There is no reason to doubt their sincerity. Gods were pervasive.

Nineteenth and early-twentieth-century writers sometimes assumed that paganism was in decline. It seemed obvious that paganism was a flawed religious system: it made no sense. These writers took on board the criticisms of Christian theologians, such as Augustine. It seemed obvious that the much admired, intelligent Romans would perceive the flaws in their own religion and reject it. For many brought up within a Judaeo-Christian tradition, religion and morality are inextricably linked. It is difficult to read the accounts of the Julio-Claudians, of Messalina, Claudius, and Nero, and not regard the age as one of gross immorality. Thus, the logic goes, religion must have been in decline as well. Further, over the chronological horizon, Christianity was hovering. Religious histories of the Empire tend to be written towards its end. We know the story becomes one of the triumph of Christianity and thus all elements of religious development and history are thought to point in that direction.

All these assumptions are questionable. The Romans did not view religion as a system. They had no significant concept of sin and so religion and morality were not so closely bound. Christianity did triumph, but the reasons for that triumph are complex and that paganism failed is not one of them. There is no evidence, as far as I can see, that religion was in decline in Rome or in any other part of the Empire. There were still religious miracles. People still claimed to have met the gods in person. People went to temples. People wrote and thought about religious issues. In the Greek world especially, writers such as Plutarch, Artemidorus, Pausanias, and Aelius Aristeides devoted much of their writing to religious themes. Temples became larger and often more ornate. Money was attracted into religious institutions. In many places, religious cults could trace their origins back not centuries but millennia. I find it difficult to believe that many would have foreseen the radical change that would befall Classical religions. Religion was changing, but it was not in decline.

Imperial cult

Almost from the moment of Octavian's victory at Actium, the imperial cult began to develop. It is started with the cities of Asia Minor petitioning for the right to build a temple to Octavian. Gradually, temples to Augustus and

Rome spread through Asia Minor and into Greece. In Egypt, the Emperor stepped into the religious shoes vacated by the Ptolemies. Oaths were taken in the name of the emperors. The emperors were depicted offering cult to the traditional gods of Egypt as the pharaohs had been shown for centuries. The complex assimilation between divine and human that had characterised Egyptian religion continued. Slowly, the cult spread to the West. Temples were built in Gaul and in Spain. Italy appears to have been reluctant to adopt the cult, but local cultic activities began in the cities of Italy and became apparent also in Rome.

Much of this activity was quite small scale. Statues to the emperor were imbued with religious significance. People were made nervous around the statues since touching or damaging them could be seen as *maiestas* (treason). The spirit of the emperor was somehow imbued in the statute as the spirits of gods existed within their statues. Cultic activities may even have developed at street level. Emperor worship in the cities appears to have been organised by local authorities. In part this becomes obvious because different cities operated the cult in slightly different ways. There was no order or plan that came out from Rome (though there must have been imitation of other cults).

In the Sebasteion (temple of the Augusti) in Aphrodisias[1] many of the emperors are depicted and the cult clearly was to all the emperors. In Alexandria, we have a very early and topographically prominent Caesareum, though there is considerable debate as to whether this was a temple of Julius Caesar (Cleopatra had been his lover and he had fathered one of her children) and whether this cult became more generalised. The Caesareum was associated with a Forum in Alexandria and was probably one of the most prominent and Roman buildings in the city. Pompeii had an imperial cult building on the Forum (there is no sense of the cult being hidden away), which may be of Augustan origin, though it was remodelled later. In several Greek cities, such as Sparta, Gortyn, Mantineia, there appear to have been very prominent double-temples associated with the imperial cult (possibly one temple to Augustus and the other to Roma).

Under Augustus, the cult was personalised: it was a cult of Augustus. Tiberius appears to have maintained that focus on Augustus. Gaius, of course, changed the rules and Claudius and later emperors were circumspect about the cult. Nevertheless, the cult continued to flourish. Slowly, the cult became generalised so that it ceased to be associated so closely with a single figure but became the cult of the Caesars. The standard procedure appears to have been that a city would vote to ask permission to build a temple or set up cult worship and that the decree would be sent to the emperor who would either accept, reject or modify the honours proposed.

To most moderns, the imperial cult seems to be one of the odder aspects of Roman religion and further evidence that such religion was formal and not a matter of belief. The problem is, however, more subtle. Imperial cult built on a pre-existing tradition of cult offerings to Hellenistic kings and sometimes even to provincial governors, and the earliest cults to Augustus date from immediately after the victory over Antony which, of course, was the first opportunity for the Eastern cities to propose these honours. Cities throughout the East very quickly began to adopt the cult. The cult made sense within the traditions of the Greek *polis* and within the somewhat different traditions of divine kingship from Egypt and the East. Those older traditions had influenced the conception of kingship in the Hellenistic period.

Yet, the imperial cult was not just a local representation of monarchic power that made sense in local cultures. It spread and it spread to the West where there was no visible pre-existing tradition of divine kingship. Further, the imperial cult became far more developed than anything offered to the Hellenistic kings (outside of Egypt). One way of thinking of the cult in the East is to put it in the context of city religion. City religion was, as we have shown, localised. It worshipped local powers who affected local events. The emperors were different. They were not local but they could affect local events. The development of imperial cult was a way of thinking about the imperial in the local context and of representing the imperial in local ceremonial. For this reason, images of the emperor or emperors were regularly carried in religious processions, involving the emperors in maintaining the divine order. There is, therefore, an obvious and logical parallel between the maintaining of political order and the maintaining of religious order. If worshipping the gods was to maintain an order that was both human and divine, both secular and religious, than the emperors needed to be part of that event and thus the imperial cult needed invention.

It is sometimes suggested that the West was more reluctant to develop the imperial cult and more cynical about its adoption. It is true that the earliest and best evidence for the adoption of the cult comes from the East, but Western communities adopted it with some rapidity and enthusiasm. We may imagine that the cult was adopted for very much the same reason in the West as it was invented in the East.

In Augustan literature the divinity of the emperor is a matter of some question. There is little that suggests that Augustus was a god (and technically he was not a god), but there are plenty of confident predictions that he would become a god. Further, his characteristics are frequently divine. He is almost divine by metaphor. That metaphorical divinity continued to be characteristic in the presentation of emperors, sometimes the metaphor being less obviously metaphoric than others (under Domitian for example). Pliny's *Panegyricus* celebrates Trajan as 'one of us' and his restraint in the matter of divine honours, but makes liberal use of comparisons with the divine.

These metaphors offer us a clue to the nature of the imperial cult. We could interpret the imperial cult as metaphoric. It represented the elevated status of the emperor for whom normal honours were insufficient and who had to be honoured *as if* he was divine. There is some evidence that contemporaries found the imperial cult problematic as a religious concept. There was cynicism concerning the elevations of Drusilla (see p. 137) and Claudius (see p. 172 and 175) and Vespasian's premonition of his own forthcoming divinity was interpreted as evidence of humour (Suetonius, *Vespasian*, 23.4). There was a certain separation between the representation of the emperors as divine and the human reality of those imperial lives.

If we consider the power of the emperor, then his association with divinity becomes clearer. Imperial control over the military, wealth, political structures and the law brought unprecedented power to a single man. This power was wielded by a man frequently remote and known only from his images. The emperor communicated to the people through symbols and they granted him honours in kind – statues, shrines, rituals and temples. The imperial cult was an organised system of symbols by which the provincials demonstrated their loyalty and through which the emperors could show their favour, and should be interpreted in parallel to all the other forms of communication between an emperor and his subjects. It was of political and religious significance. The imperial cult was one way of making sense of the emperor's power.

The division between the divine and the secular was far less certain in antiquity. We are used to all-powerful remote divinities so very different from us. The Greeks and Romans and Egyptians and others had deities which were anthropomorphic. Also, if divinities were much more like humans (if there was something human in the god), humans were also in some ways like gods (there was something divine in the human). Spirits, like gods, had powers. Everyone had a *numen* or a *genius* (we would translate both words as 'spirit') and later in the Roman period it was the *numen* of the emperor which was explicitly worshipped. There is nothing exceptional about that worship in religious terms. Everyone knew that the physical form of the emperor was mortal. The question that arose was about the emperor's spiritual essence. The Romans of the first century AD did not view the gods as inhabiting a mythological past. The omens that fill the pages of Tacitus, Suetonius and Dio are examples of manifestations of the divine. Romans of our period believed themselves as likely as Romans of earlier times to meet a god walking the street. The divine surrounded the Romans and there was nothing particularly incongruous in having one who was destined to be a god among them. The same Vespasian who seemed so cynical about his forthcoming divinity was apparently able to heal the lame by touch (Suetonius, *Vespasian,* 7.2–3). The lauding of emperors as divine figures has to be taken seriously.

Augustus became a *divus* after his death. This meant that he became deified and a recipient of cult. Julius Caesar had also been made a *divus*. The process of become divine was part of the legend that surrounded Romulus and, indeed, Hercules. Only Gaius appears to have made explicit a divine pretension which associated him with the immortals; it is difficult to know how seriously to take this divine play-acting.

From the religious perspective of antiquity, the oddity of the imperial cult rested only in the immensity of the power wielded by the emperors. It is moderns who have the religious problems.

Transported and new cults

One of the more notable features of the Imperial period is the increasing diversity of religious cult in terms of origins and, of course, the increasing prominence of Christianity, though it is not until long after the period that Christianity became the majority religion of the Empire.

Rome was eclectic in its development of cult. Foreign cult might arrive through official or unofficial channels. Sometimes, such cults provoked hostility, but we have no obvious reactions in most instances. In some instances, the cult may have come with migrants. In other cases, contact with the cult may have happened in the provinces and the cult was brought back to Rome. Cults may have continued to have migrant worshippers and one suspects that immigrants would maintain their own cults to some extent, but religion does not appear to have been ethnically closed and the religions new to a particular locale also appear to have attracted locals.

One of the most obvious instances of an imported cult is that of Isis. Isiac artefacts had made their way to Italy in some number by the third century BC. There were temples to Isis in Italy in the second century BC. Rome may have been late to adopt the cult and there is some disagreement as to when the cult arrived, but it is likely to have been a visible presence in the city by the first decades of the first century BC. The cult encountered hostility, though it is not clear why. There may perhaps have been an association with Egypt with which some were uncomfortable. Isiac priests were also specialists and not connected to the political elite in Rome. Yet, one of the first acts of the triumvirs was to build a large temple of Isis in the centre of Rome and there were other large temples within the city, probably from a similar date.

Tiberius took action against Egyptian rites in Rome (Suetonius, *Tiberius,* 36), but Caligula rebuilt the Iseum Campense and Nero introduced Isiac festivals into the Roman calendar. Domitian once more rebuilt the Iseum Campense while the Iseum at Beneventum, where his portrait as pharaoh was exhibited, may have been constructed during his reign. Rome had three large Isea: the Campense, one in Regio III and one on the Capitol; there were also smaller temples on the Caelian, Esquiline and Aventine Hills.

The fortunes of the Jewish community were also varied. The Romans were officially tolerant of established Jewish communities and extended protection to the Jews in the various cities. There were exceptions and the effectiveness of Roman protection may be doubted, especially in periods of tension such as the years of the Jewish war. Gaius' plan to place a statue of himself in the temple at Jerusalem (p. 144) and his emphasis on his own divinity placed great stress on the Jewish community. Tiberius also acted against the Jews, for reasons which are unclear, probably at the same time as he acted against those following Egyptian rites (see above). The community had been restored by the reign of Claudius, who again expelled the Jews from Rome, probably because of problems within the community concerning the emergence of Christianity and perhaps resulting violence (Suetonius, *Claudius*, 25). The Jewish revolt must have increased tension and Vespasian imposed a punitive tax on the Jewish community in the aftermath of the revolt. Domitian levied the tax with a certain barbarity (see pp. 252–53) and, although Nerva may have relaxed the methods of collection (see p. 260), the tax continued to be levied.

Modern Judaism is non-proselytising (i.e. it does not actively seek converts). Although some in antiquity saw Jewishness as being transmitted through descent from the patriarchs and thus not open to converts, there is considerable evidence of communication between pagans and Jews in religious matters and it seems possible that there was some conversion in antiquity (though this remains controversial). There was an intermediate status in some Jewish communities of 'god-fearers', who were allowed some status within the community. Their presence may have blurred distinctions between Jews and non-Jews.

Many Jews lived as ethnic minorities throughout the Empire. In the Eastern cities, these communities adopted aspects of Greek culture, and Greek seems to have been widely used alongside Aramaic (the language Jesus would have used). Hellenisation affected Jewish culture as it affected other Mediterranean cultures and our two major Jewish writers of the period, Josephus and Philo, not only wrote in Greek, but were fluent in Greek literary forms. The Jewish elite mixed easily with the Roman aristocracy. Members of the Herodian royal family were frequently in Rome and were close to Claudius and (rather strangely) Gaius. The prominence of the Jewish princess Berenice and other Jews at the courts of Vespasian and Titus may also have encouraged interest in Jewish matters in the Flavian period. Josephus was in the city and there may have been others whose behaviour during the Jewish war made their homeland 'uncomfortable'. Tiberius Julius Alexander, the former prefect of Egypt, was also prominent under Vespasian. Although not a Jew himself, he was descended from Jews and may have retained connections with the Jewish community.

The situation may, however, have been changing in the aftermath of the Jewish war. The punitive taxes introduced following the Jewish revolt probably led to the creation of a register of Jews to enable the collection of the tax. People were therefore forced to declare their Jewish identity. Those who avoided paying risked punishment. Domitian's severe enforcing of religious and fiscal regulations seems to have meant that denial of Jewish identity would not be accepted as sufficient grounds for exemption from the Jewish tax. Once registered as Jews, people had to remain Jews. Also, it probably made conversion or adopting the intermediate status more difficult, since it would appear that such behaviour would lay people open to the charge of atheism and, as the emperor was a god (or almost so), atheism was almost equivalent to treason. Domitian used atheism as a political charge, and the persecution of those who showed an interest in Judaism offers some parallels to the persecution of Christians.

Outside Rome, we have evidence of tensions and extreme violence between Jewish and other communities in the Greek East. Mostly, these issues relate to the Jewish War of 66–70. In Alexandria, however, the violence appears to have had different roots and to have been more long-lasting. The issue in Alexandria was partly about membership of the urban community. It appears to have been worsened by the prefect of the time, Flaccus, who is the target Philo identifies as carrying much of the blame (Philo, *In Flaccum*). Philo's case against Flaccus was, though, that he did not restrain those elements of the Greek community who wished to do harm to the Jews. What is less clear is why anyone would have wanted to harm the Jews of the city and Philo is not inclined to provide his opponents with rational motivations. They had after all, according to Philo, been engaged in numerous violent acts against the Jewish community, including beatings murders, and the humiliation of women (which may be euphemistic). There is debate on Greek-Jewish relations in Alexandria in Philo, *Embassy to Gaius* and in Josephus' response to a polemic against the Jews, the *Contra Apion*. Towards the end of our period, the Jews of Alexandria and Cyrene revolt and a war which is depicted in terrible terms broke out. This war may have distracted Trajan from his conquests and encouraged Hadrian to withdraw from the newly conquered territories. It seems that for 80 years, there was hostility between Greeks and Jews in Alexandria.

Explaining that hostility is difficult. There were legal issues with regard to citizenship of Alexandria, but it somehow seems unlikely that people were murdered over the technicalities of the exact legal status of Jews in the city. It seems to be more likely that the legal issues were an element of a wider dispute, a tool within the argument between the two communities. The outbreak of violence in Alexandria has been seen as the origin of modern anti-Semitism, but again this is quite difficult to believe. Modern anti-Semitism has its origins in Medieval Christian prejudices against Jews as non-Christians, as Christ-killers, as outsiders, as usurers. Other mythic elements attached to Jews, associating Jews with child murder. Later, conspiracy theories (which live on) determined the world 'Jewish conspiracy' and, as all conspiracy theories do, found its representatives everywhere. Later still, in the twenty-first century anti-Semitism was adopted by the pseudo-science of race and millions died as a result. But none of that applied to ancient Alexandria. Not a single feature that we can identify as characteristic of the theories of anti-Semitism can be paralleled in antiquity.

I suspect that the Alexandrian disturbances were primarily political. The Jewish community in Alexandria was organised and, indeed, powerful. It seems likely that this community was in competition with others in the city for political favours. That competition would likely focus on winning the support of the Roman authorities. Whereas the Jews could deploy the Herodian family, the Greeks could deploy the imperial cult. Although religion was a defining feature of identity, it seems to me likely that the violence was primarily political (in our terms) and secondarily religious.

Jews appear to have lived in relative peace elsewhere in the Empire until the Christian period. We have archaeological evidence of large and elaborately decorated synagogues, suggesting considerable wealth in the community. This is unsurprising for the area of Palestine, where Jewish communities were in the majority, but we find well-preserved synagogues at Apamea, Dura and Ostia away from Jewish heartlands. More fragmentary remains are widely distributed. There is no doubt that Jewish communities were a feature of nearly every major city of the Mediterranean.

Christianity appears to have spread quickly throughout the Empire, initially through these Jewish communities. Although there was some debate in the apostolic generation, Christianity did open its faith to non-Jews and made conversion easy. Christianity was quickly able to establish itself as a separate religious tradition and not just a Jewish sect. We have no figures for the rate of conversion or the size of Christian communities. The Christians in Rome were already notable by the reign of Claudius, and Nero instituted the first persecution.

Pliny also tells us that there had been a considerable number of Christians in Bithynia. He had started persecuting the Christian community but, in the process, uncovered more information, which led him to contact the emperor. He tells us that large numbers of people were potentially implicated, but that many had ceased to be Christians at some point before the persecution started. Tellingly, he notes that meat from sacrifices was now selling on the market (*Epistles*, 10.96). This suggests that the Christian community must have been sufficiently large to have had a noticeable effect on the market. Furthermore, it also suggests that persecution had managed to detach Christians from the community. Although Christian mythography emphasised those who stayed loyal and suffered terribly as a result, many Christians either avoided detection during persecutions or lapsed, and the lapsed were a significant problem when and if they wished to return to the Church. It seems likely that the numbers of Christians fluctuated over time rather than steadily increasing.

It is unclear how Nero's persecution was organised. He may have made Christianity illegal by decree or acted against the Christians under other legislation, perhaps in connection with the fire or with 'impiety' Pliny's letter to Trajan concerned the exact charge against the Christians. Pliny was uncertain as to the legal basis of his proceedings: was he prosecuting these people because they were Christians or because of what Christians did? If the latter, then his investigations had uncovered little criminal behaviour. Trajan wrote back to Pliny to clarify procedures. Pliny was told that he was not to hunt out Christians. He was not to respond to anonymous pamphlets. Former Christians were to be released provided that they offered prayers to the emperor. Current Christians were given the opportunity to deny the charge. If they refused, they were to be killed. No mention is made of other crimes and it is to be presumed that Christians were to be punished because they were Christians (Pliny, *Epistles*, 10.97).

Pliny was active in the law courts at Rome and his ignorance of procedure in relation to the Christians suggests that persecution of Christians was comparatively rare and one wonders whether the Bithynian persecution was a local event, inspired by our zealous and self-gratulatory governor. Local bouts of persecution rather than an organised imperial campaign do appear to have driven the oppression of Christians in the first two centuries AD and it was perhaps only in the third century that systematic persecution began. Martydoms in Lyon and Smyrna in the early second century appear to have driven by local concerns.

There has been considerable concern among historians as to why the Christians were persecuted at all. The persecutions seem without obvious legal basis (as Pliny thought) and also historians have seen them as being out of keeping with Roman toleration of cultural difference. Yet, this last aspect has been considerably exaggerated. Romans tolerated differences only to an extent. From time to time, they decided that certain cultural differences were intolerable and they persecuted. This was the case with hostility towards Jews at various points, the persecution of druids, the occasional expulsion of Egyptians, and the persecution of Christians. Yet, it seems to have been Christians who most consistently attracted popular and official anger.

Although Christians sometimes claimed in their apologies that they were persecuted for ludicrous reasons and for crimes which were easily disproved (which is a good rhetorical technique), see for example the *Octavius* of Minucius Felix, it seems likely to me that the real reason Christians were persecuted lies at the heart of Roman religion. It has to do with the city-based nature of the religion. We will return to the problem in a moment.

One of the notable features of the religious practices of the Roman and indeed late Hellenistic periods is the eclecticism. Cults crossed the Empire and although there must have been some contacts with the original region of worship, it would seem unlikely that the movement of cult simply reflected the movements of population. This might seem unproblematic at first in a polytheistic universe, but we need to ask ourselves why Roman soldiers would worship the Persian god Mithras. There is a temple to Sarapis in Roman London. There is plenty of evidence that prominent Romans took up the worship of Isis. One of the most notable and peculiar monument of Ancient Rome is the pyramid of Cestius at the Ostian gate. Why would a Roman aristocrat build himself a pyramid? This eclecticism happens all over the Empire. The Greek cities adopted many Eastern cults.

One explanation for this has been to compare the movement of cult to the trade of goods and to suppose that cults operated within a religious marketplace in the Hellenistic and Roman worlds. The worshippers would then tour looking for the best offer, the best pitch that would attract him or her into the temples. The theory reflects the heterogeneity of religious practices and the seemingly open nature of the city to diverse influences. The theory would argue that the more successful cults had better offerings. Mithras gave companionship and community. Isis offered exoticism and mysticism. Christianity offered salvation, a measure of egalitarianism, and charity. The social functions of the cults are seen as key to their success.

No doubt there is something to this idea. Christian and Islamic missionaries have long been aware that feeding the bellies of the poor is a first step to winning their minds. But this is a very secular way of looking at religion. Religion was central to the lives of the ancients. It told them who they were. It managed their relationship with the ever-present divine. It was not a consumer or fashion choice.

City cults were inextricably linked with city cultures, their politics, and their long traditions. People worshipped the same gods their ancestors had worshipped and in the same manner. Even if there had been changes, religion was profoundly conservative and innovations probably masked themselves as restored traditions. Communities were made and maintained around religious rituals. I would argue that it was profoundly significant that in the early Roman Empire especially we see religious experimentation and people looked for religious experiences beyond the conventions of the established communities. We might expect innovation among groups such as soldiers who had moved away from their homelands and had to reinvent traditions. But innovation in the Mediterranean heartlands suggests to me that there was dissatisfaction with the cults of the city. Somehow, they were starting not to work. People looked to different ways of making sense of the world and different ways of approaching the divine, ways which were not so caught up in traditions and the political order. In some small way, religious innovation was a minor rebellion against tradition and order. It was an act of resistance.

If most religious cults could easily be accepted alongside traditional civic cult, the most successful and innovatory cult could not. We may have lost sight of the radical nature of Christianity. Jesus taught some extraordinary things. People were to give up their property and follow him. Caesar's things (coinage, money, the material world) were for Caesar. The structures of community in Judaism were useless compared with the relationship with the divine. There were harder notions as well, ones that play less well today. The family should be abandoned as well as the material world. Christianity rejected many social conventions It was deeply uneasy about sex and marriage (and this unease was not derived from a Jewish tradition) and regarded virginity as a pure state. In a culture in which everyone married at the behest of their families, conversion of a son or daughter to a religion that taught celibacy was a disaster. Centuries later, even good Christian families struggled with the idea of a son or daughter becoming a celibate. It is very difficult not to see such teaching as socially disruptive: how would civilisation continue if no one had sex any more? The early Christian attitude to wealth was also revolutionary: wealth should be given up and used for the poor. Many Romans will have been surprised at such a doctrine. The decision to worship a Galilean carpenter's son was at almost every level extraordinary. It was revolutionary.

Roman religious practice tended to be conservative. The *pax deorum* was secured by following ancestral custom. Judaism was part of an established world of religious cults. The continuation of Judaism did not affect the *status quo*. Christianity, however, did alter religious practice in that those who had previously worshipped at the city altars were drawn away. This threatened the *pax deorum* and could lead to popular fears about Christianity. Conversion also caused problems. Religion was not just a matter of public cult, but there was also worship in the home and gods were asked to bless significant acts. Withdrawal from these domestic ceremonies had implications for participation in family life. Unless the whole family converted, Christianity could cause domestic rifts.

Withdrawal from public cultic activity had other implications. The public cults were closely bound to the political structures of the city and the Empire. Avoidance of participation in sacrifices would have meant that men would probably have been unable to be magistrates. Sessions of the senate, for instance, commenced with a libation (an offering of wine) and this custom may have been followed by many local councils. Christianity also ruled out participation in the imperial cult.

It seems to me that the innovations in the religious culture of the first and later centuries of the Empire were on a scale that requires a dramatic explanation. The religious traditions of antiquity were very long-lasting. There were changes and developments obviously, but for 700 years or more, the pace of change was slow. Yet, in the Roman Imperial period, the rate of change increases and towards the end of the period one of the most radical and decidedly new elements of the religious environment became dominant.

The rise of Christianity was intimately connected with the Roman Empire. I see the emergence of the cult in Judaea as a response to imperial rule. For me, early Christianity was profoundly anti-imperial. I think, but this is very controversial, that Christianity's success lay in that anti-imperialism. It was the failure of the Christians to make offerings to various gods and to a statue of Trajan which so annoyed Pliny that he felt it right to put them to death without further enquiry. Withdrawal from the imperial cult was seen as a denial of the political and religious order. This was incomprehensible to Romans. It was almost insane. In Pliny's view, such disloyalty had to be punished. In many ways, he was right. The Christians were opposed to Empire. Yet, the popularity and eventual success of Christianity should make us pause and worry and ask profound questions about the nature of imperial rule and what it does to people.

In the early first century a story started to circulate about a man who the authorities had arrested and beaten. He was tortured. He was mocked. He was nailed to a cross on a hill. He died slowly and in very great pain. He was recognised as an enemy of the state. Three centuries later, the authorities worshipped that man as God. We need to consider the profound implications of that story again and again.

Note

1   See http://www.nyu.edu/projects/aphrodisias/seb.htm. Accessed April 2013.

Chapter 17

Romanisation

This chapter concentrates on the issue of cultural change. It is also something of a conclusion. It asks the fundamental question of how Rome changed the world. Behind that question is a difficult political and moral issue, which is not one historians often tackle head on. The problem relates to civilisation. It is worth thinking about here because it does affect how people have understood the Roman Empire and how they continue to represent it. The issues are whether the spread of Roman culture meant a spread of civilisation and whether that spread of civilisation was actually a social good.

The beneficial effects of Rome have been closely related to the spread of that culture. Roman imperialism was the medium by which Classical culture was spread through most of Europe and North Africa. Classical culture has been widely admired and highly valued, and continues so to be. In the eighteenth and nineteenth centuries, the Roman Republic was valued for its imperial success and its political brilliance, but the Empire was lauded for its peace and success. Edward Gibbon, the great Roman historian whose *Decline and Fall of the Roman Empire* (1776) remains one of the most important texts in Western historical literature, saw the second century as the historical moment in which 'the condition of the human race was most happy and prosperous'. That view has been widely accepted. In the late nineteenth century, the beneficial effects of Roman imperialism helped justify European imperialism. The imperial mission was to spread civilisation. In this period a view of a ladder or typology of civilisation developed. The West was the most advanced and that advanced status required it to spread its bounty to the rest of the world. One of the reasons for Western superiority, especially in regard to 'Oriental' civilisation, was the Classical legacy. Historians of the Empire viewed the imprint of Rome as having been long-lasting and fundamental, even in places such as Britain.

Romanisation is caught up in these debates about modern imperialism, but also about the nature of culture and about whether certain cultures are better than others. Gibbon was a utilitarian. He defined the 'best' civilisation in terms of the maximisation of happiness and it is this movement that fed the emphasis in the American Declaration of Independence on the fundamental right to 'life, liberty and the pursuit of happiness'. Happiness remains difficult to measure. Yet, the fundamental questions remain: did Roman imperialism transform and improve local cultures? Did Rome leave a legacy in the West? Further, while pro-imperial writers of the nineteenth and twentieth centuries tended to see the impact of Rome as being transformational, the modern experience of post-imperial politics has led many to doubt the efficacy of imperialism and stress cultural opposition to imperial cultures and cultural continuities in the face of imperial oppression. In recent decades, a loose philosophical and political movement (post-colonialism) has revisited ideas of imperialism and had argued that although oppositional movements tended to emphasise cultural continuities and imperialists wanted to see their rejection as a return to savagery, imperialism did have significant cultural effects and that both the colonised and the colonising societies were profoundly changed by the encounter. The debate was highly political and remains so. Ghandi was often forced to debate the virtues of British imperialism and one of the counters to his demand for Indian independence was 'What about Western civilisation?', to which Ghandi supposedly responded, 'I think it would be a good idea'. Would Roman civilisation have been a good idea?

Such questions raise the issue of what we are talking about when we talk about Romanisation. At its simplest level, Romanisation is the process of change by which local cultures became more 'Roman'. Yet, we have seen in the chapter on religion that 'Roman' is actually quite difficult to define when it comes to matters religious. In the East, 'Romanisation' and 'Hellenisation' are often regarded as synonymous. Also, judgement is frequently made on the basis of material culture. But is civilisation only a matter of materialism? How does material culture relate to other aspects of culture? Further, how does culture relate to identity?

Lest one believes that is solely a modern issue to which we are made over-sensitive by contemporary concerns, one of the few ancient historians to discuss the processes of cultural change in the Empire is Tacitus. In *Agricola* 21 Tacitus writes:

> The following winter was spent on schemes of improvement. For since the men were dispersed and primitive, they were easily roused to war, and [Agricola] wished to make them quiet and peaceful through comforts. Privately, he encouraged, and publicly he helped so that they built temples, fora, and houses. He praised the eager, and castigated the slow. Thus, desire for honour supplanted force. Now, indeed, he educated the son of the chiefs in liberal arts and preferred the talent of the British to the studiousness of the Gauls, so that instead of rejecting Latin, they desired eloquence in it. Even our clothes were honoured and the toga was often worn; and little by little, they were given up to the seductions of moral weakness, the porticos, the baths, the elegant entertainments. This was called "culture" among the ignorant when it was part of their enslavement.

Tacitus is discussing what we would call Romanisation. Agricola provided the Britons with the material culture of the Roman Empire. He also provided them with an education in Classical language. Together, this was called 'culture', but only by the ignorant. The Latin word used for this concept is *humanitas*, which we could interpret as the quality of being human. We could summarise Tacitus' remark to mean that it was thought that to live as a human one needed the accoutrements of Roman civic life, when really the wise, such as Tacitus and his readers, know that such accoutrements are enslaving. We can imagine that Tacitus and Ghandi might well have a decent conversation about this.

In this final chapter, I suggest that the impact of Roman imperialism on local cultures was profound. I see the emergence of an imperial culture. There were many local variations and continuities. Imperial culture built on pre-existing traditions, but it was new and it was recognisably similar across the Roman Empire. I also suggest that the home of Empire, Rome, was profoundly changed by Empire.

The reasons for coming to this conclusion are mostly detailed in the previous chapters. The Roman Empire is marked by religious change and although many local traditions continued, they were often expressed in new forms. The Empire is marked by economic change. The material culture of many of the regions of the Empire was transformed. Pottery, wine, oil, jewellery, clothing, metalwork, and many other goods circulated throughout the Mediterranean region and beyond. Roman coinage became enormously widespread. Coins appear everywhere: at all kinds of sites and even in places where there is no obvious site. In Britain especially, there are many coin finds every year scattered all across England. We find mosaics from Hadrian's Wall to the frontiers of Syria. Statues and works of art are found in all sorts of communities, not just the wealthy, but in cities and villages, on farms and in villas. Classical-style buildings are also found throughout the Empire. Cities proliferated and grew. There can be little doubt that even at the end of our period (AD 117) the territory of the Empire was more culturally, economically, politically, and socially homogeneous than a century earlier and this process of homogenisation continued for centuries.

The development of urban centres on a Roman model is one of the most obvious facets of Romanisation. Such settlements can be seen in all the conquered lands of the West. Typically, the city centre would have a regular street plan where the intersections of the streets formed regular rectangular blocks. The two main streets (the *cardo* and *decumanus*) ran through the geometric centre of the city and, near where these streets crossed, the Forum would be situated. The Forum would have a basilica, temples, and other Roman-style buildings. The city would normally also be provided with baths.

In the countryside, the development of villas also attests the importation of Roman culture. There is some disagreement about the classification of villas. Archaeologists have tended to define as villas rural structures which have both a rectangular ground plan and stone footings. Such a definition may work for villas in Britain, but clearly cannot apply to many other areas of the Empire where the native architectural style was for rectangular stone farmhouses. Some early British villas show little sign of Roman influence other than the ground plan and building materials, though these were notable developments. In other provinces, rural properties began to develop more 'Roman' features, such as bathhouses or mosaics. In southern Gaul and Spain, structures similar in style to Italian farms developed. In Germany, northern Gaul and Britain, the style of development was rather different: corridor villas (a series of rooms connected by a passage running alongside the rooms) were common. In Gaul, the first century AD saw the development of some elaborate villas with suites of rooms arranged on three sides of a courtyard. Although problems of categorisation remain, and many buildings which have been classified as villas were built on or near the site of pre-existing native farms, few doubt that the emergence of these new architectural styles was in some way related to Roman conquest.

Language is also a crucial area of change. The preservation of large numbers of privately erected Latin inscriptions (mainly funerary inscriptions) from the Roman West and Greek inscriptions from the East would seem to attest widespread knowledge of Latin or Greek. We have many thousands of such inscriptions and we may assume that most of the inscriptions that from antiquity have been lost.

Of course, there were many others who did not record their lives or deaths in Latin or Greek inscriptions. It is very possible that the majority of our privately erected inscriptions emanate from a relatively small sector of society. A large proportion of the inscriptions from Roman Britain involve soldiers and their families. Many African inscriptions again come from a similarly military context. It is arguable that these provide us with virtually no evidence for the linguistic culture of the majority of the population. Pre-conquest languages continued in common use in Africa, Egypt and Syria and we may assume similar linguistic continuities in Celtic areas. Recent studies on the Latin in use at the Roman fort at Vindolanda on Hadrian's Wall and in the fort at Bu Njem in Tripolitania show the influence of non-Latin languages. Even in these military contexts and in contexts in which some trained scribes operated, we can detect native influences on Latin (though it seems likely that Latin was spoken at both forts).

Egyptian and Aramaic re-emerged as literary languages in Late Antiquity suggesting that both languages continued to be widely used even in periods for which there is virtually no evidence for them being spoken. Yet, this is not straightforward evidence of continuity. Egyptian literature was written in Coptic. Coptic script was heavily based on Greek. In fact, the language itself was influenced by Greek. Both Coptic and Syriac were used primarily for Christian texts and attest to the Christianisation of the Syriac- and Egyptian-speaking populations and it was through Christianisation that these populations were assimilated into the religious culture of the Roman Empire.

Even if evidence of local cultural continuities is abundant and local cultures and local cultural traditions were not eliminated, the evidence of change is overwhelming. The debate among historians has been too black and white, seeing culture as either local or Roman (or Greek). In many, many cases, ethnic labels are simply inadequate as a description of the processes that were underway. Further, they emphasise origins in a way that may well mislead. To take a modern example, my computer was manufactured in China by a Japanese firm and is running American software while I write in UK English. The origins of the artefacts that surround are less important, it seems to me, than the globalised economy (and culture) that those artefacts attest.

Rome conquered societies which had long-established cultural traditions. Those cultural traditions were embedded in local economies and political and social structures. These social forces established local identities. The Roman Empire possessed pre-industrial technology, poor systems of bureaucratic control, and information systems poor compared with that of any modern state. Rome moved very few officials or representatives into the provinces. The largest single group were soldiers, but, as we have seen, soldiers were unlikely to have caused significant cultural change (see pp. 364–66). In the East especially, Roman government relied on pre-existing political and administrative structures. Much basic business was conducted through local urban elites. The Roman state appears to have not intervened in very significant ways in provincial society, nor does it appear to have had the technical means to intervene to change cultural values. Roman imperialism largely depended on the extremely blunt instrument of military power.

The only possible explanation for the widespread change that we see in the Imperial period is that locals adopted elements of the imperial culture. Although that might sound very peaceful and utopian, we have to consider the social logic that led to the adoption of imperial cultural values. If we reduce the question to the level of the individual, it must be that individuals saw an advantage in adopting aspects of the imperial culture.

There were various possible advantages. Some of these were purely technological. Roman engineering and manufacturing was comparatively advanced. Yet, I think the advantages are more likely to have been social, political, and economic. The Roman authorities were obviously powerful in the provinces they came to control. They were able to concentrate at least some of the wealth of those provinces in the hands of their administration. Yet, they needed local support. An enterprising provincial who was able to build a relationship with a local tax collector, for example, would be able to benefit from that relationship. People did not collect tax for fun: they did it to make money. Provincials had a considerable interest in inserting themselves into the Roman structures or power and wealth. Doing so probably required familiarity with various aspects of the imperial culture.

Of course, by establishing a few contacts and with a little money, a provincial could acquire status in one's local community. One would become an individual who might get the Romans to do things. On a larger scale, we see this process operating in the cities of the Greek East, where individuals established personal relations with the imperial family. They served as representatives and ambassadors and secured favours. Those favours brought them status in the local communities and thus we see them being given honours (statues and decrees in their favour). Further down the social scale, the same processes were probably at work. Obviously, a villager would not be able to go an embassy to Rome, but he might befriend a local military officer. He might get some business. He might find work for fellow-villagers and suddenly appear to be a trusted individual.

One of the ways of exploiting that increase in status was through display. How better to advertise your Roman connections than by offering your guests some Spanish wine? You might order a mosaic. You might decide to change the architectural layout of your house, teach your sons and daughters Latin and Greek. Romans would come to see you as more Roman, a better representative of Roman power, and locals would see that power in your house. You might move to the city, to be closer to the political centre.

If all that sounds very self-improving and beneficial, we could consider other advantages that Roman culture might bring. The Romans supported wealth and the wealthy. The acquisition of wealth did, as we have seen, allow the acquisition of more wealth. Political connections may also have brought financial benefits. Building up one's wealth opened certain possibilities for political authority. Even if there was no landed aristocracy before the Roman invasions, aristocracies emerged within newly conquered provinces, gradually accumulating land. Yet, the accumulation of wealth had social effects. A rich person might decide to invest his wealth in a temple, and the temple would then become a symbol not just of the local religious continuities, but of the wealth of the person (or people) who made the investment. One does not necessarily need an inscription in a small community: everyone knows who has the money. And then, one might decide to bring in a few slaves, supported in your master status by the full weight of Roman law and of Roman social prestige. If anyone complains, your wealth has bought you friends and such complaints will be dealt with.

Roman imperial culture supported a hierarchy. It was in a person's interests to get a place in that hierarchy. The hierarchy brought wealth and power to certain individuals and provided them with an interest in engaging with the imperial culture. It was far better to be a master than a slave.

In Tacitean terms, we see the local adoption of the social values of imperial culture. The slavery (though Tacitus would not have put it this way) comes in accepting the social and political disciplines that come with the Roman imperial hierarchy. Tacitus' attribution of slavery to the material benefits of Romanisation looked to the imperial culture and the emperors' tendency to tyranny, but imperial tyranny did not directly reach the small cities of Roman Britain. Nevertheless, the mentalities of imperial corruption were widespread (as Tacitus illustrated throughout the *Annales*). The emperor might have been corrupt, but so were the senators, so were the tax collectors and the soldiers. The *Agricola* is filled with accounts of Roman corruption, at least until Agricola took over the administration of Britain. Tacitus would seem to be portraying corruption as endemic to the Roman system. To become Roman was to become corrupt.

Nevertheless, Tacitus himself was not going to abandon Roman ways or the material culture of the Empire, cross the borders to join the barbarians. The implication of the Tacitean text is that Tacitus and his contemporaries also willingly (though perhaps knowingly) accepted their slavery. There was not, after all, much of an alternative. We must remember that this slavery was imposed by Agricola and Agricola was clearly and unquestionably the hero of the hour.

Tacitus allows us to think again about the processes of cultural change within the Roman Empire and to put cultural change within the context of Roman culture and Roman imperialism in its broadest sense. Much of the latter half of this book has focused on Roman power structures. We have seen the close relationship between political power, religious authority, social status, and economic power. We have seen that power in its brutal forms in slavery and imperial violence. When we considered Roman society, we tried to think about it in terms of networks of power relations and discourses which reflected and maintained those power relations. It is these structures of power, repeated and replicated throughout the Empire, that gave the Empire its cultural and political unity.

Instead, then, of thinking about the Roman Empire as a unified state structure on analogy with our modern national states with a national culture, we should perhaps be thinking of the Empire as made up of many local political, economic, cultural, and social networks. Most of these existed with local environments, perhaps centring on local cities, though connected to imperial structures. Yet, even if there was imperial or provincial level sponsorship, it seems that it was at a local level that many of the values of Roman imperial culture were replicated. If we take the cities of the East as an example, these were not reshaped and remade in the Roman style and later Roman periods by direct Roman intervention, nor by Romans moving into the cities. Rather, the cities saw that it was to their advantage to adapt to certain imperial norms, to build temples to the imperial cult, to honour the emperors, to integrate Rome into their cultural world. They did so because individual members of the elite and perhaps the collective of the population saw the clear advantages in being more Roman.

Undoubtedly, some of those advantages were derived from political powers external to the community, from governors and the emperor. We should remember that Empire had enormous resources that they could use to benefit a city. We should also remember that individuals could benefit greatly from making political connections to members of the Roman elite. Official postings and wealth might follow a successful campaign to be noticed. Once someone was recognised as a person of importance, then the governor was likely to take that person seriously and the network of friendship would grow further and potentially be beneficial to the city. The rioting in Alexandria between the Greek and Jewish communities appears at least in some respects to have been sparked by competition to win the support of imperial level elites for these localised communities.

Yet, the urge to Romanise also looked inwards. Rome was associated with power. Those who associated with Rome would also seem powerful. The symbolic language of Roman imperial culture would work within local communities. But adopting elements of Roman culture would also enable the deployment of Roman social values, values of hierarchy in which the political elite were expected to exercise control within their communities and accumulate wealth and power. The Roman authorities had an interest in finding people to work with them in local communities and making sure that those people were powerful and wealthy and it seems certain that many in local communities could see the material benefit in working with the Romans.

If we think about the Empire in this way, we can see that the overall political unity allows for considerable local variation and for local continuities. One could go to the local temple and worship the local god, but also dress in the latest Roman styles, wear the fashionable earrings, have one's hair done in the Roman style. Such matters may seem trivial, but fashions appear to follow similar patterns in Rome and in the small cities of Middle Egypt. Egyptian mummies, in some ways the most conventional, archaic and non-Roman of burial practices, have portraits depicting men and women in the latest Roman fashions. The audience for such portraits is hardly the Egyptian prefect or the very small number of Romans who lived in the province, but locals, members of the local elites. Following the latest trend was an assertion of status in a local community.

Such adoption of Roman values works through the social system. We have seen the evidence for economic change in the various provinces. In particular, there is evidence for urbanisation and the concentration of wealth in cities. We have seen also evidence for the growth in large estates in many regions of the Empire. The estates brought with them new social and economic relationships.

It becomes evident that the Empire was a 'total' culture. It encompassed all areas of life. It spread through all political and economic structures. It was replicated because locals saw advantages in its replication and adoption. It allowed the hierarchies of imperial power to spread across the Empire. It is in this context that we can re-read Tacitus. The replication of Roman culture through the Empire meant the replication of certain social structures of domination. For Tacitus, those structures carried within them corruption. Corruption was systemic and it was only the occasional great man who could rise above that corruption. Being good in a corrupt system was, as Tacitus shows us throughout his works, very difficult.

In some cases, we do see attempts to avoid Rome. In Judaea, for example, the religious, political and economic systems of the region were not easily adapted to Roman imperial structures. Religious difference may have allowed the mobilisation of resistance to social and economic influences. Jewish resistance led to a revolt. The Jewish revolt was crushed with great brutality and the symbolic heart of Jewish identity, the Temple, was destroyed. In the last chapter, I argued that Christianity may have provided a religious home for the disaffected. Christianity was persecuted.

Ultimately, the Roman Empire was achieved by conquest and maintained by force. Cultural change was not a happy process of adaptation to a technically superior culture in order to spread happiness and contentment. It was Tacitus, not Gibbon, who captured the essence of the Roman Empire. Cultural change depended on the power that the Roman authorities controlled and exercised. It was a feature of dependency and enormous disparities of power within Roman society. It was slavery.

Glossary

amphora   pottery vessel for the transport of liquid trade goods, especially wine, olive oil, or fish sauce.

annals   the practice of writing historical accounts on a year-by-year basis.

augustales   priests of the imperial cult.

auxiliaries   support units to the legions, normally organised into groups of 500 or 1,000. Auxiliaries provided cavalry and probably light-armed troops.

canabae   settlement outside the walls of a military camp.

Capitoline Jupiter   the main god of Rome.

castris   an *origo* of the camp.

census   the procedure by which (male) citizens were registered and assigned to a property-status group.

client kingdom   a state dependent on Rome, in which the king was either appointed by or had his accession ratified by the Roman state.

collegium   a guild or religious grouping. A *collegium* appears to have been constituted by some sort of agreement between its members, who probably regularly dined together. *Collegia* sometimes had premises.

comitia centuriata   Roman assembly which passed laws and elected senior magistrates. The voting population was organised into centuries by census class.

comitia tributa   Roman assembly for the passing of laws and election of certain magistrates. The assembly was organised by tribes.

consul   the senior Roman magistrate.

consul (*ordinarius*)   the consul who was appointed on 1st January and who, together with his colleague, gave his name to the year.

consul (suffect)   a consul appointed in the middle of the year.

curator annonae (**curator of the grain-supply**)   senatorial official charged with looking after the supply of grain to Rome.

curule **chair**   chair of which a presiding magistrate sat.

Damnatio memoriae   in this process, official records of someone's life were erased and the erasure left to mark their disgrace.

democracy   rule by the people (citizens).

dictator   emergency magisterial position. The dictator was given almost unlimited power for the duration of a crisis.

donatives   gifts of money, normally to the military and normally provided at accessions and at significant moments in the reign (adoptions, major victories, etc.).

endogamy   marriage to persons within a single family.

equestrians   sometimes called the Knights, equestrians were a status group in Roman society. Equestrians were wealthy landowners. In the imperial period, some equestrians developed official roles.

exogamy   marriage to persons outside the family.

imperium   power which was derived from a magisterial position.

imperium maius   greater imperium which was granted to give emperors the ability to command provincial governors.

interpretatio Graeca   the translation of gods of a non-Greek origin into Greek equivalents.

libertus   freedman. *Liberti* had a particular status in Roman law and society.

lineage marriage   marriage to unify two lineages.

magistrates   the executive officials of Roman government (see pp. 6–7).

monarchy   rule by one.

maiestas   the charge of treason or offences against the majesty of the Roman people.

nobiles   members of the aristocracy descended from senior magistrates.

novi homines (**new men**)   those who achieved high status in Roman politics without having a senatorial ancestor.

oligarchy   rule by a few (normally a wealthy or hereditary elite).

origo   place of origin.

panegyric   praise speech, normally for the emperor. The word is also sometimes used of praise poetry.

patronus   a patronus was the person who had been the master of a slave, now freed. The institution allowed the continuation of a relation of obligation and association between a freedman and his or her former master.

plebs   non-patrician Romans. The term came to be applied specifically to the urban population of Rome.

pomerium   a boundary within the city of Rome, which had certain sacred qualities.

Pontifex Maximus   the head of the college of Pontiffs in Rome. This was one of the most important boards of priests. Under the emperors, the position came to be identified as the chief priesthood of Rome, though originally the *Pontifex Maximus* appears to have had little authority over other priestly colleges.

Prefect of Egypt   equestrian governor of Egypt.

Praefectus Fabrum (**Prefect of works**)   senior equestrian official in the Augustan and Tiberian periods.

Praefectus Urbi (**Prefect of the City**) senior political role with overall authority for Rome, often as a deputy for the emperor.

praetor the second rank magistrate in Rome. Praetors either supervised legal business in the city of Rome or served as provincial governors.

Praetorian Guard the major military force located in Rome to protect the emperor and secure the city.

Prefect of the Praetorian Guard commander of the Praetorian Guard. The post was normally held by two equestrian military officers.

Primus pilus a senior centurion in a legion.

proconsuls magistrates who served with the powers of the consul, usually as provincial governors.

procurators officials who were given a whole range of managerial tasks within the Empire. Tasks ranged from the supervision of state assets, through tax collection and provision of legal advice and judgements in the provinces to acting as a provincial governor. The officials could be freedmen of the Caesar or could be equestrians. A hierarchy of procurators evolved gradually.

proscriptions a process by which certain individuals were declared enemies of the state. Their names were posted in Rome. A reward was offered for proof of their murder, normally a portion of their property.

province a region of the Roman Empire under direct rule, normally controlled by a legate, a proprietor, a proconsul, or a procurator.

rescript judgement sent in reply to a petition.

salii a band of 'jumping' priests who performed and archaic ritual in Rome. They also sang a hymn in archaic Latin.

senate the senior assembly in Rome. The senate consisted mainly of former magistrates. Senators served for life. The senate met to advise the magistrates. In the Imperial period, the senate was given the power to make law.

sesterces One of the many coins of imperial Rome, along with the copper *as*, the silver *denarius* and the gold *aureus*. Romans normally expressed values either in *sesterces* or *denarii*.

spolia opima (**best spoils**) an honour granted to a Roman general who managed to personally kill the leader of the opposing forces in battle.

stoicism A philosophical movement current in Rome in the imperial period. Stoicism is associated with the disciplining of emotions.

subsistence agriculture an agricultural system in which the farmers produce only as much as they need to survive.

timocratic division separation of the population into groups depending on wealth.

tax farming some tax collections were let out to contract so that individuals or groups (*publicani*) would bid to collect the tax. The money would be paid into the treasury normally after the tax was collected, but a security of land was often required

tribes (Roman)　the territorial-based groups into which Roman citizens were divided for purposes of voting and military service.

tribunes of the legions　senior officers of a legion (normally six to a legion) who served under the legionary commander (the legate).

tribunes of the plebs　magistrates elected to defend the rights of the Roman people. Tribunes were able to veto certain acts of other magistrates.

tribunician power　the powers of the tribune without the office. These powers were granted to Augustus and to every subsequent emperor.

triumph　an elaborate parade with various associated religious ceremonies.

triumvirs　literally, three men. The triumvirs were the three men who took power in the Roman state in December 43 BC with dictatorial powers. They acted to 'reconstitute' the Roman state and were magistrates backed by law. The term is also applied to an informal political alliance between Caesar, Crassus and Pompey, though the use of the term in this last instance carries no implication of a magisterial position.

tyrannicide　killing a tyrant.

tyrant　an illegitimate or violent autocratic ruler.

vigiles　the night watch.

Further reading

The further reading listed here is a guide to the next stage in investigating the period. It is far from complete: a complete bibliography would be many hundreds of pages. I have organised by subject area, but also provided a list of general sites and books in the initial section. The reading focuses on books rather than articles so that the material can be accessed by those who are not able to use university libraries. I have also confined the readings to English language materials.

General

Key websites provide the majority of the important texts in the original and translation and important collections of images. For texts see, http://penelope. uchicago.edu/Thayer/E/Roman/Texts/. For images, see http://www.vroma.org/, http://www.romansociety.org/imago/home.html. The Fordham Internet History Source Book http://www.fordham.edu/halsall/ancient/asbook.asp also has very well-organised texts and extracts for Roman history. Museums now have much of their collections available for viewing on line, see, for example, http://www.britishmuseum.org/research/search_the_collection_database.aspx. The Perseus site also houses large numbers of texts and translation and archaeological images, see http://www.perseus.tufts.edu/hopper/collections.

For a general overview of the period see:

Brunt, Peter A. *Roman Imperial Themes*. Oxford: Oxford University Press, 1990.

Edwards, Catharine. *Death in Ancient Rome*. New Haven: Yale University Press, 2007.

Edwards, Catharine. *The Politics of Immorality in Ancient Rome*. Cambridge: Cambridge University Press, 1993.

Goodman, Martin. *The Roman World 44 BC–AD 180*. London and New York: Routledge, 1997.

Gowing, Alain M. *Empire and Memory: The Representation of the Roman Republic in Imperial Culture*. Cambridge: Cambridge University Press, 2005.

Patterson, John R. 'The city of Rome: from republic to empire.' *Journal of Roman Studies* 82 (1992): 157–64.

Rutledge, Steven H. *Imperial Inquisitions: Prosecutors and Informants From Tiberius to Domitian*. New York: Routledge, 2001.

Wilkinson, Sam. *Republicanism during the Roman Empire*. London: Continuum, 2012.

Winterling, Aloys. *Politics and Society in Imperial Rome*. Chichester, Wiley-Blackwell: 2009.

Woodman, Antony J. *The Cambridge Companion to Tacitus*. Cambridge: Cambridge University Press, 2010.

1 Rome before Augustus

Blois, Lukas de. *The Roman Army and Politics in the First Century Before Christ*. Amsterdam: Gieben, 1987.

Brunt, Peter A. *The Fall of the Roman Republic and Related Essays*. Oxford: Oxford University Press, 1988.

Erdkamp, Paul. *A Companion to the Roman Army*. Malden, MA: Blackwell, 2007.

Gruen, Erich S. *The Last Generation of the Roman Republic*. Berkeley, Los Angeles, London: University of California Press, 1974.

Hölkeskamp, Karl-Joachim. *Reconstructing the Roman Republic: an ancient political culture and modern research*. Princeton, N.J. and Oxford: Princeton University Press, 2010.

Hopkins, Keith. *Conquerors and Slaves*. Cambridge: Cambridge University Press, 1978.

Keaveney, Arthur. *The Army in the Roman Revolution*. Abingdon: Taylor and Francis, 2007.

Millar, Fergus. *Rome, the Greek World and the East Vol. 1: The Roman Republic and the Augustan Revolution*. Chapel Hill: University Of North Carolina Press, 2002.

Rosenstein, Nathan and Robert Morstein-Marx (eds). *A Companion to the Roman Republic,* edited by. Malden, MA, Oxford, Carlton: Wiley-Blackwell, 2006.

Wallace-Hadrill, Andrew. *Rome's Cultural Revolution*. Cambridge, Cambridge University Press: 2008.

2 Augustus

Eck, Werner. *The Age of Augustus*. Malden, MA: Blackwell Publishing, 2007.

Edmondson, Jonathan. *Augustus*. Edinburgh: Edinburgh University Press, 2009.

Galinsky, Karl. *Augustan Culture: An Interpretive Introduction*. Princeton: Princeton University Press, 1996.

Galinsky, Karl. *The Cambridge Companion to the Age of Augustus.* Cambridge and New York: Cambridge University Press, 2005.

Jones, Arnold Hugh Martin. *Augustus.* London: Chatto & Windus, 1970.

Lacey, Walter Kirkpatrick. *Augustus and the Principate: The Evolution of the System.* Leeds: Cairns, 1996.

Levick, Barbara. *Augustus: Image and Substance.* New York: Longman, 2010.

Millar, Fergus G .B. and Erich Segal. *Caesar Augustus: Seven Aspects.* Oxford: Oxford University Press, 1984.

Osgood, Josiah. *Caesar's Legacy: Civil War and the Emergence of the Roman Empire.* Cambridge: Cambridge University Press, 2006.

Raaflaub, Kurt and Mark Toher (eds). *Between Republic and Empire, Interpretations of Augustus and his Principate.* Berkeley University of California Press, 1990.

Syme, Ronald. *The Roman Revolution.* Oxford: Oxford University Press, 1939.

Wallace-Hadrill, Andrew. *Rome's Cultural Revolution.* Cambridge, New York: Cambridge University Press, 2008.

Zanker, Paul. *The Power of Images in the Age of Augustus.* Ann Arbor: University of Michigan Press, 1988.

3   Tiberius

Griffin, Miriam. 'The Senate's Story.' *Journal of Roman Studies* 87 (1997): 249–63.

Levick, Barbara. *Tiberius the Politician.* Rev. ed. London: Routledge, 1999.

Rogers, Robert Samuel. *Studies in the Reign of Tiberius: Some Imperial Virtues of Tiberius and Drusus Julius Caesar.* Baltimore, MD: Johns Hopkins Press, 1943.

Seager, Robin. *Tiberius.* Oxford: Wiley, 2008.

4   Gaius Caligula

Barrett, Anthony A. *Caligula: The Corruption of Power.* London: Routledge, 1989.

Ferrill, Arthur. *Caligula: Emperor of Rome.* London: Thames and Hudson, 1991.

Wilkinson, Sam. *Caligula.* London: Routledge, 2005.

Winterling, Aloys. *Caligula: A biography.* Translated by Deborah Lucas Schneider, Glenn W. Most, and Paul Psoinos. Berkeley, CA and London: University of California Press, 2011.

5   Claudius

Levick, Barbara. *Claudius.* London: Batsford, 1990.

Momigliano, Arnaldo. *Claudius: The Emperor and His Achievement.* Cambridge: Heffer, 1961.

Mouritsen, Henrik. *The Freedman in the Roman World.* Cambridge: Cambridge University Press, 2011.

Osgood, Josiah. *Claudius Caesar: Image and power in the early Roman empire.* Cambridge: Cambridge University Press, 2011.

Weaver, P. R. C. *Familia Caesaris: A Social Study of the Emperor's Freedmen and Slaves.* Cambridge: Cambridge University Press, 1972.

6   Nero

Barrett, Anthony A. *Agrippina: Mother of Nero.* London: Batsford, 1996.

Bartsch, Shadi. *Actors in the Audience: Theatricality and Doublespeak from Nero to Hadrian.* Cambridge, Mass: Harvard University Press, 1994.

Champlin, Edward. *Nero.* Cambridge, Mass: Belknap Press of Harvard University Press, 2003.

Elsner, Jas, and Jamie Masters. *Reflections of Nero: Culture, History and Representation.* London: Duckworth, 1994.

Griffin, Miriam T. *Nero: The End of a Dynasty.* London: Batsford, 1984.

Griffin, Miriam T. *Seneca: A Philosopher in Politics.* Oxford: Clarendon Press, 1976.

Rudich, Vasily. *Political Dissidence under Nero: The Price of Dissimulation.* London: Routledge, 1993.

Rudich, Vasily. *Dissidence and Literature under Nero: The Price of Rhetoricization.* London: Routledge, 1997.

Seneca, *De clementia.* Edited with translation and commentary by Susanna Braund. Oxford: New York: Oxford University Press, 2009.

Veyne, P. *Seneca. The Life of a Stoic,* translated by David Sullivan. New York, London: Routledge, 2003.

7   Civil wars

Ash, Rhiannon. *Ordering Anarchy: Armies and Leaders in Tacitus' Histories.* London: Duckworth, 1999.

Gallia, Andrew B. *Remembering the Roman Republic: Culture, Politics, and History under the Principate.* Cambridge University Press, Cambridge: 2011.

Morgan, Gwyn. *69 AD: The Year of Four Emperors.* New York: Oxford University Press, 2006.

Murison, Charles Leslie. *Rebellion and Reconstruction: Galba to Domitian: An Historical Commentary On Cassius Dio's Roman History Books 64–67 (AD 68–96).* Atlanta, GA: Scholars Press, 1999.

Wellesley, Kenneth. *The Year of the Four Emperors.* London: Routledge, 2000.

8   Vespasian and Titus

Darwall-Smith, Robin Haydon. *Emperors and Architecture: A Study of Flavian Rome*. Brussels: Latomus, 1996.
Dominik, William J, and A. J Boyle. *Flavian Rome: Culture, Image, Text*. Boston: Brill, 2003.
Levick, Barbara. *Vespasian*. New York: Routledge, 1999.

9   Domitian

Jones, Brian W. *The Emperor Domitian*. London: Routledge, 1992.
Jones, Brian W. *Domitian and the Senatorial Order: A Prosopographical Study of Domitian's Relationship With the Senate, A.D. 81–96*. Philadelphia: American Philosophical Society, 1979.
Newlands, Carole E. *Statius' Silvae and the Poetics of Empire*. Cambridge: Cambridge University Press, 2002.
Southern, Pat. *Domitian: Tragic Tyrant*. London: Routledge, 1997.

10   Nerva and Trajan

Bennett, Julian. *Trajan: Optimus Princeps : A Life and Times*. London: Routledge, 1997.
Grainger, John D. *Nerva and the Roman Succession Crisis AD 96–99*. New York: Routledge, 2003.
Lepper, Frank A. *Trajan's Parthian War*. London: Chatto & Windus, 1948.

11   Society

Alston, Richard and Efrossini Spentzou. *Reflections of Romanity: Discourses of Subjectivity in Imperial Rome*. Columbus: Ohio State University Press, 2011.
Alston, Richard, Edith Hall and Justine McConnell. *Ancient Slavery and Abolition: From Hobbes to Hollywood*. Oxford: Oxford University Press. 2011.
Alston, Richard, Edith Hall and Laura Proffitt. *Reading Ancient Slavery*. London, New York: Duckworth, 2010.
Beard, Mary. *Pompeii: The Life of a Roman Town*. London: Profile, 2008.
Berry, Joanne. *The Complete Pompeii*. New York: Thames & Hudson, 2007.
Bradley, K. R. *Slaves and Masters in the Roman Empire: A Study in Social Control*. New York: Oxford University Press, 1987.
Bradley, Keith R. *Slavery and Society at Rome (Key Themes in Ancient History)*. Cambridge, Cambridge University Press, 1994.
Ellis, Simon P. *Roman Housing*. London. Duckworth, 2000.
Finley, Moses I. *Ancient Slavery and Modern Ideology*. London: Chatto & Windus, 1980.

Fitzgerald, William. *Slavery and the Roman Literary Imagination*. Cambridge: Cambridge University Press, 2000.

Garnsey, Peter. *Ideas of Slavery from Aristotle to Augustine*. Cambridge, New York: Cambridge University Press, 1996.

Garnsey, Peter. *Social Status and Legal Privilege in the Roman Empire*. Oxford: Clarendon, 1970.

Hales, Shelley. *The Roman House and Social Identity*. Cambridge: Cambridge University Press, 2003.

Hasegawa, Kinuko. *The Familia Urbana During the Early Empire: A Study of Columbaria Inscriptions*. Oxford: Archaeopress, 2005.

Hope, Valerie M. *Death in Ancient Rome: A Source Book*. New York: Routledge, 2007.

Jongman, Willem. *The Economy and Society of Pompeii*. Amsterdam: Gieben, 1991.

Joshel, Sandra R. *Work, Identity and Legal Status At Rome: A Study of the Occupational Inscriptions*. Norman: University of Oklahoma Press, 1992.

Sandra R. Joshel. *Slavery in the Roman World*. Cambridge: Cambridge University Press, 2010.

Katsari, Constantina and Eduardo Dal Lago (eds). *From Captivity to Freedom: Themes in Ancient and Modern Slavery*. Leicester: Leicester University Press, 2008.

McKeown, Niall. *The Invention of Ancient Slavery* (Duckworth Classical Essays). London: Duckworth, 2007.

Mouritsen, Henrik. *The Freedman in the Roman World*. Cambridge: Cambridge University Press, 2011.

Murnaghan, Sheila and Sandra R. Joshel. *Women and Slaves in Greco-Roman Culture: Differential Equations*. New York: Routledge, 1998.

Ostia Antica: http://www.ostia-antica.org/

Petersen, Lauren Hackworth. *The Freedman in Roman Art and Art History*. New York: Cambridge University Press, 2006.

Pompeii on line: http://www.pompeionline.net/

Saller, Richard P. *Personal Patronage Under the Early Empire*. Cambridge: Cambridge University Press, 1982.

Wallace-Hadrill, Andrew. *Houses and Society in Pompeii and Herculaneum*. Princeton: Princeton University Press, 1994.

12   Economy

Alston, Richard. *The City in Roman and Byzantine Egypt*. London: Routledge, 2002.

Bowman, Alan, Peter Garnsey, and Dominic Rathbone (eds). *The Cambridge Ancient History, Volume XI, The High Empire, AD 70–192*: 2nd edn. Cambridge: Cambridge University Press, 2000.

Bowman, Alan and Andrew Wilson (eds). *Settlement, Urbanization, and Population*. Oxford: Oxford University Press, 2011.

Brunt, Peter A. *Italian manpower 225 B.C.–A.D.14*. Rev. ed. Oxford, Oxford University Press, 1987.

Cherry, John F, and Susan E. Alcock. *Side-by-side Survey: Comparative Regional Studies in the Mediterranean World*. Oxford: Oxbow, 2004.

Duncan-Jones, Richard. *Money and Government in the Roman Empire*. Cambridge: Cambridge University Press, 1994.

Duncan-Jones, Richard. *Structure and Scale in the Roman Economy*. Cambridge: Cambridge University Press, 1990.

Finley, Moses I. *Ancient History: Evidence and Models*. London: Chatto & Windus, 1985.

Finley, M. I. *The Ancient Economy*. Berkeley: University of California Press, 1999.

Garnsey, Peter. *Cities, Peasants, and Food in Classical Antiquity: Essays in Social and Economic History*. New York, USA: Cambridge University Press, 1998.

Garnsey, Peter. *Famine and Food Supply in the Graeco-Roman World*. New York: Cambridge University Press, 1988.

Greene, Kevin. *The Archaeology of the Roman Economy*. London: Batsford, 1986.

Hermansen, Gustav. *Ostia: aspects of Roman City Life*. Edmonton: University of Alberta Press, 1982.

Holleran, Claire. *Shopping in Ancient Rome: The Retail Trade in the Late Republic and the Principate*. Oxford: Oxford University Press, 2012.

Hordern, Peregrine and Nicholas Purcell. *The Corrupting Sea: A Study of Mediterranean History*. Oxford, Malden, Mass.: Blackwell, 2000.

Hopkins, Keith. 'Taxes and trade in the Roman empire, 200 BC–AD 400', *Journal of Roman Studies* 70 (1980): 101-25.

Hopkins, Keith. *Death and Renewal*. Cambridge: Cambridge University Press, 1983.

Launaro, Alessandro. *Peasants and Slaves: The Rural Population of Roman Italy (200 BC to AD 100)* Cambridge: Cambridge University Press, 2011.

Ligt, L. de. *Fairs and Markets in the Roman Empire: Economic and Social Aspects of Periodic Trade in a Pre-industrial Society*. Amsterdam: J.C. Gieben, 1993.

Morris, Ian, Walter Scheidel, and Richard P. Saller. *The Cambridge Economic History of the Greco-Roman World*. Cambridge: Cambridge University Press, 2007.

Frayn, Joan M. *Markets and Fairs in Roman Italy: Their Social and Economic Importance from the second century BC to the third century AD*. Oxford, Oxford University Press: 1993.

Nijf, Onno van. *The Civic World of Professional Associations in the Roman East*. Amsterdam: J.C. Gieben, 1997.

Smith, Christopher and Helen Parkins (eds), *Trade, Traders and the Ancient City* Hoboken: Routledge, 1998.

Rickman, Geoffrey. *The Corn Supply of Ancient Rome*. Oxford: Clarendon Press, 1980.

Reden, Sitta von and Walter Scheidel. *The Ancient Economy*. Edinburgh: Edinburgh University Press, 2002.

Wilson, Stephen G. and John S Kloppenborg. *Voluntary Associations in the Graeco-Roman World*. London: Routledge, 1996.

13   Administration and government

Jones, Brian W. *Domitian and the Senatorial Order: A Prosopographical Study of Domitian's Relationship With the Senate, A.D. 81-96*. Philadelphia: American Philosophical Society, 1979.

Lendon, J. Edward. *Empire of Honour: The Art of Government in the Roman World*. Oxford: Oxford University Press, 1997.

Lintott, Andrew. *Imperium Romanum: Politics and Administration*. London: Routledge, 1993.

Millar, Fergus. *The Emperor in the Roman World (31 BC–AD 337)*. London: Duckworth, 1977.

Millar, Fergus. *The Roman Near East, 31 B.C.–A.D. 337*. Cambridge, Mass.: Harvard University Press, 1993.

Richardson, John. *Roman Provincial Administration, 227 BC to AD 117*. Bristol: Bristol Classical Press, 1984.

Saller, Richard P. *Personal Patronage Under the Early Empire*. Cambridge: Cambridge University Press, 1982.

Sherk, Robert K. *Roman Documents From the Greek East: Senatus Consulta and Epistulae to the Age of Augustus*. Baltimore, MD: Johns Hopkins, 1969.

Talbert, Richard J. A. *The Senate of Imperial Rome*. Princeton, N.J: Princeton University Press, 1984.

14   Roman army and military policy

Alston, Richard. *Soldier and Society in Roman Egypt: A Social History*. London: Routledge, 1995.

Breeze, David, Roy W. Davies and Valerie A. Maxfield. *Service in the Roman Army*. Edinburgh: Edinburgh University Press with the Publications Board of the University of Durham, 1989.

Campbell, J. B. *The Emperor and the Roman Army: 31 BC–AD 235*. Oxford: Clarendon, 1984.

Campbell, Brian. *The Roman Army, 31 BC–AD 337: A Sourcebook*. London: Routledge, 1994.

Cascio, Elio Lo and Lukas De Blois. *The Impact of the Roman Army (200 BC–AD 476): Economic, Social, Political, Religious and Cultural Aspects: Proceedings of the Sixth Workshop of the International Network Impact of Empire (Roman Empire, 200 BC–AD 476), Capri, Italy, March 29–April 2, 2005*. Leiden: Brill, 2007.

Erdkamp, Paul. *A Companion to the Roman Army*. Chichester: Wiley, 2011.

Erdkamp, Paul. *The Roman Army and the Economy*. Amsterdam: Gieben, 2002.

Hoyos, Dexter. *A Companion to Roman Imperialism*. Leiden: Brill, 2013.

Isaac, Benjamin H. *The Limits of Empire: The Roman Army in the East*. Oxford: Oxford University Press, 1993.

Keppie, Laurence. J. F. *The Making of the Roman Army: From Republic to Empire*. London: Routledge, 1998.

Le Bohec, Yann. *Encyclopedia of the Roman Army*. Chichester: Wiley-Blackwell, 2012.

Luttwak, Edward N. *The Grand Strategy of the Roman Empire From the First Century A.D. to the Third*. Baltimore: Johns Hopkins, 1976.

Mattern, Susan P. *Rome and the Enemy: Imperial Strategy in the Principate*. Berkeley: University of California Press, 1999.

Wells, C. M. *The German Policy of Augustus: An Examination of the Archaeological Evidence*. Oxford: Clarendon, 1972.

15   Family and gender

Alston, Richard and Efi Spentzou. *Reflections of Romanity: Discourses of Subjectivity in Imperial Rome*. Columbus, Ohio State University Press, 2011.

Bradley, Keith. R. *Discovering the Roman Family: Studies in Roman Social History*. New York: Oxford University Press, 1991.

Champlin, Edward. *Final Judgments: Duty and Emotion in Roman Wills, 200 B.C.–A.D. 250*. Berkeley: University of California Press, 1991.

Dixon, Suzanne. *Childhood, Class, and Kin in the Roman World*. New York: Routledge, 2001.

Dixon, Suzanne. *Reading Roman Women*. London: Duckworth, 2001.

Foucault, Michel. *The Care of the Self: The History of Sexuality III*. London: Penguins Press, 1986.

Hallett Judith P. and Marilyn B. Skinner. *Roman Sexualities*. Princeton: Princeton University Press, 1997.

Laurence Ray and Andrew Wallace-Hadrill (eds). *Domestic Space in the Roman World: Pompeii and Beyond* edited by. Portsmouth, RI: Journal of Roman Archaeology Suppl. 1997.

Saller, Richard. *Patriarchy, Property and Death in the Roman Family*. Cambridge, Cambridge University Press, 1994.

16   Religion

Alvar Ezquerra, Jaime. *Romanising Oriental Gods: Myth, Salvation, and Ethics in the Cults of Cybele, Isis, and Mithras*. New York: Brill, 2008.

Ando, Clifford *Roman Religion*. Edinburgh: Edinburgh University Press, 2003.

Beard, Mary, John North and Simon Price. *Religions of Rome*. Cambridge: Cambridge University Press, 1998.

Bowersock, G. W. *Martyrdom and Rome*. Cambridge: Cambridge University Press, 1995.

Donalson, Malcolm Drew. *The Cult of Isis in the Roman Empire: Isis Invicta*. Lampeter, Wales: E. Mellen Press, 2003.

Esler, Philip F. *Modelling Early Christianity: Social-scientific Studies of the New Testament in Its Context*. London: Routledge, 1995.

Fishwick, Duncan. *The Imperial Cult in the Latin West: Studies in the Ruler Cult of the Western Provinces of the Roman Empire*. 2nd ed. New York: Brill, 1993.

Goodman, Martin. *Mission and Conversion: Proselytizing in the Religious History of the Roman Empire*. Oxford University Press, 1994.

Goodman, Martin. *Rome and Jerusalem: The Clash of Ancient Civilizations*. New York: Allen Lane, 2007.

Gradel, Ittai. *Emperor Worship and Roman Religion*. Oxford: Clarendon Press, 2002.

Irby-Massie, Georgia L. *Military Religion in Roman Britain*. Boston: Brill, 1999.

Lane Fox, Robin. *Pagans and Christians*. Harmondsworth: Viking, 1986.

Liebeschuetz, J. H. W. G. *Continuity and Change in Roman Religion*. Oxford: Clarendon, 1979.

Moxnes, Halvor. *Constructing Early Christian Families: Family as Social Reality and Metaphor*. London: Routledge, 1997.

North, John. A. *Roman Religion*. Oxford: Oxford University Press, 2000.

Price, Simon R. F. *Rituals and Power: The Roman Imperial Cult in Asia Minor*. Cambridge: Cambridge University Press, 1984.

Rives, J. B. *Religion in the Roman Empire*. Malden, Mass: Blackwell, 2007.

Scheid, John and Janet Lloyd. *An Introduction to Roman Religion*. Edinburgh: Edinburgh University Press, 2003.

Small, Alastair and Duncan Fishwick. *Subject and Ruler: the Cult of the Ruling Power in Classical Antiquity: Papers Presented At a Conference Held in the University of Alberta On April 13–15, 1994, to Celebrate the 65th Anniversary of Duncan Fishwick*. Ann Arbor: Journal of Roman archaeology, 1996.

Weinstock, Stefan. *Divus Julius*. Oxford: Clarendon, 1971.

17 Romanisation

Alston, Richard. *The City in Roman and Byzantine Egypt*. London: Routledge, 2002.

Ando, Clifford. *Imperial Ideology and Provincial Loyalty in the Roman Empire*. Berkeley: University of California Press, 2000.

Mattingly, David J. 'Dialogues in Roman Imperialism'. *Journal of Roman Archaeology* Suppl. Portsmouth, RI.: Journal of Roman Archaeology, 1997.

Millett, Martin. *The Romanization of Britain*. Cambridge, Cambridge University Press, 1990.

Webster Jane and Nick Cooper (eds). *Roman imperialism: post-colonial perspectives*. Leicester, Leicester University Press, 1996.

Woolf, Greg. *Becoming Roman: The Origins of Provincial Civilization in Gaul*. New York: Cambridge University Press, 1998.

Index